Practical Internet Security
by John R. Vacca

Publisher's Note

The chapters in this work were authored in principal part by the
individuals named as references for them. Their contributions are
used with permission. This work should therefore be considered
an edited volume.

ISBN-13: 978-0-387-40533-9
e-ISBN-13: 978-0-387-29844-3

Practical Internet Security

Practical Internet Security

by

John R. Vacca
USA

John R. Vacca
Author and IT Consultant
34679 TR 382
Pomeroy, Ohio 45769
e-mail: jvacca@hti.net
http://www.johnvacca.com/

Library of Congress Control Number: 2006926793

Practical Internet Security
by John R. Vacca

ISBN-13: 978-0-387-40533-9
ISBN-10: 0-387-40533-X
e-ISBN-13: 978-0-387-29844-3
e-ISBN-10: 0-387-29844-4

Printed on acid-free paper.

Printed in the United States of America.

9 8 7 6 5 4 3 2 1

springer.com

Dedication

This book is dedicated to 2nd cousin Allessandria.

Contents

Acknowledgements

There are many people whose efforts on this book have contributed to its successful completion. I owe each a debt of gratitude and want to take this opportunity to offer my sincere thanks.

A very special thanks to my Springer Publishing Editor/CS, Susan Lagerstrom-Fife, without whose initial interest and support would not have made this book possible; and, for her guidance and encouragement over and above the business of being a Publishing Editor. And, thanks to Editorial Assistant, Sharon Palleschi of Springer, whose many talents and skills are essential to a finished book. Many thanks also to Deborah Doherty of Springer Author Support, whose efforts on this book have been greatly appreciated. Finally, a special thanks to Michael Erbschloe who wrote the foreword for this book.

Thanks to my wife, Bee Vacca, for her love, her help, and her understanding of my long work hours.

Finally, I wish to thank all the organizations and individuals who granted me permission to use the research material and information necessary for the completion of this book.

Foreword

From the fundamentals to the level of advance sciences, this book explains and illustrates what individuals and organizations can do to manage Internet security. The comprehensive coverage of Internet security provides a solid education for any student or professional in a world where connectivity has become the norm.

The explanations of technology, security policies, and practical procedures are excellent. Vacca uniquely provides insight and methods on how masqueraders can infiltrate systems and what steps can be taken to prevent such occurrences and to respond them if they occur.

The book also covers another often-overlooked problems in the Internet world-eavesdropping and counterfeiting. The process of unauthorized listening and looking and how to counter eavesdropper is expertly examined as is the practices of counterfeiting forgery and how to prevent becoming a victim of such crimes.

The book also provides explanations of the most important security measures all organizations should implement including preventing and countering denial-of-service attacks, the use of firewalls, operating system security features, and securing web communications with SSL.

I highly recommend this book for networking professionals and those entering the field of network management. I also highly recommend it to curriculum planners and instructors for use in the classroom.

Michael Erbschloe
Security Consultant and Author
St. Louis, Missouri

Preface

INTRODUCTION

Enterprises today are linking their systems across enterprise-wide networks and VPNs as well as increasing their exposure to customers, competitors, browsers and hackers on the Internet. Each connection magnifies the vulnerability to attack. With the increased connectivity to the Internet and the wide availability of automated cracking tools, enterprises can no longer simply rely on operating system security to protect their valuable corporate data. Furthermore, the exploding use of Web technologies for enterprise intranets and Internet sites has escalated security risks to enterprise data and information systems. It is imperative that Web professionals are trained in techniques to effectively protect their sites from internal and external threats.

PURPOSE

The purpose of this book is to show globally how the Internet is paving the way for secure communications within enterprises and on the public Internet. In addition, the book will provide the fundamental knowledge you need to analyze risks to your system and implement a workable security policy that protects your information assets from potential intrusion, damage or theft. Through dozens of real life scenarios and/or examples, you will learn which countermeasures to deploy to thwart potential attacks. In this book, you will also gain extensive hands-on experience in securing Web communications and Web sites. You will learn the common vulnerabilities of Web sites; as well as, how to carry out secure communications across unsecured networks.

SCOPE

This book will illustrate the importance of Internet security as a method of protection for Internet and intranet based applications. In addition to commercial enterprises and governments, the book will also address, but not be limited to the following line items as part of extensive hands-on examples that will provide you with practical experience in establishing Internet security:

- Maintaining strong authentication and authenticity.
- Preventing eavesdropping.
- Retaining integrity of information.
- Minimizing the effects of denial-of-service attacks.
- Selecting a firewall topology.
- Evaluating computer and hacker ethics.
- Installing and configuring Microsoft IIS, Netscape iPlanet or Apache.
- Securing your Web browser.
- Auditing and hardening your server operating system.
- Configuring user authentication.
- Implementing host-based access restrictions.
- Using SSL to encrypt Web traffic.
- Creating a certificate authority (CA).
- Implementing a client certificate.
- Configuring your Web server to require client certificates.
- Protecting browsers and servers with a proxy-based firewall.

This book will leave little doubt that a new world infrastructure in the area of Internet security is about to be constructed. No question, it will benefit enterprises and governments, as well as their advanced citizens. For the disadvantaged regions of the world, however, the coming Internet security revolution could be one of those rare technological events that enable traditional societies to leap ahead and long-dormant economies to flourish in security.

TARGET AUDIENCE

This book is primarily targeted toward domestic and international system administrators, government computer security officials, network administrators, senior managers, engineers, sales representatives, marketing staff, WWW Developers, military senior top brass, and other Internet users. This book is valuable for those who require the fundamental skills to develop and implement security policies designed to protect their enterprise's information from attacks, including managers, network and system administrators, technical staff and support personnel. This book is also valuable for those involved in securing Web sites, including Web developers, Webmasters, and systems, network and security administrators. Some experience with Web servers and technologies is required. Basically, the book is targeted for all types of people and organizations around the world that have Internet, extranet, and intranet security concerns. In addition, the targeted audience also includes the following:

- Scientists.
- Engineers.
- Educators.

- Top Level Executives.
- Computer and network security personnel and IT/IS directors.
- Information Technology (IT) and Department Managers.
- Programmers and Technical Staff.
- The massive target market of more than 600 million Internet and intranet users around the world.

ORGANIZATION OF THIS BOOK

The book is organized into fifteen parts as well as an extensive glossary of security, wireless network and Internet networking terms and acronyms at the back. It provides a step-by-step approach to everything you need to know about Internet security. The following detailed organization speaks for itself:

Part I: Introduction To Internet Security

Part One discusses Internet technologies and basic security issues.

Chapter 1, "Internet technologies," discusses securing dynamic content on a Web server. Topics include security considerations that apply to all dynamic content in general, Server Side Includes, Common Gateway Interface, and two ways to wrapper CGI content.

Chapter 2, "Basic Security Issues," is intended to help management successfully navigate a course, by providing an overview of security principles and the technologies which are appropriate for securing the Internet and networks today.

Part II: Establishing Your Organization's Security

Part Two discusses real threats that impact security and the security policy itself, which is the foundation for your protection.

Chapter 3, "Real Threats That Impact Security," discusses, what can you do about all of these real security threats.

Chapter 4, "A Security Policy: The Foundation Of Your Protection," provides technical professionals with the information they need to explain Internet policy issues to policy makers. It provides a construct for linking high-level policy to detailed technical decisions.

Part III: Developing Your Security Policy

The third part of this book discusses the steps you can take now and how to respond to attacks.

Chapter 5, "Steps To Take Now," provides a methodology for the steps you must take now to rapidly develop a risk profile for your enterprise; and, the enterprise requirements you must adhere to in developing an Internet security policy.

Chapter 6, "Responding To Attacks," contains hypothetical sample policy statements that address Internet-based security.

Part IV: Securing The Web Client

Part Four covers threats and vulnerabilities and how to protect your web browser.

Chapter 7, "Threats And Vulnerabilities," presents an overview of these vulnerabilities and threats, and is a marked deviation from the previous Top-20 lists. In addition to Windows and UNIX categories, SANS and NIPC have also included cross-platform applications and networking products.

Chapter 8, "Protecting Your Web Browser," focuses on the security aspects, particularly the risks involved with running any web browser and how to overcome some of these security shortcomings. Internet Explorer and Firefox will be used as examples, as these are the most commonly used, and therefore the most commonly exploited.

Part V: Network Interconnections: A Major Point Of Vulnerability

Part Five covers the basic operating system and TCP/IP concepts; as well as, early system security improvements.

Chapter 9, "Basic Operating System And TCP/IP Concepts," provides you with a much better understanding of the real-world risks of TCP/IP reset attacks. In other words, to better understand the reality of this threat, the aim of this chapter is to provide some background into the basic workings of operating systems and of TCP/IP concepts, and then to build upon this foundation to understand how resets attacks work.

Chapter 10, "Early System Security Improvements," focuses on early system security improvements like DES, shadow passwords and dialback/dialer passwords.

Part VI: Deterring Masqueraders And Ensuring Authenticity

Part six covers the impersonation of users, how masqueraders can iniltrate your system and how to hold your defensive line.

Chapter 11, "Impersonating Users" focuses on the impersonation of users by stolen passwords and the borrowing of IP addresses.

Chapter 12, "How Masqueraders Infiltrate A System," deals with a broad sweep of technologies and issues connected with policing, profiling and privacy as applicable to cyber surveillance and the infiltration of masqueraders.

Chapter 13, "Holding Your Defensive Line," shows you how to thwart blended threats, where a defense-in-depth strategy is the preferred approach. Defense-in-depth relies on the premise that multiple layers of security afford more comprehensive protection than any single mechanism.

Part VII: Preventing Eavesdropping To Protect Your Privacy

Part Seven covers unauthorized listening and looking and the countering or not countering the eavesdropper.

Chapter 14, "Unauthorized Listening And Looking," describes instant messaging and offers a brief overview of some of the security threats associated with the service. It covers the unauthorized listening and looking of IM: Yeah! Eavesdropping!

Chapter 15, "Countering Or Not Countering The Eavesdropper: That's The Question?," answers that question, and provides recommendations to counter or provide support for the eavesdropper either way.

Part VIII: Thwarting Counterfeiters And Forgery to Retain Integrity

Part Eight covers the forger's arsenal and how to shield your asets.

Chapter 16, "The Forger's Arsenal," focuses on the forger's arsenal (hacking e-mail messages; censoring system logs; and, scrambling the routing tables); as well as, the enhancement of the Internet Protocol (IP), called Path Enhanced IP (PEIP), which is designed to eliminate source forgery.

Chapter 17, "Shielding Your Assets," focuses on how to shield your assets through patch management.

Part IX: Avoiding Disruption Of Service To Maintain Availability

Part Nine covers denial-of-service attacks, how to construct your bastions and the importance of firewalls.

Chapter 18, "Denial-Of-Service Attacks," provides information and defenses against Denial of Service (DoS) attacks, which cause networked computers to disconnect from the network or just outright crash due to the delivery of viruses and bombs (nukes) via the Internet and data flooding.

Chapter 19, "Constructing Your Bastions," discusses how to protect your site against the growing community of black-hat hackers, by thinking like they do and seeing the same information.

Chapter 20, "The Importance Of Firewalls," focuses on the importance of firewalls, how they work and what kinds of threats they can protect you from, how to use a packet filter to shield against bombardment, and how to use application proxies to manage Internet communications.

Part X: Configuring Operating System And Network Security

Part Ten discusses operating systems that pose a security risk and network security.

Chapter 21, "Operating Systems That Pose A Security Risk," discusses the problem of operating system security and the social and economic implications for risk management and policy.

Chapter 22, "Network Security," covers network security abuses.

Part XI: Enhancing Web Server Security

Part Eleven discusses how to control access, extend web site security functionality and how to secure web communications with SSL VPNs.

Chapter 23, "Controlling Access," explores how a comprehensive approach simplifies network access management, creates a secure, intelligent wired and wireless environment and provides affordable network security that detects all users and enforces all enterprise policies at every access point.

Chapter 24, "Extended Web Site Security Functionality," investigates spoofing and phishing attacks and present countermeasures, with regards to extended web site security functionality, while focusing on solutions that protect naïve as well as expert users.

Chapter 25, "Securing Web Communications With SSL VPNs," examines the security risks that arise from securing web communications with SSL VPNs and proposes strategies for remediation.

Part XII: Issuing And Managing Certificates

Part Twelve discusses why digital certificates are used; as well as, certificate authorities and trusting CAs in servers and browsers.

Chapter 26, "Why Digital Certificates Are Used," takes a look at digital certificates (past, present and future) and their potential for deterring phishing attacks and online fraud. It demonstrates the severe pitfalls from First Generation manual vetting of certificate holders and the inherent unreliability of the identity information they contain (which can easily be faked).

Chapter 27, "Certificate Authorities," discusses the use of CAs to verify that the site is who it claims to be.

Chapter 28, "Trusting Cas In Servers And Browsers," briefly touches on some common shared certificate configurations.

Part XIII: Firewalls And Firewall Topologies

Part Thirteen discusses how to provide protecting servers and clients with firewalls, how to choose the right firewall, firewall topologies and how to select the right firewall security topology policy.

Chapter 29, "Protecting Servers And Clients With Firewalls," presents a brief overview of firewall components, types available, and the relative advantages and disadvantages of each. It is intended to lay out a general road map for administrators who wish to publish information for public consumption with regards to protecting servers and clients, while preventing unauthorized access to their private or confidential network.

Chapter 30, "Choosing The Right Firewall," explores, in depth, the aspects of security and exemplifies several existing solutions.

Chapter 31, "Firewall Topologies," focuses on independent utilities that may be assembled to provide an in depth defense against intrusion, extrusion, and collusion.

Chapter 32, "Selecting Firewall Security Topology Policy," helps the responsible manager and firewall administrator create useful policy for the firewall.

Part XIV: Security Management Solutions And Future Directions

Part Fourteen discusses how to identify and respond to security violations; conduct real-time monitoring and auditing; how to limit damage; keep up to date on new threats and emerging technologies; and, finally the summary, conclusions, and recommendations for the book.

Chapter 33, "Identifying And Responding To Security Violations," describes Internet security tool technology (as part of Internet security management solutions and future directions); and demonstrates how it can help administrators identify potential problems; as well as, make well-informed security decisions that strengthen the Internet's security posture.

Chapter 34, "Real-Time Monitoring And Auditing," focuses on "theoretical best-practices" combined with "real-world practicality" to define a usable policy for the real-time auditing and monitoring of databases. By following the policies outlined in this chapter, you can properly implement a database system that will work well, and provide adequate security for the data it houses.

Chapter 35, "Limiting Damage," focuses on how to limit damage to your computer.

Chapter 36, "Keeping Up ToDate On New Threats," examines components of a comprehensive framework that enables enterprises to enhance their threat-mitigation capabilities, while increasing the return on investment of existing information technology infrastructures. This chapter also looks at the role of a multilayered approach to building and maintaining an effective security ecosystem for enterprises.

Chapter 37, "Emerging Technologies," examines differing views on how to deal with weaknesses in the Internet (specifically Internet security).

Chapter 38, "Summary, Conclusions And Recommendations," focuses on these security principles and presents a summary, conclusion and recommendation for each.

Part XV: Appendices

Seven appendices provide additional resources that are available for Internet security. Appendix A shows how to configure Internet authentication service on Microsoft Windows 2003 server windows 2003 / enhanced. Appendix B discusses Internet security management, resiliency and security. Appendix C contains a list of top Internet security implementation and deployment companies. Appendix D contains a list of Internet security products. Appendix E contains a list of Internet security standards. Appendix F contains a list of miscellaneous Internet security resources. The book ends with Appendix G – a glossary of Internet security related terms and acronyms.

CONVENTIONS

This book uses several conventions to help you find your way around, and to help you find important sidebars, facts, tips, notes, cautions, disclaimers and warnings. They alert you to critical information and warn you about problems.

John R. Vacca
Author and IT Consultant
e-mail: jvacca@hti.net
visit us at http://www.johnvacca.com/

PART I

INTRODUCTION TO INTERNET SECURITY

Chapter 1

INTERNET TECHNOLOGIES

INTRODUCTION

In the context of industrial information technology, the Internet and World Wide Web increasingly are seen as a solution to the problem of providing "anywhere, anytime" services. In the classical view of an Internet security-enabled IT infrastructure, services are requested and consumed by a user (a human requesting plant production data from his or her desktop); and, data are provided by an origin server (a Web server located in a plant that can authenticate users, implement encryption, serve data, and source multimedia streams). This rather simplistic view works well if the number of users is small, the complexity of services required is modest, and the real-time response requirements are lax. However, it fails to scale when one accounts for the complexities of modern networking: many simultaneous users, potentially operating in multiple languages; many complex data types, including incompatible display formats; many differing schemes for implementing privacy [6] and Internet security through many combinations of authentication and encryption [1].

THE WEB CLIENT/SERVER ARCHITECTURE

Most Internet security software applications have been developed using the classic client – server model – multiple servers hold vast quantities of information of all kinds, and clients of all types reach that information via diverse devices. Originally, this was considered an ideal architecture because all the processing occurred at the network "ends" (clients and servers), thereby allowing the network itself to remain blissfully unconcerned about the type of traffic it was transmitting. This original concept was known as the end-to-end principle of the Internet [1]. As differences in client capabilities arose (hardwired versus wireless connections [5], large monitors versus PDA screens), they were either ignored entirely by applying a "lowest common denominator" approach; or else, they were accommodated by having the server hold data in multiple formats and using special-purpose protocols to negotiate which format to deliver to which device (creating a specialized cell phone interface) [1].

As Web traffic types became more complex and as clients became more diverse, this pure client – server architecture became less attractive. Caches near the client and at network-edge delivery points were added to make operations faster; gateways (such as for wireless devices) were added to help diverse groups of clients connect; Content delivery networks (CDNs) were invented to organize the vast array of Internet content for the client [1]. All of these services operated "in the network." These services grew up independently, making extensions and new services both vendor specific and hard to manage. Developing network services became tedious and expensive. With today's evolution of diverse client devices, content providers were forced to offer data in every format necessary for every connecting device: PDAs, PCs, cell phones, laptops, e-book readers, etc. [1].

These difficulties were not limited to differing client device and connection capabilities; they also arose from differing client preferences. Client preference with regard to, say, the language of presentation leads to maintaining multiple versions of a common information store; for example, a multinational company might keep duplicate databases in English, French, German, Japanese, etc. Resolving client language preferences at the server increases Internet traffic, while maintaining multiple versions of a Website introduces the obvious difficulties of version control. Although in-the-network services can be quite diverse, they share several key similarities:

- Service detection and operation occurs at in-the-network facilities (proxies) that are in the path between client and server.
- The in-the-path service operation is frequently done with devices both inside and outside the path between client and server (called the outside-path device a "callout server").
- Similarly to a cache, these services transform and organize information but rarely "own" the content (as is done by a server) [1].

However, as noted earlier, each of these services was uniquely designed to suit a particular system and this has resulted in significant maintenance overhead for these software services. To address this problem, an industry group meeting at the Internet Engineering Task Force (IETF) proposed Open Pluggable Edge Services [1] (OPES) as an alternative, unifying architecture for these in-the-network services. OPES defines an architecture for building these stateless services that is suitable for content delivery services, client preference implementation and device adaptation. A client's request is intercepted by an in-the-net device, which is called NetEdge, and is amended (personalized) by client information retained in the edge server, and then passed to the relevant origin server(s). Servers essentially own their content; NetEdge may cache content while making presentation style changes, but NetEdge never owns the data. In the model, an origin server never reformulates its content. All content transformations occur in the NetEdge using well-defined protocols at the request of one end (server) or the other (client). Examples of value-added NetEdge services include language translation, media adaptation, rate adaptation, image transcoding, local content insertion (weather forecast), edge assembly, authentication, and virus scanning. All services benefit from the NetEdge's knowledge of its clients' preferences and capabilities [1].

Keeping the preceding in mind, this part of the chapter reviews the evolution of Internet security from its original client/server model to the new NetEdge service model. It also illustrates the type of data transformations that are best performed at the network edge, discusses the architecture and framework of an OPES server, and reviews the initial performance measurements [1].

Internet Security Evolution

A client – server architecture was adequate when data were primarily text, and client diversity meant distinguishing whether the client was connecting from a PC, MAC, or workstation. However, as the data to be delivered have become richer, and as the clients to whom it is delivered have become more diverse, Internet security architecture has evolved to cope with the changes. As shown in Fig. 1-1, media gateways are used to interface wireless clients; caches are used to improve the delivery of static information; encryption enhances the privacy of data delivered; security and authentication modules attempt to protect the enterprise infrastructure from hackers and terrorists; and, content delivery networks attempt to assemble dynamic content from databases, streaming servers, and content servers to improve performance by making accesses appear more "local [1]."

But, the proliferation of boxes that perform vendor-specific services is not an effective answer to a distributed "edge services" computing model for Internet security. A better

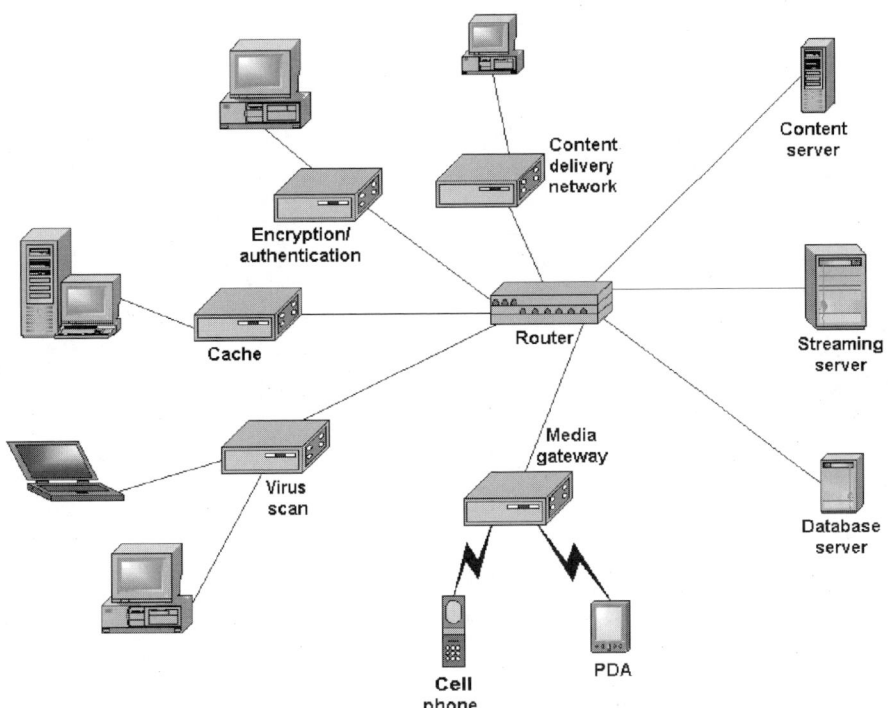

Figure 1-1. Today's plethora of Internet security interface devices.

approach is to design a common architecture for the specification and delivery of edge services. Service determination results from many factors including the request, client, and server, so the architecture logically has a programmable rule engine to identify and match in-the-network services [1]. This allows the specification and implementation of future services, and packages those services into a NetEdge box (see Fig. 1-2) [1].

> **Note:** This approach does not require that all Internet users abandon their current investments; rather, it offers an evolutionary growth path that is logical, programmable, and expandable so that it can accommodate future needs and changes.

NetEdge is not a repackaging of existing software; it is an evolution of Internet security with standard interfaces allowing for programmable technologies to be formulated and operate in a multivendor environment. It evolves these service technologies, such as Edge Side Includes, and creates a platform for the in-the network aspects of Web services using the Web Services Definition Language [1] (WSDL). Services have associated policies, security, and specifications as specified by the Intermediary Rule Markup Language (IRML) [1].

NetEdge Services

IETF has already identified numerous useful services. Users will no doubt invent more as clients become more complex and diverse [1]. Let's first show by illustration how these services might be used. Afterwards, a discussion of how services are defined and implemented will ensue.

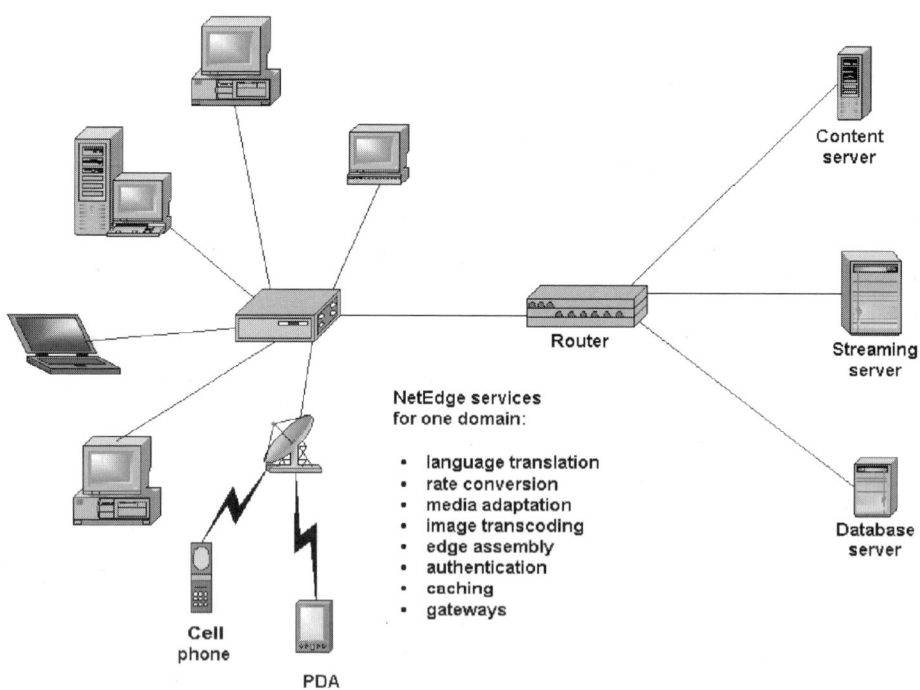

Figure 1-2. Tomorrow's Internet utilizing the NetEdge.

Language Translation

Although natural language translation by machine does not yet have the quality of human translation, it has reached a certain level of utility. In the area of factory automation, for example, one can envision a "data assistant" that translates among common languages at a level of proficiency that allows a native English speaker to read data retrieved from a plant in France (but probably not at a level sufficient to translate novels or convert legal contracts or give medical advice). Such translation services are currently available from sites such as http://www.babelfish.com/ on a manual, page-by-page basis. In other words, the NetEdge service automates and regularizes their invocation through a rule language. For example, when the nativeWeb page is in German and the viewer has expressed a preference for English, the NetEdge service invokes the German-to-English translator on the text, and the customized output is then delivered to the viewer in English. Fig. 1-3 illustrates how production data maintained in English might be translated via the NetEdge to fit user preferences for French or Spanish [1].

Media Adaptation

In a different data access scenario, assume that the user wants to purchase a product and have it shipped directly to the user. Today, that is accomplished by filling in Web forms that answer questions. Forms are needed because customers often have multiple potential answers to questions such as "which credit card?" or "which shipping address?" In this example, the customer has two credit cards, one for personal use and one for business use. Currently, selected services can keep a personal record for this client, but each Web server must determine from the client which credit card to use and the customer must keep these data updated for each service. The seller could create a dynamic Web page with the name and number of both cards, a radio button or hotlinks for each, and a header question along the lines of "Which card shall you charge?" The client's intentions are then signaled via a mouseclick on a radio button followed by clicking a "submit" button. This works as long as the viewer has a screen and a mouse. But what if the choice is being made at a computer that has only a touchscreen? What if the interaction is being done on a PDA? What if the purchaser is accessing the Website through a cell phone? To deal with all these situations, the

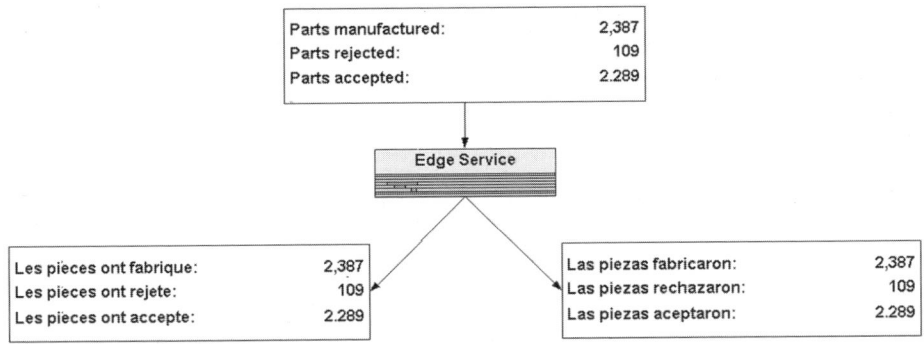

Figure 1-3. English-to-French and English-to-Spanish translation.

corporate site would have to anticipate each type of access device and write specialized code that handles responses from each device type. From the point of view of the Web server, all that needs to be answered is "which of these two cards shall you use?" But to understand that answer, the Website needs to anticipate that it might be provided by a mouseclick at the desktop, a finger touch on a touchscreen, a stylus tap on a PDA, or the spoken words "use the personal card" on the cell phone. In addition, when using this strategy all users have to maintain their personal information separately on every corporate Web service that they utilize [1].

Distributing these logical elements leads to a more extensible solution. First, you would separate the question/answer logic from the devices that support it. Second, you would centralize the personal information about the consumer by making it available for all desired consumer requests as a NetEdge service. Using XML [1], it is easy to specify the data needed for the server requests and the data options supplied by the consumer. Then, the NetEdge can take responsibility for getting the questions answered. NetEdge knows the identity of the client (from an information profile stored at the client's request) and the details of his access technology (wired or wireless, text or voice). NetEdge thus has the data to "fill in the blanks." If there are still more questions to be resolved, NetEdge can communicate directly with the consumer using the technique best matched to the access method.

How might this occur? The basic scenario is that a user wants to purchase a corporate product. Having previously registered one time with the NetEdge, the user's profile contains his or her personal information, including home and corporate shipping addresses and personal and corporate credit card numbers, all protected by modern encryption technology. The user then selects his or her product by name using his or her desktop computer. Then, the choice is made from a cell phone that utilizes voice recognition techniques. In either case, NetEdge understands the purchaser's intent, and submits the basic order to the company; the company responds with an XML table that the NetEdge must complete [1].

Using information from the profile, NetEdge fills in the known fields. When it reaches a point of ambiguity, the NetEdge must resolve the question in a way consistent with the client's capabilities. To determine the correct shipping address, NetEdge posts a Web form with clickable hotlinks for "Home" and "Corporate" shipping address if the interaction is occurring with a desktop PC. With a cell phone, the NetEdge uses voice synthesis to ask "Shall I ship to your home or corporate address?" and then uses voice recognition to parse the spoken answer "Home." For choosing the proper credit card, the actions are similar. NetEdge also posts a Web form with clickable links if the interaction is occurring from a computer, or otherwise asks the question via voice synthesis if the client is using a cell phone. With the answers in hand, the NetEdge then completes the XML form and submits it to the corporate e-commerce server to complete the order.

> **Note:** Look at the high degree of personalization that is achieved without burdening the origin server.

The NetEdge makes a dynamic decision about what mode of interaction is best suited to this client, and resolves whatever ambiguity exists to complete the order form. At the company's e-commerce server, it presents an XML form to the NetEdge and is unaware of how the client's information is gathered (from a profile or from questions) or what access mechanism the client is using. This dramatically reduces the user interface code required in the origin server.

Image Transcoding

A common industrial occurrence is that visual data stored in one format are preferably viewed in a different format for reasons of local compatibility, image compression, or availability of appropriate viewer software. With regards to teleradiology work with the University of Virginia Health Sciences Center, researchers encountered a case that begs for a NetEdge solution [1] on the server side. The context is the collection, dissemination, and interpretation of medical diagnostic imagery. In this case, the particular situation was that sonographic images (digital ultrasound) were being collected and stored in the industry standard format on the medical center's Picture Archiving and Communications System (PACS). For routine cases, the staff radiologist loads the DICOM playback software, selects a particular patient's DICOM image file, plays back the "movie" of the examination, and dictates an interpretation. That works well when all the data is local and can be exchanged via high-speed LANs (the raw imagery can be 2 GB; a severely edited DICOM-encoded examination can still be 100 MB) [1].

So, what happens when the radiologist is not co-located with the PACS? If access is achieved remotely over WANs (DSL, cable modems, telephone lines), then bandwidth is not available to shuttle large images, thus forcing image compression. But, what kind of compression does the interpreting radiologist trust will not distort the image and thus reduce diagnostic accuracy? Should it be motion JPEG, MPEG-2, MPEG-4, MPEG-7, wavelets, or fractals [1]?

An elegant solution would be for the NetEdge, using its profile of the consulting radiologist's image compression preferences, to transcode the DICOM image on-the-fly as it moves through the box. With this solution, the PACS retains only one version of the imagery (the original DICOM version), but the radiologist can dynamically choose which compression scheme best fits his or her own preferences and his/her viewing device's capabilities (resolution, contrast, bandwidth), and the imagery is transcoded enroute to fit those preferences and capabilities [1].

> **Note:** In this case, the NetEdge is on the server side, rather than the client side of the domain, because compression is needed before transmission.

Not only is it important to allow certain transcodings, but in this example, it might be equally important to disallow certain transformations. For instance, viewing an MPEG version of a DICOM movie would be acceptable medical practice if sufficient scientific testing had been done to assure that diagnostic accuracy was not reduced. But, what if the opposite were true? What if it was known that, say, JPEG compression of mammograms was inadequate because JPEG's discrete cosine transform can blur the edges of tumors, thus possibly permitting a radiologist to miss a potential cancer? If that were the case, then the NetEdge rule language could forbid using JPEG compression on mammograms. The point is that the rule-based nature of the NetEdge would allow the translation service vendor (or industry, or user, or standards body, as appropriate) to state programmatically which transformations are appropriate, and which are inappropriate, and under what conditions [1].

Other Services

Once the user sees the potential for distributing computation and conversion to the network edge, it is easy to visualize an unlimited number of additional value-added edge services, such as unicast to multicast conversion [1], content filtering, virus scanning, local content insertion (data relevant to the identify and location of the user is inserted into the delivered data stream) and various caching activities. It is a specific goal of OPES to encourage vendors to define and implement new services, install them on a NetEdge (with proper authentication and security) via an administrative interface, and make new services available to the general user community [1].

NetEdge Architecture

The NetEdge architecture consists of the operational environment located at the NetEdge device, the service interfaces typically at the "callout device" and a management component located with the systems operation software. All of the components work together to provide a suite of in-the-network services [1]. Other work such as Ninja [1] examined issues within-the-net transformation services, but did not offer the general framework for service recognition and execution provided by NetEdge.

NetEdge Environment

NetEdge architecture extends the proxy edge device to facilitate in-the-path service operations. This implementation extends the Apache proxy on Linux. The services of interest are those that transform, rather than own, data. In other words, just like a cache, there is no claim of responsibility for the content for the whole of its lifetime. Content Delivery Networks follow this model, organizing and presenting content according to the wishes of the content provider. Other services (Internet Service Vendors (ISVs), corporate gateways) provide customized content according to the preferences of the requestor (client). This particular project builds a platform to architect services that augment or transform request/reply information between the client and content providers [1].

Given information about what messages require service, the edge appliance determines if a service is required and establishes the actions needed to execute that service. The model typically has the service executed with an out-of-path or "callout" computation engine. This is present for scalability, as the edge device must address many services at essentially the same time. The objective of the NetEdge design is scalability and flexibility, particularly in how services can be invoked. The scalability focus is concerned with not overloading in-the-path agents, and the flexibility focus is concerned with executing services in different operating environments. To this end, the NetEdge appliance runs services with a multi-tiered approach, as shown in Fig. 1-4 [1].

As its core, the NetEdge appliance extends a proxy device, either as a forward proxy (in an ISV) or as a reverse proxy (in a CDN). This provides an open platform for performing services on the content passing through it [1].

Note: Researchers used an Apache proxy running on Linux for their research implementation.

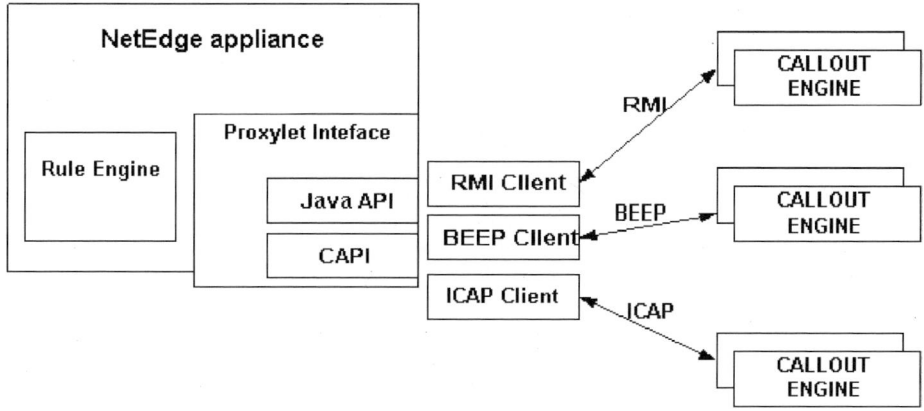

Figure 1-4. NetEdge service callout interface.

A rule engine in the edge device determines which services are needed, and when, for a given request/reply sequence (a client can choose an optional translation based upon the country indicator in the URL and the browser's language setting). As shown in Fig. 1-5 [1], the invocation of the rule engine occurs naturally at the following four points where requests and replies transit the NetEdge:

1. Point 1: User data requests enter the NetEdge.
2. Point 2: User requests, possibly after alteration by a callout invoked by a rule, are passed along to an origin server.
3. Point 3: Server data are returned to the NetEdge.
4. Point 4: Server data, possibly after personalization by a callout invoked by a rule, are forwarded to the client [1].

> **Note:** The rules are specified in IRML [1]. IRML indicates what inputs should indicate a service, at what processing points in the proxy, and what action should take place.

For any edge engine, there is a set of rules to direct its behavior. These rules offered in a language such as IRML are compiled into the rule engine that drives the recognition and actions of the edge device. The rule engine eliminates evaluating network traffic that does not require services; today, that may be a majority of the network traffic, so without a match, the traffic passes through untouched, thereby maximizing performance. When a service is required, the rule engine provides exactly the service that is needed. The connection between the rule engine and the available services is done with a code fragment called a *proxylet* that is set up to invoke a particular service under a particular set of circumstances [1].

The current proxylet interface implementation has two available APIs, one in Java and one in C/C++. If desired, service implementers can write directly to one of these APIs and have the service run directly on the local machine. However, since offloading the actual work of the service onto remote callout servers is desirable for scalability, proxylets for remote callout protocols are provided and are expected to be the main ones used [1].

The three client proxylets already in use are Remote Method Invocation (RMI) and Blocks Extensible Exchange Protocol (BEEP) [1] in Java and Internet Content Adaptation

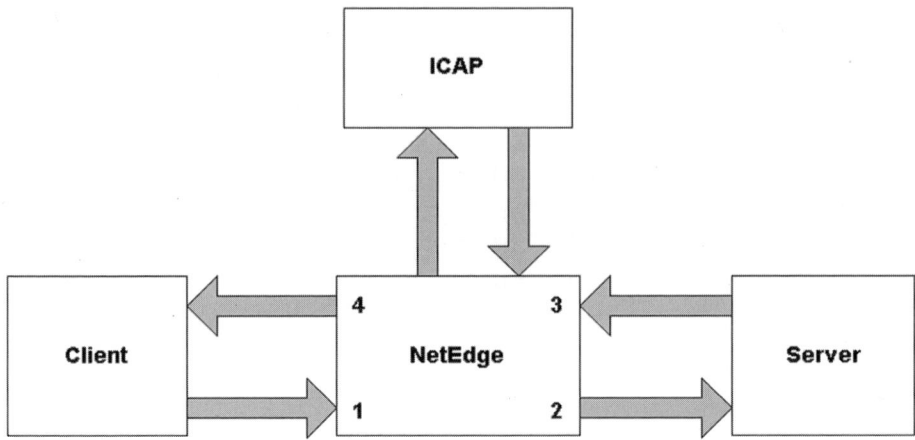

Figure 1-5. NetEdge data processing points.

Protocol (ICAP) [1] in C/C++. The language interface is chosen simply by what is most convenient for the application designer.

The RMI interface exposes a well-defined API for modifying content. The RMI interface parallels the C and Java APIs for proxylets. The two adaptation protocols provided are ICAP and BEEP. Both of these are application-layer protocols designed for specific uses. ICAP, in particular, is designed to modify HTTP requests and replies and is, therefore, very useful for Web traffic [1].

One of the benefits of this multilayered approach is the ease of supporting new protocols; for instance, the support of SOAP [1] or CORBA could be added by simply creating a Java or C proxylet to handle the new interface. A developer experienced with the NetEdge appliance and the new protocol should be able to add support in a matter of a few weeks. At this point, this architecture is an *ad-hoc* extension because today's Internet is populated with proxies (and reverse proxies) that serve as both a potential computational and caching agent for in-the- net services.

The callout service engine(s) where nearly all the data transformations are performed is any compute engine outside the basic network path. In a CDN or ISP world, this would typically be another compute engine in the rack of systems used for Web services. The NetEdge box communicates with this engine by using a standard protocol to request the service. Some environments assume control of the data traffic that is being sent back to the client and others use the NetEdge box. This is defined with the interface proxylet and control protocol between NetEdge and the callout [1].

Service administration covers the installation of services, rules, and rule consistency. Many concerns have been discussed about security and administration issues and, indeed, these issues are still being resolved. The current system does not yet resolve conflicts among rules (two or more different rules resulting from the same input recognition). This remains a research question [1].

The initial focus included only the simple rule checking and typical tools (such as FTP) for distribution of rules and services. Security issues are quite complex because there is no clean way to assure that a service will always do the right thing. This is yet another current research issue that will be thoroughly covered in this book [1].

NetEdge Performance

When comparing the network performance of the current Internet security architecture to the proposed NetEdge architecture, the user does not suffer any substantial additional delays. Extensive measurements of a client running on Windows 2003, connected over a 1.5-Mb/s DSL line to a router connected over a Fast Ethernet (100 Mb/s) to a Windows 2003 origin server, showed that the average one-way packet latency between client and server was 14.8 ms with a jitter of 3.47 ms. When the NetEdge is introduced on the Fast Ethernet, the data path becomes client to DSL to router to Ethernet to NetEdge to Ethernet to origin server, and the one-way latency increases to 21.1 ms with a jitter of 5.17 ms [1].

That increase in the average latency of 6.3 ms is, of course, attributed to the additional hop on the path between client and server. But by definition, the NetEdge appliance is always going to be located on the network edge, and thus is never far from the client. Another important measurement is packet loss. In the standard architecture, a 5-min video clip, streamed at 1.2 Mb/s, incurred no packet losses. With the addition of the NetEdge, the packet loss was also zero [1].

Throughput in the standard architecture averaged 1,635 kb/s on both the uplink and downlink. Introducing the NetEdge changed the average throughput to 1623 kb/s, a reduction of 12 kb/s, or less than 1% of the original throughout. Given the potential advantages of the NetEdge with regard to offloading the origin server, the throughput reduction is insignificant [1].

Now, let's look at the most important of the Internet Security Technologies: The Web Server. This part of the chapter details how to secure dynamic content on a Web server. Topics covered include general security issues pertaining to dynamic content, securing Server Side Includes, configuring the Common Gateway Interface, and wrappering dynamic content.

WHAT DOES THE WEB SERVER DO?

Once upon a time, the World Wide Web was a relatively static place. The Web server's sole function was to simply deliver a requested Web page, written in HTML, to a client browser. Over time, developers started looking for ways to interact with users by providing dynamic content – that is, content that displayed a form or executed a script based on user input. Thus Server Side Includes (SSI) and the Common Gateway Interface (CGI) were born [2].

A Server Side Include page is typically an HTML page with embedded command(s) that are executed by the Web server. An SSI page is parsed by the server (a "normal" Web page is not), and if SSI commands are found they are executed before the resultant output is delivered to the requesting client. SSI is used in situations that demand a small amount of dynamic content be inserted in a page, such as a copyright notice or the date. SSI can also be used to call a CGI script; however, there is a performance penalty associated with SSI. The server must parse every page designated as SSI-enabled, which is not an optimal solution on a heavily loaded Web server [2].

The CGI is a standard for communication between a program or script, written in any one of several languages, and a Web server. The CGI specification is very simple: input from a client is passed to the program or script on STDIN (standard input). The program then takes that information, processes it, and returns the result on STDOUT (standard output) to the Web server. The Web server combines this output with the requested page and returns it to the client as HTML. CGI applications do not force the server to parse every requested page; only pages containing CGI-recognized arguments involve further processing [2].

Thus, with the preceding in mind, this part of the chapter is targeted at Webmasters and system administers responsible for securing a Web server configured to provide dynamic content to clients. It details general security issues related to SSI- and CGI-enabled content, reducing CGI risks with wrappers, and some brief language-specific caveats. Also, this part of the chapter does not cover the configuration steps required to enable SSI or CGI. Configuration examples provided are based on the following assumptions:

- Your network is secure, behind a firewall [8], and the server itself is in a controlled environment.
- The operating system has been properly secured and all unnecessary services are disabled.
- The Web server user and group directives are correctly set, and appropriate permissions assigned.
- The Server Root and log directories are protected.
- User overrides are disabled.
- Default access has been disabled, and access opened for only those system directories designated "public [2]."

In other words, in order to fully absorb the material discussed in this part of the chapter, the reader should have a good working knowledge of general Web server-security; installing and configuring modules; key configuration directives; the role of access files; how to read log files; UNIX file permissions; and, basic system administration. Readers should also be familiar with the syntax, commands, and functions of whatever programming language they intend to use to create CGI applications [2].

General Considerations

The very first question a Web server administrator must confront is, "Do I really want/need to provide dynamic content from my server?" While dynamic content has allowed for a diverse range of user interaction and become a de facto standard for most large Web sites, it remains one of the largest security threats on the Internet. CGI applications and SSI-enabled pages are not inherently insecure, but poorly written code can potentially open up dangerous back doors and gaping holes on what would otherwise be a well-secured system [2]. The following are the three most common security risks CGI applications and SSI pages create:

- Information leaks: Providing any kind of system information to a hacker could potentially provide a hacker with the ammunition they need to break into your server. The less a hacker knows about the configuration of a system, the harder it is to break into.
- Access to potentially dangerous system commands/applications: One of the most common exploits used by hackers is to "take over" a service running on the server and use it for their own purposes. For example, gaining access to a mail application via an HTML form-based script, and then harnessing the mail server to send out spam or acquire confidential user information.
- Depleting system resources: While not a direct security threat per se, a poorly written CGI application can use up a system's available resources to the point where it becomes almost completely unresponsive [2].

A glance at the preceding list shows that a high percentage of security holes is invoked or leveraged through user input. One of the most common problems with applications written in C and C++ are buffer overflows. When a program overflows a buffer, it crashes. A good hacker can then take advantage of the crashed program to gain access to the system [2].

Another common problem involves a system call that opens a subshell to process a command. In Perl such a call could be made using any of the following functions: system(), exec(), piped(), open(), or eval(). The lesson here is to never trust user input, and ensure all your system calls are not exploitable. The first is typically achieved by establishing explicit rules (for example, by checking input with a regular expression) for what is acceptable and what is not. The process of sanitizing system calls is language-dependent. The trick is to always call external programs directly rather than going through a shell. Using Perl, this is accomplished by passing arguments to the external program as separate elements in a list rather than in one long string [2].

A related trick used by many hackers is to alter the PATH environment variable so it points to the program they want your script to execute, instead of the program you're expecting. This exploit can be easily subverted by invoking any programs called using full pathnames. If you have to rely on the PATH variable, get in the habit of explicitly setting it yourself at the beginning of the application [2].

A denial of service (DOS) attack occurs when an attacker makes repeated calls to one or more CGI applications. The Web server dutifully launches a CGI process and a child server process for each call. Eventually, if enough calls are made, the server runs out of system resources and comes to a grinding halt. Unfortunately, there's not a lot you can do to prevent a DOS attack beyond banning the host access to the server [2].

Later, this part of the chapter will discuss using a wrapper to limit the danger inherent in running CGI applications. Next, this part of the chapter details potential risks and solutions specific to Server Side Includes and CGI applications [2].

Securing Server Side Includes

Many Web administrators consider Server Side Includes (SSI) on a par with CGI applications when it comes to potential security risks. As noted in the preceding, any program or page that uses the exec command to call a system file presents a huge security problem if the call is made incorrectly. On the other hand, it's a remarkably simple process to disable all exec calls from an entire Web site, or allow exec calls to be made from a specific directory only [2].

A consideration administrators need to be aware of concerning SSI was briefly discussed earlier. It is not a good practice to allow SSI commands to be executed from pages with an .html or .htm file extension, especially on a high-traffic server. Remember, all SSI pages are parsed by the server. Poorly coded pages can consume system resources at an astonishing rate, and will eventually result in an unresponsive server. To avoid such a scenario, it is common practice to use a separate extension for SSI-enabled documents (typically, .shtml).

Reducing CGI Risks With Wrappers

Perfect system security is a lofty but unattainable goal. Securing any system is a dynamic process – checking for and applying operating system updates, program fixes and patches, scanning program revisions for desirable feature additions, reviewing user security and permissions, etc. When it comes to keeping a handle on CGI-related security issues, the very best solution is to not run any CGI applications at all. Unfortunately, such a course of action is rarely left to the same people tasked with actually securing the system. Administrators charged with maintaining a CGI-enabled server need to strike a careful balance: Users demand dynamic content capabilities, the potential danger inherent in CGI applications, and protecting systems that are typically exposed 24/7 to the "big bad world of the Internet [2]."

Ideally, in order to run a tight ship, every CGI application exposed to the public should be thoroughly checked by the system administrator or head developer for good coding practices and potentially dangerous system calls. Unfortunately, doing so often presents a two-fold problem: One, on a busy server, it severely strains administrative resources; and two, most system administrators often do not have time to stay current on a half-dozen different programming languages and administer their servers [2].

One common solution to reducing the risks inherent in CGI applications is to employ a wrapper program on the Web server. A wrapper allows CGI applications to be run under the user ID of the site owner – that is, the owner of the directories and documents that comprise a Web site. How does this increase system security? Simple. In a non-wrapper environment, CGI scripts are executed by the Web server user. This means the Web server user has to be a member of the same group as the site owner. It also means that anyone with a Web account on the server has the ability to execute a script in any other site directory on the server. Wrappering CGI applications restricts the damage a user can do to the user's files alone. As an added bonus, most CGI wrappers perform additional security checks before they allow a requested application to execute [2].

Although an understanding of HTTP is not strictly necessary for the development of CGI applications, some appreciation of "what's under the hood" and how hypertext documents are transferred, will certainly help you to develop them with more fluency and confidence. As with any field of endeavor, a grasp of the fundamental underlying principles allows you to visualize the structures and processes involved in the CGI transactions between clients and servers – giving you a more comprehensive mental model on which to base your programming [3].

Transferring Hypertext Documents with HTTP

Underlying the user interface represented by browsers, is the network and the protocols that travel the wires to the servers or "engines" that process requests, and return/transfer the various media. The protocol of the web is known as HTTP, for HyperText Transfer Protocol. HTTP is the underlying mechanism on which CGI operates, and it directly determines what you can and cannot send or receive via CGI [3].

HTTP Properties: A Comprehensive Addressing Scheme

The HTTP protocol uses the concept of reference provided by the Universal Resource Identifier (URI) as a location (URL) or name (URN), for indicating the resource on which a method is to be applied. When an HTML hyperlink is composed, the URL (Uniform Resource Locator) is of the general form http://host:port-number/path/file.html. More generally, a URL reference is of the type service://host/file.file-extension and in this way, the HTTP protocol can subsume the more basic Internet services [3].

HTTP is also used for communication between user agents and various gateways, allowing hypermedia access to existing Internet protocols like SMTP, NNTP, FTP, Gopher, and WAIS. HTTP is designed to allow communication with such gateways, via proxy servers, without any loss of the data conveyed by those earlier protocols [3].

Client-Server Architecture

The HTTP protocol is based on a request/response paradigm. The communication generally takes place over a TCP/IP connection on the Internet. The default port is 80, but other ports can be used. This does not preclude the HTTP protocol from being implemented on top of any other protocol on the Internet, so long as reliability can be guaranteed [3].

A requesting program (a client) establishes a connection with a receiving program (a server) and sends a request to the server in the form of a request method, URI, and protocol version, followed by a message containing request modifiers, client information, and possible body content. The server responds with a status line, including its protocol version and a success or error code, followed by a message containing server information, entity metainformation, and possible body content [3].

The HTTP Protocol Is Connectionless

Although it has just been established that the client makes a connection with a server, the protocol is called connectionless because once the single request has been satisfied, the connection is dropped. Other protocols typically keep the connection open (in an FTP session you can move around in remote directories, and the server keeps track of who you are, and where you are) [3].

While this greatly simplifies the server construction and relieves it of the performance penalties of session housekeeping, it makes the tracking of user behavior (navigation paths between local documents), impossible. Many, if not most, web documents consist of one or more inline images, and these must be retrieved individually, incurring the overhead of repeated connections [3].

The HTTP Protocol Is Stateless

After the server has responded to the client's request, the connection between client and server is dropped and forgotten. There is no "memory" between client connections. The pure HTTP server implementation treats every request as if it was brand-new (without context) [3].

CGI applications get around this by encoding the state or a state identifier in hidden fields, the path information, or URLs in the form being returned to the browser. The first two methods return the state or its id when the form is submitted back by the user. The method of encoding state into hyperlinks (URLs) in the form only returns the state (or id) if the user clicks on the link and the link is back to the originating server [3].

It's often advisable to not encode the whole state but to save it (in a file, and identify it by means of a unique identifier, such as a sequential integer). Visitor counter programs can be adapted very nicely for this – and thereby become useful. You then only have to send the state identifier in the form, which is advisable if the state vector becomes large – saving network traffic. However you then have to take care of housekeeping the state files (by periodic clean-up tasks) [3].

An Extensible And Open Representation For Data Types

HTTP uses Internet Media Types (formerly referred to as MIME Content-Types) to provide open and extensible data typing and type negotiation. For mail applications, where there is no type negotiation between sender and receiver, it's reasonable to put strict limits on the set of allowed media types. With HTTP, where the sender and recipient can communicate directly, applications are allowed more freedom in the use of non-registered types [3].

When the client sends a transaction to the server, headers are attached that conform to standard Internet e-mail specifications (RFC822). Most client requests expect an answer either in plain text or HTML. When the HTTP Server transmits information back to the client, it includes a MIME-like (Multipart Internet Mail Extension) header to inform the client what kind of data follows the header. Translation then depends on the client possessing the appropriate utility (image viewer, movie player, etc.) corresponding to that data type [3].

HTTP Header Fields

An HTTP transaction consists of a header followed optionally by an empty line and some data. The header will specify such things as the action required of the server, or the type of data being returned, or a status code. The use of header fields sent in HTTP transactions gives the protocol great flexibility. These fields allow descriptive information to be sent in the transaction, enabling authentication, encryption, and/or user identification. The header is a block of data preceding the actual data, and is often referred to as meta information, because it is information about information [3].

The header lines received from the client, if any, are placed by the server into the CGI environment variables with the prefix HTTP followed by the header name. Any characters in the header name are changed to characters. The server may exclude any headers which it has already processed, such as Authorization, Content-type, and Content-length. If necessary, the server may choose to exclude any or all of these headers if including them would exceed any system environment limits [3].

HTTP Methods

HTTP allows an open-ended set of methods to be used to indicate the purpose of a request. The three most often used methods are GET, HEAD, and POST [3].

The GET Method

The GET method is used to ask for a specific document – when you click on a hyperlink, GET is being used. GET should probably be used when a URL access will not change the state of a database (by, for example, adding or deleting information) and POST should be used when an access will cause a change. The semantics of the GET method changes to a "conditional GET" if the request message includes an If-Modified-Since header field. A conditional GET method requests that the identified resource be transferred only if it has been modified since the date given by the If-Modified-Since header. The conditional GET method is intended to reduce network usage by allowing cached entities to be refreshed without requiring multiple requests or transferring unnecessary data [3].

The HEAD Method

The HEAD method is used to ask only for information about a document, not for the document itself. HEAD is much faster than GET, as a much smaller amount of data is transferred. It's often used by clients who use caching, to see if the document has changed since it was last accessed. If it was not, then the local copy can be reused, otherwise the updated version must be retrieved with a GET. The metainformation contained in the HTTP headers in response to a HEAD request should be identical to the information sent in response to a GET request. This method can be used for obtaining metainformation about the resource identified by the request URI without transferring the data itself. This method is often used for testing hypertext links for validity, accessibility, and recent modification [3].

The POST Method

The POST method is used to transfer data from the client to the server. This method designed to allow a uniform method to cover functions like: annotation of existing resources; posting a message to a bulletin board, newsgroup, mailing list, or similar group of articles; providing a block of data (usually a form) to a data-handling process; and, extending a database through an append operation [3].

The HyperText Transfer Protocol: Next Generation

The essential simplicity of HTTP has been a major factor in its rapid adoption. But, this very simplicity has become its main drawback. The next generation of HTTP, dubbed "HTTP-NG", will be a replacement for HTTP with much higher performance, and adding some extra features needed for use in commercial applications. It's designed to make it easy to implement the basic functionality needed by all browsers, while making the addition of more powerful features such as security and authentication much simpler [3].

The current HTTP often causes performance problems on the server side, and on the network, since it sets up a new connection for every request. HTTP-NG divides up the connection (between client and server) into lots of different channels. Each object is returned over its own channel. HTTP-NG allows many different requests to be sent over a single connection. These requests are asynchronous – there's no need for the client to wait for a response before sending out a new request. The server can also respond to requests in any order it sees fit – it can even interweave the data from multiple objects, allowing several images to be transferred in "parallel" [3].

To make these multiple data streams easy to work with, HTTP-NG sends all its messages and data using a "session layer." This divides the connection up into lots of different channels. HTTP-NG sends all control messages (GET requests, meta-information, etc.) over a control channel. Each object is returned over in its own channel. This also makes redirection much more powerful – for example, if the object is a video the server can return the meta-information over the same connection, together with a URL pointing to a dedicated video transfer protocol that will fetch the data for the relevant object. This becomes very important when working with multimedia aware networking technologies, such as ATM or RSVP. The HTTP-NG protocol will permit complex data types such as video to redirect the URL to a video transfer protocol and only then will the data be fetched for the client [3].

Now, as businesses form closer relationships with customers and business partners, and as employee mobility grows, the Internet becomes an increasingly attractive medium for software distribution. Dynamic content technologies make the Internet (as well as Intranet and extranet) software distribution practical, while giving software developers, distributors, and users the options they need to secure software distribution in accordance with their requirements and preferences. It does so by adapting industry-standard technologies, originally developed to protect Web-based commerce, to the domain of software and dynamic content distribution across any IP-based network [4].

Like most aspects of the Internet, security is a dynamic field. Two prominent Internet security measures, firewalls and proxies, hardly existed 11 or 12 years ago. Now they are standard protection for corporate networks connected to the Internet. Recently, other mechanisms (public key encryption, digital signatures, digital certificates, and SSL) have begun to be used to secure Web-based commerce. This final part of the chapter describes these young security technologies and shows how dynamic content technologies have incorporated them into corporate networks, thus leading the way to secure software distribution [4].

DYNAMIC CONTENT TECHNOLOGIES

Internet security dynamic content technologies can be employed in combinations to satisfy a range of security needs. Those needs range from those that are recognized today; as well as, those that, due to changing business conditions or new developments on the Internet, will be discovered tomorrow [4].

Access Control

The first and most obvious security component is controlling access to the solution and to dynamic contents within the solution. There are three forms of access control that must be considered:

1. Administrative Access: Determines who can administrate the system.
2. Application Publishing Access: Determines who can publish applications (either for initial delivery, or updating, or for deletion) to manage.
3. Client Side Access to Applications: Determines who can download applications to use (if the administrator has decided the user can the ability to determine whether or not they run the application) [4].

Access control for any of these forms of access is provided by user authentication. The default authentication mechanism is a challenge/response authentication scheme using a username/password combination. In situations where stronger authentication is desired, client-side certificate-based authentication is also supported [4].

Multiple implementation mechanisms are available to determine the user profile information. A dynamic content list of usernames and passwords can be created with a graphical editor. Or, the usernames and passwords can be imported from an existing username/password file that's stored in the LDIF format (produced by Lightweight Directory Access Protocol (LDAP) implementations). Or, a custom authentication extension can be used to integrate into an existing user directory data store used for authentication; this can be NT Domains, Active Directory, LDAP, or an RDBMS [4].

Transport: Firewall Friendly

Firewalls were some of the first security specific technologies developed to address a unique threat that the Internet introduced: breaking into corporate networks that were attached to the Internet. Equivalent to a common burglary, hackers or crackers break into private networks attached to the Internet and vandalize or steal contents. For most companies, a firewall acts as their first line of defense against network break-ins. Corporations using the Internet to distribute and manage applications to their extended enterprise, to business partners and to customers will need a solution that is firewall friendly. This means that the communication protocols can be tracked and protected by commonly available firewalls. Solutions designed for Intranet or LAN only use often relies on proprietary protocols or heavyweight protocols that dynamically open communication ports cannot be protected or are very difficult to protect with a firewall [4].

Internet security dynamic content use the language of the web (HTTP and HTTP-S) as its' primary means of communications. This provides corporations with the following key benefits:

- Reduce network security concerns by requiring only two or three additional open ports on the network. Using HTTP means that all communications sessions can travel through the same port that a corporations' daily web activity travels through.

- Integrate with current network security architecture. Utilizing the same port as web traffic means that there are fewer security architecture modifications to consider [4].

Protect Data Transmission Using Secure Sockets Layer (SSL)

SSL (see sidebar, "SSL'), provides data encryption and data integrity so that data transmissions are protected against eavesdroppers, man-in-the-middle attack, spoofing, or any other sort of tampering or acquisition of information during transmission. SSL provides two important security mechanisms: data encryption to scramble data into information that is unreadable to unintended audiences; and, data integrity to verify that the data being transmitted was sent by a "trusted" source. Both of these mechanisms are provided using digital certificates issued by a Certificate Authority (CA) that binds the identity of a distinguished bit string (certificate) to an individual or entity (like a corporation) [4]. See sidebar, "Certificate Authority".

Secure Sockets Layer (SSL)

Secure Sockets Layer was originally developed by Netscape Communications. SSL has rapidly become the standard mechanism to secure communication between endpoints on the Internet by combining encryption and digital certificates to provide both data authentication and confidentiality. SSL is readily available in most Internet browsers and is easily integrated into today's distributed applications [4].

When SSL is deployed in an application, the SSL client will initiate contact with the server without any encryption. Once the connection has been established, the server authenticates itself by presenting a certificate to the client and answering a challenge from the client based upon that certificate. As an option, the SSL server may require the client to authenticate itself, by presenting a certificate. If the client accepts the server certificate, the two automatically negotiate a private key encryption algorithm. To encrypt the session traffic, the client then encrypts the symmetric key with the server's session key (obtained from the server certificate) and returns it to the server [4].

The symmetric key encryption algorithm established between the client and the server is used to protect messages transmitted during the remainder of the connection. The encrypted messages also carry a message digest that each side will check in order to authenticate that the messages have not been altered in transmission. SSL allows for different ciphers to be used in operations such as authenticating client and server to each other and establishing session keys [4] [7].

Certificate Authority

Digital certificates are issued and managed by impartial third parties known as Certificate Authorities (CA). To obtain a certificate, an applicant presents proof of identity along with a public key to the CA. The CA verifies the applicant's identity, then issues a certificate that has been signed with the CA's private key [4].

A certificate authority may issue several types of certificates with each type of certificate providing a different level of identity checking. For example, a certificate for an individual is typically inexpensive and minimally researched. A certificate for a server or host machine is more expensive and more thoroughly researched. Finally, a certificate for a software-signing certificate is even more carefully checked [4] [7].

Encryption

Encryption is the foundation of secure message transmission in an open medium like the Internet. To encrypt a message means to make it secret by scrambling it into what is known as cipher text. Cipher text is useless gibberish to anyone who reads it; therefore an encrypted message can be exposed without revealing its true content. A message is encrypted with a fixed algorithm and a variable called a key. The longer an encryption key, the more powerful the encryption algorithm and the harder the keys are to crack. Encryption algorithms can vary in length from 32 bits up to 1024 bits; algorithms stronger than 40 bits are commonly referred to as strong encryption. The combination of encryption, decryption and the participants combine to form a crypto system [4].

Data Integrity

Using a digital signature allows both senders and receivers to ensure that the messages being sent are in their authentic form. But what if somehow an imposter has inserted himself in the middle and is using the digital signature to send messages to an unsuspecting receiver. To combat this problem, another form of digital technology (known as digital certificates) is used to authenticate user identity. A digital certificate is a unique data structure that cannot be forged and binds a subject (person or company) and a public key. A digital certificate states that: The public key in this certificate belongs to the subject named in this certificate; and, the private key partner of the public key in this certificate also belongs to the subject named in this certificate [4].

If a receiver can correctly decrypt a message with the public key listed in a certificate, then the sender of that message must be the person holding the private key that matches the public key. Implicit in all assumptions about the security of a certificate is that the private key has not been compromised [4].

Tip: The preceding statement is true so long as the certificate subject safeguards its private key.

Application Authentication

Application authentication is a means of providing an end user with some assurance that the application is a valid and trusted source of information. Authenticating an application has been brought on by the fact that hackers have the ability to "hijack" an Internet address and the subsequent application and convince an unknowing user that the false address is valid. Application authentication is especially important if users are not familiar with the application developer and they are accessing the application across the Internet [4].

How Application Authentication Works

The process by which an application is authenticated is commonly referred to as *code signing*. The primary mechanism for performing application verification is done through the use of digital signatures (hence the term code signing). A digital signature is a unique, mathematical value that summarizes a message and is then encrypted. The signature is then appended to the original message and sent to the recipient. The message recipient also summarizes the message then decrypts the sender summary, and performs a mathematical comparison. If the comparison does not match, then the recipient will know that the message has been tampered with [4].

Trusted Channels Can Do More

A channel can be either *untrusted* or *trusted*. Untrusted channels are prevented from performing potentially dangerous operations, such as writing over a user file. By default, a channel is untrusted and prohibits these potentially harmful operations:

- Reading or writing the file system, except for a single directory.
- Connecting to any network host except the one from which it was downloaded; this prevents untrusted channels from unauthorized acquisition or disclosure of information.
- Calling non-Java code, which could perform insecure operations outside the control of the security manager. As a result, users can download a channel written by an unknown developer without worrying that the channel will damage or reveal information [4].

Finally, a developer who creates a channel that needs these capabilities must have a channel "trusted by the user." For example, a scheduling channel may need to connect to machines on the local network to check the schedules of colleagues invited to a meeting. Or a financial analysis channel may need to execute a CPU-intensive algorithm that's written in C. A channel that's designated as trusted is signed by applying a digital signature to the channel. This ensures its integrity and reliably informs prospective users of the channel developer's identity. Once a channel is granted the trusted status, the channel can run without constraint and is able to perform any capabilities in the system, like any application you would buy commercially and install manually. Several things are required to run a trusted channel carefully checked: the channel was designated as trusted by the publisher, signing it with a digital signature; and, the channel's digital signature matches a set designated as trusted by the user (by inspecting the certificate that comes with the trusted channel) [4]. When the a channel that's designated as trusted is launched, it:

- Displays a warning that the channel needs capabilities not permitted to untrusted channels
- Lists the capabilities the channel needs
- Offers to show the channel's certificate
- Asks the user to grant or deny permission [4]

SUMMARY AND CONCLUSIONS

Industrial Websites, like many commercial ones, are viewed at different times by disparate users with differing preferences for data organization, display, and access methods. Forcing the data's origin server to accommodate all possible modes and preferences of access unnecessarily burdens the Web server, increases network traffic, increases the number of versions of the database maintained, increases system complexity, and forces multiple servers to implement redundant services. The OPES concept regularizes the architecture by encouraging modularity, uniformity, adherence to standards, security, and compartmentalization of knowledge [1].

NetEdge implements a set of useful services (language translation, media independence, image transcoding) and yet provides a general framework whereby any vendor with a useful service may offer it to the user community. Standard Internet security protocols are used throughout, and the security of the services offered and the identity of their authors are assured through modern encryption and digital signature techniques. All data are passed in industry-standard XML format to permit computers to understand the semantics; as well as, the values, of the information being exchanged [1].

This chapter also discussed securing dynamic content on a Web server. Topics included security considerations that apply to all dynamic content in general, Server Side Includes, Common Gateway Interface, and two ways to wrapper CGI content. While an exhaustive discussion of securing all forms of dynamic content is beyond the scope of this chapter, hopefully this chapter has provided a basic understanding of where the most common security holes lie, and how to address them [2].

Finally, this chapter covered an array of security features that companies can selectively utilize to protect their businesses, their software, and their customers and partners. By using Internet security products for software and dynamic content distribution, companies are also positioned to respond immediately to new security requirements, whether caused by changing business conditions, altered public perceptions, or the ever-evolving Internet [4].

REFERENCES

[1] Alfred C. Weaver and Michael W. Condry. "Distributing Internet Services to the Network's Edge," IEEE Transactions In Industrial Electronics, © Copyright 2003, IEEE, IEEE Corporate Office, 3 Park Avenue, 17th Floor, New York, New York, 10016-5997 U.S.A., Vol. 50, No. 3, pp. 80-85, June, 2003.

[2] Tom Syroid. "Web Server Security," © Copyright 2002, IBM Corporation, 1133 Westchester Avenue White Plains, New York 10604 United States, September 1, 2002.

[3] "HyperText Transfer Protocol," Copyright 2006 Jupitermedia Corporation All Rights Reserved. Jupitermedia Headquarters, 23 Old Kings Highway South, Darien, CT 06820, 2006.

[4] "Marimba Desktop/Mobile Change Management Security Concepts," Copyright © 2003 Marimba, Inc. All Right Reserved. Marimba Inc., 440 Clyde Ave., Mountain View, CA. 94043, 2003.

[5] John R. Vacca, Guide to Wireless Network Security, Springer, 2006.

[6] John R. Vacca, Net Privacy: A Guide to Developing and Implementing an Ironclad ebusiness Privacy Plan, McGraw-Hill, 2001.

[7] John R. Vacca, Public Key Infrastructure: Building Trusted Applications and Web Servicess, Auerbach Publications, 2004.

[8] John R. Vacca, Firewalls: Jumpstart for Network and Systems Administrators, Digital Press, 2004.

Chapter 2

BASIC SECURITY ISSUES

INTRODUCTION

Internet security is a contradiction in terms, like the classic references to Alaskan Crab and the National Security Agency. True security can only be achieved when the information is isolated, locked in a safe, surrounded by guards, dogs and fences, and rendered inaccessible. Some would argue that even then, there is not absolute security. It simply is not possible, therefore, to render a network system completely secure, and anyone who wishes to understand and apply the principles of security to the Internet or any other network, must first understand and accept this basic tenet in order to be successful. In spite of this, managers of network systems must strive to attain this unreachable goal simultaneously [1].

The reason behind this often frustrating dilemma lies in the motivations for the development of networks. Networks were created as a remedy to the problem of data isolation in the early days of computing. "Islands of Automation" were a hindrance to conducting business successfully because critical information required by one "island" could not be accessed by others. Networks became the communication bridges by which these islands could be integrated. Since security and privacy [2] are the antithesis of sharing and distribution, Internet security must become a balance between providing appropriate access to those who need the information and safeguarding that information by denying access to those not authorized. This is all done while assuming some level of risk, which is appropriate to the sensitivity of the information that is to be guarded [1].

This is not intended to imply that Internet security is not necessary, nor that management should not strive for it. On the contrary, the explosion of information across the networks in this country and in the world has raised the specter of corporate espionage to new heights. Corporations today know that in the information age, information is power; and, those organizations which control their information appropriately, can gain a competitive advantage: those who do not are vulnerable to losing valuable trade secrets to competitive spies [1].

Equally dangerous is the possibility of loss of information or compromising that information due to acts of sabotage, such as from disgruntled employees. As employees become more mobile, and as they demand more information while they are on the road, the vulnerabilities of compromised information become more severe by an enterprise's own employees [1].

Within this perplexing situation, managers must navigate between the risks of losing information so necessary to the enterprise's operation and the costs and constraints associated with an overly aggressive security solution. This chapter is intended to help management successfully navigate this course by providing an overview of security principles and the technologies which are appropriate for securing the Internet and networks today [1].

INTERNET AND NETWORK SECURITY ISSUES:
BASIC SECURITY CONCEPTS

A good place to begin is by defining the basic concepts involved in securing any object. The key words in the security lexicon are vulnerability, threat, attack, and countermeasure. An examination of each follows [1].

Vulnerability is the susceptibility of a situation to being compromised. It is a potential, a possibility, a weakness, an opening. A vulnerability in and of itself may or may not pose a serious problem, depending on what tools are available to exploit that weakness. The classic definition of vulnerability comes from Greek Mythology, with the story of Achilles, whose heel represented his greatest vulnerability [1].

A threat is an action or tool which can exploit and expose a vulnerability and therefore compromise the integrity of a given system. Not all threats are equal in terms of their ability to expose and exploit the vulnerability. For example, the Microsoft Concept virus exploits a vulnerability in Word Macros allowing access to the users' file system, but the virus itself is relatively benign. Other similar viruses could do a lot more damage [1].

An attack defines the details of how a particular threat could be used to exploit a vulnerability. It is entirely possible that situations could exist where vulnerabilities are known and threats are developed, but no reasonable attack can be conceived to use the specific threat upon a vulnerability of the system. An example of an attack is a Trojan Horse attack, where a destructive tool such as a virus is packaged within a seemingly desirable object, like a piece of free software [1].

Countermeasures are those actions taken to protect systems from attacks which threaten specific vulnerabilities. Achilles covered his heel with a protective metal plate as a countermeasure to potential attacks to his one vulnerability. In the Internet security world, countermeasures consist of tools such as virus detection and cleansing, packet filtering, password authentication, and encryption [1].

Any security scheme must identify vulnerabilities and threats, anticipate potential attacks, assess whether they are likely to succeed or not, assess what the potential damage might be from successful attacks, and then implement countermeasures against those defined attacks which are deemed to be significant enough to counter. Therefore, you can see that security is all about identifying and managing risk, and that security is a very relative concept which must be tailored to the needs, budget, and culture of each organization. For example, a Trojan Horse attack on one organization could succeed easily and compromise extremely important information. The same attack on another organization would only result in minimal damage, perhaps because there is no sensitive data available on that particular system. Furthermore, companies have personalities just as people do, and therefore, some companies are willing to live with more risk than others. In each of these organizations, different security schemes will be employed with different countermeasures to suit their specific situations [1].

As will be discussed later, management must consider all of these factors in defining a security strategy. Management must also consider the cost of protecting against all possible attacks. Security costs money, and each organization must determine how much it will cost to institute appropriate countermeasures. Only then can an organization truly determine which of the possible spectrum of attacks should be defended, and which should be ignored [1].

Generic Internet Security Threats

In any organization, there are a number of generic security threats which must be dealt with. These include the theft of information, the compromising or corruption of information, loss of confidentiality, and the disruption of service [1].

One of the major threats which companies are dealing with is the introduction of malicious programs over the network. The term "computer virus" has been used loosely to categorize these attacks which come in Trojan Horses, worms, and logic bombs as well as true viruses [1].

A Trojan Horse is a program that conceals harmful code. It usually disguises itself as an attractive or useful program which lures users to execute it, and in doing so, damages the user's system. For example, a posting in the US Department of Energy Computer Advisory Capability page lists a known Trojan Horse in a program called AOL4FREE. While the title suggests that this program will allow you to participate in AOL without any costs, running the program will delete all of the files on your hard disk. The program hidden in the Trojan Horse can be one which causes malicious damage, or one which performs some espionage for the attacker, such as stealing the password file from the computer it invades [1].

A logic bomb is code that checks for certain conditions and when these conditions are met, it "detonates" to do its damage. Sometimes, like the Magellan virus, the trigger logic is a date, but it can be any given set of parameters, including a person's name, a bank account number, or some combination of events and parameters [1].

A worm is a self contained program which replicates itself across the network. Therefore, it multiplies its damage by infecting many different nodes [1].

A virus is code which plants a version of itself in any program it can modify. The Microsoft Concept virus is a good example: once it has "infected" Microsoft Word, all subsequent documents which are opened by the user may only be saved as template files. In all other respects, Microsoft Word continues to operate normally [1].

> **Note:** These are not mutually exclusive threats. A logic bomb could plant a virus under the specified conditions, as could a Trojan Horse deliver a worm.

Furthermore, each of these threats could have different or multiple missions. These could be the theft of data, the compromising of confidentiality, integrity or availability, or the disruption of service to the organization [1].

In addition to planting computer programs which could create these effects, there are also threats which involve the theft or compromise of information while it is in transit between endpoints of a network. One such example is called Snooping, in which an attacker simply eavesdrops on electronic communications [1].

These are the classes of threats that today's network managers must deal with, and that senior management must be aware of, since they will play a major part in determining the appropriate and tolerable cost of security to counteract these potential threats [1].

Internet Security Countermeasures

Given the preceding scenario, a reasonable question at this point might be: "What tools are available today to help mitigate the consequences of these security threats on the network?" The good news is that there are multiple technologies which can be brought to bear on the issues, and they are impressively effective [1].

Internet Security Policy

The bad news is that no amount of technology can overcome a poorly planned, poorly implemented or nonexistent Internet security policy. Consider the following story witnessed by a poster on a security newsgroup on the Internet: A customer being waited on at a public service agency (say a Registry of Motor Vehicles) requires some information from the clerk – who in turn, needs to access that information from a workstation centrally located in the area behind the window. Sitting at the workstation, the clerk yells to a co-worker "Dee, is the password still ...? [1]"

Again, the security of any information in any organization today is primarily dependent on the quality of the Internet security policy and the processes by which that organization imposes on itself. If the security procedures are lax, are not enforced uniformly, and allow gaping security holes to exist, no amount of technology will restore the security breaches. Organizations that are concerned about security on the Internet should ask themselves a few of the following questions before worrying about encryption, packet filtering, proxy servers, and other related technology solutions:

- Does the corporate policy allow passwords such as "password", employee initials, or names or initials of employees' immediate family members?
- Is there a process in place to change passwords periodically?
- Do employees keep their password written on paper under their mousepads, keyboards, monitors, etc.?
- Is there a program in place to make employees aware of the need for security and to disseminate security procedures to the employees to facilitate its implementation?
- Do employees understand the different levels of security of information and what techniques to apply to each to ensure an appropriate level of protection?

- Is the responsibility for information security assigned to a senior member of the management team, who is held accountable for maintaining appropriate security?
- Is there a set of guidelines to identify the security classification of different documents and information generated by the employees?
- Is there a process in place to classify or categorize these documents and information and secure them appropriately [1]?

It should be self evident at this point that the primary need for any organization is to get its own house in order, identify its security needs based on the types of information with which it deals and develop a security policy and plan before committing to technology. The following are some elements of a good security plan:

- Develop security requirements based on an analysis of the organization's mission, the information at risk, the threats to that information and the implications of any successful attacks.
- Appoint a security officer and delineate clearly the required job responsibilities and skills.
- Define appropriate security services and mechanisms and allocate them to components of the company's IT systems.
- Identify different measures of security appropriate for each level.
- Remember that security is not only technology; physical security and procedural security are as important as the technology used.
- Identify users who should have access to each level of security [1].

Authentication

A primary tool in securing any computer system is the ability to recognize and verify the identity of users. This security feature is known as authentication. Traditionally, special names and secret passwords have been used to authenticate users, but as the anecdote in the preceding demonstrates, the password is only as good as the users' ability to keep it secret and protect it from being abused by unauthorized users [1]. There are three generally accepted techniques for authenticating users to host machines:

1. Authentication by something the user knows
2. Authentication by something the user has
3. Authentication by physical characteristics [1]

Authentication By Something The User Knows

Authentication by something the user knows is the password/username concept described in the preceding. There are two common approaches to password authentication, known as PAP and CHAP. PAP, which stands for Password Authentication Protocol, simply asks the requester to provide a "secret" password, and if the password provided is included in the user profiles, the requester is given access. CHAP (Challenge Handshake Authentication Protocol) takes the concept one step further by challenging the requester to encrypt a response to the challenge message. This, in effect, acts as a different password for each entry. Often, the CHAP mechanism is combined with an encrypting smart card, which uses an encryption key to encode the challenge message. Only if the challenge message is correct will the requester be granted access to the system [1].

Authentication By Something The User Has

In the authentication by something the user has technique, the user is given some kind of token, such as a magnetic stripe card, key. In other sophisticated cases such as the remote access standard RADIUS (which will be discussed later), the user has a smart card equipped with a computer chip which can generate an encrypted code back to the computer system [1].

Authentication By Physical Characteristics

Here, the mechanism is to recognize some measure of the individual which ostensibly cannot be duplicated. Biometric techniques such as fingerprint ID, palm print ID, retinal scan, manual and digital signature, or voice recognition are used to validate the identity of the potential user.

Authentication is also necessary when two computers communicate with each other. For example, what should your host computer do when another computer asks to have a disk mounted which contains all of your organization's personnel data? How do you know that the requesting computer has a legitimate reason to access that information, and that it is not some external network hacker trying to steal information from your organization? In order to prevent such events, the Internet Engineering Task Force (IETF) has formed a working group by the name of IPSec (Internet Protocol Security). Additionally, there are a number of de facto standards – those which are developed by companies rather than by official committees, but which enjoy widespread acceptance. While many of these standards are under review and take some time to work their way through the approval process, two are worthy of mention here, IPSec's SKIP (Simple Key Management for Internet Protocol) and Livingston's RADIUS (Remote Authentication Dial In User Service) [1].

SKIP is a technique for providing authentication and encryption security at the IP layer of the Internet architecture. It relies on the existence of an authority in the network which can issue a certificate [3] to known trusted entities within the system. If an entity claiming to be a member of the system requests an action, the receiving computer system can have the requester present an encrypted certification that they are who they say they are. The certificate conforms to one of the methods of authentication, namely, a secret encoding technique and a secret key which are only available to trusted members of the system. The fact that SKIP operates at the very lowest protocol layers of the architecture, it has the advantage of protecting all upstream applications as well, by preventing connections between systems which are not authorized. Since potential intruders cannot even establish connections, their ability to do malicious damage is severely restricted [1].

In Fig. 2-1, the Requesting Entity first gains a certificate by requesting one from the trusted certification authority (1), who validates the trustworthiness of the Requester by granting a certificate (2) [1]. Armed with this certificate, the Requester can now petition the host and presents the certificate along with the request of the host (3). The host, upon seeing the certificate will grant the information to the requester (4).

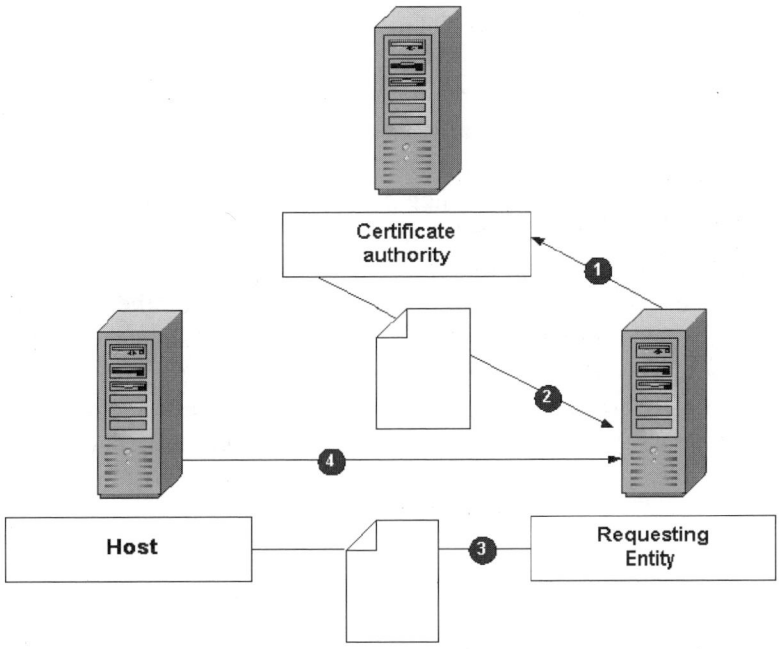

Figure 2-1. How to gain a certificate.

RADIUS is one of the more popular public network authentication protocols. The primary purpose of RADIUS is to offer centralized access control for remote dial-in users. RADIUS simplifies the administration of passwords, user names, profiles for remote users, and other security and accounting related information by placing all of the security in a central server, and issuing challenges to the user [1].

Privacy

A perpetrator may observe confidential data as it traverses the Internet. This ability is probably the largest inhibitor of business-to-business communications today. Without encryption, every message sent may be read by an unauthorized party.

Today, intruders continue to install packet sniffers on root-compromised systems. These sniffers are used to collect account names and passwords, and are frequently installed as part of a widely available kit that also replaces common system files with Trojan horse programs. These kits provide cookbook directions that even a novice or unskilled intruder could use to compromise systems.

Virtual Private Networks

The Internet Community is constantly seeking new and better mechanisms to secure the Internet. Today, there are several other relevant proposals for standards which are under review by the Internet Engineering Task Force (IETF). One proposal which is generating some potential interest is the Level 2 Tunneling Protocol (L2TP), which is under review as part of the IPSec group within the IETF. This proposal would establish a set of protocols by which compliant Internet components could create their own channel inside the Internet. This channel would be protected by authentication and encryption countermeasures. These would ensure that even though the traffic is being transmitted over the public Internet, individual sessions can be established which are private to those members allowed to work within that channel. The technology is known as tunneling because the correspondents are creating a tunnel of sorts through the public packets inhabiting the Internet, and exchanging very private communications within them. The concept comes from medieval times, where tunnels were built between fortified towns and castles to allow their inhabitants to move safely between them away from the dangers of the bands of marauders outside their gates [1].

The use of tunneling technology allows another concept to be implemented: the concept of a Virtual Private Network, or VPN. Companies who want a less expensive alternative to private Wide Area Networks can utilize tunneling within the Internet and develop their own virtual WANs, safe from unwanted intrusions, yet riding on the cost benefits of the Internet mass volumes [1].

Non Repudiation

This security concept protects against the sender or receiver denying that they sent or received certain communications. For example, when a person sends a certified or registered letter via the United States Postal Service (USPS), the recipient is supposed to prove his or her identity to the delivery person, and then confirm their receipt by signing a form. The signed form is then returned to the sender, which proves to the sender that their correspondence was delivered. This prevents the recipient (for example a debtor) from claiming that they never received the correspondence (for example a demand note) and therefore using that as an excuse for their actions (not paying the debt). In computer networks, these kinds of services are also available, and are becoming increasingly valuable as commerce on the Internet continues to gain in popularity [1]. There are three different types of non-repudiation services that are applicable in computer network messaging:

1. Non-repudiation of Delivery Service.
2. Non-repudiation of Origin Service.
3. Non-repudiation of Submission Service [1].

Non-repudiation of Delivery Service is similar to the US Post office certified mail example in the preceding. This provides the sender with proof that a message was successfully delivered to the intended recipient. Many e-mail packages offer senders the option to request a return receipt. This return receipt provides the sender with a non-repudiation of delivery service feature – the recipient can't legitimately claim they did not receive the message [1].

Non-repudiation of Origin of Service provides the recipient with proof of who originated the message and what it contains. For example, according to a usenet posting, America Online (AOL) was victimized by crackers pretending to be AOL employees and requesting passwords and credit card information from subscribers. In other words, a particular cracker armed with an AOL hacker program created a fake screen to pass himself off as an AOL employee and steal the AOL user's password. Non Repudiation of Origin of Service could have foiled this kind of attack if it had been available to AOL subscribers. If it had been available, users could have verified that the crackers were not genuinely AOL employees, and therefore would not have given away their passwords [1].

Non-repudiation of Submission Service is similar to the concept of non repudiation of delivery. This service offers proof that a given message was in fact sent from a particular sender. If you go back to the US Post Office example, when you mail important papers such as legal documents, it is considered prudent to send them via registered mail. When you do so, you get a receipt from the Postal Service and a special identification number is affixed to the return. Thus, if the recipient does not receive the documents, or contends that it was not sent on time, you have evidence that your submission did occur at a particular time [1].

Integrity

Integrity refers to the completeness and fidelity of the message as it passes through the network. The key here is making sure that the data passes from the source to the destination without undetected alteration [1].

> **Note:** The use of the word "undetected" is important here. You may not be able to thwart someone from tapping out messages and attempting to modify them as they move through the network, but you will be able to detect any attempt at modification and therefore reject the message if such a modification attempt is detectable.

If the order of transmitted data also is ensured, the service is termed connection-oriented integrity. The term anti-replay refers to a minimal form of connection-oriented integrity designed to detect and reject duplicated or very old data units [1].

Confidentiality

Confidentiality is a security property that ensures that data is disclosed only to those authorized to use it, and that it is not disclosed to unauthorized parties. The key point behind ensuring the confidentiality of information on the network is to deny information to anyone who is not specifically authorized to see it or use it. Encryption is a frequently used mechanism for guaranteeing confidentiality, since only those recipients who have access to the decrypting key are able to decode the messages. Confidentiality therefore equates to privacy [1].

Access Control

Finally, the access control concept relates to the accepting or rejecting of a particular requester to have access to some service or data in any given system. A service could be a program, a device such as a printer or a file system, and data could be a text file, an image, a collection of files, or any combination of the above. The real question is, what are the risks involved in allowing access to any of the system's services or information to individuals requesting such access? In some cases, such as the advertising Web page of an organization, the answer is that no damage could occur. The objective of such a page is precisely to spread the word about the organization, and therefore access control is not an issue. On the other hand, access control is a major issue if someone requests access to the file which contains the passwords for all of the users of the system. It is therefore necessary to define a set of access rights, privileges, and authorizations, and assign these to appropriate people within the domain of the system under analysis [1].

SUMMARY AND CONCLUSIONS

Okay, so now you've covered all of the building blocks and some examples of how they might go together. The question still might be on your mind: What should the organization do to be secure. The answer is "it depends." It depends on specific security needs and budget limitations of your organization. Very few enterprises, not even the Federal Government and the Military, can afford "security at any price." Eventually, you will be forced to stop building security features and learn to live with the residual risks of your system. Where you stop depends on how much you are willing to pay to get the amount of security appropriate to your application [1].

One typical and common sense approach is to develop a security infrastructure incrementally. Start inexpensively with packet filtering and authenticating routers as the beginning firewall [4]. Many industry analysts contend that over 90% of attacks can be successfully defended by integrated routers and firewalls. Later, if you still need more, you can add encryption and key management for further enhancements. At each point, determine where your vulnerabilities are, what the potential attacks might be, and what consequences would ensue from a successful attack. Many people find that the use of simple and inexpensive packet filtering and authentication, "move their dots" into the lower left hand quadrant of the likelihood/consequence space, and they have no further need to add more sophisticated measures. Certainly, if more is required, and the cost implications are warranted, customers can move into application coupled systems to further enhance the security. The ultimate move, of course, is to go to private networks, where one eliminates the physical connection to the network from potential hackers. Finally, use the services of agencies such as the National Computer Security Agency (NCSA) and ISS, which offer security audits of sites to help you determine vulnerabilities and countermeasures, and help you decide whether the risks facing your operations warrant further expenditures of time and money [1].

REFERENCES

[1] "Internet Security Primer," copyright 2003/2004 ZZZ Online, ZZZ Online, 2004.
[2] John R. Vacca, Net Privacy: A Guide to Developing and Implementing an Ironclad ebusiness Privacy Plan, McGraw-Hill, 2001.
[3] John R. Vacca, Public Key Infrastructure: Building Trusted Applications and Web Servicess, Auerbach Publications, 2004.
[4] John R. Vacca, Firewalls: Jumpstart for Network and Systems Administrators, Digital Press, 2004.

PART II

ESTABLISHING YOUR ORGANIZATION'S SECURITY

Chapter 3

REAL THREATS THAT IMPACT SECURITY

INTRODUCTION

The Internet provides a wonderful means of exchanging information, but no one wants sensitive information on their computers to be stolen or destroyed. Hackers and worms are constantly on the lookout for computers with security vulnerabilities connected to the Internet. Unfortunately, whether it's due to a lack of knowledge, tight budget, or sheer laziness, too many of you don't protect your own data [1].

COMMON HACKER EXPLOITS

Once a hacker finds a computer with open ports they probe further to see if the software behind each open port contains buffer overflows, outdated software or misconfigurations. If a hacker finds one of these vulnerabilities they may attack your computer. Here is a partial list of the things a hacker could do to your computer if it has vulnerabilities:

1. View Your Passwords
2. Watch Everything You Do
3. Install a Zombie
4. Copy Files From Your Hard Drive
5. Copy Files To Your Hard Drive [1]

View Your Passwords

If a hacker has access to your computer they may have access to files stored on your computer where passwords are kept. Sometimes passwords are stored in normal text and sometimes they are encrypted. Either way, a hacker can probably crack the passwords you use on your system so they can continue to access your computer [1].

If you access your enterprise's network from home then this becomes especially dangerous. The passwords you type to access your enterprise's network may be stored on your home PC. A hacker may be able to break into your enterprise's network because your home PC was not secure [1].

Watch Everything You Do

If a hacker installs remote control software then you are no longer safe. Remote control software allows a hacker to view everything on your computer as you do. If you view your personal banking information on your computer then so does the hacker. Also, remote control software allows a hacker to record keystrokes typed into your computer. So your passwords are no longer safe and should be changed [1].

Install A Zombie

Zombie software allows a hacker to make your computer attack other computers on the Internet. Once Zombie software is installed on your computer you will not know it is running. If Zombie software were installed on your computer right now you could be attacking the website of a large enterprise. The enterprise will trace the attack back to your computer and you will plead ignorance. In European countries you are now liable for damages to others if a hacker is using your computer for attack purposes [1].

Copy Files From Your Hard Drive

If you have network shares set to READ for the group EVERYONE then a hacker may be able to copy your data. If you have personal accounting data or confidential files on your computer then a hacker may have already copied that data. Accounting software, word processing, spreadsheet, and most applications don't use good password encryption schemes. Most passwords for these applications can be cracked easily [1].

Copy Files To Your Hard Drive

If you have network shares set to READ/WRITE for the group EVERYONE then a hacker may be able to copy files to your computer. Why is that a problem? This is how hackers install remote control software. Or they may decide to copy viruses to your computer, or ruin the configuration of your computer, or store pornographic material for later browsing or whatever [1].

VULNERABILITY DETECTION

What makes a computer vulnerable to hackers and worms? Whenever a computer starts a program that program uses a port. Each port has a number from 0 to 65,535. For example, most web servers listen on port 80. When you connect to a web server your web browser is really connecting to port 80 on that server [1].

Every program running on your computer opens a port and almost all programs have known vulnerabilities. Hackers and worms try to break into your computer by attacking your computer ports. Therefore, it is recommended that you turn off all unnecessary programs or services on your computer [1].

Sometimes you need to run programs on your computer and you can't simply turn them off. This is when firewalls come into play [3]. Firewalls filter all ports on your computer. This stops everyone from accessing your ports while allowing you to run as many programs as you want [1].

Sounds great!? The problem is that firewalls will often stop certain programs from running properly. Some programs will not function if their ports are blocked. A good example is web server software. If a web server is using a firewall and all access to port 80 is blocked then no one can connect to its web server. The system administrator would then open port 80 so the web server would function properly [1].

Even if you are using a firewall, a port that is open and accessible by others may have security weaknesses. A firewall doesn't provide any protection for open ports. An attacker doesn't care if you are using a firewall as long as your ports are open. And to make matters worse, many firewalls themselves have vulnerabilities since they are programs running on your computer or a device in front of your computer. See BugTraq (http://www.securityfocus.com/archive/1) for a list of vulnerabilities for any firewall, application or operating system [1].

So what can you do if you must have some open ports on your computer? The best solution is to test for vulnerabilities on your computer and see if any weaknesses are detected. Then apply the security patches provided from the vendor. This keeps your computer safe from attackers while allowing you to run the programs you desire [1].

WHAT YOUR ISP ISN'T TELLING YOU

There are many Internet Service Providers (ISPs) to choose from. Each ISP has its own customer security policies. Many ISP's do not provide their customers adequate Internet security [1].

SOFTWARE PATCHING

Misconfigured, buggy, and outdated software can all compromise your computer security. Software vendors regularly release buggy software and then issue downloadable patches (or updates) later on. It is up to the home user (or IT administrators) to regularly apply new security patches [1].

One of the most common methods for hackers and worms to gain access to a computer is by exploiting known problems in software for which patches exist. For example, Microsoft released many patches for Internet Information Server (IIS; a web server program) months or even years before the "Code Red" and "NIMDA" worms appeared. Anyone who had downloaded the patches earlier was not affected by either of these worms [1].

Achieving and maintaining computer security is a process not an event. It is recommended that frequent checks and application of security patches be made to keep your computer secure [1].

But, even after implementing the above intrusion prevention systems, is your enterprise really safe from Internet security threats? Not really!

The problem still is that spyware, viruses and hacker attacks can be devastating to small enterprises. Here's how to protect your enterprise from internet security threats [1].

ARE YOU AT RISK FROM INTERNET SECURITY THREATS?

Many small-enterprise owners assume that large enterprises are far more vulnerable to Internet security threats than they are. In truth, however, it's often the other way around. For example, the destructive Mydoom worm affected one out of three small and mid-sized enterprises – but only one out of six large enterprises, according to the Internet Security Alliance, a non-profit organization that provides a forum for information security issues [2].

Because they have a false sense of security and assume they're not at risk, many small-enterprise owners don't adequately protect their computers and networks from spyware, viruses, worms, hacker attacks, customer data theft and other security threats. In addition, with so many balls to juggle already, entrepreneurs often put computer security far down on their to-do lists – if it makes the list at all [2]. The result: Nearly half of all small and mid-sized enterprises haven't taken the most basic security precautions, such as installing antivirus and anti-spyware programs, according to industry analysts.

Why You're at Risk

There are several reasons why your computers, network and the data that resides on them are at greater risk now than ever before. Let's briefly look at some of these reasons:

- Enterprise Internet/network security is harder to breach.
- Unprotected systems are easier to find.
- Computer security threats are more sophisticated – and more damaging.
- Threats often come from within.
- The resulting impact of a security attack is greater [2].

Enterprise Internet/Network Security Is Harder To Breach

In recent years, many enterprises, impacted by Internet threats and in order to comply with strict security measures required by the Sarbanes-Oxley Act and other regulations, have significantly bolstered their Internet/network security. As a result, criminals are increasingly turning their attentions toward easier hacker targets – small enterprises [2].

Unprotected Systems Are Easier To Find

Many hackers now have software tools that constantly search the Internet for unprotected networks and computers. Once discovered, unprotected computers can be accessed and controlled by a hacker, who can use them to launch attacks on other computers or networks [2].

Computer Security Threats Are More Sophisticated And More Damaging

Spyware authors are busy creating pernicious programs that resist removal, perpetually mutate, and spread across the Internet in minutes. Meanwhile, blended threats, which assume multiple forms and can attack systems in many different ways, are on the rise. Small enterprises without adequate, updated security solutions can easily be victimized by these and other threats [2].

Threats Often Come From Within

All too often, security breaches don't come from outside the enterprise but from within, either intentionally or unintentionally. For example, an employee may unknowingly download spyware while playing an online game or visiting a web site. Small- enterprise systems are more vulnerable to employee tampering simply because they often lack the internal security precautions of a larger enterprise [2].

The Resulting Impact Of A Security Attack Is Greater

Finally, small enterprises often lack the financial resources that large enterprises have to bounce back from security attacks. Suppose you're an online retailer and a hacker launches a denial-of-service attack against your web site. Do you have the necessary insurance or funds to recover from the subsequent loss of revenue – not to mention the damage to your business's reputation [2]?

SUMMARY AND CONCLUSIONS

So, keeping the preceding in mind, what can you do about all of these real security threats? As previously discussed, there are plenty of ways to protect your enterprise from Internet security threats [2]:

- Change your thinking.
- Assess your needs.
- Cover the basics.
- Get help.
- Put it in writing.
- Keep your security updated.
- Give wireless networks extra protection.
- Don't go overboard.
- Prepare for the future [2].

Change Your Thinking

Internet security should be a fundamental part of your enterprise survival/continuity plan. Think of it this way: Many small enterprises have grown reliant on the Internet for communicating with customers and partners; selling or marketing their products or services; and more. How will your enterprise continue to perform those functions if your computers are affected by a devastating virus [2]?

Assess Your Needs

Do you have a full understanding of the security you need versus what you currently have? If you're a harried small-enterprise owner, chances are the answer's no! The good news is, you may have more protection than you realize. For instance, most home office and small-enterprise local area network (LAN) routers include a built-in firewall – technology that blocks intruders from accessing the computers on the network [2].

Cover The Basics

At a minimum, all your enterprise computers should be protected by a hardware or software firewall and antivirus and anti-spyware programs. Some Internet security suite solutions geared toward small enterprises combine all three protections, as well as offer safeguards against identity theft [4], spam, phishing scams and more [2].

Get Help

Does computer security seem like too a daunting task for you to handle? If so, hire a consultant to perform a security audit of your enterprise systems and network and make recommendations. Your network equipment reseller or technology vendor can also help you determine the security solutions you need. Another option is to outsource the job to a U.S. based corporation – not to a foreign one (see sidebar, "The U.S. Government Is Outsourcing Our National Security To Foreign Governments"). A managed service provider can design, implement and maintain your Internet/network security solution for a flat monthly fee [2].

The U.S. Government Is Outsourcing Our National Security To Foreign Governments

While governments like Singapore make efforts to support local industry, the Bush Administration is jumping on the outsourcing bandwagon. It's cutting in-house software development in favor of off-the-shelf packages from enterprises that outsource to foreign enterprises. As a result, according to industry analysts, in 2005, the U.S. imported $3.6 billion more in government services than it sold abroad. The Congressional Research Service warns of security risks because defense is one of the most heavily outsourced of activities in the federal government. That could be one reason why the Bush Administration earned a "D" for computer security from a key Congressional subcommittee. It actually should have been given a "F-." Nonetheless, the Pentagon is outsourcing the CAD (computer-aided design) for its next generation F35 fighters to an Indian company in collaboration with Dell.

Put It In Writing

A detailed, written security plan that includes policies and procedures as well as technology requirements is particularly important for enterprises with employees. If your security procedures aren't set down in writing, they're easy for an employee to dispute or disregard [2].

Keep Your Security Updated

New Internet threats are emerging daily. Your security solutions won't be effective against new viruses, worms or spyware if they're not regularly updated. Fortunately, most antivirus software and other security solutions can be updated automatically [2].

Give Wireless Networks Extra Protection

On a wireless network, data is transmitted over radio waves, which can be easily intercepted. This means a wireless network is inherently less secure than a wired one [5]. If you or your employees use a wireless connection to access company databases or files, consider taking additional security measures. For instance, a virtual private network (VPN) connection provides a secure way for mobile workers to wirelessly tap into a enterprise's network [2].

Don't Go Overboard

A house without any windows or doors would be extremely secure – but who would want to live there? By the same token, the more secure your computer or network is, the more difficult it can be to use. Find the right balance between security and usability, and stick with it [2].

Prepare For The Future

Finally, a secure network provides enterprises with benefits beyond protection from Internet threats. Inherently, a secure network is a robust network. And a robust network is an excellent foundation that can support new technologies, such as VoIP, that can greatly increase productivity and reduce operating costs [2]. Ultimately, when your enterprise is secure, it's stronger and more agile – and definitely more competitive.

REFERENCES

[1] "Internet Security Threats," copyright 2006 SecurityMetrics, Inc., SecurityMetrics, Inc., 1358 W. Business Park Drive, Orem, UT 84058, USA, 2006.

[2] Peter Alexander. "Is Your Biz Safe From Internet Security Threats?" Copyright © 2006 Entrepreneur.com, Inc. All rights reserved. Entrepreneur Media Inc., 2445 McCabe Way, Ste. 400, Irvine, CA 926 14July 11, 2005.

[3] John R. Vacca, Firewalls: Jumpstart for Network and Systems Administrators, Digital Press, 2004.

[4] John R. Vacca, Identity Theft, Prentice Hall, 2002.

[5] John R. Vacca, Guide to Wireless Network Security, Springer, 2006.

Chapter 4

A SECURITY POLICY: THE FOUNDATION OF YOUR PROTECTION

INTRODUCTION

While Internet connectivity offers enormous benefits in terms of increased access to information, Internet connectivity is dangerous for sites with low levels of security. The Internet suffers from glaring security problems that, if ignored, could have disastrous results for unprepared sites. Inherent problems with TCP/IP services, the complexity of host configuration, vulnerabilities introduced in the software development process, and a variety of other factors have all contributed to making unprepared sites open to intruder activity and related problems [1]. Enterprises are, rightly concerned about the security implications of using the Internet, and ask the following questions:

- Will hackers disturb internal systems?
- Will valuable enterprise data be compromised (changed or read) in transit?
- Will the enterprise be embarrassed [1]?

All of preceding are valid concerns. Many technical solutions are emerging to address basic Internet security concerns. However, they come at a price. Many of the solutions limit functionality to increase security. Others require significant tradeoffs in terms of ease-of-use. Others cost traditional resource-staff time to implement and operate and money to buy and maintain equipment and software [1].

The purpose of an Internet Security Policy is to decide how an enterprise is going to protect itself. The policy will generally require two parts: a general policy and specific rules (which are the equivalent of system specific policy described in the preceding). The general policy sets the overall approach to Internet Security. The rules define what is and what is not allowed. The rules may be supplemented with procedures and other guidance [1].

For Internet policy to be effective, the policy maker must understand the tradeoffs being made. The policy must also be in synchronization with other related policy issues. This chapter attempts to provide technical professionals with the information they need to explain

Internet policy issues to policy makers. It provides a construct for linking high-level policy to detailed technical decisions [1].

The Internet is a vital resource that is changing the way many enterprises and individuals communicate and do business. However, the Internet suffers from significant and widespread security problems. Many agencies and enterprises have been attacked or probed by intruders, with resultant losses to productivity and reputation. In some cases, enterprises have had to disconnect from the Internet temporarily, and have invested significant resources in correcting problems with system and network configurations. Sites that are unaware of or ignorant of these problems face a risk that network intruders will attack them. Even sites that do observe good security practices face problems with new vulnerabilities in networking software and the persistence of some intruders [1].

The fundamental problem is that the Internet was not designed to be very secure. Some of the inherent problems with the current version of TCP/IP are:

- Ease of eavesdropping and spoofing
- Vulnerable TCP/IP services
- Lack of policy
- Complexity of configuration [1]

Ease Of Eavesdropping And Spoofing

The majority of Internet traffic is not encrypted. E-mail, passwords, and file transfers can be monitored and captured using readily available software [1].

Vulnerable TCP/IP Services

A number of the TCP/IP services are not designed to be secure and can be compromised by knowledgeable intruders. Services used for testing are particularly vulnerable [1].

Lack Of Policy

Many sites are configured unintentionally for wide-open Internet access without regard for the potential of abuse from the Internet. Many sites permit more TCP/IP services than they require for their operations and do not attempt to limit access to information about their computers that could prove valuable to intruders [1].

Complexity Of Configuration

Host security access controls are often complex to configure and monitor. Controls that are accidentally misconfigured can result in unauthorized access [1].

MAJOR TYPES OF POLICY

Computer security policy means different things to different people. It can mean senior management's directives to create a computer security program, establish its goals and assign responsibilities. It can mean mid-level managerial decisions regarding issues like e-mail privacy [3] or fax security. Or it can mean low-level technical security rules for particular systems [1].

> **Note:** These are the kind of policies that are being enforced by the system's technical controls as well as its management and operational controls.

In this chapter, the term computer security policy is defined as the documentation of computer security decisions – which covers all the types of policy previously described. In making these decisions, managers face hard choices involving enterprise strategy, competing objectives, and resource allocation. These choices involve protecting technical and information resources, as well as guiding employee behavior [1].

> **Note:** In general, policy is set by a manager. However, in some cases, a group (an intra-enterprise policy board) may set it.

The essential element of policy is that it is a decision. It provides direction for an enterprise. In order for the policy to be useful, it is essential that a different direction could have been realistically selected. Because policy sets a direction, it can be used as the basis for making other lower level decisions. High-level policy should not need to be changed frequently [1].

It is also essential that the policy be implemented in such a way that the enterprise actually goes in that direction. Two common problems with organizational policy are that: The policy is a platitude rather than a decision or direction; and, the policy is not really used by the enterprise. Instead it is a piece of paper to show to auditors, lawyers, other enterprise components, or customers, but it does not affect behavior. It may be helpful to consider some examples to explain these essential elements of policy.

Example 1

An enterprise decides to have a policy promoting computer security. The policy reads something like: It is the policy of this enterprise to protect the confidentiality, integrity, and availability of data. It is passed out to employees as a memo signed by the enterprise president. However, what enterprise is going to have a policy saying that it does not care about security? And, how would an employee change his or her behavior based on this memo? Well, a policy which states a goal of protecting data and then assigns responsibility to a specific enterprise element to develop a security program; assigns significant resources to that element; and, puts good people on the program, would be more effective. The implementation of the policy, in this example, includes putting good people and other significant resources on the program. That is how the employees know that this is a real decision, not a show to appease an auditor [1].

Example 2

A technical administrator (who is male) decides that good security requires that users do not share accounts. So, the administrator gets his or her management to sign a directive requiring this (by stating that this is the generally accepted security practice). However, the users do not know how to share files without sharing accounts, so they ignore the directive.

The manager did not really understand what she or he was signing or its implication for operations. The policy did not really set a direction because the manager did not understand. A more astute manager should have asked why the technical administrator needed such a policy [1].

> **Note:** If it is good practice, why does it need a directive?

She or he would have found out, then, about the underlying problems. Also, she or he would have found out there was a real choice to be made, operate insecurely or put resources into setting up new procedures and training users [1].

Managerial decisions on computer security issues vary greatly. To differentiate among various kinds of policy, it is helpful to categorize them into three basic types:

- Program policy
- Issue-specific policies
- System-specific policies [1]

Program Policy

Program policy sets enterprise strategic directions for security and assigns resources for its implementation. Program policy is used to create an enterprise's computer security program. A management official, normally the head of the enterprise or the senior administration official, issues program policy to establish (or restructure) the enterprise's computer security program and its basic structure. This high-level policy:

1. Defines the purpose of the program and its scope within the enterprise.
2. Assigns responsibilities (to the computer security enterprise) for direct program implementation, as well as other responsibilities to related offices (such as the Information Resources Management (IRM) organization).
3. Addresses compliance issues [1].

Issue-Specific Policies

Issue-specific policies address specific issues of concern to the enterprise; whereas program policy is intended to address the broad enterprise-wide computer security program. Issue-specific policies are developed to focus on areas of current relevance and concern (and sometimes controversy) to an enterprise. Management may find it appropriate, for example, to issue a policy on how the enterprise will approach contingency planning (centralized versus decentralized) or the use of a particular methodology for managing risk to systems. A policy could also be issued, for example, on the appropriate use of a cutting-edge technology (whose security vulnerabilities are still largely unknown) within the enterprise. Issue-specific policies may also be appropriate when new issues arise, such as when implementing a recently passed law requiring additional protection of particular information. Program policy is usually broad enough that it does not require much modification over time, whereas issue-specific policies are likely to require more frequent revision as changes in technology and related factors take place [1].

In general, for issue-specific and system-specific policy, the issuer is a senior official. The more global, controversial, or resource-intensive, the more senior the issuer is [1].

System-Specific Policies

System-specific policies focus on decisions taken by management to protect a particular system. Program policy and issue-specific policy both address policy from a broad level, usually encompassing the entire enterprise. However, they do not provide sufficient information or direction, for example, to be used in establishing an access control list or in training users on what actions are permitted. System-specific policy fills this need. It is much more focused, since it addresses only one system [1].

> **Note:** A system refers to the entire collection of processes, both those performed manually and those using a computer (manual data collection and subsequent computer manipulation), that performs a function. This includes both application systems and support systems, such as a network.

Many security policy decisions may apply only at the system level and may vary from system to system within the same enterprise. While these decisions may appear to be too detailed to be policy, they can be extremely important, with significant impacts on system usage and security. These types of decisions can be made by a management official, not by a technical system administrator [1].

> **Note:** The impacts of these decisions, however, are often analyzed by technical system administrators.

> **Tip:** It is important to remember that policy is not created in a vacuum. For example, it is critical to understand the system mission and how the system is intended to be used. Also, users may play an important role in setting policy.

Technical Policy Approach

There is a fourth type of policy that is defined in Internet security literature. It is a technical approach. This chapter defines the technical approach as analysis that supports the general policy and specific rules. It is, for the most part, too technical for policy-making officials to understand. As such, it is not very useful as a policy. However, it is imperative for defining the possible solutions that will define the tradeoffs, which is an essential element of setting policy [1].

Now, let's look at what to include in a general Internet security policy. In addition, this part of the chapter will also show you how to obtain approval; how to get the policy implemented; as well as, taking a look at a high level policy statement sample.

WHAT TO INCLUDE

A useful structure for issue-specific policy is to break the policy into its basic components. The components are as follows:

- Issue Statement.
- Statement of the Organization's Position.
- Applicability.
- Roles and Responsibilities.
- Compliance.

- Points of Contact and Supplementary Information.

Issue Statement

To formulate a policy on an issue, managers first must define the issue with any relevant terms, distinctions, and conditions included. It is also often useful to specify the goal or justification for the policy–which can be helpful in gaining compliance with the policy. For Internet security policy, an enterprise may need to be clear whether the policy covers all Internet-working connections or only Internet ones. The policy may also state whether other Internet non-security issues are addressed, such as personal use of Internet connections [1].

Statement Of The Enterprise's Position

Once the issue is stated and related terms and conditions are discussed, this next step is to clearly state the enterprise's position (management's decision) on the issue. This would state whether Internet connectivity is allowed or not and under what conditions [1].

Applicability

Issue-specific policies also need to include statements of applicability. This means clarifying where, how, when, to whom, and to what a particular policy applies. Does this apply to all components of the organization? A public affairs type of office may be exempted from a restrictive policy [1].

Roles And Responsibilities

The assignment of roles and responsibilities is also needed. For a complex issue such as Internet security, technical roles to analyze the security of various architectures or management roles granting approvals may need to be defined. A monitoring role may also be needed [2].

Compliance

For some types of Internet policies, it may be appropriate to describe, in some detail, the infractions that are unacceptable, and the consequences of such behavior. Penalties may be explicitly stated and should be consistent with enterprise personnel policies and practices. When used, they should be coordinated with appropriate officials and offices and, perhaps, employee bargaining units. It may also be desirable to task a specific office within the enterprise to monitor compliance [1].

Points Of Contact And Supplementary Information

For any issue-specific policy, the appropriate individuals in the enterprise to contact for further information, guidance, and compliance should be indicated. Since positions tend to change less often than the people occupying them, specific positions may be preferable as the point of contact. For example, for some issues, the point of contact might be a line manager; for other issues it might be a facility manager, technical support person, system administrator, or security program representative. Internet rules or system specific policies should be cited. These are described in Chapter 5 [1].

OBTAINING APPROVAL

What is the enterprise? Policy (good policy) can only be written for a defined group with similar goals. Therefore an enterprise may need to divide itself into components if the parent enterprise is too big or too diverse to be the subject of an Internet security policy. For example NIST is a component agency of the Department of Commerce (DOC). NIST's mission requires a large amount of scientific collaboration in an open environment. Another component of DOC, the Census Bureau, has a requirement to maintain the confidentiality of individual census questionnaires. With such different missions and requirements, a central Internet security policy from DOC is probably not needed. Even within NIST, there are significant differences in mission and requirements, such that most Internet security policy is set at a lower level than NIST-wide [1].

Ties To Other Policy Areas

The Internet is one of many ways in which a typical enterprise interacts with external sources. Internet policy should be consistent with other policy mediating access with the outside. For example:

- Physical access to the enterprise's building(s) or campus
- Public/Media Interaction
- Electronic access [1]

Physical Access To The Enterprise's Building(S) Or Campus

In one sense, the Internet is an electronic doorway to the enterprise. Both good and bad things use the same doorway. An enterprise which has an open physical campus has, presumably, already made a risk-based decision that the openness is either essential for the enterprise's mission or that the threat is low or too expensive to mitigate. A similar logic may hold for an electronic door. However, there are important differences. Physical threats are more directly linked to physical location. Linking to the Internet is linking to the entire world. An enterprise whose physical plant is in a remote and friendly place, say Montana, might have an open physical campus, but still require a restrictive Internet policy [1].

Public/Media Interaction

The Internet can be a form of public dialogue. Many enterprises instruct employees how to work with the public or the media. These policies will probably need to be ported to electronic interactions. Many employees may not be aware of the public nature of the Internet [1].

Electronic Access

The Internet is not the only means of Internet-working. Enterprises use the telephone system (public switched network) and other public and private networks to connect external users and computer systems to internal systems. By connecting to the Internet and the telephone system, you can share some threats and vulnerabilities [1].

GETTING POLICY IMPLEMENTED

Don't assume that just because your enterprise has a lot of policies or directives or internal regulations that that is how policy is set. Look around and see if any of the formal writings are followed. If not, you can either try to re-invent your enterprise's paperwork process (generally difficult, but perhaps worthwhile) or figure out where the policy is really set [1].

> **Tip:** If you pick the second option, you will probably also need the formal writing.

Some Helpful Hints On Policy

To be effective, policy requires visibility. Visibility aids implementation of policy by helping to ensure policy is fully communicated throughout the enterprise. Management presentations, videos, panel discussions, guest speakers, question/answer forums, and newsletters increase visibility. The enterprise's computer security training and awareness program can effectively notify users of new policies. It also can be used to familiarize new employees with the enterprise's policies [1].

Computer security policies should be introduced in a manner that ensures that management's unqualified support is clear, especially in environments where employees feel inundated with policies, directives, guidelines, and procedures. The enterprise's policy is the vehicle for emphasizing management's commitment to computer security and making clear their expectations for employee performance, behavior, and accountability [1].

To be effective, policy should be consistent with other existing directives, laws, organizational culture, guidelines, procedures, and the enterprise's overall mission. It should also be integrated into and consistent with other enterprise policies (personnel policies). One way to help ensure this is to coordinate policies during development with other enterprise offices. Since, unfortunately, a study of informal policy is beyond the scope of this chapter, this very important piece of the process will not be well described. However, most policy is set by what the big boss really wants. For an enterprise's Internet security policy (or any policy) to be effective, the big boss has to understand the choice to be made and make it freely. Generally, if the big boss believes the policy, it will filter through the informal mechanisms [1].

SAMPLE HIGH LEVEL POLICY STATEMENTS

This final part of the chapter provides some sample policies. It is not meant to preclude other formats, other levels of detail, but is meant to assist the reader in understanding the principles laid out in this chapter [1].

The first is for an enterprise which chooses not to restrict Internet access in any way. While this course is fraught with many security perils, it may be the best choice for an enterprise which requires openness or requires a lack of control by management on the working level. In general, these enterprises are best advised to separate at least some data and processing from the main enterprises processing. For example, some universities and colleges need this kind of environment for student and faculty systems [1].

> **Note:** But not for administrative systems.

The second example is more a middle-of-the-road policy. Internal and public systems are separated by a firewall [2]. However, most Internet-based services are still made available to the internal users. Generally a dual-homed gateway or a bastion host would serve as the firewall. However, this approach can also be implemented through the use of cryptography to create virtual private networks or tunnels on the Internet [1].

Finally, the third example is for an enterprise that requires security more than Internet services. The only Internet service for which the enterprise sees a business case is email [1].

> **Note:** It is interesting that one factor in the business case is to provide email as a perk for employees. The enterprise still provides a public access server for the Internet, but it is not connected to internal systems.

SUMMARY AND CONCLUSIONS

This chapter was intended to help an enterprise create a coherent Internet-specific information security policy. It provided a brief overview of the Internet and its constituent protocols. It discussed the primary uses of the Internet, and the associated policy implications. Finally, it provided sample policy statements for low, medium and high risk/protection environments [1].

REFERENCES

[1] "Internet Security Policy: A Technical Guide," copyright 2006 RXN Communications, RXN Communications, Victoria, Minnesota 55386, USA, 2006.
[2] John R. Vacca, Firewalls: Jumpstart for Network and Systems Administrators, Digital Press, 2004.
[3] John R. Vacca, Net Privacy: A Guide to Developing and Implementing an Ironclad ebusiness Privacy Plan, McGraw-Hill, 2001.

PART III

DEVELOPING YOUR SECURITY POLICY

Chapter 5

STEPS TO TAKE NOW

INTRODUCTION

In today's environment of severely constrained resources (both staffing and financial) investments in security controls must show a positive return on investment. Internet security can be looked as an enabling investment, reducing operational costs or opening new revenue streams, or as a protective investment, preventing potential costs or negative business impacts. In either case, the cost of the security controls must be appropriate for the risk and reward environment faced by your enterprise [1].

In simple terms, a risk is realized when a threat takes advantage of a vulnerability to cause harm to your system. Security policy provides the baseline for implementing security controls to reduce vulnerabilities and reduce risk. In order to develop cost effective security policy for protecting Internet connections some level of risk analysis must be performed to determine the required rigor of the policy, which will drive the cost of the security controls deployed to meet the requirements of the security policy. How rigorous this effort must be is a factor of:

- The level of threat an enterprise faces and the visibility of the enterprise to the outside world
- The sensitivity of the enterprise to the consequences of potential security incidents
- Legal and regulatory issues that may dictate formal levels of risk analysis [1]

> **Note:** This does not address the value of information or the cost of security incidents. In the past, such cost estimation has been required as a part of formal risk analyses in an attempt to support measurements of the ROI of security expenditures. As dependence on public networks by enterprises and government agencies has become more widespread, the intangible costs of security incidents equal or outweigh the measurable costs. Information security management time can be more effectively spent assuring the deployment of good enough security rather than attempting to calculate the cost of anything less than perfect security.

For enterprises that are subject to regulatory oversight, or that handle life-critical information, more formal methods of risk assessment may be appropriate. This chapter provides a methodology for the steps you must take now to rapidly develop a risk profile for your enterprise; and, the enterprise requirements you must adhere to in developing an Internet security policy [1].

THREATS/VISIBILITY

A threat is any circumstance or event with the potential to cause harm to an enterprise through the disclosure, modification or destruction of information, or by the denial of critical services. Threats can be non-malicious, through human error, hardware/software failures, or natural disaster. Malicious threats can be categorized within a range going from rational (obtaining something of value at no cost) to irrational (destroying the information or reputation of others). Typical threats in an Internet environment include:

- Component Failure: Failure due to design flaws or hardware/software faults can lead to denial of service or security compromises through the malfunction of a system component. Downtime of a firewall [2] or false rejections by authorization servers are examples of failures that affect security.
- Information Browsing: Unauthorized viewing of sensitive information by intruders or legitimate users may occur through a variety of mechanisms: mis-routed electronic mail, printer output, mis-configured access control lists, group IDs, etc.
- Misuse: The use of information assets for other than authorized purposes can result in denial of service, increased cost, or damage to reputations. Internal or external users can initiate misuse.
- Unauthorized deletion, modification or disclosure of information: Intentional damage to information assets that result in the loss of integrity or confidentiality of enterprise functions and information.
- Penetration: Attacks by unauthorized persons or systems that may result in denial of service or significant increases in incident handling costs.
- Misrepresentation: Attempts to masquerade as a legitimate user to steal services or information, or to initiate transactions that result in financial loss or embarrassment to the organization. The presence of a threat does not mean that it will necessarily cause actual harm. To become a risk, a threat must take advantage of a vulnerability in system security controls (discussed later in the chapter) and the system must be visible to the outside world. Visibility is a measure of both the attractiveness of a system to malicious intruders and of the amount of information available in the public domain about that system [1].

All enterprises with Internet access are to some extent visible to the outside world, if by nothing more than through Domain Name Services. However, some enterprises are more visible than others are, and the level of visibility may change regularly or due to extraordinary events. The Internal Revenue Service is much more visible than the Migratory Bird Management Office, and the IRS is particularly visible as April 15th nears. Exxon became much more visible after the Valdez disaster and various other oil spill accidents, while MFS became much less visible after being acquired by Worldcom [1].

Since many Internet-based threats are opportunistic in nature, an enterprise's level of visibility directly drives the probability that a malicious actor will attempt to cause harm by realizing a threat. In the Internet environment, curious college students, teenage vandals, criminals, agents of espionage, or curious cyber-surfers can carry out threats. As the use of public networks for electronic commerce [5] and critical business functions increases, attacks by criminals and espionage agents (both economic and foreign) will increase [1].

SENSITIVITIES/CONSEQUENCES

Enterprises have different levels of sensitivity to risk. Security policy needs to reflect the enterprise's particular sensitivity to various types of security incidents and prioritize security investments on those areas of highest sensitivity [1].

There are two major factors that drive an enterprise's level of sensitivity. The first factor is the consequences of a security incident (see Table 5-1) [1]. Almost all enterprises have some level of cost sensitivity – security incidents can result in significant recovery and restoration costs even if no critical services are affected. However, means of transferring risk (such as insurance policies or contractual terms and conditions) may mean that a certain level of cost exposure does not change the business financial bottom line [1].

Table 5-1. Risk Profile Matrix.

Risk Profiling Matrix Threats	Rating	Visibility	Rating	Score
None identified as active; exposure is limited	1	Very low profile, no active publicity	1	
Unknown state or multiple exposures	3	Middle of the pack, periodic publicity	3	
Active threats, multiple exposures	5	Lightning rod, active publicity	5	
Consequences	**Rating**	**Sensitivity**	**Rating**	**Score**
No cost impact; well within planned budget; risk transferred	1	Accepted as cost of doing business; no organization issues	1	
Internal functions impacted; budget overrun; opportunity costs	3	Unacceptable Business Unit management impact; good will costs	3	
External functions impacted; direct revenue hit	5	Unacceptable Corporate Management impact; business relationships affected	5	
	Total Score:			

Rating: Multiply Threat rating by Visibility rating, and Consequences rating by Sensitivity rating.

Add the two values together:

- **2–10: Low Risk**
- **11–29: Medium Risk**
- **30–50: High Risk**

One important step towards determining the consequences is performing an information asset inventory, discussed in more detail in Chapter 6. While it sounds simple, keeping an accurate inventory of what systems, networks, computers, and databases are currently in use is a complex task. Enterprises should combine such an inventory with a data classification effort, discussed in Chapter 6, where the information stored on line is categorized by its importance to the goals of the business or mission [1].

More serious consequences occur when internal functions are disrupted, resulting in costs of missed opportunities, personnel down time, as well as recovery and restoration. The most serious consequences are when external functions are effected, such as delivery of products to customers or receipt of orders. These consequences are related directly to the financial impact of a security incident through disruption of services, or to a potential future impact due to loss of customer trust [1].

The second factor to consider is more a function of political or enterprise sensitivities. In some enterprise cultures upper level management may feel that an article in the mainstream press highlighting a break-in at your agency or enterprise is a major disaster, whether or not there are significant costs involved. In more open environments, such as universities and scientific research communities, management may feel that an occasional incident is preferable to any restriction on the flow of information or outside access. These factors need to be considered when determining enterprise sensitivity to security incidents [1].

INFORMATION ASSET INVENTORY

To assure protection of all information assets and so that the current computing environment may be quickly re-established following a disaster, each Network Administrator must maintain an inventory of production information systems. This inventory must indicate all existing hardware, software, automated files, databases and data communications links [1]. For each information asset, the following information should be defined:

- Type: hardware, software, data
- General Support System or Critical Application
- Designated "owner" of the information
- Physical or logical location
- Inventory item number, where applicable [1]

GENERAL SUPPORT SYSTEMS

A general support system is an interconnected set of information resources under the same direct management control which shares common functionality. Normally, the purpose of a general support system is to provide processing or communications support across a wide array of applications. General support systems consist of all computers, networks, and programs that support multiple applications, and are usually managed and maintained by a central IRM or ADP enterprise [1].

Security policy for general support systems is generally the most applicable to Internet usage, as the servers, communications software, and gateways that provide Internet connectivity are generally centrally controlled [1].

CRITICAL/MAJOR APPLICATIONS

All applications require some level of security, and adequate security for most of them should be provided by security of the general support systems in which they operate. However, certain applications, because of the nature of the information in them, require special management oversight and should be treated as major. A major or critical application is any use of computers or networks that would seriously impact the ability of the enterprise to perform its mission if that application was altered or unavailable [1].

Examples of critical applications are personnel systems, billing systems, financial or billing systems, etc. Since most users spend the majority of their computer time interacting with one of these major applications, security awareness and education should be integrated into the training and documentation for these systems [1].

Most major applications do not currently involve Internet connectivity; however, this is beginning to change. Next generation operating systems are incorporating Internet connectivity, as are groupware and publishing software programs [1].

Data Categorization

In order to develop effective information security policy, the information produced or processed by an enterprise must be categorized according to its sensitivity to loss or disclosure. Based on this categorization, policy for allowing Internet access to information or for transmitting information over the Internet can be defined [1].

Most enterprises use some set of information categories, such as Proprietary, For Internal Use Only, or ENTERPRISE Sensitive. The categories used in the information security policy should be consistent with any existing categories [1].

Data must be broken into four sensitivity classifications with separate handling requirements:

- SENSITIVE
- CONFIDENTIAL
- PRIVATE
- PUBLIC [1]

This standard data sensitivity classification system must be used throughout ENTERPRISE. The designated owners of information are responsible for determining data classification levels, subject to executive management review.

SENSITIVE

This classification applies to information that requires special precautions to assure the integrity of the information, by protecting it from unauthorized modification or deletion. It is information that requires a higher than normal assurance of accuracy and completeness. Examples of sensitive information include ENTERPRISE financial transactions and regulatory actions [1].

CONFIDENTIAL

This classification applies to the most sensitive enterprise information that is intended strictly for use within ENTERPRISE. This information is exempt from disclosure under the provisions of the Freedom of Information Act or other applicable federal laws or regulations. Its unauthorized disclosure could seriously and adversely impact ENTERPRISE, its stockholders, its business partners, and/or its customers. Health care-related information should be considered at least CONFIDENTIAL [1].

PRIVATE

This classification applies to personal information that is intended for use within ENTERPRISE. Its unauthorized disclosure could seriously and adversely impact ENTERPRISE and/or its employees [1].

PUBLIC

This classification applies to all other information that does not clearly fit into any of the preceding three classifications. While its unauthorized disclosure is against policy, it is not expected to impact seriously or adversely ENTERPRISE, its employees, and/or its customers [1].

ENTERPRISE REQUIREMENTS

Enterprises and other organizations use the Internet because it provides useful services. Enterprises choose to support (or not support) Internet-based services based on a business plan or an information technology strategic plan. In other words, enterprises should analyze their business needs, identify potential methods of meeting the needs and consider the security ramifications of the methods along with cost and other factors [1].

Most enterprises use Internet-based services to provide enhanced communications between enterprise units, or between the enterprise and its customers, or provide cost savings means of automating enterprise processes. Security is a key consideration – a single security incident can wipe out any cost savings or revenue provided by Internet connectivity [1]. There may also be a number of different technological solutions for meeting the needs of the enterprise, some that are more easily secured than others.

The rest of this chapter explains the major services provided by Internet connectivity. It also maps the security controls available to the services they can help protect. Table 5-2 shows a mapping of security controls to the Internet-based services commonly used by businesses and enterprises. The marks show which controls are most often employed to secure a given service. Some of the controls, such as incident handling, provide security for all services; the mark highlights services for which the control is essential [1].

Table 5-2. Mapping of Security Controls and Services.

	I&A	Access Control	Firewall	Software Import Controls	Encryption	Archi- tecture	Incident Handling	Adminis- trative
Remote Access	X	X	X		X			X
Electronic Mail	X			X	X			X
Info Publishing		X	X			X		X
Research		X	X	X		X		X
Electronic Commerce	X	X	X	X	X	X	X	X
High Availability						X		X
Ease of Use						X		X

Remote Access

Increasingly, enterprise require remote access to their information systems. This may be driven by the need for employees on travel to access email, or for sales people to remotely enter orders, or by a business decision to promote telecommuting. By its very nature, remote access to computer systems adds vulnerabilities by increasing the number of access points [1]. There are three major modes of remote access:

- Service Specific
- Remote Control
- In Remote Node operation

Service Specific

Service specific remote access is typically limited to remote operation of one service, often email. Products such as Lotus Notes and cc:Mail support mobile connections to these products with no provision of general network services. This mode is generally the most secure form of operation – vulnerabilities are limited [1].

Remote Control

Remote Control allows the remote user to operate a personal computer that is physically located at the enterprise location. The enterprise computer can be a special purpose system or the user's desktop computer. The remote computer is used strictly as a keyboard and a display. Remote control limits remote users to the software programs that are resident on the enterprise computer, a plus from the security point of view. Some remote control multi-user products also provide an enhanced level of auditing and logging [1].

Remote Node Operation

In Remote Node operation, the remote computer connects to a remote access server that assigns the remote computer a network address. All operating software is located on the remote computer, along with local storage [4]. Remote node operation provides all network services to remote users, unless access control software is utilized. Remote node operation is becoming the most popular form of remote access, but also introduces the highest level of vulnerability to enterprise systems. These forms of remote access can be accomplished using dial-in connections, telnet sessions, or using software products that support mobile computing. The next part of the chapter describes the vulnerabilities of the various methods of remote access [1].

Dial-in

Remote access over commercial telephone lines is still the most common form of remote access. Typically the remote computer uses an analog modem to dial an auto answer modem at the enterprise location. Security methods for protecting this connection include:

- Controlling knowledge of the dial-in access numbers
- Username/password pairs
- Advanced authentication [1]

Controlling Knowledge Of The Dial-In Access Numbers

This approach is vulnerable to automated attacks by war dialers. These are simple pieces of software that use auto-dial modems to scan blocks of telephone numbers and locate and log modems [1].

Username/Password Pairs

Since an attacker would need to be tapping the telephone line, dial-in connections are less vulnerable to password sniffer attacks that have made reusable passwords virtually useless over public networks. However, the use of network sniffers on internal networks, the lack of password discipline, and social engineering make obtaining or guessing passwords easy. For example, help desks are also used to dealing with legitimate users who have forgotten their passwords and will often release passwords to clever social engineers [1].

Advanced Authentication

There are many methods which can be used to supplement or replace traditional passwords. These methods include:

- Dial-back modems
- One Time Passwords
- Location-based [1]

Dial-Back Modems

These devices require the user to enter a username/password upon initial connection. The enterprise modem then disconnects and looks up the authorized remote telephone number for the connecting user. The enterprise modem then dials the remote modem and establishes a connection. The user then enters the username and password for the system connection.

This approach is vulnerable to call forwarding attacks, and does not provide the flexibility required to support connections from airports and hotels [1].

One Time Passwords

Cryptographic-based /response systems, such as S/Key from Bellcore, and SecurID from Security Dynamics require the user to operate a software or hardware-based password generator. These devices create a unique password for each session and require the remote user to both know the username/password information and to possess the password generator. While this method is still vulnerable to session hijacking attacks, this approach provides the minimum acceptable level of security for most remote access connections [1].

Location-based

This emerging set of authentication products takes advantage of the growing use of technologies such as the Global Positioning System to enforce location-based authentication. If a user is not connecting from an authorized location, access is denied. This technology is immature, complex and currently expensive. However, it may be appropriate for many applications. Vulnerabilities are related to the ability of an attacker to supply bogus location information. Most approaches use cryptography [3] to prevent this form of attack. Since most users don't hesitate to discuss sensitive matters over the telephone, dial-in connections are no less secure than the voice communications via telephone. While this is true from the confidentiality point of view, dial-in connections to computers provide an access point for intruders. These access point exist even if there is no Internet connection [1].

Telnet/X Windows

Telnet and the remote login commands supported by Unix provide a means for remotely logging in to computers over network connections. Many personal computers come equipped with TCP/IP software that also provides telnet capability. Telnet essentially provides a text-oriented remote control connection from the remote client to the host computer. Telnet usually requires a username/password pair be sent over the network connection in the clear – a major security weakness [1].

X Windows provides a remote control connection that supports use of graphical user interfaces, passing screen and keyboard data over the network connection. X Windows has a few security features that are often bypassed by users to simplify the connection process [1].

Mobile Computing

The use of portable computers has risen dramatically, driven by the dramatic fall in the cost, size, weight, and fragility of laptop computers. Most of the laptops in use by enterprise and government agencies come configured with high speed modems, 5 GB or larger disk drives, and a variety of pre-configured communications software. A growing trend is the use of docking stations or port extenders to allow laptop computers to be used in a desktop environment as well as in out of office situations. A less common variation is the transfer of PCMCIA card-based disk drives between portable (or remote desktop-based) computers and the home office based machine [1].

Mobile computing involves the use of portable computers to perform enterprise functions, and often involves establishing remote connections to enterprise networks. While the connection mechanisms used are the same as described in the preceding (dial-in, telnet, etc.), the use of portable computers introduces additional vulnerabilities:

- The location of the remote computer can change frequently, often on a daily basis. Dial-back modems are generally not useful for controlling access.
- The remote computer is often used in public situations, such as on airplanes, or in airports. Data and password compromise can occur through shoulder surfing.
- The remote computer is often left unattended in relatively insecure locations, such as in hotel rooms or in rental cars. Data stored on disk is vulnerable to snooping or copying.
- Remote computers are often lost or stolen while employees are in travel, making all information stored available to compromise. Employees are often reluctant to quickly report the loss, making fraudulent remote access possible. Some large enterprises (with 8,000 or more laptop computers in use) lose on average two laptop computers per week [1].
- Laptop computers use internal modems for dial-in access, with the same PCMCIA card often used as the Network Interface Card when the laptop is used in an office environment. If an analog phone line is available at the desktop, the built-in modem can be used for unapproved dial-in or dial-out connections to bulletin boards or Internet Service Providers.
- Mobile computing users also tend to be cellular phone users, and often discuss sensitive security-related matters over the cellular airwaves. Talking over a cellular phone is vulnerability to eavesdropping by a wide variety of criminals, competitors, and news organizations. The use of cellular or other radio-based modems for data communications increases the vulnerability level [1].

Electronic Mail

While the multi-media content of the World Wide Web receives most of the attention, electronic mail is what really drove the growth of the Internet. The use of Internet email to carry business-critical communications is growing exponentially. While email provides a low cost means of communicating with customers, suppliers, and partners, there are a number of security issues related to the use of electronic mail:

- Internet email addresses are easily spoofed. It is nearly impossible to be certain who created and sent an email message based on the address alone.
- Internet email messages can be easily modified. Standard SMTP mail provides no integrity checking.
- There are a number of points where the contents of an email message can be read by unintended recipients. Internet email is much like a postcard – the message is viewable at every intermediate stop.
- There is usually no guarantee of delivery with Internet email. While some mail systems support return receipts, when such receipts work at all, they often only signify that the user's server (not necessarily the user) has received the message. These weaknesses make

it important for enterprises to issue policies defining acceptable use of electronic mail for business purposes [1].

Information Publishing

The Internet greatly simplifies the task of providing information to citizens, clients, suppliers, and partners – or at least those that have computers connected to the Internet. Today in the United States, roughly 70% of the homes have personal computers, and only about 75% of those homes have the capability to connect to the Internet. It will still be several years before electronic publishing can make a very serious dent in paper-based publishing [1].

However, any use of electronic information publishing that reduces the number of requests for information via telephone or US Mail can be of significant benefit in meeting enterprise goals as budgets and head counts decline. There are two primary types of information publishing, push and pull. Subscription-based magazines are an example of push publishing – information is sent to subscribers on a regular basis. Newsstand sales are an example of pull publishing – readers must take the initiative to get the information [1].

The electronic equivalent of push publishing is the creation of a mailing list that sends information to all subscribers of the list. Typically list server software is used to send messages to the list and to provide for adding, modifying, and deleting entries on the list. List servers are relatively secure, in that the users do not need to connect to the publishing organization's network to receive information. However, there are a few vulnerabilities:

First, list server software accepts user inputs to subscribe to the list, be removed from the list, or to obtain information about the list. There is a wide variety of freeware list server software available, and some of the packages may not fully check user input. Malicious users can send Unix commands or extremely large input strings in an attempt to cause unintended operation or buffer overflows [1].

Second, if not configured correctly, list server software can make the entire list of subscriber addresses visible to each subscriber. This can provide information to support denial of service or social engineering attacks. There are two electronic equivalents of pull publishing commonly in use on the Internet: File Transfer Protocol servers and World Wide Web servers. These have pretty much supplanted the use of bulletin board systems, although some BBS are still in use in the government [1].

To provide FTP services over the Internet, about all that is needed is a computer and a connection to the Internet. FTP servers can be set up on just about any computer running the Unix operating system, and on many running Microsoft Windows. Many commercial and shareware versions of ftp software are available, often as part of a TCP/IP stack that provides the software drivers to connect to Internet services. They can allow fully anonymous login, where passwords are not required, or they can be set up to require a valid username/password pair. FTP servers provide a simple interface resembling a standard Unix file directory. Users can retrieve files and then view or execute the files later, if they have the appropriate applications [1].

If an FTP server is not configured correctly, it can provide access to any file found on the host computer, or even on the network connected to the host computer. FTP servers should be limited to accessing a limited directory space, and should require the use of passwords whenever feasible [1].

Unless you've been stranded on a remote island for the past thirteen years, you're probably familiar with the explosive growth of the World Wide Web. Web servers provide an inexpensive means of publishing information that contains text and embedded graphics, or even audio and video. The use of the HyperText Markup Language and HyperText Transfer Protocol standards allows Web-based documents to be easily retrieved and viewed by users on a wide variety of client platforms [1].

While developing a professional Web site is complicated and expensive, any computer connected to the Internet can be easily setup as a Web server. World Wide Web server software is available in both commercially-supported and freeware versions for all varieties of server and personal computer operating systems. Many of the latest versions of operating systems are including the software needed to host Web servers, along with very helpful wizard programs that automate the setup tasks [1]. Similar to FTP servers, Web servers can introduce significant security vulnerabilities to enterprise networks if not configured correctly.

Research

Doing research over the Internet generally involves using client software to search for and retrieve information from remote servers. Types of client software include:

- File Transfer Protocol: FTP software supports logging in to remote systems, browsing directory structures, and retrieving files.
- Gopher: Developed at the University of Minnesota, Gopher software essentially provides a graphical user interface to FTP-like browsing and retrieval functions.
- World Wide Web: Web browsers have pretty much conquered the market for Internet information retrieval. Web browser client software generally includes the ability to use FTP and Gopher functions, along with more advanced multi-media capabilities.
- Proprietary systems: There are still a number of Internet-based information systems that require the use of proprietary software rather than a Web browser. These generally involve access to copyrighted or proprietary information stored in relational databases [1].

Thus, the major risk related to the use of the Internet for research is the possibility of importing viruses or other malicious software. With the rise of macro viruses that can be contained in standard word processing files, downloading documents can now be as risky as downloading executable files. In addition, the availability of helper applications and downloadable applets to support viewing of special purpose formats (such as Postscript) has increased the risk of Trojan Horse programs being hidden in legitimate programs [1].

A secondary risk is the footprint that client software leaves when used to browse Internet-based information servers. Most server software has the ability to log the IP address of the client as a minimum, and Web server software can often retrieve information on the type of browser used, the last site visited, the email address in use on the browser, and other sensitive information. In addition, Web server software can store a cookie file on the browser client, thus allowing the server to track the client's visits to the server and keep track of what areas are visited [1].

Electronic Commerce

The use of computers and networks has proceeded in three major phases, or waves as often called by the pundits:

- Back office automation: The early days of the mainframe moved many financial and record keeping functions, such as billing, finance, and personnel, onto computers.
- Front office automation: The advent of the personal computer and local area networks allowed office functions, such as word processing, correspondence tracking, financial estimation, etc., to be taken over by computers.
- Customer contact automation: As the penetration of personal computers into business and homes advances, and the Internet continues to provide inexpensive, ubiquitous connectivity, the contact between enterprises and their customers (individuals, other businesses, suppliers, partners, etc.) will more and more take place via a computer-computer connection. This buyer to seller contact using computers and networks is the basic definition of electronic commerce [1].

For the purposes of exploring the relevant security issues, electronic commerce has been broken into four basic classes: electronic mail, electronic data interchange, information transactions, and financial transactions. Electronic mail was discussed in detail earlier; the following addresses the remaining three categories [1].

Electronic Data Interchange

Electronic Data Interchange (EDI) is a self explanatory term. In its simplest form, EDI is the electronic exchange of information between two enterprise concerns (referred to in the EDI world as trading partners), in a standardized format. The basic unit of exchange is a transaction set, which generally relates to a standard business document, such as Purchase Order or a Customer Invoice. Through standards bodies such as X.9 and UN/EDIFACT, the business community has developed a set of standard transactions sets for various industries [1].

Each transaction set has an extensive set of data elements required for that business document, with specified formats and sequences for each data element. If the transaction contains more than one transaction (many purchase orders sent to one vendor) several transaction groups would be preceded by a functional group header, and would be followed by a function group trailer [1].

Enterprises began to use EDI to reduce the time and cost of dealing with suppliers. Driven by automobile manufacturing, large enterprises required suppliers to use EDI for all transactions, eliminating tremendous amounts of paper and shortening the time and effort required to keep databases current. Value Added Networks (VANs) were typically used to carry EDI transactions, providing lower costs than dedicated connections such as leased lines, while offering a reliable and secure delivery service [1].

The Internet can provide the connectivity needed to support EDI at a substantial cost saving over VANs. However, the Internet doesn't provide the security services (integrity, confidentiality, non-repudiation) required for business EDI. Similar to electronic mail over the Internet, EDI transactions are vulnerable to modification, disclosure or interruption when sent over the Internet. The use of cryptography to provide the required security services has changed this, however, and many enterprises and government agencies are moving to Internet-based EDI [1].

Information Transactions

Providing information is a major and costly element of commerce. Such information may take a variety of forms:

- Static data, such as historic information, maps, etc.
- Enterprise information, such as telephone numbers, addresses, organization charts, etc.
- Produce or service information
- Fee-based information services, such as news, periodical subscriptions, data base re- trievals, stock quotes, etc. Using the Internet to provide these services is substantially less expensive that using fax, telephone, or postal mail services. Potential customers can search for and retrieve information at their own pace without requiring expensive customer support services [1].

Typically, such information services use the World Wide Web as the underlying mechanism for providing information. Integrity and availability of the information provided are key security concerns that require security controls and policy [1].

Financial Transactions

In one form or another, computers and networks have been used to process financial transactions for decades. Electronic Funds Transfers are used for bank to bank transactions, and Automated Teller Machines are used for consumer to bank transactions. Credit card authorizations and settlement processing is performed over telephone lines or data networks [1].

To maintain the security of these transactions, they have always been carried over private networks or been encrypted using the Data Encryption Standard. Similar to EDI over VANs, the connectivity options have been limited and the leased lines are expensive. Once again the Internet provides an opportunity for cost savings in electronic financial transactions [1]. There are three major classes of financial transactions and five major types of payment mechanisms as shown in Table 5-3 [1]:

Table 5-3. Financial Payments and Transactions.

	Cash	**Check**	**Debit**	**Credit**	**EFT**
Business to Business		Primary			Secondary
Business to Consumer	Primary	Secondary	Secondary	Secondary	
Consumer to Consumer	Primary	Secondary			

The use of the Internet to carry these types of transactions replaces the physical presentation or exchange of cash, checks, or debit/credit cards with the electronic equivalent:

Cash

There are a number of competing approaches to electronic cash under development. All methods use cryptography to create secure digital wallets to safely store digital currency. The transfer of electronic cash does not necessarily have to involve a financial institution as an intermediary [1].

Checks

The banking industry is developing a standard for electronic checking, defining how the information carried on physical checks should be contained in an electronic message. Electronic checks will always involve a financial institution for transferring funds [1].

Debit Cards

Smart cards and stored value cards can be loaded with electronic currency in a variety of manners. Each transaction debits the appropriate amount until the card is empty. Stored value cards do not require financial institutions as intermediaries [1].

Credit Cards

The major players in the credit card industry (Visa, Master Card, and American Express) have developed a standard for performing credit card transactions over public networks. Known as Secure Electronic Transactions, this standard supports the three-way transactions between the buyer, the seller, and the acquirer of the credit card debt, typically a bank. Electronic credit card transactions using SET will always involve a financial institution [1].

Electronic Funds Transfer (EFT)

EFT uses cryptography to secure the transfer of funds between banks and other financial institutions. Consumers can authorize banks to send and receive payments via EFT for the consumer. Each of these forms of electronic financial transactions involves the use of cryptography to provide for integrity, confidentiality, authentication, and non-repudiation [1].

High Availability

As use of the Internet becomes more critical to routine enterprise operations, security controls protecting Internet connections often need to support requirements for high availability or non-stop operations. These requirements often have a major impact on security policy, requiring business decisions between the costs of redundant configurations versus the cost of temporarily operating without security controls [1].

A simple example is the firewall. A firewall can be a single point of failure – if the firewall goes down, the entire connection to the Internet can be lost for the duration of the failure. If temporary loss of Internet connectivity does not have a major impact on enterprise operations, the policy may be to simply halt Internet operations until the firewall is restored. For low risk profile enterprises, the policy may allow the failed firewall to be bypassed for the duration of the outage. However, if the connectivity is critical, or for higher risk profile enterprises, policy may require the acquisition and use of a firewall configured as a hot or cold spare. The business or mission side of the enterprise makes the tradeoff between the costs of each approach [1].

For very large enterprises, performance may also dictate the use of multiple security controls, such as firewalls or authentication servers. For example, an enterprise supporting many thousands of external Internet users may need multiple T1 or T3 connections to the Internet, requiring multiple firewalls. Enterprises with many thousands of internal users who tend to connect to the system simultaneously (early in the morning, right after lunch, etc.) may require multiple authentication servers to keep response times to acceptable levels [1]. Some of the key efforts is supporting high availability requirements are:

- Capacity planning
- Redundancy
- Recovery

Capacity Planning

An interesting phenomenon is that as soon as a firewall is installed, users will swear the Internet connection is slower. Properly selected security controls such as firewalls will generally not be the bottleneck in system throughput. However, detailed capacity planning is critical, as security controls that do impact performance will quickly be bypassed. Firewall vendors specifications should be derated at least 50% when modeling needed capacity, and any critical security control should have its performance profiled on a test network [1].

Redundancy

For all but the lowest risk profile enterprises, an on-line backup firewall is a necessity. Similarly, the use of authentication servers or secure remote access servers generally require the ability to rapidly switch in backup servers. Synchronization of policy is the key for the use of redundant backup security servers – all updates, backups, and modifications must be implemented on both systems, and the licensing for both systems must be kept current [1].

Recovery

When a failed unit has been repaired and brought back on line, careful configuration control is a must. The hardware and software configuration must be analyzed to assure that approved, current and patched versions of all products are running and that no unneeded services have been introduced or enabled during the repair process. Any debug features or system traps used in testing should be removed or disabled [1].

Ease Of Use

The user population of many systems connected to the Internet may range from secretaries to scientists, from neophytes to nerds. A frequent enterprise requirement is often that all applications be easy to use by the typical user population. This is not an easy requirement to quantify, but from a security perspective, it often gets translated as: If security controls get in the way of people doing their jobs, you will figure out a way to bypass the security controls [1].

Two key elements of ease of use are reducing the number of times a user has to authenticate to the system and designing the interface to security controls to match the capabilities or preferences of the user population. These areas are briefly discussed next.

Single Sign-on

In the course of performing daily tasks, a user might be forced to log on to many different computers and networks. Often, each system requires the user to enter a username and password. Since remembering multiple passwords is difficult for many users, this leads to passwords being written down (and often posted on PC monitors) or forgotten. Another user reaction is to simply use the same password for all computer systems. However, different systems may have different rules for passwords, or may have different periods of validity for passwords, causing users to resort to once again writing down the various passwords [1].

Single Sign-on systems attempt to make the use of multiple passwords transparent to the user. This is accomplished in a variety of ways:

First, some SSO systems simply create scripts which contain the various username/password pairs and logon commands. This removes the burden from the user, but often transfers it to the administrative staff who often is required to maintain the scripts. Such scripts also require secure storage, as misuse would allow access to all systems for which the user has privileges [1].

Second, other approaches to Single Sign-on, such as those based on Kerberos, use cryptographic techniques to forward user privileges to each network or server the user needs to access. These systems require the establishment and operation of privilege servers, as well as the integration of the SSO technology into each system to be accessed [1].

User Interface Design

Finally, the design of the user interface to Internet security functionality should be consistent with the user interface of other applications that will be used regularly by system users. When security controls are purchased off-the-shelf, or are embedded in off-the-shelf applications, the user interface to such security functionality will be outside the control of your enterprise. For internally developed applications it is important that the user interface be designed considering the perspective of the end user, not the security enterprise [1].

SUMMARY AND CONCLUSIONS

This chapter provided a methodology for the steps you must take now to rapidly develop a risk profile for your enterprise; and, the enterprise requirements you must adhere to in developing an Internet security policy. The chapter also explained the major services provided by Internet connectivity. Finally, it also mapped the security controls available to the services the enterprise can help protect.

REFERENCES

[1] "Internet Security Policy: A Technical Guide," copyright 2006 RXN Communications, RXN Communications, Victoria, Minnesota 55386, USA, 2006.

[2] John R. Vacca, Firewalls: Jumpstart for Network and Systems Administrators, Digital Press, 2004.

[3] John R. Vacca, Satellite Encryption, Academic Press, Jul 1999.

[4] John R. Vacca, The Essential Guide To Storage Area Networks Prentice Hall, Nov 2001.

[5] John R. Vacca, Electronic Commerce, 4th edition(Networking Series), Charles River Media, Aug 2003.

Chapter 6

RESPONDING TO ATTACKS

INTRODUCTION

A series of questions will emerge from the need to support some combination of the Internet-based enterprise requirements discussed next; and, the major focus of this chapter:

- Identification and Authentication
- Software Import Control
- Encryption
- System/Architecture Level
- Incident Handling
- Administrative
- Awareness and Education [1]

What controls and procedures should be implemented to support your enterprise needs? What type of risk profile do you fall under? What is your style and culture of doing business? Who is responsible? The elements that drive the answers to such questions form the policy framework for the enterprise to respond to attacks [1].

SAMPLE POLICY AREAS

This first part of the chapter contains hypothetical sample policy statements that address Internet-based security. The policy elements are derived from the major sources of security controls (software import control, encryption [3], and system architecture). The rationale that drives the selection of certain policy is given, followed by the actual sample policy statement(s) [1].

Multiple sample policies are contained here for use at the different risk profiles as was previously discussed in Chapter 5. Some areas provide multiple examples at the same risk level to show the different presentation methods that might be used to get the message across [1].

Security policies fall into two broad categories: technical policies to be carried out by hardware or software, and administrative policy to be carried out by people using and managing the system. The following indicate each type of policy [1].

Identification And Authentication

Identification and Authentication (I&A) is the process of recognizing and verifying valid users or processes. I&A information is generally then used to determine what system resources a user or process will be allowed to access. The determination of who can access what should be part of a data categorization effort, described later in the chapter [1].

This chapter assumes that a decision has been made to allow connectivity to internal systems from the Internet. If there is no connectivity, there is no need for I&A. Many enterprises separate Internet-accessible systems from internal systems through the use of firewalls [2] and routers [1].

Authentication over the Internet presents several problems. It is relatively easy to capture identification and authentication data (or any data) and replay it in order to impersonate a user. As with other remote I&A, and often with internal I&A, there can be a high level of user dissatisfaction and uncertainty which can make I&A data obtainable via social engineering. Having additional I&A for use of the Internet may also contribute to I&A data proliferation which is difficult for users to manage. Another problem is the ability to hijack a user session after the I&A has been performed [1].

There are three major types of authentication available: static, robust, and continuous. Static authentication includes passwords and other techniques that can be compromised through replay attacks. They are often called reusable passwords. Robust authentication involves the use of cryptography or other techniques to create one-time passwords that are used to create sessions. These can be compromised by session hijacking. Continuous authentication prevents session hijacking [1].

Static Authentication

Static authentication only provides protection against attacks in which an imposter cannot see, insert or alter the information passed between the claimant and the verifier during an authentication exchange and subsequent session. In these cases, an imposter can only attempt to assume a claimant's identity by initiating an access control session as any valid user might do; and, trying to guess a legitimate user's authentication data. Traditional password schemes provide this level of protection, and the strength of the authentication process is highly dependent on the difficulty of guessing password values and how well they are protected [1].

Robust Authentication

Robust authentication mechanisms relies on dynamic authentication data that changes with each authenticated session between a claimant and verifier. An imposter who can see information passed between the claimant and verifier may attempt to record this information, initiate a separate access control session with the verifier, and replay the recorded authentication data in an attempt to assume the claimant's identity. Level 1 strong authentication protects against such attacks, because authentication data recorded during a previous session will not be valid for any subsequent sessions [1].

However, robust authentication does not provide protection against active attacks in which the imposter is able to alter the content or flow of information between the claimant and verifier after they have established a legitimate session. Since the verifier binds the claimant's identity to the logical communications channel for the duration of the session, the verifier believes that the claimant is the source of all data received through this channel [1].

Traditional fixed passwords would fail to provide robust authentication because the password of a valid user could be viewed and used to assume that user's identity later. However, one-time passwords and digital signatures can provide this level of protection [1].

Continuous Authentication

Continuous authentication provides protection against impostors who can see, alter, and insert information passed between the claimant and verifier even after the claimant/verifier authentication is complete. These are typically referred to as active attacks, since they assume that the imposter can actively influence the connection between claimant and verifier. One way to provide this form of authentication is to apply a digital signature algorithm to every bit of data that is sent from the claimant to the verifier. There are other combinations of cryptography that can provide this form of authentication, but current strategies rely on applying some type of cryptography to every bit of data sent. Otherwise, any unprotected bit would be suspect [1].

General Internet I&A Policies

Although passwords are easily compromised, an enterprise may find that a threat is not likely, would be fairly easy to recover from, or would not affect critical systems (which may have separate protection mechanisms). Low authentication is required for access to corporate systems from the Internet. The minimum standard for authentication is passwords. Medium Internet access to XYZ category of information and processing (low impact if modified, unavailable, or disclosed) requires a password and access to all other resources requires robust authentication [1].

Telnet access to enterprise resources from the Internet requires the use of robust authentication. High Internet access to all systems behind the firewall requires robust authentication. Access to ABC information and processing (high impact if modified, unavailable, or disclosed) requires continuous authentication [1].

Password Management Policies

The following discussion covers general password policies applicable for Internet use. Passwords and user logon IDs will be unique to each authorized user:

- Passwords will consist of a minimum of 6 alphanumeric characters (no common names or phrases). There should be computer-controlled lists of proscribed password rules and periodic testing (letter and number sequences, character repetition, initials, common words, and standard names) to identify any password weaknesses.

- Passwords will be kept private (not shared, coded into programs, or written down).
- Passwords will be changed every 90 days (or other period). Most systems can enforce password change with an automatic expiration and prevent repeated or reused passwords.
- User accounts will be frozen after 3 failed logon attempts. All erroneous password entries will be recorded in an audit log for later inspection and action, as necessary.
- Sessions will be suspended after 15 minutes (or other specified period) of inactivity and require the password to be reentered.
- Successful logons should display the date and time of the last logon and logoff.
- Logon IDs and passwords should be suspended after a specified period of disuse.
- For high risk systems: After excessive violations, the system should generate an alarm and be able to simulate a continuing session (with dummy data, etc.) for the failed user (to keep this user connected while personnel attempt to investigate the incoming connection [1].

Robust Authentication Policy

The decision to use robust authentication requires an understanding of the security gained and the cost of user acceptance and administration. User acceptance will be dramatically improved if users are appropriately trained on why the robust authentication is being used and how to use it [1].

There are many technologies available that provide robust authentication including dynamic password generators, cryptography-based challenge/response tokens and software, and digital signatures and certificates. If digital signatures and certificates are used another policy area is opened up – what are the security requirements for the certificates [1]?

Users of robust authentication must receive training prior to use of the authentication method. Employees are responsible for safe handling and storage of all enterprise authentication devices. Authentication tokens should not be stored with a computer that will be used to access enterprise systems. If an authentication device is lost or stolen, the loss must be immediately reported to security so that the device can be disabled [1].

Digital Signatures And Certificates

If I&A makes use of digital signatures, then certificates are required. They can be issued by the enterprise or by a trusted 3rd party. Commercial PKI infrastructures are emerging within the Internet community. Users can obtain certificates with various levels of assurance [1].

Example Of Different Levels For A PKI

Level 1 certificates verify electronic mail addresses. This is done through the use of a personal information number that a user would supply when asked to register. This level of certificate may also provide a name as well as an electronic mail address; however, it may or may not be a genuine name (it could be an alias) [1].

Level 2 certificates verify a user's name, address, social security number. It also verifies other information against a credit bureau database [1].

Level 3 certificates are available to enterprises. This level of certificate provides photo identification (for their employees) to acENTERPRISE the other items of information provided by a Level 2 certificate [1].

Once obtained, digital certificate information may be loaded into an electronic mail application or a web browser application to be activated and provided whenever a web site or another user requests it for the purposes of verifying the identity of the person with whom they are communicating. Trusted certificate authorities are required to use such systems effectively, otherwise fraudulent certificates could easily be issued [1].

Many of the latest web servers and web browsers incorporate the use of digital certificates. Secure Socket Layer (SSL) is the technology used in most Web-based applications. SSL supports strong authentication of the Web server and added client side authentication. Once both sides are authenticated, the session is encrypted, and provides protection against both eavesdropping and session hijacking. The digital certificates used are based on the X.509 standard and describe who issued the certificate, the validity period, and other information [1].

Oddly enough, passwords still play an important role even when using digital certificates. Since a digital certificate is stored on a computer, they can only be used to authenticate the computer, rather than the user, unless the user provides some other form of authentication to the computer. Passwords or passphrases are generally used; smart cards and other hardware tokens will be used in the future. Any enterprise systems making limited distribution data available over the Internet should use digital certificates to validate the identity of both the user and the server. Certificates may only be issued by ENTERPRISE-approved Certificate Authorities. Certificates at the user end will be used in conjunction with standard technologies such as Secure Sockets Layer to provide continuous authentication to eliminate the risk of session hijacking 1].

Access to digital certificates stored on personal computers should be protected by passwords or passphrases. All policies for password management must be followed [1].

Software Import Control

Data on computers is rarely static. Mail arrives and is read. New applications are loaded from floppy, CDROM, or across a network. Web-based interactive software downloads executables that run on a computer. Each modification runs the risk of introducing viruses, damaging the configuration of the computer, or violating software-licensing agreements. Enterprises need to protect themselves with different levels of mechanisms depending on the sensitivity to these risks [1]. Software import control provides an enterprise with several different security challenges:

- Virus and Trojan Horse Prevention, Detection, and Removal
- Controlling Interactive Software (Java, ActiveX)
- Software Licensing [1]

Each challenge can be categorized according to the following criteria:

- Control: Who initiates the activity, and how easily can it be determined that software has been imported

- Threat type: Executable program, macro, applet, violation of licensing agreement
- Cleansing Action: Scanning, refusal of service, control of permissions, auditing, deletion [1]

When importing software onto a computer one runs the risk of getting additional or different functionality than one bargained for. The importation may occur as a direct action, or as a hidden side-effect which is not readily visible. Examples of direct action are:

- File Transfer: Utilizing FTP to transfer a file to a computer
- Reading E-mail: Causing a message which has been transferred to a computer to be read, or using a tool (Word) to read an attachment
- Downloading software, from a floppy disk or over the network can spawn indirect action. Some examples include: Reading a Web page which downloads a Java applet to your computer; and, executing an application such as Microsoft Word, and opening a file infected with a Word Macro Virus [1].

> **Warning:** Viruses imported on floppy disks or infected vendor media will continue to be a major threat.

Virus Prevention, Detection, and Removal

The most common carrier of viruses has been the floppy disk, since sneaker net was the most common means of transferring software between computers. As telephone-based bulletin boards became popular, viruses traveled more frequently via modem. The Internet provides yet another channel for virus infections, one that can often bypass traditional virus controls [1].

For enterprises that allow downloading of software over the Internet (which can be via Internet email attachments), virus scanning at the firewall can be an appropriate choice – but it does not eliminate the need for client and server based virus scanning, as well. For several years to come, viruses imported on floppy disks or infected vendor media will continue to be a major threat [1].

A virus is a self-replicating program spread from executables, boot records, and macros. Executable viruses modify a program to do something other than the original intent. After replicating itself into other programs, the virus may do little more than print an annoying message, or as damaging as deleting all of the data on a disk. There are different levels of sophistication in how hard a virus may be to detect [1].

Simple viruses can be easily recognized by scanning for a signature of byte strings near the entry point of a program, once the virus has been identified. Polymorphic viruses modify themselves as they propagate, therefore have no signature, and can only be found (safely) by executing the program in a virtual processor environment. Boot record viruses modify the boot record such that the virus is executed when the system is booted [1].

Applications that support macros are at risk for macro viruses. Macro viruses are commands that are embedded in data. Vendor applications, such as Word, Excel, or printing standards such as Postscript are common targets. When the application opens the data file the infected macro virus is instantiated [1]. The security service policy for viruses has three aspects:

- Prevention: Policies which prevent the introduction of viruses into a computing environment
- Detection: Determination that an executable, boot record, or data file is contaminated with a virus
- Removal: Deletion of the virus from the infected computing system may require reinstallation of the OS from the ground up, deleting files, or deleting the virus from an infected file [1].

There are various factors that are important in determining the level of security concern for virus infection of a computer. Viruses are most prevalent on DOS, Windows (3.x, 95), and NT operating systems. However there are also some UNIX and even LINUX viruses [1].

The frequency that new applications or files are loaded on to the computer is proportional to the susceptibility of that computer to viruses. Configuration changes resulting from exposure to the Internet, exposure to mail, or receipt of files from external sources are more at risk for contamination [1].

The greater the value of the computer or data on the computer, the greater the concern should be for insuring that virus policy as well as implementation procedures are in place. The cost of removal of the virus from the computing environment must be considered within your enterprise as well as from customers you may have infected. Cost may not always be identified as monetary; enterprise reputation and other considerations are just as important [1].

> **Note:** Viruses are normally introduced into a system by a voluntary act of a user (installation of an application, FTP of a file, reading mail, etc.). Prevention policies can therefore focus on limiting introduction of potentially infected software and files to a system. This also indicates in a high-risk environment that virus-scanning efforts should be focused on when new software or files are introduced to maximize protection.

Low Risk

Software import control policies for low risk environments should concentrate on educating users on their responsibilities for regularly scanning for viruses. For example, let's look at a few [1]:

Prevention

Users will be trained about the possibility of receiving viruses and other malicious code from the Internet. They will also be trained on the use of virus scanning tools [1].

Detection

Off the shelf virus-scanning tools will be used to scan computers weekly. No auditing of virus scanning tool records is necessary [1].

Employees will inform the system administrator of any virus detected, configuration change, or different behavior of a computer or application. When informed that a virus has been detected, the system administrators will inform all users with access to the same programs or data that a virus may have also infected their system. The users will be informed of the steps necessary to determine if their system is infected and the steps to take to remove the virus. Users will report the results of scanning and removal activity to the system administrators [1].

Removal

Any machine thought to be infected by a virus will immediately be disconnected from all networks. The machine will not be reconnected to the network until the system administration staff can verify that the virus has been removed. When applicable, off-the-shelf virus scanning tools will be used to remove a virus from an infected file or program. If virus-scanning software fails to remove the virus, all software on the computer will be deleted including boot records if necessary. The software will then be reinstalled for uninfected sources and re-scanned for viruses [1].

Medium Risk

Software import control policies for medium risk environments should dictate more frequent scanning for viruses. This also includes the use of server and email virus scanners [1].

Prevention

Software will be downloaded and installed only by network administrators (who will scan or test software). Anti-virus software will be installed in file servers to limit the spread of viruses within the network. Scanning of all files and executables will occur daily on the file servers. Workstations will have memory resident anti-virus software installed and configured to scan data as it enters the computer. All incoming electronic mail will be scanned for viruses. Programs will not be executed; as well as, files opened by applications prone to macro viruses without prior scanning [1].

> **Note:** Employee security training will include information about virus infection risks:

Virus scanning software is limited to the detection of viruses that have been previously identified. New and more sophisticated viruses are being developed constantly. Virus scanning software must be updated on a regular (monthly or quarterly) basis to maintain currency with the latest viruses. It is important to inform the system administrator of any different or out of the ordinary behavior a computer or application exhibits. It is important to immediately disconnect a computer that is infected or thought to be infected from networks to reduce the risk of spreading a virus [1].

Detection

Off the shelf virus-scanning tools will be used to scan computers on a daily basis. The virus scanning tools will be updated on a monthly basis. All software or data imported onto a computer (from floppy disk, e-mail, or file transfer) will be scanned before being used [1].

Virus scanning logs will be recorded, reported and examined by the system administration staff. Employees will inform the system administrator of any virus that is detected (configuration change or different behavior of a computer or applications) [1].

When informed that a virus has been detected the system administrators will inform all users who may have access to the same programs or data that a virus may have also infected their system. The users will be informed of the steps necessary to determine if their system is infected and the steps to take to remove the virus. Users will report the results of scanning and removal activity to the system administrators [1].

Removal

Any machine thought to be infected by a virus will immediately be disconnected from all networks. The machine will not be reconnected to the network until system administration staff can verify that the virus has been removed. When applicable, off-the-shelf virus scanning tools will be used to remove a virus from an infected file or program. If virus-scanning software fails to remove the virus, all software on the computer will be deleted including boot records if necessary. The software will then be reinstalled with uninfected sources and rescanned for viruses [1].

High Risk

High security level systems contain data and applications that are critical to the enterprise. Infection will cause considerable loss of time, data, and potentially harm the reputation of the enterprise. Large numbers of computers may be involved. All reasonable measures possible to prevent virus infection must be taken [1].

Prevention

The CIO/Security Administrator must approve all applications before they can be installed on a computer. No unauthorized applications may be installed on a computer. Software configurations will be scanned on a monthly basis to validate that no extraneous software has been added to a computer [1].

Software will be installed only from approved internal servers to limit exposure to contaminated software. No software will be downloaded from the Internet onto any computer. File transfer gets from external sources will not be permitted [1].

Anti-virus software will be installed in file servers to limit the spread of viruses within the network. Scanning of all files and executables will occur daily on the file servers. Workstations will have memory resident anti-virus software installed and configured to scan data as it enters the computer. Programs will not be executed, nor files opened by applications prone to macro viruses without prior scanning [1].

All incoming mail and files received from across a network must be scanned for viruses as they are received. Virus checking will be performed if applicable at firewalls that control access to networks. This will allow centralized virus scanning for the entire enterprise, and reduce overhead by simultaneously scanning incoming messages that have multiple destinations. It also allows for centralized administration of the virus scanning software, limiting the locations on which the latest virus scanning software needs to be maintained [1].

In addition, employee security training will include the following information about virus infection risks:

- Virus scanning software is limited to the detection of viruses that have been previously identified.
- New viruses and more sophisticated viruses are being developed constantly.
- Virus scanning software must be updated on a regular (monthly or quarterly) basis to maintain currency with the latest viruses.
- It is important to inform the system administrator of any different or out of the ordinary behavior a computer or application exhibits.
- It is important to immediately disconnect a computer that is infected or thought to be infected from networks or reduce the risk of spreading a virus [1].

Failure to follow the preceding policies may result in punishment according to ENTERPRISE standards [1].

Detection

All software must be installed on a testbed and tested for viruses before being allowed on an operational machine. Only after receiving approval from the CIO/Security Administrator may software be moved to operational machines [1].

Use off-the-shelf scanning software will be enhanced by state of the art virtual machine emulation for polymorphic virus detection. All other new virus detection methods will be incorporated into the detection test bed. To keep abreast of the latest viruses which have been identified, scanning software will be updated monthly or as updates arrive [1].

Virus scanning of all file systems on a daily basis is mandatory. Virus scanning results will be logged, automatically collected, and audited by the system administration staff [1].

All data imported on a computer (from floppy disk, e-mail, or file transfer) will be scanned before being used. Employees will inform the system administrator of any virus that is detected, configuration changed, or different behavior of a computer or application [1].

When informed that a virus has been detected, the system administrators will inform all users who may have access to the same programs or data that a virus may have also infected their system. The users will be informed of the steps necessary to determine if their system is infected and the steps to take to remove the virus [1].

Removal

Any machine thought to be infected by a virus will immediately be disconnected from all networks. The machine will not be reconnected to the network until system administration staff can verify that the virus has been removed. When applicable, off-the-shelf virus scanning tools will be used to remove a virus from an infected file or program. If virus-scanning software fails to remove the virus, all software on the computer will be deleted including boot records if necessary. The software will then be reinstalled with uninfected sources and rescanned for viruses [1].

Controlling Interactive Software

A programming environment evolving as a result of Internet technology is Interactive Software, as exemplified by Java and ActiveX. In an Interactive Software environment, a user accesses a server across a network. The server downloads an application (applet) onto the user's computer that is then executed. There are significant risks involved in this strategy. Fundamentally, one must trust that what is downloaded will do what has been promised [1].

There have been various claims, now effectively debunked, that when utilizing languages such as Java it is impossible to introduce a virus because of restrictions within the scripting language for file system access and process control. Because of these significant risks, there are several levels of trust that a user must have before employing this technology:

- The server can be trusted to download trustworthy applets
- The applet will execute in a limited environment restricting disk reads and writes to functions which do not have security
- The applet can be scanned to determine if it is safe
- Scripts are interpreted, not precompiled. As such, there is a risk that a script can be modified in transit and not perform its original actions [1].

Java And ActiveX Security Models

Java is a programming language developed by Sun Microsystems in order to provide a mechanism for allowing software programs to be downloaded over the Internet and run on a variety of workstations and personal computers. Java is interpreted at run time, and actually runs on top of software called the Java Virtual Machine. The JVM runs on Unix, Windows, Macintosh, or other operating systems to allow Java applets to run identically across heterogeneous environments [1].

Java's security model is to tightly control the environment in which applets can operate, creating a safe sandbox for applet processing. Applets can only communicate with the server from which they were downloaded and are prohibited from accessing local disks or network connections. However, many bugs have been discovered in Java that allow clever programmers to create applets that can easily escape the sandbox. Sun has responded by making the walls of the sandbox higher, but new vulnerabilities are still regularly found [1].

ActiveX is an outgrowth of Microsoft's Object Linking and Embedding technology, which allows programs to communicate with functions within standard applications, such as word processors and spreadsheets. ActiveX allows applications to communicate over the Internet, and for applets to be downloaded to a user machine and access local resources [1].

Microsoft's ActiveX security model is quite different than Sun's Java model. ActiveX allows the user to specify the trust relationship with the server that downloads the applet. If the server is trusted, and its identity verified by the use of digital certificates, an ActiveX applet can be downloaded and operate much like any other piece of software on the user computer. Digital signatures can be used, called Authenticode, which verifies that the code came from a trusted developer and was not modified [1].

Neither security model is clearly superior. The Java approach limits the damage a malicious applet can cause – if all bugs in Java are found and addressed. The ActiveX approach mirrors the way businesses buy and install commercial software, but it places a large degree of authority with the individual user. Some firewall vendors support blocking or authenticating applets at the firewall [1].

> **Note:** A user may not be aware that an applet is being downloaded and executed on his/her computer. As such, security measures must be set up in advance to prevent such an occurrence.

Low Risk

Users should be trained about the risks of Interactive Software. This also includes how to configure their browsers to prevent downloading of applets [1].

Medium Risk

If possible, firewalls will be configured to block the reception of applets from external sources and block the distribution of applets outside of internal networks unless authentication technology is used to protect it from untrusted sources. Users will configure their browsers to accept applets only from trusted servers. If this not possible, then browsers will be configured to not accept applets. If appropriate, use of applets will be restricted only to development networks and not permitted on operational networks [1].

High Risk

Use of Interactive Software is prohibited. Web browsers, and where applicable, firewalls, will be configured and the configurations audited by the system administration staff to inhibit the downloading of applets. Failure to comply with this policy will result in disciplinary action against the employee [1].

Software Licensing

The Internet has allowed many software enterprises to use new means of distributing software. Many enterprises allow the downloading of trial versions of their products, sometimes limited versions (crippleware) or versions that only operate for a limited period of time. However, many enterprises take a shareware approach, allowing fully functional copies of software to be downloaded for trial use and requiring the user to register and pay for the software when used for commercial purposes [1].

When users forget or decline to properly register software downloaded over the Internet, the enterprise can be in violation of software licenses. This may put an enterprise at severe risk of penalties, or loss of reputation if discovered. The Business Software Alliance and the Software Publishing Alliance actively audit corporate licensing and pursue violators. Internet security policy should detail enterprise policy on downloading commercial software [1].

Low Risk

Vendor licensing regulations will be followed for all commercial software downloaded over the Internet. Trial versions of programs should be deleted after the trial period, or the software should be procured through approved procedures [1].

Medium/High Risk

Commercial software should not be downloaded over the Internet without approval of system administration. All software to be used on ENTERPRISE computers can only be installed by system administration, following all licensing agreements and procedures. The system administration staff will inspect the computers periodically to verify that only approved and licensed software has been installed. Violation of this policy may result in disciplinary action [1].

Encryption

Encryption is the primary means for providing confidentiality services for information sent over the Internet. Encryption can be used to protect any electronic traffic, such as mail messages or the contents of a file being downloaded. Encryption also can protect information in storage [4], such as in databases or stored on computer systems where physical security is difficult or impossible (such as on laptop computers that may be left in hotel rooms) [1].

There are a number of management issues related to encryption use: First of all, the United States government currently imposes export controls on strong cryptography, currently defined as any encryption system with an encryption key longer than 40 bits that does not provide for key recovery. There are no restrictions on encryption for domestic use. For use in foreign countries, or in networks that include nodes in a foreign country, each use must receive export approval. In addition, some countries such as France and China impose their own set of controls on domestic use of encryption. Any use of encryption involving foreign countries needs to be thoroughly researched [1].

Management ability to monitor internal communications or audit internal computer systems may be impacted by the use of encryption. If employees encrypt outgoing email messages, or the content of the hard drive on their desktop computer, system administrative personnel will be unable to audit such messages and files. In addition, if the decryption keys are lost or damaged, the data may be permanently lost. If this level of monitoring or disaster recovery is important to your enterprise operations, policy should mandate the use of encryption systems that support some form of key recovery [1].

There are a bewildering array of encryption algorithms and encryption key lengths. Policy should mandate the use of algorithms that have been in use commercially long enough to provide some assurance of security. The length of the encryption keys used should be driven by the value of the data to be encrypted. In general, given the state of the technology, encryption using keys of 40 or fewer bits is only acceptable for use behind the firewall – for keeping the honest people honest. Leading cryptographers recommend enterprises use key lengths of at least 75 bits, with 90 bits being preferable. The Data Encryption Standard uses 56 bit keys, which is still acceptable for near term use. NIST has developed a new standard, the Advanced Encryption Standard. Triple DES, which provides an effective key length of 112 bits, is still being used [1].

General Encryption Policy

To assure interoperability and consistency across the enterprise, corporate policy should mandate standards to which encryption systems must comply, specifying algorithms and parameters to be used. To assure interoperability and reduce life cycle costs, standard products should be selected for enterprise use. While many easy to use and strong COTS products are available, enterprises still need to understand the overhead involved with encryption. The secure generation, storage, and transmission of keys; as well as, ensuring interoperability and, if needed, key recovery, will require significant resources [1].

> **Note:** In general, key recovery is not an issue for Internet use, except for very high-risk enterprises, but the same encryption will probably be used for local storage.

Medium-High

Encryption should be used for information that will be stored in non-secure locations or transmitted over open networks such as the Internet. Any encryption of other enterprise information must be approved in writing. Where encryption is used, enterprise-approved standard algorithms and standard products must be used. The minimal encryption key length for sensitive or confidential data is 56 bits – 75 bit keys are recommended. The security of any encryption system is very dependent on the secrecy of the encryption keys used – procedures for secure generation and management of those keys are critical. (A specific office is responsible for developing procedures for encryption use and for training users [1].

The use of hardware-based random number generators is required for generating keys for encryption of enterprise information. Use of a software-based random number generator will require written approval. Encryption keys should be considered sensitive information and access to those keys must be restricted on a need to know basis. For symmetrical or secret key systems, such as DES, keys must only be transmitted via secure means. Since any compromise of these secret keys will make any use of encryption useless, security policy must detail acceptable means of distributing such keys. When encryption is to be used, secure means must be used for all distribution of secret keys. Acceptable approaches include:

- Use of public key exchange algorithms
- Double wrapped internal mail
- Double wrapped courier mail [1]

Encryption keys must not be sent via electronic mail, unless the electronic mail is encrypted using keys that have been previously exchanged using secure means. The keys used to encrypt information must be changed at the same frequency as the passwords used to access the information. Data that has been encrypted can be lost forever if the decryption key is lost or damaged. Given that encryption will generally be used to protect valuable information, the loss of decryption keys can result in considerable damage. A number of approaches to assure accessibility of decryption keys have been proposed and are appearing in commercial products. As this technology is in its early stage, there are likely to be interoperability issues between products – enterprise security staff should maintain a list of acceptable technologies or products. All encryption products used must support some form of technology to make encryption keys available to management for all encryption of stored enterprise information. Where encryption is used, enterprise-approved key recovery implementations must be used. Any use of encryption without such technology must be approved in writing. The use of public key encryption technologies requires both a public key and a private key to be created and maintained for each user. Public keys must be distributed or stored in a manner that they are accessible to all users. In advanced applications, digital certificates may be used to distribute public keys via Certificate Authorities. Secret keys are similar to passwords, and must be kept private by each user. Enterprises may choose to require that all employees' secret keys be available to management [1].

The ENTERPRISE Certificate Authority server will maintain all valid public keys for authorized encryption users. For secure communications with external entities, the ENTER-PRISE will accept Digital Certificates only from approved Certificate Authorities [1].

User secret keys must be kept private and should be treated the same as passwords. Any potential compromise of a user secret key must be reported to the security department immediately [1].

Low-Medium

Encryption keys should be considered synonymous with the ENTERPRISE's most sensitive category of information and access to those keys must be restricted on a need to know basis. The keys to be used for encryption must be generated by means that are not easily reproducible by outside parties.

Low

The ENTERPRISE will maintain listings of public keys for authorized encryption users. These lists will be stored on the authentication server or distributed via email. User secret keys must be kept private and should be treated the same as passwords [1].

Remote Access

Enterprises use both dial-in lines and the Internet to provide remote access. Both types of connections can be monitored, but it is much more likely for Internet connections. The entity monitoring a session can read all the traffic including downloaded or uploaded files, email, and authentication information. If enterprises encrypt the entire session, it will address both the authentication and confidentiality issues. For medium-high security environments, encryption can be used to prevent unauthorized viewing of the information flowing during remote access connections [1].

Medium-High

All remote access to the ENTERPRISE computer systems, whether via dial-up or Internet access, must use encryption services to protect the confidentiality of the session. ENTERPRISE approved remote access products must be used to assure interoperability for remote access server encryption technologies [1].

Information regarding access to enterprise computer and communication systems, such as dial-up modem phone numbers, is considered confidential. This information must not be posted on electronic bulletin boards, listed in telephone directories, placed on business cards, or made available to third parties without the written permission of the Network Services Manager. The Network Services Manager will periodically scan direct dial-in lines to monitor compliance with policies and may periodically change the telephone numbers to make it more difficult for unauthorized parties to locate enterprise communications numbers [1].

Virtual Private Networks

Encryption is also used to create virtual private networks on the Internet. This is discussed in more detail later in the chapter.

System/Architecture Level

Connecting to the Internet will involve a number of system architectural decisions that impact overall system security. One initial consideration will be the architecture of the firewall and the connection to the Internet. Other architectural choices that require policy decisions include the use of the Internet to connect physically separate networks (Virtual Private Networks) providing remote access to systems connected to the Internet, and provided access to internal databases from the Internet. The security issues and sample policy statements related to these areas are detailed next [1].

Virtual Private Networks

Many enterprises have local area networks and information servers spread across multiple locations. When enterprise-wide access to information or other LAN-based resources is required, leased lines are often used to connect the LANs into a Wide Area Network. Leased lines are relatively expensive to set up and maintain, making the Internet an attractive alternative for connecting physically separate LANs [1].

The major shortcoming to using the Internet for this purpose is the lack of confidentiality of the data flowing over the Internet between the LANs, as well as the vulnerability to spoofing and other attacks. Virtual Private Networks use encryption to provide the required security services. Typically encryption is performed between firewalls, and secure connectivity is limited to a small number of sites [1].

Security isn't the only issue with using the Internet to connect LANs. The Internet today provides no performance or reliability guarantee. Files or messages may be delayed or not delivered at all, depending on the overall state of the network and the state of individual routers, servers, and networks that make up the Internet [1].

Medium-High

Virtual Private Networks between sites must not use the Internet to carry time critical traffic. Where the level of reliability typically provided by the Internet is not sufficient to guarantee the required level of service to users, other means of interconnection must be used [1].

High

When the Internet is used to provide Virtual Private Network connections between sites, means of rapidly providing backup connections must be maintained to return service in the event of an Internet outage or denial of service. One important consideration when creating Virtual Private Networks is that the security policies in use at each site must be equivalent. A VPN essentially creates one large network out of what were previously multiple independent networks. The security of the VPN will essentially fall to that of the lowest common denominator – if one LAN allows unprotected dial-up access, all resources on the VPN are potentially at risk. The establishment of Virtual Private Networks (VPNs) over the Internet between enterprise networks requires written approval of the CIO. Adding networks to an existing VPN also requires written approval of the CIO. A review and update of the security policies in use at each site to be connected to the VPN must be performed before operation will be authorized.

Trusted Links

The firewall encrypts all traffic destined for the remote host or network and decrypts all traffic it receives from. Traffic flows between hosts in a Trusted VPN relationship freely, as if there were no firewalls in between. The traffic is effectively routed by the firewalls involved, bypassing the proxies and thus not requiring any authentication at the firewall itself. Any two hosts who are part of a VPN Trusted Link have full network connectivity between them, and may communicate using any TCP/IP services that they support. Trusted Links are often used to connect geographically separate networks belonging to the same enterprise, each with their own connections to a local Internet service provider, into a seamless single virtual network in a secure fashion [1].

Private Links

The traffic is encrypted between the firewall and the remote host or network just as it is for the Trusted Link. However, traffic from remote hosts in a Private Link relationship is not freely routed, but must be proxied by the firewall and connections authenticated there as dictated by the firewall's usual proxy access policies. This relationship provides authentication of the network source of the traffic and confidentiality for the data, but the two networks maintain distinct network security perimeters, and only services which the firewall is configured to proxy can be used through it. Private Links are often used between the networks of enterprises that do not wish to allow full access between their networks, but need confidentiality of the traffic between them [1].

Pass-Through Links

Pass-through links are used to forward encrypted traffic between hosts on opposite sides of the firewall who are members of their own VPN peer relationship. This allows a firewall situated between two other VPN peers to be configured to route that encrypted data across. The intermediate firewall does not decrypt this traffic, nor does it need to know the encryption key used, it merely needs to know the addresses of the hosts on both sides of the link so it knows to allow the encrypted packets to pass. This pass-through arrangement means that the intermediate firewall is simply used as a router for this type of traffic [1]. So, for all Virtual Private Connections over the Internet, ENTERPRISE firewalls must operate in the Private Link mode, encrypting VPN traffic and requiring the use of firewall proxies limiting the services available to remote VPN hosts.

Low-Medium

For all Virtual Private Connections over the Internet, ENTERPRISE firewalls must operate in the Trusted Link mode. This also includes encrypting VPN traffic, but not requiring the use of firewall proxies for VPN traffic [1].

Remote System Access

While Internet-based attacks get most of the media attention, most computer system break-ins occur via dial-up modems. As discussed in section Chapter 5, there are a variety of configurations for supporting remote access via dial-up lines and other means. In general, the major security issue is authentication – making sure that only legitimate users can remotely access your system. The use of one-time passwords and hardware tokens is recommended for most enterprises [1].

Another issue is the enterprise's ability to monitor the use of remote access capabilities. The most effective approach is to centralize the modems into remote access servers or modem pools [1].

Low

All users who access the enterprise system through dial-in connections periodically change their passwords. Direct dial-in connections to enterprise production systems must be approved by the Network Services Manager [1].

Medium-High

All users who access the enterprise system through dial-in connections must use one-time passwords. Direct dial-in connections to enterprise production systems must be approved by the Network Services Manager and the Information Security Manager. The use of desktop modems to support dial-in access to enterprise systems is prohibited [1].

Low-Medium-High

Information regarding access to enterprise computer and communication systems, such as dial-up modem phone numbers, is considered confidential. This information must not be posted on electronic bulletin boards, listed in telephone directories, placed on business cards, or made available to third parties without the written permission of the Network Services Manager. The Network Services Manager will periodically scan direct dial-in lines to monitor compliance with policies and may periodically change the telephone numbers to make it more difficult for unauthorized parties to locate enterprise communications numbers [1].

Access to Internal Databases

Another key architectural decision is how to securely support external access to internal databases. For small, relatively static user populations (enterprise employees) that answer may be to create a VPN whose perimeter includes all users who need to access the internal database. For large or frequently changing user populations, such as the general public, some other means of securing access needs to be provided [1].

One solution is to host the database outside the enterprise firewall. This poses the lowest risk to internal systems but makes the database vulnerable to outside attack and may require connectivity through the firewall to allow internal access or updates. This architecture is not workable in many cases, where the database needs to be accessed frequently by internal legacy systems [1].

Another approach is to provide connectivity from an external (outside the firewall) server through the firewall to an internal database. Many firewalls now support SQL proxies to limit the risk of providing this connectivity. The use of these proxies is fairly complex and requires training and expertise to assure a secure configuration. Allowing such connections through the firewall greatly increases risk and should be avoided whenever possible [1].

Low-Medium

All connections between external users and internal databases must be through the appropriate proxies on the ENTERPRISE firewall. Only proxies approved by the Network Services Manager will be installed on the firewall [1].

High

No connections between external users and internal databases will be allowed. Where applications require Internet or Web access to ENTERPRISE databases, the databases will be hosted external to the ENTERPRISE firewall. Updates to these databases will be via air gap means, such as using floppy disks or other portable media. Any sensitive or confidential information to be stored on an external server will be encrypted [1].

Use Of Multiple Firewalls

Virtual Private Networks is one example of the use of multiple firewalls. Bandwidth, availability or other performance requirements often dictate the use of multiple parallel firewalls, as well. Since the firewalls are in parallel, the security policy implemented by each firewall must be identical, or the resultant level of security provided would be that of the least secure firewall. When multiple firewalls are used in parallel for availability or performance reasons, the configuration of each firewall should be identical and under the control of a single firewall administrator. The Network Services Manager must approve any change to any firewall in this type of configuration. Multiple internal firewalls may also be used to segment networks to provide access control to sensitive data and support detailed logging of such access. Known as Intranet firewalls, this type of configuration is often used by medium-high security enterprises to wall off human resource or financial systems on internal networks [1].

Medium-High

Any sensitive or confidential information made accessible on internal networks that are connected to the Internet must be protected by a ENTERPRISE-approved firewall. The firewall should be configured to limit access to such data to only authorized internal users. Load balancing is the process whereby network traffic flowing through a network goes through more than one firewall in order to have a high network throughput. This is analogous to having more than one route to a city. The reason for doing this is twofold: load sharing and firewall backup (in case of the failure of one firewall, security will be maintained). Therefore, a site that wishes to include this policy might write one as follows: More than one firewall may be deployed so that in case of one firewall failure, access into your network is still controlled by a firewall, or that network load is shared among these firewalls. In such a configuration, the operational parameters of all firewalls should be identical to assure a consistent security configuration [1].

Incident Handling

An incident is defined as an event that has actual or potentially adverse effects on computer or network operations resulting in fraud, waste, or abuse; compromise of information; or loss or damage of property or information. Examples include penetration of a computer system, exploitation of technical vulnerabilities, or introduction of computer viruses or other forms of malicious software (as defined by FIRST – Forum of Incident Response and Security Team) [1].

Although the focus on securing a connection to the Internet is often on protecting from external threats, the misuse of the Internet connection by internal users is often a significant threat as well. Internal users may now have wide open access to internal databases via Virtual Private Networks or intranets that never existed before. Internal users may also be tempted to explore other systems over the Internet, causing your computer system to be the launching point for Internet attacks. Incident handling needs to address internal incidents as well as those instigated by external threats [1].

Intrusion Detection Overview

Intrusion detection plays an important role in implementing an enterprise security policy. As information systems grow in complexity, effective security systems must evolve. With the proliferation of the number of vulnerability points introduced by the use of distributed systems, it is not enough to just bolt the doors and hope the locks hold. Some type of assurance is needed that the network is secure that all the doors are closed, they are strong and the locks are working. Intrusion detection systems can provide part of that assurance [1].

Intrusion detection provides two important functions in protecting information system assets. The first function is that of a feedback mechanism which informs the security staff as to the effectiveness of other components of the security system. In this sense intrusion detection is like a report card for perimeter defense sub-systems such as firewalls and dial-up access control systems. The lack of detected intrusions is an indication that the perimeter defenses are working, if a robust and effective intrusion detection system is in place. The second function is to provide a trigger or gating mechanism that determines when to activate planned responses to an incident [1].

This part of the chapter presents an overview of different methods that may be used to detect intrusions into a computer information system. This is a representative list of the tools that various enterprises are using today, hence there will always be new tools evolving. Not all of these tools are used within all network environments, nor should they be. Instead, the tools which are appropriate within the context of asset valuation, risk assessment, cost justification, and resources available, should be selected for each situation [1].

Security is normally enforced through a combination of technical and traditional management methods. A decision must be made on the role technology will play in enforcing or supporting the policy. The methods listed tend to be technology based, although some discussion is provided of management tasks relative to these technologies [1]. This part of the chapter on intrusion detection also contains some sample policy statements, ranging from the lowest security to the highest security afforded [1].

Methods

Intrusion detection can be implemented in different ways, and the choice of implementation method should be made based on the type of network being protected, the perimeter defense systems used, and the level of protection required by local policy. There are a number of methods for performing intrusion detection [1].

Regardless of the method chosen, an enterprise should have a defined Incident Response Capability. This may simply be a designated point of contact for users to report suspected incidents to, or it may be as formal as a team that uses proactive methods and tools to prevent incidents [1].

One method is passively waiting for complaints from users or others. Typical complaints might be that files have been modified or removed, or that disk volumes on servers are full for no apparent reason. The benefit of this method is that it is easy to implement. There are several disadvantages to this method. Obviously this method adds little protection to information systems or assurance to the security policy. Sophisticated attackers generally will not create such obvious symptoms. By the time it is apparent that the network has been attacked, it is too late to prevent damage. In extreme cases, the first indication that something is wrong may be when law enforcement investigators, or worse, newspaper reporters arrive on the premises [1].

Another method is reviewing audit logs periodically, searching for exceptional events. The events, which are of interest, could be excessive failed authentication attempts, excessive permission violations, unusual traffic patterns, etc. This method offers some additional protection beyond passive complaint based detection. Depending upon the frequency of the audit review, it may provide sufficient information to limit the impact of an attack. Generally, all modern computer and network systems will provide the required level of audit capability as a standard feature. Often, this feature is disabled by default and must be explicitly enabled. This method will require administrative efforts on an ongoing basis. Its effectiveness is dependent upon consistent and frequent manual review of log records. If the log function built into the underlying operating system or application is used (and that system or application is not sufficiently hardened against attacks), this method may be circumvented by sophisticated attackers who cover their tracks. They cover their tracks by disabling logging functions during their unauthorized activities, or by editing the log files to remove incriminating evidence [1].

Other monitoring tools can easily be constructed using standard operating system software, by using several, often unrelated, programs together. For example, checklists of file ownership's and permission settings can be generated and stored off-line. These lists can then be reconstructed periodically and compared against the master. Differences may indicate that unauthorized modifications have been made to the system [1].

It is important to vary the monitoring schedule. System administrators can execute many of the commands used for monitoring periodically throughout the day. In addition, by running various monitoring commands at different times throughout the day, it becomes harder for an intruder to predict your actions. For example, if an intruder knows that each day at 5:00 p.m. the system is checked to see that everyone has logged off, he or she will simply wait until after the check has completed before logging in. But if the system administrator performs routine monitoring at random times of the day, an intruder cannot guess when this will happen, and thus a greater risk of detection [1].

Integrity-monitor tools for UNIX systems such as Tripwire perform a checksum of a file or file system, so that subsequent checksum results of the same system can be compared in order to detect modifications. These tools require installation by skilled system administrators. Ongoing administrative time is required to ensure that the integrity checks are consistent. Since the security mechanism is not part of the underlying operating systems or applications, it is much less likely that an attacker can cover the tracks left by their activities. Unfortunately, these tools may only be effective at indicating attacks where system modules are modified and may not detect other types of attacks, such as those where information is stolen by copying files [1].

Alarms and alerts from perimeter access control systems can indicate that a suspected attack is underway. Some perimeter access control systems such as firewalls or dial-up access control systems may be configurable to provide alarms if certain access rules are violated, error thresholds are exceeded, etc. These alarms may be audible, visual, email, pager, or messages to higher level management systems (SNMP traps). Once implemented, this type of detection may be relatively inexpensive from a management perspective, as the system may configured to send alerts to the network management staff who are already monitoring other aspects of network status (dedicated personnel are not required). However, only intrusions that traverse the known perimeter systems will be detected. Intrusion from external networks via covert or unknown channels will not be detected, nor will unauthorized access of sensitive hosts or servers by employees or other valid network users. Another factor to consider is that if an attacker is capable of penetrating these perimeter access control systems, there is no assurance that they will not also disable any alarm functions provided by those systems [1].

Automated tools exist which perform real-time analysis of data traffic, and employ advanced logic to detect patterns of activity that indicate that an intrusion attack is underway. These tools can be host based, installed on each host system that is deemed critical, or network based, installed at centralized data traffic locations to allow all traffic to be monitored. These tools may be deployed so that attacks from both internal and external sources may be detected. Since they are independent of both host/server operating systems and perimeter access control systems, they are less likely to be subverted by attackers who successfully penetrate those systems. The success of these systems is dependent upon accurate foreknowledge of behavior patterns that indicate an intrusion, and this may not be possible. If overly specific patterns are defined, actual observed intrusive behavior may not match the target behavior. If less specific patterns are defined, excessive false alarms may result. This type of approach requires sophisticated heuristics that may overly complicate the use of the tool [1].

Tools also exist which regard statistical anomalies as a possible indication of an intrusion. This is done by maintaining a statistical profile of various network entities such as individual users, groups of users, applications, servers, etc., and then comparing the observed behavior of a member of one of these classes of entities. If the observed behavior falls outside of the range of the statistical profile, then this is an indication of a possible intrusion. This type of approach requires sophisticated heuristics that may overly complicate the use of the tool [1].

Use of sophisticated software forensics may identify authorship of various code modules. By routinely analyzing modules on protected systems, substitution of valid software by intruders can be detected. This esoteric approach theoretically offers protection against attacks which would not be detected by network perimeter defenses, such as those which use covert channels, or attacks by internal users where those users are knowledgeable and sophisticated enough to circumvent normal host security. The possible benefit of this method must be balanced against the normally low probability of such an attack and the complexity of the defense, as well as its limitation to detecting software modification such as introduction of Trojan horse programs [1].

Incident Response

The computer security policy should define the approach to be taken when dealing with a suspected intrusion. The procedures for dealing with these types of problems must be written down. A number of questions must be addressed before an incident occurs, so that the answers result from a calm, business-like consideration rather than the possible panic that may arise during the excitement of the incident. Some of the questions that must be addressed include:

- Who has authority to decide what actions will be taken?
- When should law enforcement be involved?
- Should your enterprise cooperate with other sites in trying to track down an intruder?

- Should the intrusion be stopped immediately upon detection, or should the suspected intruder be allowed to continue? By allowing the suspected intrusion to continue, additional evidence may be gathered in order to understand the method of attack to prevent a recurrence, as well as for possible use in tracking down the intruder(s) and for bringing civil and/or legal action against them.

Answers to these questions should be part of the incident handling procedures. If incident handling procedures are not in place, they need to be developed. The intrusion detection systems and procedures outlined here are only one part of an overall security program. While some limited utility may be derived from any one component of a security program (access control, intrusion detection, incident response, etc.) for best results, all components should be implemented in a unified approach based on a security policy developed for the specific site. For example, if server-based alarms are forwarded to the client/server support group, but firewall alarms are handled by the network support group, the extent of an intrusion may be underestimated or missed entirely (see sidebar, "Intrusion Detection Policy Risk Levels") [1].

Intrusion Detection Policy Risk Levels

Intrusion Detection Policy: Low Risk

Implementation:

- Operating system and application software logging processes should be enabled on all host and server systems.
- Alarm and alert functions, as well as logging, of any firewalls and other network perimeter access control systems should be enabled.

Administration:

- System integrity checks of the firewalls and other network perimeter access control systems must be performed on a routine basis.
- Audit logs from the perimeter access control systems should be reviewed daily.
- Audit logs for servers and hosts on the internal, protected network should be reviewed on a weekly basis.
- Users should be trained to report any anomalies in system performance to their system administration staff, as well as relevant network or information systems security staff.
- All trouble reports received by system administration personnel should be reviewed for symptoms that might indicate intrusive activity. Suspicious symptoms should be reported to Network or Information Systems security personnel.

Intrusion Detection Policy: Medium Risk

Implementation:

- Normal logging processes should be enabled on all host and server systems.
- Alarm and alert functions, as well as logging, of any firewalls and other network perimeter access control systems should be enabled.
- All critical servers should have additional monitoring tools such as tripwire or appropriate software wrappers installed, as a supplement to the activity logging process provided by the operating system. Examples: Domain Name Servers, authentication servers, security servers in the Unix environment, domain controllers and Exchange servers in the Windows NT environment, and any application server which is considered to be mission critical should be afforded this protection.

Administration:

- System integrity checks of the firewalls and other network perimeter access control systems must be performed on a routine basis.
- Audit logs from the perimeter access control systems should be reviewed daily.
- Audit logs for servers and hosts on the internal, protected network should be reviewed on a weekly basis.
- User education should be provided in order to train end users of computing systems to report any anomalies in system performance to their system administration staff, as well as relevant network or information systems security staff.
- All trouble reports received by system administration personnel should be reviewed for symptoms that might indicate intrusive activity. Suspicious symptoms should be reported to Network or Information Systems security personnel.
- Host based intrusion tools such as tripwire will be checked on a routine basis.
- The IRC or network security personnel will establish relationships with other incident response enterprises, such as other IRCs within the organization or FIRST (FIRST maintains contact with many IRCs (see http://www.first.org)) and share relevant threats, vulnerabilities, or incidents.
- Unless critical systems have been compromised, the enterprise will first make an attempt to track intruders before correcting systems. (Name of specific person or office) has the authority to make decisions concerning closing security holes or attempting to learn more about the intruder. This person must be well training in legal issues surrounding incident handling.

Intrusion Detection Policy: High Risk

Implementation:

- Normal logging processes should be enabled on all host and server systems.
- Alarm and alert functions, as well as logging, of any firewalls and other network perimeter access control systems should be enabled.
- All servers should have additional monitoring tools such as tripwire or appropriate software wrappers installed, as a supplement to the activity logging process provided by the operating system.
- All critical servers should have redundant intrusion detection tools installed, which operate on a different principle from the primary tool that is installed on all servers. For examples: If the primary IDS tool is tripwire, which uses a checksum based approach to ensuring system integrity, then the critical servers will also have expert systems IDS tools which use a statistical anomaly approach.
- At logical network concentration points, IDS tools will be installed which monitor for traffic patterns consistent with known attacks.

Administration:

- System integrity checks of the firewalls and other network perimeter access control systems must be performed on a routine basis.
- Audit logs from the perimeter access control systems should be reviewed daily.
- Audit logs for servers and hosts on the internal, protected network should be reviewed on a daily basis.
- User education should be provided in order to train end users of computing systems to report any anomalies in system performance to their system administration staff, as well as relevant network or information systems security staff.
- All trouble reports received by system administration personnel should be reviewed for symptoms that might indicate intrusive activity. Suspicious symptoms should be reported to Network or Information Systems security personnel.
- Host based intrusion tools such as tripwire, will be checked on a daily basis.
- Network traffic monitoring IDS systems will be checked on a periodic basis for proper function and configuration.
- The IRC or network security personnel will establish relationships with other incident response enterprises, such as other IRCs within the enterprise or FIRST (FIRST maintains contact with many IRCs (see http://www.first.org)) and share relevant threats, vulnerabilities, or incidents.
- The enterprise will attempt to prosecute intruders but will not allow security holes to go uncorrected in order to learn more about the intruder [1].

Administrative

Internet security policy must be closely integrated with the day-to-day use of the Internet by its users and the day-to-day management of the network and computer systems. It must also be adopted into the organization's culture and environment through education. This document concentrates on areas of technical policy. However, administrative decisions such as assigning security responsibility are, often, more important in the long run. This part of the chapter addresses additional aspects of Internet security that need to be considered as administrative issues [1].

In addition to the myriad technical and administrative responsibilities of the network administrator for internal operations, there are responsibilities related to Internet connectivity. This part of the chapter covers areas not addressed in other chapters:

- Assigning security responsibility.
- Resolving violations/establishing penalties.
- Appropriate use, including restricting access to specific WWW sites or Usenet newsgroups, etc., in accordance with ENTERPRISE policy. Appropriate use of email is covered later in this chapter.
- Establishing a privacy policy, specifically including email privacy and network monitoring. Email privacy is included later in the chapter on Email [1].

Assigning Security Responsibility

The success of any security policy depends more on the motivation and skill of the people administering the policy than it does on any sophisticated technical controls. Effective Internet security begins with the network administrator(s) (often called the LAN or System administrator). The network administrators are responsible for implementing LAN security as it pertains to the Internet. If there are multiple network administrators, it is important that roles be coordinated. For example, an attack on a ENTERPRISE's Web site may involve contingency plans for response and restoring to be carried out by a Web administrator; as well as, an increase in the local auditing and monitoring of the internal network by the LAN administrator and increased surveillance of the firewall by a Firewall administrator. It is an enterprise decision, often having to do with size, whether or not to group various network administration functions together [1].

The enterprise should specifically name the person or office responsible for the day to day security of the Internet connection. This duty will often be given to the network or LAN administrator but may also be given to a separate security enterprise. In this case, it is imperative that the network administrator and the security officer coordinate closely and that the security officer be well-versed in Internet protocols [1].

The person or office responsible for Internet security is the person or entity whom you designate him or her or it to be. The person responsible for Internet security may have considerable technical power to configure the firewall, create and suspend userIDs and review audit reports. The actions of this person should be monitored by using separation of duties (if there are multiple network administrators) or through careful screening of the individual. A disgruntled or malicious network administrator is a significant problem [1].

Higher risk enterprises may wish to use the following policies: A personnel screening process should be in place for critical roles. And, critical roles such as system and LAN administrators, security personnel, and other sensitive positions as determined by senior management must satisfactorily complete the screening before being given system manager privileges [1].

Furthermore, system and LAN administrators and other privileged roles are given incremental access. In other words, newly hired system administrators are not given full system privileges if their job function does not require it. More privileges are given as the breath of their job function increases, and consequently, their level of trust [1].

Managers of critical roles are responsible for determining job function and scope so that broad system and network privileges are not excessively given. Unfortunately, system policy will not always be followed. For any of the specific policies discussed in this chapter, it may be appropriate for an enterprise to state penalties for non-compliance. For the most part, this is only necessary if the penalty is severe or could be construed as severe. Other violations can be dealt with on a case-by-case basis using the procedures the enterprise uses for other personnel problems [1].

> **Note:** Many enterprises have stated penalties which are severe for software copyright violations, because employees viewed the act as minor; whereas, the enterprise and the copyright holder viewed it as major.

The LAN Administrator may temporarily suspend access privileges of any user if deemed necessary to maintain the integrity of the computer or network. A more strict policy may cite the need for authorization from the Security Officer or System Manager prior to the system administrator taking or restoring system privileges [1].

Appropriate Use

Similar to policies for appropriate use of the telephone, enterprises need to define appropriate use of the Internet and the World Wide Web. While it is tempting to simply state that any such use must be for business purposes only, it is generally recognized that this type of policy is completely unenforceable. If a policy cannot be consistently enforced, non-compliance is inevitable and the policy will have no force as a basis for punitive action. Acceptable use of electronic mail as well as the related privacy concerns is identified later in the chapter [1].

Higher risk enterprises that cannot tolerate a more flexible attitude toward casual use of the Internet might consider some alternative solutions that may fit better into the ENTERPRISE culture and are enforceable. A separate public access server with a commercial Internet service provider or other link to the Internet, could be set up for employee use. This service would not be connected to any internal systems and could be used for incidental purposes in accordance with the ENTERPRISE's appropriate use policy [1].

Software tools such as a firewall can be used to block access to all Internet sites except those that the enterprise has approved. No matter what the risk environment, certain uses of the ENTERPRISE connection to the Internet can never be sanctioned. The use of the ENTERPRISE connection to the Internet is inappropriate when that use:

- Compromises the privacy of users and their personal data.
- Damages the integrity of a computer system, or the data or programs stored on a computer system.
- Disrupts the intended use of system or network resources.
- Wastes resources that are needed for business use (people, network bandwidth, or CPU cycles).
- Uses or copies proprietary software when not authorized to do so.
- Uses a computer system as a conduit for unauthorized access attempts on other computer systems.
- Uses a government, enterprise, or university-owned system for private purposes or for purposes not in the direct interest of the government, enterprise, or university.
- Consists of unauthorized and excessive snooping, probing, or otherwise connecting to a node or nodes in a manner that is deemed not to be of an authorized nature.
- Results in the uploading, downloading, modification, or removal of files on any node in the network for which such action is not authorized [1].

Whether an enterprise's policy on acceptable use of the Internet is flexible, tolerant, or severe, education is the key to influencing user behavior. Users need to be educated on how they are a part of the ENTERPRISE's reputation and how Internet use can affect that reputation. Users should know that every visit to an Internet site leaves a footprint and why the ENTERPRISE reserves the right to monitor its resources. Administrators need to know their responsibilities regarding the implementation of tools and technical controls (blocking access to sites, monitoring, and reporting) – so that the ENTERPRISE's acceptable use policy can be enforced [1].

Internet Usage Policy: Low Risk

The Internet is considered a valuable ENTERPRISE asset. Users are encouraged to make use of the Internet and explore its uses. With such open access, employees must maintain a diligent and professional working environment [1].

Employees may not use the Internet for personal commercial purposes, may not access any obscene or pornographic sites, and may not access or use information that would be considered harassing. Employees abusing such privileges will be subject to monitoring of their computer system activity and disciplinary action, ranging from verbal reprimands to termination or legal prosecution [1].

Access to the Internet from a ENTERPRISE-owned home computer or through ENTERPRISE-owned connections must adhere to all the same policies that apply to use from within ENTERPRISE facilities. Employees should not allow family members or other non-employees to access ENTERPRISE computer systems [1].

> **Tip:** Users posting to Usenet newsgroups, Internet mailing lists, etc. must include a ENTERPRISE disclaimer as part of each message.

It is impossible to define all possible unauthorized use, therefore disciplinary action may occur after other actions if the circumstances warrant it. Examples of other behavior deemed unacceptable which would result in disciplinary action include:

- Unauthorized attempts to break into any computer.
- Using ENTERPRISE time and resources for personal gain.
- Theft or copying electronic files without permission.
- Sending or posting ENTERPRISE confidential files outside the ENTERPRISE or inside the ENTERPRISE to unauthorized personnel.
- Refusing to cooperate with a reasonable security investigation.
- Sending chain letters through e-mail [1].

Internet Usage Policy: Medium Risk

A ENTERPRISE's computer systems and networks are provided for enterprise use only. Occasional, reasonable personal use is allowed. Any use perceived to be illegal, harassing, offensive, in violation of other ENTERPRISE policies, or any other uses that would reflect adversely on the ENTERPRISE can be the basis for disciplinary action up to and including termination or judicial action. All employees are expected to conduct their use of these systems with the same integrity as in face-to-face or telephonic enterprise operations [1].

Another approach to stating the above might be: ENTERPRISE communications systems and equipment; including electronic mail and Internet systems; along with their associated hardware and software, are for official and authorized purposes only. Managers may authorize incidental use which: does not interfere with the performance or professional duties; is of reasonable duration and frequency; serves a legitimate ENTERPRISE interest, such as enhancing professional interests or education; and, does not overburden the system or create any additional expense to the ENTERPRISE [1].

> **Tip:** Users posting to Usenet newsgroups, Internet mailing lists, etc. must include a ENTERPRISE disclaimer as part of each message.

Personal accounts on on-line services should not be used from ENTERPRISE computers. A ENTERPRISE subscription for commercial Internet services or fee-for-use services must be in place prior to using ENTERPRISE-owned equipment to access these commercial services [1].

Passwords to ENTERPRISE systems are provided in order to protect sensitive information and messages from unauthorized use or viewing. Such passwords are not intended to prevent appropriate review by ENTERPRISE management. ENTERPRISE management reserves the right to periodically monitor employees' use of any computer systems or network [1].

> **Note:** Managers are responsible for ensuring that assigned personnel understand Internet acceptable use policy.

Access to the Internet from a home computer must adhere to all the same policies that apply to use from within ENTERPRISE facilities. Employees should not allow family members or other non-employees to access ENTERPRISE computer systems [1].

Internet Usage Policy: High Risk

The ENTERPRISE is fully interconnected with the Internet and other networks. In general, valid users enjoy unrestricted network access. However, access from the Internet or other sites to or through ENTERPRISE Internet resources is only authorized when that access is in conjunction with valid work or project-related requirements [1].

A separate public access server to the Internet is provided for an employee's personal use. This service is to be used with professional discretion. Only those sites to which the ENTERPRISE has approved access are available through this service [1].

All employees are expected to conduct their use of these systems with the same integrity as in face-to-face or telephonic business operations. Any use perceived to be illegal, harassing, and offensive or in violation of other ENTERPRISE policies can be the basis for disciplinary action up to and including termination or judicial action [1].

> **Tip:** Users posting to Usenet newsgroups, Internet maillists, etc. must include a ENTERPRISE disclaimer to their message.

> **Note:** ENTERPRISE management reserves the right to periodically monitor employees' use of any computer systems or network.

Access to the Internet from a home computer must adhere to all the same policies that apply to use from within ENTERPRISE facilities. Employees should not allow family members or other non-employees to access ENTERPRISE computer systems [1].

Privacy

The privacy policy for Internet usage should be consistent with other privacy policies. Just because it is (technically) easy to monitor employees does not mean it is always a good idea. Employee morale is a significant factor to security, as well as productivity. Employees should be made aware that network records are subject to release for conditions outside the enterprise's control, such as a subpoena or, for Government agencies, a Freedom of Information Act request [1].

Low And Medium Risk

The Internet connection is an enterprise resource. Activities may be subject to monitoring, recording, and periodic audits to insure they are functioning properly and to protect against unauthorized use. In addition, the enterprise may access any user's computer accounts or communication. The enterprise will disclose information obtained through such auditing to appropriate third parties, including law enforcement authorities or FOIA requesters. Use of resources is expressed consent by the user to such monitoring, recording and auditing [1].

Awareness And Education

Most enterprises' computer users generally fall into one of three camps: those that are Internet wizards; those that are somewhat knowledgeable, but haven't had much experience with it; and, those that have heard of it, know that great stuff is out there, but have no notion as to how to proceed. Most users are generally aware that there are security risks related to Internet use, but don't necessarily understand what the security issues are. They often do not know how to recognize a security problem or how to include Internet security procedures (rules of behavior) into their daily computer lifestyles. They may not know the consequences for inappropriate or unauthorized actions [1].

Making computer system users aware of their security responsibility and teaching them correct practices helps users change their behavior. Users cannot follow policies they do not know about or understand. Training also supports individual accountability, which is one of the most import ways to improve computer security. Without knowing the necessary security measures and how to use them, users cannot be truly accountable for their actions. Training is also needed for network administrators who need special skills to understand and implement the technology needed to secure Internet connections. The risks of Internet connectivity should be emphasized to upper management to ensure their support is obtained [1].

All users, managers, and administrators who are given Internet access should receive initial and periodic security awareness and training appropriate for their use of the Internet. Training for experienced users should focus on acceptable use issues. The reasons why the ENTERPRISE has adopted a policy, for instance, against certain newsgroups needs to be understood. Personal postings or replies to postings that include the "ENTERPRISE.com" header, whether disclaimers are used or not, immediately reflect the ENTERPRISE. This might be a shock to such users if they have come from a university setting. Emphasis should be placed on roles and responsibilities, along with technical security issues. Technical administrators should be trained in their responsibilities for implementing technical policy on their system and networks as previously described [1].

Users that are somewhat knowledgeable need to be educated to the methods and ways of the Internet. These users may be more familiar with bulletin board type systems and must be informed that their postings now span worldwide, rather than the US or a local community. These users need to be patient: they should browse and watch for awhile before jumping in to a discussion group. They should not download software or subscribe to information until the knowledge base improves – it could cause the ENTERPRISE to be at risk. Somewhat knowledgeable users need to be educated as to how to become experienced Internet users in addition to the acceptable use, responsibilities, technical and security issues [1].

Inexperienced users need the full array of help. They must be educated as to what the Internet is, kinds of services that are available, what the community is, and how to interact with it. They must learn about Internet mailing lists, newsgroups, search engines and etiquette on the Internet to name a few. They must also receive the education given to experienced and partly knowledgeable users [1].

Internet Security Education: Low Risk

It is the policy of enterprises to provide periodic security awareness training to all managers, operators, and end users. Such training will be augmented with the very new and rapidly changing issues regarding security and the Internet. Users are encouraged to scan security-related lists, keep up with security issues and technology and share security relevant information with the Security Department [1].

Internet Security Education: Medium Risk

There is a fairly liberal culture on the use of the Internet; however, more knowledge needs to be gained on how to effectively use the Internet capabilities and its security implications. The following policies are in addition to the policy listed for low risk enterprises. Internet security training should include combined or separate training sessions from the regular security education curriculum, news flashes or tips via the system, memos, computer incident alerts, and other appropriate training as determined by the enterprise. Issues and topics covered may include firewall training, downloading of information and software, Applet software (Java, ActiveX), email, mail lists, home pages, browsers, acceptable use of Internet, etc [1].

Network and firewall administrators and staff, and technical managers of networks with an Internet connection should receive training on managing network security, tradeoffs, and costs to various approaches, kinds of attacks that can occur, network architecture, and security policy issues. LAN and system administrators should receive technical hands-on Firewall training [1].

Certain system and network configuration and scanning tools (pingall, SATAN) have become a must for security reviews in terms of identifying active systems and IP address, current configuration parameters, etc. Additionally virus and vulnerability scanning tools both in the public and commercial domain (SATAN, ISS, NETProbe, PINGWARE, COPS, Tripwire, etc.) are extremely useful for exposing system vulnerabilities. All network and system administrators will be educated in their uses. They will also be required to keep up-to-date on such technologies [1].

New users will receive an orientation to the Internet which will include hands-on training, and a review of its security considerations. All users will sign an Internet Acceptable Use agreement [1].

Internet Security Education: High Risk

The enterprise would like to increase the availability of the Internet to its users, but in a conservative manner and only after the users are knowledgeable and competent regarding Internet security issues. The following policies are in addition to the policy listed for medium risk enterprises. Users will also receive continuous security training in the form of news flashes, security alerts or tips via the system, memos, computer incident alerts, and other appropriate training as determined by the enterprise. Issues and topics covered may include firewall training, downloading of information and software, Applet software issues (Java, ActiveX), e-mail, mail lists, home pages, browsers, acceptable use of Internet, encryption, etc. [1].

INTERNET FIREWALL POLICY

Many enterprises have connected or want to connect their private LAN's to the Internet so that their users can have convenient access to Internet services. Since the Internet as a whole is not trustworthy, their private systems are vulnerable to misuse and attack. A firewall is a safeguard one can use to control access between a trusted network and a less trusted one. A firewall is not a single component, it is a strategy for protecting an enterprise's Internet-reachable resources. A firewall serves as the gatekeeper between the untrusted Internet and the more trusted internal networks [1].

The main function of a firewall is to centralize access control. If outsiders or remote users can access the internal networks without going through the firewall, its effectiveness is diluted. For example, if a traveling manager has a modem connected to his or her office PC that he or she can dial into while traveling, and that PC is also on the protected internal network, an attacker who can dial into that PC has circumvented the firewall. If a user has a dial-up Internet account with a commercial ISP, and sometimes connects to the Internet from their office PC via modem, he or she is opening an unsecured connection to the Internet that circumvents the firewall. Firewalls can also be used to secure segments of an enterprise's intranet, but this part of the chapter will concentrate on the Internet aspects of firewall policy. Firewalls provide several types of protection:

- They can block unwanted traffic.
- They can direct incoming traffic to more trustworthy internal systems.
- They hide vulnerable systems which can't easily be secured from the Internet.
- They can log traffic to and from the private network.
- They can hide information like system names, network topology, network device types, and internal user ID's from the Internet.
- They can provide more robust authentication than standard applications might be able to do. Each of these functions are described in more detail next [1].

As with any safeguard, there are trade-offs between convenience and security. Transparency is the visibility of the firewall to both inside users and outsiders going through a firewall. A firewall is transparent to users if they do not notice or stop at the firewall in order to access a network. Firewalls are typically configured to be transparent to internal network users (while going outside the firewall); on the other hand, firewalls are configured to be non-transparent for outside network coming through the firewall. This generally provides the highest level of security without placing an undue burden on internal users [1].

Authentication

Router-based firewalls don't provide user authentication. Host-based firewalls can provide these kinds of authentication:

- Username/password: This is the worst kind, because the information can be sniffed or shoulder-surfed.
- One-time passwords: One-time passwords using software or hardware tokens, generate a new password for each session. This means that old passwords cannot be reused if they are sniffed or otherwise borrowed or stolen.
- Digital Certificates: Digital certificates use a certificate generated using public key encryption [1].

Routing Versus Forwarding

A clearly defined policy has to be written as to whether or not the firewall will act as a router or a forwarder of Internet packets. This is trivial in the case of a router that acts as a packet filtering gateway: the firewall (router in this case) has no option but to route packets. Applications gateway firewalls should generally not be configured to route any traffic between the external interface and the internal network interface, since this could bypass security controls. All external to internal connections should go through the application proxies [1].

Source Routing

Source routing is a routing mechanism whereby the path to a target machine is determined by the source, rather than by intermediate routers. Source routing is mostly used for debugging network problems but could also be used to attack a host. If an attacker has knowledge of some trust relationship between your hosts, source routing can be used to make it appear that the malicious packets are coming from a trusted host. Therefore, because of this security threat, a packet filtering router can easily be configured to reject packets containing source route option. Thus, a site that wishes to avoid the problem of source routing entirely should write that policy [1].

IP Spoofing

IP spoofing is when an attacker masquerades his or her machine as a host on the target's network (fooling a target machine that packets are coming from a trusted machine on the target's internal network). Policy regarding packet routing has to be clearly written so that they will be handled accordingly if there is a security problem. It is necessary that authentication based on source address be combined with other security schemes to protect against IP spoofing attacks [1].

Types Of Firewalls

There are different implementations of firewalls which can be arranged in different ways. The various firewall implementations are discussed next and example policies presented. Table 6-1 depicts several firewall architectures and their ratings as they would apply to low, medium and high risk processing environments [1].

Packet Filtering Gateways

Packet filtering firewalls use routers with packet filtering rules to grant or deny access based on source address, destination address and port. They offer minimum security but at a very low cost, and can be an appropriate choice for a low risk environment. They are fast, flexible, and transparent. Filtering rules are not often easily maintained on a router, but there are tools available to simplify the tasks of creating and maintaining the rules [1]. Filtering gateways do have inherent risks including:

- The source and destination addresses and ports contained in the IP packet header are the only information that is available to the router in making a decision whether or not to permit traffic access to an internal network.
- They don't protect against IP or DNS address spoofing.
- An attacker will have a direct access to any host on the internal network once access has been granted by the firewall.
- Strong user authentication isn't supported with some packet filtering gateways.
- They provide little or no useful logging [1].

Table 6-1. Firewall Security Risk.

Firewall Architecture (if any one of these is being implemented)	High Risk Environment (Hospital)	Medium Risk Environment (University)	Low Risk Environment (florist shop)
Packet filtering	0	1	4
Application Gateways	3	4	2
Hybrid Gateways	4	3	2
Here are rating numbers, from recommended to unacceptable, for various firewall types:			
4 recommended choice			
3 effective option			
2 acceptable			
1 minimal security			
0 unacceptable			

Application Gateways

An application gateway uses server programs (called proxies) that run on the firewall. These proxies take external requests, examine them, and forward legitimate requests to the internal host that provides the appropriate service. Application gateways can support functions such as user authentication and logging [1]. Because an application gateway is considered as the most secure type of firewall, this configuration provides a number of advantages to the medium-high risk site:

- The firewall can be configured as the only host address that is visible to the outside network, requiring all connections to and from the internal network to go through the firewall.
- The use of proxies for different services prevents direct access to services on the internal network, protecting the enterprise against insecure or misconfigured internal hosts.
- Strong user authentication can be enforced with application gateways.
- Proxies can provide detailed logging at the application level [1].

Application level firewalls should be configured such that out-bound network traffic appears as if the traffic had originated from the firewall (only the firewall is visible to outside networks). In this manner, direct access to network services on the internal network is not allowed. All incoming requests for different network services such as Telnet, FTP, HTTP, RLOGIN, etc., regardless of which host on the internal network will be the final destination, must go through the appropriate proxy on the firewall. Applications gateways require a proxy for each service, such as FTP, HTTP, etc., to be supported through the firewall. When a service is required that is not supported by a proxy, an enterprise has three choices:

- Deny the service until the firewall vendor has developed a secure proxy: This is the preferred approach, as many newly introduced Internet services have unacceptable vulnerabilities.

- Develop a custom proxy: This is a fairly difficult task and should be undertaken only by very sophisticated technical enterprises.
- Pass the service through the firewall: Using what are typically called plugs, most application gateway firewalls allow services to be passed directly through the firewall with only a minimum of packet filtering. This can limit some of the vulnerability but can result in compromising the security of systems behind the firewall [1].

Low

When an in-bound Internet service not supported by a proxy is required to pass through the firewall, the firewall administrator should define the configuration or plug that will allow the required service. When a proxy is available from the firewall vendor, the plug must be disabled and the proxy made operative [1].

Medium-High

All in-bound Internet services must be processed by proxy software on the firewall. If a new service is requested, that service will not be made available until a proxy is available from the firewall vendor and tested by the firewall administrator. A custom proxy can be developed in-house or by other vendors only when approved by the CIO [1].

Hybrid Or Complex Gateways

Hybrid gateways combine two or more of the preceding firewall types and implement them in series rather than in parallel. If they are connected in series, then the overall security is enhanced; on the other hand, if they are connected in parallel, then the network security perimeter will be only as secure as the least secure of all methods used. In medium to high risk environments, a hybrid gateway may be the ideal firewall implementation [1].

Firewall Architectures

Firewalls can be configured in a number of different architectures, and provide various levels of security at different costs of installation and operation. Enterprises should match their risk profile to the type of firewall architecture selected. This part of the chapter describes typical firewall architectures and sample policy statements [1].

Multi-Homed Host

A multi-homed host is a host (a firewall in this case) that has more than one network interface, with each interface connected to logically and physically separate network segments. A dual-homed host (host with two interfaces) is the most common instance of a multi-homed host [1].

A dual-homed firewall is a firewall with two network interfaces cards (NICs) with each interface connected to a different networks. For instance, one network interface is typically connected to the external or untrusted network, while the other interface is connected to the internal or trusted network. In this configuration, a key security tenet is not to allow traffic coming in from the untrusted network to be directly routed to the trusted network – the firewall must always act as an intermediary. Routing by the firewall should be disabled for a dual-homed firewall so that IP packets from one network are not directly routed from one network to the other [1].

Screened Host

A screened host firewall architecture uses a host (called a bastion host) to which all outside hosts connect, rather than allow direct connection to other, less secure internal hosts. To achieve this, a filtering router is configured so that all connections to the internal network from the outside network are directed towards the bastion host. If a packet filtering gateway is to be deployed, then a bastion host should be set up so that all connections from the outside network go through the bastion host to prevent direct Internet connection between the ENTERPRISE network and the outside world [1].

Screened Subnet

The screened subnet architecture is essentially the same as the screened host architecture, but adds an extra strata of security by creating a network which the bastion host resides (often call perimeter network) which is separated from the internal network. A screened subnet can be deployed by adding a perimeter network, in order to separate the internal network from the external. This assures that if there is a successful attack on the bastion host, the attacker is restricted to the perimeter network by the screening router that is connected between the internal and perimeter network [1].

Intranet

Although firewalls are usually placed between a network and the outside untrusted network, in large enterprises or organizations, firewalls are often used to create different subnets of the network, often called an Intranet. Intranet firewalls are intended to isolate a particular subnet from the overall enterprise network. The reason for the isolation of a network segment might be that certain employees can only access subnets guarded by these firewalls only on a need-to-know basis. An example could be a firewall for the payroll or accounting department of an enterprise [1].

The decision to use an Intranet firewall is generally based on the need to make certain information is available to some but not all internal users, or to provide a high degree of accountability for the access and use of confidential or sensitive information. For any systems hosting ENTERPRISE critical applications, or providing access to sensitive or confidential information, internal firewalls or filtering routers should be used to provide strong access control and support for auditing and logging. These controls should be used to segment the internal ENTERPRISE network to support the access policies developed by the designated owners of information [1].

Firewall Administration

A firewall, like any other network device, has to be managed by someone. Security policy should state who is responsible for managing the firewall. Two firewall administrators (one primary and secondary) should be designated by the Chief Information Security Officer (or other manager); and should be responsible for the upkeep of the firewall. The primary administrator should make changes to the firewall and the secondary should only do so in the absence of the former so that there is no simultaneous or contradictory access to the firewall [1]. Each firewall administrator should provide their home phone number, pager number, cellular phone number and other numbers or codes in which they can be contacted when support is required.

Qualification Of The Firewall Administrator

Two experienced people are generally recommended for the day to day administration of the firewall. In this manner, availability of the firewall administrative function is largely insured. It should be required that information about each firewall administrator be written down so that he or she may be contacted in the event of a problem [1].

Security of a site is crucial to the day to day business activity of an enterprise. It is therefore required that the administrator of the firewall have a sound understanding of network concepts and implementation. For instance, since most firewalls are TCP/IP based, a thorough understanding of this protocol is compulsory [1].

An individual that is assigned the task of firewall administration must have a good hands-on experience with networking concepts, design, and implementation, so that the firewall is configured correctly and administered properly. Firewall administrators should receive periodic training on the firewalls in use and in network security principals and practices [1].

Remote Firewall Administration

Firewalls are the first line of defense visible to an attacker. By design, firewalls are generally difficult to attack directly, causing attackers to often target the administrative accounts on a firewall. The username/password of administrative accounts must be strongly protected [1].

The most secure method of protecting against this form of attack is to have strong physical security around the firewall host and to only allow firewall administration from an attached terminal. However, operational concerns often dictate that some form of remote access for firewall administration be supported. In no case should remote access to the firewall be supported over untrusted networks without some form of strong authentication. In addition, to prevent eavesdropping, session encryption should be used for remote firewall connections [1].

Low

Any remote access over untrusted networks to the firewall for administration must use strong authentication. For example, this would be such as one time passwords and/or hardware tokens [1].

Medium

The preferred method for firewall administration is directly from the attached terminal. Physical access to the firewall terminal is limited to the firewall administrator and backup administrator [1].

Where remote access for firewall administration must be allowed, it should be limited to access from other hosts on the ENTERPRISE internal network. Such internal remote access requires the use of strong authentication, such as one time passwords and/or hardware tokens. Remote access over untrusted networks such as the Internet requires end to end encryption and strong authentication to be employed [1].

High

All firewall administration must be performed from the local terminal – no access to the firewall operating software is permitted via remote access. Physical access to the firewall terminal is limited to the firewall administrator and backup administrator [1].

User Accounts

Firewalls should never be used as general purpose servers. The only user accounts on the firewall should be those of the firewall administrator and any backup administrators. In addition, only these administrators should have privileges for updating system executables or other system software. Only the firewall administrator and backup administrators will be given user accounts on the ENTERPRISE firewall. Any modification of the firewall system software must be done by the firewall administrator or backup administrator and requires approval of the Network Services Manager [1].

Firewall Backup

To support recovery after failure or natural disaster, a firewall like any other network host has to have some policy defining system backup. Data files as well as system configuration files need to be have some backup plan in case of firewall failure. The firewall (system software, configuration data, database files, etc.) must be backed up daily, weekly, and monthly so that in case of system failure, data and configuration files can be recovered. Backup files should be stored securely on a read-only media so that data in storage is not over-written inadvertently and locked up so that the media is only accessible to the appropriate personnel. Another backup alternative would be to have another firewall configured as one already deployed and kept safely so that in case there is a failure of the current one, this backup firewall would simply be turned on and used as the firewall, while the previous is undergoing a repair. At least one firewall should be configured and reserved (not-in-use) so that in case of a firewall failure, this backup firewall can be switched in to protect the network [1].

Network Trust Relationships

Enterprise networks frequently require connections to other enterprise networks. Such connections can occur over leased lines, proprietary Wide Area Networks, Value Added Networks, or over public networks such as the Internet. For instance, many local governments use leased lines or dedicated circuits to connect regional offices across the state. Many business use commercial VANs to connect business units across the country or the world [1].

The various network segments involved may be under the control of different enterprises and may operate under a variety of security policies. By their very nature, when networks are connected, the security of the resulting overall network drops to the level of the weakest network. When decisions are made for connecting networks, trust relationships must be defined to avoid reducing the effective security of all networks involved [1].

Trusted networks are defined as networks that share the same security policy or implement security controls and procedures that provide an agreed upon set of common security services. Untrusted networks are those that do not implement such a common set of security controls, or where the level of security is unknown or unpredictable. The most secure policy is to only allow connection to trusted networks, as defined by an appropriate level of management. However, business needs may force temporary connections with business partners or remote sites that involve the use of untrusted networks [1].

High

All connections from the ENTERPRISE network to external networks must be approved by and managed by the Network Services Manager. Connections will be allowed only with external networks that have been reviewed and found to have acceptable security controls and procedures. All connections to approved external networks will pass through ENTERPRISE-approved firewalls [1].

Low-Medium

All connections from the ENTERPRISE network to external networks must be approved by the Network Services Manager. All connections to approved external networks will pass through ENTERPRISE-approved firewalls. To eliminate a major vulnerability, all connections and accounts related to external network connections should be periodically reviewed and deleted as soon as they are no longer required. Audit trails and system logs for external network connections should be reviewed weekly. Any accounts related to these connections that are not used on a monthly basis should be deactivated. The Network Services Manager will ask functional managers to validate the need for all such connections on a quarterly basis. When notified by the Network System Manager that the need for connection to a particular network is no longer valid, all accounts and parameters related to the connection should be deleted within one working day [1].

Virtual Private Networks (VPN)

Virtual Private Networks allow a trusted network to communicate with another trusted network over untrusted networks such as the Internet. Since some firewalls provide VPN capability, it is necessary to define policy for establishing VPNs. Any connection between firewalls over public networks should use encrypted Virtual Private Networks to ensure the privacy and integrity of the data passing over the public network. All VPN connections must be approved and managed by the Network Services Manager. Appropriate means for distributing and maintaining encryption keys must be established prior to operational use of VPNs. Firewall-based VPNs can be established in a number of different configurations [1].

DNS And Mail Resolution

On the Internet, the Domain Name Service provides the mapping and translation of domain names to IP addresses, such as mapping server1.acme.com to 123.45.67.8. Some firewalls can be configured to run as a primary, secondary, or caching DNS server [1].

Deciding how to manage DNS services is generally not a security decision. Many enterprises use a third party, such as an Internet Service Provider, to manage their DNS. In this case, the firewall can be used as a DNS caching server, improving performance but not requiring your enterprise to maintain its own DNS database [1].

If the enterprise decides to manage its own DNS database, the firewall can (but doesn't have to) act as the DNS server. If the firewall is to be configured as a DNS server (primary, secondary, or caching), it is necessary that other security precautions be in place. One advantage of implementing the firewall as a DNS server is that it can be configured to hide the internal host information of a site. In other words, with the firewall acting as a DNS server, internal hosts get an unrestricted view of both internal and external DNS data. External hosts, on the other hand, do not have access to information about internal host machines. To the outside world all connections to any host in the internal network will appear to have originated from the firewall. With the host information hidden from the outside, an attacker will not know the host names and addresses of internal hosts that offer service to the Internet [1].

> **Tip:** A security policy for DNS hiding might state: If the firewall is to run as a DNS server, then the firewall must be configured to hide information about the network so that internal host data are not advertised to the outside world.

System Integrity

To prevent unauthorized modifications of the firewall configuration, some form of integrity assurance process should be used. Typically, checksums, cyclic redundancy checks, or cryptographic hashes are made from the runtime image and saved on protected media. Each time the firewall configuration has been modified by an authorized individual (usually the firewall administrator), it is necessary that the system integrity online database be updated and saved onto a file system on the network or removable media. If the system integrity check shows that the firewall configuration files have been modified, it will be known that the system has been compromised. The firewall's system integrity database should be updated each time the firewall is configuration is modified. System integrity files must be stored on read only media or off-line storage. System integrity should be checked on a regular basis on the firewall in order for the administrator to generate a listing of all files that may have been modified, replaced, or deleted [1].

Documentation

It is important that the operational procedures for a firewall and its configurable parameters be well documented, updated, and kept in a safe and secure place. This assures that if a firewall administrator resigns or is otherwise unavailable, an experienced individual can read the documentation and rapidly pick up the administration of the firewall. In the event of a break-in, such documentation also supports trying to recreate the events that caused the security incident [1].

Physical Firewall Security

Physical access to the firewall must be tightly controlled to preclude any authorized changes to the firewall configuration or operational status, and to eliminate any potential for monitoring firewall activity. In addition, precautions should be taken to assure that proper environment alarms and backup systems are available to assure the firewall remains online. The ENTERPRISE firewall should be located in a controlled environment, with access limited to the Network Services Manager, the firewall administrator, and the backup firewall administrator [1].

The room in which the firewall is to be physically located must be equipped with heat, air-conditioner, and smoke alarms to assure the proper working order of the room. The placement and recharge status of the fire extinguishers should be checked on a regular basis. If uninterruptible power service is available to any Internet-connected systems, such service should be provided to the firewall as well [1].

Firewall Incident Handling

Incident reporting is the process whereby certain anomalies are reported or logged on the firewall. A policy is required to determine what type of report to log and what to do with the generated log report. This should be consistent with the Incident Handling policies. The following policies are appropriate to all risk environments [1].

The firewall should be configured to log all reports on daily, weekly, and monthly bases so that the network activity can be analyzed when needed [1]. Firewall logs should be examined on a weekly basis to determine if attacks have been detected. The firewall administrator should be notified at anytime of any security alarm by email, pager, or other means so that he or she may immediately respond to such alarm.

The firewall should reject any kind of probing or scanning tool that is directed to it so that information being protected is not leaked out by the firewall. In a similar fashion, the firewall should block all software types that are known to present security threats to a network (such as Active X and Java) to better tighten the security of the network [1].

Restoration Of Services

Once an incident has been detected, the firewall may need to be brought down and reconfigured. If it is necessary to bring down the firewall, Internet service should be disabled or a secondary firewall should be made operational – internal systems should not be connected to the Internet without a firewall. After being reconfigured, the firewall must be brought back into an operational and reliable state. Policies for restoring the firewall to a working state when a break-in occurs are needed. In case of a firewall break-in, the firewall administrator(s) are responsible for reconfiguring the firewall to address any vulnerabilities that were exploited. The firewall should be restored to the state it was before the break-in so that the network is not left wide open. While the restoration is going on, the backup firewall should be deployed [1].

Upgrading The Firewall

It is often necessary that the firewall software and hardware components be upgraded with the necessary modules to assure optimal firewall performance. The firewall administrator should be aware of any hardware and software bugs; as well as firewall software upgrades that may be issued by the vendor. If an upgrade of any sort is necessary, certain precautions must be taken to continue to maintain a high level of operational security. Sample policies that should be written for upgrades may include: To optimize the performance of the firewall, all vendor recommendations for processor and memory capacities should be followed [1].

The firewall administrator must evaluate each new release of the firewall software to determine if an upgrade is required. All security patches recommended by the firewall vendor should be implemented in a timely manner [1].

Hardware and software components should be obtained from a list of vendor-recommended sources. Any firewall specific upgrades should be obtained from the vendor. NFS should not be used as a means of obtaining hardware and software components. The use of virus checked CDROM or FTP to a vendor's site is an appropriate method [1].

The firewall administrator(s) should monitor the vendor's firewall mailing list or maintain some other form of contact with the vendor, in order to be aware of all required upgrades. Before an upgrade of any of the firewall component, the firewall administrator must verify with the vendor that an upgrade is required. After any upgrade, the firewall should be tested to verify proper operation prior to going operational [1].

Revision/Update Of Firewall Policy

Given the rapid introduction of new technologies, and the tendency for enterprises to continually introduce new services, firewall security policies should be reviewed on a regular basis (see sidebar, "Example Policies). As network requirements change, so should the security policy [1].

Example Policies

All enterprises should employ at least the low-level policies. Medium-level should add the medium-level policies. High should add low, medium and high.

Low

User

All users who require access to Internet services must do so by using ENTERPRISE-approved software and Internet gateways. A firewall has been placed between your private networks and the Internet to protect your systems.

Employees must not circumvent the firewall by using modems or network tunneling software to connect to the Internet.

Some protocols have been blocked or redirected. If you have a business need for a particular protocol, you must raise the issue with your manager and the Internet security officer.

Manager

A firewall should be placed between the ENTERPRISE's network and the Internet to prevent untrusted networks from accessing the ENTERPRISE network. The firewall will be selected by and maintained by the Network Services Manager.

All other forms of Internet access (such as via dial-out modems) from sites connected to the ENTERPRISE WAN are prohibited. All users who require access to Internet services must do so by using ENTERPRISE-approved software and Internet gateways.

Technician

All firewalls should fail to a configuration that denies all services, and require a firewall administrator to re-enable services after a failure. Source routing should be disabled on all firewalls and external routers.

The firewall should not accept traffic on its external interfaces that appear to be coming from internal network addresses. The firewall should provide detailed audit logs of all sessions so that these logs can be reviewed for any anomalies.

Secure media should be used to store log reports such that access to this media is restricted to only authorized personnel. Firewalls should be tested off-line and the proper configuration verified.

The firewall should be configured to implement transparency for all outbound services. Unless approved by the Network Services manager, all in-bound services should be intercepted and processed by the firewall. Appropriate firewall documentation will be maintained on off-line storage at all times. Such information should include but not be limited to the network diagram, including all IP addresses of all network devices, the IP addresses of relevant hosts of the Internet Service Provider (ISP) such as external news server, router, DNS server, etc. and all other configuration parameters such as packet filter rules, etc. Such documentation should be updated any time the firewall configuration is changed.

Medium

User

Strong authentication using ENTERPRISE-approved one-time passwords and hardware tokens is required on all remote access to internal systems through the firewall.

Manager

The network security policy should be reviewed on a regular basis (every three months minimum) by the firewall administrator(s) and other top information (security) managers. Where requirements for network connections and services have changed, the security policy should be updated and approved. If a change is to be made, the firewall administrator should ensure that the change is implemented and the policy modified. The details of the ENTERPRISE internal trusted network should not be visible from outside the firewall.

Technician

The firewall will be configured to deny all services not expressly permitted and will be regularly audited and monitored to detect intrusions or misuse. The firewall should notify the system administrator in near-real-time of any item that may need immediate attention such as a break-in into the network, little disk space available, or other related messages so that an immediate action could be taken.

The firewall software will run on a dedicated computer – all non-firewall related software, such as compilers, editors, communications software, etc., will be deleted or disabled. The firewall will be configured to deny all services not expressly permitted and will be regularly audited and monitored to detect intrusions or misuse.

High

User

All non-business use of the Internet from ENTERPRISE systems is forbidden. All access to Internet services is logged. Employees who violate this policy are subject to disciplinary action.

Your browser has been configured with a list of forbidden sites. Any attempts to access those sites will be reported to your manager.

Manager

All non-business use of the Internet from ENTERPRISE systems is forbidden. All access to Internet services is logged. Employees who violate this policy are subject to disciplinary action.

Technician

All access to Internet services is logged [1].

Logs And Audit Trails (Audit/Event Reporting And Summaries)

Most firewalls provide a wide range of capabilities for logging traffic and network events. Some security-relevant event that should be recorded on the firewall's audit trail logs are: hardware and disk media errors; login/logout activity; connect time; use of system administrator privileges; inbound and outbound e-mail traffic; TCP network connect attempts; and, in-bound and out-bound proxy traffic type [1].

Example Service-Specific Policies

Connecting to the Internet makes a wide range of services available to internal users and a wide range of system accesses available to external users. Driven by the needs of the business or mission side of the enterprise, policy has to be clearly written to state what services to allow or disallow to both inside and outside networks [1].

There is a wide range of Internet services available (see Table 6-2) [1]. The most popular services are the FTP, telnet, HTTP, etc. Other common services are detailed here also [1].

BSD "r" commands, such as rsh, rlogin, rcp, etc., are designed to allow UNIX system users to execute commands on remote systems. Most implementation do not support authentication or encryption and are very dangerous to use over the Internet [1].

Post Office Protocol (POP) is a client-server protocol for retrieving electronic mail from a server. POP is a TCP-based service that supports the use of nonreusable passwords for authentication, known as APOP. POP does not support encryption – retrieved email is vulnerable to eavesdropping [1].

Table 6-2. Managerial-level concerns.

Purpose	Protocols	What	Why
Email		Users have a single external email address	* Does not reveal business info.
	SMTP	* A single server or cluster of servers provides email service for organization	• Centralized email is easier to maintain. • * SMTP servers are difficult to configure securely.
	POP3	* POP users must use AUTH identification.	* Prevents password sniffing.
	IMAP	* Groups are encouraged to transition to IMAP.	* Better support for travel, encryption.
USENET news	NTTP	* blocked at firewall	* no business need
WWW	HTTP	* directed to www.my.org	• Centralized WWW is easier to maintain. • * WWW servers are difficult to configure securely.
*	all others	routed	

Network News Transfer Protocol (NNTP) is used to support Usenet newsgroups. NNTP is a TCP-based service that implements a store and forward protocol. While NNTP is a relatively simple protocol, there have been recent attacks against common NNTP server software. NNTP servers should not be run on the firewall, but standard proxy services are available to pass NNTP [1].

Finger and whois are similar functions. Finger is used to retrieve information about system users. Finger often gives out more information than is necessary – for most enterprises, finger should be disabled or limited at the firewall. Whois is very similar and should also be disabled or limited at the firewall [1].

The UNIX remote printing protocols lp and lpr allow remote hosts to print using printers attached to other hosts. Lpr is a store and forward protocol, while lp uses the rsh function to provide remote printing capabilities. In general, lp and lpr should be disabled at the firewall unless vendor supplied proxies are available [1].

Network File System (NFS) allows disk drives to be made accessible to users and systems across the network. NFS uses a very weak form of authentication and is not considered safe to use across untrusted networks. NFS should not be allowed through a firewall [1].

Real Audio provides for the delivery of digitized audio over TCP/IP networks. To take advantage of the multimedia capabilities of the World Wide Web, a number of new services have been developed [1].

Which Internet services to allow or deny must be driven by the needs of the enterprise. Sample security policy for some of these Internet services that might be required by a typical enterprise are illustrated in Table 6-3 [1].

An enterprise may wish to support some services without using strong authentication. For example, an anonymous FTP server may be used to allow all external users to download open information. In this case, such services should be hosted outside the firewall or on a service network not connected to enterprise networks that contain sensitive data. Table 6-4 that follows summarizes a method of describing such policy for a service such as FTP [1].

Table 6-3. Sample Internet Security Policy.

	Policy				
Service	Inside to Outside	Outside to Inside	Sample Policy		
	Status	Auth	Status	Auth	
FTP	y	n	y	y	FTP access should be allowed from the internal network to the external. Strong authentication should be required for FTP access from the outside to the inside.
Telnet	y	n	y	y	Telnet access should be allowed from the inside network to the outside network. For the telnet from the outside to the inside network, authentication should be required.

Rlogin	y	n	y	y	rlogin to ENTERPRISE hosts from external networks requires written approval from the Network Services Manager and the use of strong authentication.
HTTP	y	n	n	n	All WWW servers intended for access by external users will be hosted outside the ENTERPRISE firewall. No inbound HTTP will be allowed through the ENTERPRISE firewall.
SSL	y	n	y	y	Secure Sockets Layer sessions using client side certificates is required when SSL sessions are to be passed through the ENTERPRISE firewall.
POP3	n	n	y	n	The ENTERPRISE Post Office Protocol server is to be hosted inside the ENTERPRISE firewall. The firewall will pass POP traffic only to the POP server. The use of APOP is required.
NNTP	y	n	n	n	No external access will be allowed to the NNTP server.
Real Audio	n	n	n	n	There is currently no business requirement for supporting streaming audio sessions through the ENTERPRISE firewall. Any business units requiring such support should contact the Network Services Manager.
Lp	y	n	n	n	Inbound lp services are to be disabled at the ENTERPRISE firewall
finger	y	n	n	n	Inbound finger services are to be disabled at the ENTERPRISE firewall
gopher	y	n	n	n	Inbound gopher services are to be disabled at the ENTERPRISE firewall
whois	y	n	n	n	Inbound whois services are to be disabled at the ENTERPRISE firewall
SQL	y	n	n	n	Connections from external hosts to internal databases must be approved by the Network Services Manager and used approved SQL proxy services.
Rsh	y	n	n	n	Inbound rsh services are to be disabled at the ENTERPRISE firewall
Other, such as NFS	n	n	n	n	Access to any other service not mentioned above should be denied in both direction so that only Internet services you have the need for and you know about are allowed and all others are denied.

* Status (Y/N) = whether users can use the service.

* Auth (Y/N) = whether any form of authentication (strong or otherwise) is performed before the service can be used.

Table 6-4. Summarized Security Policy.

Policy	Non-Anonymous FTP service	Anonymous FTP service
Put server machine outside the firewall	N	Y
Put server machine on the service network	N	Y
Put server machine on protected network	Y	N
Put server machine on the firewall itself	N	N
Server will be accessed by everyone on the Internet	N	Y

WORLD WIDE WEB (WWW)

The Internet, as described in the introductory part of Chapter 4, is a network of networks, providing the infrastructure for communication and sharing of information. It provides a number of services including e-mail, file transfer, login from remote systems, interactive conferences, news groups, and the World Wide Web [1].

The World Wide Web (known as "WWW', "Web" or "W3") is the universe of Internet-accessible information. The World Wide Web began as a networked information project at CERN, the European Laboratory for Particle Physics. The Web has a body of software, and a set of protocols and conventions used to traverse and find information over the Internet. Through the use hypertext and multimedia techniques, the web is easy for anyone to roam, browse, and contribute to [1].

Web clients, also known as web browsers, provide a user interface to navigate through information by pointing and clicking. Web servers deliver Hyper Text Markup Language (HTML) and other media to browsers through the Hyper Text Transfer Protocol (HTTP). The browsers interpret, format, and present the documents to users. The end result is a multimedia view of the Internet [1].

Web servers can be attacked directly, or used as jumping off points to attack an enterprise's internal networks. There are many areas of Web servers to secure: the underlying operating system, the Web server software, server scripts and other software, etc. [1].

Browsers also introduce vulnerabilities to an enterprise, although generally less severe than the threat posed by servers. The following policy samples provide for the use of World Wide Web browsers, servers, and for publishing information on World Wide Web home pages (see sidebar, "Example Browsing Policies"):

- Browsing the Internet
- Example Browsing Policies
- Web Servers
- Example Web Server Policies [1]

Browsing The Internet

There are a number of risks related to the use of WWW browsers to search for and retrieve information over the Internet. WEB browsing programs are very complicated and getting more complicated all the time. The more complicated a program is, the less secure it generally is. Flaws may then be exploited by network-based attacks [1].

Example Browsing Policies

Low Risk

User

- Software for browsing the Internet such as WWW, Gopher, WAIS, etc. is provided to employees primarily for enterprise use.
- Any personal use must not interfere with normal enterprise activities, must not involve solicitation, must not be associated with any for-profit outside business activity, and must not potentially embarrass the ENTERPRISE.
- ENTERPRISE Internet users are prohibited from transmitting or downloading material that is obscene, pornographic, threatening, or racially or sexually harassing.
- Users of the WWW are reminded that Web browsers leave "footprints" providing a trail of all site visits.

Manager

   Approved sources for licensed WWW software will be made available to users.

Technical

   A local repository of useful WWW browsers, helper applications and plug-ins will be maintained and made available for internal use.

Medium Risk

User

- Software for browsing the World Wide Web is provided to employees for enterprise use only.
- All software used to access the WWW must be approved by the Network Manager and must incorporate all vendor provided security patches.
- Any files downloaded over the WWW should be scanned for viruses, using approved virus detection software.
- Due to the non-secure state of the technology, all WWW browsers should disable the use of Java, JavaScript, and ActiveX
- Only ENTERPRISE approved versions of browser software may be used or downloaded. Non-approved versions may contain viruses or other bugs.
- All WEB browsers should be configured to use the firewall http proxy.

- When using a form, ensure that the SSL or Secure Sockets layer or other such mechanism is configured to encrypt the message as it is sent from the user's browser to the Web server.

High Risk

User

- Users may browse the Internet using World Wide Web (WWW), Gopher, WAIS, etc., for the sole purpose of their research or job function.
- No sites known to contain offensive material may be visited.
- Any user suspected of misuse may have all transactions and material logged for further action.
- URLs of offensive sites must be forwarded to the ENTERPRISE Web security contact.

Manager

- A ENTERPRISE-wide list of forbidden sites will be maintained. WWW software will be configured so that those sites cannot.
- Internet sites containing offensive material will be immediately blocked by network administrators.
- Contractors must follow this policy after explicit written authorization is given for access to the Internet.

Technical

All sites visited are logged.

Web browsers should be configured with the following rules:

- They will only access the Internet through the firewall HTTP proxy.
- They will scan every file downloaded for viruses or other malign content.
- Only ActiveX controls signed by the ENTERPRISE may be downloaded.
- Only Java signed by the ENTERPRISE may be downloaded.
- Only JavaScript signed by the ENTERPRISE may be downloaded.

Web pages often include forms. As with e-mail, data sent from a Web browser to a Web server passes through many interconnecting computers and networks before reaching its final destination. Any personal or valuable information sent using a Web page entry may be eavesdropped on [1].

Web Servers

Many enterprises now support an external WWW Web site describing their ENTER-PRISE or service. For security reasons, servers are usually posted outside the ENTERPRISE firewall (see sidebar, "Example Web Server Policies"). Web sites range from home-spun notices, to carefully developed and designed marketing vehicles. Enterprises may spend a considerable amount of money and effort into developing a Web site that is informational yet non-cumbersome, or that creates the right ENTERPRISE logo or style. In a sense, an enterprise's Web site forms a piece of the ENTERPRISE's image and reputation [1].

Example Web Server Policies

Low Risk

User

- No offensive or harassing material may be made available via ENTERPRISE Web sites.
- No personal commercial advertising may be made available via ENTERPRISE Web sites.

Manager

- Managers and users are permitted to have a Web site.
- The personal material on or accessible from the Web site is to be minimal.
- No offensive or harassing material may be made available via ENTERPRISE Web sites.
- No ENTERPRISE confidential material will be made available.

Technical

A local archive of Web server software and authoring tools will be maintained and made available for internal use.

Medium Risk

User

- Users are not permitted to install or run Web servers.
- Web pages must follow existing approval procedures regarding ENTERPRISE documents, reports, memos, marketing information, etc.

Manager

Managers/Users are permitted to have Web pages for a enterprise-related project or function.

Technical

- The Web server and any data to be accessed by the general public must be located external to the ENTERPRISE firewall.
- Web servers should be configured so users cannot install CGI scripts.
- All network applications other than HTTP should be disabled (SMTP, ftp, etc.)
- Information servers should be located on a screened subnet to isolate itself from other site systems. This reduces the chance that an information server could be compromised and then used to attack site systems.
- If using a Web administrative tool, restrict access to only authorized systems (via IP address, rather than hostname). Always change default passwords.

High Risk

User

- Users are forbidden to download, install or run Web server software.
- Network traffic will be monitored for unapproved Web servers, and operators of those servers will be subject to disciplinary action.

Manager

- The CIO must approve the operation of any other web server to be connected to the Internet in writing.
- All content on ENTERPRISE WWW servers connected to the Internet must be approved by and installed by the Web Master.
- No confidential material may be made available on the Web site.
- Information placed on the Web site is subject to the same Privacy Act restrictions as when releasing non-electronic information. Accordingly, before information is placed on the Internet, it must be reviewed and approved for release in the same manner as other official memos, reports, or other official non-electronic information. Copyrights must be protected and permission obtained before placing copyrighted information on the Web site Contact public affairs or legal authorities for advice and assistance.
- All publicly accessible Web sites must be thoroughly tested to ensure all links work as designed and are not "under construction" when the site is opened to the public. Under construction areas are not to appear on publicly accessible Web sites.

Technical

- There should be no remote control of the Web server (from other than the console.) All administrator operations (security changes) should be done from the console. Supervisor-level logon should not be done at any device other than the console.
- The Web server software, and the software of the underlying operating system, should contain all manufacturer recommended patches for the version in use.
- Incoming HTTP traffic will be scanned, and connections to unapproved Web sites will be reported.
- Restricting user access to addresses ending in .GOV or .COM provides a minimal level of protection for information not cleared for release to the public. A separate server or partition may be used to separate restricted use information (internal ENTERPRISE information or internal Web site) from information released to the public.
- All Web sites may be monitored as part of the ENTERPRISE's network administration function. Any user suspected of misuse may have all their transactions logged for possible disciplinary action.
- On UNIX systems, Web servers should not be run as root.
- The implementation and use of CGI scripts should be monitored and controlled. CGI scripts should not accept unchecked input. Any programs that run externally with arguments should not contain metacharacters. The developer is responsible for devising the proper regular expression to scan for shell metacharacters and should strip out special characters before passing external input to the server software or the underlying operating system.
- All ENTERPRISE WWW servers connected to the Internet will have a firewall between the Web server and internal ENTERPRISE networks. Any internal WWW servers supporting critical ENTERPRISE applications must be protected by internal firewalls. Sensitive, confidential, and private information should never be stored on an external WWW server [1].

The creation, management, and maintenance of a ENTERPRISE's external Web site should be assigned. In larger enterprises, Internet Web site responsibilities may be spread across several position groupings. For example, a Director of online business development may be responsible for identifying and implementing new business opportunities while the Web site manager oversees the overall strategy of the Web site including coordinating content preparation, distribution, and budget monitoring. A Director of on-line sales/marketing may be responsible for advertising revenue generation related to the Web site. A Web site engineer or Webmaster would responsible for the technical aspects of the Web site, including development, connection, Intranet, e-mail, and firewall security. There would most likely be programmers for the operational aspects of the Web site, including installations, design, coding, debugging, and documentation of the Web site. A Web site artist may create the graphic and content aspects [1].

In a smaller enterprise, a Web site engineer or Webmaster may assume most of the preceding responsibilities and report to a marketing or Public Relations manager. In the smallest of enterprises, a system analyst or system/LAN administrator may be given the additional role. Whatever manner the Web site is administered, this role or series of roles enforces ENTERPRISE policy that is defined by management. Senior management, such as the Director of online enterprise development in the preceding large ENTERPRISE example, should be the designated authority to approve new or revised external Web sites prior to posting [1].

Additionally, internal ENTERPRISE Web sites which are inside the ENTERPRISE firewall are often used for posting ENTERPRISE information to employees. Information such as birthdays, enterprise calendars, phone directories, etc., are often posted. Internal Web sites are also used for internal project information, providing a central point of reference for the project team. Although internal Web sites do not carry the same visibility as external pages, they do need to be managed with system specific guidance and procedures. The project leader generally takes on this responsibility [1].

Anyone can create a Web site for posting information that is non-ENTERPRISE related. A ENTERPRISE must determine whether they will allow personal home pages through the ENTERPRISE's Internet service, or whether employees may only do so through their own Internet service provider [1].

As described earlier, most enterprises deploying an Internet do so to offer information or services to the public. Because they are presenting information, rather than hiding it, they often describe the web site a public web site; nothing confidential is on the web server, so there is no danger or threat there. The problem with this attitude is that while the information may be publicly available, the web site is an extension of the enterprises that own it and must be a secure form of vandalism [1].

Public web sites of MGM/Universal Studios, the Nation of Islam, The U.S. Department of Justice, and the U.S. Central Intelligence Agency can identify with this statement. They all had break-ins to their public sites. The attackers exploited weaknesses in the base operating systems on which the web servers ran. They broke into these sites with apparent ease, modified information, in some instances added pornographic photos, and in one case inserted hateful language [1].

While public embarrassment may be the only consequence in these cases, this may be significant enough not to want to bear the consequence a second time! Had the attackers modified a ENTERPRISE's statements of services, falsified prices, etc., the consequences could be more severe [1].

ELECTRONIC MAIL

Electronic mail or email is one of the most popular uses of the Internet. With access to Internet email, one can potentially correspond with any one of millions of people world-wide. Proprietary email systems can be gatewayed to Internet email, which expands the connectivity of email many fold [1].

In addition to one-to-one communication, email can support email address lists, so that a single individual or enterprise can send email to a list of addresses of individuals or enterprises. Sometimes email lists have entries which point to other email lists, so that a single message can end up being delivered to thousands of people [1].

A variation on email lists are email-based discussion groups. Participants send email to a central mailing list server, and the messages are broadcast to the other participants. This allows subscribers, who may be in different timezones or different continents, to have useful discussions. With the appropriate software, people can subscribe or unsubscribe from the list without human intervention. These discussion list servers often provide other services such as archives of list traffic, discussion digests, and retrieval of associated files. USENET newsgroups are an elaboration of the email discussion group [1].

Electronic mail is increasingly critical to the normal conduct of business. Enterprises need policies for email to help employees use electronic mail properly, to reduce the risk of intentional or inadvertent misuse, and to assure that official records transferred via electronic mail are properly handled. Similar to policies for appropriate use of the telephone, enterprises need to define appropriate use of electronic mail [1]. Organizational polices are needed to establish general guidance in such areas as:

- The use of email to conduct official business
- The use of email for personal business
- Access control and confidential protection of messages
- The management and retention of email messages [1]

Email Primer

The principle Internet email protocols (not including proprietary protocols which are tunneled or gatewayed to the Internet) are SMTP (Simple Mail Transport Protocol), POP (Post Office Protocol) and IMAP (Internet Mail Access Protocol). Let's look at them next in greater detail [1].

SMTP

SMTP is a host-to-host email protocol. An SMTP server accepts email messages from other systems and stores them for the addressees. Stored email can be read in various ways. Users with interactive accounts on the email server machine can read the email using local email applications. Users on other systems can download their email via POP or IMAP email clients [1].

UNIX hosts have been the most popular SMTP email platform. Some commonly used SMTP servers are Sendmail, Smail, MMDF, and PP. The most popular UNIX SMTP server is Sendmail. Sendmail supports queuing of messages, rewriting of headers, aliases, email lists, etc. It is usually configured to run as a privileged process. This means that if it can be subverted somehow, an attacker can cause damage beyond deleting email [1].

POP

POP is the most popular email retrieval protocol. A POP server allows a POP client to download email that has been received via another email server. Clients can download all messages or just unread messages. It does not support deleting messages before downloaded based on message attributes like sender or subject. POP supports authenticating the user with a password, which is transmitted in the clear (not encrypted) to the server [1].

POP also supports an additional authentication method called APOP, which hides the password. Some POP implementations support Kerberos for authentication [1].

IMAP

IMAP is a newer, and as yet, less popular email retrieval protocol. As stated in the RFC: IMAP4rev1 includes operations for creating, deleting, and renaming mailboxes; checking for new messages; permanently removing messages; setting and clearing flags; [RFC-822] and [MIME-IMB] parsing; searching; and selective fetching of message attributes, texts, and portions thereof. IMAP is more convenient for reading email while traveling than POP, since the messages can be left on the server, without having to keep the local list and server list of read email messages in sync [1].

MIME

MIME stands for Multipurpose Internet Mail Extensions. As stated in RFC 2045, it redefines the format of email messages to allow for:

1. Textual message bodies in character sets other than US-ASCII
2. An extensible set of different formats for non-textual message bodies
3. Multi-part message bodies
4. Textual header information in character sets other than US-ASCII [1].

It can be used to support security features like digital signatures and encrypted messages. It also facilitates mailing virus-infected executables and malign active content [1]. Much like helper applications for World Wide Web browsers, mail readers can then be designed to automatically invoke helper applications to address certain MIME message types [1].

Potential Email Problems: Accidents

It is easy to have email accidents. An email message can be sent instantly with no hope of retrieval. A single keystroke or mouse-click can misroute the message. Email messages may be archived for years, so that an ill-considered remark can return to haunt the sender later. Email folders can grow until the email system crashes. Misconfigured discussion group software can send messages to the wrong groups. Errors in email lists can flood the subscribers with hundreds of error messages. Sometime errors messages will bounce back and forth between email servers, multiplying until they crash the servers [1].

When an enterprise's internal email system is connected to the Internet, the effect of accidents can be multiplied a thousandfold. Some ways to prevent accidents are to:

- Train users what to do when things go wrong, as well as how to do it right.
- Configure email software so that the default behavior is the safest behavior.
- Use software that follows Internet email protocols and conventions religiously. Every time an online service gateways their proprietary email system to the Internet, there are howls of protest because of the flood of error messages that result from the online service's misbehaving email servers [1].

Personal Use

Since email is usually provided as an enterprise tool, like a telephone, facsimile machine or photocopier, non-business use would normally be limited or forbidden (depending on the enterprise). While it is tempting to simply state that all use of email must be for enterprise purposes only, it is generally recognized that this type of policy is difficult to enforce. If a policy can not be consistently enforced, non-compliance is inevitable and the policy will have no force as a basis for punitive action. It is much more effective to define policy that places clear limits on personal use of email, in the same manner as personal use limits are defined for telephones and fax machines [1].

If you use your ENTERPRISE telephone to check on your drycleaning, even if the drycleaner has CallerID&tm; it is unlikely to interpret the order as an official ENTERPRISE request. But sending email from the enterprise's address can be likened to sending a letter on ENTERPRISE letterhead, using the ENTERPRISE's postage meter. If the sender use their ENTERPRISE account to send email to an email discussion list, suddenly it appears as though the ENTERPRISE endorses whatever opinions the sender put in their last message [1].

Marketing

In the past, when the Internet was a research network, purely commercial uses were forbidden. Also, since relatively few enterprises and people had Internet email, there was relatively little temptation to use it for commercial purposes. Gradually, as the Internet expanded and non-research uses were permitted, enterprises began maintaining email lists to communicate with their customers. In general, customers had to request to be put on the email lists. When the major online services gatewayed their email systems to the Internet, suddenly there was a convenient means to reach a large affluent audience. Unsolicited direct email marketing on the Internet was born [1].

People wrote software to automate the population and maintenance of email lists, and started enterprises to collect and sell lists of email addresses to marketers. Since the cost of sending email is nominal compared to paper mail, there is little incentive to be selective about the list of addresses sent to, the size of the message, or the frequency of the mailings [1].

Email Threats

The most common mail transfer protocols (SMTP, POP3, IMAP4) do not typically, include provisions for reliable authentication as part of the core protocol, allowing email messages to be easily forged. Nor do these protocols require the use of encryption which could ensure the privacy of email messages. Although extensions to these basic protocols do exist, the decision whether to use them needs to be established as part of the mail server administration policy. Some of the extensions use a previously established means of authentication whiles others allow the client and server to negotiate a type of authentication that is supported by both ends [1].

Impersonation

The sender address on Internet email cannot be trusted, This is because the sender can create a false return address, or the header could have been modified in transit, or the sender could have connected directly to the SMTP port on the target machine to enter the email [1].

Eavesdropping

Email headers and contents are transmitted in the clear. As a result, the contents of a message can be read or altered in transit. The header can be modified to hide or change the sender, or to redirect the message [1].

Mailbombing

Mailbombing is an email-based attack. The attacked system is flooded with email until it fails. A system will fail it in different ways, depending on the type of server and how it is configured [1].

Some ISPs give temporary accounts to anyone who signs up for a trial subscription, and those accounts can be used to launch email attacks. Here are typical failure modes:

- Email messages are accepted until the disk where email is stored fills up. Subsequent email is not accepted. If the email disk is also the main system disk, it may crash the system.
- The incoming queue is filled with messages to be forwarded until the queue limit is reached. Subsequent messages can't be queued.
- Some email systems set a maximum number of email messages or total size of messages that a user can receive at one time. Subsequent messages are refused or discarded.
- A particular user's server disk quota can be exceeded. This prevents subsequent mail from being received, and may keep them from getting other useful work done. Recovering may be difficult for the user, since they may need to use more disk space just to delete the email.
- The volume of mail may make it difficult for the system administrator to spot other warnings or error reports.
- Mailbombing an email list may cause subscribers to unsubscribe [1].

Junk And Harassing Mail

Since anyone in the world can send you email, it can be difficult to stop someone from sending it to you. People can get your address from ENTERPRISE email directories, or subscriber lists, or Usenet postings. If you give your email address to any Web site, they can resell to your address to junk mailers. Some web browsers volunteer your email address when you visit a web site, so you may not realize who you've given it to. Most mail systems have some provision for filtering email, that is, searching the email header or body for particular words or patterns, and then filing or deleting the email. However, many users don't know how to use the filtering mechanism. Also, client-side filtering usually only takes place after the email has been received or downloaded, so large messages or large numbers of messages can't be discarded [1].

Anonymous remailers can be used an attack and a safeguard. Someone sending junk or harassing email can hide their identity behind an anonymous remailer. Someone who wants to send email without exposing their home address to junkmailers or harassers can use addresses from anonymous remailers. If they start receiving unwanted email at an address, they can drop it and start a new one [1].

One common remedy used by some USENET users is to configure their news client software to put an unusable REPLY-TO address in their USENET postings, and then putting their real email address in their signature lines or in the body of the message. That way, junk emailers who automatically compile email address lists from the REPLY-TO field of USENET postings get unusable addresses [1].

There are several bills in Congress to restrict junk email. One proposal would adopt sto-plists like those used for junkmail. It would also require advertisements to put advertisement on the subject line of messages [1].

Another proposal would treat junk email like junk faxes. That is, any unsolicited advertisements would be illegal [1].

Email Safeguards: Impersonation

Impersonation can be prevented by using encryption algorithms to digitally sign the email message. One popular method uses public key encryption. A one-way digital hash of the message is encrypted using the private key of the sender. The receiver uses the public key of the sender to decrypt the hash, then checks the hash against the received message. This ensures that the message really was written by the sender, and that the message wasn't changed in transit. The U.S. Federal Government is required to use the Secure Hash Algorithm (SHA) and the Digital Signature Standard, where applicable. The most popular commercial software uses RSA's RC2, RC4, or RC5 algorithms [1].

Eavesdropping

Eavesdropping can be prevented by encrypting the contents of the message or the channel that it's transmitted over. If the channel is encrypted, system administrators at the sending or receiving end could still read or alter the messages. Various email encryption schemes have been proposed, but none has reached a critical mass. One relatively popular application is PGP (which stands for Pretty Good Privacy). In the past, PGP was somewhat controversial, because the encryption it uses is strong enough to be covered by the munitions control regulations. The commercial version of PGP includes plug-ins for several popular email clients, which makes it more convenient to sign and encrypt email within the client. Recent versions of PGP use a licensed version of the RSA public key encryption algorithm [1].

Acceptable Use Of Electronic Mail

All employees are to use electronic mail as they would any other type of official EN-TERPRISE communications tool. This implies that when email is sent, both the sender and the reader should assure that the communications complies with normal communications guidelines. No communications via email should be unethical, be perceived to be a conflict of interest, or contain confidential information [1].

Protection Of Electronic Mail Messages And Systems

The protection provided for electronic mail messages, systems, and software should be consistent with the value of the information that will be transmitted over networks. In general, there should be centralized control of electronic mail services. Policies should be defined to specify the level of protection to be implemented (see sidebar, "Example Email Policy") [1].

Example Email Policy

Low

User

- Use of electronic mail services for purposes constituting clear conflict of ENTER-PRISE interests or in violation of ENTERPRISE information security policies is expressly prohibited, as is excessive personal use of email.
- Use of ENTERPRISE email to participate in chain letters or moonlighting is not acceptable.
- The ENTERPRISE provides electronic mail to employees for enterprise purposes. Limited personal use is acceptable as long as it doesn't hurt the ENTERPRISE.
- The use of email in any way to facilitate the conduct of a private commercial purpose is forbidden.

Manager

- All employees will have an email account.
- Email address directories can be made available for public access.
- If the ENTERPRISE provides access to electronic mail to external users such as consultants, temporary employees, or partners, they must read and sign the email policy statement.
- The contents of email messages will be considered confidential, except in the case of criminal investigations.

Technical

The POP server will be configured to except plaintext passwords from local machines.

Medium

User

- Electronic mail is provided by the ENTERPRISE for employees to conduct ENTERPRISE business. The use of email for personal business is not allowed.
- Confidential or ENTERPRISE proprietary information will not be sent by email.
- Only authorized email software may be used.
- Anonymous remailer software cannot be installed.
- Employees may not use anonymous remailers for any purpose.

Manager

- Confidential or ENTERPRISE proprietary information will not be sent by email.
- Employees found to be deliberately misusing email will be disciplined appropriately.

Technical

- The email system will provide a single externally accessible email address for employees. The address will not contain the name of internal systems or groups.
- A local archive of approved MIME-compatible viewers will be maintained and made available for internal use.

High

User

- Electronic mail is provided by the ENTERPRISE for employees to conduct ENTERPRISE business. No personal use is allowed.
- All electronic messages created and stored on ENTERPRISE computers or networks are the property of the ENTERPRISE and are not considered private.
- The ENTERPRISE retains the right to access employee electronic mail if it has reasonable grounds to do so. The contents of electronic mail will not be accessed or disclosed other than for security purposes or as required by law.
- Users must not allow anyone else to send email using their accounts. This includes their supervisors, secretaries, assistants and any other subordinates.
- The ENTERPRISE reserves the right to review all employee email communications. Email messages may be retrieved by the ENTERPRISE even though they have been deleted by the sender and the reader. Such messages may be used in disciplinary actions.

Manager

- Directories of employee email addresses will not be made available for public access.
- If confidential or proprietary information must be sent via email, it must be encrypted so that it is only readable by the intended recipient, using ENTERPRISE-approved software and algorithms.
- No visitors, contractors, or temporary employees may use ENTERPRISE email.
- Encryption should be used for any information classified sensitive or confidential that will be transmitted over open networks such as the Internet.
- Outbound messages will be spot-checked to ensure that this policy is being followed.

Technical

- Incoming messages will be scanned by viruses and other malign content.
- Email servers should be configured to refuse email addressed to non-ENTERPRISE systems.
- Email server logs files will be scanned by unapproved versions of email client software, and the users will be reported.
- Email clients will be configured so that every message is signed using the digital signature of the sender [1].

Retention Of Electronic Mail Messages

The National Archives and Records Administration (NARA) has issued standards for management of Federal records created or received on electronic mail. These standards require Agencies to manage such records in accordance with the provisions pertaining to adequacy of documentation, record keeping requirements, agency record management responsibilities, and records disposition (36 CFR parts 1220,1222, and 1228) [1].

Retention Policy For Federal Agencies

When an electronic mail message is determined to be part of the official records, the storage and retention of that message must comply with the following guidelines:

- Some transmission data (names of sender and addressee(s) and date the message was sent) must be preserved for each electronic mail record in order for the context of the message to be understood. Agencies should determine if any other transmission data is needed for purposes of context.
- Agencies that use an electronic mail system that identifies users by codes or nicknames (or, identifies addressees only by the name of a distribution list), should instruct the staff on how to retain names on directories or distributions lists, in order to ensure the identification of the sender and addressee(s) of messages that are records.

- Agencies that use an electronic mail system that allows users to request acknowledgments or receipts showing that a message reached the mailbox or inbox of each addressee (or that an addressee opened the message), should issue instructions to e-mail users specifying when to request such receipts or acknowledgments for record keeping purposes and how to preserve them.
- Agencies with access to external electronic mail systems should ensure that Federal records sent or received on these systems are pre-served in the appropriate record keeping system and that reasonable steps are taken to capture available transmission and receipt data needed by the agency for record keeping purposes.
- Some e-mail systems provide calendars and task lists for users. These may meet the definition of Federal record. Calendars that meet the definition of Federal records are to be managed in accordance with the provisions of General Records Schedule 23, Item 5.
- Draft documents that are circulated on electronic mail systems may be records if they meet the criteria specified in 36 CFR 1222.34.
- Agencies should consider the following criteria when developing procedures for the maintenance of electronic mail records in appropriate record keeping systems, regardless of format.
- Record keeping systems that include electronic mail messages must:
  - Provide for the grouping of related records into classifications according to the nature of the enterprise purposes the records serve
  - Permit easy and timely retrieval of both individual records and files or other groupings of related records
  - Retain the records in a usable format for their required retention period as specified by a NARA-approved records schedule
  - Be accessible by individuals who have a business need for information in the system
  - Preserve the transmission and receipt data specified in agency instructions
  - Permit transfer of permanent records to the National Archives and Records Administration (see 36 CFR 1228.188 and 36 CFR 1234.32(a)) [1].

Agencies should also not store the record keeping copy of electronic mail messages that are Federal records only on the electronic mail system, unless the system has all of the features specified in the preceding. If the electronic mail system is not designed to be a record keeping system, agencies should instruct staff on how to copy Federal records from the electronic mail system to a record keeping system [1].

Furthermore, agencies that maintain their electronic mail records electronically should move or copy them to a separate electronic record keeping system unless their system has the features previously described. Because they do not have the features specified in the preceding, backup tapes should not be used for record keeping purposes. Enterprises may retain records from electronic mail systems in an off-line electronic storage format (such as optical disk or magnetic tape) that meets the requirements described at 36 CFR 1234.30(a) [1].

In addition, Agencies that retain permanent electronic mail records scheduled for transfer to the National Archives, should store them in a format and on a medium that conforms to the requirements concerning the transfer at 36 CFR 1228.188. They should also be able to maintain the ability to convert the records to the required format and medium at the time the transfer is scheduled [1].

Next, Agencies that maintain paper files as their record keeping systems should print their electronic mail records and the related transmission and receipt data specified by the agency. Electronic mail records may not be deleted or otherwise disposed of without prior disposition authority from NARA (44 U.S.C. 3303a). This applies to the original version of the record that is sent or received on the electronic mail system and any copies that have been transferred to a record keeping system. See 36 CFR part 1228 for records disposition requirements [1].

When an agency has taken the necessary steps to retain the record in a record- keeping system, the identical version that remains on the user's screen or in the user's mailbox has no continuing value. Therefore, NARA has authorized deletion of the version of the record on the electronic mail system under General Records Schedule 20, Item 14, after the record has been preserved in a record keeping system along with all appropriate transmission data [1].

The disposition of electronic mail records that have been transferred to an appropriate record keeping system is governed by the records schedule or schedules that control the records in that system. If the records in the system are not scheduled, the agency should follow the procedures at 36 CFR part 1228 [1].

Commercial Retention Policy

Official ENTERPRISE records communicated through email must be identified, managed, protected, and maintained as long as needed for ongoing operations, audits, legal actions, or any other known purpose. Where email is the only communications means for official ENTERPRISE records, the same procedures should be followed as would be required if the message were transmitted via hard copy [1].

To prevent premature deletion of records, employees should forward a copy of any such record to the appropriate official file or archive. Both outgoing and incoming messages and attached files should be stored. Any email message containing a formal approval or constituting any commitment by the ENTERPRISE to any outside enterprise must be copied to the appropriate file (in hard copy if required) to support accountability and audits [1].

Finally, the retention period for all messages should be defined by the legal department. If messages are retained too long, the enterprise may be required to make such information public in a court action [1].

SUMMARY AND CONCLUSIONS

This chapter contained hypothetical sample policy statements that address Internet-based security. The policy elements were derived from the major sources of security controls (software import control, encryption, and system architecture). The rationale that drives the selection of certain policy was given, followed by the actual sample policy statement(s) [1].

Firewalls can also be used to secure segments of an enterprise's intranet. This chapter concentrated on the Internet aspects of a firewall policy [1].

Browsers also introduce vulnerabilities to an enterprise, although generally less severe than the threat posed by servers. This chapter also provided the following policy samples for the use of World Wide Web browsers, servers, and for publishing information on World Wide Web home pages: Browsing the Internet, example browsing policies, Web servers and example Web server policies [1].

Finally, electronic mail or email is one of the most popular uses of the Internet. With access to Internet email, one can potentially correspond with any one of millions of people world-wide [1].

REFERENCES

[1] "Internet Security Policy: A Technical Guide," copyright 2006 RXN Communications, RXN Communications, Victoria, Minnesota 55386, USA, 2006.
[2] John R. Vacca, Firewalls: Jumpstart for Network and Systems Administrators, Digital Press, 2004.
[3] John R. Vacca, Satellite Encryption, Academic Press, Jul 1999.
[4] John R. Vacca, The Essential Guide To Storage Area Networks, Prentice Hall, Nov 2001.
[5] John R. Vacca, Electronic Commerce, 4th edition(Networking Series), Charles River Media, Aug 2003.
[6] Forensics
[7] Privacy
[8] Wireless
[9] Identity
[10] PKI

PART IV

SECURING THE WEB CLIENT

Chapter 7

THREATS AND VULNERABILITIES

INTRODUCTION

Six years ago, the SANS Institute [1] and the National Infrastructure Protection Center (NIPC) at the FBI released a document summarizing the Ten Most Critical Internet Security Vulnerabilities, with regards to securing the Web client. Thousands of enterprises used that list, and the expanded Top-20 lists that followed one, two, and three years later, to prioritize their efforts so they could close the most dangerous holes first. The vulnerable services and the threats that they posed, led to worms like Blaster, Slammer, Code Red and many others, that have been on these lists [1].

This chapter presents an overview of these vulnerabilities and threats, and is a marked deviation from the previous Top-20 lists. In addition to Windows and UNIX categories, SANS and NIPC have also included cross-platform applications and networking products. The change reflects the dynamic nature of the evolving threat landscape and the vulnerabilities that attackers target. Unlike the previous Top-20 lists, this list is not cumulative in nature. SANS and NIPC have only listed critical vulnerabilities and threats from 2005 and 2006. If you have not patched your systems for a length of time, it is highly recommended that you first patch the vulnerabilities listed in the Top-20 2005 list [1].

SANS and NIPC have made a best effort to make this list meaningful for most enterprises. Hence, the Top-20 is a consensus list of vulnerabilities and threats that require immediate remediation. It is the result of a process that brought together dozens of leading security experts. They come from the most security-conscious government agencies in the UK, US, and Singapore; the leading security software vendors and consulting firms; the top university-based security programs; many other user enterprises; and the SANS Institute [1].

The SANS Top-20 is a living list. It includes step-by-step instructions and pointers to additional information useful for correcting the security flaws. SANS and NIPC will update the list and the instructions as more critical vulnerabilities and more current or convenient methods of protection are identified, and they welcome your input along the way. This is a community consensus list – your experience in fighting attackers and in eliminating the vulnerabilities and threats, can help others who come after you [1].

TOP THREATS AND VULNERABILITIES IN WINDOWS SYSTEMS

The family of Windows Operating systems supports a wide variety of services, networking methods and technologies. Many of these components are implemented as Service Control Programs (SCP) under the control of Service Control Manager (SCM), which runs as Services.exe. Vulnerabilities in these services that implement these Operating System functionalities are one of the most common avenues for exploitation [1].

Windows Services

Remotely exploitable buffer overflow vulnerabilities continue to be the number one issue that affects Windows services. Several of the core system services provide remote interfaces to client components through Remote Procedure Calls (RPC). They are mostly exposed through named pipe endpoints accessible through the Common Internet File System (CIFS) protocol, well known TCP/UDP ports and in certain cases ephemeral TCP/UDP ports. Windows also contains several services which implement network interfaces based on a variety of other protocols, including several Internet standards such as SMTP, NNTP etc. Many of these services can be exploited via anonymous sessions (sessions with null username and password) to execute arbitrary code with SYSTEM privileges [1].

Description

Earlier versions of the operating system, especially Windows NT and Windows 2000, enabled many of these services by default for better out of the box experience. These non essential services increase the exploit surface significantly. The critical vulnerabilities were reported in the following Windows Services in 2005 and 2006:

- MSDTC and COM+ Service
- Print Spooler Service
- Plug and Play Service
- Server Message Block Service
- Exchange SMTP Service
- Message Queuing Service
- License Logging Service
- WINS Service
- NNTP Service
- NetDDE Service
- Task Scheduler [1]

Exploit code is available for most of these vulnerabilities and has been seen in the wild. Zotob worm and its variants exploited the buffer overflow in Plug and Play service [1].

Operating Systems Affected

Windows NT Workstation and Server, Windows 2000 Workstation and Server, Windows XP Home and Professional, and Windows 2003 are all potentially vulnerable. But, how can you determine if these operating systems are really at risk; as well as, how can you protect against the Windows Services Vulnerabilities? The following sidebar, "Risk Determination And Protection" shows you how [1].

Risk Determination And Protection

How to Determine If You Are at Risk

- Use any Vulnerability Scanner
- You can also verify the presence of a patch by checking the registry key mentioned in the Registry Key Verification section of the corresponding security advisory. Additionally, it is advisable to also make sure the updated file versions mentioned in the advisory are installed on the system.
- To check if your system is vulnerable to an issue in an optional service, you need to determine if the service is enabled. This can be done through the Service Manager interface, which can be invoked from the Start->Run menu by typing services.msc. The column "Start Type" shows if the service is configured for start or "disabled". The "Status" column in the UI shows if a service is currently running.

How To Protect Against The Windows Services Vulnerabilities

- Keep the systems updated with all the latest patches and service packs. If possible enable Automatic Updates on all systems.
- Use Intrusion Prevention/Detection Systems to prevent/detect attacks exploiting these vulnerabilities.
- Determine if the vulnerability exists in a non essential component that can be removed. For example if your environment does not require message queuing services (CVE-2005-0059), it can be removed using control panel -> add remove programs -> windows components interface. Please take caution when determining this as it could break functionality if there is other software that depends on this.
- In some cases, exposure to the vulnerability could be removed by disabling the corresponding service. For example License Logging Service (CVE-2005-0050) could be disabled in many environments. Type services.msc in the start->run menu to invoke the service manager interface. Locate the required service and right click after highlighting it. Invoke the properties option in the popup menu. The "Startup Type" of the service can be modified to disable the respective service.

- In some cases, null session access to the vulnerable interface could be re-moved as a work-around. For example the spools vulnerability (CVE-2005-1984) could be mitigated on Windows 2000 by removing SPOOLSS from the registry value HKEY_LOCAL_MACHINE\SYSTEM\CurrentControlSet\Services\ LanmanServer\Parameters\NullSessionPipes. It is a good practice to review your current RestrictAnonymous settings and keep it as stringent as possible based on your environment.
- Many of these vulnerabilities (CVE-2005-1984, CVE-2005-1983, CVE-2005-1206, CVE-2005-0045 etc.) are found on interfaces offered through CIFS, and blocking ports 139 and 445 at the perimeter is essential for preventing remote attack scenarios. It is also a good practice to block inbound RPC requests from the Internet to ports above 1024 to block attacks to other RPC based vulnerabilities using firewalls [2].
- XP SP2 and Windows 2003 SP1 comes with several security enhancements, including the Windows firewall. It is highly advisable to upgrade to these service packs and enable the Windows firewall [1].

Internet Explorer

Microsoft Internet Explorer is the most popular browser used for web surfing and is installed by default on each Windows system. Internet Explorer contains multiple vulnerabilities that can lead to memory corruption, spoofing and execution of arbitrary scripts. The most critical issues are the ones that lead to remote code execution without any user interaction when a user visits a malicious webpage or reads an email. Exploit code for many of the critical Internet Explorer flaws are publicly available [1].

Description

These flaws have been widely exploited to install spyware, adware and other malware on users' systems. The spoofing flaws have been leveraged to conduct phishing attacks. In many cases, the vulnerabilities were 0-days (no patch was available at the time the vulnerabilities were publicly disclosed). In 2005 and 2006, Microsoft has released the following multiple updates for Internet Explorer:

1. Cumulative Security Update for Internet Explorer
2. JView Profile Remote Code Execution
3. Windows Shell Remote Code Execution [1]

> **Note:** The latest cumulative update for Internet Explorer includes all the previous cumulative updates.

Operating Systems Affected

The following operating systems affected: Internet Explorer 5.x and 6.x running on Windows 98/ME/SE; Windows NT Workstation and Server; Windows 2000 Workstation and Server; Windows XP Home and Professional; and, Windows 2003, are all potentially vulnerable. But, how can you determine if these operating systems are really at risk; how can you protect against these vulnerabilities; as well as, how can you secure Internet Explorer? The following sidebar, "Risk Determination, Protection And Security" shows you how [1].

Risk Determination, Protection And Security

How to Determine If You Are at Risk

- Use any Vulnerability Scanner.

How to Protect against These Vulnerabilities

- If you are using Internet Explorer on your system, the best way to remain secure is to upgrade to Windows XP Service Pack 2. The improved operating system security and Windows Firewall will help mitigate risk. For those unable to use Windows XP with Service Pack 2, it is strongly recommended that another browser be used.
- Keep the systems updated with all the latest patches and service packs. If possible enable Automatic Updates on all systems.
- To prevent exploitation of remote code execution vulnerabilities at Administrator level, users' tools like Microsoft DropMyRights can be used to implement "least privileges" for Internet Explorer.
- Many spyware programs are installed on a system as a Browser Helper Objects. A Browser Helper Object or BHO is a small program that runs automatically every time Internet Explorer starts and extends its functionalities. Browser Helper Objects can be detected by AV scanners. Another choice is to periodically review your BHOs using BHO-Daemon or Microsoft AntiSpyware.
- Use Intrusion Prevention/Detection Systems and Anti-virus and Malware Detection Software to block malicious HTML script code.

How to Secure Internet Explorer

To configure the Security settings for Internet Explorer:

- Select Internet Options under the Tools menu.
- Select the Security tab and then click Custom Level for the Internet zone.
- Most of the flaws in IE are exploited through Active Scripting or ActiveX Controls.
- Under Scripting, select Disable for Allow paste operations via script to prevent content from being exposed from your clipboard.
- Select Disable for Download signed and unsigned ActiveX Controls. Also select Disable for Initialize and script ActiveX Controls not marked as safe.

- Java applets typically have more capabilities than scripts. Under Microsoft VM, select High safety for Java permissions in order to properly sandbox the Java applet and prevent privileged access to your system.
- Under Miscellaneous select Disable for Access to data sources across domains to avoid Cross-site scripting attacks.
- Please also ensure that no un-trusted sites are in the Trusted sites or Local intranet zones as these zones have weaker security settings than the other zones [1].

Note: Disabling Active Scripting may cause some web sites not to work properly. ActiveX Controls are not as popular but are potentially more dangerous as they allow greater access to the system.

Windows Libraries

Windows applications leverage a large number of system libraries often packaged in DLL files. These libraries are used for many common tasks such as HTML parsing, image format decoding, protocol decoding etc. Local as well as remotely accessible applications use these libraries [1].

Description

A critical vulnerability in a library usually impacts a range of applications from Microsoft and third-party vendors that rely on that library. Often the exploitation is possible via multiple attack vectors. For instance, the flaws in image processing libraries can be exploited via Internet Explorer, Office and image viewers. In most cases, the libraries are used by all flavors of Windows operating systems, which increases the number of systems available for attacks. The critical libraries affected during 2005 and 2006 are as follows:

1. Windows Graphics Rendering Engine Remote Code Execution
2. Microsoft DirectShow Remote Code Execution
3. Microsoft Color Management Module Remote Code Execution
4. HTML Help Remote Code Execution
5. Web View Remote Code Execution
6. Windows Shell Remote Command Execution
7. Windows Hyperlink Object Library Remote Code Execution
8. PNG Image Processing Remote Code Execution
9. Cursor and Icon Processing Remote Code Execution
10. Windows Compressed Folder Remote Code Execution
11. JPEG Processing Remote Code Execution [1]

For most of these vulnerabilities, exploit code is publicly available. Attacks exploiting these vulnerabilities have been seen in the wild. An example of a large-scale attack reported involved exploiting the Cursor and Icon Handling flaws to install malware on users' systems. Trojan Phel.A was reported to exploit the flaw in the HTML Help Library [1].

Note: For some libraries such as HTML Help and Windows Shell, a newer update includes the older updates. Hence, only the latest update needs to be applied for yet unpatched systems.

Operating Systems Affected

The following operating systems affected are as follows: Windows NT 4, Windows 2000, Windows XP, and Windows 2003. But, how can you determine if these operating systems are really at risk; as well as, how can you protect against these Windows Libraries vulnerabilities? The following sidebar, "Windows Libraries Risk Determination and Protection" shows you how [1].

Windows Libraries Risk Determination and Protection

How to Determine If You Are Vulnerable

These flaws can usually be best resolved by patching, since work-arounds are complicated due to multiple attack vectors. One can use Vulnerability Scanners to check if the appropriate update has been installed.

How to Protect against Windows Libraries' Vulnerabilities

- Ensure that your Windows system has all the latest security patches installed.
- Block the ports 135-139/tcp, 445/tcp and other ports used by Windows systems at the network perimeter. This prevents a remote attacker from exploiting the vulnerabilities via shared file systems.
- Use TCP/IP Filtering available in both Windows 2000 and XP, or the Internet Connection Firewall in Windows XP systems to block inbound access to the affected ports. Using a properly configured personal/network firewall will also solve the problem.
- Due to a large number of attack vectors, Intrusion Prevention/Detection Systems as well as Anti-virus and Malware Detection Software are very helpful in protecting from these vulnerabilities.
- If you are running third-party applications on customized Windows 2000/XP platforms, please ensure that an appropriate patch from the vendor has been applied.
- Follow the principle of "Least Privilege" to limit worms and Trojans from getting a foothold on any systems. Further details about limiting access to certain registry keys, executables and directories are available in the NSA guides at http://www.nsa.gov/snac/index.cfm?MenuID=scg10.3.1.
- Use system hardening guidelines (such as those from CISecurity) to make systems more resistant to remote and local attacks [1].

Microsoft Office And Outlook Express

Microsoft Office is the most widely used email and productivity suite worldwide. The applications include Outlook, Word, Powerpoint, Excel, Visio, Frontpage, Access etc. Vulnerabilities in these products can be exploited via following attack vectors:

- The attacker sends the malicious Office document in an email message. Viruses can exploit this attack vector.
- The attacker hosts the document on a web server or shared folder, and entices a user to browse the webpage or the shared folder. Hence, browsing the malicious webpage or folder is sufficient for the vulnerability exploitation.
- The attacker runs a server such as News server that sends malicious responses to trigger a buffer overflow in email clients [1].

> **Tip:** Internet Explorer automatically opens Office documents.

> **Note:** Outlook Express, a basic email client, is installed on all versions of Microsoft Windows starting with Windows 95.

Description

The critical flaws that were reported in2005 and 2006 in Office and Outlook Express are:

1. Cumulative Security Update for Outlook Express
2. Microsoft OLE and COM Remote Code Execution
3. Microsoft Office XP Remote Code Execution [1]

Exploit code and technical details are publicly available for all these vulnerabilities. A flaw in the Office Access component is yet unpatched and reportedly being exploited by a Trojan.

Operating Systems Affected

The operating systems (OS) affected: Windows NT Workstation and Server, Windows 2000 Workstation and Server, Windows XP Home and Professional, and Windows 2003 are all potentially vulnerable. So, how do you determine if you are at risk; as well as, how to protect the OS against these vulnerabilities? Sidebar "Risk And Protection" shows you how [1].

Risk And Protection

How to Determine If You Are at Risk

The Office and Outlook Express installations running without the patch referenced in the Microsoft Bulletins previously listed are vulnerable. The simplest way is to use a Vulnerability Scanner.

How to Protect against These Vulnerabilities

- Keep the systems updated with all the latest patches and service packs. If possible enable Automatic Updates on all systems.
- Disable Internet Explorer feature of automatically opening Office documents.
- Configure Outlook and Outlook Express with enhanced.
- Use Intrusion Prevention/Detection Systems and Anti-virus and Malware Detection Software to prevent malicious server responses and documents from reaching the end users [1].

Windows Configuration Weaknesses

The configuration weaknesses in Windows systems are still being exploited by newer families of bots and worms. These weaknesses typically fall under the following : Weak passwords on Windows accounts or network shares; and, default configuration/passwords for servers [1].

Weak Passwords On Windows Accounts Or Network Shares

In the last four years, the weak authentication scheme in Windows has made it to the Top 10 windows vulnerabilities. LAN Manager (LM) hashes are known to be weak and are replaced by various versions of NTLM (NTLM AND NTLMv2) authentication. Although most current Windows environments have no need for LAN Manager (LM) support, Microsoft Windows locally stores legacy LM password hashes (also known as LANMAN hashes) by default on Windows NT, 2000 and XP systems [1].

Since LM uses a much weaker encryption [3] scheme than more current Microsoft approaches (NTLM and NTLMv2), LM passwords can be broken in a relatively short period of time by a determined attacker. Even passwords that otherwise would be considered strong can be cracked by brute-force in under a week on current hardware. A hacker can either try known defaults, or check for common passwords or use a brute force attack also called a dictionary attack to guess the password of users' accounts. Tools like THC's Hydra can be used to remotely crack passwords. LophtCrack and John the Ripper are other well known password cracking or auditing programs [1].

Many families of worms or BOT Zombies like GaoBot, PhatBot and AgoBot spread through network shares that have weak passwords. These worms use a list of hardcoded passwords in an attempt to match the victim's password, enabling them to spread [1].

Default Configuration/Passwords for Servers

When installing Microsoft Data Engine (MSDE) or Microsoft SQL Server Desktop (MSDE2000), the default SQL Administrator account or sa account has a default blank password and uses SQL authetication. MSDE ships as a component of several applications such as Microsoft Office 2000 and other third party applications. This blank or Null password leaves it vulnerable to a worm. For instance, worms like Voyager Alpha Force, SQL Spida and Cblade use the preceding vulnerability [1].

IIS Servers by default have settings that make them vulnerable to attacks. Some accounts that are created by default at installation like IUSR_computername account have write access privileges even for anonymous users. Permissions on such accounts should be modified for restricted access [1].

IIS services such as FTP, NNTP or SMTP are enabled by default and are a ripe source of attacks. These IIS services should be disabled [1].

Operating Systems Affected

The following operating systems are affected: Windows NT, Windows 2000, Windows XP and Windows 2003. How to protect against these vulnerabilities are as follows:

- Enforce strong password policy by accepting passwords that have a minimum number of characters (12 or higher if possible). Use tools like L0phtcrack or John The Ripper to audit accounts with weak passwords.
- Prevent Windows from storing the LM hash in Active Directory or SAM database by following the instructions posted by Microsoft.
- Tweak the registry to restrict Anonymous access to network shares.
- Modify default configuration settings on IIS servers and MS-SQL servers [1].

TOP THREATS AND VULNERABILITIES IN CROSS-PLATFORM APPLICATIONS

Backup software is a valuable asset for any enterprise. The software typically runs on a large number of systems in an enterprise [1].

Backup Software

In recent years with the growth in data size, the trend has been to consolidate the backup function into few servers, or even a single server. The hosts requiring the backup service communicate with the backup server over the network. This may be a push where the client sends data to the server or a pull where the server connects to each client in turn, or a combination of both [1].

Description

During 2005 and 2006, a number of critical backup software vulnerabilities have been discovered. These vulnerabilities can be exploited to completely compromise systems running backup servers and/or backup clients. An attacker can leverage these flaws for an enterprise-wide compromise and obtain access to the sensitive backed-up data. Exploits have been publicly posted and several malicious bots are using the published exploit code [1].

Operating Systems and Backup Software Affected

All operating systems running backup server or client software are potentially vulnerable to exploitation. The affected operating systems are mainly Windows and UNIX systems. The following popular backup software packages are known to be affected by vulnerabilities:

- Symantec Veritas NetBackup/Backup Exec
- Symantec Veritas Storage Exec [4]
- Computer Associates BrightStor ARCServe
- EMC Legato Networker
- Sun StorEdge Enterprise Backup Software (formerly Solstice Backup Software)
- Arkeia Network Backup Software
- BakBone Netvault Backup Software [1]

How to determine if you are vulnerable, and how to protect against these vulnerabilities are shown in sidebar: "Backup Software Vulnerability And Protection."

Backup Software Vulnerability And Protection

How to Determine If You Are Vulnerable

- Use any Vulnerability Scanner to detect vulnerable backup software installations.
- If you are using aforementioned backup software, it is recommended to update to the latest version. Monitor your backup software vendor site and subscribe to the patch notification system if they have one, and some of general security related sites such as US-CERT, CERT, SANS (Internet Storm Center) for new vulnerability announcements relating to your chosen backup software.
- The typical ports used by backup software:
  - Symantec Veritas Backup Exec
  - +TCP/10000 TCP/8099, TCP/6106
  - CA BrightStor ARCServe Backup Agent
  - +TCP/6050, UDP/6051, TCP/6070, TCP/41523, UDP/41524
  - Sun and EMC Legato Networker
  - +TCP/7937-9936
  - Arkeia Network Backup
  - +TCP/617
  - BakBone Netvault Backup
  - +TCP/20031 and UDP/20031

How to Protect against These Vulnerabilities

- Ensure the latest vendor supplied software patches are installed on the clients and servers.

- The ports being used by backup software should be firewalled from any untrusted network including the Internet.
- Data should be encrypted when stored on backup media and while being transported across the network.
- Host/Network based firewalls should be run to limit the accessibility of a systems backup software to ensure that only the appropriate backup hosts can communicate on the backup server ports
- Segregate network to create a separate backup network VLAN.
- Backup media should be stored, tracked and accounted like other IT assets to deter and detect theft or loss.
- Backup media should be securely erased, or physically destroyed at the end of its useful life [1].

Anti-virus Software

Anti-virus software is seen as a required basic tool within the defense-in-depth toolbox to protect systems today. Anti-virus software is now installed on almost all desktops, servers and gateways on various platforms to combat virus outbreaks [1].

Description

In 2006, there has been a shift in focus to exploit security products used by a large number of end users. This includes anti-virus and personal firewall software. The discovery of vulnerabilities in anti-virus software is not limited to just desktop and server platforms. Gateway solutions could also be affected. Compromising a gateway could potentially cause a much larger impact since the gateway is the outer layer of protection and the only protection against some threats in many small enterprises [1].

Multiple buffer overflow vulnerabilities have been discovered in the anti-virus software provided by various vendors including Symantec, F-secure, Trend Micro, Mcafee, Computer Associates, ClamAV and Sophos. These vulnerabilities can be used to take a complete control of the user's system with limited or no user interaction [1].

Anti-virus software has also been found to be vulnerable to evasion attacks. By specially crafting a malicious file, for instance, an HTML file with an exe header, it may be possible to bypass anti-virus scanning. The evasion attacks can be exploited to increase the virus infection rate [1].

Operating Systems Affected

Any system installed with anti-virus software or virus scan engine meant to scan malicious code could be affected. This includes solutions installed on desktops, servers and gateways. Any platform could be affected including all Microsoft Windows and Unix systems.

How To Determine If You Are Vulnerable And How To Protect Against Anti-Virus Software Vulnerabilities

If you are running any release of any anti-virus software that has not been updated to the latest version, you are likely to be affected. You can protect against anti-virus software vulnerabilities by doing the following:

- Ensure that all of your antivirus software is regularly and automatically updated.
- Regularly check your vendor website for upgrades, patches and security advisories.
- If you have deployed anti-virus software on gateway and desktops, it is recommended that you use different anti-virus vendor solutions for gateway and desktop. In the event one is vulnerable, it will not result in a single point of failure [1].

PHP-based Applications

PHP is the most widely used scripting language for the web. According to some reports, 50% of the Apache servers world-wide have PHP installed [1].

Description

A large number of Content Management Systems (CMS), portals, Bulletin Boards, Discussion Forums are written in PHP. There has not been a single week in 2006 that a problem was not reported in some software using PHP. The typical vulnerabilities that have been exploited during 2006 are:

1. Vulnerabilities in the PHP package itself. Exploit code is available for some of these vulnerabilities.
2. Remote File include vulnerabilities in the applications using PHP. These are very common and easy to exploit. These flaws allow an attacker to run code of his orher choice on the vulnerable web server.
3. Remote Command Execution vulnerabilities in the applications using PHP. These are easy to exploit and the discoverers typically post a proof of concept code on the Internet. Santy worm resulted from such a vulnerability in the popularly used bulletin board-phpBB.
4. SQL Injection vulnerabilities in the applications using PHP. These are easy to exploit and are actively used to recover password hashes for administrators of the PHP applications.
5. Remote Code Execution vulnerabilities in libraries implemented using PHP. For instance, PHP XML-RPC and Pear XML-RPC libraries are used by a number of software projects. Lupper worm is exploiting remote code execution vulnerabilities in these libraries [1].

The last three types of the preceding vulnerabilities result from lack of sanitization of user-supplied input. The availability of web scanning tools has automated the process of finding these vulnerabilities [1].

Affected Software

Web servers that are not running the latest version of PHP package. If you are running other PHP software that is not at its latest version, the web server is most likely vulnerable [1].

How to Determine If You Are at Risk

Scanning the web servers periodically with Vulnerability Scanners is your best bet since the number of vulnerabilities in PHP applications reported every week can be difficult to keep track of, and especially if you are running a large number of PHP-based applications on your servers. You can protect against PHP vulnerabilities by doing the following:

- Apply all vendor patches for PHP and PHP-based applications.
- Frequent web scanning is recommended in environments where a large number of PHP applications are in use.
- Use the following PHP Configuration that is safer:
  - register_globals (should be off)
  - allow_url_fopen (should be off)
  - magic_gpc_quotes (should be off for well written software, should be on for poorly written PHP 3 and PHP 4 scripts)
  - safe_mode and open_basedir (should be enabled and correctly configured)
- Configure Apache mod_security and mod_rewrite filters to block PHP attacks.
- Use tools like Paros Proxy for conducting automated SQL Injection tests against your PHP applications.
- Upgrade to PHP 5 as it will eliminate many latent PHP security issues.
- Follow the Least Privilege principle for running PHP using tools like PHPsuExec, php_suexec orsuPHP from suPHP.
- Use any Intrusion Prevention/Detection Systems to block/alert on malicious HTTP requests [1].

Database Software

Databases are a key element of many systems storing, searching or manipulating large amounts of data. They are found in virtually all businesses, financial, banking, customer relationship and system monitoring applications [1].

Description

Due to the valuable information they store such as personal or financial details, the databases are often a target of attack. Since databases are extremely complex applications and are normally a collection of a number of programs, this results in a large number of attack vectors. The most common vulnerabilities in most database systems found today can be classified into:

- Buffer overflows in processes that listen on well known TCP/UDP ports
- SQL Injection via the web front end of the database

- Databases running in default configuration with default usernames and passwords
- Databases running with weak passwords for privileged accounts [1]

There are many different database systems available. Some of the most common are Microsoft SQL Server (proprietary, runs on Windows), Oracle (proprietary, runs on many platforms), IBM DB2 (proprietary, runs on multiple platforms), MySQL and PostgreSQL (both open source and available on many platforms) [1].

All modern relational database systems are port addressable, which means that anyone with readily available query tools can attempt to connect directly to the database, bypassing security mechanisms used by the operating system. For example, Microsoft SQL server can be accessed via TCP port 1433, Oracle via TCP port 1521, IBM DB2 via ports 523 and 50000 up, MySQL via TCP port 3306, and PostgreSQL via TCP port 5432 [1].

In 2006, Oracle has issued cumulative updates that patch hundreds of vulnerabilities. Hence, even if all the vulnerabilities corrected via a cumulative patch are not of critical nature, the administrators are forced to apply the patches to correct a few critical issues [1]. Proof of concept exploits for many database flaws are readily available on the Internet.

Operating Systems Affected

The open source databases are available on virtually every operating system in common use today. Most commercial DBMS also run on multiple platforms [1].

How to Determine If You Are Vulnerable

Because databases are often distributed as components of other applications, it is possible for a database to have been installed without administrators realizing it. Databases may therefore remain unpatched or in vulnerable default configurations. It is not sufficient to check a simple list of the applications that have been installed! This was graphically demonstrated when the SQL Slammer worm attacked the Microsoft Data Access Component (MDAC), which is included in many applications [1].

Perform a vulnerability scan on systems to determine whether DBMS software is available, accessible and vulnerable. You can use any vulnerability scanners or tools from database vendors such as MySQL Network Scanner and/or Microsoft SQL server tool. Thus, you can protect against database vulnerabilities by doing the following:

- Ensure that all DBMS are patched up to date. Unpatched or outdated versions are likely include vulnerabilities. Check vendor sites for patch information. Remain up to date with the vulnerabilities and alerts announced by the vendors:
  - Oracle Security Alerts (http://otn.oracle.com/deploy/security/alerts.htm)
  - MySQL (http://lists.mysql.com/)
  - PostgreSQL (http://www.postgresql.org/community/)
  - Microsoft SQL (http://www.microsoft.com/technet/security/bulletin/notify.mspx)
  - IBM DB2 (http://www-306.ibm.com/software/data/db2/udb/support/)
- Ensure that the DBMS and applications have been secured:
  - Use minimal privileges.

- Remove/change default passwords on the database's privileged and system accounts before deploying the system on the network.
- Use stored procedures where possible.
- Remove/disable unnecessary stored procedures.
- Set length limits on any form fields.
- There are several useful resources to help secure DBMS mentioned in the references section.
- Use firewalls or other network security devices to restrict network access to the ports associated with database services.
- Do not trust user input! Ensure that the applications linked to databases clean all user input at the server side to avoid attacks such as SQL injection (see http://www.sans.org/rr/whitepapers/securecode/23.php) [1]

File Sharing Applications

Peer to Peer File Sharing Programs (P2P) are used by a rapidly growing user base. These applications are used to download and distribute data such as music, video, graphics, text, source code etc. P2P applications are also used legitimately for distribution of OpenSource/GPL binaries and ISO images of bootable Linux distributions. However, often times the data is either of a questionable nature or is copyrighted [1].

Description

P2P programs operate through a distributed network of clients, sharing directories of files or entire hard drives of data. Clients participate by downloading files from other users, making their data available to others and coordinating file searches for other users [1].

Most of the P2P programs use a set of default ports (see Table 7-1), but they can automatically or manually be set to use different ports if necessary to circumvent detection, firewalls, or egress filters. The trend seems to be moving towards the use of http wrappers and encryption to easily bypass enterprise restrictions. The main risks arising from P2P software are:

- Remotely exploitable vulnerabilities in P2P applications that can be used to compromise P2P clients or servers.
- Viruses and bots use P2P shared folders for spreading by copying malicious files into these folders with enticing filenames.
- P2P software is generally bundled with spyware and adware software. This increases the spyware/adware infection in an enterprise.
- Attackers can masquerade malicious files as legitimate music or video files. When the users download these files, their system can be infected and used as a bot.
- P2P shares typically have no passwords or weak passwords, a flaw that can be exploited to infect the share with malicious files.
- An enterprise can be liable to lawsuits for copyright infringement.
- P2P traffic can contribute substantially to overall bandwidth and make other mission-critical applications slower. This can be especially threatening to quality of service for voice and video traffic in an enterprise [1].

Table 7-1. Common protocols and ports used by peer-to-peer applications.

P2P Service	Default/primary port or port range, TCP	Default/primary port or port range, UDP
BearShare	6346	
Bittorrent	2181, 6881-6999	
Blubster		41170-41350
eDonkey	4661-4662	5737
eDonkey2000	4661-4662	4665
eMule	4661-4662,4711	4665,4672
Gnutella	6346/6347	6346/6347
Grouper	8038	8038
Kazaa	1214	1214
Limewire	6346/6347	6346/6347
Morpheus	6346/6347	6346/6347
Shareaza	6346	6346
WinMx	6699	6257

Exploit code is available for some of the buffer overflow vulnerabilities in the P2P software. According to Symantec's research, in the second half of 2004, 6% of Internet attacks tried to exploit vulnerabilities in eDonkey and another 5% in Gnutella. The number of threats using P2P, IM, IRC, and CIFS within Symantec's top 50 malicious code reports has increased by 39% over the previous six-month period [1].

Operating Systems Affected

There are versions of P2P software available for all Windows operating systems currently in use, along with versions for Linux, UNIX and MacOS systems. Sidebar, "File Sharing Applications Vulnerabilities And Protection" will help you determine if you are vulnerable and the type of protection that you need [1].

File Sharing Applications Vulnerabilities And Protection

How to Determine If You Are Vulnerable

Detecting P2P activity on the network can prove to be challenging. The following are the vulnerabilities:

- It is possible to detect P2P software running on your network by monitoring traffic for common ports used by the software or by searching traffic for certain application layer strings commonly used by P2P software. Please see Table 7-1 for a listing of ports often used by P2P.

- There are a number of applications and services that can assist in detection or prevention of P2P traffic. Some host based intrusion prevention software can prevent the installation or execution of P2P applications.
- Network based Intrusion Detection/Prevention products can detect/prevent P2P traffic from entering or leaving the network or monitor the P2P traffic.
- Monitoring your WAN connections with applications such as NTOP can also reveal P2P traffic.
- You may also wish to scan network storage locations for content commonly downloaded by users, including *.mp3, *.wma, *.avi, *.mpg, *.mpeg, *.jpg, *.gif, *.zip, *.torrent, and *.exe.
- Monitoring volumes for sudden decreases in free disk space can also be useful.
- Scanners often have a plug-in to detect running P2P applications, and for Microsoft Windows machines, SMS can be used to scan for executables that are installed on workstations.

How to Protect against P2P Software Vulnerabilities

- Regular users should not be permitted to install software, especially peer to peer applications. To prevent regular users from installation of unauthorized software, it is recommended to deny Administrative level privileges for regular users. To prevent accidental installation of unauthorized software by Administrator level users, tools like Microsoft DropMyRights can be used for securing of any Web browsers and mail clients. In Active Directory environments, Software Restriction Group Policies can be used in order to block known types of binaries from execution.
- Egress filtering should restrict access to any ports not required for business purposes, although as more P2P applications move to http, this will prove less effective.
- Monitor your network for P2P traffic and address violations of policy through appropriate channels. That can be achieved by monitoring of firewall, IDS logs. Enterprise solutions are available for detection and blocking of unauthorized P2P and IM connections.
- On individual workstation tools like Microsoft PortQry and Port Reporter can be used to monitor and log unusual network activity.
- Use enterprise-wide anti-virus and antispyware products and ensure that updates are performed daily.
- Use host-based firewalls in addition to perimeter firewalls. Windows XP and Windows 2003 include Windows firewall, which provides adequate protection if properly configured. A variety of third-party host based firewalls (ZoneAlarm, Sygate, Outpost) provide additional functionality and flexibility. Windows 2000, XP and 2003 systems can use IPSec policies in order to provide port filtering of unnecessary network traffic. In Active Directory environments, IPSec policies and Windows Firewall configuration (for Windows XP SP2 and Windows 2003 SP1) can be managed centrally through Group Policies.

- Disable Simple file sharing feature of Windows XP, if not explicitly required: Start – Settings – Control Panel – Folder Options – Tab View – Disable (uncheck) setting Use Simple File Sharing – Apply – OK.
- Monitor systems for presence of unknown executables and unauthorized modification of system files. Software products like Tripwire (there are commercial and open source versions of the product) can be used to detect changes in files [1].

DNS Software

The Domain Name System (DNS) is a critical Internet mechanism that primarily facilitates the conversion of globally unique host names into a corresponding globally unique Internet Protocol address using a distributed database scheme. The DNS relies on a confidence model developed in an era of mutual trust that is vastly different from today's generally hostile Internet [1].

Description

Because of the changed nature of the Internet, the DNS is prone to many types of transaction attacks that take advantage of that trust, including cache poisoning, domain hijacking, and man-in-the-middle redirection. In 2006, DNS cache poisoning vulnerabilities were exploited to redirect users to malicious domains to install malware on users' systems. Open recursive DNS servers are actively being used as DDoS reflectors providing a huge amplification factor. The affected software follows:

- Symantec Gateway Security
- Symantec Enterprise Firewall
- Symantec VelociRaptor
- DNSmasq DNS Server
- Windows NT and Windows 2000 (prior to SP3) DNS servers in the default configuration
- Windows DNS server forwarding requests to a BIND DNS server running version 4.x or 8.x
- Windows DNS server forwarding requests to another vulnerable Windows DNS server [1]

How to Determine If You Are at Risk

All Internet users are at risk of having incorrect data being returned from DNS queries. If scanning the DNS servers under your control shows that the current version or patch(es) released by the appropriate DNS software vendor have not been installed, your DNS server(s) are at risk [1].

A proactive approach to maintaining the security of any DNS server is to subscribe to one of the customized alerting and vulnerability reports, such as those available from SANS, Secunia, and others, or by keeping up with advisories posted at the Open Source Vulnerability Database (http://www.osvdb.org). In addition to security alerts, an updated vulnerability scanner can be highly effective in diagnosing any potential vulnerabilities in DNS servers [1].

How to Protect against DNS Vulnerabilities

As with any software package, updates and patches to DNS server software must be applied as soon as they are available; and, have been tested for any impact to local network operations. To generally protect against DNS vulnerabilities, you must do the following:

- Apply all vendor patches or upgrade DNS servers to the latest version.
- Apply appropriate firewall rules for any DNS servers inside a network that are not required to be accessible from the Internet.
- To secure the zone transfers between a primary and a secondary DNS server in a cryptographic way, configure the servers to use the DNS Transaction Signatures (TSIG).
- Jail: In Unix, to prevent a compromised DNS service from exposing one's entire system, restrict the service so that it runs as a non-privileged user in a chroot()ed directory.
- Do not allow your recursive DNS servers to be used except by your own network blocks unless required. Firewalls or DNS configurations files can prevent this scenario in most cases. Disabling recursion and glue fetching assists in defending against DNS cache poisoning.
- Consider signing your entire zone using DNS Security Extensions (DNSSEC).
- On most systems running BIND, the command "named -v" will show the installed version enumerated as X.Y.Z where X is the major version, Y is the minor version, and Z is a patch level. Currently the two major versions for BIND are 8 and 9. The Internet Systems Consortium recommends that all BIND users migrate to version 9 as soon as possible.
- DNS servers are integrated into many common products such as firewalls, enterprise network servers, and security appliances. All Internet-facing servers, appliances, and systems must be checked to ensure that any embedded DNS software is updated and maintained per the vendor's recommendations.
- Servers that are not specifically designed to support DNS transactions (for example, mail, web, or file servers) should not be running a DNS server application or daemon unless absolutely necessary [1].

Media Players

Media players are popularly used and have an install base of millions of systems. The increase in broadband connections has facilitated more content being downloaded in the form of multimedia files such as movies, video or music. This content is embedded into Web pages, presentations, or integrated into multimedia applications [1].

Description

Media players can end up on systems through default installations or bundled with other software. Typically browsers are set up to conveniently download and open media files without requiring user interaction [1].

A number of vulnerabilities have been discovered in various media players during 2006. Many of these vulnerabilities allow a malicious webpage or a media file to completely compromise a user's system without requiring much user interaction. The user's system can be compromised simply upon visiting a malicious webpage. Hence, these vulnerabilities can be exploited to install malicious software like spyware, Trojans, adware or keyloggers on users' systems. Exploit code is publicly available in many instances. Some of the more popular media players include:

- Windows: Windows Media Player, RealPlayer, Apple Quicktime, Winamp, iTunes
- Mac OS: RealPlayer, Quicktime, iTunes
- Linux/Unix: RealPlayer, Helix Player [1]

The operating systems affected include: Microsoft Windows, Unix/Linux and Apple Mac OS X [1].

How To Determine If You Are At Risk

If you run any of these players, and you are not running the most recent version with all applicable patches, you are vulnerable to the associated attacks. Periodic system reviews of installed software can be used to track unintended media player installations [1].

How to Protect against These Vulnerabilities

The following are some common approaches to protect against these vulnerabilities:

- Keep the media players updated with all the latest patches. Most players support updating via the help or tools menus.
- Carefully review default installations of operating systems and other products to ensure they do not include unwanted media players. Configure operating systems and browsers to prevent unintentional installation.
- Use Intrusion Prevention/Detection Systems and Anti-virus and Malware Detection Software to block malicious media files [1].

Instant Messaging Applications

Instant Messaging (IM) applications are being used today by millions of users both for personal and business purposes. IM applications are available for virtually all platforms including the handheld devices. Today's most popular IM applications are: Yahoo! Messenger, AOL Instant Messenger, MSN Messenger, Jabber, Trillian, Skype and IRC. GoogleTalk has just been released and is also gaining ground [1].

Description

A web version of many of these IM applications is also available whereby a user does not need to install the IM client on his or her system. These applications provide an increasing security threat to an enterprise. The major risks are the following:

1. Vulnerabilities in IM applications that could be used to compromise a user's system. During 2006, buffer overflows were discovered in the AIM URI handler as well as MSN Messenger PNG Image Processing. Exploit code is available for these vulnerabilities.
2. Most of these applications have the capability of transferring files. This feature is being currently exploited by many IM worms to infect users' systems with malware.

3. The file transfers can also result in leaking sensitive information.

4. Many worms and bots use IRC channels to communicate with the attacker. The IRC channels can also be used for launching DDoS attacks.

5. Some of these applications can carry voice data, which in addition to file transfers, may result in rogue bandwidth utilization [1].

Operating Systems Affected

Instant Messaging applications are available for all platforms including Windows, UNIX and Mac OS. You can protect against IM vulnerabilities by doing the following:

- Establish enterprise policy outlining appropriate IM usage within the enterprise. Run routine audits of Firewall and Proxy logs to enforce IM usage policy.
- Restrict the end users' ability to install software on the client workstation. Can be done by revoking workstation admin rights.
- Ensure that any installed messenger software such as Yahoo, MSN, AOL, Trillian etc is up to date with all vendor patches.
- Configure any Intrusion Prevention/Detection Systems to alert on any file transfers that use any of the messaging programs.
- If the site security policy permits:
  - Block the following ports at the firewall. Note that this does not offer a complete protection since some of these applications can bypass firewall rules.
    - 1503/tcp: MSN Messenger Application Sharing
    - 1863/tcp: Microsoft .NET Messenger, MSN Messenger
    - 4443/tcp: Yahoo Messenger File Sharing
    - 5050/tcp: Yahoo Messenger
    - 6891/tcp: MSN Messenger File Transfers
    - 5190-5193/tcp: AOL Instant Messenger
    - 13324-13325/tcp: MSN Messenger Audio and Video Conferencing
    - 5222-5223/tcp: Google Talk
    - 4000/udp – ICQ
  - Block access to webpages containing links with URLs such as "aim:" or "ymsgr:." This can prevent exploitation of the flaws in the URI handlers. Another option is to carefully remove just these registry keys in the "HKEY_CLASSES_ROOT."
  - For AOL block the following destination: oscar.login.aol.com
  - For Google Talk, block the following destination: talk.google.com
  - Yahoo Instant Messenger will tunnel its traffic over a variety of ports, including finger, discard, chargen and smtp. To be effective, block the following destination in addition to its ports above: cs.yahoo.com & scsa.yahoo.com
  - Use software restriction policies or other mechanisms to prevent execution of the instant messenger clients such as msmsgs.exe, aim.exe, ypager.exe, icq.exe, trillian.exe.
- Filter all HTTP traffic through an authenticating proxy server. A proxy server will give you additional abilities to filter IM traffic [1].

Mozilla And Firefox Browsers

Mozilla Firefox version 1.0 was officially released in November 2004. Mozilla and Firefox have emerged as viable alternatives to Internet Explorer and have been steadily gaining the browser market share [1].

Description

With increased usage, the browsers have come under greater scrutiny by security auditors and hackers alike, resulting in multiple vulnerabilities discovered during 2006. Many of the flaws discovered are critical in nature and allow a malicious webpage to completely compromise a client system. Exploit code for leveraging these vulnerabilities is publicly available as well [1].

Operating Systems Affected

The operating systems affected include Mozilla and Firefox browsers on Windows and Linux systems. In order to determine if you are at risk and the protection that is needed against these vulnerabilities, you need to perform the following:

- If you are running Firefox or Mozilla without the latest version, you are at risk. Firefox now has both an automated and manual tool that you can use to check for updates. However, you should visit the Firefox site regularly to ensure timely application of patches.
- Use any Vulnerability Scanner to detect vulnerable installations.
- Use Intrusion Prevention/Detection Systems and Anti-virus and Malware Detection Software to block malicious HTML script code [1].

Other Cross-platform Applications

This part of the chapter includes the Top-20 lists vulnerabilities in widely deployed products that cannot be classified into the other categories. In most cases, these vulnerabilities can be exploited for remote code execution [1].

Description

Some of the vulnerabilities may even allow an enterprise-wide compromise. Exploit code is available on the Internet and large-scale scanning for the vulnerable systems has been observed in the following:

1. Computer Associates License Manager Overflows
2. Novell eDirectory iMonitor and ZENWorks Buffer Overflows
3. Computer Associates Message Queuing Vulnerabilities
4. Sun Java Security Vulnerabilities
5. HP Radia Management Software Overflows
6. Snort BackOrifice Preprocessor Buffer Overflow
7. RSA SecurID Web Agent Overflow [1]

TOP THREATS AND VULNERABILITIES IN UNIX SYSTEMS

Most of the Unix/Linux systems include in their default installation a number of standard services. Over the years, security savvy administrators have either been turning the non-required services off or firewalling them from the Internet. The reference section points to detailed write-ups about secure UNIX configurations in general [1].

UNIX Configuration Weaknesses

Of particular interest in 2006 were attacks against SSH. SSH is an interactive service that is available on most UNIX systems. Since the service encrypts data when it traverses the network, if the SSH version is fully patched, the service is generally assumed to be safe. However, this was one of the services very popularly targeted in 2006 using brute-force password-guessing attacks. Systems with weak SSH passwords for typical user accounts were actively compromised; privilege escalations were then used to gain root access, and install root-kits to hide the compromise [1].

Description

It is important to know that brute forcing passwords can be another technique to compromise even a fully patched system. It is recommended to use public key authentication mechanism offered by most SSH implementations like OpenSSH to thwart such attacks. These attacks can be extended to other interactive services like telnet, ftp etc. [1]

Affected Versions

All versions of UNIX are potentially at risk from improper and default configurations. All versions of UNIX may be affected by accounts having weak or dictionary-based passwords for authentication. You can be protected against these vulnerabilities by doing the following:

- Don't use default passwords on any accounts.
- Don't use weak passwords or passwords based on dictionary words. Audit your machines to ensure your password policy is being adhered to. Install the latest vendor patches regularly to mitigate vulnerabilities in exposed services. Patch management is a critical part of the risk management process.
- Limit the number of login attempts to exposed services.
- Limit the accounts that can log in over the network; root should not be one of them. Consider employing firewall rules to limit where any remote logins, such as SSH, can occur from.
- Prohibit shared accounts and don't use generic account names like tester, guest, sysadmin, admin, etc.
- Log failed login attempts. A large number of failed logins to a system may require a further check on the system to see if it has been compromised.
- Consider using certificate based authentication.

- If your UNIX system allows the usage of PAM authentication modules, implement PAM modules that check for password's strength.
- Firewall services that do not require access to the Internet.
- Use The Center for Internet Security benchmarks from www.cisecurity.org for your OS and services you use. Also consider using Bastille to harden Linux and HP-UX based hosts from www.bastille-linux.org.
- Consider moving services from their default port where possible [1].

Mac OS X

Multiple questions have been submitted asking whether the entire MacOS is a security risk. Of course not, any more than the entire Internet Explorer is a security risk. MacOS includes software that has critical vulnerabilities and Apple has a patch policy, described next, that do not allow you to be more specific in identifying the elements of MacOS that contain the critical vulnerabilities [1].

Description

The Mac OS X was released by Apple in 2001 as a solid UNIX-based Operating System. Although Mac OS X has security features implemented out of the box such as a built-in personal firewall, unnecessary services turned off by default and easy ways to increase the OS security, the user still faces many vulnerabilities [1].

Mac OS X also includes the Safari web browser. Multiple vulnerabilities have been found in this browser and in certain cases exploit code has also been posted publicly [1].

Apple frequently issues Mac OS X cumulative security updates that tend to include fixes for a large number of vulnerabilities with risk ratings ranging from critical to low. This complicates the tracking of vulnerabilities for this OS, and the best way to ensure security is to apply the latest cumulative patch [1].

How To Determine If You Are Vulnerable

Any default or unpatched Mac OS X installations should be presumed to be vulnerable. The following procedure will check if there are new packages available. If you do not see any important packages patches available, you may be safe:

1. Choose System Preferences from the Apple Menu.
2. Choose Software Update from the View menu.
3. Click Update Now.
4. Check the items available [1]

To aid in the process of vulnerability assessment, you can leverage any vulnerability scanner. You can also be protected against Mac OS X vulnerabilities by doing the following:

- Be sure to stay current and have all security updates for Apple products applied by turning on the Software Update System to automatically check for software updates released by Apple. Although different schedules are possible, it is recommend that you configure it to check for updates on a weekly basis at least. For more information about how to check and run the Software Update System, see the Apple Software Updates webpage – http://www.apple.com/macosx/upgrade/softwareupdates.html

- To avoid unauthorized access to your machine, turn on the built-in personal firewall.
- If you have authorized services running in your machine that need external access, be sure to explicitly permit them [1].

TOP THREATS AND VULNERABILITIES IN NETWORKING PRODUCTS

Cisco's Internetwork Operating System (IOS) is Cisco's standard router and switch operating system. While not all of Cisco's routers and switches run IOS, there is an effort to transition them to IOS at the earliest possible opportunity [1].

Cisco IOS And Non-IOS Products

IOS is by far the most common enterprise router and switch operating system in the world, powering nearly 85% of the global Internet backbone. IOS has often enjoyed a reputation for security and robustness [1].

Description

It has long been believed that, as embedded devices, Cisco routers and switches were immune to severe security vulnerabilities. However, serious security research in 2006 has revealed several vulnerabilities that can result in denial-of-service conditions or remote code execution vulnerabilities. The critical vulnerabilities that appeared in Cisco IOS in 2006 are:

1. Remote Denial-of-Service in BGP Processing
2. Remote Denial-of-Service in SNMP Processing
3. Remote Denial-of-Service in OSPF Processing
4. Remote Code Execution in IPv6 Processing
5. Remote Code Execution in Firewall Authentication Proxy [1]

While most of Cisco's network hardware runs Cisco's Internetwork Operating System, some lines of hardware run different, more application-specific operating systems. Primary examples include the CatOS-based Catalyst line of switches, the PIX firewall, and the Cisco CallManager systems. While these systems form a minority of Cisco's product line, they still have very high penetration into the enterprise switching, firewall, and voice markets. The critical vulnerabilities that appeared in non-IOS-based Cisco products in 2006 are:

1. Remote Code Execution in Cisco CallManager
2. Hardcoded Username and Password in Cisco Wireless LAN Solution Engine
3. Hardcoded SNMP Community Strings in Cisco IP/VC
4. Remote Code Execution in Cisco Collaboration Server [1]

The critical vulnerabilities that appeared in IOS as well as non-IOS-based Cisco products in 2006 are: Cisco Devices IPSec Handling Vulnerabilities – PROTOS IPSec Test Suite. The versions affected included:

- Cisco IOS versions 11.1 through 12.4 are vulnerable.
- Cisco CallManager (CCM) 3.2 and earlier, 3.3 before 3.3(5), 4.0 before 4.0(2a)SR2b, and 4.1 4.1 before 4.1(3)SR1 are vulnerable.
- Cisco wireless LAN Solution Engine versions 2.0 through 2.5 are vulnerable.
- Cisco IP/VC Videoconferencing Systems 3510, 3520, 3525 and 3530 are vulnerable.
- UploadServlet in Cisco Collaboration Server (CCS) running ServletExec before 3.0E are vulnerable [1].

   Tip: Exploit code is available for some of these flaws.

How to Determine If You Are at Risk

The Cisco systems running without the patched versions of IOS are vulnerable. A network-management application, such as CiscoWorks (http://www.cisco.com/en/US/ products/sw/cscowork/ps2425/) can ease IOS version auditing [1].

How to Protect against These Vulnerabilities

The following are some common approaches to protect against the preceing vulnerabilities:

- Apply access lists on all interfaces. These access lists should only allow the minimum of traffic necessary. Access lists on externally-facing interfaces should be especially stringent.
- Disable unnecessary services on the router or switch. View the running configuration of the router by using the show running-configuration command.
- If the system must run SNMP, try to run at least SNMP version 2, and preferably version 3. If possible, be sure to use SNMP signatures and encryption. On both versions 2 and 3, be sure to change the default SNMP community string. If possible, disable SNMP write access entirely. Many management applications need only read access to perform their functions.
- Be sure to run the latest available version of IOS that supports the necessary feature set.
- Disable Cisco Discovery Protocol if possible, as this allows for information disclosure and is contributory to vulnerability [1].

Juniper, CheckPoint and Symantec Products

Juniper's Operating System (JunOS) is Juniper's standard router OS. JunOS is the second most common backbone Internet router. CheckPoint and Symantec solutions like VPN and Firewalls also enjoy a wide deployment [1].

Description

Vulnerabilities were announced in 2006 in these products that could be exploited to reboot Juniper routers and compromise the Symantec and CheckPoint Firewall/VPN devices. Exploit code is available for some of these flaws. The versions affected include:

- Juniper routers that are running an older JunOS version.
- CheckPoint VPN-1/FireWall-1 NG with Application Intelligence R54, R55 or R55W
- CheckPoint VPN-1/FireWall-1 Next Generation FP3
- CheckPoint VPN-1/FireWall-1 VSX FireWall-1 G
- Symantec Firewall/VPN Appliance 100, 200/200R (firmware builds prior to build 1.63)
- Symantec Gateway Security 320, 360/360R (firmware builds prior to build 622) [1]

So, in order to protect against these vulnerabilities, you must do the following:

- Upgrade to the latest JunOS version for Juniper routers.
- Apply patches supplied by CheckPoint and Symantec.
- Disable "Aggressive Mode IKE" on VPN devices whenever possible.
- Audit network devices for default SNMP community strings. Scanners usually include SNMP testing suite with a variety of commonly used default community strings.

Cisco Devices Configuration Weaknesses

Cisco's Internetwork Operating System (IOS) provides a myriad of configuration options. There are several configuration options that are not secure by default [1].

Description

This part of the chapter enumerates some of the more insecure default configurations on Cisco's IOS for 2006. They are as follows:

1. No Remote Logging By Default
2. Default SNMP Community Strings
3. Default or Nonexistent Default Passwords
4. IP Source Routing Enabled
5. TCP and UDP Small Services
6. Finger Service
7. IP Directed Broadcast Enabled
8. HTTP Configuration [1]

Versions Affected

As a rule, more recent versions of IOS have a more secure default configuration. However, even the most recent versions still are lacking certain security measures in their default configurations [1].

How to Determine If You Are at Risk

Generally, it is necessary to know what version of IOS a device is running to determine its default configuration. A network-management application, such as CiscoWorks (http://www.cisco.com/en/US/products/sw/cscowork/ps2425/) can ease IOS version auditing. The running and saved configurations in IOS can be displayed with the show running-config and show startup-config commands, respectively.

How to Protect against These Vulnerabilities

The following are some common approaches to protect against these vulnerabilities:

- Enable remote logging. To do this, make sure a secure syslog server is available. Configure the router to log to this device by issuing the logging server ip addressand logging on commands.
- Disable SNMP if possible, or change the default community strings. SNMP can be disabled entirely with the no snmp-server command. For systems that need SNMP, the default community strings can be changed with the snmp-server community command. If possible, SNMPv3 should be used, and configured to use encryption and signatures.
- An encrypted enable (supervisor) password should be configured with the enable secret command. Passwords should also be set on the console, aux, and vty ports. Use the password command in the line configuration mode for each line. Line configuration mode can be accessed via the line command.
- IP Source Routing allows traffic originators to specify the path traffic will take through the network. This is generally not used for legitimate purposes on real networks, and should be disabled with the no ip source-route command.
- IOS provides numerous small services via TCP and UDP, such as echo and chargen. These services are generally not used and provide holes for potential attacks. They can be disabled with the no service tcp-small-servers and no service udp-small-servers commands.
- IOS provides a finger service to list the users currently logged into the router. This allows for information disclosure as well as a potential for attacks. It should be disabled with the no service finger command.
- IP Directed Broadcasts allow for unicast IP packets to be converted to link-layer broadcasts once they reach a specified subnet. These are generally only used maliciously, especially for so-called "smurf" attacks. Directed broadcasts should be disabled with the no ip directed-broadcast command.
- IOS allows for web-based configuration using an HTTP server embedded in the operating system. This HTTP server has been known to host security problems in the past, and is generally not needed. It should be disabled with the no ip http command [1].

Finally, see sidebar, "Top-20 Risks Mitigation And Identification" for products for identifying and mitigating the Top-20 Risks.

Top-20 Risks Mitigation And Identification

Vulnerability Scanners and Patch Management Systems

A Microsoft Baseline Security Analyzer can be used for identifying vulnerable Windows systems. Open-source scanners as well as commercial vulnerability scanners and patch management systems are available from a number of vendors as well, and can help identify vulnerable systems and/or automatically download patches to the vulnerable systems.

Intrusion Prevention/Detection Systems and Firewalls

- Network and Host-based Intrusion Prevention Systems can be used to prevent exploits targeted at vulnerabilities. These systems provide a "virtual" patch until the vendor patch is installed on the vulnerable systems.
- Network-based Intrusion Detection Systems can be used as an alarm on suspicious network activity and exploits.
- Network-based Firewalls can be used to appropriately block the unwanted TCP/UDP ports at the network perimeter and inside.
- Host-based firewalls can be used to allow access to only selected services on a host.

Anti-virus and Malware Detection Software

Anti-virus and Anti-spyware software can be used to remove viruses, spyware, adware, Trojans and backdoors from infected systems. Gateways running these software can be used to stop the malware from entering an enterprise [1].

SUMMARY AND CONCLUSIONS

This chapter has discussed the new threat and vulnerabilities landscape, that is shown to be increasingly dominated by attacks and malicious code that are used to commit cybercrime, criminal acts that incorporate a computer or Internet component. Attackers have moved away from large, multipurpose attacks on network perimeters and toward smaller, more focused attacks on client-side targets.

Finally, the threat and vulnerabilities landscape is coming to be dominated by emerging threats such as bot networks and customizable modular malicious code. Targeted attacks on Web applications and Web browsers are increasingly becoming the focal point for cybercriminals. Whereas traditional attack activity has been motivated by curiosity and a desire to show off technical virtuosity, many current threats are motivated by profit. They often attempt to perpetrate criminal acts, such as identity theft [5], extortion, and fraud, for financial gain.

REFERENCES

[1] "The Twenty Most Critical Internet Security Vulnerabilities (Updated) ~ The Experts Consensus," Version 6.01 November 28, 2005 Copyright (C) 2005, SANS Institute, The SANS Institute, 8120 Woodmont Avenue, Suite 205, Bethesda, Maryland 20814 2006.

[2] John R. Vacca, Firewalls: Jumpstart for Network and Systems Administrators, Digital Press, 2004.

[3] John R. Vacca, Satellite Encryption, Academic Press, Jul 1999.

[4] John R. Vacca, The Essential Guide To Storage Area Networks, Prentice Hall, Nov 2001.

[5] John R. Vacca, Identity Theft, Prentice Hall, 2002.

Chapter 8

PROTECTING YOUR WEB BROWSER

INTRODUCTION

There has been much debate lately between two different browsers, namely Microsoft's Internet Explorer and the Mozilla Project's Firefox web browser. Security is in the center of this debate, accompanied by features and usability. This chapter focuses on the security aspects, particularly the risks involved with running any web browser and how to overcome some of these security shortcomings. Internet Explorer and Firefox will be used as examples, as these are the most commonly used, and therefore the most commonly exploited [1].

The browser debate going on today will probably continue throughout the well into 2007 and beyond. There may even be a full-blown Browser War status in the near future. Regardless of the outcome, and regardless of who wins, the bottom line is that you will need to secure your web browser. This may not always translate into actual browser or operating system configuration, but may mean being aware of your web browsing behavior. There are certainly some good tips to securing your web browser that you can configure. This chapter covers some in them briefly. However, you will find less malware (spyware, adware, and viruses) on your computer by changing your browsing habits and being more aware of your clicking. Almost all the browser exploits require that you click on something. Now, lets come back to reality and realize that people are going to click stuff, children especially, that could trigger malicious software to run on your computer. So your strategy is two fold: maintain a secure environment and be an educated user. The goal of this chapter is to help you in both of these areas. First, the chapter shows examples of the more common threats, and then moves on to the defensive measures. The weaknesses shown here are not the most critical, but they will help you to understand the basics of how web browser exploits work and how they are used in attacks [1].

BROWSER WEAKNESSES

As previously stated, this chapter focuses on the risks involved with running Internet Explorer and Firefox. These browsers are the most commonly exploited; because they are the most commonly used [1].

Internet Explorer

Internet Explorer has had its share of problems. In 2005 alone, Microsoft released numerous updates that fixed various security problems. These are the vulnerabilities that have been recognized by Microsoft. Vulnerabilities that have not yet been fixed by Microsoft also exist and pose an even greater threat, because there is no patch for them, yet [1].

The example chosen here is of a unpatched Internet Explorer vulnerability that will be explained in detail. The vulnerability deals with the status bar, which is the space in Internet Explorer (and all other browsers) in the lower left hand corner that displays, among other things, the destination of the hyperlink that you currently have your cursor positioned over. Due to a bug in Internet Explorer it is possible to construct a link that will display one web site link in the status bar, but really take you to a different web site [1].

This vulnerability poses a threat because you may think that you are being taken to your bank's web site, but in reality you are going to a web site created by an attacker attempting to gather your personal information through a phishing attack. It is important to note that this vulnerability also exists in MS Outlook Express [1].

Mozilla Firefox

Firefox has gained popularity as a web browser very quickly. It is a trimmed down version of the Mozilla web browser. It does have some security advantages, however it does not include support for technologies such as MS ActiveX, which coincidentally has posed many security issues for Internet Explorer. Not all web sites/applications will work in Firefox, but most agree it works well for general web browsing. Of course, just as any software, Firefox has its share of security problems too. It contains a similar bug that was previously explained with Internet Explorer, using a slightly different exploit. It too will allow a malicious user to "spoof" the real destination of a link in a web site. This time it only works when hovering over the link, right clicking, and choosing "Save Link As…" [1].

This exploit only works with Firefox version 1.0.1 and appears to have been fixed in later versions. If you ry it with 1.0.3 and 1.0.4, you can see the "hidden" link to "http://www.google.com" if you clicked and held the mouse button down on the link or right clicked and chose "Save Link As…". For fun, go to http://www.google.com – using Internet Explorer and notice that it spoofs the status bar successfully [1].

It's interesting to see that a vulnerability originally released for Firefox seems to work better in Internet Explorer. Even so, there still is not an exploit that works well with both [1].

UNIVERSAL STATUS BAR SPOOFING?

The preceding examples use two different ways to implement the URL status bar spoofing in pure HTML. Using JavaScript, you can construct an exploit that works equally well with the latest versions of Internet Explorer and Firefox. Remember, clicking the link in either example does not take you to http://www.defensiveintuition.com, but to http://www.google.com. Go to the following link to try it with your favorite web browser [1]:

http://www.defensiveintuition.com/allbrowsers.html

The exploit in the preceding link works differently depending on which browser you are using. Next is an example of how it works in Firefox [1]:

In Firefox, it will display the spoofed site in the text bubble when you hover over the link. Firefox does not display the spoofed link the status bar because it will not allow the contents to be modified by JavaScript. Internet Explorer appears to be completely fooled. The spoofed site appears in both the text bubble and the status bar [1].

URL status bar spoofing is not as critical a vulnerability as some other web browser vulnerabilities. It allows an attacker to trick users into going to a web site to perform a phishing attack. However, it shows that browsers contain vulnerabilities that may go unpatched, and how the exploits for these vulnerabilities are morphed to maintain effectiveness. There are many other exploits for both browsers, some patched and some not. All software will contain vulnerabilities sooner or later; it is the responsiveness of the vendor/author of the software that matters. If you use Firefox for general web browsing, you might only use Internet Explorer for sites that don't work in Firefox. Firefox seems to have less security problems. It is better at handling all those web-browsing annoyances, like pop-ups and banner ads. Regardless of your web browser choice you should implement the tips in the remainder of this chapter to help protect you from being vulnerable, whether they are patched vulnerabilities, unpatched vulnerabilities, or behavior-based vulnerabilities [1].

KEEP YOUR SYSTEM UPDATED

This is the most fundamental step to securing your computing environment. You should run windows update automatically and have it check for updates daily. Remember, be certain to reboot after you have run Windows updates. In Firefox you will need to look for an arrow-type icon in the upper right hand corner and click on it when it appears. This will guide you through installing the latest version of the web browser [1].

CONFIGURE SECURITY IN YOUR WEB BROWSER

There are many steps you can take to tighten the security of your web browser. Some of these may cause web sites and applications not function.

Disclaimer: Use following tips at your own risk:

- Disable JavaScript: This can be done in most browsers and will prevent certain attacks, such as the universal URL status bar spoofing.
- Disable Java: This falls in the same category as JavaScript.
- Use a pop-up blocker: Sometimes sites will use pop-ups to execute malicious code, plus they are pretty annoying.
- Don't cache your passwords or saved form information: Caching means that this information can be stored on your computer where other people could collect it [1].

KEEP YOUR BROWSER IN CHECK

A step often left out in the patching process is testing the system to see if the patches actually applied. This is difficult for the average user, as the best way to do this is to actually attempt to exploit the vulnerability after each patch. An easier way to test is to visit either of these two great web sites that will check your web browser software and configuration for vulnerabilities. You should visit them each time you apply a patch [1]:

http://bcheck.scanit.be/bcheck/
http://browsercheck.qualys.com/index.php

PRINCIPAL OF LEAST PRIVILEGE

Many users ignore this rule when setting up their personal PC. If it can be helped, you should be logged in as a user that does not have administrative rights. Mac OS X is a good example of this model, when you need to do something that requires administrative privileges, you are prompted for the administrative password. To translate this to Windows, you should use the "Run As..." feature. The excuse by users for running as an administrator, is they need to install software. The solution is to download the software you wish to install, right click on the icon, choose "Run As..." from the menu, and enter the administrative credentials. It requires a little more extra effort than OS X, but will help prevent a malicious web site from installing software without your knowledge on your computer. This tactic is especially useful for children [1].

ANTI-SPYWARE

Every system should have at least one Anti-Spyware package installed. It should be run on a regular basis to remove unwanted spyware and adware. It is best to do this while running in Windows Safe Mode (while booting windows press the F8 key when the Windows XP splash screen appears), as Anti-Spyware software will be able to remove spyware more easily. The following are some of the more popular Anti-Spyware packages:

- MS Anti-Spyware: This generally works really well. It constantly monitors your system for spyware, automatically updates its definitions, and even allows you to easily secure your web browser using its advanced features. This is, so far, a free product from Microsoft.

- Ad-Aware: This is a commercial product that in generally well known and good at removing spyware.
- Spybot: This is a free Anti-Spyware product that is also well known and good at removing Spyware.
- HiJackThis: A very advanced spyware removal tool that gives you more control, but uses less discretion than the above tools [1].

ANTI-VIRUS

No computer system should be without anti-virus software. It helps to protect your system against malware, and newer versions even detect spyware and adware. The following are two of the easiest to use:

- Clamwin: This is a free anti-virus program that features auto-updating and a large support base. It was the February 2005 project of the month and seems to be gaining wider support.
- Symantec Anti-Virus: With each version, this software package seems to get smarter. Newer versions contain more protection from spyware, adware, and browser injected malware than ever before. It features automatic updates and numerous other features [1].

THINK BEFORE YOU CLICK!

Finally, as previously stated, you can prevent malware from being installed on your computer, and phishers from getting your personal information by changing your habits. Here are some general guidelines to follow:

- Do not follow links sent to you via email
- View email in plain text, not HTML
- Use a separate credit card for Internet purchases (with a low limit)
- If it sounds too good to be true, it probably is
- If you do your banking online, only do it from one computer you trust
- Open attachments only if you are expecting them
- Always type in the web site manually if you are going to enter personal information
- Never trust the status bar [1]!

SUMMARY AND CONCLUSIONS

This chapter focused on the security aspects, particularly the risks involved with running any web browser and how to overcome some of these security shortcomings. There were certainly some good tips to securing your web browser that you could configure. This chapter covered some in this briefly [1].

Finally, it was determined that your security strategy was two fold: maintain a secure environment and be an educated user. The goal of this chapter was to help you in both of these areas. The chapter showed some examples of the more common threats, and then moved on to the defensive measures [1].

REFERENCES

[1] Paul Asadoorian, "Web Browser Insecurity," © SANS Institute 2000–2005 [Author retains full rights.], The SANS Institute, 8120 Woodmont Avenue, Suite 205, Bethesda, Maryland 20814 2006.

PART V

NETWORK INTERCONNECTIONS: A MAJORPOINT OF VULNERABILITY

Chapter 9

BASIC OPERATING SYSTEM AND TCP/IP CONCEPTS

INTRODUCTION

A vulnerability in TCP/IP (the transmission control protocol/Internet protocol), continues to be a serious Internet security problem. The goal of this chapter is to provide you with a much better understanding of the real-world risks of TCP/IP reset attacks. In other words, to better understand the reality of this threat, the aim of this chapter is to provide some background into the basic workings of operating systems and of TCP/IP concepts, and then to build upon this foundation to understand how resets attacks work [1].

TCP/IP OVERVIEW

The first part of this chapter aims at providing some basic information about TCP/IP. Much of the detail has been intentionally glossed over, focusing primarily on that which is relevant to understanding TCP/IP reset attacks. If you already have a good understanding of TCP/IP, you may want to skip directly to the part of the chapter that discusses how reset attacks work. Please realize that this chapter only focuses on the aspects of TCP/IP necessary to understand reset attacks. If you don't already have a good understanding of TCP/IP, don't expect to be an expert after reading this chapter [1].

TCP/IP is an abbreviation for the Transmission Control Protocol, defined in RFC 793 which was released in September of 1981. TCP/IP is a connection oriented protocol that can reliably get information from one host to another across a network/Internet. By reliable, TCP/IP guarantees all data will arrive uncorrupted at the remote host, automatically detecting dropped or corrupted packets and resending them as needed. Every TCP/IP packet includes a header, which is defined by the RFC as shown in Fig. 9-1 [1].

Programs utilize TCP/IP by passing it buffers of data. TCP/IP breaks this data into packages known as segments, and then uses IP to further package these segments into

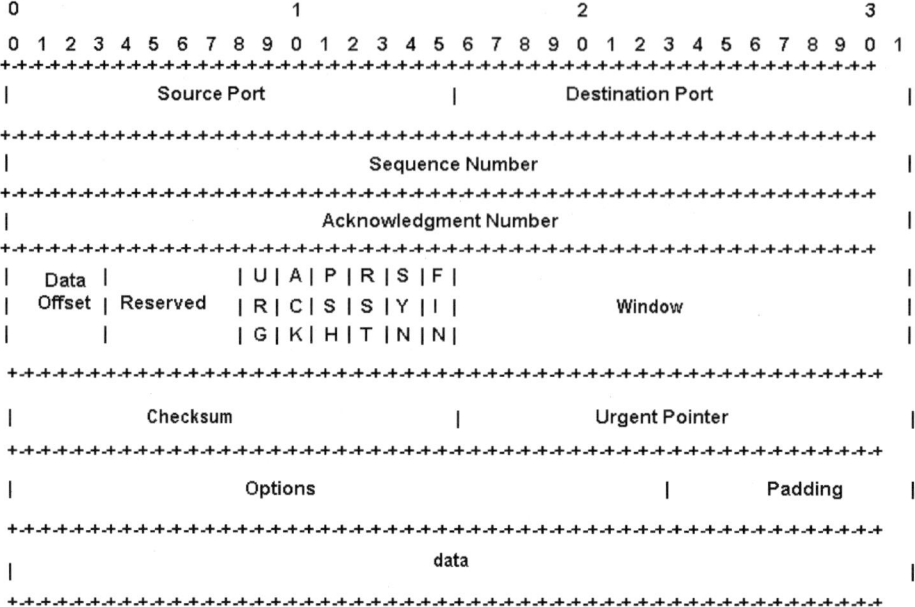

Figure 9-1. TCP/IP packet header.

datagrams. Finally, the datagrams are embedded into a network packet which can be routed across a network [1].

When the packet arrives at its destination, the IP stack on the remote host extracts the datagram from the packet, then the segment from the datagram. The segment is then passed up to the TCP/IP stack, where it can be validated. Ultimately the TCP/IP stack can reassemble all the segments into the complete buffer which is then passed to the application. TCP/IP provides two way communication, so this same process occurs in both directions [1].

Sequence Numbers

With data having been broken into segments which are then routed as separate packets over a network, it is quite possible for packets to arrive at their destination out of order. A field in the TCP/IP header provides for a 32-bit sequence number, a value that starts at an arbitrary integer then increments sequentially with each transmitted packet. Using these sequence numbers, the receiving TCP/IP stack is able to properly reorder the received segments [1].

Windows

TCP/IP also provides a mechanism for hosts to tell each other how much data they want to receive at a time. This is known as a window, defined by a 16-bit field in the TCP/IP header. Once defined, a host will generally only receive data that is within its specified window, dropping anything else. Being within the window means that the sequence number of the packet is a number that is within the range of data that one end of the connection told the other end it was willing to receive at any one point in time. If a receive queue gets full, the host can declare a window of size 0, telling the other endpoint not to send anything and giving the backed up host a chance to catch up [1].

Control Bits

There are six control bits defined in TCP/IP, one or more of which is defined in each packet. The control bits are 'SYN', 'ACK', 'PSH', 'URG', 'RST', and 'FIN'. TCP/IP uses these bits to define the purpose and contents of a packet. For the purposes of this chapter, the SYN, ACK and RST flags are of primary interest, though they will all be briefly defined [1].

The SYN bit is used in establishing a TCP/IP connection to synchronize the sequence numbers between both endpoints. The ACK bit is used to acknowledge the remote host's sequence numbers, declaring that the information in the acknowledgment field is valid. The PSH flag is set on the sending side, and tells the TCP/IP stack to flush all buffers and send any outstanding data up to and including the data that had the PSH flag set. When the receiving TCP/IP sees the PSH flag, it too must flush its buffers and pass the information up to the application. The URG bit indicates that the urgent pointer field has a valid pointer to data that should be treated urgently and be transmitted before non-urgent data. The RST bit tells the receiving TCP/IP stack to immediately abort the connection. And the FIN bit is used to indicate that the client will send no more data (but will continue to listen for data) [1].

For example, a TCP/IP connection is usually initiated with a three-way handshake. That is, host A will send a packet to host B, setting only the SYN control bit, and putting a randomly generated number into the sequence number field of the packet's TCP/IP header. This randomly generated sequence number is the ISN, or initial sequence number [1].

Host B receives the packet with only the SYN bit sent, and therefor knows that host A is trying to establish a connection, currently trying to synchronize sequence numbers. Host B therefor replies by sending a packet back to host A, setting both the SYN and ACK bits. Host B generates its own random sequence number and puts it into the sequence number field of the packet's TCP/IP header. Host B also puts Host A's ISN +1 into the acknowledgment field, indicating the next sequence number expected from Host A [1].

Host A receives this packet with both the SYN and the ACK bits set. It verifies that the number in the acknowledgment field is correct, then generates a third packet, this time with only the ACK control bit set. In the acknowledgment field of this third packet goes the sequence number +1 from the previous packet, acknowledging to Host B that the SYN ACK packet was received and indicating which sequence number is next expected. When this done, the three way handshake is complete and a TCP/IP connection is now established between host A and host B. At this point, data can be transmitted in both directions between the hosts [1].

The three way handshake that's been described is the most common mechanism for opening a TCP/IP connection. However, the RFC does not require that communication begin this way, and therefor it is perfectly legal to add in other control bits during the initiation of communication [1].

> **Note:** Many of the problems with TCP/IP have originated from the fact that the RFC really divides the protocol into two separate parts, the first being connection establishment and breakdown, and the second being data flow.

This has resulted in weird stuff like SYN|ACK|FIN exchanges being possible. Some people will say it is wrong, but it is explicitly left open in the RFCs. Nothing says you can't attempt to move data in your first packet [1].

Ports

In addition to allowing hosts to carry on bidirectional communication within one connection, TCP/IP also allows hosts to maintain more than one TCP/IP connection at a time. This is done using ports. A port is a unique integer from 1 through 65,535. All TCP/IP connections originate on a source port within the preceding range, and terminate on a destination port within the same range [1].

For most common TCP/IP connections, the destination port is a well known established value. For example, a web browser usually connects to destination port 80, a mail client sending email connect to destination port 25, and an ssh client connects to destination port 22. The reason these clients connect to specific ports is that their respective servers are known to be listening on those ports. The complete list of officially assigned port numbers is maintained by IANA [1].

The source of TCP/IP connections, however, can usually originate from any port, though certain lower port numbers are reserved and unavailable for use as a source port. In particular, ports 1-1024 are reserved for well known and privileged processes. There can only be one outgoing TCP/IP connection from each port at a time, allowing the TCP/IP server to differentiate between multiple TCP/IP connections from the same host [1].

When a TCP/IP connection is made, the combination of the source port and IP address and the destination port and IP address results in a unique fingerprint that can be used to differentiate between all active TCP/IP connections. With this minimal understanding of how TCP/IP works, it is now possible to understand what reset attacks are and how they work [1].

TCP/IP RESET ATTACKS

The primary idea behind a TCP/IP reset attack is to falsely terminate an established TCP/IP connection. Let's imagine an established TCP/IP connection from host A to host B. Now, a third host, C, spoofs a packet that matches the source port and IP address of host A; the destination port and IP address of host B; and, the current sequence number of the active TCP/IP connection between host A and host B. Host C sets the RST bit on the spoofed packet, so when received by host B, host B immediately terminates the connection. This results in a denial of service, until the connection can be reestablished. However, the severity of such an attack is different from application to application [1].

Applications and protocols that require lengthy sustained connections are most vulnerable. Perhaps the most affected is Cisco's BGP, or Border Gateway Protocol, the latest version of which is defined in RFC 1771. BGP is so vulnerable as it relies on a persistent TCP/IP session being maintained between peers. If the connection gets terminated, it then takes time to rebuild routing tables and remote hosts may perform route flapping. A route flap is any routing change that results in a BGP table being changed. A router that is constantly loosing its connection and causing route flapping on other BGP routers will eventually suffer route dampening, or suppression. As BGP is used on large border routers, this could have a significant impact on a large number of users [1].

As described earlier in this chapter, TCP/IP utilizes sequence numbers to determine whether or not a packet with valid endpoints (IP addresses and ports) applies to the current active session. This both allows TCP/IP to both properly reassemble even out of order packets into the original data buffer, as well as to ignore potentially spoofed packets [1].

Slipping In The Window

TCP/IP connections are more susceptible to this type of attack than was previously thought. Specifically, in previous calculations it was assumed that a brute force attack would have to try every sequence number from 1 up to the maximum of 4,294,967,295. However, the number of required attempts is significantly less than this, due to TCP/IP windows [1].

For example, if the TCP/IP stack on host A has defined a 16K window, the stack must accept any packet that has a sequence number that falls within this range, as the packets may be arriving out of order. Hence, someone that is performing a TCP/IP reset attack doesn't have to send a RST packet with every possible sequence number, instead he or she only has to send a RST packet with a sequence number from each possible window. In other words, there is still the assumption that in a 16K window size, an attacker would have to send 4,294,967,295 / 16,384, or 262,143 packets to exhaust all possible windows [1].

A number like 262,143 may sound like a large number, though when considering a RST attack, it is possible that an attacker will be able to generate tens of thousands of packets per second, depending on their bandwidth. What more, an attack could be distributed among many hosts, thus being an aggregation of all their bandwidths. However, assuming the attacker has a single DSL at their disposal, they will be able to generate about 250 packets per second. Thus, a single DSL would be able to exhaust all possible windows in just over 17 minutes. However, with a T1 at 4,370 packets a second, the attacker would be able to exhaust all possible windows within only 60 seconds [1].

The example here assumed a 16K window size, however the TCP/IP RFC provides a 16 bit field for the window, allowing it to be as large as 64K. If the full window size is utilized, an attacker would only have to send 4,294,967,295 divided by 65,535, or 65,537 packets. With this window size, it would take a DSL about 4 minutes, and a T1 only about 15 seconds. And remember that these times assume that you would have to try every single window before finding a match, when by the law of averages you could expect it to take closer to half that time [1].

At DSL speeds against a host using 64K windows, you can use brute force to (on average) generate a reset in within 3 minutes; however, some of the attacks may take only a few seconds to be successful. At T1 speeds, you can blindly tear down a session in less than 8 seconds. With a connection faster than a T1, the time to brute force a matching RST attack can quickly become insignificant [1].

At this point one may wonder why anyone would specify a large window, as it obviously decreases the security of the TCP/IP stack. The reason is, larger window sizes generally provide higher performance. For this reason, RFC-1323 was defined in 1992 and titled: "TCP/IP Extensions for High Performance." Among other features, this RFC defines window scaling, a widely supported TCP/IP extension that effectively increases the available window size from 16 bits to 30 bits. Thus, against an application or protocol using window scaling which is open to the maximum range, an attacker would only have to send 4,294,967,295 divided by 1,073,741,824, or 4 packets. That's right, it would only take 4 spoofed packets to generate a matching RST packet against an application that fully utilized window scaling. Again, an example that uses window scaling is Cisco's BGP, which frequently utilizes window scaling to improve performance [1].

Source Ports

All of the preceding examples assume that the attacker already knows the destination port and IP address as well the source port and IP address. The destination port and IP address are easy, as they are generally published. The source IP address is also generally easy, as this is simply the client that is being spoofed. The only piece that can frequently be difficult to find is the source port [1].

For example, if an operating system randomly assigns source ports from a pool that ranges from 1025 through 49,152 (such as OpenBSD), this increases the difficulty of performing a reset attack 48,127 times as the attacker would have to try their sequence attack with every possible port number. In the first example with 16k windows, it was determined that with known endpoints it would require 262,143 packets to guarantee a successful reset attack. However, if using random ports as has been described, it would now require 262,143 times 48,127, or 12,616,156,161 packets. An attack of that size would all but certainly be detected and dealt with before a brute force reset would occur [1].

Realizing the security added by using randomized source ports, you would expect that most operating systems employ this defensive strategy. Unfortunately, most operating systems allocate source ports sequentially, including Windows and Linux. A notable exception is OpenBSD, which began randomizing source port allocation in 1996 [1].

SYN Attacks

A reset attack can be performed indirectly without setting the RST bit. Instead, the attacker can set the SYN bit, otherwise identically performing the brute force attack as described earlier. On most TCP/IP stack implementations, a duplicate SYN will cause a RST to be sent in reply with the provided sequence number. If the SYN is within the window of the active matching session, in addition to sending a RST in reply, it will cause the local end of the connection to be immediately torn down. This action is by design, intended to handle system reboots during a TCP/IP connection [1].

In response to the threats of reset attacks, the IETF is now recommending that when TCP/IP stacks receive an in-window SYN packet, they should instead reply with an ACK. If the SYN was truly from the remote client attempting to re-establish communication after a reboot, then it will not expect the ACK packet and will reply with a valid (in-window) RST, causing the now stale connection to be torn down. If the SYN was instead spoofed by an attacker, the ACK will be ignored. However, this may be even more problematic, as if the attacker keeps spoofing valid SYN packets the continuous flood of generated ACK packets could become a serious problem [1].

> **Note:** Nowhere is the IETF telling anyone that this is dangerous. Every SYN you spoof onto one of your sessions, you will send an ACK over your peer link. If you have 1GB to spoof to you, but your link to your peer is a T1, you can hurt your T1. These types of things are called reflectors. They are bad.

For these reasons, SYN based reset attacks are actually more serious than RST based reset attacks. Not only can using the SYN bit tear down a connection, but based on the latest IETF recommendations, it can also result in the generation of more packets, potentially flooding a connection. Think of it this way: Some systems have SYN behaviors that can interact badly with RST behaviors on other systems [1].

Blind Data Injection

Finally, a third related attack is called blind data injection, and again relies an brute force to find a matching sequence number. Essentially, instead of simply sending empty RST or SYN packets, the attacker could send data packets. The attack would commence as has been already described, except now instead of tearing down a connection, the attacker may instead corrupt the connection, invalidating the data that was being exchanged [1].

SUMMARY AND CONCLUSIONS

At this point, you should have a decent understanding of what a reset attack is, and how it works. The goal of this chapter was to better understand if the threat is real, and indeed it seems to be. Lots of people are saying this is not a problem, but its clearly evident that you will see a worm using it one day. Worms can effectively perform distributed attacks, greatly increasing the speed at which a reset attack could be conducted [1].

It is not possible to fully protect against a brute force TCP/IP reset attack, but there are many things that can be done to harden TCP/IP stacks. The TCP/IP RFC is not a narrow definition, leaving many design decisions up to each operating system's implementation. It is perhaps because of this fact that many popular operating systems are quite susceptible to reset attacks, though there are published methods for hardening against them. The fact is, critical server systems with these poor TCP/IP behaviors will stay around for quite some time [1].

Finally, choices made in the implementation of a TCP/IP stack can significantly affect an attacker's ability to efficiently perform reset and other types of attacks. Hopefully other operating systems will follow this lead, further hardening themselves against such attacks [1].

REFERENCES

[1]   Jeremy Andrews, "Understanding TCP Reset Attacks, Part I," (c)2002–2005 KernelTrap, KernelTrap.org, Florida, USA, 2006.

Chapter 10

EARLY SYSTEM SECURITY IMPROVEMENTS

INTRODUCTION

Due to the current popularity of international commerce on the Internet, the topic of computer security has moved quickly from being a low priority for enterprises and government agencies to a high priority. This interest has been heightened by computer break-ins at places like Los Alamos National Laboratories and NASA. Admissions by the United States government that many attempted military computer break-ins were successful has only added fuel to the fire. Your computer systems are at risk, but the good news is that you can do something about it [1].

The creators of the Internet never envisioned that it would become the hub of international commerce. They designed the Internet for the open and free exchange of research information between universities and government. They did not design it to be secure and Internet firewalls [4] were an afterthought. Some firewalls are good and others are not. Are proxy firewalls better than filtering firewalls? Nobody really knows and maybe both are necessary depending on the risks involved. However, firewalls may not be enough protection. Secure network routers are coming on line, but they have yet to prove themselves. Potential security problems exist anytime a government or an enterprise computer is connected to the Internet. Furthermore, fragments of previously deleted e-mail and files may linger for years in the heart of a computer's hard disk drive and discarded floppy diskettes. Computer secrets never go away. Many crooks have learned this lesson the hard way. However, things may not be as bad as they appear from a computer security standpoint [1].

Through the implementation of proper computer security policies and strategies, network connections to the Internet can be made more secure and sensitive data can be secured by using file encryption [5]. Also, computer storage media [6] can be effectively cleansed of sensitive information. Knowing the risks up front makes the job much easier for computer users and security policy makers. Firewalls and secure network routers haven't come of age yet and security tied to them may not be adequate protection for trade secrets and sensitive computer data. However, these technologies have their place and only a fool would connect a computer network to the Internet without some sort of a firewall [1].

Given enough time, desire and resources, it is a safe bet that almost any computer security system can be broken. The only totally secure computer system is one locked in a room, without people and without connections to other computers. Since such a security strategy is impractical, other security strategies and policies must be implemented. Government and enterprise management cannot ignore the Internet just because of potential Internet security problems. The wealth of free information available on the Internet and inexpensive worldwide E-mail access can result in significant cost savings and increased productivity. Don't forget. You do live in the information age. An enterprise cannot remain competitive if it doesn't take advantage of all available technologies [1].

Internet firewalls serve a very good purpose. Much like the perimeter fence at a military base, firewalls act as the first important line of defense. However, they are not the total answer. Encryption should be wisely used to protect sensitive information from unauthorized eyes. It is no secret that foreign competitors of large U S enterprises gainfully employ former Eastern Block intelligence agents. You see, it is more cost effective to steal the secrets of your competition than it is to spend millions of dollars for research and development. Unless good encryption is employed, they can make copies of the computer secrets without leaving any trace or clue that they even compromised such secrets. Lets face it. Most written communications today are created on computers. Most of these computers are not secure and to make matters worse many computers involved are portable notebook computers. File encryption helps here also [1].

An Internet firewall is essentially one or more systems that control access between computer networks. In this regard, the Internet is nothing more than a very large computer network. An installed firewall on a computer network serves two basic purposes: it controls access to the network from outside servers, and it also controls the transfer of information from the network to outside servers. It is not enough to just install an Internet firewall. The type of firewall(s) needed is usually dictated by the needs of the enterprise and the level of risk involved. The most important thing to remember about a firewall is that it creates an access control policy for the enterprise. Executive management and the computer security staff must be involved in defining what the access policy will be prior to purchase and installation. Absent of such planning, the enterprise will set its security policy based on the on the whim of the installer, or worse, the default configuration of the manufacturer. Let's not forget that hackers love default security settings [1].

Once the mysterious focus of spy stories and movies, encryption is really nothing more than the scrambling of data to make it unreadable. There is strong encryption and weak encryption, and an entire chapter could be written on the topic. Most word processing, spreadsheet and database applications that provide encryption as an option, are not secure. In fact, commercial applications exist which can be used to quickly defeat the security afforded by these applications. For the purposes of this chapter, standalone file encryption products will be discussed. To keep things simple, let's just say that the longer the encryption key the stronger the security. This assumes, of course, that a solid encryption algorithm has been employed. Unfortunately there are several algorithms to choose from. With the preceding in mind, the rest of this chapter will focus on early system security improvements like DES, shadow passwords and dialback/dialer passwords [1].

DES

The most secure encryption algorithms, implemented by software, have a key length of 128 bits or more. These include IDEA, Triple DES, 128 bit RC4 and 128 bit SEAL. A relatively new algorithm that seems secure is Blow Fish. The lesser strength, but still relatively secure algorithms include 80 bit RC5 and 64 bit RC5 encryption schemes. The Data Encryption Standard (DES), developed back in the 70's is currently the standard used by the federal government regarding the encryption of sensitive but unclassified data. It deals with a 56 bit key length and is on the edge of what is breakable using today's technology and about $250,000 worth of computer hardware [1].

Currently, the United States government restricts the export of encryption software that relies strong encryption algorithms. However, there is heated controversy regarding this issue between government and software enterprises. Because of the potential loss of international technology trade by US enterprises, Congress will probably support the export of more powerful encryption products in the future. If they don't, this country could lose billions of dollars in foreign trade, over the next few years, to countries like Japan and China. If they do, it could create more problems for governments law enforcement and intelligence agencies. There are good arguments in both directions [1].

How difficult is it to break encryption? The answer involves the speed of the computer used to perform the task, the length of the key involved and how much money you have to throw at the problem. However, calculating how much time it takes to break a specific key length is simple. Given current technology, approximately 90 million DES key combinations or five million RC4 key combinations can be processed per second. The cost of the computer hardware to accomplish this is approximately $50,000–$75,000. In other words, for about $50,000, given current technology, it would take only a second or so to break encryption tied to a key length of 26 bits. It would take approximately one hour to break a key length of 38 bits. A 40 bit key could be broken in about four hours, a 48 bit key in about one month, and a 56 bit key (Full DES) in 30 years or so. Up the price to about $1 million and DES can be broken in approximately 10 days. I think you get the idea. Security tied to a 128 bit encryption algorithm is very secure, given the state of technology today and the expected state of technology for the next 30 years [1].

SHADOW PASSWORDS

Shadow passwords are a means of keeping your encrypted password information secret from normal users. Recent versions of both Red Hat and Debian Linux use shadow passwords by default, but on other systems, encrypted passwords are stored in /etc/passwd file for all to read. Anyone can then run password-guesser programs on them and attempt to determine what they are. Shadow passwords, by contrast, are saved in /etc/shadow, which only privileged users can read. In order to use shadow passwords, you need to make sure all your utilities that need access to password information are recompiled to support them [2].

DIALBACK/DIALER PASSWORDS

Before you install the remote access software, you should create a security plan for remote users dialing in to your network. This involves selecting the type of access security you want to implement and whether the restrictions will be placed globally or for selected users only [3].

Types Of Access Security

Remote access provides the following levels of access security:

- Default Security
- User-, Port-, and Service-Level Security
- Global Security for All Users
- User-Specific Security
- Service-Specific Security
- Third-Party Security [3]

Default Security

Default security is in effect when you first install and set up a basic configuration. The default security for each service is explained in Table 10-1 [3]. The default security parameters specify the following:

- All users have access to all services and ports.
- All services have access to all ports at all times.
- Users can remain connected for an unlimited amount of time.
- Users cannot use the dialback feature.
- User sessions can remain idle for an unlimited amount of time.
- Users can dial out to any number.
- There are no restrictions on defining Remote Client passwords [3].

Table 10-1. Default Security Requirements.

PPP Remote Node Service	AppleTalk Remote Access Service	NASI Connection Service
NetWare username and NetWare password	NetWare username and Remote Client password	NASI, Win2NCS, or Mac2NCS workstation: NetWare password Remote workstation: NetWare username and Remote Client password

After the remote client establishes a connection, the remote client must log in to the NetWare network. The system does not prompt for a NetWare login until the user runs the login command [3].

User-, Port-, and Service-Level Security

As an administrator, you can customize the level of security by restricting the following:

- Users from accessing certain ports
- Users from accessing specific services
- Ports to a particular service for a specified time [3]

Global Security for All Users

You can define the following security options globally for all users:

- Maximum connection time
- Idle time before disconnection
- Password restrictions
- Dialback
- Dial-out restrictions [3]

Maximum Connection Time

You can limit the time online for all users. If you set this value to 0 minutes, remote access will immediately disconnect the user when the user dials in. If you set this value to −1, there is no limit. Connections that are already established are not affected [3].

Idle Time Before Disconnection

Remote access disconnects a user after the connection has been idle for a specified amount of time, in minutes. This helps you manage line usage costs by disconnecting inactive connections. This option is not valid for ARAS connections [3].

Password Restrictions

These restrictions apply to the Remote Client password that is set for each user. You can specify the number of times a user can enter an incorrect password, as well as the minimum length of the password [3].

Dialback

You can require users to specify a dialback number at connection time. Or, you can allow users to request dialback at connection time [3].

Dial-Out Restrictions

You can restrict users from dialing out to a specific number by specifying a list of authorized numbers. Dial-out restrictions apply only to modem-independent ports [3].

> **Note:** Frame=26:/2.0 internal insetSetting is a value for a security option for user overrides, in order, the nearest container, remote access server, and global settings for that option.

User-Specific Security

You can define remote access security for each user. If you have more than one remote access server on the network, you can customize user security from a single server console. You can configure the following options for each user:

- Maximum connection time
- Idle Timeout
- Dialback
- Dial-out restrictions
- Remote Client password [3]

Maximum Connection Time

You can limit the time online for a user. If you set this value to 0 minutes, remote access will immediately disconnect the user when the user dials in. If you set this value to -1, there is no limit. Connections that are already established are not affected. This parameter overrides any global defaults [3].

Idle Timeout

Remote access disconnects the user after a connection has been idle for a specified amount of time. You can set the idle timeout value for a user or a container. This option is not valid for ARAS connections [3].

Dialback

Forced dialback enables you to enforce maximum security by preconfiguring a dialback number for each caller. You can also require users to specify a dialback number at connection time, or you can allow users to choose to dial back and specify a dialback number at connection time [3].

Dial-Out Restrictions

You can restrict a user from dialing out to any number by creating a list of authorized numbers for that user. Dial-out restrictions apply to modem-independent ports [3].

Remote Client Password

You can set a Remote Client password for ARAS, NCS, and PPPRNS clients using the PAP or CHAP method of authentication. By default, there is no Remote Client password, and ARAS, NCS, and PPPRNS services are denied without a password. The NetWare password is still required for PPPRNS with NWCAP selected [3].

You can set the password to be valid for a specific number of days and require users to change their passwords when they expire. Remote access provides users with the tools to change their Remote Client passwords [3].

Once a user's Remote Client password has expired, the user must use these tools to change the Remote Client password. The user is allowed three grace logins after the password has expired. If the user logs in using the three grace logins without changing the password, the user is denied logon to remote access. The administrator must then use NIASCFG or the NetWare Administrator utility in Windows to assign a new password to the user [3].

Note: However, you must specify dial-out restrictions on each remote access server.

Service-Specific Security

You can configure service-specific security options for each of the following services:

- PPP Remote Node Service
- NASI Connection Service
- AppleTalk Remote Access Service [3]

PPP Remote Node Service

You can disable PPPRNS security. Or, you can enable one or more of the three supported protocols used to establish a connection:

- NetWare Connect Authentication Protocol (NWCAP)
- Password Authentication Protocol (PAP)
- Challenge Handshake Authentication Protocol (CHAP) [3]

NetWare Connect Authentication Protocol (NWCAP)

This type of authentication is the default method for maintaining network security. With this method, users must specify the NetWare password to successfully establish a connection. This type of authentication is supported by the PPPRNS client for the remote access dialer. The NetWare password is encrypted and is not sent in plain text across the wire [3].

> **Note:** The PPPRNS client for DOS (DOSDIAL) and Windows (Windows Dialer) NetWare Connect^{TM} dialers are also supported.

Password Authentication Protocol (PAP)

This type of authentication offers minimum security. It is not enabled by default. If you enable this protocol, users must specify the Remote Client Password to successfully establish a connection. The Remote Client password is sent in plain text across the wire [3].

This method is supported by the PPPRNS client for the remote access dialer. Enable this option if you have UNIX clients that support PAP, such as the LAN WorkPlace® software [3].

> **Note:** The PPPRNS client for DOS (DOSDIAL) and Windows (Windows Dialer) NetWare Connect dialers are also supported.

Challenge Handshake Authentication Protocol (CHAP)

This type of authentication allows third-party PPP clients that support CHAP to connect to remote access. It is disabled by default, and is used by Windows 2003 and Windows NT. This method is not supported by the PPPRNS client that is shipped with Novell Internet Access Server [3].

This method of authentication requires users to specify the Remote Client password to establish a connection. The Remote Client password is used for encryption and is not sent across the wire [3].

If the default NWCAP authentication is enabled, users must specify a NetWare username and password. If you enable PAP or CHAP, users must specify Remote Client passwords [3].

PPPRNS negotiates the security modes in the following order (when enabled): CHAP, PAP, and NWCAP. For example, the server is configured to support both NWCAP and

CHAP. If the client supports CHAP, CHAP is used. If the client supports NWCAP, NWCAP is used. If the client supports both CHAP and NWCAP, CHAP is used because it is negotiated first [3].

When PAP or CHAP is used, a Remote Client password must be defined to allow users access. To allow users access without Remote Client passwords, either turn off PPPRNS security or use the Set PPPRNS AdmitNoConfig=ON command at the server console to validate users without Remote Client passwords. So, if security is disabled at the server side, the remote client must specify None for the security type [3].

NASI Connection Service

For NASI Connection Service (NCS), you apply security to the network workstation dialing out and to the remote workstation dialing in. Enabling security for the network workstation means that NASI workstations must specify a password. Enabling remote security means that remote workstations must specify a username and a Remote Client password [3].

AppleTalk Remote Access Service

For AppleTalk Remote Access Service (ARAS), you can restrict access to AppleTalk zones globally for all users. Or, you can restrict access to AppleTalk zones on a per-user basis [3].

Third-Party Security

Remote access supports third-party security products that implement token-based challenge/response types of security. These products have both hardware and software components. Remote access supports the software by providing a configuration option in the configuration utility. The hardware components are installed between the remote access port and the modem [3].

When third-party security is enabled, PPPRNS and NCS users must be validated through third-party security. After third-party security passes, call selection takes place. Any configured security for a service is applied to the call before the session is established [3].

PPPRNS users must configure their dialers to enter terminal mode to process the third-party security validation and transfer the call to PPP mode. If the dialer is configured incorrectly, that is, the call goes into PPP mode right away, the call will be rejected [3].

When the services available on a port are PPPRNS, NCS, or both, the incoming call executes third-party security as soon as the call is received. If additional services (such as ARAS) are also available on a port, the usual call selection will take place first. This enables services that do not support third-party security to accept calls even when third-party security is enabled. After the initial call selection, third-party security is executed [3].

Finally, if third-party security passes, a second call selection process takes place to determine which service the call is destined for. If PPPRNS clients are configured incorrectly and the call is selected during the initial call selection process, the call is terminated. In addition, if you have services other than PPPRNS or NCS selected, you can minimize the call establishment time for PPPRNS and NCS calls by restricting ARAS (and other services that do not support third-party security) to using specific ports [3].

SUMMARY AND CONCLUSIONS

This chapter's message to you is this: Fear of the Internet is unfounded if proper security measures are implemented as part of a well-designed security strategy. Firewalls have their place in the security design, but enterprise trade secrets and sensitive government data need to be encrypted at a high level of security. To avoid the threat of destruction of data by hackers, make regular and periodic backups and store copies off site. That might sound pretty basic; but today, there are still many major federal agencies and large enterprises that don't backup critical data files on a regular basis. To put it mildly, they are playing with cyber fire!

REFERENCES

[1] Michael Anderson, "Internet Security – Firewalls & Encryption The Cyber Cop's Perspective," © 2005 Armor Forensics, All Rights Reserved, Armor Forensics, 13386 International Parkway, Jacksonville FL 32218, 2005.
[2] Kevin Fenzi and Dave Wreski, "Linux Security HOWTO," ibiblio.org, Chapel Hill, North Carolina, U.S.A., January 2004.
[3] "Remote Access Security," © 2006 Novell, Inc. All Rights Reserved. Novell, Inc., 1177 Avenue of the Americas, 35th Floor, New York, New York, 2006.
[4] John R. Vacca, Firewalls: Jumpstart for Network and Systems Administrators, Digital Press, 2004.
[5] John R. Vacca, Satellite Encryption, Academic Press, Jul 1999.
[6] John R. Vacca, The Essential Guide To Storage Area Networks, Prentice Hall, Nov 2001.

PART VI

DETERRING MASQUERADERS AND ENSURING AUTHENTICITY

Chapter 11

IMPERSONATING USERS

INTRODUCTION

Identity theft is one of the fastest growing crimes in the United States. The loss to consumers was more than $700 million in 2006 [1].

But, what about the loss to enterprises, institutions and government bodies from identity theft that results in unlawful access to buildings that house physical assets and the IT network that house mission-critical, digital assets or the costs associated with trying to secure those buildings and the Internet against intrusion. Simply stated, identity theft is the unlawful acquisition of an individual's personal information by someone who uses that information to assume the identity of his or her victim for personal gain or to cause harm [1].

WHAT'S AT RISK?

For most enterprises, potential threats include:

- Subversive attacks, in which an intruder manipulates the system into non-legitimate activities, like transferring money.
- Disruptive attacks, which compromise business data and/or systems and interrupts activity.
- Privacy attacks, in which outside individuals gain access to private information.
- Physical attacks, in which outsiders gain access to a building and cause harm to property or people or steal assets [1].

Because identity theft has become so pervasive, enterprises and institutions are faced with three major, but separate security issues: physical access control, time & attendance control and logical access control, but all rely upon a common task – identity and access management [1].

IDENTITY AND ACCESS MANAGEMENT

The fire service uses a triangle to explain fire. Heat + Fuel + Oxygen = Fire. Remove any element and the triangle collapses and the fire dies. Security can be described in much the same way. Identity Management + Access Management = Security. Compromise either and security fails [1].

Traditionally, there have been only two methods by which identity and access have been controlled; what one knows and what one has. If you know something that only you are supposed to know, like your mother's maiden name, a four-digit personal identification number (PIN), or a secret password, then you must be who you say your are. If you have something that only you are supposed to possess, like an office key, car key, ATM card, swipe card or token, then you must be the valid owner [1].

IT'S NOT WHAT YOU KNOW THAT COUNTS

As illogical as this seems in today's world, these two methodologies continue to be the methods of choice for many enterprises, though banks have made the process more robust by implementing a two-challenge protocol. Anyone using an ATM card is required to know his or her four-digit PIN and to have his or her ATM card. Yet, as robust as this security challenge appears, it is frequently compromised when an ATM card is lost or stolen. Not only because a four digit PIN is relatively easy to guess, but also because many people write their PIN number on the back of their card or have actually shared their PIN number with the person that has stolen their card [1].

In most security breaches, whether physical or logical, it is the human factor that enables the breach to occur. In fact, according to CERT/CC1 84% of all Internet security breaches result from a password that has been stolen or shared. Passwords are the weakest link! Why? See the following reasons:

- Password weaknesses are well known and easily exploited. Passwords that are based on simple words that users can easily remember are also easy for hackers to guess. Simple password cracking programs can find many whole word passwords quickly.
- As passwords become more complex or increase in number, users tend to write them down.
- Passwords are subject to social engineering attacks. According to industry analysts, four out of five employees give their passwords to someone else within the company if asked. A persuasive outside caller is often able to extract passwords over the phone.
- To avoid remembering many passwords, people often use the same password across many systems, including unsecured websites where passwords may be sent in a clear text format. A single password, once cracked, may open many doors.
- Some e-mail viruses send password information back to the originator of the virus [1].

The main threats to security include outsiders who gain access by impersonating authorized users and legitimate users who impersonate other users with different authorization levels [1].

The underlying problem with passwords is that humans aren't perfect. They cannot be relied upon to maintain a strong password process that is highly rules based while other more job-related processes compete for their attention. Putting the onus of password protection on the employee is a certain path to failure. The less convenient security is, the more likely it is to be bypassed by a user. Yet, because user authentication is the gateway to your data center infrastructure, the potential risks associated with security breaches are significant. Your information system is only as secure as your least responsible user [1].

Passwords that contain many and various kinds of characters are harder to crack. They are also harder to remember. As a result, passwords have evolved into pass phrases, containing a mixture of upper and lowercase letters, symbols and numbers. Instead of using a pet's name, "Hunter", as a password, it is safer to use a pass phrase like, "My2DogsAreNamedHunter&Pluto" [1].

Enterprises routinely create and manage user identities and access privileges across 25 or more individual applications and systems, forcing users to remember upwards of 20 enterprise passwords. But not every password administrator within the enterprise embraces the same password convention. Some enterprise passwords are restricted in length while some are restricted in case. Some enterprise password conventions require a password change quarterly while some require a change monthly. These disparities add to the robust character of the security convention. If all passwords were the same, one password failure would be sufficient to compromise the security on every system to which that user has access [1].

As password conventions become more robust, the need to support users grows. This increases costs and adds considerable burden to the IT help desk staff. Several industry analysts claim that it takes up to 28 hours to set up a single user account. Gartner Group, a well-respected industry analyst, has indicated that 19% of IT budgets or approximately $600 to $750 per employee per year is wasted on password support. Strong passwords result in more help desk calls for forgotten or expired passwords, in addition to increasing employee downtime. Today, a password request help desk call costs a company between $70 and $100 and accounts for up to 49% of calls received by the help desk [1].

Yet, enterprises of every type and size are increasingly adopting an e-business infrastructure as the primary platform for conducting business. As a result, there has been a significant increase in access requirements, resulting from a growing number and type of users, and access methods. In order to increase and strengthen strategic relationships while lowering costs, enterprises are opening their information assets to customers, partners, suppliers and employees and inadvertently exposing their enterprises to significant risk [1].

ELIMINATE VULNERABLE, PASSWORD-BASED SYSTEMS

Unfortunately, these same enterprises find themselves struggling and often failing to manage user identities, and access rights in a way that serves both their business goals and their security requirements. The fundamental problem is a decentralized approach to user management and security, which was first developed 42 years ago, coupled with an escalating and variable cost of password support. In other words, enterprises are relying on people instead of technology to safeguard their business [1].

YOUR IDENTITY IS THE KEY

Biometric authentication strategies avoid many of these security flaws. In particular, they are less susceptible to human error. A biometric, such as a fingerprint or retinal scan, cannot be guessed or shared and the user doesn't have to think up a strong fingerprint, so the security of the metric doesn't depend on human effort. People can't forget their fingerprints – eliminating a common source of help desk calls. Biometric keys are not susceptible to social engineering attacks and cannot be shared or stolen [1].

Because biometrics uses a physical characteristic, instead of something to be remembered or carried around, it is convenient for users and less susceptible to misuse than other user-dependent authentication measures. Biometrics technologies (those that use human characteristics such as fingerprint, voice and face recognition) will be the most important IT innovations of the next several years. Passwords will soon be a thing of the past, replaced by biometric and smart-card technology. A major problem for identity systems is the weakness of passwords [1].

Time/Attendance Management

Biometric devices are used to authenticate an employee's identity, track when they signed in and out, prevent buddy punching and confirm who is on site at any given time. Used when employees must account for their time and presence, it lowers the costs of record keeping and improves efficiencies. When enterprises are 100% certain that an individual is who he or she says he or she is, they can be 100% certain of that person's attendance record [1].

Physical Access Security Management

Biometric devices are used to authenticate an individual's identity and are capable of controlling electronic door locks to prevent access to anyone that is not authorized to have access. When used with a web camera, this solution also has the ability to snapshot or monitor in real time who has opened the door and who has walked through [1].

Internet Access/Logical Access Security

Biometric devices are used to authenticate an employee's identity and permit access to the Internet infrastructure. Enterprises achieve single sign on functionality at a fraction of the cost of password-based conventions [1].

Though improved security is a result of deploying a biometric identity management and access control solution, many enterprises are looking for solutions that also lower their operating costs. When an employee is terminated, as an example, there is no longer a need to change the locks. Simply deactivate that employee. If specified groups of people have their access restricted to a single door, simply write a rule in the system to deny them access except through the approved door. If an employee does not have the authority to look at payroll records, simply create a challenge at the payroll record access point that can only be answered by a biometric. As in all biometric identity management solutions, a person never needs to know their logon name or password and no longer carries a key. Cost reductions are realized by the elimination of the need for the enterprise to support outdated, user-dependent methodologies [1].

WHAT'S THE COST?

In today's economy, every new solution considered must deliver a measurable return on investment and significantly impact operating cost-reduction programs consistent with good enterprise strategies. It is pointless to implement a new solution that does not contribute to lowered costs or improved productivity.

Finally, according to industry analysts, biometric technology has been shown to lower the costs associated with security management by thirty-nine to sixty-nine percent. Biometric solutions enable enterprises, institutions and government agencies to anticipate potential breach points and enhance or fine-tune the systems and policies that govern their security practices and procedures while lowering the on-going and escalating costs associated with password management systems. Biometric solutions deliver a more restrictive threat model than passwords and remove the burden of security from the users and the staff that support them. Your biometric is more unique to you than any password and it cannot be shared, lost or stolen [1].

SUMMARY AND CONCLUSIONS

This chapter focused on the impersonation of users by stolen passwords and the borrowing of IP addresses. To solve those problems, tomorrow's security is actually here today. Today, your signature serves to identify you in the world of paper-based transactions. Finally, biometrics offers the same level of convenience, with added security and ensured privacy, which is necessary and expected in a world of digital transactions and interactions [1].

REFERENCES

[1] Guy R. Martino, "Secure or Vulnerable? Your Identity is the Key," © 2002–2004 Biometric Technology Solutions, LLC, All rights reserved. Biometric Technology Solutions, LLC, 2005.

Chapter 12

HOW MASQUERADERS INFILTRATE A SYSTEM

INTRODUCTION

As a sequel to the phenomenal expansion of cyberspace, growth of information technology in its varied facets and coming of age of e-civilization, new challenges have been thrown up, particularly with regard to policing the Internet; profiling cyber terrorists and criminals; and, privacy of the citizens [5]. Cyber surveillance has assumed importance in the context of the rampant misuse and abuse of the Internet; unauthorized access to data; forgery of digital signatures; infringement of intellectual property rights covering patents and trademarks; fraudulent subversion of electronic payment systems; wars over domain names; browsers and portals; and, a growing menace of intruders, masqueraders, and saboteurs [1].

This chapter deals with a broad sweep of technologies and issues connected with policing, profiling and privacy as applicable to cyber surveillance and the infiltration of masqueraders. Presently, there is a perceptible bias against technology and technologists becaU.S.e the decision-makers are of the generalist hue and, exceptions notwithstanding, pride themselves on technological indifference. Therefore terms, which are everyday vocabulary elsewhere and the forte of terrorists in their application and exploitation, are foreign to most of U.S. This chapter is not a primer, but its rationale and thrust would be lost if technologies and methodologies used for policing cyberspace of:

- Packet-sniffing bots
- E-mail forgery
- Carnivore
- Omnivore
- Black bag jobs
- Pen register
- Trap and trace
- Intrusion detection system
- Creating effective and responsive databank
- Global Information Base (GIB)

- Knowledge-Aided Retrieval in Activity Context (KARNAC)
- "Junglee"
- The fail-proof and foolproof system for sifting, archiving, and mining data for profiling of terrorists, hackers, and criminals [1]

are not understood [1].

Does the government have powers only to investigate cyber offenses after these are committed and be unmindful of preventing crime is the moot question that you must ask yourselves before castigating the authority. This chapter also discusses the security versus privacy and legality issues of wiretapping; and, the laws of other countries of interest. It is the burden of this chapter that privacy comes a poor third in the hierarchy of reckoning after social welfare and security. Security flows from eternal surveillance, so get a good radar and keep it sweeping [1]!

PREPARING FOR THE NEW WORLD ORDER

It was way back in the 1960s that the U.S. strategic think tank, Rand Corporation, did some serious. thinking on the U.S. command-and-control setup in a nuclear scenario and how the U.S. authorities could communicate after the first nuclear strike. A dilemma that confronted them was that post-nuclear America would need a C3 (command, control and communications) network, linking city-to-city, state-to-state and base-to-base. A nuclear attack would render any conceivable network in tatters, no matter how meticulous the planning for network protection was to make it nuclear and EMP proof. Baffled by the problem of control, the Rand Corporation discarded the concept of centralized authority over the network on the reasoning that such a network would be the first to be targeted and eliminated by an enemy missile attack [1].

In a highly secret meeting, Rand came out with a novel and bold solution, perhaps a wicked one, too. It suggested, let there be no central authority, assume the network to be vulnerable at all times; design the network from the very beginning to operate while in tatters, and perhaps with tongue in cheek, let the friends and allies share the electronic vulnerability and also feel the pinch [1].

More than 42 years later, there is no central authority over the Internet, the network is bare and exposed to its marrow, continues to be in tatters and its vulnerabilities, though it be of a different kind, are a concern of the entire civilized world. It is a paradise for masqueraders, criminals, terrorists and anarchists [1].

Let U.S. shed crass naiveté. The Internet was an instrument of the Cold War and still figures high in U.S. security concerns. It was created to serve Uncle Sam's globalization agenda, more of the info-dominance and less than any humane munificence. Its roots are in ARPANET. ARPA stands for Advanced Research Projects Agency, which is part of the U.S. Department of Defense. One of the goals of ARPANET was research in distributed computer systems for military purposes. The emphasis is deliberately on military purposes, because that is how the Internet in its infancy bore a hierarchical structure [1].

Cyberspace has become the new arena to masquerade, show muscle, peddle crime, terrorism, and even anarchism. You now face the roughs and the menace of new kinds of wars with hitherto unparalleled diversity, intensity and perversity, like domain wars, portal wars, content wars, flame wars, hacker wars, cyber wars and ironically wars of endies, reminding the U.S. of the holy wars of yore. These have sharpened the bite of familiar conventional, unconventional and proxy wars. Then there are the less-abuses of the likes of spying, spoofing, sniffing, spinning (spin doctoring), spamming, stalking, sleazing and seeding (viruses, worms and Trojans). The technologies are converging and unifying the techniques and the artifacts; the societies are diverging and dividing the humans; herein lies the rub, and the intra-conflict of e-civilization [1].

Let there be no doubt that Chinese and U.S. think-tanks take their homework seriously. Both nourish the perception that the Internet provides the chance to dominate the rest of the world through means other than the military. The Internet is the high ground and a first-termer at the National Defense Academy will know that in tactics the first lesson that one learns is to occupy the high ground and hold it under all costs [1].

The new world-disorder is the most apparent, yet least talked of, consequence of the technology marvel – call it the anti-marvel of the day. The very paradigm shifts in the defining technologies of the last decade have been very rapid, accelerating, and penetrating, as has been their wont. Perspectives on revolution in military affairs and ipso facto e-civilization are in a flux; so are the dynamics of political, social, and economic sinews that interplay [1].

Till the 9/11 terrorist attack, the U.S. had unchallenged supremacy over the Internet, its projection of credentials, the prime virtues of universality of access and equitable stake-holding, notwithstanding. The information-coordinated, cyber-enabled terrorist attacks on the World Trade Center, the Pentagon, and the aborted one on the White House simply shattered this facade of supremacy. Among the many nagging questions that have confronted the U.S. authorities in the wake of 9/11 is, what precisely was the nature of support that cyber access lent the terrorists? And, what could be done to plug those holes, and what steps should be taken on the cyber front to prevent recurrence of this kind of tragedy? Could government's increased use of cyber-surveillance technologies have helped [1]?

The art of cyber-snooping and packet-sniffing has reached such an acme of sophistication that nothing is hidden from prying eyes, be these of law enforcement community, be these of hostile intelligence agencies, or even terrorists and criminals. Technologies exist that allow intelligence or counter-intelligence to eavesdrop on voice and electronic communications. This also includes 10 sniff e-mails; matching peoples' faces with those in a database as they pass by cameras; and, voice-analyzer tapes, as they are played on al Jazeera. Or, to capture keystrokes as they are punched in a PC. You have then, metaphorically, a network of eyes in the sky satellites that view the opponent's turf with amazingly high-resolution cameras [1].

The new world-disorder has unabashedly compromised the Intellectual Property Regime (IPR), and intensified technology denial and counter proliferation regimes. It would be naive to be dismissive in the adverse of influence, like infringement of sovereignty and information apartheid, that it would inevitably entail. Then there are other exploitative policies like bias towards capitalism, monopoly, concentration of content, discriminatory standards, patent regimes, copyrights and sui generis databases, besides application of U.S. domestic laws on other countries in respect of regulatory, privacy and security issues. New terms have been coined (domainism, which implies prejudice on the basis of Internet address and infra dig commercial online credentials) [1].

Cyber Terrorism

What is terrorism? Is cyber terrorism a hype or for real? What incidents have happened so far that impact security in cyberspace? What is likely to happen in the future? And what lessons can you draw from the cyber-enabled terrorism targeted against you and other countries and societies, not forgetting that the threat is often the laptop for attack [1].

According to the National Information Protection Center (NIPC), Cyber terrorism is an act through computers that results in violence, death and/or destruction and creates terror for the purpose of coercing a government to change its policies. A little differently worded definition from the FBI states, Cyber terrorism is the premeditated, politically motivated attack against information, computer systems, computer programs, and data, which results in violence against noncombatant targets by sub national groups or clandestine agents. Both of the definitions talk of violence, death and destruction, but the blow and brunt of cyber terrorism are more psychological than physical [1].

Cyber terrorism is the cheapest way of hacking belief systems, and destroying data that supports them. It is the most ubiquitous. way of hacking the cerebrum at the individual level, psyche at the collective level, and inducing fear. It's what's also now termed as waging cognitive war on the one hand; and, on the other hand, denial of service attacks and mass mailing malicious codes, worms and virus, of the Sobing and Bugbear variety that eat the vitals of cyber systems. Cyber anarchy is a vested interest. It is a veritable psychological war zoom that promotes and spreads syndromes. The impact of Anthrax, SARS and Melissa is more psychological than physical. So is that of cyber infraction. It creates paralysis and dysfunction in decision-making [1].

Terrorists have taken to cyberspace like fish to water. They use it to manage a worldwide Internet enabled terror information infrastructure (InfoInfra). They also:

- Issue terror threats
- Conduct propaganda and psychological operations
- Communicate through e-mail-enabled crypto, stegano, and PGP (Pretty Good Privacy) messages
- Launder money (the most popular of which is hawala operations)
- Obtain WMD (weapons of mass destruction) intelligence
- Carry out technology snooping
- Make contacts with hackers, crackers, and criminals
- Plan proxy operations
- Transact, shop, and schedule covert supplies of contrabands, drugs and weapons
- Arrange clandestine meetings and RVs through ICQ (the acronym stands for "I seek you"), IRC (Internet Relay Chats) and for postings on bulletin boards in short what constitutes the jugular vein of terror [1].

Cyber terrorism has emerged as the most potent threat vector. It has prospered under the tutelage of hacking. In the past, motives were political, socio-religious, and even anarchical and the acts are pulled off in such a way that the perpetrators hogged maximum publicity. Now, the motives remain much the same but the execution has become exceedingly typified by anonymity. The cyberspace is a delight for hacking, more so for anonymous and remote-controlled surreptitious operations. It is because both the perpetrator and the victim deny the impact if not the criminal or terror act, and the former to repeat the modus operandi and the latter to conceal the shame and economic consequences of being cuckolded [1].

Asymmetric warfare anchors on the unpredictable, the unknown unknown. And, cyberspace lends it the environment to execute and coordinate through remoteness and randomness, yet unbelievable but true, with synchronization bordering on precision. Scenarios are aplenty, varied and beyond the much touted war-gaming. Consider for instance a virtual attack coinciding with the real one; imagine mayhem if Code Red and 9/11 were mounted simultaneously [1].

The two most serious consequences of cyber terrorism are threats to critical infrastructure and loss of sensitive data. The infrastructure threat is to the cybernated and computerized systems of railways, dams, hospitals, oil pipelines, TV and AIR stations, telecommunications, air traffic, or any other networked system. Although this is most potent of the cyber attacks, one tends to dismiss it as the least probability. Even in the U.S. and that too after 9/11, the threat has been downplayed. For example, the Massachusetts Water Source Authority indicates that cyber terrorism to them is a lower-level threat. And, this is despite the fact that hacker, Vitek Borden, succeeded in releasing one million gallons of sewage into the water supply in Australia. He was at it for years, and that he had made 44 previous attempts that remained undetected, is a telling account of concern for cyber surveillance [1].

Compromising critical computer systems to steal or irreversibly damage vital data is the second objective of cyber terrorism. The vulnerable targets are ministries, nuclear establishments, military, R&D, defense production and other sensitive data. The greater the criticality of data, the more vulnerable it is [1].

Before closing the discussion on cyber terrorism, it would be prudent to remember that terror is a psychological condition. To succeed, it has to be communicated. The key to winning war against terror is to disrupt the terrorist's communications and protect your own. The gurumantra is to keep them under electronic cyber surveillance, wireless, cellular [4], short message service (SMS), and to ferret out terrorist information signatures before they strike. This is called "Total Information Awareness," although the term is shrouded in secrecy and has invited the wrath of privacy groups [1].

Cyber Surveillance

Cyber surveillance could be defined as a systematic observation of cyberspace by surfing, sniffing, and snooping. Or, by other means, with a view to locating, identifying, determining, profiling, and analyzing, by all available and predictable means the transmission of e-mail, movement of packets, file transfer, e-money transactions and subversive activities of criminals, cyber terrorists, hostile regimes and intelligence agencies. It equally applies to watching over friendly elements to anticipate and prevent cyber crime and social abuse, carry out counter surveillance, and find holes in our own procedures and systems of cyber security [1].

Cyberspace attacks mounted by different actors are indistinguishable from each other, in so far as the perceptions of the target personnel are concerned. In this cyberspace world, the distinction between crime and warfare is blurred. This blurring between crime and warfare also blurs the distinction between police responsibilities to protect societal interests from criminal acts in cyberspace, and military responsibilities to protect societal interests from acts of war in cyberspace. A corollary to this is the undefined division of the responsibility of conducting cyber surveillance between the security forces, like the:

- Military, paramilitary and police
- The intelligence and investigative agencies like RAW, IB, CBI and those of the three services
- Between private and public sectors
- A host of other divides that dare and defy the divide-less cyberspace [1].

CHINESE CHECKERS

A complete chapter has been devoted to China's exploitative presence and forays in cyberspace in Yashwant Deva's Secure or Perish. Since then, the Chinese have come a long way and PLA's capabilities to spy in cyberspace are next only to Echelon and their capabilities to wage cyber war and protect their cyber assets next only to NATO [1].

The scope of Chinese Information warfare spreads over a wide canvas – military, social, economic and political, and encompasses electronic warfare attacks, tactical deception, strategic deterrence, propaganda warfare, psychological warfare, network warfare, structural sabotage, and trade warfare [2]. And, of greater significance, attacks on human cognitive systems. Much stress is laid on the last two, besides network security and offensive and defensive maneuvers. The Chinese have no compunctions whatsoever about employing dubious tactics, machinations, and subterfuge such as, invasion of adversaries' financial systems through the use of computer viruses or human sabotage, disrupting enemies' economies, or spreading rumors over the Internet and thus psychologically impacting society [1].

China has an unparalleled experience in fighting cyber wars, first against Taiwan in 1999 when Web sites on either side of Taiwan Strait became high-tech battlegrounds in a new kind of conflict. And then, against the U.S. in April to May of 2001. It is believed that during the cyber dueling with Taiwan, the Americans were helping the Taiwanese and testing their own systems of cyber attacks developed by the Pentagon to penetrate enemy networks in time of war [1].

In July 1999, China's Liberation Army Daily indicated that the country needs to go all out to develop high-quality Internet warriors. It exhorted that this warrior community should include human resource development in exclusive universities, as well as work on attracting some private computer aces to take part in Internet combat. A follow-up chapter warned of breaches in Chinese computer security: The wolf has already come. Pick up your hunting rifle [1]!

The most serious attack has been that of the Chernobyl virus., written by a Taiwanese computer-engineering student, Chen Ing-hao. The virus, released on the Internet in 1998, lay dormant until April 26, 2003, when it got activated and wreaked havoc on computers around the globe. It reportedly impaired 360,000 computers in China and caused damage of up to $120 million, according to the official New China News Agency. Whereas China accused Taiwan of complicity, the Taiwanese authorities maintained that it was an individual act of crime. The Guaangzhou Military Region, which includes the South China Sea Fleet and the Second Artillery units, was hit with a computer virus throughout its entire network, linking 85 strategic and combat bases. In the morning hours of April 26, 2003, the entire system was paralyzed. The Central Military Commission and the Headquarters of the General Staff had no alternative but to declare a state of emergency in order to mobilize the command system and military defenses. At the same time, Jiang Zemin immediately signed an emergency order placing the Nanjing Military Region and the East China Sea Fleet on second-degree combat readiness. This was the first time China's military entered a second degree combat readiness since the death of Deng Xiaoping in February 1997. According to an internal military announcement, it was discovered that computer operations of the Chinese Central Command had been severely disrupted. After the incident, the State Council and the Central Committee Military Commission promptly ordered the formation of a task force composed of the General staff Intelligence Department; General staff Technology and Communications Department; Ministry of Defense Technological Intelligence Department; Institute of Military Sciences' Special Technologies Department (also known as Department 553); and, the Ministry of Security's Security Bureau. Later, this task force prepared detailed plans to cripple the civilian information infrastructures and financial banking, electrical supply, water, sewage, and telecom networks of Taiwan, U.S., India, Japan and South Korea – should the need so arise [1].

The Chinese take training in information warfare very seriously. The PLA has conducted several field exercises in recent years. An informaticised people's warfare network simulation exercise was conducted in the Echeng district of Hubei province. Five hundred soldiers simulated cyber-attacks on the cybernated infrastructures of the likely adversaries. In another exercise in the Xian in Jinan Military Region, rehearsals were carried out in planting information mines; conducting information reconnaissance; changing network data; releasing information bombs; dumping information garbage; disseminating propaganda; applying information deception; releasing clone information; organizing information defense; and establishing network spy stations. The macabre prospects and scary reach of these preparations should spur you to action, should you be on the wrong side of the Chinese bludgeon [1].

INTERCEPTION

Almost all types of electronic communications can be intercepted and that, too, without much expertise or expensive equipment. Surveillance hardware and software are not difficult to access. The former are available in many electronic stores across the globe and the latter easily downloadable for the asking. Even LTTE had a string of electronic workshops along the eastern coastline where they were making radio controlled Improvised Explosive Devices (IEDs), bugs, and other such gadgetry [1].

Most of the world's Internet capacity lies within the U.S. or connects to the U.S. Communications in 'cyberspace' normally travel via the United States, or through intermediate sites within the U.S. The traffic is broken into packets and routes taken by each depend on the origin and destination of the data, the systems through which it enters and leaves the Internet, and a myriad other factors including time of day. Even short distance traffic, say from New Delhi to Chennai, may travel via routers and Internet exchanges in California or elsewhere in the U.S. It, therefore, follows that a large proportion of international and domestic communications is readily accessible to the National Security Agency (NSA), so that it can listen to telephone conversations of its own citizens; as well as, those of other countries. So, what's in skip zone, is also covered by the other partners of Echelon [1].

For readers not familiar with Echelon, it is the name given to the global electronic surveillance system in which five partners cooperate, like NSA of the U.S., General Communication Headquarters of the UK, Communications Security Establishment (CSE) of Canada, Defense Signals Directorate (DSD) of Australia and the Government Communications Security Bureau of New Zealand. It sits between the world's well-known information and wild paranoid speculation. On one hand, you know that the NSA's mission is electronic surveillance. On the other hand, you don't know how far the abilities of NSA extend. The NSA is forbidden by law from conducting surveillance within the United States; but, it violates the law anyway, due to the arrogance and complete disregard for the law by the Bush administration. In theory, it is also not allowed to monitor the activities of U.S. citizens abroad; but again, all new passports now have a RFID chip (radio frequency identification chip) embedded within them (see sidebar, "Hacking With RFID Tags"), which allows the NSA to monitor its own citizens abroad. Can you smell "1984's" Big Brother anywhere?

Hacking With RFID Tags

Hackers can use RFID tags to infect the middleware and back-end databases that power RFID systems with worms and viruses, researchers recently found. RFID tags provide a conduit for exploiting back-end systems with buffer overflows, malicious code and bogus SQL commands. RFID applications that use Web protocols to query back-end databases could even be susceptible to the same types of security exploits as Web browsers. The potential for RFID viruses will cause developers to be more cautious in the design and implementations of RFID systems.

A lot of RFID deployments are highly proprietary, so open systems would seem to pose the most interesting targets for hackers. The key to avoiding RFID exploits is to modify RFID database processing code to ensure the integrity of data that's passed from the tag to the back-end database. When only valid data is passed through to the database itself, there should be no concern for SQL or buffer overflow or similar attacks.

While VARs indicate that they see the potential for RFID-based attacks, there is some disagreement. RFID tags don't operate on software and don't have executable code, which means it's not possible to infect them with viruses.

The notion of programming a virus into an RFID tag also is impossible due to storage limitations. You can't build an executable code out of 96 bits.

However, the small memory space of an RFID tag as a barrier to the future development of RFID viruses doesn't seem to exist at this time. It's surprising that any vendors dismissed the possibility of RFID viruses by indicating that the amount of memory in the tags is too small.

It is therefore recommended that developers of the wide variety of RFID-enhanced systems take steps to add stronger security to limit the potential damage from the coming wave of hackers experimenting with RFID exploits, RFID worms and RFID viruses on a larger scale. Research on RFID viruses is important because it highlights the importance of designing future architectures for RFID systems that can analyze data and filter out malicious code. As this technology evolves, you need to keep in mind that more complex tags need to have strong security features and protocols [3].

Today, the Bush administration is spying on all Americans full time. However, there was a time in the not too distant past that allowed NSA to have (and still has) extensive exchange agreements that are mutually convenient to overcome the legalities. For example, there is an agreement where the UK spies upon the U.S., and then shares with the NSA some of the information it gathers. In the past, even though the NSA was unable to legally spy on Americans, it could still can get intelligence on Americans through this exchange agreement. It is widely accepted that the NSA and the National Reconnaissance Office (NRO) operate surveillance satellites, including those for electronic surveillance as well as photographing the earth's surface. These satellites can monitor terrestrial microwave as well as cell-phone traffic. The NSA, likewise, has numerous ground stations spread throughout the world (the NSA operates one in communist China for the purpose of monitoring Russian activities. The party line of the Civil Libertarians indicates that the Echelon system is a whole new critter; it doesn't monitor the communications of the post-Soviet purveyors of glow-in-the-dark explosives; nope, the Echelon system keeps an eye on everybody [1].

In 2006, it was estimated that the amount of Internet traffic flowing through cables beneath the Atlantic was roughly 1,200 gigabits/second. While this is 70 million times faster than a dialup connection, it is well within the range and capability of the NSA to intercept. In the same year, the company Network ICE was selling Internet monitoring equipment where a single machine costing roughly $25,000 to run its software could monitor roughly 7-gigabit/second. This means that the NSA has acquired the ability to monitor all cross-Atlantic traffic with a small investment of only $70-million in hardware [1].

Packets or data grams include numbers that represent their origin and their destination, called IP addresses, which are unique to each computer. Therefore, tracing them is not difficult at all. Handling, sorting and routing millions of such packets each second is fundamental to the operation of major Internet centers. The same facilities and processes could be used for interception too. Internet traffic can be accessed either from international communications links entering the U.S., or when it reaches major Internet exchanges. Both methods have advantages. Access to communications systems is likely to remain clandestine – whereas access to Internet exchanges might be more detectable, but provides easier access to more data and simpler sorting methods [1].

Technologies And Methodologies

New technologies (packet sniffers, computerized voice recognition and keystroke biometrics that can automate surveillance) are being actively developed by many countries, both of the West and the East. A packet sniffer is a wiretap device that plugs into a computer network and eavesdrops on the network traffic. Like a telephone wiretap that allows an intelligence agency to listen in on conversations, a sniffer program lets someone listen in on computer conversation. Carnivore is one such packet sniffer or packet filter. According to a former employee, NSA had, by 1995, installed sniffer software to collect such traffic at nine major Internet exchange points (IXPs) [1].

Equipment for covert collection is highly specialized, selective and miniaturized. One major NSA supplier "The IDEAS Operation" now offers micro-miniature digital receivers, which can simultaneously process Sigint (Signal Intelligence) data from eight independent channels. This radio receiver is the size of a credit card. It fits in a standard laptop computer. IDEAS claim, reasonably, that their tiny card performs functions that would have taken a rack full of equipment not long ago [1].

The Ottawa Citizen reported that CSE had spent over $1.1 million to 'isolate key words and phrases from the millions of signals to create a speaker identification system. A joint NSA/CIA "Special Collection Service" manufactures equipment and trains personnel for covert collection activities. One major device is a suitcase-sized computer processing system, called Oratory. It is, in effect, a miniaturized version of the Dictionary system, capable of selecting non-verbal communications of interest from a wide range of inputs, according to pre-programmed selection criteria [1].

The amount of information monitored by the NSA is huge; for it's processing, the NSA uses a keyword dictionary. Massive supercomputers sift through the traffic looking for these keywords. These dictionaries are updated almost daily according to world conditions. Dictionary sorting and selection can be compared to using search engines, which select Web pages containing key words or terms and specifying relationships. The forwarding function of the Dictionary computers may be compared to e-mail. When requested, the system provides lists of communications matching each criterion for review, analysis, gisting or forwarding. It may be a wild speculation, but is possible that al-Qaeda could have rigged up a Dictionary of their own. How else is it possible to keep track of so much intelligence today that they exhibit without much ado, and without being afflicted by a zero-error syndrome [1].

Although the term black-bag operation has originated in the U.S. and specific to their context, intelligence agencies the world over have taken to it and widely use it. It is a secret break-in by a law-enforcement or intelligence organization. In other words, it is designed to secretly search the location, copying files or other materials, and to plant bugs, wiretaps, or key-loggers. The Federal Intelligence Surveillance Court (FISC) in the U.S. holds hearings to approve break-ins for national security reasons. The Bush administration spied and is spying on Americans without the benefit of such hearings.

In the year 2000, the FBI secretly entered the office of Nicodemo Scarfo and installed a keylogger. The FBI was able to capture Scarfo's password and decrypt his PGP-encoded e-mail. The 1971 Watergate goof up was an illegal black-bag operation. In October 1993, Attorney General Janet Reno authorized the FBI to enter the home of Aldritch Ames, a suspected CIA mole. This was after months of electronic and physical surveillance, including searches of his trash [1].

Network wiretap comes with a feature called protocol analysis, which allows it to decode the computer traffic and make sense of it. Network sniffing has a distinct advantage over telephone wiretaps as many networks use shared media, dispensing the need to break into a wiring closet to install the wiretap. This can be done from any network connection and is called promiscuous mode sniffing. However, this shared technology is fast changing to switched technology, which implies that to be effective, the sniffer would be obliged to actively tap the wire [1].

Carnivore is a type of sniffer written by the FBI that scans Internet traffic looking for e-mail messages. It profiles the suspects after analyzing the From: and To: identities of e-mail messages, matching cyber to the real and storing the e-mail messages to the disk. Seemingly Carnivore is a legal instrument, which cannot be installed on a network without a court order and a search warrant for the ISP to comply; however, ISPs have been known to have given sniffing access to the FBI. In the wake of the 9/11 hijacking and air assault, major Internet Service Providers (ISPs) in the U.S. extended total and unqualified cooperation to the federal authorities in the conduct of the investigation of the terrorist attacks [1].

Like NSA, the Carnivore watches the packets go by, then saves a copy of the ones it is interested in. Carnivore was a hush hush affair. The news of its existence broke in July 2000, leading to public furor. The FBI claimed that the Carnivore was designed to conduct efficient wiretaps of e-mail and online communications involving suspected hackers, terrorists, and other criminals [1].

Carnivore is packed in a slim laptop and is described as a tool within a tool that enables the FBI, in cooperation with an Internet Service Provider, to collect counter-intelligence by tapping e-mails or other electronic communications of a targeted user. This is supposed to be done on court orders – something that the Bush administration purposely ignored. Carnivore is used in two ways, like as a content-wiretap and a trap-and-trace, pen-register. Carnivore box consists of a commercial-off-the-shelf (COTS) Windows NT or Windows 2003 box with 256-megabytes of RAM, a Pentium V or higher, 8 to 36 gigabytes of disk space, and a 4G Jaz drive where evidence is something missing. The box has no TCP/IP stack, and therefore, it is hack-proof. A hardware authentication device to control access to the box, and preventing personnel from breaking into the device without leaving telltale signs, is incorporated [1].

Carnivore comes in two pills, the Red one and the Blue one. The former is administered when the ISP claims that it cannot or will not comply with the court order. The Blue Pill is a sophisticated Carnivore program that scans only e-mails where the ISP cooperates for an investigation [1].

Immediately after 9/11, the FBI administered the Red Pill (served EarthLink with a search warrant to gather electronic information relating to national security). With the exception of Earthlink, no one demurred let alone protested when provisions of Foreign Intelligence Surveillance Act (FISA) – which provides guidelines for sensitive investigations by the FBI, CIA, NSA and a handful of other federal organizations, were put into operation. Even Carnivore boxes were installed on servers for the FBI to monitor electronic correspondences of suspected criminals, privacy or no privacy [1].

Earlier, the FBI was using Carnivore in a mode they call Omnivore: capturing all the traffic to and from the specified IP address. DARPA's Genoa Carnivore is now known as DCS 1000. Its effectiveness is yet to be proved, though it is a cutting-edge search engine, a sophisticated information harvesting program, and adopts peer to peer computing methodology [1].

Carnivore can also be used to monitor Internet traffic other than e-mail. Besides e-mail, one common use is to monitor Web traffic: where Web sites are visited, as well as tracking which people might be accessing a particular Web site [1].

There are a number of ways Carnivore and other sniffers can be defeated and Web surfing made anonymous (establishing an SSL connection to proxies), anonymization service and resorting it to remailers, but that would be beyond the scope of this chapter. However, it must be mentioned that cyber tactics is as important a subject as military tactics and it would be wise to teach and learn the tricks of the trade in a formal way [1].

Another equipment of surveillance that merits familiarization with is Real-Time Surveillance System (RTSS). It provides round-the-clock, non-stop, one-window operation with several digital cameras, supporting as many simultaneous camera displays with video recording, synchronized audio recording, motion detection recording and playback with facility for backup. Significantly, it supports live video via dial-up, high bandwidth Internet and LAN. It alarms alerts and has Pan-Tilt-Zoom-Iris-Focus (PTZIF) controls with a remote facility. It also permits networking with several RTSS units, and provides Internet access and surveillance video at 2/3 frames per second. Video watermark technology and passwords make it tamper proof [1].

Today in the e-market, spyware is available that can capture and record every conversation on the Internet Relay Chat (IRC), every transaction and other banking information, passwords, mouse-clicks and keystrokes on the computer, exposing private information to unauthorized public view. Some of the software products have the ability to send this information clandestinely via the e-mail. This spyware is downloadable, worth 80 dollars or so. It can keep a home PC under surveillance from the workplace or vice versa, with salient features of remote keystroke viewing, desktop viewing, application and task management, and open windows management. A good example is that of SpyBuddy, which has features like:

- Internet conversation logging
- Disk activity logging
- Window activity logging
- Clipboard activity logging
- Web site activity monitoring
- Print document logging

- Keystroke monitoring
- Screen shot capturing
- Web-watch keyword alerting
- Remote capture
- Remote system information viewing
- Remote file system navigation
- Remote locking control
- Remote Internet connection monitoring
- Document history viewing
- Mouse freeze control
- Remote Web site launching
- Remote application launching
- Remote shut down and the ability to log chat conversations
- Record all changes made to the hard drive (directories and files), which are created, deleted or renamed.

Fantastic is the world of cyber-spying [1].

Then, there is a variety of anti-spy software (SpyCop, X-Cleaner, Anti-keylogger, NitroU.S. Anti-spy, Evidence Eraser software of the likes of Window washer, Evidence Eliminator Pro and Evidence Terminator). The SpyCop can find:

- Computer monitoring programs used for spying
- Allows renaming any suspect files
- Minimizes software while scanning so that the computer is free to do the other tasks
- Facilitates exploring for hostile spyware by a right click
- Provides a single file-scan function built in complete with browse capability
- Saves results to a text file for future reference
- Prints results directly from the software
- Finds when a spy program was installed
- Checks if a spy program is detectable with database search
- Conducts live updates to a database without re-downloading
- Is unrecognizable to most spy programs
- Has a screensaver, which scans the system when the user is absent [1].

Finally, the purpose of describing the facilities claimed by e-marketed spy and anti-spy software is to impress that in spite of the kind of intelligence and surveillance games that are being played in cyberspace, the vulnerabilities have neither abated, nor cyber security made fail proof and foolproof. Another purpose is to show how technology has completely overshadowed the 007 image of spying and changed its nature from real to virtual (like the Alias and 24 TV shows), and the sweep near to remote. Virus scanners do not detect spyware, and firewalls [6] do not stop their ingress. The one that needs access to the target computer to install spy software is just not true. There are hybrid versions that can be sent just like a virus in e-mail [1].

SUMMARY AND CONCLUSIONS

The U.S. and China take cyber surveillance very seriously. Therefore, let the U.S. get on with it. Finally, that's the only way of becoming a superpower.

REFERENCES

[1] Yashwant Deva, "Cyber Surveillance: Threats and New Technologies," Aakrosh, Forum for Strategic and Security Studies, [Strategic Affairs (Stratmag.com) is an unofficial Defence website, which is not endorsed or recognized by any Government or its institutions. All the material published on this site is in the public domain. The views represented in this site are those of the authors alone.], 2004.

[2] John R. Vacca, Computer Forensics: Computer Crime Scene Investigation, 2nd Edition, Charles River Media, 2005.

[3] Kevin McLaughlin, "RFID Tags May Provide New 'In' For Hackers," CRN, Copyright © 2006 CMP Media LLC, CMP Media LLC, 600 Community Drive, Manhasset, New York 11030, page 57, March 27, 2006.

[4] John R. Vacca, Guide to Wireless Network Security, Springer, 2006.

[5] John R. Vacca, Net Privacy: A Guide to Developing and Implementing an Ironclad ebusiness Privacy Plan, McGraw-Hill, 2001.

[6] John R. Vacca, Firewalls: Jumpstart for Network and Systems Administrators, Digital Press, 2004.

Chapter 13

HOLDING YOUR DEFENSIVE LINE

INTRODUCTION

The Internet is a two-edged sword for most enterprises. On the positive side, the web provides easy access to information, fosters collaboration among partners and vendors, and can increase employee productivity. The web augments established distribution channels for many enterprises and is the sole distribution channel for others. Most enterprises could not exist today without a web presence and with a substantial portion of their workforce provisioned to use Internet resources as part of their daily work [1].

With so many employees accessing the web, IT leaders are becoming increasingly familiar with the problems and risks of unfettered Internet access that add up to a significant down side. Employees may spend too much time surfing the web for personal use, reducing productivity.

> **Note:** According to industry analysts, the average computer-enabled employee spends 12.6 hours per week accessing the Internet with 3.6 to 6 hours spent on non-work activity.

Worse, they may visit inappropriate sites that may present legal liabilities. They may link to sites that are the source of malware, inadvertently downloading spyware and keyloggers. Employees who download music or videos from Peer-to-Peer (P2P) file-sharing sites risk involving the enterprise in lawsuits filed by copyright owners. Even legal purchases of music and videos from authorized sites may consume a disproportionate amount of the enterprise's external bandwidth, driving up costs [1].

Employees may also discuss enterprise-confidential business over unsecure Instant Messaging (IM) services or open infected IM attachments that unleash malware behind the perimeter firewall [2]. The situation has become critical. Enterprises need the web in order to conduct their business, yet they are losing employee productivity and are threatened by new web-borne attacks that may cause significant damage. The drain on employee time and network resources is well known: In one industry analyst survey, a quarter of enterprises reported terminating workers for Internet misuse. A solution is needed that will allow managers and their employees to use Internet resources with appropriate measures of flexibility and responsibility. The enterprise needs to hold its defensive line (hiding passwords; implementing packet filters; adopting strong authentication with Kerberos and other tools; and, authenticating users with public key encryption) against employees who would allow masqueraders to infiltrate its systems [1].

TROUBLE ARRIVES ON PORTS 80 AND 443

To facilitate web connections and content delivery, Port 80 is the designated port for web traffic using HTTP. Similarly, Port 443 is the conduit for HTTPS traffic which is HTTP encrypted using SSL, the Secure Sockets Layer built into all standard web browsers. The result is that Ports 80 and 443 are always open on most enterprise firewalls. There is generally no attempt by perimeter firewalls to inspect, analyze, or otherwise impede the flow of traffic through these ports [1].

Knowing that these ports are open, vendors have designed their products to use them to communicate with locations behind the firewall. For example, most Instant Messaging protocols default to Port 80 if their designated port is blocked. The same is true for many P2P file-sharing protocols. These web ports have become four-lane off-ramps from the information superhighway [1].

INCREASINGLY SOPHISTICATED CRIMINALS/MASQUERADERS TARGET THE INTERNET

Criminals/masqueraders have also recognized that Ports 80 and 443 are open doors and have devised clever ways to exploit this vulnerability. While early attacks added malware extensions to P2P protocols or Instant Messages, more recent attacks have been perpetrated using:

- False web sites that take advantage of mis-keyed URLs
- Phishing scams that send phony e-mails directing people to counterfeit sites where they must enter financial information to update their accounts
- Pharming frauds in which an enterprise's DNS servers are corrupted so that even users who enter valid URLs are unknowingly redirected to fake sites
- Drive-by downloads in which merely visiting a URL can automatically download unwanted applications including keyloggers and Trojan horses
- Unintended linkages to sites with hard-to-eradicate pop-up ads and spyware [1]

> **Note:** Spyware is a broad category of malicious software intended to intercept or take partial control of a computer's operation without the user's informed consent. While the term taken literally suggests software that surreptitiously monitors the user as a spy would, it has come to refer more broadly to software that subverts the computer's operation for the benefit of a third party (see: http://en.wikipedia.org/wiki/Spyware).

The purpose of attacks has changed as their level of sophistication has increased. Early malware was aimed at creating problems or causing disruption – exploits that became a hacker's bragging rights. Today's attacks are mostly criminal, aimed at disabling a web-based business or stealing identities or Personal Identifiable Information (PII) that can be used for financial gain [1].

> **Tip:** The current price for a stolen but valid credit card sold on the Internet is between $40.00 and $80.00, depending on type and expiration date. See http://www.usdoj.gov/opa/pr/2004/October/04_crm_726.htm, for more information on Internet criminal activities.

BLENDED THREATS RAISE THE BAR

Blended threats are another step up in sophistication because they combine methods to maximize the speed of contagion and severity of damage. For example, an attack might have characteristics of both viruses and worms that exploit vulnerabilities in computers, networks, or other physical systems. A virus might be sent in an e-mail attachment along with a Trojan horse embedded in an HTML file meant to damage the recipient's computer. Nimda, CodeRed, and Bugbear exploits were blended threats [1].

To thwart blended threats, a defense-in-depth strategy is the preferred approach. Defense-in-depth relies on the premise that multiple layers of security afford more comprehensive protection than any single mechanism. The layers of defense typically include technological, procedural, and policy techniques [1].

The National Security Agency (NSA) states that defense-in-depth is a best practices strategy in that it relies on the intelligent application of techniques and technologies that exist today. The agency's recommendations focus on three areas: people, technology and operations [1].

The NSA technological arsenal includes firewalls, Intrusion Detection and Intrusion Prevention systems (IDS/IPS), anti-virus and anti-spam applications. The NSA recommends using multiple firewalls, installed at the perimeter and in front of key applications. The perimeter and application firewalls should implement different technologies, the NSA suggests. Typically this is accomplished by using a stateful inspection firewall at the perimeter and an application-layer firewall including content filtering for web traffic in front of user LANs and mission-critical applications [1].

WEB PROXIES ACCELERATE CONTENT DELIVERY, WEB FILTERS ADD SECURITY

As the use of the web has increased, enterprises have worked to manage and reduce bandwidth costs by employing web proxies. A web proxy is a server that sits close to the Internet, storing common web pages and even entire websites visited by network users. By storing frequently accessed sites such as microsoft.com and espn.com, response times for users are lessened, thereby saving time and hopefully helping the content consumers be more productive. Since content served from local resources does not have to traverse the Internet (particularly the link to the organization's Internet Service Provider) web proxy servers conserve external bandwidth. When deployed in a large enterprise, web proxies can provide significant savings [1].

Web filters allow or disallow access to specific websites and screen inbound content. A web filter can be set to examine Port 80/443 traffic in a number of important ways:

- Does the requested URL link to a website prohibited by the enterprise's Acceptable Use Policy (AUP) – such as a pornographic, gambling, or file-sharing site?
- Is the requested URL attempting to return disallowed attachments or spyware?
- Is access to this category of URL allowed during this time period?
- Do downloads from the site meet additional AUP specifications which might prohibit music, images, or restrict file size?
- Is the traffic from disallowed IM or P2P services?
- Is the requested URL to a valid site or a phishing look-alike?
- Is the requested content coming from the URL that the user intended to reach, or is it from a redirect established as a pharming scam [1]?

DEFENSE-IN-DEPTH SOLUTIONS TO WEB-BORNE THREATS

Recognizing the need for additional protection to combat the increasing sophistication and frequency of web based attacks, web caching vendors have added significant defensive capabilities to their offerings. Simultaneously, CIOs and IT Directors have encouraged vendors to provide their solutions in an appliance format to reduce the total cost of ownership (TCO) by making the systems easy to set up and maintain [1].

Microsoft® was one of the original vendors to offer a web caching solution. The company's first proxy server has evolved to include robust application filter and firewall capabilities, now available as Microsoft Internet Security and Acceleration (ISA) Server 2004 [1].

ISA Server not only provides superior web caching capabilities, but it can also act as an application-layer firewall to protect mission critical Microsoft applications such as Exchange, Internet Information Services (IIS), and SharePoint® Portal Server. With its tight integration with Active Directory® (AD), ISA makes it convenient for administrators to use strong authentication methods to grant granular access to web resources using AD as the hub of network security [1].

Today, enterprises need web security software, which provides content filtering plus web security tools that protect against current and emerging web-based threats. This should include real-time updates and advanced configuration and reporting tools. When integrated with ISA, the web security software should be able to implement its access controls according to the user/group/role assignments maintained in Active Directory, enabling comprehensive federated policy management for access to internal and external resources [1].

ISA IN A SINGLE AUTO-UPDATING APPLIANCE

Today, enterprises also need a single auto-updating appliance. Based on a hardened Windows® 2003 Operating System, the combined solution provides comprehensive security that meets today's growing need for a defense-in-depth security architecture. It should augment traditional security solutions with deep packet inspection across inbound and outbound HTTP/HTTPS traffic and provides additional layers of security to address user-based threats such as spyware, keyloggers, and fraud-based attacks. The solution should also secure core applications such as Microsoft SharePoint, Exchange, IIS, and Outlook®Web Access (OWA), as shown in Fig. 13-1 [1].

These appliances should be able to streamline the deployment and management of web caching, policy management, updates, and directory services. They should be able to provide enterprises with a rapidly deployable, scalable, high-availability security solution that meets the needs of growing enterprises, including functionality that addresses branch office deployments and remote employee security (see sidebar, "High-Availability Security Solution" [1].

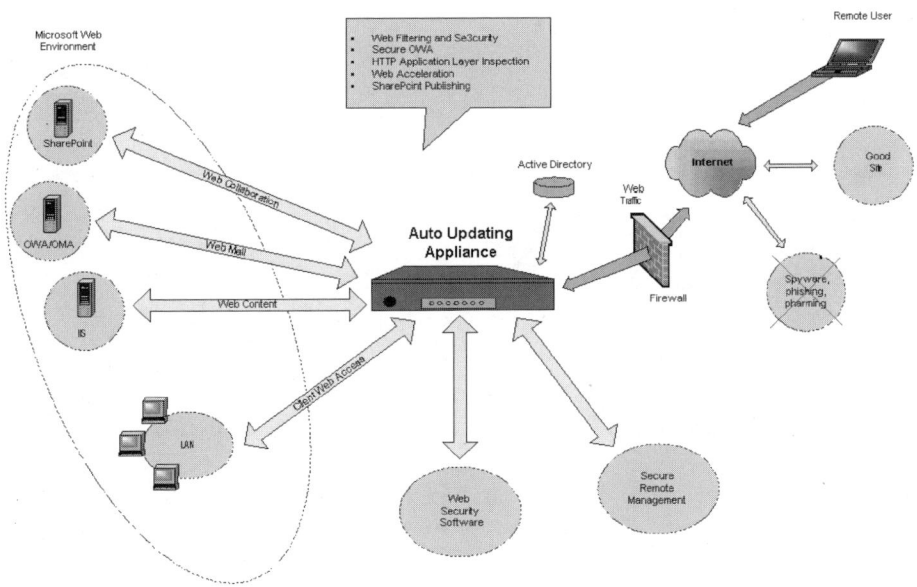

Figure 13-1. Security for core applications.

High-Availability Security Solution

Microsoft ISA Server 2004

- Proxy-based HTTP/HTTPS deep packet inspection
- Web authentication delegation
- Secure publishing of Outlook Web Access, Exchange
- Federated policy management through Active Directory
- IIS, SharePoint, and other web-facing applications
- Reverse and forward proxy cache
- Integrated forms-based authentication
- Incoming/outgoing filtering by protocol and application

Web Security Software

- Spyware, keylogger, mobile malicious code, pharming
- Network bandwidth management and control and phishing mitigation
- Website access restriction
- IM/P2P protection
- Detailed logs and reports
- Real-time security updates
- Granular policy settings by user/group/role/network/
- Web content classification, filtering, and management protocol when federated with Active Directory through ISA

Single Auto Updating Appliance Integration

- Automated updates distributed via web
- ISP connection failover
- Secure remote administration
- Options for hot-swap mirrored disk drives and power supplies
- Automatic 1:1 hardware failover
- Integrated MOM agent for use with Microsoft Operations Manager [1]

Installed behind a perimeter firewall and in front of web servers, enterprises should have a single auto updating appliance with Web security software implemented in the best-practice line of defense-in-depth. The single auto updating appliances should provide an important extra layer of protection for traffic passing through the perimeter firewall on Ports 80/443, screening and filtering it in accordance with enterprise policies. Finally, with authentication and access integrated with Active Directory, real-time updates supplied by the Web security software, and pre-tested system upgrades delivered via e-mail from single auto updating appliances, should enable enterprises to integrate web security into a comprehensive federated network security architecture with minimal time and attention from the IT staff [1].

SUMMARY AND CONCLUSIONS

Enterprises rely on the Internet to compete effectively, yet the risks associated with its use are increasing. Web-borne threats are increasingly fast, sophisticated, and criminal in their intent. As a best-practice security policy, line of defense-in-depth should protect client devices and mission-critical applications, especially those that face the Internet. Installed behind a perimeter firewall, single auto updating appliances should simplify the implementation of line of defense-in-depth. Finally, single auto updating appliances should integrate an application layer firewall with web caching and content filtering provided by the Web security software and enable federated policy management through the Active Directory to control access to both internal and external resources [1].

REFERENCES

[1] Robert Mannal, "Implementing Web Security in a Defense-in-Depth Architecture," Copyright © 2006 Network Engines, Inc., Network Engines, Inc., 25 Dan Road Canton, MA 02021-2817, 2006.
[2] John R. Vacca, Firewalls: Jumpstart for Network and Systems Administrators, Digital Press, 2004.

PART VII

PREVENTING EAVESDROPPING TO PROTECT
YOUR PRIVACY

Chapter 14

UNAUTHORIZED LISTENING AND LOOKING

INTRODUCTION

Instant messaging is an increasingly popular method for communicating over the Internet. Instant messaging (IM) is a real-time supplement to and, in some regards, a replacement for e-mailing. Unlike e-mail, instant messaging allows users to see/look whether a chosen friend or co-worker is connected to the Internet. Typically, the instant messaging service will alert a user if somebody on the user's list of correspondents is on-line. Instant messaging also differs from e-mail in that messages are exchanged directly almost instantly, allowing for a two-way communication in real-time [1].

Because of the almost immediate two-way nature of communication, many users feel that the use of instant messaging in the workplace leads to more effective and efficient workplace communications and, therefore, to higher productivity. As a result, IM is increasing in popularity in both professional and personal applications. However, as with most things Internet based, the increasing use of instant messaging has led to an associated increase in the number of security risks [1].

This chapter describes instant messaging and offer a brief overview of some of the security threats associated with the service. It covers the unauthorized listening and looking of IM: Yeah! Eavesdropping!

HOW DOES INSTANT MESSAGING WORK?

Instant messaging networks consist of clients and servers. A user installs a client that connects to a server operated by the instant messaging network vendor, such as AOL or ICQ, or Yahoo Messenger [1].

> **Note:** Because they use different protocols, the different instant messaging services are not interoperable. Therefore, ICQ users can only communicate with other ICQ users, not with users of other instant messaging services.

All users that sign up for instant messaging are given a unique identifier, which can be either a name or a number. The user then gives out the unique identifier to people that he or she wants to communicate with via the instant messaging network [1].

The user starts an instant messaging session by authenticating to the server. When two authenticated users want to communicate, the following sequence occurs:

- Shana instructs the instant messaging client to send a text-message to Bernard. The client creates a packet containing the message and sends it to the server.
- The server looks at the packet and determines that the recipient is Bernard. The server then creates a new packet with the message from Shana and sends it to Bernard [1].

Most instant messengers will continue to send all following messages via the central server. However, some instant messengers create a direct connection between the users after the first message. The use of a central server is beneficial in many ways. For example, Shana is only required to know the unique identifier for Bernard. Furthermore, she can send messages to Bernard even if he is not on-line. The server will store the message until Bernard authenticates with the server, at which time it is sent to him [1].

Furthermore, most instant messaging clients have the ability to create buddy lists, or lists of preferred people the user wants to communicate with that keeps track of whether those people are available for instant messaging. For example, when Bernard sends Shana his unique identifier, Shana can save it in her buddy list. From then on, whenever Shana authenticates with the instant messaging server, she can see Bernard in her buddy list; therefore, she is not required to remember Bernard's unique identifier. She will also be notified if he is on-line, off-line, away from his desk, etc. [1].

INSTANT MESSAGING SECURITY THREATS

Instant messaging networks provide the ability to not only transfer text messages, but also the transfer of files. Consequently, instant messengers can transfer worms and other malware. Instant messengers can also provide an access point for backdoor trojan horses. Hackers can use instant messaging to gain backdoor access to computers without opening a listening port, effectively bypassing desktop and perimeter firewall [2] implementations. Furthermore, finding victims doesn't require scanning unknown IP addresses, but rather simply selecting from an updated directory of buddy lists. In addition to client-initiated file transfers, all the major instant messaging networks support peer-to-peer file sharing where one can share a directory or drive. This means that all the files on a computer can be shared using the instant messaging client, leading to the spread of files that are infected with a virus or other malware. As you shall see, this characteristic also makes information being communicated along IM vulnerable to unauthorized viewing and listening [1].

Worms

Email worms are part of daily life for any computer security professional. However, these threats can be dealt with swiftly by effective gateway monitoring and by installing desktop

AV protection. Therefore, once detection is available for a particular worm, infected emails will be stopped at the gateway. In the case of instant messaging, however, antivirus software does not currently monitor traffic at the gateway level. If a worm starts to spread using instant messaging, it cannot be stopped before it reached the user's computer [1].

The number of instant messaging worms is rising steadily. Despite the growing threat, there are still no antivirus applications that directly monitor instant messaging traffic on a server level [1]. This is due to the difficulty in finding Instant Messaging traffic, as it is often embedded inside HTTP packets. However, a few antivirus applications plug in to instant messaging clients, scanning files as they are received. The lack of applications scanning instant messaging network traffic is partly due to the difficulty in monitoring instant messaging traffic, as well as the constant modifications to the clients and the protocols they use. Unfortunately, this makes instant messengers an open door to the computer, as unscanned traffic will bypass most server-based security measures. Only the antivirus product running at the desktop level can catch the worms [1].

The way in which these worms replicate varies. Some of the worms spread via email as well as instant messaging. Others spread only via instant messaging. However, currently instant messaging worms all still require user interaction for execution. None make use of an exploit to allow auto-execution upon receipt. Therefore, if instant messaging users are more aware of the threats and how to prevent them, the success of these worms would be significantly reduced [1].

Backdoor Trojan Horses

One can share every file on another person's computer using an instant messenger. All the popular instant messengers have file sharing capabilities or the ability to add such functionality by applying patches or plug-ins. As the instant messaging clients allow peer-to-peer file sharing, a trojan horse can configure the instant messaging client to share all files on the system with full access to everyone, and in this way gain backdoor access to the computer. The benefit for a hacker using an instant messenger to access files on a remote computer instead of installing a backdoor trojan horse is that even if the computer is using a dynamic IP address, the screen name will probably never change. Furthermore, the hacker will receive a notification each time the victim's computer is on-line. Keeping track of and accessing infected computers will therefore be very easy for the hacker. In addition, the hacker does not need to open new suspicious ports for communication, but can instead use already open instant messaging ports [1].

There are currently a handful of trojan horse programs that target instant messaging. Some modify configuration settings so file sharing is enabled for the entire hard drive. These types of trojans pose a large threat, as they allow anyone full file access to the computer [1].

There are also classic backdoor trojan horses that utilize instant messengers to send messages to the author of the trojan, giving the hacker information about the infected computer. This information includes things such as system information, cached passwords, and the IP address of the infected computer. In addition, the hacker can send messages to the infected computer via instant messaging instructing it to perform some unauthorized action [1].

Backdoor trojan horses that allow access to the computer by utilizing instant messenger clients may be harder to prevent than classic backdoor trojans. Classic backdoor trojans open an outgoing listening port on the computer, forming a connection with a remote machine. This can effectively be blocked by a desktop firewall. However, if the trojan operates via the instant messaging client, it does not open a new port. As a result, the user has generally already created an allow rule in their desktop firewall products for instant messaging traffic to be outbound from their machine, thereby allowing the backdoor trojan horse using the same channel to go unblocked. The number of backdoor trojan horses utilizing instant messengers is increasing steadily [1].

Hijacking and Impersonation

Hackers can impersonate other users in many different ways. The most frequently used attack is simply stealing the account information of an unsuspecting user [1].

To get the account information of a user, the hacker can use a password-stealing trojan horse. If the password for the instant messaging client is saved on the computer, the attacker could send a trojan to an unsuspecting user. When executed, the trojan would find the password for the instant messaging account used by the victim and send it back to the hacker. The means for sending back the information to the hacker varies. They include using the instant messenger itself, IRC, and email [1].

Furthermore, since none of the four major instant messaging protocols encrypt [3] their network traffic, attackers can highjack connections via man-in-the-middle attacks. By inserting messages into an ongoing chat-session, a hacker could impersonate one of the chatting parties [1].

Though more difficult, one can also highjack the entire connection by using a man-in-the-middle attack. For example, a disconnect message, which appears to come from the server, can be sent to the victim from the hacker. This will cause the client to disconnect. The hacker can also use a simple denial of service exploit, or other unrelated exploits, to keep the client disconnected. Since the server keeps the connection open and does not know that the client has been disconnected, the hacker can then impersonate the victim user [1].

Stolen account information for any instant messenger can obviously be very damaging. Because the hacker can use this information to disguise him- or herself as a trusted user, the people on the victim's buddy list will trust the hacker and may therefore divulge confidential information or execute malicious files. Losing a password for an instant messenger account can therefore be dangerous for more people than just the user who lost the password [1].

Denial of Service

Instant messaging may make a user's computer vulnerable to denial of service (DoS) attacks. These attacks may have different end results: some DoS attacks make the instant messaging client crash, others will make the client hang, and in some cases consume a large amount of CPU power, causing the entire computer to become unstable [1].

There are many ways in which a hacker can cause a denial of service on an instant messenger client. One common type of attack is flooding a particular user with a large number of messages. The popular instant messaging clients contain protection against flood-attacks by allowing the victim to ignore certain users. However, there are many tools that allow the hacker to use many accounts simultaneously, or automatically create a large number of accounts to accomplish the flood-attack. Adding to this is the fact that once, the flood-attack has started and the victim realizes what has happened, the computer may become unresponsive. Therefore, adding the attacking user accounts to the ignore list of the instant messenger client may be very difficult. Even though denial of service attacks are more of an annoyance than they are dangerous, they can be used in combination with other attacks, such as the hijacking of a connection [1].

Unauthorized Disclosure of Information

Information disclosure could occur without the use of a trojan horse. Since the data that is being transmitted over the instant messaging network is not encrypted, a network sniffer, which can sniff data on most types of networks, can be used to capture the instant messaging traffic. By using a sniffer, a hacker could sniff the packets from an entire instant messaging session. This can be very dangerous, as he or she may gain access to privileged information. This is particularly dangerous in the enterprise environment, in which proprietary or other confidential information may be transmitted along the instant messaging network [1].

Information Disclosure: A Case Study

Some instant messaging clients allow all communication to be saved in log-files. Even though this is a feature that is often requested and required by enterprises, it can sometimes be very dangerous to keep logs, as the logs may include sensitive enterprise data. This was made evident in a case where a hacker stole logs from an instant messaging client belonging to the CEO for an enterprise. The hacker posted the logs to several places on the Web, thereby creating one of the worst possible enterprise nightmares. The logs included sensitive enterprise data regarding business partners, employees and affiliate websites. After the posting of the logs, several members of the senior staff resigned [1].

The preceding case shows how dangerous it can be if a hacker is able to monitor instant messaging sessions. Even though the log-files were stolen in this case, sniffing the data-packets could have caused the same damage [1].

BLOCKING INSTANT MESSAGING

The most effective way of preventing instant messaging to jeopardize the security of a network and the machines upon it is to deny it access to the network in the first place. Preventing the use of instant messaging is difficult. Simple port blocking firewalls will not be effective because clients can use common destination ports such as HTTP port 80 and FTP port 21. Most of the clients will even auto-configure themselves to use other ports than the default one if they are unable to communicate over the default port [1].

Firewalls with protocol analysis may prevent instant messaging clients from communicating via common destination ports, such as port 80, because instant messaging traffic is different from HTTP traffic. However, the latest versions of all the various clients embed the traffic data within an HTTP request, bypassing protocol analysis [1].

The client and responses essentially prepend an HTTP header to each packet sent, thereby circumventing any protocol analysis firewall. With some clients, such as ICQ and AIM, HTTP headers are added only when an HTTP proxy is being used. However, AOL provides access to such a proxy for free, and the clients auto-configure themselves to use this proxy if direct access is being blocked on all ports [1].

Even though, in the case of AIM and ICQ, blocking the address can prevent access to the proxy, there are many other proxy servers freely available on the Internet. A simple search on the Internet will return hundreds of freely available proxy servers. Keeping up with blocking each one is an administrative nightmare. Enterprise policies are the best way to prevent employees within enterprises from using instant messaging. In order to ensure that instant messaging does not jeopardize the security of the enterprise's systems, it should be clearly stated in any and all security policies that instant messaging will be permitted only with the express knowledge and consent of the enterprise [1].

Securing Instant Messaging

That said, many enterprises would prefer to give their employees access to instant messaging, particularly as it can be a valuable communications tool. In this case, it is vital that the enterprise ensure that the IM service that is employed is as secure as possible. Securing instant messaging is not an easy task. One of the best ways to secure the information being transmitted along an IM network is to encrypt it. There are currently several enterprises that offer encrypted instant messaging communication. There are also instant messaging clients available that are compatible with some of the major networks that apply encryption to the instant messaging traffic [1].

In addition to encrypting the communication, the main thing an enterprise should do to secure instant messaging is to keep logs. However, as seen in the previous case study, it is absolutely vital to keep the logs secure. Furthermore, if file transfer via the instant messaging network is not required, then an instant messaging system that does not allow for files to be transferred should be utilized [1].

SUMMARY AND CONCLUSIONS

Because hackers generally target specific computer systems, they aren't the biggest threat for any instant messaging network as a whole. On the other hand, worms are non-discriminate and target all computer systems of a particular network. As a result, they appear to pose the biggest threat for the future. You have seen worms that use security exploits and become widespread in a very short amount of time. Code Red and Nimda are examples of worms that used security exploits to spread themselves quickly [1].

It is unlikely that instant messaging will exceed email as the primary vector of infection in the near future, as far more people use email than instant messaging. Furthermore, the major instant messaging networks still use proprietary protocols so that a worm that spreads via one service, such as MSN Messenger, will not affect users of another service, such as Yahoo! Messenger. However, this does not mean one can disregard the threat that instant messaging poses. As you have seen, there are already worms in the wild that spread via instant messaging. And, if clients become interoperable, or users primarily utilize one network, instant-messaging worms may become more widespread [1].

The number of worms for instant messaging is increasing each month, and looking at the success of some of these worms, clearly instant messaging is an up and coming platform for malicious threats. Furthermore, there are many exploits available for the various clients. As a result, security professionals and end users alike need to be aware of the security issues involved with instant messaging. As with any Internet-based technology, the best way to ensure the security of instant messaging services is to educate users of the risks involved and the means of mitigating those risks, preferably before a serious incident occurs [1].

REFERENCES

[1] Neal Hindocha, "Instant Insecurity: Security Issues of Instant Messaging," Copyright 2005, SecurityFocus, SecurityFocus Symantec Corporation, Suite # 1000, 100 4th Avenue S.W., Calgary, AB T2P 3N2, Canada, January 13, 2003.

[2] John R. Vacca, Firewalls: Jumpstart for Network and Systems Administrators, Digital Press, 2004.

[3] John R. Vacca, Satellite Encryption, Academic Press, Jul 1999.

Chapter 15

COUNTERING OR NOT COUNTERING
THE EAVESDROPPER: THAT'S THE QUESTION?

INTRODUCTION

Countering or not countering the eavesdropper: that's the question? It all depends on who it is – the FBI, NSA, CIA, etc. ... or is it the wily hacker or terrorist? This chapter will answer that question, and provide recommendations to counter or provide support for the eavesdropper either way.

Wiretaps have been used since the invention of the telegraph and have been a legal element of the US law enforcement arsenal for more than a quarter century. In keeping with law enforcement's efforts to keep laws current with changing technologies, in 1994 the US Congress passed the Communications Assistance for Law Enforcement Act (CALEA). The law proved to be controversial because it mandated that digitally switched telephone networks must be built wiretap enabled, with the US Department of Justice in charge of determining the appropriate technology standards [1].

The law provided a specific exclusion for information services. Despite that explicit exemption, in response to a request from the US Federal Bureau of Investigation (FBI), in August 2005, the Federal Communications Commission (FCC) ruled that broadband voice over IP (VoIP) must comply with CALEA. Civil-liberties groups and the industry immediately objected, fearing the ruling's impact on privacy and innovation. There is another community that should be very concerned. Applying CALEA to VoIP requires embedding surveillance technology deeply into the protocol stack. The FCC ruling undermines network security and, because the Internet and private networks using Internet protocols support critical as well as noncritical infrastructure, national security as well. The FCC ruling is a step backward in securing the Internet, a national (and international) priority [1].

CALEA'S HISTORY

In 1992, the FBI was struggling. What had been a boon for telephony (the split-up of AT&T (Ma Bell), which previously had a monopoly of the US market), was a serious problem for the bureau. Instead of implementing wiretaps by working with a single service provider and phone company, the FBI found itself facing a plethora of suppliers of services and telephones. Even worse from the FBI's perspective were the new telecommunications technologies: cell phones, call forwarding, call waiting, and speed dialing. That same year, the FBI put forth the Digital Telephony proposal, which would have required wiretapping standards to be included as part of the design of digital-switching telephone equipment [1].

The FBI claimed that the advanced calling features impeded court-authorized wiretaps. However, The Washington Post investigated and discovered that, FBI officials have not yet fumbled a criminal probe due to the inability to tap a phone. At this news, Computer Professionals for Social Responsibility, a public – interest group, initiated Freedom of Information Act litigation; in response, the FBI released a four-page list of impeded cases in which, citing national security, all information was blacked out [1].

Digital Telephony Proposal

The FBI's Digital Telephony proposal represented a sharp change in the government's approach to wiretapping. Instead of letting service providers determine how to configure their systems to accommodate wiretaps, the proposal put government in the middle of telephone-equipment design. In fact, this bill placed the US Attorney General, a position not generally known for technical expertise, into the process of standards design of equipment used by the general public. Industry and civil-liberties groups opposed the FBI proposal, and no one in Congress would sponsor it [1].

In 1994, the FBI reintroduced the bill, and this time, events played out differently. Over the course of the Congressional session, the bill's scope changed, narrowing down to common carriers (rather than all electronic communication service providers), adding some protections for transactional information (the first time such information was afforded protection in wiretapping law) and eliminating a clause requiring telephone companies to decrypt encrypted conversations [2], regardless of whether they had an encryption key. There was also a sweetener for the telecommunications companies: a US$500 million authorization to help carriers update their networks to comply with the law's requirements. Although other civil-liberties groups had continued to oppose the bill, the Electronic Frontier Foundation's support of the final version (now renamed CALEA) helped persuade the telephone companies to support it. This time, the bill passed. Though the law governed just the US, its impact was far broader. The FBI pressed other nations to adopt similar laws. In any case, because the law applied to the US telecom market, much of the rest of the world was forced to adopt the standards that CALEA dictated [1].

Implementing CALEA

The law ran into trouble almost immediately. The telephone companies believed that negotiations on the bill had left them in a position in which standards would be determined through consultation with the FBI. After passage however, the FBI took the stance that the law allowed it to set requirements without consultation [1].

The FCC, which has jurisdiction over telecommunications regulations, and the courts, have generally upheld the FBI's interpretation – even in cases in which CALEA excluded the FBI's proposed standards. Even though CALEA required telephone companies to meet the government's standards by 1998, disagreements between telecommunications companies and the FBI on appropriate standards meant the deadline could not be met. Congress was unhappy with the delay, and several Congressmen, including Senator Patrick Leahy (D-Vermont) and Representative Bob Barr (R-Georgia), pointed the finger at the FBI [1].

These disputes (and delays) concerned CALEA's application to telephony. CALEA's language specifically exempted information services: The term telecommunications carriers – (A) means ... a common carrier for hire; and (B) includes (i) ... commercial mobile service; or (ii) ... service that is a replacement for a substantial portion of local telephone exchange service ...; but (C) does not include ... information services. Nonetheless, in late 2003, the FBI served notice to the FCC that VoIP providers would be subject to CALEA [1].

As was the case in 1992 with the Digital Telephony proposal, the FBI did not provide any examples of problems found in conducting law enforcement wiretaps on VoIP calls. In March 2004, the FBI, the US Department of Justice, and the US Drug Enforcement Agency submitted a joint petition to the FCC requesting that it rule on CALEA's applicability to VoIP. Over the next year, computer enterprises joined the anti-CALEA coalition of civil-liberties groups and telecommunications providers that formed in the 1990s. None objected to the idea of wiretapping voice calls (indeed, many enterprises were involved in determining appropriate ways to enable the tapping of VoIP calls) but all objected to the idea that the government should be involved in setting standards for interception on the packet-switched Internet. In August 2005, the FCC announced that broadband providers of VoIP must comply with CALEA.4 CALEA, which mandates government role in standards design, is an oddity in U.S. wiretap law, which will be briefly examined [1].

U.S. WIRETAP LAWS

Wiretaps have had a long and complex history in U.S. jurisprudence. Their first use was in the mid 19th century, in response to the invention of the telegraph. Shortly afterward, they appeared in war: Confederate General Jeb Stuart traveled with his own wiretapper to tap Union army lines. Wiretaps came into their own during Prohibition, the period between 1920 and 1933 in which the manufacture and sale of alcohol was illegal. Federal law-enforcement agents discovered the value of wiretaps in both investigating and prosecuting bootlegging cases. The Olmstead case set the stage for the next 40 years of U.S. wiretap law [1].

A Form Of Search

In the 1920s, Roy Olmstead had a major bootlegging operation in Seattle. Federal agents wiretapped Olmstead and his co-conspirators, placing taps in the basement of his office building and on telephone poles outside private houses. Olmstead's lawyers argued their case on the basis of the Fourth Amendment within the U.S. Constitution: The right of the people to be secure in their persons, house, papers and effects against unreasonable searches and seizures shall not be violated, and no Warrants shall issue but upon probable cause, supported by Oath or affirmation, and particularly describing the place to be searched, and the persons or things to be seized [1].

The U.S. Supreme Court held that wiretaps were not a form of search, and thus didn't require search warrants. But, the most well-known opinion in the Olmstead case isn't that of the majority, but of Justice Louis Brandeis's dissent. He indicated that wiretaps were a special type of search [1]:

The evil incident to invasion of privacy of the telephone is far greater than that involved in tampering with the mails. Whenever a telephone line is tapped, the privacy of persons at both ends of the line is invaded, and all conversations between them upon any subject, and although proper, confidential, and privileged, may be overheard. Moreover, the tapping of one man's telephone line involves the tapping of the telephone of every other person whom he may know or who may call him. As a means of espionage, writs of assistance and general warrants are but puny instruments of tyranny and oppression when compared with wiretapping [1].

—Olmstead v. United States

A decade later, citing the 1934 US Federal Communications Act, which prohibited the interception and divulgence of wired communications, the U.S. Supreme Court overturned the Olmstead decision in the Nardone cases. In a series of cases over the next 30 years, the Supreme Court also slowly narrowed the circumstances under which law enforcement could perform electronic bugging without a warrant, until 1967, in Charles Katz v. United States, when the Court concluded that an electronic bug in even so public a place as a phone booth, was indeed a search and therefore should be protected under the Fourth Amendment [1].

The Court's rulings of the 1930s did not end law enforcement wiretapping; instead, tapping went underground figuratively as well as literally. After the Nardone rulings, law enforcement didn't publicly divulge wiretapped information (or, it did, but not the fact that the information came from wiretaps). This legal never-never land led to abuses by FBI director J. Edgar Hoover's agents, including the wiretapping (and bugging) of political dissidents, Congressional staffers, and US Supreme Court Justices. The FBI's extensive records on political figures was well known, and this information, some of which was salacious, ensured that Congress conducted little oversight of the FBI. When, in reaction to the Katz decision, Congress decided to pass a wiretapping law, the national legislature was quite concerned about preventing Hoover-era abuses. Evidently, that didn't carry over to the Bush administration, which has shown total disregard to Federal wire tapping laws, by spying on its citizens without their knowledge and presenting the proper wiretap warrants. One can only speculate (like Nixon's which had been conducted for political purposes) what this illegal spying was all about. As Mark Phelps (alias "Deep Throat") said to Woodward and Bernstein in 1974, "Follow the Money!"

Changing Views

The complications of investigating organized crime (including victims' reluctance to testify, so-called victimless crimes (such as prostitution), and the corruption of local law enforcement) make electronic surveillance a particularly valuable tool. In 1967, a presidential commission investigating organized crime concluded, legislation should be enacted granting carefully circumscribed authority for electronic surveillance to law enforcement officers. In response, US President Lyndon Johnson signed the Omnibus Crime Control and Safe Streets Act of 1968, of which Title III legalized law enforcement wiretaps in criminal investigations. Because of wiretaps' invasive nature, the act listed only 26 crimes that could warrant wiretap investigations, including murder, kidnapping, extortion, gambling, counterfeiting, and the sale of marijuana. The US Judiciary Committee's report explained that each offense was chosen because it was intrinsically serious or because it is characteristic of the operations of organized crime [1].

Congress decided that stringent oversight of wiretapping should require a federal district court judge to review each federal wiretap warrant application. Although President Johnson had used wiretaps on civil-rights leader Martin Luther King Jr. during the 1964 Democratic Party convention and on US Vice President Hubert Humphrey in 1968, publicly, the president was ambivalent about wiretaps. Even as he described the Title III provisions for wiretapping as undesirable, he signed the wiretapping provisions into law [1].

Title III

For criminal investigations (the only kind Title III addresses), wiretap warrants are more difficult to obtain than normal search warrants. The judge must determine that there's probable cause to believe:

- An individual is committing, has committed, or is about to commit an indictable offense
- Communications about the offense will be obtained through the interception
- Normal investigative procedures have been tried and either have failed, appear unlikely to succeed, or are too dangerous
- The facilities subject to surveillance are being used or will be used in the commission of the crime [1].

Title III covers procedures for obtaining wiretaps for law enforcement investigations. In 1972, in a court case involving domestic national security issues, the US Supreme Court ordered an end to warrantless wiretapping, even for national security purposes. Domestic national security cases had fueled a large number of inappropriate investigations of Americans, including:

- The US Central Intelligence Agency opening and photographing nearly a quarter of a million first-class letters without search warrants between 1953 and 1973
- The 300,000 individuals indexed on CIA computers and CIA files on 7,200 individuals

- The US National Security Agency obtaining copies of millions of private telegrams sent to and from the US from 1947 to 1975 without search warrants through an arrangement with three US telegraph companies
- US Army Intelligence keeping files on 100,000 Americans [1].

Because of the public outcry over the discovery of numerous Nixon administration national security wiretaps that had been conducted for political purposes, it took until 1978 for Congress to craft the Foreign Intelligence Surveillance Act (FISA), which authorizes procedures for national security wiretapping. Congress considered it extremely important that safeguards be in place to prevent such illegal surveillance in the future. As it turned out, they were wrong [1].

FOREIGN INTELLIGENCE SURVEILLANCE ACT

In contrast to Title III's requirements that a judge determine whether there's probable cause to believe that an individual is involved in committing an indictable offense, in FISA cases, the judge, a member of an FISA court, must determine whether there's probable cause that the target is a foreign power or agent of a foreign power. The purpose of the surveillance is to obtain intelligence information. The law provides that no United States person may be considered a foreign power or an agent of a foreign power solely upon the basis of activities protected by the first amendment to the Constitution of the United States [1].

The requirements for foreign intelligence wiretaps are less stringent than those for law enforcement. United States versus United States District Court, held that domestic national security wiretapping must be conducted under a search warrant, and the U.S. Supreme Court stated that, Different standards (for gathering intelligence) may be compatible with the Fourth Amendment if they are reasonable both in relation to the legitimate need of Government for intelligence information and the protected rights of the citizens. National security investigations are more typically concerned with preventing future crimes rather than prosecuting previous ones, and the ability to present a case in court is often orthogonal to the real concerns of national security cases [1].

Title III and FISA form the basis for U.S. wiretap law. State statutes also exist, with approximately half of all wiretaps for criminal investigations in the U.S. performed using state wiretap warrants. The rules governing state wiretaps must be at least as restrictive as those governing Title III. There have been several updates and modifications to the federal wiretap statutes, including the Electronic Communications Privacy Act, CALEA, and the PATRIOT Act. In this chapter, the focus is solely on CALEA [1].

COMMUNICATIONS IN AN AGE OF TERROR

US wiretap laws were passed during an era in which the national threats were organized crime and civil unrest. In evaluating the efficacy of applying a CALEA-like law to the Internet, it's important to put today's threats into context and understand the new communications context [1].

Law Enforcement And Terrorism

The war on terror is the US's most pressing security concern, but it isn't actually a war on terror: it's a war against violent religious fundamentalists who use terror as a weapon. However, it's also used by the Bush administration (like in George Orwell's "1984") as a political weapon (like phony terror threats and incidents which always end up not being credible) to divert the public's attention away from the domestic- (high gas prices, border security, illegal immigration, etc. ...) and international (Iraq War, Iran's nuclear program, etc. ...) problems that are causing the administration's poll numbers to plummet.

As a society, you have become accustomed to using war to refer to situations to which the word doesn't properly apply: the war on drugs, the war on poverty, even the war on spam. In the case of violent fundamentalists (for Osama bin Laden and al Qaeda, this means violent Muslim fundamentalists), this is indeed a war [1].

Law enforcement concerns have governed domestic approaches to this war. In part, this is because you know how to catch so-called bad guys. The FBI's successful investigations of the Lockerbie plane crash over Scotland in 1988 and the first World Trade Center bombing in 1993, led the public and policymakers into believing the tools of law enforcement were appropriate for combating terrorism. But the war against violent religious fundamentalists won't be won by law enforcement, which provides the wrong tools and the wrong incentives. For example, one of the most important functions of law enforcement is its deterrent value, but law enforcement isn't a deterrent to terrorists. Rather, violent fundamentalists often view a jail sentence as a form of martyrdom and an increased opportunity for recruiting [1].

Even more basic to the distinction between law enforcement and national security investigations is that law enforcement and national security investigations have substantively different purposes. Law enforcement sees the solving of a crime as a success. Yet, when terrorism is concerned, prevention is the only real measure of success. Law enforcement seeks a level of proof that will convict a criminal in a court of law, which is inappropriate in a war against terrorists. The type of intelligence work needed for national security investigations seeks different outcomes than those of criminal investigations, which are measured by arrests made and convictions obtained.

The events of September 11th, 2001 make it dreadfully clear that the law enforcement focus is inadequate for this war. National security's emphasis on prevention is the critical aspect of this war [1].

Computer Security And Terrorism

What does all of this have to do with computer security? The Internet has proved a boon to many industries, and the last decade has seen a massive shift to it as the preferred form of conducting business. But the Internet is insecure. The network was originally designed to share resources, and neither security nor wiretapping were considerations in its initial design. Security is a serious concern for Internet users, which include many private industries that form part of critical infrastructure: energy companies and the electric-power grid, banking and finance, and health care. That's why applying CALEA to VoIP is a mistake: the insecurities that will result are likely to extend well past VoIP to other aspects of the Internet, and the end result will be greater insecurity [1].

ENTER NEW TECHNOLOGY: THE INTERNET

Although it might look like a duck, walk like a duck, and quack like a duck, Internet telephony is not, in fact, a duck. It's a very different species from the circuit-switched telephony of Ma Bell [1].

Telephony Versus The Internet

At its bottom level (metal wires, optical fibers, microwave relays, and satellite channels) the public-switched telephone network (PSTN) and the Internet use the same resources, but the way they manage those resources is quite different. In circuit-switched telephony, a dedicated, end-to-end circuit is established for the call. Calls have time multiplexing, which means several calls may share a line. Either each call has a dedicated timeslot in every frame (called synchronized multiplexing) or there's an asynchronous version of the slots, in which each timeslot includes the call's identifier [1].

In the pre-computer telephone network, the route a call took was represented by the states of mechanical switches in the telephone offices through which the call passed. In a computerized network, the call is represented by table entries that show which incoming line is connected to which outgoing line. This is a commitment of resources that represents a significant cost for the network, a cost related to the traditional cost of a three-minute phone call. In digital terms, the resource commitment is optimized for communications that send thousands or millions of bits at a time [1].

The route that packets on the Internet take is determined not by entries in the network's tables, but by addresses carried in the packets. Packet progress through the network is affected by routing tables; these tables reflect the network's characteristics and not that of the individual communications. In theory (though less so in practice), each packet of a VoIP call can use a distinct path to reach its destination. This is the first problem that Internet wiretapping poses. On the Internet, routing control is distributed. It's impossible to determine a priori the routing of the packets the communication is broken into – this is determined by the routing tables, which change depending on the network traffic. Thus, unless the communication is tapped at the endpoints (at the user, or at the Internet service provider if the user always accesses the same provider), it's impossible to guarantee 100 percent access to all communication packets. From a privacy viewpoint, and to address law enforcement's minimization requirement (that wiretapping be of a designated target (and not someone else using the line) and that the tapped call be related to the investigation), a further difficulty is posed by the fact that many other pieces of traffic travel along portions of the same path as the communication to be tapped. Thus, tapping anywhere but at the endpoints exposes other communications; this was one of the problems of the FBI's Carnivore (now renamed DCS-1000) system for tapping email [1].

> **Note:** Carnivore was an FBI Internet monitoring system designed to be installed at an ISP. The system filtered Internet communications and delivered target communications to a remote site, namely the law-enforcement agency. According to the FBI, only those communications that were subject to the wiretap order were forwarded to the FBI. The FBI has since shifted to using commercial software to conduct such investigations.

Intelligence At The Endpoints

The PSTN was architected throughout the system to have high quality for its most important application: voice transmission. The endpoints (the phone receivers) are dumb. In considering the issue of architecting wiretaps into communications channels, a crucial difference between the PSTN and the Internet is that intelligence is at the endpoints for the Internet. The underlying network is deliberately simple, leaving the endpoints able to deploy complex systems [1].

The Internet design paradigm was chosen for flexibility: The function in question can completely and correctly be implemented only with the knowledge and help of the application standing at the endpoints of the communications system. Therefore, providing that questioned function as a feature of the communication system itself is not possible [1].

The principle of letting the endpoints implement the function rather than having low-level function implementation be part of the underlying communication system is known as the end-to-end argument in system design. It is fundamental to Internet design [1].

Intelligence at the endpoints enables versatility. Applications can be developed far beyond what the original designers of the communication system envisioned. Indeed, innovation on the Internet has flourished precisely because of applications. The flexibility afforded by the Internet design paradigm means there are few barriers to entry for a novel service, and the Internet boom of the late 1990s was greatly enabled by the low barrier to entry for new applications [1].

The layered approach to network design (application, transport, network, link, and physical) doesn't itself preclude wiretapping. It simply requires that wiretapping, an application, be handled in the application layer, or at the target's network connection. The whole issue of applying CALEA to VoIP exists to achieve 100 percent compliance with court-authorized wiretaps, but such compliance is impossible to guarantee at the application layer. Service providers do (and will) seek to comply with court-authorized wiretaps, but an end user who is determined to thwart a wiretap, perhaps through a complicated scheme of directing in which streams the traffic will run, will be able to do so. Without pushing wiretapping capabilities deeper into the protocol stack, it will be impossible to achieve 100 percent success for court authorized VoIP wiretaps. And pushing wiretapping capabilities further into the network stack violates the end-to-end principle, which, although not sacrosanct, has proved quite valuable [1].

Building Wiretapping Into Protocols

There is nothing inherent in the design of a communications network that rules out security or wiretapping, and indeed there are defense communications networks that provide both security and the capability of tapping. Had security or wiretapping been part of the Internet's core requirements, the functionality could have been built in from the beginning. There are secure government communication systems which, at (government) customer request, are capable of doing key recovery, thus enabling data recovery (wiretapping). The difficulty in designing these capabilities into the Internet occurs in attempting to securely implement wiretapping ex post facto into the current network architecture. The FBI petition to apply CALEA to VoIP is nothing less than a request to redesign Internet architecture [1].

In 2000, an Internet Engineering Task Force (IETF) Network Working Group studying the issue of designing wiretap requirements into Internet protocols observed that any protocol designed with built-in wiretapping capabilities is inherently less secure than the protocol would be without the wiretapping capability. Adding wiretapping requirements into network protocols makes protocols even more complex, and the added complexity is likely to lead to security flaws. Wiretapping is a security breach, and no one wants to see those breaches, deliberately architected or not. The IETF Network Working Group decided not to consider requirements for wiretapping as part of the IETF standards process [1].

The IETF's warning is clear: Internet wiretapping can be used not only by those interested in protecting US interests, but also by those who oppose them. A technology designed to simplify Internet wiretapping by US intelligence presents a large target for foreign intelligence agencies. Breaking into this one service might give them broad access to Internet communications without the expense of building an extensive intercept network of their own [1].

In the spirit of modern computer-based industries, it seems likely that any intercept capability built into Internet facilities will be capable of the same remote management that's typical of the facilities themselves. This was the case, for example, with Carnivore. System vulnerabilities are thus as likely to be global as local. Were foreign intelligence services to penetrate and exploit Internet wiretapping technology, massive surveillance of US citizens, residents, and enterprises might follow. Used in combination with inexpensive automated search technology, this could lead to an unprecedented compromise of American security and privacy. Of course, Internet protocols govern the entire Internet (and not a US version) and thus the impact of CALEA on VoIP, were it to succeed, would be international in scope. Across the globe, Internet security and privacy would be put at risk [1].

At present, there's a struggle to achieve adequate security on the Internet without intentional security compromises in its design. Although it might one day be possible to incorporate surveillance into packet-switched networks with sufficient security that the overall safety of society is increased rather than decreased, it's hard to see how this could be less difficult than the unfinished task of developing a scalable and economical secure network. At the very least, built-in wiretapping would require secure communications of its own to carry the intercepted information to the customers for which it's collected [1].

This problem is made worse by the unreasonable effectiveness of the Internet as a communications channel. Building surveillance capabilities into the Internet infrastructure, and not into the application endpoints, would expose to eavesdropping not only current applications, but also future ones, including, for example, the billions of small devices such as radio-frequency identification (RFID) tags and sensors that communicate via the Internet. The concern expressed earlier that security holes built into the Internet for wiretapping that are used in combination with inexpensive automated search technology could lead to serious security breaches applies here as well [1].

Over the past several years, the US government sought improvements in civilian communications infrastructure security even though some of those improvements were likely to impede law enforcement investigations. Intelligence agencies clearly supported the shift, which found that the advantages provided to society through increased information security outweighed the disadvantages to intelligence and law enforcement. In 2000, the US Department of Commerce relaxed its cryptographic export-control regulations, which simplified the deployment of communications security in commercial equipment. This action marked a substantial change in direction on the civilian sector's use of strong cryptography. Similarly, in recent years, the US government, instead of restricting the use of strong cryptography, has encouraged several cryptographic efforts, including the development of the 128-bit Advanced Encryption Standard and the deployment of Elliptic Curve Cryptosystems [1].

Finally, these changes don't mean that Internet communications can't be wiretapped. The Internet's insecurity is well known, and few communications are routinely protected (for example, encrypted end to end). As the IETF Network Working Group observed, the use of existing network features, if deployed intelligently, provide extensive opportunities for wiretapping [1]. But exploiting current insecurities and actually building them into Internet protocols have significantly different effects on society's communications security. There's an arguement against the latter; but no issue is taken with the former [1].

SUMMARY AND CONCLUSIONS

From the very early days of the republic, the US has treated communications as something of the people, for the people, and by the people. The US Postal Act of 1792 established two fundamental principles: privacy of the mails (postal officials weren't allowed to open mail unless it was undeliverable) and low rates for newspapers, thereby encouraging the dissemination of political information. In these two decisions, the US acted very differently from Britain and France, which neither guaranteed the privacy of the mails nor encouraged the use of the mails for political communication. Indeed, in Europe, the postal service was a system of government surveillance. By contrast, the US Post Office was seen as a facilitator of democracy rather than a controller of the people and, as a result, it was one of the few strong federal institutions established in the nascent US. A bedrock reason for the growth of telecommunications in the US has been the privacy afforded to communications. This spawned trust in the use of communication systems and a growing dependence on them. The FBI's efforts on CALEA run completely contrary to the US's 222-year history of developing its communication systems [1].

The attempt to apply CALEA to VoIP poses much risk to the US economy through the potential loss of enterprise information, to US national security through the provision of cost-effective massive intelligence gathering, and to privacy and thus the freedom of US citizens [1].

Society has seen such risks before. In 1999, a report prepared for the European Parliament revealed that the US (as part of a surveillance program known as Echelon, conducted jointly with the United Kingdom, Australia, Canada, and New Zealand) was targeting commercial communication channels. In response, European governments decided to liberalize their cryptographic export-control policy, even though the US had pressed for tighter controls on cryptographic exports.

Note: The US, in part so as not to lose trade to Europe, liberalized its cryptographic export-control policies shortly afterward.

Finally, to law enforcement, it might seem obvious that wiretap laws should automatically be updated with each change in communications technology. Looking at the issues more broadly, this is not a clear proposition. Wiretap laws were passed at a particular time to satisfy a particular set of problems. As technology and society change, so must laws. Society's security needs aren't enhanced by requiring that VoIP implementations be developed as CALEA-enabled, and CALEA requirements applied to the Internet are likely to cause serious harm to security, industrial innovation, and the political efforts in the war against radical terrorists. Applying CALEA to VoIP is likely to decrease, rather than increase security. Security requirements should follow the medical profession's Hippocratic oath: First, do no harm. The proposed CALEA requirements don't pass this test, and shouldn't be approved [1].

REFERENCES

[1] Susan Landau, "Security, Wiretapping, and the Internet," IEEE Security & Privacy, Copyright ©2006, IEEE, Inc. All rights reserved. IEEE, Inc., IEEE Corporate Office, 3 Park Avenue, 17th Floor, New York, New York, 10016–5997 U.S.A., vol. 3, no. 6, November/December 2005, pp. 26-33.

[2] John R. Vacca, Satellite Encryption, Academic Press, Jul 1999.

PART VIII

THWARTING COUNTERFEITERS AND FORGERY TO RETAIN INTEGRITY

Chapter 16

THE FORGER'S ARSENAL

INTRODUCTION

Communication in the Internet works by sending packets from one place to another. Each packet, like a post card, contains a source address and a destination address. The Internet fulfills the role of the post office, delivering packets to their specified destination addresses. It is interesting to notice that only the destination address is used to deliver the packet. In most cases, however, the sender wants the destination to reply. The source address is used by the destination to address the reply [1].

Unfortunately, considerable mischief can be caused by sending packets with incorrect source addresses. First, it is very likely that those sending such unwanted messages would also like to avoid being identified by the recipients. Even worse, a recipient who believes the forged source address will blame the owner of that address for the unwanted message [1].

Some of the worst attacks in the Internet today involve sending packets that cause automatic replies. Typically, in this case, neither the party that receives the original packet nor the party that receives the reply would object to a few such packets, but the attacker arranges for them to get huge numbers. Each feels like he or she is being attacked by the other. Alternatively, a large number of places are sent a smaller number of packets and the replies all converge on a victim who sees an attack that appears to come from a large number of places. Even if the attack is coming from a large number of places, that number can be made to appear much larger by reflecting the packets off many innocent intermediaries [1].

INGRESS FILTERING

The commonly recommended solution is called ingress filtering. In the post-office analogy, ingress filtering corresponds to the local post office only accepting letters with its own zip code in the return address. A potential attacker can still successfully use valid return addresses that belong to his or her neighbors, or even non-existent addresses with that zip code. However, if these letters cause trouble, the range of possible suspects is relatively small. If the attacker sends many such letters, the local post office is likely to find out that the letters came from him or her [1].

All of the preceding statements hold for the Internet as well as the post office. The local post office corresponds to an ISP. The ISP knows that all of the packets it sends out should have source addresses in a given range. Ingress filtering simply refuses to forward those packets with source addresses outside that range [1].

> **Note:** The post office actually does have something just as good as this. The postmark shows where
> a letter entered the system. The recipient can compare the return address to that postmark.

There are a few problems with ingress filtering. First, as noted, it is still hard to tell when an attacker forges the address of his or her neighbor. More important, the Internet, unlike the post office, has no central authority that can force all of the ISPs to check the source addresses of outgoing packets. Finally, this extra effort does not really help the ISP that exerts the effort. It helps the rest of the world by preventing source forgery originating from that ISP, whereas the customers who pay the ISP for service get no direct benefit. In light of this, perhaps it is not so surprising that, in spite of all of the preceding recommendations (and their appeals to the spirit of cooperation), few, if any, ISPs actually do ingress filtering [1].

DISCERNING TRUE PACKET SOURCES

Unlike the post office, the Internet consists of a large number of different carriers who forward packets to each other. If things work correctly, then each forward operation brings a packet closer to its destination until it finally arrives there. When a packet arrives, each forwarder can normally tell who sent it the packet, but not where that party, in turn, got the packet, or anything more about the path the packet took through the different carriers. It is therefore recommended that each forwarder add to the packet an indication of who gave the packet to it. Each packet will then arrive with a complete forwarding path [1].

Again, this is not a new idea. The advantage of this scheme is that the path is not controlled by the sender. A forger is now in the position of writing a return address of New York when the receiver can plainly read a postmark that says Chicago! This is really a proposal to change the communication protocol used in the Internet. The new protocol is viewed as an enhancement of the Internet Protocol (IP), and is referred to as Path Enhanced IP, or PEIP [1].

The indication in the preceding of where the packet came from does not have to be an IP address. That would take much more space than necessary, space that could otherwise be used for real data. In PEIP, space is saved by encoding the paths. The encoding scheme and some additional reasons to save space are mentioned next [1].

A forwarder that can receive packets from ten different places will add to the path a number between one and ten. This, naturally, means that a receiver needs a way to decode the path. However, a separate protocol will be needed to decode the path into a sequence of IP addresses. This protocol requires each machine along the path to take the data that it (supposedly) added, and find the IP address of the neighbor for which it would have added that data. The mappings between neighbors and added data are expected to remain reasonably stable. In other words, within reason, it should be possible to trace the path of a packet that was received in the past [1].

For reasons that will become clear next, it is desirable for the path to include one explicit IP address, generally the address of the first router to forward the packet. The rule is that if a forwarder cannot be sure who gave it the packet, as is typically the case when it comes out of a LAN, then it must discard any path that came with the packet. In effect, the forwarder is taking responsibility for the packet. The originator of a packet likewise should send it with an empty path, meaning he or she did not get it from anywhere else [1].

> **Note:** The final recipient is typically in a LAN, but he or she will not discard the path. He or she will use it to see where the packet come from. The recipient that puts the first element in a path (which implies that he or she is sure who sent him the packet) starts the path with the actual IP address of the sender. In effect there are two cases.

A packet that comes from a LAN goes to the router connected to the LAN which forwards it with an empty path. The recipient then starts the path with the IP address of that router, which is the one that allowed the packet into the network [1].

A packet that is created by a router is sent with an empty path. The recipient then puts the IP address of that router in the path indicating that the packet is the responsibility of the originating router [1].

It is therefore recommended that ingress filtering be not only universally adopted, but actually enforced. This involves both a technical and a social component. Source tracing is the technical component. Its role is to make apparent to all where forged packets enter the network and who was foolish enough to trust those places. The social component involves shunning those places that forward forged packets. Source tracing provides the accountability that both justifies denying service to the guilty party (since his or her guilt is evident) and forces his or her provider to take this action (otherwise, he or she appears to act as an accomplice) [1].

Ideally, the allowable source addresses should be part of the agreements between ISPs (ISP A agrees to accept and forward from ISP B traffic with the following IP source addresses). Then both ISPs should filter traffic with non-conforming source addresses [1].

If necessary, the paths themselves can be used to filter offending traffic. Suppose Alice gets traffic from Bob who gets it from Charlie. Alice sees that this traffic has forged the source addresses (or is objectionable to her for some other reason). She can complain to Bob and ask him to stop accepting packets from Charlie, or at least stop forwarding them to her. However, even before she can contact Bob, and later, even if Bob refuses, Alice can filter the packets from Bob with paths indicating that he got them from Charlie. In general this filtering can be done anywhere along the path. The explicit IP address at the end of the path will turn out to be especially useful for this kind of filtering [1].

NEED FOR TWO PATHS

The paths in the preceding show where a packet came from. However, there is an important class of attacks for which additional data would be very useful. These attacks involve sending packets with forged source addresses to an intermediate host, causing it to reply to those forged source addresses. For instance, if attacker Albert sends a request to intermediate host Harry with the source address of victim Victor, Harry will have no reason to suspect that the source address is forged. If Harry simply replies (or, more important, if he and a million others reply) then Victor gets a reply from Harry (and a million others like him). Victor can tell where the replies came from but this does not help him. What would be more useful is the source of the original request packet [1].

For this reason, it is recommended that all replies to packets that could easily have been forged contain the path that the original packet took from its sender to its receiver, who is now replying. That is, Harry sends the path from Albert to Harry along with the reply. Victor now gets three things: the unsolicited reply, the path from Harry to Victor and the path from Albert to Harry. Victor can now not only trace back to Harry, but, by concatenating the path from Albert to Harry to the path from Harry to Victor, he can trace the path all the way back to Albert [1]!

> **Note:** In this case, the explicit IP address at the end of the path from Albert to Harry is likely to be the most important piece of data.

Of course, it would be preferable for Albert's ISP, Isaac, to find and punish Albert. It is also reasonable to blame Isaac for failing to filter packets with Victor's address as their source. In fact, one would hope that Isaac's service provider, in turn, will threaten to stop carrying traffic for Isaac unless he starts filtering his packets. And so on... [1].

Although many different types of packet satisfy the description of those that should send double paths, most of the packets actually sent in the Internet do not need to. In particular, most TCP packets reply to (acknowledge) a previous packet that could not have been sent by an attacker unless he or she either made a very lucky guess or happened to control a router that forwarded an earlier packet in the same connection (in which case he or she is already in position to do a lot of damage). These packets therefore need not send a second path. On the other hand, a TCP packet that results in a no-such-connection error response could be sent by an attacker using a forged source address, so the no-such-connection response should contain the extra path. Similarly a SYN packet could contain a forged source address, so the SYN-ACK response should contain an extra path [1].

USE OF EXPLICIT IP ADDRESSES

The attack described earlier motivates the inclusion of the explicit IP address at the end of the path. Albert sends packets to a huge number of intermediate hosts, causing them all to reply to Victor. Victor sees unsolicited packets coming from all sorts of addresses by all sorts of paths. Without the explicit IP address he can see the source of the attack by tracing the paths of a few unsolicited packets. What he cannot easily do is recognize (and thereby filter, or ask his upstream providers to filter) all of the paths from Albert via all possible intermediaries. On the other hand, it is easy to recognize the packets containing secondary paths ending with a particular IP address, in this case that of the router that allowed Albert's packets into the network [1].

The inclusion of one explicit IP address is a compromise based on the assumption that, routers are much less likely than normal hosts to be controlled by attackers. If Albert controlled a router he could have it send packets with arbitrary paths, including random IP addresses at the ends. Then Victor would no longer be able to easily identify the attack packets. However, if paths were completely unencoded, the IP address of the attacking router would be in the secondary path of every attack packet, and could therefore be used to filter those packets. The cost, of course, is the space required by unencoded paths, 100 bytes in IPv4 and 400 bytes in IPv6 for 25 hops. With encoded paths, the only way to stop such an attack is to get the neighbors of the attacking router to stop forwarding its packets. The problem of identifying the attacking router is addressed later in the chapter [1].

The packets arriving with secondary paths should be replies to packets sent by the recipient. Therefore the secondary paths ought to end with the addresses of routers that are neighbors of that recipient. This should make it easy, at least for places close enough to the ultimate destination, to filter out packets that reply to requests with forged source addresses. However, it is hoped that source forgery will be sought out and punished, not just filtered near the victim. As an aside, it is interesting to notice that a single ping followed by a single trace operation would generate the equivalent of a round trip traceroute [1].

HOW EXPENSIVE IS PEIP?

The longest paths in the Internet are currently about 25 hops. The average is actually much less. The routers that forward packets are typically connected to no more than 16 other routers. Therefore a typical hop should take no more than 4 bits. This gives a total of about 16 bytes for the longest paths in IPv4 (including the 4 byte explicit address) and 28 bytes in IPv6 (where the explicit address is 16 bytes) [1].

Of course, in packets with an extra path, the expense could be twice as high. However, as noted in the preceding, these packets make up a small fraction of the traffic in the Internet. To give an idea of the value of the bandwidth being used, it is relevant to mention that the smallest possible IPv6 header is 40 bytes, whereas the smallest possible IPv4 header is 20 bytes. Most IPv4 headers are actually the minimum length. Anyone who wants to move from IPv4 to IPv6 therefore must be willing to pay 20 bytes per packet [1].

The time it takes a router to add its data to the path is a small constant. This should not pose a serious problem. If expanding a packet is problematic for specific routers, it would be possible to pre-allocate space. A more serious problem is that this extra data might require fragmentation. For non-attack traffic this does not seem like a major problem. TCP traffic, which comprises most of the traffic in the Internet, avoids this problem by using non-fragmentable packets to find a Path MTU. Attack traffic is discussed next [1].

A reasonable question is what maximum size of paths must be supported. Both IPv4 and IPv6 limit paths to 255 hops. As noted in the preceding, this is far more than any real paths.

Of course, legitimate paths must not be cut off since that prevents source tracing. On the other hand, there are good reasons to limit the length to the maximum realistic path length. Something in the range of 30 hops or 16 bytes (for IPv4) seems like a reasonable limit [1].

PROBLEMS CAUSED BY PEIP

This part of the chapter represents an attempt to anticipate problems that might be caused by adoption of PEIP. Feedback from Beta testing of PEIP implementations and reviewers of PEIP documents will result in modifications to this part of the chapter [1].

Small Packet Networks

The term small packet networks is used in RFC791 (IPv4) where it discusses fragmentation of packets. Clearly IP requires a lower level transport mechanism that is capable of carrying packets of some reasonable size. In particular, fragmentation would not help if the maximum packet size is less than the size of the IP header, since every fragment has to carry a header. It is preferable for every fragment to also carry a path. This effectively increases the minimal requirement by the maximum path size. That is one reason for keeping this maximum path size within reasonable bounds (far less than 255 bytes). This does not seem to be a problem with current or future technology [1].

RFC791 (IPv4) states that all hosts must be prepared to accept datagrams of up to 576 octets (whether they arrive whole or in fragments). RFC2460 (IPv6) states that "IPv6 requires that every link in the Internet have an MTU of 1280 octets or greater. It is not clear what might go wrong if these requirements were violated. This includes the path in the data that is to be sent within these limits, and that might result in failure of some other feature that requires that much data of its own. The alternative is to raise these limits to include the maximum amount of path data. That means that some implementations that satisfy the current requirements would fail to satisfy the new ones [1].

PMTU Discovery

The Path Maximum Transmission Unit (PMTU) in both IPv4 and IPv6 is defined as the minimum MTU of all links in a path. The discovery algorithm specified in RFC1191 (for IPv6) and RFC1981 (for IPv6) is indeed a straight forward algorithm for finding that quantity. Unfortunately, that is not what is needed if one is going to extend the path at each hop. The result will be that (a sender tries to send a packet of length 999 and gets back an error response complaining) the link can only send packets of up to size 1004! However, in both cases, the error response includes at least part of the original packet that provoked the response. If this includes enough data to compute both the length of the original IP packet and the length of the path at that link, then the sender will be able to adjust the PMTU correctly [1].

The preceding is one of several considerations that influence the choice of PEIP format. Since the error response, like other ICMP replies, includes the beginning of the packet that causes the reply, it would be convenient to put the path at the beginning of the packet and (re)define the data returned by ICMP to include this path. Another motivation for limiting the path length is that these ICMP replies carry only a limited amount of data from the original packet. The space devoted to the path is therefore deducted from that available for other data [1].

> **Tip:** Paths would be useful to detect (and thereby defeat) the attacks mentioned in RFC1981 in which the attacker sends Packet Too Big messages.

VULNERABILITIES OF PEIP

A key claimed advantage of PEIP is that the path is not controlled by the sender. Of course, this is not entirely true because paths can be forged too. While the sender cannot control the path that is recorded after the packet leaves him or her, he or she is able to control the path by which the packet supposedly reached him or her in the first place. That is, assuming no other router on the way alters the path, the recipient can definitely tell that the packet came via the sender, but the sender can, for whatever reason, claim that he or she got it from somewhere else by altering that part of the path [1].

There are really two cases to consider. The normal case is that an attacker controls a machine at the edge of the network. This turns out to be the easy case, as shown next. The more dangerous case is that the attacker controls a router that forwards traffic from many different places. He or she could then alter the paths of any packets forwarded by that router, or for that matter, manufacture new packets at that router with forged paths [1].

In many cases (probably the vast majority) it is easy to tell that this information is falsified. Suppose Alice traces the path of a packet she got from Bob. Bob says he got it from Charlie. Now suppose Alice sends a message to Charlie and he replies. One would expect that his reply would be marked with the same path as the original packet. If it is not then either someone forwarded differently than before (a different route), someone lied in answering the trace request, or someone forged the path of the original packet. In this case Alice knows that she got the original from Bob, so Bob is the only suspect. If Bob does not want to be caught by that sort of check then he has to claim that the packet at least came from someone who, given a packet addressed to Alice, would have forwarded it to Bob [1].

Suppose Bob can find such a neighbor. In fact, suppose it is actually Charlie. Bob can then send Alice packets that appear to come from Charlie. If Alice does not like these packets she cannot be sure whether they really come from Bob or Charlie. She can complain to both of them. She can also tell them both that she will filter out all packets she gets from Bob with a path indicating that they came to Bob from Charlie. Bob has now denied the service of communication from Charlie to Alice. Of course, he could have done that anyway by simply not forwarding packets from Charlie to Alice. The solution is for Charlie to stop sending his packets for Alice through Bob. He has to find a new path to Alice. If Bob now sends Alice a packet claiming to come from Charlie, the previously described check shows Alice that Bob is the forger, since replies from Charlie no longer come through Bob [1].

Of course, it is hoped that the case where a router is controlled by an attacker is very rare. Attackers who control routers can very likely cause even worse damage than forging source addresses. More likely, the attacker controls his or her own machine inside a LAN. He or she can try to send a packet with an arbitrary path, but the router that forwards that packet out of the LAN is required to discard that path [1].

> **Tip:** Of course, it should also filter the packet if the source address is not inside the LAN.

Even if the router fails to do this, the check in the preceding will always show that this path is a forgery. The reason is that nobody should be forwarding packets into the LAN in order to reach a location outside the LAN. No matter where (outside the LAN) the attacker claims he or she got the packet, the replies from that place will come back along a different route [1].

It is, of course, possible to forward outside traffic through a LAN. The fact that this makes it impossible to reliably trace the source of such packets seems sufficient justification for disallowing this. Technically, the router that accepts such packets must take the responsibility for those packets. It is supposed to do this by deleting the paths coming from the LAN. The alternative is to trust the machines in the LAN to provide accurate paths. If they prove untrustworthy then the router that accepts their paths will be seen to be cheating, which is more than adequate cause for shunning that router [1].

Secondary Path Forgery

Notice that the packets with two paths mostly originate from hosts, and these hosts might well be controlled by attackers. These attackers might therefore forge the second path. Even easier, they could forge both a source address and a (primary) path in a packet sent to a host in their own LAN. That host would then reply to the forged source address with the attacker's forged path as the second path. This is regarded as secondary, rather than primary, path forgery, since the ultimate objective is to send a packet with an incorrect secondary path. This sort of attack is relatively easy to counter by simply filtering the offending packets, all of which come from the network of the attacker [1].

For the sake of completeness, it is also possible to attack other machines in one's own LAN with forged primary or secondary paths. Of course, the administrator who is able to look at the traffic coming into or going out of the LAN will see immediately that these attacks are coming from the inside [1].

Example Attacks

An attacker who controls routers can simulate any of the attacks shown next. The means of identifying the attacking router was described in the preceding. That class of attack will be disregarded next. Instead, other attacks will be examined, and focus placed on how to distinguish one from another and how to filter the attack packets. It is not always possible to tell just from the paths in the attack packets who the attacker is. That is, one kind of attack can simulate another. The attack techniques considered are:

- Source: Forged source address (allowed by a router with ingress filtering misconfigured; failure to delete paths from the packets where this is required is regarded as worse than misconfigured, but actually attacking). Source forgery without use of an intermediary to reply to the forged source address is ignored since this seems comparatively trivial.

- Path2: Forged secondary paths (including forged paths inside a LAN). In this case there is no intermediary (or it is in the attacker's LAN).
- Slaves: Control over a large number of slaves to do the preceding [1].

Attackers, intermediate hosts and victims will always be labeled A, H and V, with subscripts to indicate multiple instances, as shown in Fig. 16-1 [1]. It's like Attack 2, but the same fake path (from possibly fake address x) is always used. The interesting point is that A3 and A4 are not distinguishable without contacting places that are (supposedly) sending the attack packets to H [1].

Slaves can give rise to much more ambiguity. The diagrams shown in Fig. 16-1, unfortunately, start to get unwieldy. In general the ambiguity arises from restricting the attack so that V gets the same sort of paths as would arise from a different attack, or of course, a restriction of another attack. These restrictions do not make it any harder to filter the attacks. Rather they show that it will require additional communication in order to be sure about the source of the attack, and therefore in order to punish it [1].

Slaves Doing Variants Of Attack 1

As a starting point, the slaves could all do attack 1. This attack is straight forward to filter, but more inconvenient since it has to be done for each slave. If efforts to enforce ingress filtering meet with success, this sort of attack will become very difficult to execute

Attack	Diagram	Path at victim	Filter
1. Source	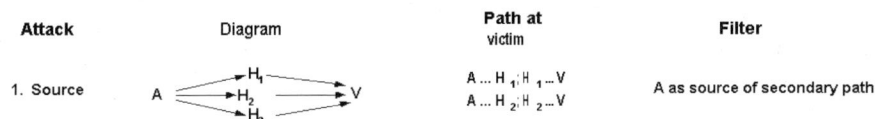	$A \ldots H_1 ; H_1 \ldots V$ $A \ldots H_2 ; H_2 \ldots V$	A as source of secondary path

A sends packets to many different hosts, all with V's address as the source. V sees a lot of different double paths, but all originate from A.

2. Path2		$x \ldots ; H \ldots V$ $y \ldots ; H \ldots V$	H as source of primary path

A sends packets to many different (primary) paths and V's address as the source to host H on his own LAN. (Equivalently, he could manufacture replies with forged second paths.) V sees many different secondary paths, but all packets share the same primary path from A's LAN.

3. Restricted Source		$A \ldots H ; H \ldots V$ $A \ldots H ; H \ldots V$ ...	A as source of secondary path OR H as source of primary path

Like Attack 1 but the same intermediate host is always used.

4. Restricted Path2		$x \ldots ; H ; \ldots V$ $y \ldots ; H ; \ldots V$ ...	x as source of secondary path OR H as source of primary path

Figure 16-1. Subscripts to indicate multiple instances.

and will be effectively limited to a small number of slaves. As an example of a restriction, the slaves could all use the same set of intermediate hosts. This would appear to V the same as attack 2. However, after each slave has sent one such packet either the attack must end or the secondary paths must start repeating, which is different from attack 2. Another problem with this attack is that it is likely to catch the attention of H who now seems to qualify as the victim since he is suffering at least as much as V [1].

Unfortunately, the fact that the restricted attack 5 can be distinguished from attack 2 is not very useful, since a restriction of attack 2 looks the same as the restricted attack 5. In this case the attacker simply reuses the same set of forged secondary paths over and over. Yet another approach is for the slaves to do this restriction of attack 2 [1].

Slaves Doing Variants Of Attack 2

The slaves could also do attack 2. In this case ingress filtering is no obstacle. This attack is again straight forward to filter, but inconvenient since it has to be done for each slave. The obvious restrictions include the slaves doing attack 4, or all of the slaves using the same set of forged secondary paths. All of these result in sets of paths arriving at V that have multiple interpretations [1].

Fragmentation

The fact that packets grow along the forwarding path suggests that attackers could send packets that will require fragmentation somewhere along the path. This is not a problem in IPv6 since routers do not do such fragmentation. In IPv4, however, they do. In a region where all links have the same MTU this could be used to force one router to do a lot of fragmentation where it never had to do any before. This would cause it to use more resources of various sorts, which could cause it to drop more packets, or for that matter could cause it to crash. The commonsense solution is that routers should limit the rate at which they are willing to do this (and all other expensive operations) so that they drop the expensive packets if necessary rather than the others. This is not regarded as an additional requirement for a router, since routers should already do this [1].

Flooding the Source Tracing Facility

Finally, the fact that a new service is proposed for decoding paths opens up new avenues for attack. Routers have to be able to respond to these requests. An attacker might attempt to overload a router with such requests. Of course, this is nothing new. The attacker could send all sorts of other packets to routers. The obvious answer is that the routers have to limit the amount of resources they expend on these requests to ensure that they can still do their primary job. The fact one attacker might try to use up this limit is to deny service to others is also a familiar problem. The solution to this and many other similar attacks is to use paths to allocate effort [1].

SUMMARY AND CONCLUSIONS

Source address forgery is widely recognized as one of the biggest security problems in the Internet today. This chapter focused on the forger's arsenal (hacking e-mail messages; censoring system logs; and, scrambling the routing tables); as well as, the enhancement of the Internet Protocol (IP), called Path Enhanced IP (PEIP), which is designed to eliminate source forgery. Specifically, PEIP makes it possible to recognize packets with forged source addresses, see where they come from, and, if necessary, even filter them. Ingress filtering, the much recommended but little used partial solution to source forgery, is still beneficial in the presence of PEIP. Furthermore, PEIP actually improves prospects for enforcement of ingress filtering. Finally, elimination of source forgery makes PEIP a more solid foundation than IP for a robust and secure Internet infrastructure [1].

REFERENCES

[1] Donald Cohen, K. Narayanaswamy and Fred Cohen, "Changing IP to Eliminate Source Forgery," Cs3, Inc., 5777 W Century Blvd., Suite 1185, Los Angeles, CA 90045, 2006.

Chapter 17

SHIELDING YOUR ASSETS

INTRODUCTION

Many enterprises, especially small and midsize enterprises, can afford neither the security products nor the requisite expertise to derive full benefits from them. What they need is an effective perimeter solution that does not require hardware, software or installation [1].

THE BUSINESS ISSUES

Internet-perimeter security is a high-wire act in which enterprise owners and executives must balance the price of security versus the risks and costs of failure. The price of security can run into tens of thousands of dollars for capital expenditures (CAPEX) and ongoing investments in:

- Security hardware such as firewalls, intrusion detection/prevention devices and sensors that must be installed, monitored and maintained
- Security software that must be installed, configured, and managed for updates and patches
- Full-time employees to install, monitor and manage the equipment and software around the clock
- Consultants using specialized security expertise to adapt these security solutions to the needs of the business [1]

The costs of failure are even more painful and include:

- Damage to the enterprise and its networked systems from threats such as worms, viruses, Distributed Denial of Service (DDoS), identity theft, phishing, directed and undirected attacks and unforeseen zero day threats
- Network downtime resulting in lower operations productivity and reduced employee efficiencies
- Lost revenue and lost customers from the interruption in enterprise continuity

- Damage to enterprise brand image and reputation that could lead to loss of credibility among stakeholders both inside (board of directors, employees) and outside (customers, partners, regulators, media) of the enterprise
- Legal consequences (stiff fines and jail time) stemming from non-compliance with government regulations that require enterprises (regardless of size) to protect the privacy and integrity of customer and employee data and other digital assets [1]

To attain and sustain Internet-perimeter security is especially challenging for small and midsize businesses (SMBs). For these enterprises, achieving levels of security that are comparable to that of a Fortune 500 enterprise may seem unrealistic. The costs of failure, however, are unacceptable (with less margin for error than many larger enterprises have) and include everything from the consequences outlined in the preceding to the potential demise of the enterprise. Today, SMBs must work hard to find the right balance of security investment and cyber-risk for their enterprises [1].

What is the typical security profile of an SMB? It depends. SMB security solutions are as varied as the businesses themselves. The SMB market covers a broad spectrum and means different things to different people: SMBs generally are considered to have from 100 to 5,000 employees. Their security setup may be as simple as having a firewall and a network administrator to having an array of equipment and a Network Operations Center (NOC) supporting multiple networks across geographically dispersed locations [1].

Even with this broad range of SMB security environments, there is still common ground in the security issues with which these enterprises must deal. SMBs all have needs, issues and challenges, pertaining to computer security that include:

- Security policy set-up, management, and governance
- Vulnerability shielding of assets and patch management
- Security resources, including in-house security expertise (or lack of same)
- The challenge of keeping up to date with infrastructure updates
- The difficulty of staying current on the dynamically changing threat environment
- Validation and remediation of security events
- Regulatory compliance (the need to satisfy the requirements of governmental regulations such as Sarbanes-Oxley Act of 2002, the Gramm-Leach-Bliley Act (GLBA), the Health Insurance Portability and Accountability Act (HIPAA), the Family Educational Rights and Privacy Act (FERPA), the Statement on Auditing Standards (SAS-70), California Senate Bill 1386 (SB1386), ISO 7009 and Canada's Personal Health Information Privacy Act (PHIPA))
- Pressure from various entities, including the enterprise's board, auditors, competitors, media and regulators [1]

CONVENTIONAL SECURITY SOLUTIONS

What choices do SMBs have when it comes to protecting their networked systems from Internet-based threats such as worms and viruses? Historically, small and midsize enterprises

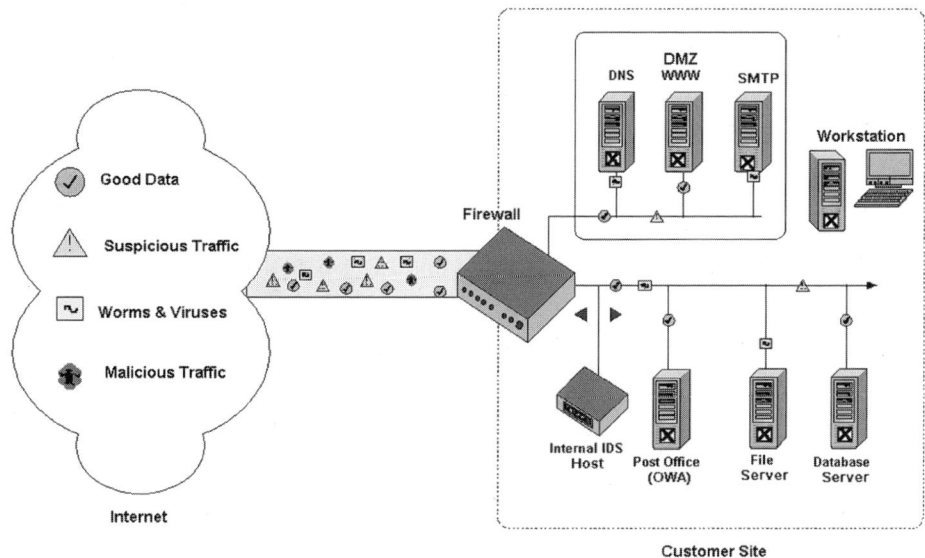

Figure 17-1. Conventional perimeter security.

have had limited affordable choices when protecting their information assets, managing threat profiles and safeguarding the full perimeter of their networked systems [1].

One option, as a starting point, is to conduct a security risk assessment to identify key security issues and vulnerabilities. Based upon the results of this assessment, the enterprise is likely to develop a security plan that includes installing hardware devices in conjunction with security software to protect both their internal and external (public facing) computer systems [1].

Depending on the enterprise's size, its financial and organizational resources, and how it chooses to prioritize security as a business issue, the security plan may end up as a relatively simple checklist or highly complex security strategy (see Fig. 17-1) [1]. For example, elements of the plan for perimeter security might include:

- Firewalls
- Encrypting files and messages
- Intrusion Detection Systems
- Using digital signatures to protect transactions: PGP/MD5
- Intrusion Prevention Systems
- Protecting logs with immutable files
- A demilitarized zone (DMZ)
- Adopting advanced routing protocols
- Patch and vulnerability management systems [1]

Installation and configuration of such premises-based equipment typically require CAPEX investments of tens of thousands of dollars, plus costly annual charges for maintenance of the equipment. Additionally, the enterprise needs expertise to understand the security event data, as well as for 24x7 monitoring. Around-the-clock security monitoring typically requires at least five to seven full-time employees who are certified security experts to understand, manage, and respond to security events. The enterprise could pay its Internet Service Provider (ISP) or hire a Managed Security Services Provider (MSSP) to do this monitoring and reporting. For many SMBs, MSSPs make sense because that can provide 24x7 coverage and protection for a fraction of the cost of internal resources. In addition, MSSPs see such a broad range of threats from all over the Internet (for many different clients and geographies), and they have the experience and expertise to act upon that data and prevent emerging threats, including worms and viruses [1].

MINIMAL RESOURCES = MINIMUM SECURITY

But what about SMBs with limited resources? Unfortunately, many small and midsize enterprises lack the requisite expertise and cannot afford to outsource security monitoring. These enterprises may rely on the network firewall as their primary enforcement point for their security policy. The firewall is intended to both protect the enterprise from malicious, Internet based activity and to facilitate business with others that are connected to the Internet. The firewall is a necessary component for any enterprise providing Internet-accessible services and for the safe and secure utilization of these services. A firewall, however, is only the first line of defense in a layered security program [1].

By definition, if an enterprise is to provide its employees, partners, suppliers and other stakeholders with Internet-accessible services, some paths or doors to these services must remain open to incoming traffic. As these business services increase and more doors are unlocked, firewall systems may become more open than originally intended. Unfortunately, in many cases, the burden of day-to-day network and systems operations does not allow for regular review and re-evaluation of enterprise services requirements and Internet security policies and practices. In these situations, the firewall can and will become an easily circumvented border on the perimeter of the network [1].

Although conventional firewalled networks may seem to be protected, many security compromises occur because of misconfigured firewalls or unpatched systems. Indeed, rigorous patch management has emerged as a fundamental driver for ensuring business continuity and network security. In today's environment, the time between recognition of a security vulnerability and exploitation of that vulnerability (via worms, viruses, or hackers) is accelerating to the point that zero day threats (that is, exploits occurring on the same day that a vulnerability is discovered) are a real possibility for every business [1].

Sole reliance on the firewall may leave these businesses exposed to vulnerabilities, undirected attacks, exploits from hackers, worms and viruses. Considering these vulnerabilities, SMBs cannot afford to be without some additional form of perimeter protection to augment the firewall [1].

THE NEXT GENERATION OF PERIMETER SECURITY

What many enterprises need (both large and small) is a fully functional layer of security in front of the existing IT security infrastructure. Ideally, this solution would be easy to use and require no changes to the enterprise's network infrastructure. In an ideal world, much of this security could be provided by the enterprise's Internet Service Provider. The ISP could analyze and filter the Internet traffic provided to their clients BEFORE the client sees the threat. Of course, because ISPs are organized and run as common carriers of telecommunications services, they are not likely (under their current business model) to interrupt or filter any of the network traffic that they provide. Thus, the mitigation of Internet-borne threats and risks are left to the individual enterprises [1].

These Internet-connected enterprises need the next generation of perimeter security (a buffer zone between their networked systems and the Internet to provide the same type of analysis and malicious Internet traffic filtering and blocking that could be performed at their ISP) before it is sent to their enterprise systems. This next generation of perimeter security (the buffer zone) should be designed to provide multiple layers of protection that work simultaneously to deliver [1]:

- Protection of information assets through a variety of security safeguards such as intrusion detection and prevention, early worm prevention, and distributed denial of service avoidance – without the need for additional hardware or software purchases
- Automated blocking of malicious traffic and known exploits and worms
- Proactive, vulnerability-shielding capability that blocks unforeseen threats and provides additional time to install critical patches from software vendors
- Clean Internet connections for optimized bandwidth
- Anti-virus and spam filtering for e-mail
- URL, content and application filtering
- A central repository for correlation, reporting and auditing of security-related activities (for regulatory compliance and data analysis)
- Simple and rapid implementation for full protection of the perimeter within minutes, rather than in days or weeks
- Real-time access and control to all security information events and response mechanisms, so that enterprise users can maintain ownership of their security
- Scalability to accommodate enterprise growth
- True affordability for small and midsize enterprises [1]

Finally, the next-generation of perimeter security should be priced so any size enterprise can afford to be secure. This next generation security solution should also be easy to activate – requiring no hardware to install, no software to configure, no devices to tune, no equipment to maintain, no training to implement and no expertise to operate. In short, the next generation of perimeter security should deliver enterprise-class perimeter security in a simple, affordable and effective manner (one that is particularly pain free to the SMBs that have very limited resources) but is scalable for enterprises of all sizes [1].

SUMMARY AND CONCLUSIONS

Ideally, Internet security should be built in by an enterprise's Internet Service Provider. An enterprise should be able to establish a public Internet presence and shield its information systems and critical assets in minutes – with no security hardware, no security devices, no security sensors, no security software, no security consultants and no installation of any of these security solutions. Unfortunately, in the real world, Internet-perimeter security solutions require expensive equipment and time-consuming installation by a team of full-time security experts. These conventional solutions require intensive capital expenditures for equipment and software, as well as significant investments in full-time employees or outside consultants to handle installation, maintenance, and monitoring. Finally, worst of all, conventional perimeter security solutions are typically of limited effectiveness [1].

REFERENCES

[1] "Internet-Perimeter Security With No Hardware, No Software and No Installation," © 2004 VigilantMinds Inc., VigilantMinds Inc., 4736 Penn Avenue, Pittsburgh, Pa 15224, 2004.

PART IX

AVOIDING DISRUPTION OF SERVICE TO MAINTAIN AVAILABILITY

Chapter 18

DENIAL-OF-SERVICE ATTACKS

INTRODUCTION

DoS attacks are very common but they are not a joking matter. In the US, they can be a serious federal crime under the National Information Infrastructure Protection Act of 1996 (http://www.usdoj.gov/criminal/cybercrime/compcrime.html) with penalties that include years of imprisonment, and many countries have similar laws. For example, Jeffrey Lee Parson, the 19 year old who wrote a variant of the Blaster worm and used it to attack 48,000 computers, was sentenced to 18 months in prison in January 2005, and had to pay a substantial fine. At the very least, offenders can lose their Internet Service Provider (ISP) accounts, get suspended or fired if school/work resources are involved, etc. [1].

Often the victims are people on Internet Relay Chat (IRC) (http://www.irchelp.org/), but DoS attacks do not involve IRC servers in any way, so IRC operators (IRC ops) (http://www.irchelp.org/irchelp/ircd/opermyth.html) cannot stop or punish the offenders. If you are attacked, try not to take it personally and do not retaliate, or else you will be breaking the law yourself and probably just inviting a much more determined new attack. Instead, read this chapter thoroughly to learn more about these attacks, make sure your computer is patched against known weaknesses, and if necessary consider getting some protective firewall software. Denial of service should not be confused with other attacks (http://www.irchelp.org/irchelp/security/trojanterms.html) like viruses, Trojan Horses, and cracking or hacking. There are two types of DoS attacks, both of which are described in the next:

1. Operating System attacks, which target bugs in specific operating systems and can be fixed with patches.
2. Networking attacks, which exploit inherent limitations of networking and may require firewall protection [1].

OPERATING SYSTEM ATTACKS

These attacks exploit bugs in a specific operating system (OS), which is the basic software that your computer runs, such as Windows XP or 2003. In general, when these problems are identified, they are promptly fixed by the company such as Microsoft, so if you frequently apply the latest security patches, you greatly reduce this vulnerability. All Windows users should regularly visit Microsoft's Windows Update Site (http://update.microsoft.com/windowsupdate/v6/thanks.aspx?ln=en&&thankspage=5) which automatically checks to see if you need any updates. If possible, set your PC to check for updates automatically and at least weekly [1].

NETWORKING ATTACKS

These attacks exploit inherent limitations of networking to disconnect you from the IRC server or your ISP, but don't usually cause your computer to crash. Generally it doesn't matter what kind of operating system you use, and there is essentially nothing you can do personally to defend against the attacks. Even large companies like Yahoo, Amazon, and Microsoft have been crippled by such large scale attacks. Network attacks include outright floods of data to overwhelm the finite capacity of your connection. This is a spoofed unreach/redirect aka "click" which tricks your computer into thinking there is a network failure and voluntarily breaking the connection; and, a whole new generation of distributed denial of service attacks (although these are seldom used against individuals unless you've really upset somebody) [1].

Just because you got disconnected with some unusual error message such as the ubiquitous "Connection reset by peer" (external link (http://trout.snt.utwente.nl/ubbthreads/showflat.php?Cat=&Board=connectionissues&Number=38665)) for Windows users doesn't mean you got attacked. Almost all disconnects are due to natural network failures. On the other hand, you should feel suspicious if you get disconnected repeatedly, especially if it happens only when you frequent certain IRC channels or talk to certain people [1].

> **Note:** If that's the case, shouldn't you really just avoid these troublemakers?

What can you do about networking attacks? If the attacker is flooding you, you essentially must have a better connection than he or she does, or get your ISP involved in protecting you [1].

IRC users can hide their actual hostname/IP by connecting indirectly via a relay or proxy, which is a separate account or computer which acts as an intermediary so that you appear to be using a different account entirely. This can be effective against small attacks especially if you run a relay on a shell service account which tends to have more bandwidth than the attacker's connection. Of course, the attacker can still use many different accounts to conduct a distributed DoS attack, just like how they took down the major e-commerce enterprises repeatedly in recent years [1].

> **Note:** There is no such thing as a free proxy – those are just unsecured computers whose owners didn't set up their proxy security properly, or worse yet, the machine has been compromised. Using

those machines is both illegal and inappropriate – after all, would you like it if dozens of random strangers were stealing your processor, memory, and bandwidth?

So what can your ISP to do to help? Your ISP can set up a firewall which stops the flood before it ever gets to you. If the attacks are serious enough, your ISP may even involve law enforcement to help catch the attackers. Unfortunately, many ISPs are understaffed or inexperienced at handling the huge number of both false and legitimate complaints filed, so customers get ignored and nothing is done. If that is the case, you essentially need to steer clear of the attacker and wait for them to get bored (a surprisingly effective technique) or change ISPs [1].

Finally, what about setting up your own firewall? This is one of the most frequently misunderstood issues in network security. Having your own personal firewall is useless against an external flood. At best, it may let you record the source of the attacks. If the attacker is dumb enough to be using his or her own account to attack you, then you may be able to get his account shut down. In most cases, however, the attacks come from tens or hundreds of computers which have been hijacked through viruses, so the best you can do is share those logs with your ISP and hope they can block the attacks for you. That is why it is not recommend that average users go and download personal software firewalls blindly! The subject of firewalls is covered later in this book [1].

SUMMARY AND CONCLUSIONS

The purpose of this chapter was to provide information and defenses against Denial of Service (DoS) attacks, which cause networked computers to disconnect from the network or just outright crash due to the delivery of viruses and bombs (nukes) via the Internet and data flooding. Finally, These attacks are sometimes also called "nukes", "hacking", or "cyber-attacks", but in this chapter, the technically correct term of DoS attacks was used [1].

REFERENCES

[1] Joseph Lo, "Denial of Service or "Nuke" Attacks," © IRCHELP.ORG, Duke Advanced Imaging Labs (DAILabs) of the Department of Radiology of Duke University Medical Center, March 12, 2005.

Chapter 19

CONSTRUCTING YOUR BASTIONS

INTRODUCTION

The largest security team at the largest enterprise is still many orders of magnitude smaller than the population attempting to break into the enterprise's network. Why? The Internet [1]!

In most cases, would-be intruders use a number of small programs to probe your host computer for weaknesses. When malicious hackers find a hole, they use other tools to exploit the vulnerability and gain access to your network. To protect yourself from these black hats, it's important to see your own system from the perspective of a person with the necessary tools. Only then can you effectively fortify your network against probing and potential attacks [1].

HOST PROBING

When probing a host machine, the goal is to find out as much information as possible about the machine. Using that information, black hats can further probe and even attack the remote machine. The most critical pieces of information found during a probe include the host's operating system and the available applications on the computer. With that information, the crackers can discern which vulnerabilities to exploit [1].

With each probing tool and its respective countermeasures, the machine becomes more secure, as it is more difficult for probing software to see it. The less information someone can get about your machine, the better [1].

PORT SCANNING

To learn which applications are potentially exploitable on a machine without having to log into the machine, an intruder can use a port scanner. The port scanner steps through all the network ports on a remote machine, attempting to establish a connection to each one, producing a brute-force report that lists which services are running and accessible to the machine doing the probing [1].

While there are many port scanning tools, you may want to use one that is free. It could be a simple Unix program that gives feedback on which ports it was able to connect to and, if possible, which protocols are related to those ports. The protocols often indicate that a potentially exploitable application is connected to that port. For example, Web servers (which use the HTTP protocol) are connected to port 80 on most computers. If the scanning tool can establish a connection to port 80, you can generally assume that the HTTP protocol is related to that port on that machine [1].

OS FINGERPRINTING

The second step is to learn which operating system the remote machine is running, using a technique called OS fingerprinting. It was once the case that, to determine the OS running on a remote machine, one could use a primitive tool like telnet. Connecting to another computer with this utility would yield basic information regarding the remote system's available services. From that information, you could infer, with some degree of accuracy, which OS was running on it [1].

To take the guesswork out of fingerprinting, developers invented a new generation of tools that use creatively formed IP packets to test for behavioral patterns in a remote machine's IP stack. The software sends packets with particular characteristics that cause only certain operating systems to handle them in predictable ways. Each packet/response pair further limits which operating systems the remote machine could be, until the tool has no further ability to narrow the OS options and it reports back one or more choices [1].

The best tool for this type of OS fingerprinting is one that incorporates multiple techniques used in the area of packet-based OS detection and now looks for particular signatures associated with operating systems that can be used to classify types of remote machines. If the software responds with multiple OS choices, it will probably be the same base OS and different version numbers [1].

The last step in securing your system from host probing, after port scanning and OS fingerprinting, is to learn which exploits exist for those combinations and which countermeasures can defend against them. Many applications on a given OS have known vulnerabilities [1].

For example, you can further explore port 25, the standard port for the Simple Mail Transport Protocol (SMTP), using the relaycheck.pl utility. By doing so, you'll find out whether the system uses the sendmail Mail Delivery Agent (MDA), and whether that agent is misconfigured. You can also determine if the agent can be used as an SMTP relay, and whether it's running sendmail 8.9.3. From there, it's possible to use the agent to send spam or even get access to the system [1].

Further checks might uncover that the phf (phone book) utility resides in the cgi-bin/ directory. Determining which vulnerabilities exist and how to patch them is a matter of doing your research. One good place to start is the SecurityFocus site (http://www.securityfocus.com/). You'll find exploits organized by OS, and other information on common tools and code used by black hats. The exploits are provided there to help secure a site, not to break into it. However, these exploits, like any tool, can also be put to bad use [1].

COUNTERMEASURES

To counter potential attacks, for example, you can install IP Filter (http://coombs.anu.edu.au/~avalon/) to mask some of the remote packet OS fingerprinting. The IP Filter utility is a kernel network module that intercepts and analyzes incoming and outgoing packets on a host and determines whether the packets are supposed to be received by or sent from the host. IP Filter also looks for poorly formed packets, illegal packet types, and packets from impossible networks – like the loopback network, for instance. It is, in some ways, a host-based firewall package [1].

Another way to safeguard your machine is to turn off the inetd program. Standard Unix installations often include inetd and cause it to be started automatically when you turn the machine on. The inetd program supports standard telnet and FTP servers; however, a secure, external server doesn't need it. If you disable inetd, you can ensure that both telnet and FTP capabilities are still there by installing a public domain FTP server and sshd (secure remote access software (http://erdelynet.com/2004/08/30/cygwin/see-cygwincom-for-cygwin-ssh-docs/)) [1].

A public domain FTP server's strength is that the FTP daemon runs like a daemon; for example, it doesn't require another program running in the back- ground. The sshd's strength is that it uses encrypted sessions for remote management, whereas telnet transmits passwords in plain text [1].

Hackers frequently exploit applications through odd packet types sent to them in their native form. This introduces another scenario: IP stack smashing. This is the practice of sending some type of IP packet to a host that causes the host's OS to either crash the network kernel module, run a program encapsulated in the packets or make a change through a buffer overflow. You can sidestep stack smashing by making some additions to your ipf.conf file to note that packets with any extra options set should be blocked and logged. Per the IP specification, IP packets have header data that includes option fields for the packets themselves. For instance, applications can set the transmission priority of various packets by modifying the option fields. These option fields were originally meant for flexibility in a developing protocol. In practice, they remain unused and can be blocked without significant side effects [1].

THE BOTTOM LINE

To protect your site against a growing community of black-hat hackers, you have to think like they do and see the same information. By following a few short steps, you can fortify what was once an insecure machine, making it secure from the inside.

Finally, protecting your system is often about appearances. In the same way that a blinking car-alarm light and a sticker on the window notifies potential thieves that the automobile is protected, a server with few available applications and an OS that can't be detected shows attackers that your site is secure. You're increasing the chances the attacker will move on. But if there's plenty of available data, the attacker will be that much more dedicated to breaking the site [1].

SUMMARY AND CONCLUSIONS

From computer viruses to identity theft to hacker attacks and beyond, the Internet's benefits (and risks) expand as more and more information moves online. Do you have an inside track on the technology to use to protect your enterprise and your customers? What cool new tools protect your enterprise? What keeps you up at night? Finally, do you imagine the cracker horde peeking over your firewall, ready to storm the bastions with smart MUAs, anti-virus toolsets and the imposing of quotas on processes, files and accounts? This chapter answered all of those questions [1].

REFERENCES

[1] John Stewart, "SD Secure Start: January 2004 – Outside Looking In," Copyright © 2006 CMP Media, LLC, CMP Media LLC, 600 Community Drive, Manhasset, NY 11030, May 14, 2004.

Chapter 20

THE IMPORTANCE OF FIREWALLS

INTRODUCTION

If you have been using the Internet for any length of time, and especially if you work at a larger enterprise and browse the Web while you are at work, you have probably heard the term firewall used. If you have a fast Internet connection into your home (either a DSL connection or a cable modem), you may have found yourself hearing about firewalls for your home network as well. It turns out that a small home network has many of the same security issues that a large enterprise network does. You can use a firewall to protect your home network and family from offensive Web sites and potential hackers as shown in Fig. 20-1 [1].

Basically, a firewall is a barrier to keep destructive forces away from your property. In fact, that's why its called a firewall. Its job is similar to a physical firewall that keeps a fire from spreading from one area to the next. As you read through this chapter, you will learn more about the importance of firewalls, how they work and what kinds of threats they can protect you from, how to use a packet filter to shield against bombardment, and how to use application proxies to manage Internet communications [1].

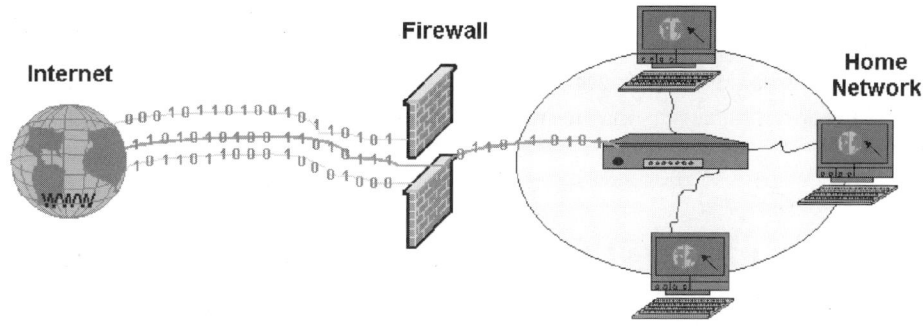

Figure 20-1. Protecting your home network.

WHAT IT DOES

A firewall is simply a program or hardware device that filters the information coming through the Internet connection into your private network or computer system. If an incoming packet of information is flagged by the filters, it is not allowed to get through [1].

By now, you probably know a good bit about how data moves on the Internet, and you can easily see how a firewall helps protect computers inside a large enterprise. Let's say that you work at an enterprise with 500 employees. The enterprise will therefore have hundreds of computers that all have network cards connecting them together. In addition, the enterprise will have one or more connections to the Internet through something like T1 or T3 lines. Without a firewall in place, all of those hundreds of computers are directly accessible to anyone on the Internet. A person who knows what he or she is doing can probe those computers, try to make FTP connections to them, try to make telnet connections to them and so on. If one employee makes a mistake and leaves a security hole, hackers can get to the machine and exploit the hole [1].

With a firewall in place, the landscape is much different. An enterprise will place a firewall at every connection to the Internet (for example, at every T1 line coming into the enterprise). The firewall can implement security rules. For example, one of the security rules inside the enterprise might be: Out of the 500 computers inside this enterprise, only one of them is permitted to receive public FTP traffic. Allow FTP connections only to that one computer and prevent them on all others [1].

An enterprise can set up rules like this for FTP servers, Web servers, Telnet servers and so on. In addition, the enterprise can control how employees connect to Web sites, whether files are allowed to leave the enterprise over the network and so on. A firewall gives an enterprise tremendous control over how people use the network [1]. Firewalls use one or more of three methods to control traffic flowing in and out of the network:

- Packet filtering: Packets (small chunks of data) are analyzed against a set of filters. Packets that make it through the filters are sent to the requesting system and all others are discarded.
- Proxy service: Information from the Internet is retrieved by the firewall and then sent to the requesting system and vice versa.
- Stateful inspection: A newer method that doesn't examine the contents of each packet but instead compares certain key parts of the packet to a database of trusted information. Information traveling from inside the firewall to the outside is monitored for specific defining characteristics, then incoming information is compared to these characteristics. If the comparison yields a reasonable match, the information is allowed through. Otherwise it is discarded [1].

MAKING THE FIREWALL FIT

Firewalls are customizable. This means that you can add or remove filters based on several conditions. Some of these are:

- IP addresses
- Domain names
- Protocols
- Ports
- Specific words and phrases [1]

IP addresses

Each machine on the Internet is assigned a unique address called an IP address. IP addresses are 32-bit numbers, normally expressed as four "octets" in a "dotted decimal number." A typical IP address looks like this: 216.27.61.137. For example, if a certain IP address outside the enterprise is reading too many files from a server, the firewall can block all traffic to or from that IP address [1].

Domain Names

Because it is hard to remember the string of numbers that make up an IP address, and because IP addresses sometimes need to change, all servers on the Internet also have human-readable names, called domain names. For example, it is easier for most of you to remember www.howstuffworks.com than it is to remember 216.27.61.137. An enterprise might block all access to certain domain names, or allow access only to specific domain names [1].

Protocols

The protocol is the pre-defined way that someone who wants to use a service talks with that service. The someone could be a person, but more often it is a computer program like a Web browser. Protocols are often text, and simply describe how the client and server will have their conversation. The http in the Web's protocol. Some common protocols that you can set firewall filters for include:

- IP (Internet Protocol): The main delivery system for information over the Internet
- TCP (Transmission Control Protocol): Used to break apart and rebuild information that travels over the Internet
- HTTP (Hyper Text Transfer Protocol): Used for Web pages
- FTP (File Transfer Protocol): Used to download and upload files
- UDP (User Datagram Protocol): Used for information that requires no response, such as streaming audio and video
- ICMP (Internet Control Message Protocol): Used by a router to exchange the information with other routers
- SMTP (Simple Mail Transport Protocol): Used to send text-based information (e-mail)
- SNMP (Simple Network Management Protocol): Used to collect system information from a remote computer
- Telnet: Used to perform commands on a remote computer [1]

An enterprise might set up only one or two machines to handle a specific protocol and ban that protocol on all other machines [1].

Ports

Any server machine makes its services available to the Internet using numbered ports, one for each service that is available on the server. For example, if a server machine is running a Web (HTTP) server and an FTP server, the Web server would typically be available on port 80, and the FTP server would be available on port 21. An enterprise might block port 21 access on all machines but one inside the c enterprise [1].

Specific Words And Phrases

This can be anything. The firewall will sniff (search through) each packet of information for an exact match of the text listed in the filter. For example, you could instruct the firewall to block any packet with the word "X-rated" in it. The key here is that it has to be an exact match. The "X-rated" filter would not catch "X rated" (no hyphen). But you can include as many words, phrases and variations of them as you need [1].

Built In Firewall

Some operating systems come with a firewall built in. Otherwise, a software firewall can be installed on the computer in your home that has an Internet connection. This computer is considered a gateway because it provides the only point of access between your home network and the Internet [1].

Hardware Firewall

With a hardware firewall, the firewall unit itself is normally the gateway. A good example is the Linksys Cable/DSL router. It has a built-in Ethernet card and hub. Computers in your home network connect to the router, which in turn is connected to either a cable or DSL modem. You configure the router via a Web-based interface that you reach through the browser on your computer. You can then set any filters or additional information [1].

Hardware firewalls are incredibly secure and not very expensive. Home versions that include a router, firewall and Ethernet hub for broadband connections can be found for well under $100 [1].

WHAT IT PROTECTS YOU FROM

There are many creative ways that unscrupulous people use to access or abuse unprotected computers. Some of the items in the following list are hard, if not impossible, to filter using a firewall. While some firewalls offer virus protection, it is worth the investment to install anti-virus software on each computer. And, even though it is annoying, some spam is going to get through your firewall as long as you accept e-mail [1].

- Remote login
- Application backdoors
- SMTP session hijacking
- Operating system bugs
- Denial of service
- E-mail bombs
- Macros
- Viruses
- Spam
- Redirect bombs
- Source routing [1]

Remote Login

Remote Login is when someone is able to connect to your computer and control it in some form. This can range from being able to view or access your files to actually running programs on your computer [1].

Application Backdoors

Some programs have special features that allow for remote access. Others contain bugs that provide a backdoor, or hidden access, that provides some level of control of the program [1].

SMTP Session Hijacking

SMTP is the most common method of sending e-mail over the Internet. By gaining access to a list of e-mail addresses, a person can send unsolicited junk e-mail (spam) to thousands of users. This is done quite often by redirecting the e-mail through the SMTP server of an unsuspecting host, and making the actual sender of the spam difficult to trace [1].

Operating System Bugs

Like applications, some operating systems have backdoors. Others provide remote access with insufficient security controls or have bugs that an experienced hacker can take advantage of [1].

Denial Of Service

This type of attack is nearly impossible to counter. What happens is that the hacker sends a request to the server to connect to it. When the server responds with an acknowledgement and tries to establish a session, it cannot find the system that made the request. By inundating a server with these unanswerable session requests, a hacker causes the server to slow to a crawl or eventually crash [1].

E-mail Bombs

An e-mail bomb is usually a personal attack. Someone sends you the same e-mail hundreds or thousands of times until your e-mail system cannot accept any more messages [1].

Macros

To simplify complicated procedures, many applications allow you to create a script of commands that the application can run. This script is known as a macro. Hackers have taken advantage of this to create their own macros that, depending on the application, can destroy your data or crash your computer [1].

Viruses

Probably the most well-known threat is computer viruses. A virus is a small program that can copy itself to other computers. This way it can spread quickly from one system to the next. Viruses range from harmless messages to erasing all of your data [1].

Spam

Typically harmless but always annoying, spam is the electronic equivalent of junk mail. Spam can be dangerous though. Quite often it contains links to Web sites. Be careful of clicking on these because you may accidentally accept a cookie that provides a backdoor to your computer [1].

Redirect Bombs

Hackers can use ICMP to change (redirect) the path information takes by sending it to a different router. This is one of the ways that a denial of service attack is set up [1].

Source Routing

In most cases, the path a packet travels over the Internet (or any other network) is determined by the routers along that path. But the source providing the packet can arbitrarily specify the route that the packet should travel. Hackers sometimes take advantage of this to make information appear to come from a trusted source or even from inside the network! Most firewall products disable source routing by default [1].

Establishing The Level Of Security

The level of security you establish will determine how many of these threats can be stopped by your firewall. The highest level of security would be to simply block everything. Obviously that defeats the purpose of having an Internet connection. But a common rule of thumb is to block everything, then begin to select what types of traffic you will allow.

You can also restrict traffic that travels through the firewall so that only certain types of information, such as e-mail, can get through. This is a good rule for enterprises that have an experienced network administrator that understands what the needs are and knows exactly what traffic to allow through. For most of you, it is probably better to work with the defaults provided by the firewall developer unless there is a specific reason to change it [1].

One of the best things about a firewall from a security standpoint is that it stops anyone on the outside from logging onto a computer in your private network. While this is a big deal for enterprises, most home networks will probably not be threatened in this manner. Still, putting a firewall in place provides some peace of mind [1].

PROXY SERVERS AND DMZ

A function that is often combined with a firewall is a proxy server. The proxy server is used to access Web pages by the other computers. When another computer requests a Web page, it is retrieved by the proxy server and then sent to the requesting computer. The net effect of this action is that the remote computer hosting the Web page never comes into direct contact with anything on your home network, other than the proxy server [1].

Proxy servers can also make your Internet access work more efficiently. If you access a page on a Web site, it is cached (stored) on the proxy server. This means that the next time you go back to that page, it normally doesn't have to load again from the Web site. Instead it loads instantaneously from the proxy server [1].

There are times that you may want remote users to have access to items on your network. Some examples are:

- Web site
- Online business
- FTP download and upload area [1]

In cases like this, you may want to create a DMZ (Demilitarized Zone). Although this sounds pretty serious, it really is just an area that is outside the firewall. Think of DMZ as the front yard of your house. It belongs to you and you may put some things there, but you would put anything valuable inside the house where it can be properly secured [1].

Setting up a DMZ is very easy. If you have multiple computers, you can choose to simply place one of the computers between the Internet connection and the firewall. Most of the software firewalls available will allow you to designate a directory on the gateway computer as a DMZ.

Finally, once you have a firewall in place, you should test it. A great way to do this is to go to http://www.grc.com and try their free Shields Up! security test. You will get immediate feedback on just how secure your system is [1]!

SUMMARY AND CONCLUSIONS

Finally, as you read this chapter, you learned about the importance of firewalls. This included how they work and what kinds of threats they can protect you from, how to use a packet filter to shield against bombardment, and how to use application proxies to manage Internet communications [1].

REFERENCES

[1] Jeff Tyson, " How Firewalls Work," © 1998–2006 HowStuffWorks, Inc., HowStuffWorks.com, c/o Convex Group, Inc., One Capital City Plaza, 3350 Peachtree Road, Suite 1500, Atlanta, GA 30326, 2006.

PART X

CONFIGURING OPERATING SYSTEM AND NETWORK SECURITY

Chapter 21

OPERATING SYSTEMS THAT POSE SECURITY RISKS

INTRODUCTION

The threats to international security posed by operating systems (OSs) are significant, and must be addressed quickly. This chapter discusses here in turn the problem in principle, OSs and its actions in relation to those principles, and the social and economic implications for risk management and policy [1].

THE PROBLEM IN PRINCIPLE

Computing is essential to industrialized societies. As time passes, all societal functions become more deeply dependent on it: power infrastructure, food distribution, air traffic control, emergency services, banking, telecommunications, and virtually every other large scale endeavor is today coordinated and controlled by networked computers. Attacking national infrastructures is also done with computers – often hijacked computers. Thus, threats to computing infrastructures are explicitly and inherently risk harm to those very societies in proportion to those society's dependence on them. A prior history of catastrophe is not required to make such a finding. You should not have to wait until people die to address risks of the scale and scope discussed here. So, with the preceding in mind, this part of the chapter focuses on the following:

- Your society's infrastructure can no longer function without computers and networks.
- The sum of the world's networked computers is a rapidly increasing force multiplier.
- A monoculture of networked computers is a convenient and susceptible reservoir of platforms from which to launch attacks; these attacks can and do cascade.
- This susceptibility cannot be mitigated without addressing the issue of that monoculture.
- Risk diversification is a primary defense against aggregated risk when that risk cannot otherwise be addressed; monocultures create aggregated risk like nothing else.
- The growth in risk is chiefly amongst unsophisticated users and is accelerating.

- Uncorrected market failures can create and perpetuate societal threat; the existence of societal threat may indicate the need for corrective intervention [1].

Regardless of where or how it is used, computing increases the capabilities and the power of those who use it. Using strategic or military terminology that means what it sounds like, computing is a force multiplier to those who use them – it magnifies their power, for good or ill. The best estimates of the number of network connected computers show an increase of 50% per year on a worldwide basis. By most general measures what you can buy for the same amount of money doubles every eighteen months ("Moore's Law"). With a conservative estimate of a four year lifetime for a computer (in other words, consumers replace computers every four years on average) the total computing power on the Internet therefore increases by a factor of 2.7 per annum (or doubles every 10 months). If a constant fraction of computers are under threat of misuse, then the force available to misusers will thus double every 10 months [1]. In other words, the power available to misusers (computer hackers, in popular parlance) is rising both because what they can buy grows in power per dollar spent and because the total number of networked computers grows, too [1].

> **Note:** This analysis does not even include attacks enabled by storage capacity, which doubles in price-performance twice as fast as CPU (doubles every nine months rather than eighteen).

Internetworked computing power makes communication feasible. Communication is of such high value that it has been the focus of much study and much conjecture and not just recently. For one-way broadcast communication, the value of the network itself rises proportionally to N, the potential number of listeners ("Sarnoff's Law"). By way of example, advertisers pay for television time in rough proportion to the number of people viewing a given program [1].

For two-way interactive communications (such as between fax machines or personal email) the value of the network rises proportionally to N2, the square of the potential number of users ("Metcalfe's Law"). Thus, if the number of people on email doubles in a given year, the number of possible communications rises by a factor of four [1].

Growth in communications rises even more when people can organize in groups, so that any random group of people can communicate with another. Web pages, electronic mailing lists and online newsgroups are good examples of such communications. In these cases, the value of the network rises proportionally to 2N, the potential number of groups being an exponential growth in N ("Reed's Law") [1].

Assume for now that the Internet is somewhere between the Metcalfe model, where communications vary according to the square of the number of participants (N^2), and the Reed model, where communications vary according to two raised to the Nth power (2^N) [1].

If you make this assumption, then the potential value of communications that the Internet enables will rise somewhere between 1.52 = 2.3 and 21.5 = 2.8 times per annum. These laws are likely not precisely accurate. Nonetheless, their wide acceptance and historic record show that they are good indicators of the importance of communication technology [1].

To extend this simple mathematical model one final step, you have to assume so far that all communications are good, and assigned to the value of the network a positive number. Nonetheless, it is obvious that not all communications (over computer networks, at least) are positive. Hackers, crackers, terrorists and garden-variety criminals use the network to defraud, spy and generally wreak havoc on a continual basis. To these communications you should assign a negative value [1].

The fraction of communications that has positive value is one crucial measure, and the absolute number of negative communications is another. Both are dependent on the number of networked devices in total. This growth in the number of networked devices, however, is almost entirely at the "edges" of networked computing – the desktop, the workstation, the home, the embedded system, the automated apparatus. In other words, the growth in "N" is not in the core infrastructure of the Internet where highly trained specialists watch over costly equipment with an eye towards preventing and responding to attacks. Growth, rather, is occurring mostly among ordinary consumers and non-technical personnel who are the most vulnerable to illegal intrusions, viruses, Trojan horse programs and the like. This growth at the periphery, furthermore, is accelerating as mobile, wireless devices come into their own and bring with them still more vulnerabilities [1].

Viruses, worms, Trojan horses and the like permit malicious attackers to seize control of large numbers of computers at the edge of the network. Malicious attackers do not, in other words, have to invest in these computers themselves – they have only to exploit the vulnerabilities in other people's investments [1].

Barring such physical events as 9/11, an attack on computing is a set of communications that take advantage of latent flaws already then present in those computers' software. Given enough knowledge of how a piece of software works, an attacker can force it to do things for which it was never designed. Such abuse can take many forms; a naturalist would say that attacks are a broad genus with many species. Within this genus of attacks, species include everything from denial of service, to escalation of authority, to diversion of funds or data, and on. As in nature, some species are more common than others [1].

Similarly, not all attacks are created equal. An annoying message that pops up once a year on screen to tell a computer user that he or she has been infected by Virus XYZ is no more than that; an annoyance. Other exploitations cost society many, many dollars in lost data, lost productivity and projects destroyed from data crashes. Examples are many and familiar including the well known ILOVE YOU, NIMDA, and Slammer attacks not to mention taking over users' machines for spamming, porn distribution, and so forth. Still other vulnerabilities, though exploited every day and costing society substantial sums of time and money, seldom appear in the popular press. According to industry analysts, global damage from malicious software inflicted as much as $507 billion in global economic damage in 2006. The the SoBig worm, which helped make August, 2003, the costliest month in terms of economic damage, was responsible for nearly $30 billion in damage alone [1].

For an attack to be a genuine societal-scale threat, either the target must be unique and indispensable (a military or government computer, authoritative time lookup, the computer handling emergency response (911) calls, airport flight control), or the attack must be one which once triggered uncontrollably cascades from one machine to the next. The NIMDA and Slammer worms that attacked millions of Windows-based computers were examples of such "cascade failure" – they spread from one to another computer at high rates. Why? Because, these worms did not have to guess much about the target computers, because nearly all computers have the same vulnerabilities [1].

Unique, valuable targets are identifiable, so you, as part of society, can concentrate force around them. Given enough people and training (a tall order to be sure), it is possible to protect the unique and core assets. Advanced societies have largely made these investments, and unmitigated failures do not generally occur in these systems [1].

Not so outside this core: As a practical and perhaps obvious fact, the risk of cascade failure rises at the edges of the network where end users are far more likely to be deceived by a clever virus writer or a random intruder. To put the problem in military terms, you are the most vulnerable when the ratio of available operational skill to available force multiplication is minimized and thus effective control is weakest. Low available skill coupled to high potential force multiplication is a fair description of what is today accumulating on the periphery of the computing infrastructures of every advanced nation. In plainer terms, the power on the average desktop goes up very fast while the spread of computers to new places ensures the average skill of the user goes down. The average user is not, does not want to be, and should not need to be a computer security expert any more than an airplane passenger wants to or should need to be an expert in aerodynamics or piloting. This very lack of sophisticated end users renders society at risk to a threat that is becoming more prevalent and more sophisticated [1].

Regardless of the topic (computing versus electric power generation versus air defense) survivability is all about preparing for failure so as to survive it. Survivability, whether as a concept or as a measure, is built on two pillars: replicated provisioning and diversified risk. Replicated ("redundant") provisioning ensures that any entity's activities can be duplicated by some other activity; high availability database systems are such an example in computing just as backup generators are in electric power. The ability of redundant systems to protect against random faults is cost effective and well documented [1].

By contrast, redundancy has little ability to protect against cascade failure; having more computers with the same vulnerabilities cannot help if an attack can reach them all. Protection from cascade failure is instead the province of risk diversification – that is, using more than one kind of computer or device, more than one brand of operating system, which in turn assures that attacks will be limited in their effectiveness. This fundamental principle assures that, like farmers who grow more than one crop, those of you who depend on computers will not see them all fail when the next blight hits. This sort of diversification is widely accepted in almost every sector of society from finance to agriculture to telecommunications. In the broadest sense, economic diversification is as much the hallmark of free societies as monopoly is the hallmark of central planning [1].

Governments in free market societies have intervened in market failures – preemptively where failure was to be intolerable and responsively when failure had become self evident. In free market economies as in life, some failure is essential; the "creative destruction" of markets builds more than it breaks. Wise governments are those able to distinguish that which must be tolerated as it cannot be changed from that which must be changed as it cannot be tolerated. The reapportionment of risk and responsibility through regulatory intervention embodies that wisdom in action. If governments are going to be responsible for the survivability of your technological infrastructure, then whatever governments do will have to take Microsoft's dominance into consideration [1].

MICROSOFT

Near-monopoly dominance of computing by Microsoft is obvious beyond the findings of any court. That percentage of dominance is at peak in the periphery of the computing infrastructure of all industrial societies. According to industry analysts, Microsoft Windows represented 98 percent of the consumer client software sold in the United States in 2006. Industry analysts estimates Microsoft Windows' market share exceeds 101 percent. Its Internet Explorer and Office Suite applications share similar control of their respective markets. The tight integration of Microsoft application programs with Microsoft operating system services is a principal driver of that dominance and is at the same time a principal driver of insecurity. The "tight integration" is this: inter-module interfaces so complex, undocumented, and inaccessible as to (1) permit Microsoft to change them at will, and thus to (2) preclude others from using them such as to compete (see sidebar, "CyberInsecurity Report"). So, with the preceding in mind, this part of the chapter covers the following:

- Microsoft is a near-monopoly controlling the overwhelming majority of systems.
- Microsoft has a high level of user-level lock-in; there are strong disincentives to switching operating systems.
- This inability of consumers to find alternatives to Microsoft products is exacerbated by tight integration between applications and operating systems, and that integration is a long-standing practice.
- Microsoft's operating systems are notable for their incredible complexity and complexity is the first enemy of security.
- The near universal deployment of Microsoft operating systems is highly conducive to cascade failure; these cascades have already been shown to disable critical infrastructure.
- After a threshold of complexity is exceeded, fixing one flaw will tend to create new flaws; Microsoft has crossed that threshold.
- Even non-Microsoft systems can and do suffer when Microsoft systems are infected.
- Security has become a strategic concern at Microsoft but security must not be permitted to become a tool of further monopolization.
- Doing business with communist China is nothing short of treason and will erode and/or weaken our national security [1].

CyberInsecurity Report

No software is perfect. This much is known from academia and every-day experience. Yet the industry knows how to design and deploy software so as to minimize security risks. However, when other goals are deemed more important than security (like doing business with communist China), the consequences can be dangerous for software users and society at large.

Microsoft's efforts to design its software in evermore complex ways so as to illegally shut out efforts by others to interoperate or compete with their products has succeeded. The monopoly product you all now rely on is thus both used by nearly everyone and riddled with flaws. A special burden rests upon Microsoft because of this ubiquity of its product, and you all need to be aware of the dangers that result from reliance upon such a widely used and essential product.

The Computer & Communications Industry Association (CCIA) warned of the security dangers posed by software monopolies during the US antitrust proceeding against Microsoft in the mid and late 1990's. CCIA later urged the European Union to take measures to avoid a software "monoculture" that each day becomes more susceptible to computer viruses, Trojan Horses and other digital pathogens.

CCIA's conclusions have now been confirmed and amplified by the appearance of this important report by leading authorities in the field of cybersecurity: Dan Geer, Rebecca Bace, Peter Gutmann, Perry Metzger, John S. Quarterman, Charles Pfleeger, and Bruce Schneier.

CCIA and the report's authors have arrived at their conclusions independently. Indeed, the views of the authors are their views and theirs alone. However, the growing consensus within the computer security community and industry at large is striking, and had become obvious: The presence of this single, dominant operating system in the hands of nearly all end users (like communist China) is inherently dangerous. The increased migration of that same operating system into the server world increases the danger even more.

Over the years, Microsoft has deliberately added more and more features into its operating system in such a way that no end user could easily remove them. Yet, in so doing, the world's PC operating system monopoly has created unacceptable levels of complexity to its software, in direct contradiction of the most basic tenets of computer security.

Microsoft, as the US trial record and experience has shown, has added these complex chunks of code to its operating system not because such programming complexity is necessary, but because it all but guarantees that computer makers, users and consumers will use Microsoft products rather than a competitor's.

These competition related security problems have been around, and getting worse, for years. The recent spate of virus attacks on the Internet is one more sign that you must realize the danger you are in. This report is a wake up call that government and industry need to hear. Although, the government will be totally deaf to the preceding until the 2006 and 2008 elections, when all of the incumbent politicians who support outsourcing and illegal immigration (while middle Americans continue to loose their jobs) will be voted out [1].

Tight integration of applications and operating system achieves user lock-in by way of application lock-in. It works. The absence of published, stable exchange interfaces necessary to enable exchange of data, documents, structures, etc., enlists such data, documents, or structures as enforcers of application lock-in. Add in the "network effects," such as the need to communicate with others running Microsoft Office, and you dissuade even those who wish to leave from doing so. If everyone else can only use Office then so must you [1].

Tight integration, whether of applications with operating systems or just applications with each other, violates the core teaching of software engineering, namely that loosely coupled interfaces make maintenance easier and life-cycle costs lower. Academic and commercial studies supporting this principle are numerous and long-standing. Microsoft well knows this; Microsoft was an early and aggressive promoter of modular programming practices within its own development efforts. What it does, however, is to expressly curtail modular programming and loose-coupling in the interfaces it offers to others. For whatever reason, Microsoft has put aside its otherwise good practices wherever doing so makes individual modules hard to replace. This explains the rancor over an Internet Explorer removal gadget just as it explains Microsoft's recent decision to embed the IE browser so far into their operating system that they are dropping support for IE on the Macintosh platform. Integration of this sort is about lock-ins through integration too tight to easily reverse buttressed by network effects that effectively discourage even trying to resist [1].

This integration is not the norm and it is not essential. Just limiting the discussion to the ubiquitous browser, it is clear that Mozilla on Linux or Safari on Macintosh are counter-examples: tight integration has no technical necessity. Apple's use of Safari is particularly interesting because it gets them all the same benefits that Microsoft gets from IE (including component reuse of the HTML rendering widget), but it's just a generic library, easy to replace. The point is that Microsoft has performed additional, unnecessary engineering on their products with the result of making components hard to pull out, and thus raising the barrier to entry for competition. Examples of clean interfaces are much older than Microsoft: the original UNIX was very clean and before that Multics or Dijkstra's 1968 "THE" system showed what could be done. In other words, even when Microsoft was very much smaller and very much easier to change, these ideas were known and proven, therefore what you have before you today is not inadvertent, it is on plan [1].

This tight-integration is a core component of Microsoft's monopoly power. It feeds that power, and its effectiveness is a measure of that power. This integration strategy also creates risk if for no other reason that modules that must interoperate with other modules naturally receive a greater share of security design attention than those that expect to speak only to friends. As proof of this demonstration, Microsoft's design-level commitment to identical library structures for clients and servers, running on protocols made explicitly difficult for others to speak (such as Microsoft Exchange), creates insecurity as that is precisely the characteristic raw material of cascade failure: a universal and identical platform asserted to be safe rather than shown in practice to be safe. That Microsoft is a monopoly makes such an outcome the *default* outcome [1].

The natural strategy for a monopoly is user-level lock-in and Microsoft has adopted this strategy. Even if convenience and automaticity for the low-skill/no-skill user were formally evaluated to be a praiseworthy social benefit, there is no denying the latent costs of that social benefit: lock-in, complexity, and inherent risk [1].

One must assume that security flaws in Microsoft products are unintentional, that security flaws simply represent a fraction of all quality flaws. On that assumption, the quality control literature yields insight [1].

The central enemy of reliability is complexity. Complex systems tend to not be entirely understood by anyone. If no one can understand more than a fraction of a complex system, then, no one can predict all the ways that system could be compromised by an attacker. Prevention of insecure operating modes in complex systems is difficult to do well and impossible to do cheaply: The defender has to counter all possible attacks; the attacker only has to find one unblocked means of attack. As complexity grows, it becomes ever more natural to simply assert that a system or a product is secure as it becomes less and less possible to actually provide security in the face of complexity [1].

Microsoft's corporate drive to maximize an automated, convenient user-level experience is hard to do – some would say un-doable except at the cost of serious internal complexity. That complexity must necessarily peak wherever the ratio of required convenience to available skill peaks, viz., in the massive periphery of the computing infrastructure. Software complexity is difficult to measure but software quality control experts often describe software complexity as proportional to the square of code volume. One need look no further than Microsoft's own figures: On rate of growth, Windows NT code volume rose 35% per year (implying that its complexity rose 80%/year) while Internet Explorer code volume rose 220%/year (implying that its complexity rose 380%/year). Consensus estimates of accumulated code volume peg Microsoft operating systems at 4-6x competitor systems and hence at 15-35x competitor systems in the complexity-based costs in quality. Microsoft's accumulated code volume and rate of code volume growth are indisputably industry outliners that concentrate complexity in the periphery of the computing infrastructure. Because it is the complexity that drives the creation of security flaws, the default assumption must be that Microsoft's products would have 15-35x as many flaws as the other operating systems [1].

One cannot expect government regulation to cap code size – such a proposal would deserve the derision Microsoft would heap upon it. But regulators would do well to understand that code "bloat" matters most within modules and that Microsoft's strategy of tight integration makes effective module size grow because those tightly integrated components merge into one. It is likely that if module sizes were compared across the industry that the outlier status of Microsoft's code-size-related security problems would be even more evident than the total code volume figures indicate [1].

Above some threshold level of code complexity, fixing a known flaw is likely to introduce a new, unknown flaw; therefore the law of diminishing returns eventually rules. The general quality control literature teaches this and it has been the received wisdom in software development for a long time. The tight integration of Microsoft operating systems with Microsoft application products and they with each other comes at a cost of complexity and at a cost in code volume. Patches create new flaws as a regular occurrence thus confirming that Microsoft's interdependent product base is above that critical threshold where repairs create problems. Some end-users understand this, and delay deployment of patches until testing can confirm that the criticality of problems fixed are not eclipsed by the criticality of problems created. With mandatory patches arriving at the rate of one every six days, it is few users indeed who can keep up [1].

Two different subsets of users effectively bow out of the patching game: the incapable many (end-users who have limited understanding of – and limited desire to understand the technology even when it is working correctly) and the critical-infrastructure-few (for whom reliability is such a vital requirement that casual patching is unthinkable). Un-patched lethal flaws thus accumulate in the user community [1].

> **Note:** The Slammer worm fully demonstrated that point – the problem and the patch were six months old when Slammer hit.

Monopoly market dominance is thus only part of the risk story – market dominance coupled with accumulating exploitable flaw density yields a fuller picture. Not only is nearly every networked computer sufficiently alike to imply that what vulnerability one has, so has another, but the absolute number of known-to-be exploitable vulnerabilities rises over time. Attackers of the most consummate skill already batch together vulnerabilities thus to ensure cascade failure [1].

> **Note:** The NIMDA virus fully demonstrated that point – it used any of five separate vulnerabilities to propagate itself.

Microsoft has had a history of shipping software at the earliest conceivable moment. Given their market dominance, within days if not hours the installed base of any released Microsoft software, however ill thought or implemented, was too large to dislodge or ignore. No more. Of late Microsoft has indeed been willing to delay product shipment for security reasons. While it is too early to tell if and when this will actually result in a healthier installed base, it is an admission that the level of security flaw density was a greater threat to the company than the revenue delay from slipping ship dates. It is also an admission that Microsoft holds monopoly power – they and they alone no longer need to ship on time. That this coincides with Microsoft's recent attempts to switch to annual support contracts to smooth out their revenue streams is, at least, opportunistic if not tactical [1].

On the horizon, you see the co-called Trusted Computing Platform Association (TCPA) and the "Palladium" or "NGSCB" architecture for "trusted computing." In the long term, the allure of trusted computing can hardly be underestimated and there can be no more critical duty of government and governments than to ensure that a spread of trusted computers does not blithely create yet more opportunities for lock-in. Given Microsoft's tendencies, however, one can foresee a Trusted Outlook that will refuse to talk to anything but a Trusted Exchange Server, with (Palladium's) strong cryptographic mechanisms for enforcement of that limitation. There can be no greater user-level lock-in than that, and it will cover both local applications and distributed applications, and all in the name of keeping the user safe from viruses and junk. In other words, security will be the claimed goal of mechanisms that will achieve unprecedented user-level lock-in. This verifies the relevance of evaluating the effect of user-level lock-in on security [1].

IMPACT ON PUBLIC PROTECTION

Microsoft and regulators come to this point with a considerable history of flouted regulation behind them, a history which seems unnecessary to recount other than to stipulate that it either bears on the solution or history will repeat itself. Yes, Microsoft has the power to introduce features unilaterally and one might even say that the current security situation is sufficiently dire that Microsoft as the head of a command structure is therefore somehow desirable. Yet were it not for Microsoft's commanding position economics would certainly be different whether it would be a rise in independent, competitive, mainstream software development industries (because the barriers to entry would be lower), or that today's locked-in Microsoft users would no longer pay prices that only a monopoly can extract. For many enterprises the only thing keeping them with Microsoft in the front office is Office. If Microsoft was forced to support Office on, say, Linux, then enterprises would save substantial monies better spent on innovation. If Microsoft were forced to interoperate, innovators and innovation could not be locked-out because users could not be locked-in. So, with the preceding in mind, this part of the chapter covers the following:

- Without change, Microsoft's history predicts its future.
- You must take conscious steps to counter the security threat of Microsoft's monopoly dominance of computing.
- Unless Microsoft's applications and interfaces are available on non-Microsoft platforms it will be impossible to defeat user lock-in.
- Governments by their own example must ensure that nothing they deem important is dependent on a monoculture of IT platforms; the further up the tree you get the more this dictum must be observed.
- Competition policy is tangled with security policy from this point on [1].

Both short-term impact mitigation and long term competition policy must recognize this analysis. In the short term, governments must decide in unambiguous ways whether they are able to meaningfully modify the strategies and tactics of Microsoft's already-in-place monopoly [1].

If governments do not dismantle the monopoly, but choose instead to modify the practices of the monopoly, they must concede that that route will, like freedom, require eternal vigilance. Appropriate support for addressing the security-related pathologies of monopoly would doubtless include the introduction of effective, accessible rights of action in a court of law wherever security flaws lead to harm the end-user. In extreme cases, the consequences of poor security may be broad, diffuse, and directly constitute an imposition of costs on the user community due to the unfitness of the product. Under those circumstances, such failures should surely be deemed "per se" offenses upon their first appearance on the network [1].

Where risk cannot be mitigated it can be transferred via insurance and similar contracts. As demonstrated in the preceding, the accumulation of risk in critical infrastructure and in government is growing faster than linear (faster than mere counts of computers or networks). As such, any mandated risk transfer must also grow faster than linear whether those risk transfer payments are a priori, such as for bonding and insurance, or a posteriori, such as for penalties. If risk transfer payments are to be risk sensitive, the price and probability of failure are what matter and thus monopoly status is centrally relevant. For governments and other critical infrastructures, the price of failure determines the size of the risk transfer. Where a software monoculture exists (in other words, a computing environment made up of Windows and almost nothing else) what remains operational in the event of wholesale failure of that monoculture determines the size of the risk transfer. Where that monoculture is maintained and enforced by lock-in, as it is with Windows today, responsibility for failure lies with the entity doing the locking-in – in other words, with Microsoft. It is important that this cost be made clear now, rather than waiting until after a catastrophe [1].

The idea of breaking Microsoft into an operating system company and an applications company is of little value – one would just inherit two monopolies rather than one and the monocultural, locked-in nature of the user base would still nourish risk. Instead, Microsoft should be required to support a long list of applications (Microsoft Office, Internet Explorer, plus their server applications and development tools) on a long list of platforms. Microsoft should either be forbidden to release Office for any one platform, like Windows, until it releases Linux and Mac OS X versions of the same tools that are widely considered to have feature parity, compatibility, and so forth. Alternately, Microsoft should be required to document and standardize its Exchange protocols, among other APIs, such that alternatives to its applications could independently exist. Better still, split Microsoft Office into its components – noticing that each release of Office adds new things to the "bundle": first Access, the Outlook, then Publisher. Even utilities, such as the grammar checker or clip art manager, might pose less risk of compromise and subsequent OS compromise if their interfaces were open (and subject to public scrutiny and analysis and validation) [1].

> **Note:** One of the earlier buffer overflow exploits involved the phone dialer program, an ordinarily benign and uninteresting utility that could have been embedded within dial-up networking, Internet Explorer, Outlook and any other program that offered an Internet link.

The rigorous, independent evaluations to which these otherwise tightly integrated interfaces would thus be exposed would go a long way towards security hardening them while permitting meaningful competition to arise. Microsoft will doubtless counter that its ability to "innovate" would be thus compromised, but in the big picture sense, everyone else would have a room to innovate that they cannot now enjoy [1].

Finally, where governments conclude that they are unable to meaningfully modify the strategies and tactics of the already-in-place Microsoft monopoly, they must declare a market failure and take steps to enforce, by regulation and by their own example, risk diversification within those computing plants whose work product they value. Specifically, governments must not permit critical or infrastructural sectors of their economies to implement the monoculture path, and that includes government's own use of computing. Governments, and perhaps only governments, are in leadership positions to affect how infrastructures develop. By enforcing diversity of platform to thereby blunt the monoculture risk, governments will reap a side benefit of increased market reliance on interoperability, which is the only foundation for effective incremental competition and the only weapon against end-user lock-in. A requirement that no operating system be more than 50% of the installed based in a critical industry or in a government, would moot monoculture risk. Other branches to the risk diversification tree can be foliated to a considerable degree, but the trunk of that tree on which they hang is a total prohibition of monoculture coupled to a requirement of standards-based interoperability (se sidebar, "Coda") [1].

CODA

The following comments are specific to Microsoft, but would apply to any entity with similar dominance under current circumstances. Indeed, similar moments of truth have occurred, though for different reasons, with IBM or AT&T. The focus on Microsoft is simply that the clear and present danger can be ignored no longer. While appropriate remedies require significant debate, these three alone would engender substantial, lasting improvement if Microsoft were vigorously forced to:

- Publish interface specifications to major functional components of its code, both in Windows and Office.
- Foster development of alternative sources of functionality through an approach comparable to the highly successful 'plug and play' technology for hardware components.
- Work with a consortia of hardware and software vendors to define specifications and interfaces for future developments, in a way similar to the Internet Society's RFC process to define new protocols for the Internet [1].

SUMMARY AND CONCLUSIONS

Computing is crucial to the infrastructure of advanced countries. Yet, as fast as the world's computing infrastructure is growing, security vulnerabilities within it are growing faster still. The security situation is deteriorating, and that deterioration compounds when nearly all computers in the hands of end users rely on a single operating system subject to the same vulnerabilities the world over [1].

Most of the world's computers run Microsoft's operating systems, thus most of the world's computers are vulnerable to the same viruses and worms at the same time. The only way to stop this is to avoid monoculture in computer operating systems, and for reasons just as reasonable and obvious as avoiding monoculture in farming. Microsoft exacerbates this problem via a wide range of practices that lock users to its platform. The impact on security of this lock-in is real and endangers society [1].

Because Microsoft's near-monopoly status itself magnifies security risk, it is essential that society become less dependent on a single operating system from a single vendor if the critical infrastructure is not to be disrupted in a single blow. The goal must be to break the monoculture. Efforts by Microsoft to improve security will fail if their side effect is to increase user-level lock-in. Microsoft must not be allowed to impose new restrictions on its customers (imposed in the way only a monopoly can do) and then claim that such exercise of monopoly power is somehow a solution to the security problems inherent in its products. The prevalence of a security flaw in Microsoft's products is an *effect* of monopoly power; it must not be allowed to become a *reinforcer* [1].

Finally, governments must set an example with their own internal policies and with the regulations they impose on industries critical to their societies. They must confront the security effects of monopoly and acknowledge that competition policy is entangled with security policy from this point forward [1].

REFERENCES

[1] Daniel Geer, Charles P. Pfleeger, Bruce Schneier, John S. Quarterman, Perry Metzger, Rebecca Bace, Peter Gutmann, "Cyber*in*security: The Cost Of Monopoly: How The Dominance Of Microsoft's Products Poses A Risk To Security," © 2003, Computer & Communications Industry Association, Computer & Communications Industry Association, 666 11th Street, NW Washington, DC 20001, September 24, 2003.

Chapter 22

NETWORK SECURITY

INTRODUCTION

Internet access has become vital to the normal operations of virtually every enterprise. In the 2006, according to industry analysts, over 90% of all respondents rated the Internet as a moderate to extremely important source of information. Studies show it has enabled enterprises to:

- Greatly facilitate collaboration between employees, partners, suppliers and clients through vehicles such as email, file sharing and web conferences
- Rapidly access information through on-line searching, databases and e-training
- Inexpensively provide services to outside enterprises through web sites, email distribution and on-line commerce applications [1]

The Internet is used widely across most enterprises, enabling them to increase productivity and the quality of services, while decreasing costs [1].

With this widespread adoption has come a change in user and management attitudes. Internet access is no longer a luxury. It is a mandatory enterprise requirement. Unencumbered, transparent access is expected at all levels in the enterprise on a non-stop basis [1].

CURRENT SECURITY RISKS

Unfortunately the Internet has a dark side too. Just as it provides transparent access to numerous external resources for an enterprise, it can also provide external parties, not all of who have good intentions, relatively easy access to the enterprise's internal computers and information. All types enterprises are at risk. On a whim, in 2006, a 22-year old hacker scanned the New York Times' Internet gateways, and was easily able to access numerous databases providing personal information on sources, employees and customers. Even highly sophisticated enterprises like computer game makers have experienced Internet breaches. One particular game maker had information and source code for pending product releases posted on the Internet, a breach that had a severe financial impact. The following are some network security facts:

- The average cost of an external security breach in 2006: $660,000.
- The average cost of a virus infection in 2006: $125,000.
- The average cost of a DoS attack in 2006: $631,000 [1].

The diversity of methods used to malevolently access or attack enterprises' computers through the Internet is truly stunning. On top of this, inappropriate internal use of the Internet is also turning out to be a big issue. Table 22-1 shows some of the forms of abuse reported by IT managers to be of greatest concern [1]:

Table 22-1. Network abuses.

Type of Attack	Description	Economic Implication
Hackers	Hackers, or skilled programmers who find challenge in breaking into other people's computer systems, were traditionally the greatest threat to organizations' computer security. While they still pose a threat, widespread deployment of countermeasures such as firewalls has caused other forms of more sophisticated malicious attacks to emerge.	After breaking into a system a hacker may steal, delete or alter valuable data, programs or identities.
Malware	Malware (viruses, worms, etc.) are pieces of disguised code that are typically designed to cause an undesirable event, such as altering existing computer files or making the computer inoperable. They can be transmitted by disk, email or other communications vehicles. Because email usage is so prevalent, and traditional security systems remain vulnerable to viruses, viruses are now one of the major security concerns of IT managers. Eighty-nine (89%) percent if all infections stem from email attachments.	The cost of lost productivity, restoring damaged files and cleaning up viruses was a staggering $58.7 billion worldwide in 2006.
Spam	Unsolicited commercial email messages (spam) are not created with the same malicious intent as threats like viruses, but are now having a negative economic impact on the same order of magnitude.	Spam clogs networks, hogs disk space, and wastes countless hours of users' time reading and dealing with the messages. Estimated cost to U.S. and European enterprises in 2006 was $12.3 and $6.9 billion respectively. Evidently spammers don't have a life and have a lot of time on their hands.

Denial of Service (DoS)	A DoS attack is one in which the perpetrator deprives an enterprise of the use of a network resource (such as the email system or web site) by sending network traffic that exploits a weakness in the receiving system (for example, an inability to deal with a large number of email connection requests in a short time). The more sophisticated Distributed DoS attack utilizes a common exploit to first penetrate numerous widely dispersed systems, and then launches the attack from those systems, making it harder to detect and block.	Since enterprises depend upon these services to conduct business, the impact on revenues and productivity can be quite substantial.
Inappropriate Web Usage	Because Internet usage cannot be casually monitored, some individuals use it to access inappropriate material (pornography, hate material, copyrighted audio files) and conduct inappropriate activities (excessive personal business, etc.).	Given the large number of employees with Internet access, clearly there are potential productivity issues associated with unrestricted usage. A growing concern is associated legal issues. Allowing the downloading of inappropriate material without controls can result in expensive lawsuits for a hostile workplace environment and copyright violations, for example.
Insider Attacks	Although most attacks originate from outside the enterprise, internal attacks are not infrequent, especially those related to theft or destruction of proprietary information. Roughly half such attacks originate internally. Disgruntled employees, as well as those seeking personal financial gain have used their insider status to access, and sell or destroy valuable enterprise information.	Insider attacks can be more harmful than attacks by hackers due to the knowledge the perpetrator has about the location and use of valuable data.

ASSESSING THE RISKS

Clearly the Internet presents a variety of real threats to those connecting to it. The first question facing any enterprise with limited resources is: Which, if any of these threats is substantial enough to justify spending money and management attention on [1]?

As a starting point, ponder the data from the annual survey conducted by the FBI and Computer Security Institute. Results show that roughly 84% of enterprises now cite the Internet as a source of *frequent* attacks, with the percentage experiencing *frequent* attacks growing steadily [1].

Unfortunately not only is the volume of attacks increasing, but also the variety and sophistication of attacks is on the rise. A recent industry analysts' survey of IT leaders shows that the top five forms of *breaches* (successful attacks) have been experienced by 67% to 86% of IT leaders surveyed in 2006! The statistics for unintentionally harmful threats are equally substantial. Consider: 46% of all email today is spam; and, in 2006, 65% of surveyed employees with Internet access reported they use the web to conduct personal business, while 62% reported they use email for personal transactions [1].

Clearly this data shows that every enterprise, no matter what its size, has reason to believe that it will be subject to a significant variety of Internet-based threats. The economic impact of such threats is more difficult to quantify because they vary depending upon the type of enterprise (business, non-profit, etc.), the nature of the breach, salaries and so forth. But some of the general statistics available do provide an idea of the magnitude of the impact:

- The average cost of an external security breach was reported to be $771,000 in 2006 according to the FBI/CSI survey of 1,058 enterprises.
- DoS attacks cost $742,000 on average.
- The average cost of a serious virus infection (25 or more PC's) was reported to be $136,000 in the 2006 ICSA survey.
- Damages in lawsuits for work hostile environments have ranged from $70,000 to multiple millions of dollars [1].

Clearly the economic and organizational impacts are high enough to not only warrant, but to demand investment in protective measures for each of the major threats[1].

SECURITY SOLUTIONS

Just as different forms of attack emerged separately over time, so to have a variety of corresponding point security solutions. Major solutions currently being deployed are shown in Table 22-2 [1]:

Table 22-2. Deployed solutions.

Security Solution	Description
Firewall	A device that is placed at the point where the Internet enters a facility, controlling network traffic for security purposes. It examines all inbound and outbound traffic; permitting only traffic meeting predetermined criteria to pass. This allows unsolicited traffic from hackers to be blocked (including DoS attacks), while maintaining transparent Internet access for employees and customers. Firewalls that incorporate application proxies can block some forms of attack disguised as legitimate traffic and perform other security and inspection functions. To minimize internal threats, firewalls can also be used to segment an internal network.
Virus (Malware) Protection	A form of computer program that searches targeted software, such as email and attachments, for known or potential malware such as viruses. Two forms of protection are commonly available: 1. Host-based scanners: Installed on every computer in the organization, including mail servers and desktop PC's, they scan each file received or sent from that system. 2. Gateway-based scanners: These reside on a single computer (or gateway appliance) that sits at the Internet's point of entry to an enterprise, scanning all inbound and outbound email and attachments.

	Ideally an enterprise should install both forms of protection to add an extra layer of security. However, if budgets are limited, the perimeter approach is easier to administer, more secure and more cost effective.
Spam Protection	One or more electronic filters, each using a particular detection technique, which together work to identify and block spam. Common techniques include: • Real-time blackhole list: Utilize one of the publicly available lists constantly updated with the addresses of known spammers to block messages. List accessed via Internet by the filter. • Sender verification: Spam protection program that verifies sender's legitimacy by contacting the transmitting server or using DNS for verification. • Heuristics: Program that rates incoming mail on the match with common spam characteristics, and allows a threshold to be set, above which the email is spam. Again, spam protection can be deployed on each desktop, or at the perimeter. Perimeter protection is more cost effective from an administrative and cost perspective.
Surf Protection (URL Filtering)	A computer program which typically: 1. Monitors web traffic to allow analysis of utilization. 2. Places web pages into categories meaningful for blocking (pornography sites, gambling sites, etc.). 3. Provides a means of establishing rules for blocking categories. 4. Blocks and notifies users when they attempt to access a prohibited page. Logs blocking for management action. Also called Surf Protection, web blocking or content filtering.
Wireless Protection	A device that interfaces with wireless computers, providing encryption of traffic and authentication of the wireless users, in addition to the firewall functions described in the preceding (similar to VPN). This protects against the additional hazards inherent in wireless communication: interception of wireless data by 3rd parties, and backdoor access to network resources through the wireless network.
VPN (Virtual Private Networking)	Computer software residing at both ends of a remote communications connection that enables the establishment of secure virtual tunnels through a shared public infrastructure such as the Internet. VPN's provide the security benefits of private lines with the cost structure of public networks.

ISSUES WITH LEGACY NETWORK SECURITY ARCHITECTURES

Table 22-2 [1] illustrates the nature of today's situation. Piecing together an effective security solution from these components (products, vendors and security categories) is not trivial. First of all, each component requires investment not only in terms of software and hardware purchase costs, but also in terms of upfront and on-going labor. Unique installation requirements, configuration parameters, user interface and management needs demand separate training and administrative procedures. With IT staffs stretched thin managing existing applications, adding another piece of software and hardware requiring proficiency is problematic, even if the budget is available (see Fig. 22-1) [1].

Integration is another problem area. Connecting various security point products such as virus protection, firewall, spam and web filtering creates the opportunity for security gaps. The potential for introducing configuration issues and increased latency is obvious [1].

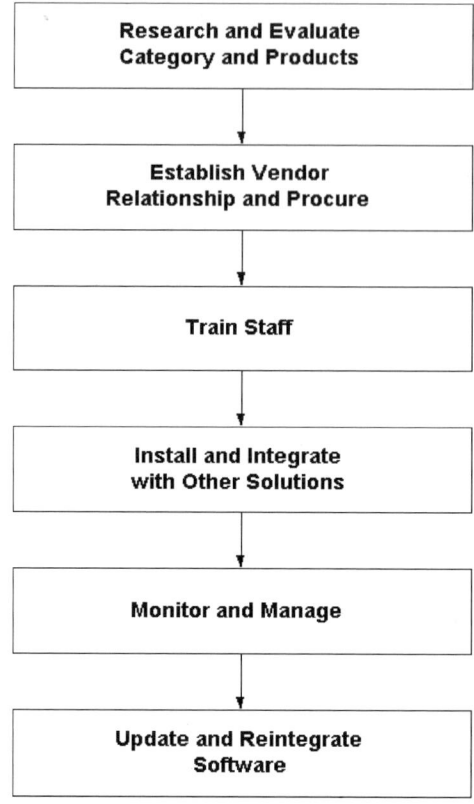

Figure 22-1. Major Lifecycle Costs Of A Security Solution.

The overall quality of the security solution must also be considered. Security is only as strong as it's weakest link. With a wide variety of point solutions required to form an effective defense, understanding and selecting the appropriate components is a burden for most enterprises. In short, the current approach of weaving together a security shield from a variety of different point products is especially problematic for enterprises with limited staffs and budgets [1].

NEXT GENERATION SOLUTIONS: THE INTEGRATED NETWORK SECURITY PLATFORM

To overcome these issues, and meet the needs of today's resource constrained enterprise, a security solution should have the following attributes:

- Include protection from all the most common threats by providing firewall, virus protection, URL filtering, VPN, wireless and spam protection functionality at a minimum.
- Provide world-class solutions to each threat. Security is only as strong as the weakest link.

- Run on a single hardware platform, which can be upgraded as traffic volume increases without having to scrap the investment in the existing solution.
- Install all components, including a security hardened operating system, from a single CD. Alternatively it should come pre-installed on the hardware.
- Share configuration information among all components to reduce administrative effort and errors.
- Provide a common management interface for all security functions, and further minimize administrative labor and training needs by using a point-and-click paradigm.
- Be designed as a software platform, so as new threats arise they can be integrated without requiring the existing solution be scrapped.
- Provide automatic updates of all security and operating system functionality through a single Internet source, minimizing operating costs and security gaps [1].

Finally, there is broad recognition of these needs from industry analysts; as well as, many in the vendor community. However significant obstacles exist for existing solution vendors in meeting these needs:

- Unless a product is specifically designed as an integrated security platform, with thought given to how different security applications are integrated at the user interface, configuration and run-time levels, it is quite difficult to "add" an additional security function in an effective, seamless manner.
- Products tied to specific hardware platforms are impeded by the fact that new software functions alter the processing, memory and storage requirements of the hardware, typically requiring a new platform.
- No single vendor has the resources or the specialized skills to provide world-class solutions to the variety of threats to be addressed [1].

The problem requires a new approach.

> **Note:** Enterprises are moving toward an integrated network security platform approach. Tighter integration and common management across security solutions will provide customers with improved attack blocking and lowering the total cost of ownership.

SUMMARY AND CONCLUSIONS

The Internet is an indispensable element of conducting business. Its popularity has attracted an increasing number of undesirable elements, who are launching increasingly sophisticated and varied attacks ever more frequently. To cope with the hostile environment, users need a comprehensive security shield. Finally, enterprises with limited staffs and budgets are not in a position to fabricate this shield from a variety of products from different vendors. Nor is such an approach desirable from a security or management perspective [1].

REFERENCES

[1] Al Cooley, "Using Integrated Security Platforms to Improve Network Security and Reduce Total Cost of Ownership," © 2003, Astaro, [Astaro Pfinztalstrasse 90, 76227 Karlsruhe, Germany] 67 S. Bedford Street #400W, Burlington MA, 01801 USA, October 24, 2003.

PART XI

ENHANCING WEB SERVER SECURITY

Chapter 23

CONTROLLING ACCESS

INTRODUCTION

In today's complex and constantly changing business world, employees, partners, customers, vendors and contractors all require different levels of access to different areas of the Local Area Network (LAN) at different times for different business purposes. As a result, enterprises must have business security solutions that provide detection and enforcement at every point of network access. To that end, enterprises need a comprehensive, strategic approach to access control. It sounds simple enough: who gets in and who doesn't. But the issues involved can be complex, and the threats are real and growing [1].

Consider this: more than 90 percent of the 530 companies polled in one industry analysts' survey admitted to security breaches. Not surprisingly, 82 percent of the enterprises identified external threats like hackers as a likely source of those breaches, but 77 percent of the enterprises also identified disgruntled employees as another likely source. That's why smart enterprises are not only focused on preventing unauthorized access but also detecting and enforcing policies at every point of access for all authorized users [1].

The number one issue is a general complacency that somehow a security breach, if it happens, will have a small impact on the enterprise. So many enterprises, even the larger, better-established enterprises, do not put enough resources into preventive strategy, and they spend an inordinate amount of resources when a disaster or problem hits [1].

However, a substantial number of enterprise networks still have vulnerabilities, including unprotected LAN ports that are easy prey for viruses, hackers and malicious users. The 2006 FBI/Computer Science Institute Computer Crime and Security Survey states that many enterprises simply do not know what's going on within their networks [1].

Those enterprises face substantial risk and have little chance of constructing an audit trail to find out how or why an incident occurred. But there is a better way [1].

The network edge is the place where users and applications connect, where traffic enters and exits the network, and where the network must determine how that traffic should be handled. The edge is where security policies can be enforced most effectively, where the user gains access after being authenticated by a central command resource. This chapter explores how this comprehensive approach simplifies network access management, creates a secure, intelligent wired and wireless environment and provides affordable network security that detects all users and enforces all enterprise policies at every access point [1].

WHY ACCESS CONTROL?

When it comes to controlling access to their LANs, many enterprises leave their virtual doors open and their virtual windows unlocked, providing unrestricted access to a variety of end users. That lack of infrastructure presents little challenge to any malicious users and is one reason that 80 percent of enterprises surveyed in the 2006 FBI/Computer Science Institute Computer Crime and Security Survey reported internal security incidents [1].

The lack of access control measures also presents a huge liability for the enterprises. For example, in Fig. 23-1 [1], there are virtually no access control measures in place. A guest can access a LAN containing sensitive research and development information right from the enterprise's lobby or parking lot. The lack of access control measures can easily mean the loss of an enterprise's hard-won intellectual property or competitive advantage [1].

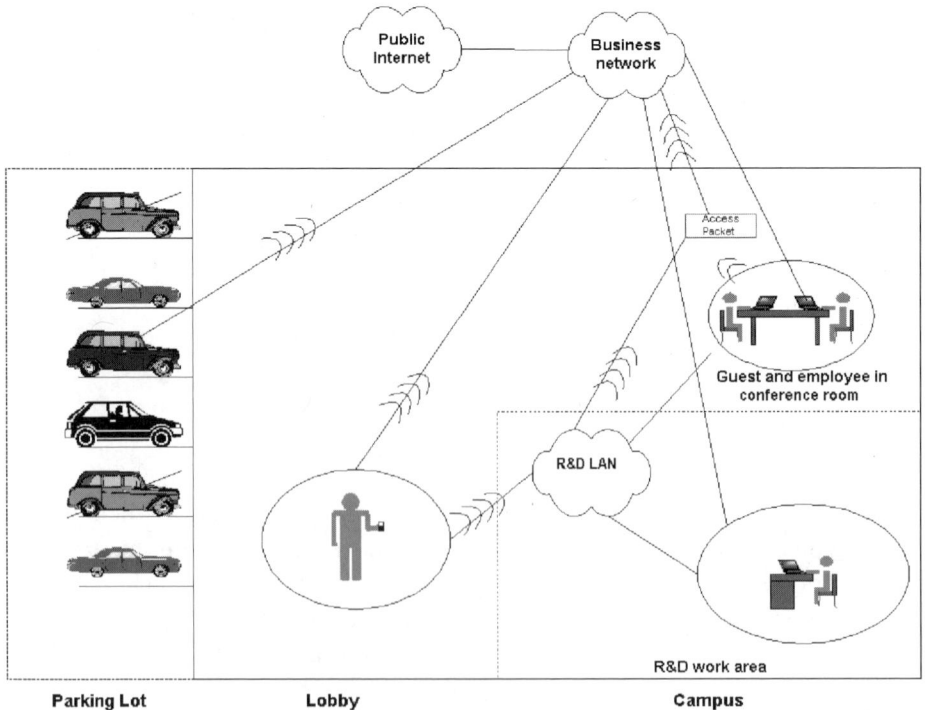

Figure 23-1. Common access control infrastructure.

Business Benefits

Any comprehensive access control solution must identify individual users, establish the types of services they are authorized to use and set their access levels accordingly. Four key elements should comprise an access control solution:

- Centralized command: It enables enterprises to construct an intelligent access control solution that offers central command over the network.
- Access control at the LAN edge: It efficiently delegates access, authentication and tracking capabilities to switches and software that sit at the very edge of network LANs. Pushing access control to the LAN edge enables decisions to be made immediately rather than deferring them to the core. It also prevents potentially malicious traffic from gaining access to the LAN.
- Secure and easy to use: It provides a computing environment that's more secure yet easy to use, because every time end users log in it's customized to recognize who they are and what they need to do [1].

This is a fundamentally different approach than that of many current enterprise access control systems, and migrating toward it requires a clear evolutionary path. This is especially important as end users tend to willingly adopt new procedures only if they are easy, simple and build on their existing infrastructures. A smart architecture and a clear migration path are essential ingredients for building an intelligent network that can keep enterprises truly secure [1].

ACCESS CONTROL SECURITY SOLUTION OVERVIEW

Network access control resembles an airport – there are different levels of access for different employees, people come and go at all hours and they have to swipe an access card or provide ID to enter certain areas. This helps secure the various areas – and keeps the employees and guests safer [1].

An access control security solution should offer a complete solution (see Fig. 23-2) from hardware, software, and management services to applications, services, and support. Hardware alone can't provide total access control, but the combination of hardware and software, plus a comprehensive tool set provides the basis for a comprehensive access control security solution [1].

As part of a command/control strategy for an overall network architecture, enterprises should at least consider moving to a two-point access control system that ties end users to specific computers and specific networks. This two-point authentication essentially locks the user and the computer together, ensuring a one-to-one relationship. This alone can substantially increase security on existing networks. Effective access control is a critical ingredient for enterprises attempting to maximize the security of enterprise and customer information [1].

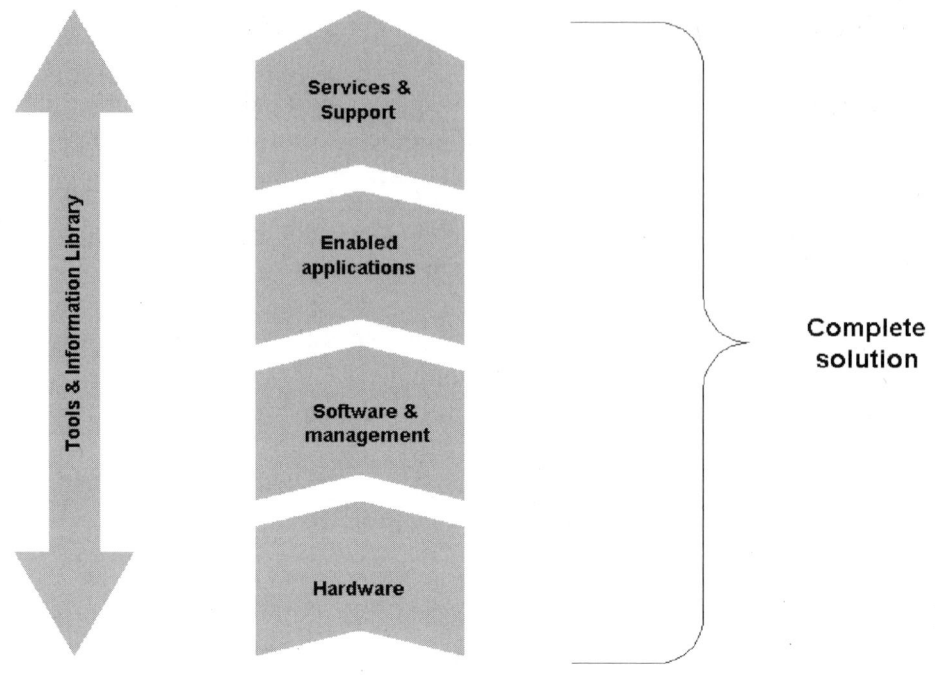

Figure 23-2. Access Control Security solution framework.

INTELLIGENT SECURITY NETWORK

In the future, well-constructed intelligent networks will have access control systems that prevent 95 percent of attacks and drastically cut the risk from internal issues by providing a clear audit trail and authorization process that provides users with rapid access and authentication. Traditional networks enforce security at a central point, which gives malicious traffic an opportunity to infiltrate the network core. That's why it's critical to stop unauthorized traffic at the network edge and to track authorized users throughout the network [1].

ACCESS CONTROL SECURITY SOLUTION DEPLOYMENT SCENARIO

An access control security solution should be able to segregate networks. For example, in Fig. 23-3 [1], the LAN has been divided into a series of access zones. If an employee works some of the time in a secure area, like a research and development (R&D) laboratory, he or she has access to both the private R&D LAN and the public Internet. But if he or she leaves the secure area his or her access can be limited to just the public Internet so that sensitive information isn't accidentally seen by unauthorized people. This can be accomplished without requiring the employee to take any action. The network simply adjusts based on his or her location. Also, if a guest visits the enterprise 's lobby before 9 a.m., she

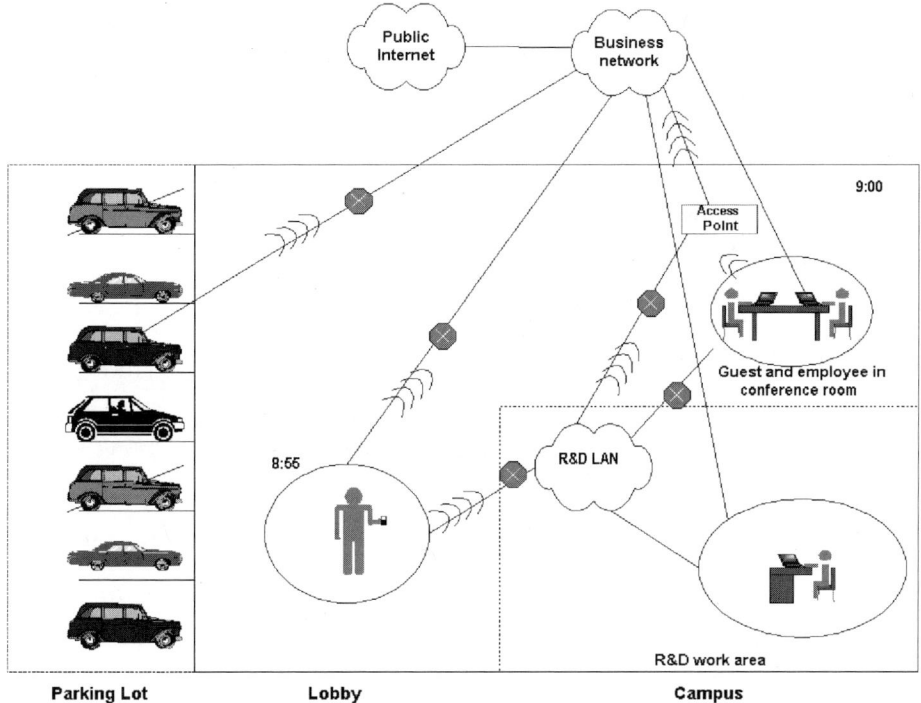

Figure 23-3. Authorization and access right boundaries.

or he can't access the public Internet or the enterprise's LAN. At 9 a.m., the guest can access the public Internet but she or he still cannot access the enterprise's LAN [1].

Finally, in this scenario, the access control security solution allows the enterprise's network administrator to authenticate its LAN users based on a variety of factors, including membership in a particular group, individual identity, time of day, physical location and job roles or responsibilities. The bottom line – more productive end users and a more secure network [1].

SUMMARY AND CONCLUSIONS

There's a curious dissonance when 90 percent of enterprises report security breaches but many of them don't have any idea what's going on within their networks. It's time to face facts: the need for comprehensive access control solutions has never been more urgent. The good news is that access control is a solvable problem for enterprises [1].

To solve this problem and protect their LANs, enterprises must essentially build a series of electronic "doors" that lead authorized users into appropriate "zones" of information and services – and nowhere else. Those doors and zones will prevent unauthorized use and enforce enterprise policies at all times and in all locations. Comprehensive access control systems architected this way can build on existing infrastructures and ultimately provide the most secure access control possible to enterprise LANs [1].

> **Note:** The new model for controlling access to a network calls for protecting data wherever it is and trusting no one completely wherever they are.

Finally, how do enterprises get there from here? Controlling access to networks is a huge task – and will remain so as the trends of the Internet, mobile computing and convergence continue to change how enterprises work [1].

REFERENCES

[1] "ProCurve Networking Access Control Security Solution," © 2006 Hewlett-Packard Development Company, L.P., Hewlett-Packard Company, 3000 Hanover Street, Palo Alto, CA 94304-1185 USA, 2006.

Chapter 24

EXTENDED WEB SITE SECURITY FUNCTIONALITY

INTRODUCTION

The web site is the medium for an increasing amount of business and other sensitive transactions, for example for online banking and brokerage. Virtually all browsers and servers deploy the SSL/TLS protocols to address concerns about security. However, the current usage of SSL/TLS by browsers, still allows extended web site functionality spoofing (misleading users by impersonation or misrepresentation of identity or of credentials) [1].

Indeed, there is an alarming increase in the amount of real-life web site-spoofing attacks, usually using simple techniques. Often, the swindlers lure the user to the spoofed web site (impersonating as financial institution, by sending her or him spoofed e-mail messages that link into the spoofed web-sites); this is often called a phishing attack. The goal of the attackers is often to obtain user-ID's, passwords/PINs and other personal and financial information, and abuse it (for identity theft). A recent study by industry analysts found that about six million users gave such information to spoofed web sites, and estimate 5.6B$ direct losses to U.S. banks and credit card issuers during 2006; other estimates of yearly damage due to phishing and spoofing attacks are between $900 million to $1.4 billion. Spoofing attacks, mostly using the phishing technique, are significant threats to secure e-commerce [1].

This chapter investigates spoofing and phishing attacks and present countermeasures, with regards to extended web site security functionality, while focusing on solutions that protect naïve as well as expert users. These attacks are not easy to deploy, as they require technical sophistication, and are sensitive to changes in browsers, operating systems and their configurations [1].

In fact, practical web site-spoofing attacks deployed so far, do not use such techniques, or use just basic scripts and browser vulnerabilities (to present fake location bar. Almost all of the many reported attacks left significant clues for the expert, attentive user, such as the lack of use of SSL/TLS (indicated by an open padlock icon, or by the lack of a padlock icon), and/or the use of a URL from a domain not owned by the victim web site. Such attacks will therefore succeed, even when using countermeasures [1].

Still, these simple attacks are very effective. It is argued that this is due to several weaknesses in the user interface of the current popular browsers, and suggests simple extensions to browsers, that should prevent many or most of these attacks. The goal here is to improve browser security-related user interface (UI), and protect (even) naïve, inattentive web users [1].

The first principle establishes the importance of default settings related to security, such as the list of certification authorities trusted by browsers. This is a special case of the unmotivated user principle and of the path of least resistance principle [1].

SECURE UI PRINCIPLE I: SECURITY SHOULD BE DEFAULT, AND DEFAULTS SHOULD BE SECURE

Default settings should provide adequate security, and only globally-trusted, obviously trustworthy parties may be trusted by default. Even if defaults are secure, users may overrule them and disable security features, if they are overly disruptive to normal work and annoying, and in particular if their importance is not sufficiently clear to the users, and especially if disabling is easy. For example, many browsers, by default, warn users if an unprotected web page contains a form (whose contents will be sent in the clear). However, most web-forms, currently, are not protected; therefore this message pops up very frequently and almost all users disable it (do not display this warning any more). This leads to the next principle [1]:

SECURE UI PRINCIPLE II: SECURITY MUST BE USABLE TO BE USED

Users will avoid or disable security mechanisms which are hard to use, disruptive or annoying. Secure usage should be the most natural and easy usage [1].

The next secure UI principle follows from well-known user-interface design principles such as recognition rather than recall principle. Its relevance to security was noted by observing that users tend to click thru textual warning messages (the unprotected form warning previously mentioned). Also, important sites such PayPal, Microsoft's Passport, Yahoo!, e-Bay and Chase, all ask users to enter passwords and/or other sensitive information in insecure web pages; this shows that not only users, but also web site designers and auditors did not notice the lack of protection [1].

SECURE UI PRINCIPLE III: ALERTS SHOULD WAKE-UP

Indicate security alerts (potential security exposures), using a clear, interruptive audio/visual signal. Alerts should not only be noticeable and interruptive, they (and other security indicators, settings etc.) should also be clear and understandable to all (or at least most) users. This leads to the third principle, which follows from usability Blooper 35 [1]:

SECURE UI PRINCIPLE IV: CRYPTOGRAPHY IS IN GREEK

Security and trust indicators and terms should be clear to all (naïve) users; avoid technical icons and jargon. To prevent web spoofing, trust indicators should be fixed at the top of the browser window to display (validated) logos or names, of the web site owner and of the authority that identified the owner of the site. It is recommend that commercial and enterprise web sites present secure logo only in the trust indicators, and do so in all of their web pages. This will protect the integrity of all of the web pages, and increase the likelihood of users detecting a spoofed (sensitive) web page, by noticing the lack of the appropriate logo and/or credentials in the trust indicators [1].

Cryptographic mechanisms should be used to validate the logos and credentials in the trust indicators. Specifically, you should bind the site's public key to the logo by signing both of them in a certificate, possibly as in [RFC3709], and use the (existing, widely available) SSL/TLS protocols to validate that the site has the private key corresponding to the public key [1].

RELATED REAL-LIFE WEB SITE-SPOOFING ATTACKS

Web Spoofing attacks were first really noticed in 1997. There, the adversary uses browser features to make it appear as if the browser displays the SSL-protected victim web page, while in fact it is displaying a cloned page. Some of these attacks are very simple, yet effective. For example, in one deployed attack, the attacker opens two browser windows: a small one, which clones for example, a Citibank™ login screen and contains no status information or bars, inside a larger one, which is simply the regular Citibank™ web site. Such sites can be extremely convincing; most users will not realize that they are entering their password into a separate, insecure pop-up window, whose URL is not even displayed. In another deployed attack, a bug in many Internet Explorer™ browsers is exploited, allowing the attacker to cause false information to be displayed in the location bar. Trust indicators can foil such attacks [1].

Chapter 25 shows that users, and even designers, do not notice the lack of protection on sensitive web pages. Several examples of sensitive yet unprotected web pages are given, asking for passwords, including PayPal, Yahoo!, Chase, E-Bay, Amazon and Microsoft's Passport. Attacks against Passport are also presented [1].

Several works presented even more elaborate web spoofing attacks, using scripts and/or Java applets, to make it even harder for users to detect the cloning. These works also propose solutions, by disabling (important) browser and extended web site functionalities, or using enhancements to the browser UI to make it hard or impossible for the attacker to display spoofed versions of important browser indicators. However, these proposals rely on users' understanding their signals, which are (even) more elaborate than the existing location bar and SSL indicator. Therefore, these proposals are not appropriate for most (naïve, inattentive) users. In fact, the current indications of location and protection (SSL) are not sufficiently visible and significant to most users [1].

Logo certificates should be used, possibly using the format in the draft standard 'X.509 certificate extension for logotypes' [RFC3709], whose goals include identifying web sites and other purposes. In particular, the logo should be displayed from such certificates in the browser interface, as protection against web spoofing. The work presented here extends the web site functionality and security, in particular, displaying the name or logo of the certificate authority that identified the site and making the trust indicator mandatory in all browser windows (which prevents attacks). A significant difference is that the design here is user-centric, and in particular allows users to select the logo, image or text for protected sites. Users can also select pet-names to identify web sites; but must be limited to textual names [1].

Finally, adoption of trust indicators may provide an incentive for protecting more web sites, compared to the current practice of protecting only very few web pages. Protecting web pages with SSL/TLS involves substantial overhead; this may be a problem for some sites. This may motivate adoption of more efficient mechanisms to protect web pages [1].

SUMMARY AND CONCLUSIONS

This chapter focused on preventing spoofed (fake) web sites (spoofing attacks. This included the very common phishing spoofing attacks, where the user reaches the spoofed web site by following a link in a spoofed e-mail message he or she receives [1].

So, the focus of this chapter was on ensuring security even for naïve web users; however, even expert, cautious users cannot be absolutely protected, unless browsers are extended with security measures. However, cautious users can increase their security, even before the site incorporates enhanced security measures, by following the following guidelines:

1. Use a trust indicator-enhanced browser, using its opportunistic logo identification mechanism to establish logos for each of your sensitive web-pages.
2. Always contact sensitive web sites by typing their address in the location bar, using a bookmark or following a link from a secure site, preferably protected by SSL/TLS.
3. Never click on links from e-mail messages or from other non-trustworthy sources (such as shady or possibly insecure web sites). These could lead you to a URL-forwarding a man-in-the-middle attack, which may be hard or impossible to detect, even if you follow guideline 1.
4. Be very careful to inspect the location bar and the SSL icon upon entering to sensitive web pages. Preferably, set up your browser to display the details of the certificate upon entering your most sensitive sites (most browsers can do this); this will help you notice the use of SSL and avoid most attacks. Do not trust indications of security and of the use of SSL when they appear as part of the web page, even when this page belongs to trustworthy enterprises.
5. If possible, restrict the damages due to spoofing by instructing your financial services to limit online transactions in your account to cover only what you really need. Finally,

consider using sensitive online services that use additional protection mechanisms beyond SSL [1].

REFERENCES

[1] Amir Herzberg and Ahmad Gbara, "TrustBar: Protecting (even Naïve) Web Users from Spoofing and Phishing Attacks," Department of Computer Science, Bar-Ilan University, Ramat Gan, 52900, Israel, 2006.

Chapter 25

SECURING WEB COMMUNICATIONS WITH SSL VPNS

INTRODUCTION

Over the years the trend toward utilizing virtual private networks (VPNs) and the Internet for remote access connectivity has grown dramatically – and shows no sign of slowing down. At a time when most enterprises need to do more with less, today's enterprise users need every bit of productivity that technology can offer. Remote access to e-mail, applications, collaborative tools and information can extend the day when users are traveling or working from home after hours. The convenience and flexibility of anywhere, anytime access give users a needed productivity boost, as well as a sense of empowerment. Greater job satisfaction and higher morale result. Remote access also facilitates on-demand information and application sharing with business partners via extranets – a meaningful way to streamline operations and improve customer service [1].

The demand for flexible remote access is being met by the increasing deployment of secure sockets layer (SSL) VPNs, browser-based technology that supports access from laptops and desktops, home computers, Internet kiosks and personal digital assistants – anywhere an Internet connection exists. Compared with other solutions, SSL VPNs can deliver cost savings, simpler administration and easier connections with partners. Where traditional VPNs are not required, expect immediate value from investments in SSL VPNs in the form of easier deployment and support [1].

However, the very success of SSL VPN delivering flexible access from a diverse set of endpoints is also its weakness. Because SSL VPNs extend remote access to nearly any unmanaged endpoint, they can expose the enterprise to a variety of security threats. If not understood and managed properly, these threats could threaten the enterprise's performance and even its very existence. This chapter examines the security risks that arise from securing web communications with SSL VPNs and proposes strategies for remediation [1].

THE BUSINESS OF SECURE REMOTE ACCESS

As SSL VPNs provide connectivity to internal computing resources, common sense suggests that sensitive information and systems should be secured. But it goes beyond common sense. New U.S. regulations such as Gramm-Leach-Bliley and Sarbanes-Oxley mandate that customer data and other sensitive information must be secure, properly stored and easily retrievable – at the risk of severe fines and even criminal prosecution [1].

In healthcare, the Health Insurance Portability and Accountability Act (HIPAA) sets out security, privacy and access guidelines for patient medical records – a challenge for IT administrators when the remote computers of physicians are beyond their direct control. In commerce, security must extend to extranet communications among trading partners, where sensitive pricing and inventory information is constantly exchanged. Unauthorized access could put the enterprise at risk, yet manufacturers cannot control the remote computers of partners [1].

Security concerns extend beyond the confidentiality of information downloaded. Unmanaged SSL VPN endpoints expose the internal network to security risks from infiltrated systems. Since they exist outside the corporate perimeter and are dependent on the choices of individual users, remote endpoints form the weakest link in the security chain [1].

REMOTE ACCESS REQUIRES COMPREHENSIVE SECURITY

Day extenders accessing enterprise resources via SSL VPN connections pose higher security risks than employees working on site – especially if teleworkers provide their own, nonstandard equipment. Home-based users may share systems with other family members, making it impossible to enforce security policies or approved configurations. Internet connection sharing could allow unknown systems to access enterprise resources over SSL VPNs, and wireless home networks are notoriously insecure. To protect remote SSL systems, the users themselves must take on more of the security burden than their in-house counterparts. Yet such users tend to be the least technologically savvy and SSL VPN solutions must include some capability to check the security state of the endpoint [1].

The SSL VPN gateway poses another security concern. Although SSL encryption provides a level of data privacy and integrity, it does not confer access rights. SSL VPN solutions must allow administrators to limit access to those authorized and no one else. And just because users can establish SSL VPN tunnels does not mean they should have access to all resources. VPN users are considered *trusted* users, yet much damage, both unintentional and intentional, has been done by trusted users. Though SSL encryption does a good job of preventing others from reading private information, it provides no guarantee of information passing through the VPN [1].

SSL VPNs generally rely on the browser to access Web, fileshares or e-mail applications via their included Web portal. However, most SSL VPN solutions today offer the capability to provide full native network-level access. For access to clientserver applications, SSL VPNs employ Java browser plug-ins as agents. Because Java has been used as a vehicle for attack, such sessions could subject internal servers to attacks from compromised endpoints.

Given that today's worms include scanning capability to look for hosts to infect, this network level connectivity represents a new vector for worms. IT administrators must be vigilant in providing policies and technology solutions that address the security threats posed by unmanaged SSL VPN endpoints [1].

ENDPOINT SECURITY CONSIDERATIONS

What exactly are the threats to remote-access endpoints using SSL VPN facilities over an Internet connection, such as cable, DSL or satellite feed? Always-on broadband connections are ripe targets for hackers looking for backdoors into an enterprise to steal and destroy data, disable systems and perform other malicious activities. Malware such as viruses, worms, trojan horses, spyware and blended threats can exploit unprotected clients and use network access to infest an enterprise with catastrophic results. As an example, in January 2004, the MyDoom blended threat attacked systems worldwide that were exposed through a backdoor. Damage has been estimated at $23 billion in the U.S. alone, according to industry analysts. Today's malware is so sophisticated that an entire network can be infected within minutes after the initial breach [1].

The proliferation of malware has led industry analysts to raise their estimate of the probability of a catastrophic global attack in 2006, with damage surpassing $400 billion, from 2.5 percent to 70 percent. Such estimates are hardly surprising given recent statistics: that one in three computers was infected, and the typical system houses 26.5 separate spyware programs [1].

Appearing as harmless applications, trojan horses are designed to steal computer data or destroy host systems. They can give attackers unrestricted access to online computers, including file transfers and adding or deleting files. System monitors can capture a user's keystrokes, emails and application sessions; the results are stored in encrypted log files for later retrieval. A well-known attack occurred in September 2003 when, using keystroke loggers and other spyware, hackers intercepted email at game developer Valve Software and stole source code for Half-Life 2, a popular game. As a result, a pirated version was posted on the Internet and the official release was delayed several months [1].

The perils of spyware are many. As an IT professional, you can't ignore it: It slows down your users' systems, impacts your end users' productivity, and could even degrade performance of your networks and network apps. Spyware can change system or registry settings, redirect users or reset home pages to specific Web sites, sneak trojans onto PCs and much more. The danger isn't only from users opening infected attachments or visiting questionable Web sites. Any computer connected to the Internet can expect to log some form of digital attack attempt roughly every 30 seconds. Clearly, unmanaged SSLVPN endpoints are at risk from spyware and other malware [1].

THE COLLABORATIVE PROCESS OF VPN SECURITY

To make SSL VPNs secure, IT administrators should engage in a collaborative process with end users. One approach is to institute an enterprise policy requiring that all users deploy third-party security software such as anti-virus and personal firewalls. Such measures help ensure that endpoints will not serve as a conduit for attacks on the enterprise network through the VPN. And they are effective [1].

All antivirus programs that are tested successfully detect and prevent known viruses, if the virus definitions are kept current. Personal firewalls complement anti-virus by defending against both inbound and outbound attacks, even some "day zero" attacks that might pass the anti-virus shield. Still, anti-virus and personal firewall protection can be difficult to ensure on unmanaged SSL VPN endpoints. Personal firewalls offer many user-defined settings and access rights that must be configured properly. And operating software, browsers and other applications must be kept current and patched with the latest security releases. If they are not, the entire enterprise is at risk. As an example, in August, 2003, the Blaster worm infected between 8 million and 16 million Windows systems worldwide – despite a patch being released a month earlier [1].

IT administrators must also control the residual data from remote access sessions over SSL VPNs. Browser-based SSL VPN sessions are "notorious for littering the local hard disk with information about where you've been and what you've done. Cookies, URL histories, user credentials, page caches and files are all captured on SSL VPN endpoints as varied as Internet kiosks, home computers and business workstations. To secure such data, SSLVPN software should control the caching of information by encrypting all data and automatically deleting it after the session [1].

Even recycling the hard drives of SSL VPN endpoints is a concern. An insurer, for instance, thought it had erased the hard drives on retired PCs – until it received blackmail threats from someone who bought one of those systems. Because the breach involved customer data, it must be disclosed to the customers under California law. SSL VPN users can also put information assets at risk if they forget to log out from public endpoints such as kiosks. One solution is non-intrusive timeouts and periodic re-authentication [1].

Given the overall responsibility that IT personnel have for the safety of the network, it is essential to enforce rigorous security policies on SSL VPNs. Automatic security controls should check the underlying configurations, patch levels and status of antivirus and firewall software running on SSL endpoints – and deny access if a minimal level of security is not met [1].

SECURING THE GATEWAY

By providing true network-level access to internal resources, SSL VPNs can offer users the same access as direct-connect LAN users. This requires strong security controls at the gateway. Given that the clientless nature of SSL VPN limits the depth to which an endpoint can be secured and inspected, it becomes increasingly critical that SSL VPN provide some screening functionality within the gateway itself. And access must be restricted to necessary data only. Content screening, application inspection and verification, and other attack controls work to guarantee that both inbound and outbound SSL VPN data adheres to security policies and does not contain malicious content that could be used to inject an attack into the network or steal private information [1].

As an example of the need for gateway protection, Web based applications are susceptible to hackers "injecting" SQL query commands to pull data from backend databases. Using this technique, it has been reported that a rogue employee "accidentally" obtained a list of passwords from the database server. In another example, PHPnuke, a widely used Web portal system, contained an injection bug that allowed attackers to gain control of the administrative side of the system. While such vulnerabilities should be addressed by patching the application code, robust security at the SSL VPN gateway provides a further and needed level of protection [1].

You have already seen how SSL VPNs provide agent-level network connectivity through ActiveX or Java controls, putting the network at risk from worms and blended threats if the gateway isn't protected. In fact, today's sophisticated malware uses multiple points of attack and multiple methods of propagation, including search engines to scan for victims and wreak havoc on information resources. The Sasser worm, for instance, used automatic scanning techniques via network-level access to infect more than 10 million systems and inflict approximately $15 billion in damages worldwide [1].

Finally, the most serious security breaches often come from within – data attacks initiated by cyber-criminals, rogue users or disgruntled employees to steal confidential credit card numbers, identity information, customer and supplier profiles, intellectual property and transaction histories. In a world where security and privacy are outsourced overseas, and increasingly fall under government regulation and the criminal code, it is crucial to monitor both inbound and outbound SSL VPN traffic for malicious intent and content [1].

SUMMARY AND CONCLUSIONS

As enterprise users move inside and outside traditional boundaries, SSL VPNs for remote access provide substantial benefits in productivity and convenience. Yet anywhere, anytime access can greatly increase the network's vulnerability to a range of security threats. Deadly attacks can be launched from unsecured or compromised SSL VPN endpoints, so it is essential to ensure their security before granting them network access. Most important, because network-based SSL tunneling can bypass perimeter security, it exposes the network to many of the same threats seen at the perimeter. Finally, your SSL VPN solution must have the capability to inspect Web, ActiveX and other types of traffic for malicious content [1].

REFERENCES

[1] Amir Herzberg and Ahmad Gbara, "SSL VPNS: The Challenge Of Delivering Both Flexibility And Security," Copyright 2004 © Check Point Software Technologies Ltd. All rights reserved. Check Point Software Technologies Inc., 800 Bridge Parkway, Redwood City, CA 94065, 2004.

PART XII

ISSUING AND MANAGING CERTIFICATES

Chapter 26

WHY DIGITAL CERTIFICATES ARE USED

INTRODUCTION

More and more people are looking for solutions to the massive growth in phishing and other consumer fraud on the Net. Digital certificates, already vital for securing web sites and encrypting communications with consumers so they can't be intercepted and read in transmission, will be a major part of the solution. But how will this happen [1]?

Digital certificates that secure web sites (SSL server certificates) contain certain information submitted by the site that bought the certificate from a public Certification Authority (CA). Some have suggested greater display and reliance on this information to help consumers detect fraud. Can this work, or will it instead give rise to new phishing opportunities and even greater incidents of consumer fraud [1]?

This chapter takes a look at digital certificates (past, present and future) and their potential for deterring phishing attacks and online fraud. It demonstrates the severe pitfalls from First Generation manual vetting of certificate holders and the inherent unreliability of the identity information they contain (which can easily be faked). These certificates could create serious legal liability for the writers of browser software and for CAs if the identity information they contain is presented to end users as reliable data. Finally, this chapter lays out a path for the future, with a description of higher assurance Second Generation automated vetting of Web identities, and discusses ongoing enhancements that will provide a better solution for online identity authentication and reduction of consumer fraud [1].

UNDERSTANDING FIRST GENERATION DIGITAL CERTIFICATES

The technology surrounding SSL server certificates and Public Key Infrastructures has been well known since the 1970s, and will not be covered here. What's important for this chapter are the two main things that digital certificates can do to secure web sites and help avoid consumer fraud: They encrypt communications between the web site owner and consumer, and they provide certain identity data about the web site owner [1].

As Internet use expanded during the 1990s from universities and the defense industry (a closed community) to online commerce and broad consumer use, the encryption function has worked brilliantly, but the identity function has not. Consumers have learned to trust the padlock symbol for sites protected by an SSL server certificate as meaning they can safely transmit their personal and financial data to complete a transaction. For the majority of consumers, they have never clicked on the lock to look "inside" the certificate at the limited identity data stored there by the issuer. A number of browser software makers are considering extracting that identity data and displaying it in the browser toolbar, but that is a flawed approach considering the inherent unreliability of that data [1].

So, where did the rules around digital certificates come from? Who made the rules?

The development of digital certificate and PKI protocols over the past 28 years was focused primarily on technical syntax and overall system structure and design, and paid only scant attention to the specific authentication steps to be followed by CAs prior to certificate issuance. The limited discussion of authentication processes during this period:

1. Was written mostly by technical PKI experts, and not by commercial users of PKI or by CAs themselves
2. Recognized that different authentication steps will be appropriate for different uses and communities (closed communities of enterprises who knew each other versus open worldwide communities)
3. Was very vague in nature, reflecting the limited expertise of the authors in business and commercial practices [1].

Early industry documents establishing digital certificate and PKI protocols skipped over specific authentication steps to be used prior to issuance of digital certificates, or made only general reference to some sort of authentication process.

> **Note:** See the early standards stated at the IETF's RFC 791 (1981), RFC 822 (1982), and RFC 1422 (1993). The standards for authentication were very weak and delegated. For example, RFC 1422 provides in part: 3.4.1.2 User Registration: Most details of user registration are a local matter, subject to policies established by the user's CA and the PCA (Policy Certification Authority) under which that CA has been certified. The CA will employ some means, specified by the CA in accordance with the policy of its PCA, to validate the user's claimed identity and to ensure that the public component provided is associated with the user whose distinguished name is to be bound into the certificate.

The technical experts who set up digital certificates and PKI as are known today worked only on the technical aspects and architecture; they "punted" on ultimate identity issues, leaving it to closed communities and public CAs to decide what authentication steps they would take before issuing a certificate to an enterprise or individual. They probably thought this was the easiest part of the online identity equation; in fact, it's the hardest [1].

> **Note:** RFC 2459, "Internet X.509 Public Key Infrastructure Certificate and CRL Profile" (1999), which set X.509 v3 standards for certificates in use today, likewise did not prescribe particular authentication standards: Requirements and assumptions: A certificate user should review the certificate policy generated by the certification authority (CA) before relying on the authentication

or non-repudiation services associated with the public key in a particular certificate. To this end, this standard does not prescribe legally binding rules or duties.

Now, what data's in a digital certificate? Where do you find it? How did it get there [1]? Under X.509 v3 standards, a digital certificate is set up with the following data fields about the certificate holder:

- CN: Common Name (the web address, such as www.geotrust.com)
- O: Organization
- OU: Organization Unit (can be a division, department, etc.)
- L: Locality
- S: State or Province
- C: Country [1]

However, public CAs do not all follow the same naming conventions (except for the CN field, which must be uniform across all providers), and do not always use all the fields. They also commonly put other information and phrases in the fields for their own purposes, such as "Subject to CPS (Certification Practice Statement) found at www.address.com" or "Liability Limited" – items that provide no identity information.

So, where do you find this information? It isn't easy. In Internet Explorer, for example, you must double click on the padlock, then choose Details, then Subject. Consumers are generally unaware the data is in there, and have never relied on it for identity purposes. That's why the data field vulnerabilities discussed next have never made a difference before. No one has ever looked at or relied on the data before. This will all change if certificate identity data is pulled out and displayed on the browser GUI in the future; browser users will get a false sense of security, and trust a displayed identity that is totally false – a perfect phishing environment for the coming decade. The one exception is the CN or Common Name field – for reasons explained next, the field must be unique, correct and verified, and can be relied upon by consumers to know which web site they are at [1].

How did the data get inside the certificate? During the early 1990s, each public CA came up with its own First Generation manual vetting process. The process typically requires only the most minimal checking of documents and records, and is prone to mistakes and forgery. Most often you can find an extremely brief and cryptic description of the manual vetting process being used in the CPS (Certification Practice Statement) published by the CA and buried in its online archives. It's hard to make sense of the process – and CAs are quick to state in legal language that they make no promises about the identity of the certificate holder and won't be held legally liable for any fraud or mistakes [1].

So, what are the phishing and fraud vulnerabilities in manual vetting? More specifically, First Generation manual vetting usually involves an online application from the domain holder with the faxing of a few basic business documents (copies of articles of incorporation, local business license, etc.) in an attempt to show identity, which are then briefly checked against light-weight third party enterprise databases. All this can be forged or faked by a certificate applicant intent on phishing or fraud as described next, meaning the identity data in an issued certificate may be completely wrong and misleading. This vetting process is all the more prone to error considering that each state, province, and country has its own set of enterprise documentation, which no single CA can verify worldwide [1].

Well, who's in charge of how manual identity vetting is done? Who makes sure identity in certificates is done right [1]?

Basically no one. Some years ago, the major browser makers required public CAs who wanted to maintain their trusted roots in the browser store of trusted roots (see next) to obtain an annual American Institute of Certified Public Accountants (AICPA) WebTrust audit – but those audits do not establish any standards for how identity is established in certificates. Instead, the auditors just look at what the CA says it does in the vetting process in the CA's CPS, then conducts spot checks of past vetting to see if the CA has been following its own rules [1].

> **Note:** The basic WebTrust audit rule is "say what you do, and do what you say."

If the CA has been fooled by phony documents or the process is flawed, the CA will still receive a clean audit. Even worse, some public CAs outsource the entire identity verification process to others, without any checking or auditing of the process. The "subcontractors" can (and sometimes do) vouch for the identity of a certificate applicant without doing any checking at all. This flawed identity data is then transmitted back to the public CA, who inserts it in the certificate and signs it with the CA's key for distribution and use by the applicant. Because WebTrust doesn't reach these outsourced subcontractors, they are never audited and their shoddy practices are not discovered. Imagine letting consumers rely on that kind of unverified identity data if it is prominently displayed in a browser GUI [1].

The problem is likely to get much worse in the near future, especially if browser GUIs are changed to display certificate data to consumers for identity reliance and trust purposes. There are literally dozens of "trusted" root certificates already pre-loaded in the browser software currently used by hundreds of millions of consumers around the world [1].

> **Tip:** As one example, open Internet Explorer (go to Tools / Internet Options / Certificates / Trusted Root Certification Authorities) and you'll find over 100 trusted root certificates listed.

Any certificate issued off of one of these trusted roots (or off a sub-root or a root that has been signed by a trusted root) will be treated as a "trusted" certificate. It will also be automatically accepted by a consumer's browser software [1].

Many of these trusted roots have been sold over the years, and many chained subroots have been issued to third parties. If any one of these third parties (who may be in any country of the world) decides to use the root to issue phony or unverified certificates to enterprises intent on phishing or fraud, and the identity data is prominently exposed to the unwary consumer in the browser GUI, there could be an explosion in phishing attacks. Perhaps worse, after the first public exposure of this new kind of phishing, consumers might no longer trust secured Web sites at all, as the flaws in the SSL technology used to secure the sites would no longer be trusted [1]. There have been some attempts to come up with strict authentication standards that would apply to all public CAs, but these are years from completion and for the reasons discussed next, will likely not scale nor work in a worldwide environment.

Now, let's look at some examples of how First Generation manual authentication certificates can contain identity data that is faked or inaccurate. Unfortunately, there are all too many examples. Here are just some:

- Fraudulent documents: With current design software and scanners, applicants can create convincing (but fake) enterprise and other identity documents.
- Real documents, fraudulently presented: Fraudsters can easily get copies of real enterprise identity documents from public records and present them to public CAs.
- Shell enterprises and empty business data accounts: In many states and provinces, an enterprise can be formed in 10 minutes for less than $100 using pre-printed forms. Creating an account with a business data agency (such as Dun & Bradstreet) can be done online in minutes. For many public CAs, a newly-created shell enterprise with an "empty" business data account would be sufficient for certificate authentication purposes.
- Duplicate names and naming conventions (XYZ Corp, XYZ Ltd., XYZ LLC): There can be 50 distinct "Acme Corporations" in the fifty states, with more in other countries. In addition, consumers are generally unfamiliar with the exact enterprise name for a trusted company (Co., Corp., Ltd.) opening other opportunities for fraudulent imitation. Certificates might be issued in all these names. Which is real, and which is used by an imposter?
- Worldwide scalability: These enterprise identity problems multiply exponentially for other countries. Is a Société Anonyme in France the same as a Fideicomiso in Mexico or a Joint Stock Company of the Closed Type in Russia? Who would set the standards for authentication for these international entities? No authoritative body does it at present. The process doesn't scale. And what if an apparently valid certificate is issued to a shell US subsidiary of a foreign enterprise, and all the consumer data provided to the US subsidiary is instantaneously transmitted to the foreign owner for phishing purposes?
- No common O field vetting among public CAs: There are no common First Generation manual vetting procedures among the top public CAs, and will not be for many years to come, if ever.
- Non-corporate enterprises (partnerships, sole proprietorships): There are many legitimate enterprise entities that don't have to be officially registered anywhere, such as partnerships and sole proprietorships. Public CAs don't have the ability to determine their validity.
- Enterprises may be dissolved, sold, merged, etc., but the data in their old certificate remains unchanged and therefore be misleading.
- The owner of the domain shown in O field of a certificate may have nothing to do with owner of the enterprise using the site: Many Web hosting enterprises and Internet service providers will secure multiple independent sites using a single digital certificate in the top level domain name, which can't contain any confirmed identity information about the individual sites being secured [1].

In addition, many sites outsource certain functions (web-based purchasing and billing) to other sites that are branded to look like the original site. The identity data in the outsourced site will not relate to or be the same as the original site. Consider the needs of small enterprises (Yahoo's merchant sites, for example) or the needs of a large enterprise (such as United Airlines) where outsourcing is used. This creates a serious potential for confusing the consumer and opens tremendous phishing holes [1].

Many more examples could be cited. All illustrate the intrinsic unreliability of the identity data contained in the O, OU, L, S, and C fields of digital certificates obtained though First Generation manual vetting, and demonstrate why the data can't be used for identity and trust purposes. The one consistent exception is data in the CN field, which can be trusted and is at the center of modern Second Generation automated vetting [1].

Are there any examples of fake or inaccurate data inside a certificate from a public CA? Unfortunately, yes. False certificates have been obtained on a number of occasions from multiple public CAs without ever submitting any false information in the process [1].

So, how are misleading certificates obtained? On several occasions, there have been examples where a certificate was easily obtained that contained inaccurate or potentially fraudulent identity information. These were obtained from multiple public CAs without ever submitting any false information in the process. Again, phishers and fraudsters haven't bothered to obtain fake digital certificates to date because consumers have never looked at or relied upon the identity information in the certificate (they don't even know it's there) – but this will all change if next-generation browser GUIs extract and display certificate data in an attempt to provide users with site identity information for trust decision purposes. There is a better way (Second Generation automated vetting) as discussed next [1].

This is frustrating – how did this happen? It happened because of a fundamental misconception by the early designers of Internet and digital certificate protocols – that authentication of enterprise entities was easy and that universal credentials (not just credentials for closed environments) could be created using manual identity vetting as currently practiced. The designers of the system were engineers without experience or interest in the legal and policy issues surrounding verified enterprise identity issues. And phishing and other identity fraud on unsuspecting consumers was not a problem [1].

Why didn't anyone notice before? Because no one has ever looked at or relied upon the identity data found inside digital certificates. That could all change if the data is given prominent browser display in the future [1].

First Generation manually vetted certificates can cost as much as $1,495.00 from some CAs, and take days to obtain. Why does anyone put up with it [1]?

One can only guess that certificate buyers put up with old-style, expensive manual vetting because their technical people grew up with it (it was something you just had to do) and didn't realize the serious flaws with the vetting process and the data contained in a certificate. More and more enterprises have migrated to the newer, Second Generation automated vetting process for their digital certificates, saving money and time. In fact, a recent industry analyst survey data from April 2006, shows that Second Generation automated certificates outsold First Generation manual certificates better than 2-to-1 over the past six months [1].

So, what about legal liability from faked or inaccurate identity data in manually vetted certificates? An enterprise can face major legal liability today in surprising ways. Consider the following example. Recently, a woman sued the local Yellow Pages directory publisher in Portland, Oregon and won an astounding jury award of $1,600,000 [1]. The woman had gone to a physician (a dermatologist) who was listed in a Yellow Pages ad under the heading "Plastic and Reconstructive Surgery." His ad said he was "Board Certified" – but he was only board certified as a physician and dermatologist, and not as a plastic surgeon [1].

After problems with the surgery, the woman discovered the doctor was not certified as a plastic surgeon and sued the Yellow Pages saying she was misled by the ad. The Yellow Pages said they publish thousands of ads, and couldn't possibly know whether individual ads are true or not [1].

Note: A representative of the publisher was quoted as saying "We publish 260 directories in 14 states. We don't validate every claim."

The jury didn't agree, and hit the Yellow Pages for $1,600,000 in damages. The case is currently being appealed to a higher court, but in the meantime the Yellow Pages must post a bond for the full judgment amount [1].

There could be a similar legal liability for browser makers, and perhaps others, if digital certificate data is displayed in a browser GUI and relied upon by a consumer for identity and trust purposes. As noted above, most identity data inside First Generation manually vetted certificates is inherently unreliable, a fact that will be instantly attractive to phishers. A consumer may say, "I thought this was my bank's real web site because I saw my bank's name displayed by the browser as confirmed identity information. A phisher then stole and used my personal data as a result" [1].

There are, in fact, known examples of certificates wrongly issued by public CAs in the name of a bank or other legitimate enterprise. If consumers are phished by means of one of these false certificates displayed on the browser GUI, they may argue that the browser maker is responsible for misleading them as to the web site's identity, and major legal liability could result. Courts may choose to ignore the language in browser User Agreements (the "fine print") that says the browser maker can't be sued for false information, saying that's not fair to consumers and that the browser maker encouraged the consumer to rely on the data by its prominent display [1].

Note: Bottom line: First Generation manual vetting is inherently flawed, and digital certificate identity data (except for the CN common name field showing the Web address, which can't be faked and is unique) is too unreliable to be used for identity purposes.

SECOND GENERATION AUTOMATED VETTING: CHEAPER, FASTER AND THE KEY TO IDENTITY VERIFICATION IMPROVEMENTS FOR THE NEXT DECADE

Consumers are desperate for better identity solutions to avoid phishing and online fraud. They once trusted email messages that claimed to be from familiar senders, until they learned the senders could be phishers in disguise who were only interested in stealing their data. Later, they stopped trusting familiar Internet addresses (long, complicated addresses that started with a familiar and trusted web address, but ended with a different phisher's address). And, after that, stopped trusting web pages set out in the spitting image of a trusted web page belonging to their bank, favorite auction site or credit card provider. Now, many people will not trust any unsolicited email, even when validly sent by their actual enterprise partner [1].

Again, this is really frustrating – the Internet is growing exponentially, and needs a better identity trust framework. What is to be done [1]?

The answer to the growing online identity problem starts with an increased use of SSL and digital certificates generally to secure web sites and verify their actual Internet address in a way that can't be faked or entered in error. This will be accomplished as public CAs gradually abandon their 1990s First Generation manual vetting processes (which cost a lot in time and money without adding any reliable and trusted identity data) and move to Second Generation automated processes. This has already started to happen [1].

The second major part of the solution is greater use and browser display of the web site's confirmed Internet address. This is important because all public CAs treat verification of the CN field in the same way, and any discrepancy between the web site's actual Internet address and the confirmed Internet address as stated in the CN common name field of a certificate will automatically generate a significant warning to the consumer via a pop-up notice. This avoids such dangerous phishing methods, as the use of long complicated address strings that start with a valid address but end with a direction to a phony site used for phishing. The prominent display of the CN field in the browser GUI will help users know where they are and learn which sites to trust. Put another way, the CN field (web address) is the only piece of data in a digital certificate that's confirmed, guaranteed to be unique, and is registered with an official public domain registry. The third major part of the solution is the automatic use and display of other trust information that is useful to the consumer, including the following:

- The name and logo of the CA who issued the certificate. Consumers will soon learn from news reports which CAs to trust and which CAs use sloppy procedures and should not be trusted.
- Automated checking against "black lists" for reported bad Web sites.
- The display of trusted and verified seals such as TRUSTe and Better Business Bureau Online.
- The display of user rating data on sites like the enterprise data compiled by BizRate and others.
- Active use of CRLs (Certificate Revocation Lists) and OCSP (Online Certificate Status Protocol) responders to check the revocation status of all certificates. This could be accomplished most easily if browser makers set the default for the CRL checking function to "on." False certificates would then no longer be accepted once revoked.
- Cooperation by Public CAs in working together to find common solutions. This could include creation of black lists available to all.
- Most important, the application of sophisticated algorithms and progressive heuristic techniques by the issuing CA for ongoing fraud detection. These can be changed hourly as needed based on new reports of phishing an identity fraud. Suspicious certificate issuance can be blocked, and already issued certificates can be revoked and entered on a black list for immediate warning display in a browser GUI [1].

The results of all these tests can be displayed via the browser GUI to help consumers decide which web sites to trust, which to be cautious of, and which to avoid entirely.

Enhancing Trust Capabilities

Various browser plug-ins and toolkits are already available for this purpose. There are other components of future solutions as well. For example, consumers can "vote on" the trustworthiness and credibility of a given SSL-secured site and report phishing and fraud attempts related to the site. Browser interfaces can then display in real time the cumulative result of that consumer feedback. Sites that have too few responses or too many negative results will deserve caution and little trust, while other sites with many positive results will deserve strong trust from the consumer. This is how eBay, Amazon and Yahoo establish trust relationships across millions of unknown buyers, sellers, and other users every day – not by means of any First Generation manual vetting process. Such a process will democratize trust decisions and create a distributed trust environment [1].

Another potential solution is for trusted SSL secured sites to "vouch" for their critical companion sites by means of a displayed and verifiable hyperlink. Consider the example of United Airlines. When a consumer visits the main United page, http://www.united.com and clicks on "Flights", the consumer is immediately redirected to a secured page at the address http://www.itn.net that has the same look-and-feel of a United page. Who is itn.net? A search of the relevant WhoIs registry for the domain and related domains shows a confusing array of names in various cities (itn.net, Travelocity.com Internet Services, alston.com; GetThere.com, etc.). Who are consumers really dealing with? The system works today because the consumer is relying on the look-and-feel of the site (branded as United Airlines) and previous successful transactions initiated through a trusted initial Internet address, http://www.united.com. But this won't work for unknown web sites that are new to a viewer. Consumer confidence in redirected web pages might be increased if the original site includes a legend on the redirected page stating as follows: "You are now at a trusted partner's site to complete your transaction with us. We vouch for the trustworthiness of this site. To confirm, please click here: https://www.originaldomainname.com/trusted partners" [1].

At that point, the consumer could confirm that the site is included in a list of trusted partners by clicking on the hyperlink and seeing that the original site has listed the partner and its address on a secured page in the original domain. This would create a transitive trust environment and enhance the user experience [1].

Finally, with the addition of other identity security techniques, sophisticated algorithms, and trust practices, it is possible (it's happening now with many browser makers, public CAs, and application providers), so long as the Internet industry moves away from the First Generation manual vetting processes initially designed in the early 1990s, and does not try to rely in the inherently inaccurate identity information contained inside the data fields (O, OU, L, S, and C) of those certificates, as a means of creating a universal credential. That old process is generally a waste of time and money, and increased reliance on the flawed data it produces will create vast new opportunities for phishing and other online identity fraud. Instead, with the use of Second Generation automated vetting of identities tied to the CN common name field that can't be faked, additional identity and anti-fraud techniques can be layered in depth to help consumers make more sophisticated trust decisions that simply are not possible today [1].

SUMMARY AND CONCLUSIONS

Be wary of supposed "confirmed" identity information contained inside First Generation manually vetted digital certificates – a process developed with little thought in the early 1990s. The manual vetting process is inherently vulnerable to mistakes and fraud, and no public CA takes responsibility for the actual identity of a certificate holder.

Note: Some public CAs don't even bother to vet the enterprise entity information before issuing a certificate.)

This creates the perfect environment for new and potentially devastating phishing attacks if the data is now displayed in browser GUIs for identity verification purposes [1].

Finally, Second Generation automated vetting is gaining rapid acceptance among certificate buyers and many public CAs, outselling First Generation manual certificates better than 2-to-1 in 2006. This lowers the cost and time for certificate issuance, and helps expand the use of SSL to secure the web. By relying on the CN or common name for web sites that can't be faked, Second Generation automated vetting establishes the groundwork for the layering of other new, sophisticated algorithms and trust techniques and browser displays to help consumers make better informed trust decisions. It's the growing trend for the next decade [1].

REFERENCES

[1] Kirk Hall, "Vulnerability of First-Generation Digital Certificates and Potential for Phishing Attacks and Consumer Fraud," © 2005 GeoTrust, Inc. All Rights Reserved. GeoTrust, Inc., 117 Kendrick Street, Suite 350, Needham, MA 02494, April 2005.

Chapter 27

CERTIFICATE AUTHORITIES

INTRODUCTION

Have you ever used a credit card to buy something on the Internet? Then you've probably used both a CA and PKI, without even knowing it. The PKI comes in because you really need somebody to confirm that the site you're on is the site you think it is. That is, say the site claims to be amazon.com. How do you know it really is the one and only amazon.com? Otherwise you might be on a phishing site typing your card info in for the convenience of somebody who'd like nothing better than spending your hard-earned money. You trust the CA to verify that the site is who it claims to be (see sidebar, "What Are Certificate Authorities?"). Ah, but how do you know to trust the CA? Well, your browser knows to trust it because it has a copy of its public key installed with the browser. How can you trust your browser? Well, you did get it from a reputable source, didn't you? This may seem a bit paranoid, but that's the first rule in thinking about security and trust [1].

What Are Certificate Authorities?

In cryptography, a certificate authority or certification authority (CA) is an entity which issues digital certificates for use by other parties. It is an example of a trusted third party. CA's are characteristic of many public key infrastructure (PKI) schemes.

There are many commercial CAs that charge for their services. Institutions and governments may have their own CAs, and there are free CAs.

Issuing A Certificate

A CA will issue a public key certificate which states that the CA attests that the public key contained in the certificate belongs to the person, enterprise, server, or other entity noted in the certificate. A CA's obligation in such schemes is to verify an applicant's credentials, so that users (relying parties) can trust the information in the CA's certificates. The usual idea is that if the user trusts the CA and can verify the CA's signature, then they can also verify that a certain public key does indeed belong to whoever is identified in the certificate.

If the CA can be subverted, then the security of the system breaks down. For example, suppose an attacker, Mallory, manages to get a certificate authority to issue a false certificate tying Alice to the wrong public key, which corresponding private key is known to Mallory. If Bob subsequently obtains and uses the public key in this certificate, the security of his communications could be compromised by Mallory – for example, his messages could be decrypted, or he could be tricked into accepting forged signatures.

Security

The problem of assuring correctness of match between data and entity when the data are presented to the CA (perhaps over an electronic network), and when the credentials of the person/company/program asking for a certificate is likewise presented, is difficult. This is why commercial CAs often use a combination of authentication techniques including leveraging government bureaus, the payment infrastructure, third parties databases and services, and custom heuristics. In some enterprise systems, local forms of authentication such as Kerberos can be used to obtain a certificate which can in turn be used by external relying parties. Notaries are required in some cases to personally know the party whose signature is being notarized; this is a higher standard than can be reached for many CA's. According to the American Bar Association outline on Online Transaction Management, the primary points of federal and state statutes that have been enacted regarding digital signatures, has been to "prevent conflicting and overly burdensome local regulation and to establish that electronic writings satisfy the traditional requirements associated with paper documents." Further the E-Sign and UETA code help ensure that:

1. A signature, contract or other record relating to such transaction may not be denied legal effect, validity, or enforceability solely because it is in electronic form.
2. A contract relating to such transaction may not be denied legal effect, validity or enforceability solely because an electronic signature or electronic record was used in its formation.

In large-scale deployments Alice may not be familiar with Bob's certificate authority (perhaps they each have a different CA), so Bob's certificate may also include his CA's public key signed by a different CA_2, which is presumably recognizable by Alice. This process typically leads to a hierarchy or mesh of CAs and CA certificates [2].

Thawte and Verisign are two of the commercial CAs on the Internet. Commercial or government sites pay for managed PKI services, basically a healthy fee for each computer that is authenticated. Thawte and Verisign vouch for the identity of computers within those enterprises. The computers in question might just be e-commerce Web servers, or it might be all users (or now, Cisco IP phones) within the enterprise [1].

Under the hood, here's what's going on. Each computer has to be issued a certificate, an electronic file digitally signed by the CA saying in effect "by the authority vested in me, you can believe this is John Doe's computer and its public key." The digital signature ties together identity and a public encryption key. This scheme also uses hash coding of the signature, and encryption to detect alterations. The online CA can then be used to confirm that the digital signature is valid, that it did in fact issue the certificate. If somebody obtains the computer's certificate and puts it on another computer, then they might be able to have another computer pretend to be John Doe's computer. This is somewhat like having your driver's license or ID card copied [1].

So a Certificate Authority (CA) is just the entity that issues and vouches for digital certificates. Public Key Infrastructure (PKI) is the technology and processes that do the work. You create a public and a private key, and a certificate containing identity info and your public key. You submit it to the PKI. The PKI verifies your identity, stores the identity info and public key (think directory or phone book), digitally signs the certificate, and returns it to you. That CA digital signature confirms that your identity is associated with the public key in the certificate. The certificate gives you a way to digitally sign things by using your private key (proving they really come from you and not someone masquerading as you). The public and private keys also give you a convenient way to automatically and securely negotiate a 3DES or AES key over public networks. But let's not get seduced into the marvels of public/private key crypto right now [1].

You trust the CAs signature since you have the CA's public key from a trusted source (your browser vendor). Since you also trust the CA, you can then trust the certificates it has signed. Stolen or lost certificates are in essence handled somewhat like stolen credit cards, using a "certificate revocation list." There are lots of intricate protocol details lurking here, but let's not get sidetracked into them either [1].

HOW SECURE IS THE CA?

There are differing degrees for need and security when interacting with a CA. This is like someone who you trust in some matters but not others [1].

If you want to work in your lab, perhaps to gain familiarity with PKI, you might use the free Simple CA on Windows or the free software at the "Set up your own" link. Anybody else using certificates you issue is trusting you, your identity verification process, and the physical and network security controls you have instituted over your lab computer. The certificates probably cannot be verified online (unless you set up a server for that), so Web or e-mail users may have to trust your signing authority or your certificate (say, based on calling to check with you) [1].

What this lacks is convenient large-scale administration. It's very manual. You have to create certificates. You have to distribute them. You have to confirm that you issued them. It's also not well enough integrated that non-technical people can really be expected to use it [1].

For example, Microsoft's implementation has more automation and appears adequate for most enterprise purposes. It ties into Active Directory, which may well be the enterprise repository of employee info. It can use US to digitally sign certificates, if you're willing to trust Microsoft user logins/Web authentication as adequate verification of identity. Probably good enough for most enterprise purposes, but how much money would you be willing to pay out based on such a certificate? Convenient, fairly secure. An enterprise might use Microsoft CA to confirm identities within the enterprise. Should outsiders have that need, then external access would be needed for checking certificates. The Microsoft CA would probably be in a server room. Some provision for redundancy and high availability might be made. That would make the CA fairly trustworthy (for internal e-mail and encryption) [1].

If you're allergic to Microsoft in some fashion, there is ongoing work in the open source and university communities to create open source, free tools for a PKl that scales to a good size. So there are alternatives for those who like getting their hands into the software. One can make a case that auditing the code improves ability to trust in the PKI. Web certificate signing based on Web logins (student ID, password) is usually considered good enough for universities, particularly due to the costs of doing identity verification more rigorously [1].

If you're thinking money and e-commerce, that's where Thawte and Verisign come in. They're well-known and fairly trusted. They claim to have put in a lot of due diligence securing their servers, people, processes, etc. As long as DNS isn't subverted, you can trust that your Web browser is talking to the real Verisign, say, when checking a certificate they issued. Yes, that's a gap: DNS is not yet secured, and there are ways to compromise local DNS [1].

If you're talking banking and large amounts of money, then you're into another whole world, where the procedures used to set up a CA in a vault, etc., matter greatly and have to be properly managed, with proper records. One key element is making sure no one was alone in position to potentially compromise the security of the CA server. You may well issue certificates offline (by courier?) in a situation like this. You want very good verification of identity, so you don't wire-transfer millions to an offshore bank account. The U.S. Federal Reserve checks banks that set up CAs, and doing it right costs at least $4–5 million [1].

What's the point here? The PKI is only as good as the security. If somebody can tap into the CA server, it's like somebody stealing a list of people, credit cards, and expiration dates. They can then pretend to be you (or worse, amazon.com, or yet worse, some bank). So tight physical and logical access controls, audit trails, etc. relate to how secure the server is. When you get to the banking level, you need to think about process, because perhaps the person installing the OS on the server left a back door, so they could get in from outside 5 or 10 years later [1].

SOME TERMINOLOGY

Technically, a certificate is a digitally signed statement binding together identity information and public key, signed by the issuer, the Certificate Authority. Enrollment is the process whereby a CA verifies identity, stores certificate information, and signs the certificate [1].

On the other hand, PKCS-IO is a standard for the certificate request message; while, X.509 is the most prevalent standard for certificates. PGP and GPG can also issue certificates, which may not meet the X.509 standard [1].

Certificate hierarchy is a chain of CAs from root to issuing CA. For instance, your enterprise CA might have a certificate from Verisign. In effect, Verisign vouches that ca.corp.com (or whatever) is Corp Go's enterprise certificate authority, and then that CA may vouch for Corp Go's employees, internal Web server, etc. This is generally simpler than having to decide individually if you trust ca.a.com and ca.b.com, etc. The top CA in this hierarchy is of course the root CA. Generally, having only a few root CAs makes life simpler [1].

WHY DO PKI IN A ROUTER?

Fore example, the Cisco IOS Certificate Server feature embeds a simple certificate server, with limited certification authority (CA) functionality, into the Cisco IOS software. Thus, the following benefits are provided to the user: Easier public key infrastructure (PKI) deployment by defining default behavior; and, the user interface is simpler because default behavior are predefined. That is, you can leverage the scaling advantages of PKI without all of the certificate extensions that a CA provides, thereby allowing you to easily enable a basic PKI-secured network [1].

Direct Integration With Cisco IOS Software

Reading a little into this, more and more Cisco devices need to authenticate themselves to each other, or send encrypted traffic. Shared keys and CiscoSecure ACS can be used for this (as with WDS for WLAN and WLSE) but it starts getting painful as it scales up. It could also be more secure. For devices such as the Cisco IP phones, the scaling could become an issue. So a clean scalable solution is needed [1].

What's really going on here, is that the dependency on the external PKI is a barrier to using certificates in a couple of ways. If your enterprise still hasn't moved to Active Directory, well, upgrades to future Microsoft OSs may start getting painful, but that's an issue for the server folks. But it sure means you can't use certificates yet. The second side to this is something usually seen in network management in large shops. The network staff finds that getting DNS and other changes done quickly and correctly by the systems administrators is hard. So they much prefer to have their own network device DNS server. But, the reality is that local administration control is sometimes needed, since otherwise, the changes you needed yesterday just don't happen [1].

So, a simple PKI in the Cisco IOS gives control of certificates for the networking device use back to network staff, should that be deemed appropriate or necessary. If you have Active Directory and want to use it, or some other CA, fine. But if you want something to facilitate quick PKI deployment for network device security, this is a nice alternative. And since all the program code is from Cisco, one can hope it'll be solidly interoperable [1]!

Finally, the Cisco CA code uses SCEP, Simple Certificate Enrollment Protocol, over HTTP. This does require enabling the Cisco IOS Web server. It provides a uniform automated way for other devices to enroll with the CA. You can always disable the Cisco 1OS Web server after a large-scale rollout and use manual certificate enrollment, if you wish to tighten security [1].

SUMMARY AND CONCLUSIONS

There are two particular concerns when setting up a CA. The identity/public key bindings take effort to create. Deploying PKI to user PCs is well known to be labor intense. So having a solid database to store the info in is important. Securely and reliably backing up the data is also important. Finally, both are mildly challenging for a router, since it has no hard drive to store such information on [1].

REFERENCES

[1] Peter J. Welcher, "Certificate Authorities," Copyright Publications & Communications, Inc., Nov 2004, Provided by ProQuest Information and Learning Company. All rights Reserved. [Copyright © 2006 FindArticles™] FindArticles, 625 Second Street, San Francisco, CA 94107, November 2004.

[2] "Certificate Authority," Wikipedia® is a registered trademark of the Wikimedia Foundation, Inc., Wikimedia Foundation Inc., 200 2nd Ave. South #358, St. Petersburg, FL 33701-4313, USA, 2006.

Chapter 28

TRUSTING SSL CAS IN SERVERS AND BROWSERS

INTRODUCTION

The practical means of implementing PKI and digital signatures are via Web server certificates that enable authentication and SSL encryption. SSL certificates form the basis of an Internet trust infrastructure by allowing websites to offer safe, secure information exchange to their customers. SSL server certificates satisfy the need for confidentiality, integrity, authentication and nonrepudiation [1].

SSL DEFINED

Secure Sockets Layer (SSL), originally developed by Netscape Communications, is an information technology for securely transmitting information over the Internet. The SSL protocol has become the universal standard on the Web for authenticating websites to Web browser users and for encrypting communications between browser users and Web servers [1].

Server certificates are available from Certificate Authorities (CAs) such as trustworthy, independent third parties that issue certificates to individuals, enterprises and websites. CAs use thorough verification methods to ensure that certificate users are who they claim to be before issuing them. CA's own self-signed SSL digital certificates are built into all major browsers and Web servers, including Netscape Communicator and Microsoft Internet Explorer, so that simply installing a digital certificate on a Web server enables SSL capabilities when communicating with Web browsers. SSL server certificates fulfil two necessary functions to establish e-commerce trust: SSL server authentication and SSL encryption [1].

SSL Server Authentication

Server certificates allow users to confirm a Web server's identity. Web browsers automatically check that a server's certificate and public ID are valid and have been issued by a certificate authority (CA) included in the list of trusted CAs built into browser software. SSL server authentication is vital for secure e-commerce transactions in which users, for example, are sending credit card numbers over the Web and first want to verify the receiving server's identity [1].

SSL Encryption

SSL server certificates establish a secure channel that enables all information sent between a user's Web browser and a Web server to be encrypted by the sending software and decrypted by the receiving software, thus protecting private information from interception over the Internet. In addition, all data sent over an encrypted SSL connection is protected with a mechanism for detecting tampering: that is, for automatically determining whether the data has been altered in transit. This means that users can confidently send private data, such as credit card numbers, to a website, trusting that SSL keeps it private and confidential [1].

HOW SSL SERVER CERTIFICATES WORK

SSL Certificates take advantage of SSL to work seamlessly between websites and visitors' Web browsers. The SSL protocol uses a combination of asymmetric public key encryption and faster symmetric encryption [1].

The process begins by establishing an SSL "handshake" – allowing the server to authenticate itself to the browser user and then permitting the server and browser to cooperate in the creation of the symmetric keys used for encryption, decryption and tamper detection. The following steps show the process flow:

1. A customer contacts a site and accesses a secured URL: a page secured by a SSL Certificate (indicated by a URL that begins with "https:" instead of just "http:" or by a message from the browser). This might typically be an online order form collecting private information from the customer, such as address, phone number and credit card number or other payment information.
2. The customer's browser automatically sends the server the browser's SSL version number, cipher settings, randomly generated data and other information the server needs to communicate with the client using SSL.
3. The server responds, automatically sending the customer's browser the site's digital certificate, along with the server's SSL version number, cipher settings etc.
4. The customer's browser examines the information contained in the server's certificate and verifies that:
   a. The server certificate is valid and has a valid date
   b. The CA that issued the server been signed by a trusted CA whose certificate is built into the browser

c. The issuing CA's public key, built into the browser, validates the issuer's digital signature

d. The domain name specified by the server certificate matches the server's actual domain name

If the server cannot be authenticated, the user is warned that an encrypted authenticated connection cannot be established.

5. If the server can be successfully authenticated, the customer's Web browser generates a unique "session key" to encrypt all communications with the site using asymmetric encryption.
6. The user's browser encrypts the session key itself with the site's public key so that only the site can read the session key and sends it to the server.
7. The server decrypts the session key using its own private key.
8. The browser sends a message to the server informing it that future messages from the client will be encrypted with the session key.
9. The server then sends a message to the client informing it that future messages from the server will be encrypted with the session key.
10. An SSL-secured session is now established. SSL then uses symmetric encryption, (which is much faster than asymmetric PKI encryption) to encrypt and decrypt messages within the SSL-secured "pipeline."
11. Once the session is complete, the session key is eliminated [1].

It all takes only seconds and requires no action by the user.

The Netscape Navigator and the Microsoft Internet Explorer browsers have built-in security mechanisms to prevent users from unwittingly submitting their personal information over insecure channels. If a user tries to submit information to an unsecured site (a site without an SSL server certificate), the browsers will show a warning by default [1].

In contrast, if a user submits credit card or other information to a site with a valid server certificate and an SSL connection, the warning does not appear. The secure connection is seamless, but visitors can be sure that transactions with a site are secured by looking for the following cues:

• The URL in the browser window displays "https" at the beginning, instead of http.
• In Netscape Communicator, the padlock in the lower left corner of the Navigator window will be closed instead of open.
• In Internet Explorer, a padlock icon appears in the bar at the bottom of the IE window [1].

SSL Strengths: 40-bit And 128-bit SSL

SSL comes in two strengths, 40-bit and 128-bit, which refer to the length of the session key generated by every encrypted transaction. The longer the key, the more difficult it is to break the encryption code. The 128-bit SSL encryption is the world's strongest: according to RSA Labs, it would take a trillion trillion years to crack using today's technology. The 128-bit encryption is approximately 3 X 1026 stronger than 40-bit encryption [1].

Microsoft and Netscape offer two versions of their Web browsers, export and domestic, which enable different levels of encryption depending on the type of SSL server certificate with which the browser is communicating. The first is the 40-bit SSL server certificates that enable 40-bit SSL when communicating with export-version Netscape and Microsoft Internet Explorer browsers (used by most people in the U.S. and worldwide) and 128-bit SSL encryption when communicating with domestic-version Microsoft and Netscape browsers. Second, 128-bit SSL server certificates enable 128-bit SSL encryption (the world's strongest) with both domestic and export versions of Microsoft® and Netscape® browsers [1].

In order to fully enable 128-bit encryption with a Global Server ID, it is important to generate the right kind of private key during the process of obtaining an SSL Certificate. An important step in the process is generating a Certificate Signing Request within the Web server software. In generating a CSR, Web server administrators should be careful to select a 1024-bit private key, which enables the Global Server ID to establish 128-bit SSL encryption, rather than a 512-bit private key, which enables only 40-bit encryption. Netscape users can follow these steps to see what level of encryption is protecting their transactions:

1. Go to the secure Web page you want to check.
2. Click the Security button in the Navigator toolbar. The Security Info dialogue box indicates whether the website uses encryption.
3. If it does, click the Open Page Info button to display more information about the site's security features, including the type of encryption used.
4. You can also check to see which level of SSL is activated on your Web server by following these steps:
   a. Using a 128-bit client, such as the domestic version of the Netscape Navigator, click on Options/Security Preferences.
   b. Under the enable SSL options, click on Configure for both SSL 2 and SSL 3. Make sure acceptance for the 40 and 56 bit encryption ciphers are turned off.
   c. Try to access the site. If it using less than 128 bit security, then you will receive an error in your browser window: "Netscape and this server cannot communicate securely because they have no common encryption methods [1]."

IE users can find out a website's encryption level by following these steps:

1. Go to the website you want to check.
2. Right-click on the website page and select Properties.
3. Click the Certificates button.
4. In the Fields box, select "Encryption type." The Details box shows you the level of encryption (40-bit or 128-bit) [1].

E-businesses may choose to simplify the process of certificate checking for site visitors by describing the security measures they have implemented in a Security and Privacy statement on their sites. Sites that use VeriSign SSL Certificates can also post the Secure Site Seal on their homepage, security statement page and purchase pages. The Seal is a widely recognized symbol of trust that enables site visitors to check certificates in real time from VeriSign with one click [1].

SGC And 128-Bit Step-Up

To ensure that strong 128-bit encryption protects e-commerce transactions for all users, enterprises should install 128-bit IDs on their servers. However, the export browsers that permit only 40-bit encryption with 40-bit SSL server certificates, will allow strong 128-bit encryption when interacting with 128-bit server certificates, because these certificates are equipped with a special extension that enable "Server Gated Cryptography (SGC)" for Microsoft browsers, and "International Step-Up" for Netscape browsers [1].

The extension enables 128-bit encryption with export-version browsers by prompting two "handshakes" when a user's browser accesses a page protected by a Global Server ID. When an export-version Netscape or Microsoft browser connects to the Web server, the browser initiates a connection with only a 40-bit cipher. When the server certificate is transferred, the browser verifies the certificate against its built-in list of approved CAs. Here, it recognized that the server certificate includes the SGC or International Step-Up extension, and then immediately renegotiates the SSL parameters for the connection to initiate an SSL session with a 128-bit cipher. In subsequent connections, the browser immediately uses the 128-bit cipher for full-strength encryption [1].

SECURING MULTIPLE SERVERS AND DOMAINS WITH SSL

As enterprises and service providers enhance their websites and extranets with newer technology to reach larger audiences, server configurations have become increasingly complex. They must now accommodate:

- Redundant server backups that allow websites and extranets to maximize site performance by balancing traffic loads among multiple servers
- Enterprises running multiple servers to support multiple site names
- Enterprises running multiple servers to support a single site name
- Service providers using virtual and shared hosting configurations [1]

However, in complex multiserver environments, SSL server certificates must be used carefully if they are to serve their purpose of reliably identifying sites and the enterprises operating them to visitors, and encrypt e-commerce transactions – establishing the trust that customers require before engaging in e-commerce. When used properly in an e-commerce trust infrastructure equipped with multiple servers, SSL server certificates must still satisfy the three requirements of online trust:

1. Client applications, such as Web browsers, can verify that a site is protected by an SSL server certificate by matching the "common name" in a certificate to the domain name (such as www.verisign.com) that appears in the browser. Certificates are easily accessible via Netscape and Microsoft browsers.
2. Users can also verify that the organization listed in the certificate has the right to use the domain name and is the same as the entity with which the customer is communicating.

3. The private keys corresponding to the certificate, which enable the encryption of data sent via Web browsers, are protected from disclosure by the enterprise or ISP operating the server [1].

The Certificate Sharing Problem

Finally, it is recommended that, to satisfy the requirements of Internet trust, one SSL server certificate needs to be used to secure each domain name on every server in a multi-server environment and that the corresponding private keys be generated from the hosting server. Some enterprises or ISPs practice certificate sharing or use a single SSL server certificate to secure multiple servers. Organizations use certificate sharing in order to secure back-up servers, ensure high-quality service on high-traffic sites by balancing traffic among several servers or, in the case of ISPs and Web hosts, provide inexpensive SSL protection to price-sensitive customers. However, certificate-sharing configurations do not satisfy the fundamental requirements of Internet trust [1].

SUMMARY AND CONCLUSIONS

This chapter briefly touched on some common shared certificate configurations. The following are conclusions and recommendations for addressing the implementation of SSL on multiple servers to most effectively reinforce an e-commerce trust infrastructure:

- Fail-Safe Backup
- Load Balancing: Multiple sites with different common names on multiple servers
- Load Balancing: Multiple sites with the same common name on multiple servers
- ISP Shared SSL
- Name-Based Virtual Hosting [1]

Fail-Safe Backup

Here, redundant servers are not used simultaneously. Certificate sharing is permissible. However, when the back-up server is not under the same control as the primary server, the private key cannot be adequately protected and a separate certificate should be used for each server [1].

Load Balancing: Multiple Sites With Different Common Names On Multiple Servers

To prevent browsers from detecting that the URL of the site visited differs from the common name in the certificate and to protect the security of private keys, a different certificate should be used for each server/domain name combination [1].

Load Balancing: Multiple Sites With The Same Common Name On Multiple Servers

Instead of jeopardizing private key functionality by copying the key for multiple servers, a different certificate should be used for each server. Each certificate may have the same common name and organizational name but slightly different organizational unit values [1].

ISP Shared SSL

Here, one certificate is issued to an ISP's domain, and used on multiple servers by multiple Web sites. This prevents site visitors from verifying that the site they are visiting is the same as the site protected by the certificate and listed in the certificate itself. Each site's server should have its own certificate. Or merchants must inform their customers that site encryption is provided by the ISP, not the merchant, and the ISP must guarantee the services of all the hosted enterprises whose sites use shared SSL [1].

Name-Based Virtual Hosting

An ISP or Web Host provides each hosted customer with a unique domain name, such as customername.isp.com. If the same certificate is used for each domain name, browsers will indicate that the site domain name does not match the common name in the certificate. Finally, to solve this problem, a "wildcard" certificate of the form *.isp.com is required to properly serve the multi-hostname configuration without creating browser mismatch error messages.

REFERENCES

[1] "Building An E-Commerce Trust Infrastructure," © 2003–2004 VeriSign UK Limited. All rights reserved. VeriSign UK Limited, 2nd Floor, Waterfront, Chancellors Road, Hammersmith Embankment, London, W6 9RU, 2004.

PART XIII

FIREWALLS AND FIREWALL TOPOLOGIES

Chapter 29

PROTECTING SERVERS AND CLIENTS
WITH FIREWALLS

INTRODUCTION

As previously explained in Chapter 20, a firewall puts up a barrier that controls the flow of traffic among domains, hosts and networks. The safest firewall would block all traffic, but that defeats the purpose of making the connection. According to a logical security policy, you need strict control over selected traffic. Enterprises typically put a firewall between the public Internet and a private and trusted network. A firewall can also conceal the topology of your inside networks and network addresses from public view, here, as well as elsewhere. But, that's only the beginning [4].

This chapter is intended to present a brief overview of firewall components, types available, and the relative advantages and disadvantages of each. It is intended to lay out a general road map for administrators who wish to publish information for public consumption with regards to protecting servers and clients, while preventing unauthorized access to their private or confidential network [4].

The information presented in this chapter is intended to simplify what can sometimes be intimidating or complex security and network setups. This chapter was not intended to be a complete manual on firewall types. Unfortunately the nature of firewall technology does not allow for a uniform "drop-in" installation setup, so every private network should research the topic of firewalls and network security to find a personalized solution or type that best fits their needs. This chapter should not be used as a replacement for knowledgeable network or security administrators [4].

Conceptually, there are three types of firewalls. Let's briefly discuss all three.

TYPES OF FIREWALLS

Now, let's start off with a brief review of basic firewall types: As previously mentioned, there are three types of firewalls:

- Simple Packet Filtering: IP or Filtering Firewalls – block all but selected network traffic.
- Application-layer Firewalls: Proxy Servers – act as intermediary to make requested network connections for the user.
- Stateful multilayer-inspection firewalls [1].

The preceding firewall types are not as different as you might think, and the latest technologies are blurring the distinction to the point where it's no longer clear if either one is "better" or "worse." As always, you need to be careful to pick the type that meets your needs (for further information, see Chapter 30, "Choosing The Right Firewall") [4].

Which is which depends on what mechanisms the firewall uses to pass traffic from one security zone to another. The International Standards Organization (ISO) Open Systems Interconnect (OSI) model for networking defines seven layers, where each layer provides services that "higher-level" layers depend on. In order from the bottom, these layers are physical, data link, network, transport, session, presentation, application [4].

The important thing to recognize is that the lower-level the forwarding mechanism, the less examination the firewall can perform. Generally speaking, lower-level firewalls are faster, but are easier to fool into doing the wrong thing [2].

Simple Packet Filtering: IP Or Filtering Firewalls

An IP filtering firewall works at the simple IP packet level. It is designed to control the flow of data packets based on their header information (source, destination, port and packet type) [3].

In other words, these types of firewalls generally make their decisions based on the source, destination addresses and ports in individual IP packets. A simple router is the "traditional" packet filtering firewall, since it is not able to make particularly sophisticated decisions about what a packet is actually talking to or where it actually came from. Modern simple packet filtering firewalls have become increasingly sophisticated, and now maintain internal information about the state of connections passing through them, the contents of some of the data streams, and so on. One thing that's an important distinction about many simple packet filtering firewalls is that they route traffic directly though them, so to use one, you either need to have a validly assigned IP address block or use a "private Internet" address block. Simple packet filtering firewalls tend to be very fast and tend to be very transparent to users [4].

In Fig. 29-1, a simple packet filtering firewall, called a "screened host firewall," is represented [4]. In a screened host firewall, access to and from a single host is controlled by means of a router operating at a network layer. The single host is a bastion host; a highly-defended and secured strong-point that (hopefully) can resist attack.

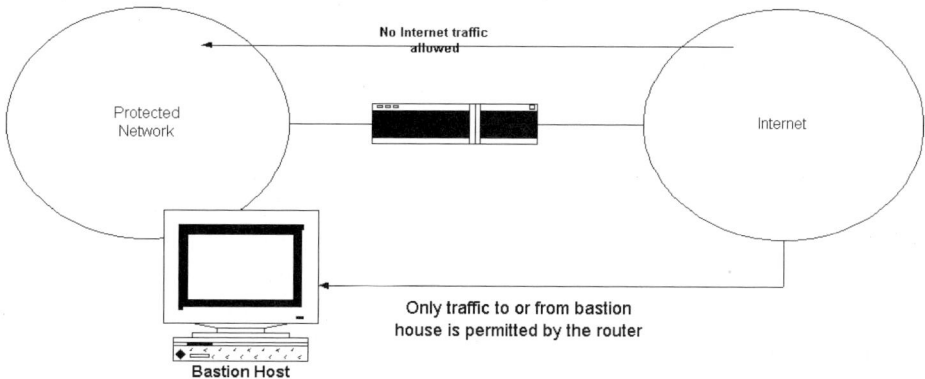

Figure 29-1. Screened Host Firewall.

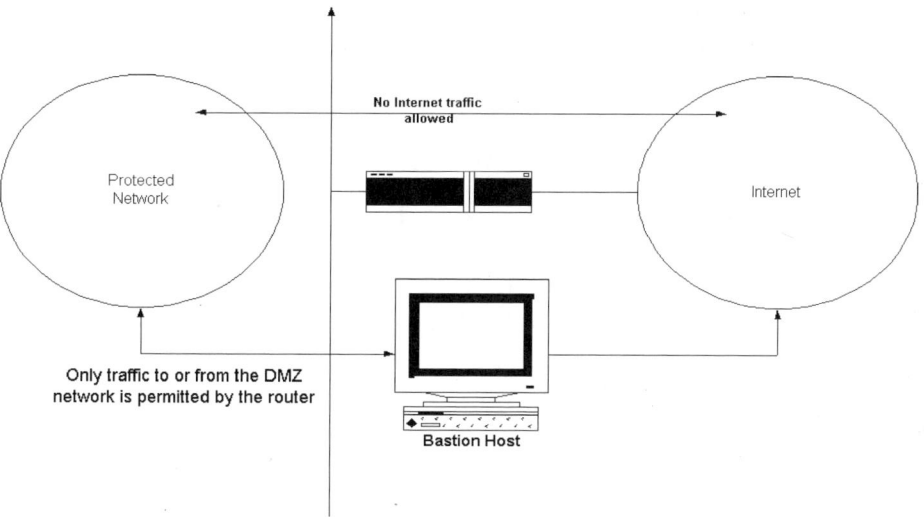

Figure 29-2. Screened Subnet Firewall.

Example Of Simple Packet Filtering Firewall

In Fig. 29-2, a simple packet filtering firewall called a "screened subnet firewall" is represented [4]. In a screened subnet firewall, access to and from a whole network is controlled by means of a router operating at a network layer. It is similar to a screened host, except that it is, effectively, a network of screened hosts.

A filtering firewall is more secure, but lacks any sort of useful logging. It can block the public from accessing a private system, but it will not indicate what connections have been made to the Internet from the inside [4].

Filtering firewalls are absolute filters. They do not support individual access control. So, a private server cannot be made accessible to a particular outside user without opening it up to the entire public [4].

Now, packet filters work by distinguishing packets based on IP addresses or specific bit patterns. Packet filters are unable to protect against application-level attacks and may be susceptible to sophisticated IP fragmentation and IP source routing attacks, because of the limited information accessed. This kind of firewall is typically found in routers, so they're economical and fast. There usually is no extra charge, since you probably need a router to connect to the Internet in the first place. You'll probably find that it will install any filter you want, even if the router belongs to your network service provider. Or, your router can simply be a computer that runs an operating system like Windows NT or Novell NetWare and contains two network interface cards (a dual-homed system) [3].

> **Note:** Most security policies require finer control than this.

Application-Layer Firewalls: Proxy Servers

Application layer firewalls generally are hosts running proxy servers, which permit no traffic directly between networks, and which perform elaborate logging and auditing of traffic passing through them. Since the proxy applications are software components running on the firewall, it is a good place to do lots of logging and access control. Application layer firewalls can be used as network address translators, since traffic goes in one "side" and out the other, after having passed through an application that effectively masks the origin of the initiating connection. Having an application in the way in some cases may impact performance and may make the firewall less transparent. Early application layer firewalls such as those built using the Trusted Information Systems (TIS) firewall toolkit (http://www.tis.com/), are not particularly transparent to end users and may require some training. Modern application layer firewalls are often fully transparent. Application layer firewalls tend to provide more detailed audit reports and tend to enforce more conservative security models than simple packet filtering firewalls [4].

Example Application Layer Firewall

In Fig. 29-3, an application layer firewall called a "dual homed gateway" is represented [4]. A dual homed gateway is a highly secured host that runs proxy software. It has two network interfaces, one on each network, and blocks all traffic passing through it.

By acting as an intermediary between the private network and the outside, proxy servers allow indirect Internet access. All network requests made by an internal computer to an outside source are intercepted by the proxy server, which logs the request, and then passes it along to the outside. Similarly, data passed back to an internal user from the outside is received by the proxy server, logged, and then passed along [4].

Furthermore, application-layer firewalls, or gateways, focus on the application layer of the Open System Interconnection (OSI) reference model of network architecture. Working at this level allows them to use dedicated security proxies to examine the entire data stream for every connection attempt. A virtual "air-gap" exists in the firewall between the inside and the outside networks. And, proxies bridge this gap by working as agents for internal or external users. The proxies are specific for applications such as FTP or Telnet or protocols such as Internet Inter-ORB Protocol (IIOP) and Oracle's SQL*Net. In the application approach,

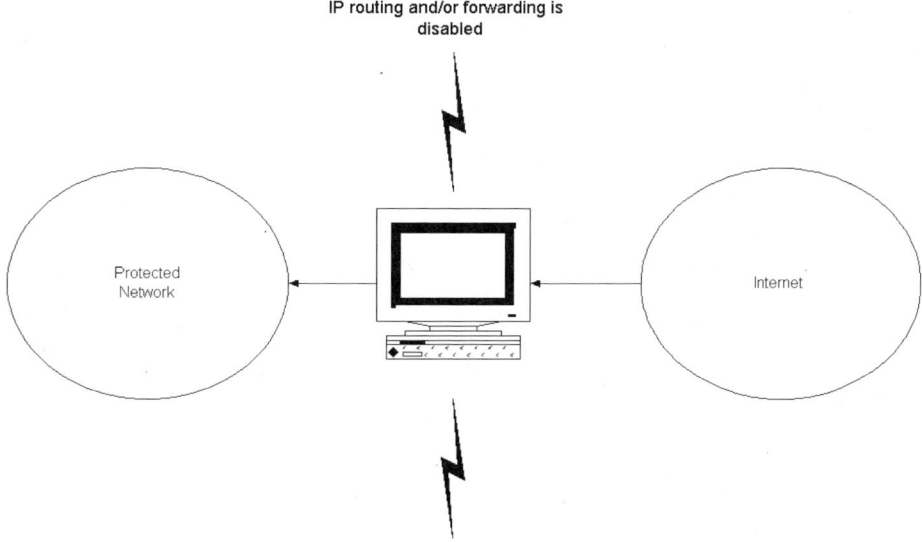

Figure 29-3. Dual Homed Gateway.

information flows through the firewall, but no outside packets do – thus, providing a virtually "fail safe" architecture. Typically, they support security policies that require fine-grain control [4].

Stateful Multilayer-Inspection Firewalls

Stateful multilayer-inspection firewalls extract the relevant communication and application state information and analyze all packet communication layers. They keep state information about connections in the operating system kernel and parse IP packets. The firewalls compare the bit patterns to packets that are already known to be trusted, instead of examining the contents of each packet. Stateful multilayer-inspection firewalls can be faster than application-layer firewalls (the proxy mechanism is at a lower level), but they are also more complex. They also have some of the advantages and shortcomings of each of the previous two firewall types [4].

UNDERSTANDING FIREWALL TYPES

Now, you are probably asking yourself, which of the preceding three different types of firewalls is more secure and delivers the best performance? As is so often the case, this question can only be answered on a case-by-case basis after you consider the topology of your network, the services you plan to use, and the services you plan to offer. In limited circumstances, a simple packet-filtering router can be just as secure as a firewall costing 10 or 20 times as much. The reverse is also true; buying an expensive firewall will give little security if it is not properly configured [4].

FIREWALL TYPES DRAWBACKS

The problem with filtering firewalls is that they inhibit access to the private network from the Internet. Only services on systems that have pass filters can be accessed. With a proxy server, users can login to the firewall and then access the private network. Also, the rapid growth of network client/server technology makes supporting and controlling developing network services a constant challenge [4].

Finally, the future of firewalls lies someplace between simple packet filtering firewall and application layer firewalls. It is likely that simple packet filtering firewall will become increasingly "aware" of the information going through them, and application layer firewalls will become increasingly "low level" and transparent. The end result will be a fast packet-screening system that logs and audits data as it passes through. Increasingly, firewalls (simple packet filtering and application layer) incorporate encryption so that they may protect traffic passing between them over the Internet. Firewalls with end-to-end encryption can be used by organizations with multiple points of Internet connectivity to use the Internet as a "private backbone" without worrying about their data or passwords being sniffed [4].

SUMMARY AND CONCLUSIONS

As previously explained in Chapter 20, a firewall an a computer network is a device which protects a private local network from the rest of the world (public parts of the same network, or the Internet at large). The role of a firewall is typically filled by a computer (or computers) that can reach both the private network and the Internet – thus, allowing it to restrict the flow of data between the two. The protected network therefore cannot reach the Internet, and the Internet can not reach the protected network, unless the firewall computer allows it. For someone to reach the Internet from inside the protected network, they must login to the firewall (via telnet, rlogin, etc.), and use the Internet from there [4].

With the preceding in mind, a dual homed system (a system with two network connections) is the simplest form of a firewall. A firewall can be setup with IP forwarding or gatewaying turned off, and accounts can be given to everyone on the network – that is, if system users can be trusted. The users can then login to the firewall and run their network services (ftp, telnet, mail, etc.) from there. Thus, the only computer on the private network that knows anything about the outside world is the firewall with this setup. Therefore, a default route is not needed by the other systems on the protected network [4].

Such a system relies entirely on all users being trusted, and that's its greatest weakness. It is therefore not recommended [4].

Nevertheless, firewalls are indispensable assets in most organizations today. However, like all technologies, firewalls can create problems of their own. Imagine the case where your organization's Web server publishes a Java applet that makes calls to a Java Database Connectivity (JDBC) client. It then sends messages to a JDBC server (a Transmission Control Protocol (TCP) service) running on a particular port of a host at your site. As the administrator of your site, you configure your firewall for detailed information to allow this traffic in either direction. But, you may have neither knowledge nor control of the remote site whose browser downloaded your applet. If a firewall at that site is configured to deny traffic destined for this same port, you have a problem. Here's an instance where an intranet over which you have control can provide a more certain solution than the Internet, over which you have relatively little control [4].

Finally, implicit in this whole discussion has been the notion that the firewall is positioned to protect internal hosts (like a Data Base Management Systems (DBMSs)) from outsiders. But, an Internet firewall is only a controlled gateway. It cannot stop attacks from malicious insiders, nor can it take the place of education and security policies and procedures. An Internet firewall is part of an overall security plan. Since the majority of network and system attacks occur from inside of the corporate networks and are launched by "inside" or trusted people, you may also want to consider additional firewalls behind the perimeter ("bastion") firewall defense. Chapter 30 will show you how to choose the right firewall to do this [4].

REFERENCES

[1] John Wack, Ken Cutler and Jamie Pole, "Guidelines on Firewalls and Firewall Policy: Recommendations of the National Institute of Standards and Technology," Computer Security Division, MIS Training Institute, Information Technology Laboratory, National Institute of Standards and Technology, U.S. Department of Commerce, Gaithersburg, MD 20899-8930, January 2002.

[2] "Information Security: Mechanisms And Techniques," Information Security: Technical Solutions, Computer Security Division, MIS Training Institute, Information Technology Laboratory, National Institute of Standards and Technology, U.S. Department of Commerce, Gaithersburg, MD 20899-8930, January 2002.

[3] Shirley Radack, Editor, "Selecting Information Technology Security Products," Computer Security Division, Information Technology Laboratory, National Institute of Standards and Technology, U.S. Department of Commerce, Gaithersburg, MD 20899-8930, 2004.

[4] John R. Vacca and Scott R. Ellis, Firewalls: Jumpstart for Network and Systems Administrators, Digital Press, 2005.

Chapter 30

CHOOSING THE RIGHT FIREWALL

INTRODUCTION

As the topology and threatscape of modern networks becomes increasingly complex, enterprise and administrative resources have become stretched ever thinner. Corporations and businesses are increasingly reliant on both the internal resources of the network as well as on external communications for day-to-day business functions. More and more of these functions are relegated to automation, with things like faxing, scanning, and document management integrating with network resources. Networks have truly emerged in this century as the cornerstone, if not the foundation, of critical business operations [1].

When the Internet is down, when the server is down, if faxing is offline, or if the network copier is on the blink, business literally grinds to a halt. And, typically, the reason that these things happen is because malicious software has wormed its way into the network, somewhere, and somehow. There are many avenues of intrusion, and there are many things that can ostensibly be implemented to fortify against such occurrences. But implementing all of them, and then maintaining patches, product updates, definitions, etc, for a slew of devices and products is not at the top of any network administrator's list of favorite things to be doing. The most rewarding and creative part of a Network Administrators job is to introduce and manage change, in ways that are beneficial to business, improve the ability to do business, and streamline business functions [1].

Playing babysitter to a bunch of equipment and software programs, and subsequently playing checkpoint police + border guard, doesn't fit into a philosophy of network change designed to improve competitiveness. As a result of the overwhelming market demand, most security firms that create firewall and other security products have moved toward a Secure Content Management (SCM) approach [1].

In these times, everyone (from the local florist to small law firms to multinational corporations) everyone is prey to harvesters seeking to build their own personal empires of subjugated computers around the world. With cracker-hackers-jackers running IP address scanners and automated cracking software, and with so many DSL install techs leaving the default username and password for router access, it is actually a rather simple matter to crack into small networks. This chapter explores, in depth, the aspects of security and exemplifies several existing solutions [1].

Firewalls, from policy development through to deployment, have a wide variety of incarnations. Interestingly enough, physical firewalls (those things that are used to actually stop the spread of fire in the firefighting and fire prevention professions) are closely analogous to information security firewalls. Just as fire needs fuel, heat, and oxygen, security attacks are also dependent on several factors, each of which can be addressed by a single unit or by a more elaborate, specialized system. Such a system brings together best of breed products in a serialized approach to examining network activity, traffic, habits, and characteristics to determine if, in fact, an attack is in progress, and to prevent known types of attacks, viruses, worms, email, spam, etc, from ever entering the network [1].

Such systems are those that are discussed in this chapter. Systems that, through a single appliance or several appliances, are capable of noticing and controlling an intrusion, regardless of its methods. This chapter also highlights single products that are part of a larger whole, or collective, of products that is marketed within a firewall context. This context is referred to by some as a Secure Content Management (SCM) offering. Central management of a host of firewall duties is the goal, something intended to de-stress the life of the network administrator and simplify security controls [1].

Some sources (Task Force on Information Warfare and Information Assurance) estimate that over 40 million people on this planet are equipped with, and knowledgeable in the use of, cracking tools. It's no surprise, then, that in the last few years, permutations in methods of attack have telescoped like a power function while the solutions and varieties of methods to repulse them have experienced little growth. They have, in fact, experienced a contraction, or convergence, of sorts [1].

CONVERGENCE

As attack methods grow in complexity and sophistication, it is almost beyond the ability, if not the scope, of one manufacturer to present a solution that can effectively strip the ground, evacuate the villages, provide aerial extinguishment, patrol surrounding areas for additional threats, provide crowd control, perimeter security and damage control. Such an operation invariably requires the efforts and cooperation of multiple platforms of proficiency. Spam. Viruses. Trojans. Spyware, adware, and malware. Critical updates and Patches. Packet filtering. Forces beyond anyone's ability to control are creating virtual conflagrations on an epoch scale – they have free-reign and are here to stay for as long as there is an Internet [1].

The Criminal MeagerMind

Cyber Crime is the highway robbery of the next generation criminal, and with its high cash payoffs, light sentencing (if caught), and book and movie consultation deals, it doesn't take a mastermind to figure out how to run a scam that will lift sessions cookies and steal credit card data from unsuspecting users. Many, many sites setup their own shopping cart systems. Most of them play the numbers and hope for a break – after all, it is the credit card companies that will be left holding the bag. Consumers pay for it with higher interest rates and higher prices; it's rare these days that a credit card company will actually be able to pinpoint where the theft originated. Attackers are diverse and wily in their approaches – getting greedy will surely kill the goose. Why steal a thousand credit cards from one database when you can steal a hundred thousand from a hundred thousand? Theirs is an economy of scale. The 100,000 credit card numbers charged varying amounts, diverted to hundreds of different accounts, can yield a multi-million dollar payoff. And insecure, open systems, with no true firewall policy, are the key to many of these schemes. Harvesting information, hijacking, creating identities, stealing identities, and assembling a powerful, ensnared network with the sole purpose of cracking open a secure location is the strategic objective. Creating a base of operations, a safe harbor with both the computing power, the anonymity, and the available bandwidth necessary to engage in a broad spectrum of elicit activities, from wandering nomad warez and codez sites, to waystations for pornographic sneakware installing popups, to spam servers, to DoS slaves, to personal file servers, to . . . anything imaginable! There is a war raging on the Internet, these systems are the pawns [1].

The firewall technologies of today and tomorrow are best of breed *solutions* that manage a pool of resources and allow for simplified grouping of such things as desktop anti-virus definition updates, email virus attachment filtering, web site filtering, spam detection, and intrusion prevention. Some of these systems consolidate function to one appliance, others provide distributed management tools. Consolidation of these resources onto one appliance provides convenient and low cost manageability, but may to consider scalability or planned redundancy. Placing an email server, a web server, a file server, virus protection, packet filtering, and intrusion detection into one appliance may seem like a great idea, and it is a great idea for a small law firm or a small consulting practice sitting on one or two DSL lines, but it can have consequences that need to be considered:

- Loss of Connectivity means no services – contingency planning a must
- Bandwidth usage is only going to go up.
- Backups and restorations of complex and proprietary appliances can be difficult to access. Failover alternatives will double the cost [1].

Considerations

Some things to be sure to consider when building out a firewall policy framework include explanations that require a broad range of historical and explanatory background. Terminology and nomenclature are often intermingled. Protocol names are bandied about with little or no explanation, and the avenues of attack, while clear and understood by the attack originator, are frequently misused and under explained by Firewall and Security marketing concerns. This part of the chapter clearly explains the terminology and the concepts that are needed to establish a firm grasp of security requirements [1].

Zero-day Attacks

The shear percentage of attacks and outages that are a result of zero-day attacks both frightens and amazes. Typically, for the most widespread of attacks that are virus based, the anti-virus companies create and release countermeasures within hours. However, the period during that free reign period, before countermeasures are released, is known as the zero-day of an attack. It is a period that may span hours, days, or even months for tortoise-like logic bomb attacks that move at such slow speeds with little or no observed impact. These "zero-day attacks" can compromise resources and inflict definitive damage [1].

> **Tip:** Intrusion detection and prevention is the KEY. During these times in which we live, it is critical that the product protecting your network be capable of intrusion detection and prevention; this will be the only defense, the only way that the firewall will be able to discern between legitimate and intruder activity. Intrusion prevention AND detection is the top priority. Don't get caught without it.

Intrusion Detection and Prevention

The best intrusion detection software provides monitoring of ports, of network traffic, and can match these activities to known threats. It won't just log the even, or send an email, or show a pretty graph – it will actually halt the intrusion. There are firewalls available that can not only prevent it, but can go so far as to provide forensic evidence that can hold its weight in a court of law. IDP can also provide a toolset that will allow administrators to tune sensitivity to reduce false positives, or to merely focus the tool n a particular area. Triggers can be established for any number of unusual activities:

- Excessive login attempts
- Bandwidth spiking
- Stateful Signature
- Denial of Service
- Protocol Anomaly
- Traffic Anomaly [1]

Password Cracking

Dictionary attack: software that will automatically attempt thousands (if not millions) of password attempts to gain access. Available for order online, and delivered by UPS, is a CD with 20+ human language dictionaries, including mangled words and common passwords, lists of common passwords, unique words for all the languages. A software called "John the Ripper" is included. Technically, this software falls into the category of a security tool, used for detecting and strengthening weak passwords. John the Ripper is a part of Owl, Debian GNU/Linux (GNU, a recursive acronym for "GNU's Not UNIX", is pronounced "guh-noo"), Linux, EnGarde Linux, Gentoo Linux, Mandrake Linux, and SuSE (Gesellschaft für Software und Systementwicklung mbH, rhymes with "moose"). It is in the ports/packages collections of FreeBSD (Berkeley Software Development), NetBSD, and OpenBSD [1].

Keyboard Loggers (Physical And Software)

These devices and softwares are used for the sole purpose of capturing keystrokes. A physical device will be readily visible as a small unit that attaches between the keyboard and the PC. Software will run in the background, and will do everything from harvesting specific passwords to actually gathering and transmitting them to locations unknown [1].

Viruses

Can be used to install, and spread throughout the internal network, "sneaks" that will send outgoing traffic guised as emails containing passwords, login names, and information about internal IP addresses. Mail is picked up at a pre-arranged drop that may or may not change according to an algorithm. Some will attempt to disable antivirus, antispam, or anti-spyware software. For example, the Cool Web Search virus is known to disable Spybot once it is removed [1].

Worms

Worms are self-replicating, malicious pieces of code that leverage weaknesses in either firewalls or operating systems. Upon the discovery of an exploit, someone releases a piece of code which then propagates throughout the Internet. A "Code Red" worm, for example, randomly locates port 80 on a server and attempts to exploit a known vulnerability in IIS servers. Once an exploitable machine was located, the Code Red worm would then execute, deface web page requests, disable certain types of routers, and continue it's search for more machines to infect. As a result, many machines were infected multiple times. Some machines on the Internet are still infected, and the Code Red Worm has been around for over three years. New worms and new exploits seem to appear and be discovered daily – many of them don't make it very far since they are poorly written or are merely experimental [1].

Packet Attacks

On April 2, 2004, iDEFENSE issued a warning related to a newly discovered remote exploitation leveraging systems' memory allocations when a particular combination of fragmented TCP, UDP, ICMP, etc, packets with specific offsets are sent to a host. This combination of packets causes the system to allocate memory – if enough packets are sent, the system under attack may allocate large portions of memory and can result in system failures. Many operating systems are capable of handling fragmented packets – these systems are vulnerable and include Windows 2000, XP , Windows Server 2000 and 2003, Unix, Linux, BSD, and Mac OS [1].

Logic Bombs

A logic bomb is a piece of software that is triggered by an event, such as a date or a particular event. Typically, when triggered, a logic bomb executes malicious code, such as the deletion of critical system files, the reformatting of a hard drive, or simply doing something annoying, such as resetting the system clock on a continuous and random basis. Once installed these buggers can be very difficult (some claim impossible) to detect and de-vein. Software such as Tripwire is excellent for prevention of this sort of attack but comes with a sacrifice of system resources and at the price of intensive configuration – Tripwire is nor for the feint of heart [1].

Session Hijacking

This is a form of "sniffing" prior visited sites session ID's and hijacking user accounts in this manner. It is not particularly relevant to this discussion; however, certain industries will encapsulate web security within their firewall policy and certainly the development or installation of software that can detect these sorts of attacks is meaningful [1].

(Remote Access) Trapdoor

Or RAT, a very common, and recent, method of exploitation that leverages social engineering to trick users into installing software on their computers that will allow remote access of the PCAnywhere or Terminal Services variety. In these cases, the Hacker can actually watch desktop activity, load and upload files, copy files, run software, and anything else a computer can do. Home and small network users not adequately protected by a firewall policy, such as a small firm that may only be protected by a NAT router, are particularly and almost exclusively susceptible to these types of attacks. Larger corporations with comprehensive firewalls are not usually vulnerable to this sort of activity. There is no way through the firewall for this particular type of activity without first establishing a VPN (Virtual Private Network). RAT crawlers are known to search known dialup, cable, and DSL (Digital Subscriber Line) IP (Internet Protocol) address pools, searching for either security flaws or existing trapdoors, such as BackOrifice or NetBus. With the explosion in the past three years of "always-on" internet connections, of MS Windows exploits, and the millions of users who don't even take the most basic of security precautions, small offices, networks, and homes are being constantly probed. Being online without a firewall setup on a bastion server is peril incarnate [1].

Phantoms and Honey Pots

These are all methods that various firewalls and security products use to distract or decoy attackers. A phantom is a cache of fake information about a user that actually replaces existing information in software systems for the sole purpose of allowing it to be taken. A honey pot is similar, but it is more likely to exist as a false service that tricks the hacker into thinking he has accessed a system when, in fact, he hasn't. This allows the firewall to detect the origination of an attacker and prevent further attempts [1].

Terminology in the world of computer security can be obfuscating, however. Some viruses make use of a "phantom," in which case the phantom results from the virus actually partitioning and reformatting a portion of a hard drive [1].

Blended Threats

Last, and in no way least, are blended threats. As illustrated in Fig. 30-1, a typical (successful) attack is a blended threat – one that is multi-faceted, and may even be tailor designed for a particular type of network system or firewall, a specific IP address, or a specific range of IP addresses [1]. A single attack may or may not be limited to any (or all) of the previously described methods.

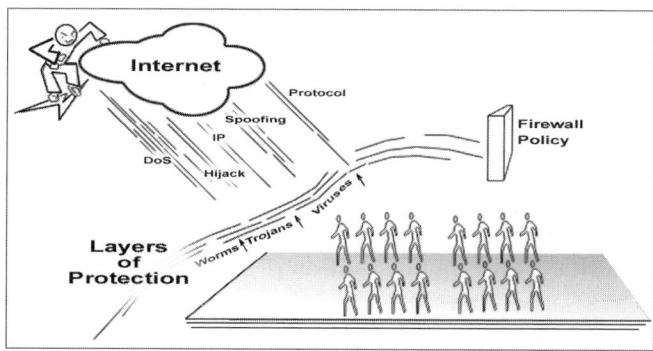

Figure 30-1. An Attacker literally generates a storm of malicious activity on the Internet, raining down bogus requests, port scans, and crack attempts upon a broad spectrum of IP addresses.

Products

There are many, many products available and more seem to emerge every day. In fact, or in odd coincidence, solutions seem to emerge with almost the same frequency as new threats – you draw your own conclusions, however, and don't let the paranoia of this author sway you. Each product has a primary focus, an area where the product is truly strong, as well as subsidiary foci that work to shore up the defenses of the primary focus, making the product more attractive and increasing market traction. They all claim to be the answer, but each truly has its own strengths and weaknesses – an efficient firewall policy will usually incorporate multiple solutions leveraged to protect and harden vital areas with respect to security, and will address multiple venues of the threatscape that may be transports for the multiple prongs of a well engineered, blended threat [1].

The Challenge

There are currently on the market, or on their way to market, many applications for business productivity that are purposed for real time use and, as a result of being on the bleeding edge of technology, many of them implement protocols that today's firewalls and security systems are either not aware of yet, or simply do not support. This is for a plethora of reasons, many of them good. Many times, these productivity enhancing applications utilize parallel channels of UDP or TCP communications and as a result they require the use of the opening and closing of a broad spectrum of logical ports. This is the crux of the matter: some protocols, by virtue of whom they are, wish to have multiple, insecure doors opened for them. Just like any software, they are designed by people and, as a result, act just like them [1].

With this in mind, then, it may be desirable to purchase a firewall that can manage the introduction of new and complex softwares that are used for real time business communication. This may be especially useful to some administrators where there is high volatility in the application base [1].

Intrusion Prevention

True intrusion prevention is in the eye of the beholder, so where is the common ground? How does today's IT Generalist know where product creators have actually developed true intrusion prevention or have merely re-labeled their intrusion detection wares as "Intrusion Prevention" to align themselves with a shifting market paradigm? True intrusion prevention can be determined with a simple series of litmus tests:

- Can it block known attacks without disruption in service?
- Can it respond to attacks within milliseconds?
- What is its system resource load? You will know if it is too much for your environment.
- A network based system should not introduce excessive drag on the network and a host based system should not overwhelm local resources. Business as usual should continue.
- False positives – 5% is an acceptable number [1].

Every network is unique, and each has its own set of quirks and foibles, and each seems to have its own set of special little friends who are trying, daily, to hack access. It follows, then, that every firewall shall perform differently, and it can be expected that even a top-of-the-line product may have issues under extreme and constant duress [1].

Host or Network based?

Host based systems are typically installed on servers and are designed only to protect a particular machine. A true network system must embrace the following aspects:

- Perform packet inspection with no loss of performance (speed)
- Include stateful packet inspection, protocol anomaly analysis, protocol awareness, signature analysis and behavior analysis as methodologies of packet inspection. To be generic, they should provide anomaly detection in each of the three areas:
- Behavioral
- Traffic
- Protocol [1]

Drop malicious sessions – don't simply reset connections.

ABOUT PACKET INSPECTION

Before investing in a firewall appliance or software that claims to provide packet level intrusion prevention, it is important that certain nuances of terminology be clarified (so you know what you're getting). Trying to pass a set of "words" to a vendor is useless without clarity of definitions. What do all these terms mean (see Sidebar, "Terminology Introspective") [1]?

Terminology Introspective

The following packet level intrusion prevention terms are defined as follows:

Packets:

Packets are the little bundles of information that, when pieced together at the end of a transfer, compromise a file, a request, a validation, a confirmation, etc, that other packets were received or transmitted successfully.

Stateful packet inspection:

Most modem/routers provide some level of stateful packet inspection. Packets come in through the modem from the internet, are passed outward through internal switches and routers, and the firewall device "inspects" each one. Simply put, packets that don't match known protocols are discarded and "good" packets are passed. Unfortunately, the constraints for determining what is a good packet have very little to do with the overall purpose of what will be assembled at the application level . . . stateful inspection is merely the inspection of packets with the knowledge of the protocol and the ability to categorize the packets' current states.

Deep packet inspection:

May involve a certain level of modeling and be connected with larger resources that require continuous threat updates.

Protocol:

A protocol of the transport layer of a network, it is the predefined means whereby packets are organized, sequenced, received and interpreted. A protocol is, essentially, a regulatory method for information packets to be received and interpreted and it ensures that each packet reaches its intended destination intact. Most simply put, it is the agreed upon format for the transmission of data from one device to another. It dictates the type of error checking (such as handshake or checksum).

Protocol analysis:

A generic term that can be grouped with "protocol analyzer", "Packet Sniffing" and Network Analysis, protocol analysis is the process of collecting packets and differentiating the type of packet stream protocol, such as UDP, TCP, FTP, SPP, or HTTP.

Protocol anomaly analysis/detection:

A piece of software through which a packet stream passes, is inspected, it is compared to existing and packets that do not match known protocols are identified. This can be as specific as determining if a particular packet stream is unusual in a certain environment. This is accomplished by knowing what is good. Because knowing what is bad would require a definition set that would require updating almost daily. Protocol anomaly analysis is to packet streams as white-lising is to email. Because it does not require updates but is based uon existing standards, packet analysis is one of the first tiers of defense and is often the only defense against zero-day attacks.

Application protocol modeling:

Utilizes a dictionary of protocol specifications and variations for the purpose of comparing a flow and locating anomalous behavior based on delta deviation that is outside an acceptable width.

Protocol decoding:

When a network analyzer gathers and reads data from the network, it needs to interpret the information and provide an understandable interface to the user about the data. Protocol decoding is the human act of studying and interpreting results from packet analysis.

Signature analysis:

Not dissimilar to virus signature analysis, protocol signature analysis attempts to match protocols to known, malicious protocols.

Behavior analysis:

Capturing and analyzing packets is almost an art form. Some softwares will capture and log packets, other software will analyze them, and some will do both. Typically, one or the other can be obtained as freeware, but when software offers both tasks, it is not free. Ethereal is a great packet analysis software, it is free, and it is open source [1].

Selecting A Firewall

A clear threatscape defense architecture begins to emerge, one that portrays / depicts a firewall collective as an array of security tools – that is manageable under one roof with software and servers working in concert to provide a secure computing environment. The following part of the chapter will aptly examine the strengths and weaknesses of ach of the Sun iForce components. Ultimately, what remains to be seen and what is the pass/fail indicator of any of these systems is: How well does it handle attacks unknown? How well can it defend, can it recognize, and can it respond? Any system connected to the Internet is subjected to daily attempts to access; it's ports are scanned, probed, and checked perhaps hundreds of times per day, even per hour [1].

What To Expect

What can a firewall do against all this? Many routers provide basic packet filtering. But, as I have mentioned to one and to many clients, this is only the foundation of a good system. A router's packet filtering is usually quite simple and it is expected that it will only at as a subsidiary firewall device. As has been mentioned before in this book, a firewall is a *policy* that encapsulates the entire security philosophy. "Firewall" is also a word, marketed by marketers (who else?) as a single device, usually a computer, that straddles a network connection and prevents all that is "bad" on one side (the outside) from getting through to the other. How does it do this [1]?

Controlling Protocols

Most firewalls will allow the administrator to configure the most common, known protocols that are known by the administrator to be used in the firewall environment. If there are DNS Servers, Ftp, web, file, email, etc servers sitting behind the firewall, it is possible to use the firewall as a sort o traffic cop – it will map the correct traffic to the IP address that it is intended to reach. Likewise, it will allow the target IP address to respond in like. Should a hacker manage to access the web server, through it's protections, the firewall would prevent enslavement of the Web server for other types of attacks, merely by limiting the type of traffic to HTTP. Furthermore, the firewall could be configured with a quota so that, should it be hijacked and should abnormal amounts of traffic begin to issue forth, the quota would be reached and service terminated [1].

Packet Inspection

Much has already been said about packet inspection in this chapter. IN most networks, packet inspection and protocol control should, typically, be conducted on separate machines, with the packet inspection coming first. It's probably a bad idea for bad packets to even reach the back side of an Internet Router. Most firewall products, however, do boast of some "stateful" packet inspection. And Packet states are well known (it is infrequent that a stateful packet inspection would need to be updated with "definitions") and even should it need it, because it is such a rare thing, these engines are rarely updatable. Since this is something that occurs in the transport layer, a firmware or hardware update would likely be needed to accomplish significant reform to the processing rules [1].

Attack Response

"In the event of an emergency, please break glass." It's not quite like that, but close. In the event of an attack, a system needs to know what to do. The more elaborate the system, the more expensive the system, the more appropriate and effective shall be the response. And this response varies from complete system shutdown, to selective restriction, to IP address blocking, IP block blocking, forensics, tracing, reporting, and actually going to the house of the hacker and arresting him. Well, that's not available yet but we can all dream. Modern firewalls can (and should) tel the difference between a legitimate connection and one that is specifically designed to arm wrestle a server into the dirt. Nobody, except the attacker (and sometimes not even then) wants an operating system to be overwhelmed by invalid requests as is the case in the infamous DoS attacks of the early part of this century [1].

File Examination

This is, perhaps, one of the single greatest performance and latency introducing aspects of traffic monitoring. File examination is the process of reviewing each and every file that passes through, whether on FTP, HTTP, VPN, etc., and attempting to detect nasty executables, disallowed file types, known viruses, worms, logic bombs, or otherwise embedded and malicious scripts. Hughes Systems Satellite firewall, at least the portion that they cordon off for se by home users, introduces approximately 10–60 seconds of latency to traffic transfer and requests and diminishes the performance and ability of any user of their satellite network to the point that the system is, effectively, useless. Companies such as Earthlink and DirecWay are resellers of the Hughes Satellite services and, while highly secure, the system is under such continuous threat that it is constantly changing and its service is completely unpredictable. Such latency can be a scourge, is avoidable, and in the process of building out a secure firewall policy that spans several networks, internal, external, corporate, etc, latency will be the primary consideration. VPN's are highly sensitive to latency – this is good because if a VPN connection begins to lag it simply assumes it is being hijacked and disconnects. This can be highly annoying to your Superintendent when he or she is trying to download his or her favorite videos of his or her toy poodle from his or her home network; and, can't maintain a VPN connection for more than 30 seconds because he or she is going through 6 stages of firewall just to reach the Gateway [1].

Firewall Solutions

The following firewall solutions have been selected for review because of their best-of-breed approach, their scalability, an their approach to central management. Each solution boasts weaknesses and strengths and may or may not be suitable to some environments. When selecting a firewall solution, be sure to evaluate all of the variables that are unique to the network being protected [1].

Esoft

Esoft is an emerging market leader in the area of firewall appliances and managed solution. Setting up an ESoft Instagate Appliance or SCM (Secure Content Management) solution can solve many of the security concerns of any small to medium sized business concern that has a budget of less than 5K to spend on security policy. HIPAA certified, the ESoft product line is also a wise choice for many types of medical professional services (see sidebar, "ESoft CASE STUDY") for details on an actual Instagate implementation. In particular, this author finds that the EX2 line is ideal for very small businesses that simply want to protect their server from what is, essentially, an open door if all that is sitting on their pipe to the Internet is a modem. It is a step above the competition with enhanced scalability and SoftPak portability options. The EX2 provides protocol filtering and stateful packet inspection while at the same time offering a full range of product consolidation [1].

ESoft CASE STUDY

This was an interesting case because it started with a request by the clients for a backup DSL line – they had just been without service for 4 days across a weekend and that was far too long (and this was the third time in three months an outage had occurred). I told them that there were no guarantees, even with a second line from a different provider, and that if there was an area-wide outage, no amount of redundancy (except maybe a satellite dish – with its own set of problems) would help them. After noticing that the client had no firewall setup, one thing that I could guarantee was that their intrusion risk on the Internet would double with the addition of another gateway. A firewall had been something they had not wanted to purchase in the past, but with the increased risk, and the additional bonus of VPN technology that would enable work-at-home, they agreed See firewalls and Load Balancing Dual DSLs for shared offices in Fig. 30-2 [1].

We chose eSoft's InstaGate Pro appliance for a number of reasons. Primarily, it offers the easiest access to product updates, definitions, configurations, and rules management. The web interface is very easy to use and offers an entire suite of tools that allow you to configure the device remotely. Secondly, the price was right. Even with licensing for up to 100 users, the price was perfect and beat the competition.

After getting the local phone company to come out and install the additional line and DSL modem, the most difficult part of this project was getting the addressing scheme setup in such a way as to not conflict with the DHCP server sitting behind the firewall. Originally, one of the DSL routers had a configuration in the 10.xx.xx.xx range. One phone call to XO and they were happy to change it to the 192.xx.xx.xx range so that it wouldn't conflict with the internal network. To ensure full firewall protection of the network, we interfaced the firewall behind the load balancer, it provides bottleneck security on both lines – the load balancer is lynch-pin to this setup because, without it, we would have needed two firewall appliances. Since the load balancer is relatively transparent, we are able to "see through" it to the InstaGate; this allows VPN functionality as well as remote updates of the device. And we got the additional bonus of a honeypot-like subnet sitting between the load balancer and the routers. If someone does get through, they won't see anything but a single piece of hardware – the load balancer, which is password protected and adds another layer of security in that it hides the internal LAN addressing scheme. Remarkably, since the installation of the firewall, the internal network is running more smoothly, they have not experienced a single outage, and virus infections are down [1].

A multilayer defense against the complexity of today's threatscape requires the development of an additional security application environment. The key to an integrated and effective security environment is no longer contingent on a single appliance or piece of software, such as a firewall, but in a secure applications management approach that brings together the multifaceted points of a distributed firewall policy. It depends upon the *layering* of defenses. InstaGate's approach to secure content management, called Instagate SCM™,

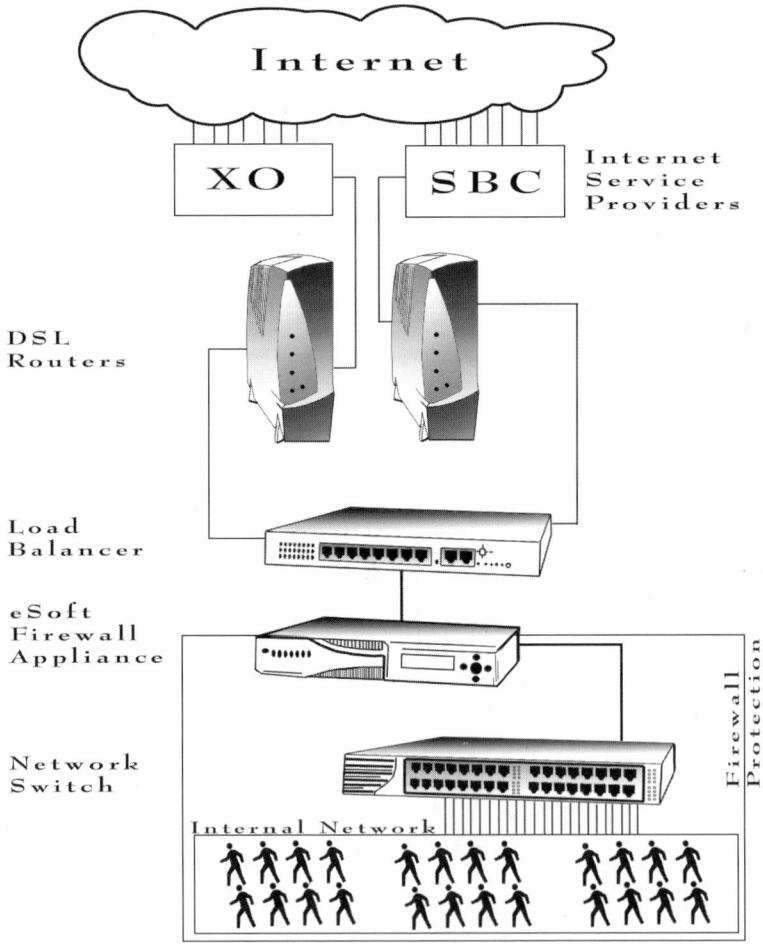

Figure 30-2. Dual DSL routers, a load balancer, and a firewall bring durable, high speed, and secure WAN access and capabilities to a small (30 Employees) office.

brings together all the points of a secure computing environment through the leverage of a single management tool/catalog that permits the implementation of various security SoftPaks™ [1].

> **Tip:** The diversity, and the purchase-only-what-you-need approach, of Secure Content Management engenders a security environment tailored to the needs of a single organization while, at the same time, permits scalability.

The most difficult aspect of security control is adapting to user habits and combating social engineering. Users will, in general, click on anything that moves. If it is a cute animation and it promises to help with something, many users will think they are being helpful to their probably overburdened IT support staff and will click on it. NetSky is possibly one of the biggest offenders (see sidebar "Social Engineering: 'These People Will Click on ANYTHING'") [1].

Social Engineering: "These People Will Click on ANYTHING" (overheard being muttered by an antagonized network administrator)

Lazaro, an attorney for a mid-sized, Midwest law firm, recently received an email from his wife. Attached to the email was an attachment. He opened it. The zip file opened, and in it was yet another attachment. He clicked on it, too, and a window opened on his screen and it told him that he could protect his computer against viruses by clicking a button. Now, Laz is not entirely to blame. A consultant working on the site was in the process of upgrading all the users to a SCM style desktop anti-virus solution, but a number of other issues had delayed her implementation by several days and, meanwhile, Laz's existing virus protection had expired. As a consultant, she was aware that several of the user's virus protection was expiring or had expired. But, with a firewall in place, it had given her a false sense of security – she felt that nothing could get in and that the user base had enough training at this point, and enough experience, not to click on anything suspect. She failed to account for the combination of multiple events – daily popups that told Laz his virus protection had expired, and an email from Laz's wife that contained a promised solution.

And then, when you factor in that Laz and the consultant are married to each other . . . Of course, you may realize by now that the email did not come from Laz's wife, the consultant. It didn't even come from her computer. It came from one of her client's computers, who had her email address in his address book, because he had received a similar email from his supervisor, who had received it from his wife, who had received it from her brother, and so on and so on, all the way back to a newsgroup where someone clicked on a NetSky-A infected file that promised free and unlimited virus protection . . . . This is what "social engineering" is all about. Creating a set of social circumstances to optimize the probability that a certain event will occur.

And in a distorted way, the NetSky variants a through m delivered as promised and removed any instances of the Bagel virus. But it only did this because the author of the NetSky variants is in a distance contest with the author of the Bagel viruses to see who can infect and dominate more computers. They do, in fact, hate each other and frequently leave messages within their code that deride and insult each other.

The moral of this story is that an unforeseeable combination of events can create a situation where even a normally smart and savvy user will click on anything. IT CAN HAPPEN TO ANYONE.

The above story is true. Here is a sample communication from the network administrator concerning the opening of socially engineered attachments, sent 2 weeks before the above story transpired:

——Original Message——

From: The Client

Sent: Wednesday, March 03, 2004 9:54 AM

To: Network Administrator

Subject: FW: Notify about your e-mail account utilization.

I opened this by mistake. Anything you recommend?

——Original Message——

From: noreply@.theClient.com [mailto:noreply@theClient.com]

Sent: Wednesday, March 03, 2004 8:30 AM

To: The Client

Subject: Notify about your e-mail account utilization.

Dear user of theClient.com gateway e-mail server,

We warn you about some attacks on your e-mail account. Your computer may contain viruses, in order to keep your computer and e-mail account safe, please, follow the instructions.

For details see the attached file.

For security reasons attached file is password protected. The password is "54215".

Cheers,

The theClient.com team

http://www.theClient.com

Network Admin RESPONSE:

—-Original Message——

From: Network Admin

Sent: Monday, March 15, 2004 9:57 AM

To: Everyone

Subject: For the record

In light of the recent outbreak of hoax and virus emails, I have composed the following in an effort to clarify and establish policy: I will never send you an email with an attachment asking you to configure or reconfigure anything.

If I do send you an email (such as this one), it will be purely informational and I will never ask you to reconfigure your account information.

I will never ask you for your account information via email.

You will never receive a legitimate notification regarding your account or internet connection from anyone other than "Scott Ellis".

Should you accidentally find yourself in a situation where your computer is asking you to install software, call me before proceeding. If you can't reach me, cancel the operation.

I will not, except in very rare circumstances and on an individual basis, will not ask you to click on any links to visit a web site or to download anything and install it on your computer.

You will never receive any legitimate email from me from any theClient.com email address, such as admin@theClient.com or accounts@theClient.com or support@theClient.com. These email addresses do not even exist on the the-Client.com email system.

In the rare case where I do send you an email with an attachment, it will be something that you are expecting because you asked me for it, or we already discussed it and determined that you needed it. And it will be from this email address.

Thank You

Network Administrator

IT Support [1]

Stories such as those illustrated by the Social Engineering sidebar exemplify and underscore the need, the requirement, for a more comprehensive security solution that that which can be provided by any, single, device. Here is a checklist of the items that are provided within an ESoft SCM deployment:

- Mail content security – utilizes virus scanning of email attachments and spam filtering to reduce the possibility of attack. Requires the installation of a mail server and a static IP address/domain name mapping in either the MX record or individual forwards.
- Servers:
- Desktop Anti-virus
- Internal fileserver
- POP and SMTP
- VPN
- Dial-In
- Web
- FTP
- DNS
- Web content security: Can provide site filtering to limit employee access to the web.
- Integrated management: Deployable to a single server, with management and automation tools that allow configuration and monitoring from any location. Supports RADIUS and LDAP authentication.
- The SoftPak Director, a part of the SCM, may contain the following SoftPaks, some with yearly fees, some with one time fees.
- Web server
- FTP server
- Desktop anti-virus
- Spam Filter
- Email Antivirus
- VPN Client
- Webmail
- Site Filter
- VPN Manager
- App Filter [1]

Sun iForce Perimter Security Solution

"The iForce Perimeter Security Solution provides multi-layer internet security to protect vital business information networks from today's threats. Combining seven essential components, the Perimeter Security Solution provides increased prevention, detection and response. This is achieved by integrating applications from industry-leading iForce and SunTone Certified Partners: Check Point Software, Symantec, Trend Micro, Tripwire, Sanctum and eSecurity" – www.sun.com [1].

The keystone of Sun's IForce Perimeter Security Solution rests in what Sun describes as a "Rock Solid Foundation" of Sun Microsystem servers. Running Sun Solaris, a flavor of UNIX, Sun provides a reliable and secure interface that can be placed between LAN and WAN environments. These servers that are grouped together in the iForce configuration are all running Sun Microsystems' Trusted Solaris Operating System (SMTSOS) – a hardened version of Sun Solaris (see sidebar, "Key iForce Components Explained"). This iForce configuration, a *collective* firewall, is a deployment of the following technologies across multiple servers:

- VPN/Firewall security through Check Point VPN-1/FireWall-1 software.
- Virus detection and scanning with Trend Micro InterScan VirusWall.
- While, for Intranet, Internet, and Extranet applications, Sanctum AppShield Web application firewall provides cookie snapping/session hijacking.
- The SUN company has developed what can only be described as a *hardened kernel* approach to the SMTSOS.
- Intrusion detection and forensics are handled by Symantec Corporation ManHunt and ManTrap threat management software.
- Data Integrity assurance with Tripwire software.
- Security event correlation management with e-Security e-Sentincl and e-Wizard products [1].

Key IForce Components Explained:

The iForce system, as a collective, comprises multiple components.

CheckPoint VPN-1: The foundation of the iForce collection of best-of-breed products, the Checkpoint firewall vpn, in addition to offering weak and strong encryption, embodies the crisp aromas and flavors of the most rarefied of mountain ranging blended units. Just kidding, this author has had way too much coffee.

Trend Micro InterScan VirusWall: This detects the presence of viruses and worms in email, ftp, and http traffic

Sanctum AppSHield: Protects web servers

SMTSOS: Each server in the iForce collection is loaded with Solaris Operating Environment and subsequently, after all patches are installed, is hardened with the Sun Solaris Security Toolkit. This is a process of eliminating or disabling non-essential services (for example, ftp services running or even installable on a web server may not be desirable), modification of user and directory permissions, and installation of any necessary tools need for the system of secure TCP wrappers used by the security solution to facilitate collective crosstalk.

Symantec Manhunt: Detect unusual behavior in network traffic.

Tripwire: A longtime Unix component on many versions of UNIX, this can require EXCESSIVE overhead as it uses a cryptographic checksum auditing method to determine if a file has been changed in a way that it shouldn't have. This software requires an extremely high level of expertise to setup properly. Otherwise, many false alarms will ensue as the software is indiscriminate and it logs whatever it is told to log. SUN offers the management expertise needed to configure this software properly on certain servers, but it is not recommended for deployment in areas of high customization.

> Professional Guidance: Part of the iForce solution includes support from Sun security experts [1].

Sana Security

Can a firewall be more than just a prophylactic barrier? The future of effective security may very well lie within the realm of application security and intrusion prevention. Host-based firewall software released by Sana Security:

- Can adapt to changes in application behavior.
- Detects and prevent known and unknown attacks.
- Provide centralized management.
- Shield custom and in-house developed applications.
- Does not require fulltime or extensive management.
- Deploys in minutes without requiring a restart.
- Protects applications that may be unable to protect themselves [1].

"Primary Response" monitors internal systems, understands the normal behavior, and shuts down any abnormal or strange behavior. It operates on an immune system analogy. They call it an application security agent, "Primary Response [1]."

Application Security

Primary Response was developed on a signatureless approach to infiltration detection. Rather, it is dependent upon intensive configuration to specific environments and is based upon research into how the human immune system repels viruses. The key to SANA's success is in the software's ability to learn and relearn independently of human interaction. This software observes and learns normal behavior for software, it watches coed paths, learns what is acceptable for those applications, and then continues to monitor the system for abnormal change. It is in this manner that Primary Response reduces time and effort spent on security [1].

It is a known and common trick of virus and stealth authors to write code that closely mimics applications, from masquerading as a notepad executable to actually replacing portions of legitimate executables with spoolers and SMTP engines, there is no known end to their chicanery. Once infiltration is successful, there are often few options to root them out and the impact can be as random and chaotic as trying to pick up the pieces and put a house together after it is hit by a hurricane. Often, rebuilding it is the only option. Tripwire-styled systems like First Response are excellent "backyard" watchdogs suitable for targeted Enterprise deployment across a conglomerate of small to medium sized networks where extremely high levels of security are REQUIRED [1].

First Response, among others in this genre of firewall technology, positions itself in the marketplace as an Enterprise grade, stand alone solution; with the ability to provide support for up to 7,000 agents per management server, it comes in as a close runner to the Lucent Brick-10000 solution. It provides role-based user management, agent management groups, and third party management systems integration. These features are among those of the SANA system that put it at the forefront of Host based firewall technology:

- Prevents vulnerability exploits
- Based on a unique, viral metaphor technology
- Automated patch updates
- Protects existing and developed applications
- Requires no signature subscription
- Provides comprehensive forensics [1]

SOCKS

Not to be confused with footwear, SOCKS (SOCKetS) is to firewalls as 802.11x is to wireless – it is a standard. It is a networking proxy protocol that allows servers on each side of a network barrier to communicate with each other. It is often used as a firewall that straddles the network barrier and permits the communication. David Koblas is the author of the two major versions of SOCKS, SOCKSv4 and SOCKSv5. v5 supports UDP, v4 does not [1].

Most proxy technologies, such as NAT (Network Address Translation) only support uni-directional proxy – they only allow one way communication. SOCKS delivers the proxy mechanism at the transport layer which allows it the flexibility to manage access based on application, user, address, etc. .... SOCKS is a good place to start for those who wish to gain an understanding of the core, underlying principles of a firewall, or for those interested in developing their own custom solutions [1].

SOCKS Implementations

It is not easily determined exactly what the underlying principle of a firewall is. Wading through the marketing hype seldom reveals the true nature of a firewall. Permeo, for example, makes no mention of their use of SOCKSv5 as their substrate logic, but the SOCKS web site clearly (and often) points to them as a prime example of a company that makes broad use of the standard. Whether or not a firewall maker uses SOCKS, a proprietary method, or some other standard, is often times a matter of conjecture. Chances are good, if the firewall under review exhibits the following aspects, it is either SOCKS or something very similar:

- Support for an unusually broad range of TCP protocols with the ability to add and manage protocols easily
- A broad range of supported IP-based applications.
- Weighs in on the side of application security as opposed to network security
- Controls outbound and inbound access.
- Is proxy based
- SOCKS is UDP and TCP only – ICMP (tracert and ping) applications will not work.
- Client security driver required to intercept and route communications through a SOCKS server [1].

SOCKS Support

As technology evolves, new products emerge, and new methods of threatening security present themselves, it's apparent that something as limited in focus as SOCKS will never penetrate a wide market application. Rather, it is more and more an item that finds specialized use as a firewall/vpn tool for application proxies [1].

Permeo

Ongoing support for SOCKS is questionable. ON the Permeo SOCKS web site, there is a FAQ about whether or not the software is Y2K compliant – draw your own conclusions. The site copyright is 1998–2002 [1].

Distinct

Security software firm that provides a SOCKS client for Yahoo! Paging users that allows them to connect through SOCKS firewalls. Again, this site has a questionable copyright date [1].

SSH Tectia

A managed security middleware solution, SSH is an industry leader in financial and government, managed security solutions. While the white paper makes little mention of SOCKS, descriptions and naming conventions within the framework suggest a high degree of parallelism to SOCKS. This is not to say that SSH is SOCKS. It is to say, however, that there are powerful similarities, and SSH may have SOCKS at its core with additional administrative capabilities that are custom SSH value add-ons. There are also similarities between the old SOCKS NEC site and the SSH Tectia white paper that leave one with an overwhelming sense of déjà vu [1].

Hummingbird

Hummingbird is a classic example of a specialized use of Socks to coordinate application communications through firewall devices. The Hummingbird SOCKS Client, in tandem with SOCKS V4/V5 servers on gateways, authenticates users, authorizes requests, and establishes a proxy connection. This creates a conduit whereby data passes transparently between the destination and the requesting client [1].

SOCKS Methodology

In Fig. 30-3, communication with the destination (far right) is initiated by the left-hand, Client device (P.C., Server, or handheld) [1]. Two additional mechanisms, or components, are introduced by SOCKS for the purposes of, well, "socksifying" and enabling SOCKS. These are the SOCKS library, introduced at the Client, or requesting, device, and the gateway component installed on, of all places, the gateway . . . (yes, the terminology can be a little obfuscated by indiscriminate redundancy).

The gateway is purposed with intercepting and replacing client application socket APIs and DNS name resolving APIs – these are the components of software that are responsible for establishing and controlling communication between different software. IE Software A and Software B both have APIs that allow Software A to send and receive information from Software B, with Software B residing either locally or remotely [1].

"Gateway" on the Gateway, is an enhanced SOCKS server. As such, it provides protocol translation services in a relaying fashion, between protocol X and the Destination protocol Y [1].

The SOCKS Library communicates with the Gateway through the SOCKS protocol, SOCKSv5, is a unique connection, special to SOCKS, and therefore is called a "SOCKsi-fied" connection and is, consequently, homogenous. This allows the limitation, in a sense,

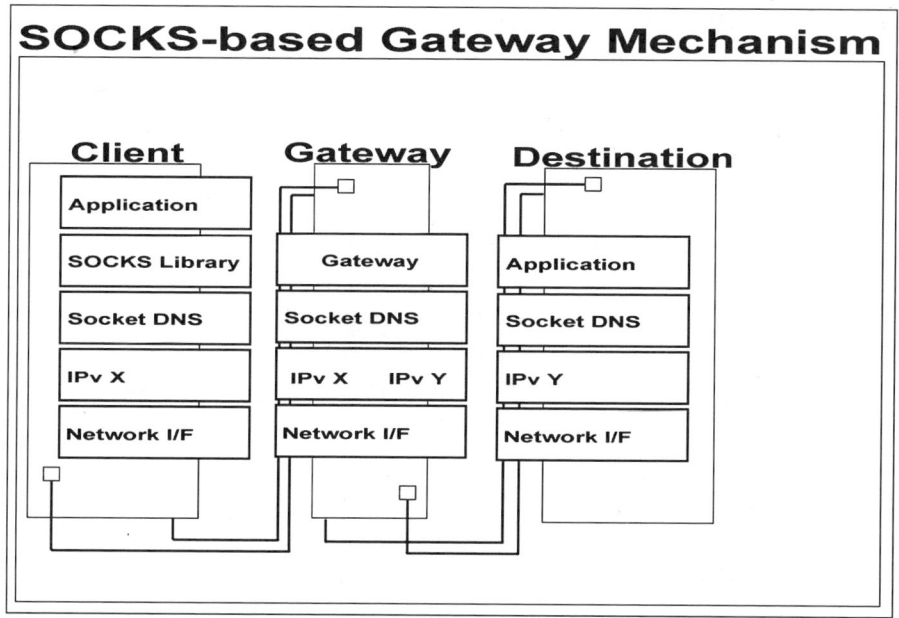

Figure 30-3. A gateway server provides SOCKS v4/5 support and acts as the relay mechanism for secure communication between a client and a destination.

of communication to a single protocol. This connection also permits the exchange of control information, information that details location and destination information. The SOCKSv5 implementation introduced support for IPv6 as well as enhanced security to the SOCKS standard (See sidebar, "SOCKS Advantage And Differences"). Once through the firewall, in the LAN sphere, the connection between the gateway and the destination is a normal one [1].

SOCKS Advantage And Differences

Internet Protocol, Version 6 (IPv6) offers several new improvements and enhancements to IPv5 that extend the protocol's capabilities: Some of the primary, and advantageous, differences in IPv6 compared to 5 and 4 include:

- "Anycast" addressing to provide a method of sending messages to several of the nearest gateways so that, conceptually, they may manage the forwarding of packets to others, updating routing tables along the line.
- IP addresses increase in length from 32 to 128 bits.
- Tasking is relegated to the destination, thereby speeding delivery and decreasing latency.
- Identification of packets as members of a particular "stream" is possible.

- Increased security is possible with the addition of extensions to this version that allow for the indication of an authenticating or specifying authority/mechanism to allow the verification of point of origin [1].

Lucent-Enterasys Secure Networks Solution

In the same vein as many other secure network market leaders, Lucent has entered into a partnership that integrates the Enterasys security product and network management tools with Lucent's firewall products. In this new market space for Lucent dwells a software portfolio and service offering with capabilities designed to address many of the critical security demands detailed in this chapter. Much like the SUN system, Lucent-Enterasys offers a wide variety of products grouped together under a single umbrella-like management philosophy [1].

Lucent VPN Firewall Brick

Finally, a carrier-grade solution, this product lineup hits hard in the arena of firewalls. Lucent claims the throughput and manageability of as many as a million concurrent VPN sessions, bandwidth management tools, and mobile data service. There are, however, multiple produce levels, from the entry level Brick-80 appliance to the advanced enterprise Brick – 1000 that boasts 1.5 Gbps throughput and is actually more like the size and dimension of a cinder-block than a brick. Each of the firewalls in the product line claim to "stretch your investment dollars" and provide carrier-grade IP services with 7500 concurrent VPN tunnels. It's unclear how the "million" VPN tunnels is formulated, perhaps on a carrier-grade Internet connection in a service center equipped with 150 Brick 1000 appliances. In fact, the Brick 1000 allows for central management of up to 1000 Brick devices and 10,000 IPSec clients. The Brick 1000 features:

- 9 10/100 ethernet ports and 4 fiber gigabit ports
- 4094 VLANS
- VPN clocking in at 400Mbps
- Content security
- DoS protection
- SYN flood protections
- Intelligent Cache management
- Stateful packet Inspection
- TCP and IP packet validation
- Virus scanning
- Strong Authentication
- Runs on Bell Labs' Inferno operating system
- 1.5 GBs throughput
- VitalQIP DNS/DHCP/IP Management Software
- Navis/Radius Authentication Server
- Network Security Assessment Service
- Security Policy Development
- Security Incident Response [1]

SUMMARY AND CONCLUSIONS

Simply setting up a firewall and then walking away, and relying on product updates and equipment upgrades to completely manage and protect your system is not entirely wise. Users arc often the first to notice attacks – while IT management and staff are busy repairing, replacing, upgrading, and planning, users are actually using the system. They will likely notice performance degradation before anyone else. In these cases, a cadre of tools in the IT Manager's war-chest will serve to detect and neutralize attempts. An informed complaint to a firewall manufacturer/support will enable quick and effective response. Packet sniffers, such as TCPDUMP, can be set to watch for particular patterns [1].

The difficulty inherent in packet analysis is characterized by an inability to accurately gage the deleterious impact of anomalous packets. Its overwhelming failure is that any types of attack looks perfectly innocent to even the best of packet analyzers. After all an email, apparently from your best friend, that contains a link to a malicious web site is, for all inspective purposes, perfectly legitimate traffic. To expect that the packet analyzer (or any firewall device) will assemble the email, open it, follow the link, download and inspect all the material from the link, test it, check it against a database of known offenders, validate IP addresses, etc. . . anyone can see that it may be a while before the email reaches its definition if it has to undergo security procedures of airport proportions [1].

At the end of the war that rages on the Internet, where security is the primary concern of administrators who must defend against unknown attackers who are simply attacking *because they can,* throughput will be king. The system that can do the most, can dig deep enough, and can do it with lightning speed, will reign. The impact of the results of socially engineered attacks can be mitigated and reduced, it remains to see if they can ever be prevented [1].

Finally, selecting the most suitable firewall for an organizational need depends, in large part, on the firewall policy. Certain organizations will have needs that cannot be met by the smaller, less redundant products. Others will have need that will be suited just fine by an "out-of-box" solution. The best solutions are tailor made by a network admin who understands and anticipates the needs and demands of his client. He creates a defense that includes a combination of firewall policy, effective technology, and a program of training and education [1].

REFERENCES

[1] John R. Vacca and Scott R. Ellis, Firewalls: Jumpstart for Network and Systems Administrators, Digital Press, 2005.

Chapter 31

FIREWALL TOPOLOGIES

INTRODUCTION

From hardware to software, there are myriad arrays of choice in the realm of security wares that provide the cast of supporting characters on the firewall stage. A firewall is more than just a single piece of equipment; as the authors of this fine book have asserted, a firewall is a policy; it is often a well-documented policy that encapsulates equipment, software, and usage policies. No one piece of equipment should be or could be acting as your entire firewall. For example, having a policy in place of changing your passwords frequently would be part of your firewall. However, where the focus of the previous chapter centered on actual firewalls and the often accompanying softwares bundled with them, this chapter's intent is to focus on independent utilities that may be assembled to provide an in depth defense against intrusion, extrusion, and collusion. Two major areas in this defense involve network topology, especially in terms of the Wide Area Network (WAN). These two areas, how they are handled, how they are managed, and how they are secured, are the measures of success of any firewall security policy. Coincidentally, the implementation and subsequent user leveraging of these security resources greatly improves work force life quality and productivity. It also makes managing remote networks from a central location a very real possibility [1].

VPN – VIRTUAL PRIVATE NETWORK

One of the first areas to cover then becomes one of intentionally opening "holes" in the firewall to allow *desirable* traffic through. One such hole through a firewall is the Virtual Private Network (VPN) as shown in Fig. 31-1 [1].

Often times, when presenting the concept of a VPN as a solution to clients coworkers, customers, there will be some resistance. VPN technology is relatively straightforward and

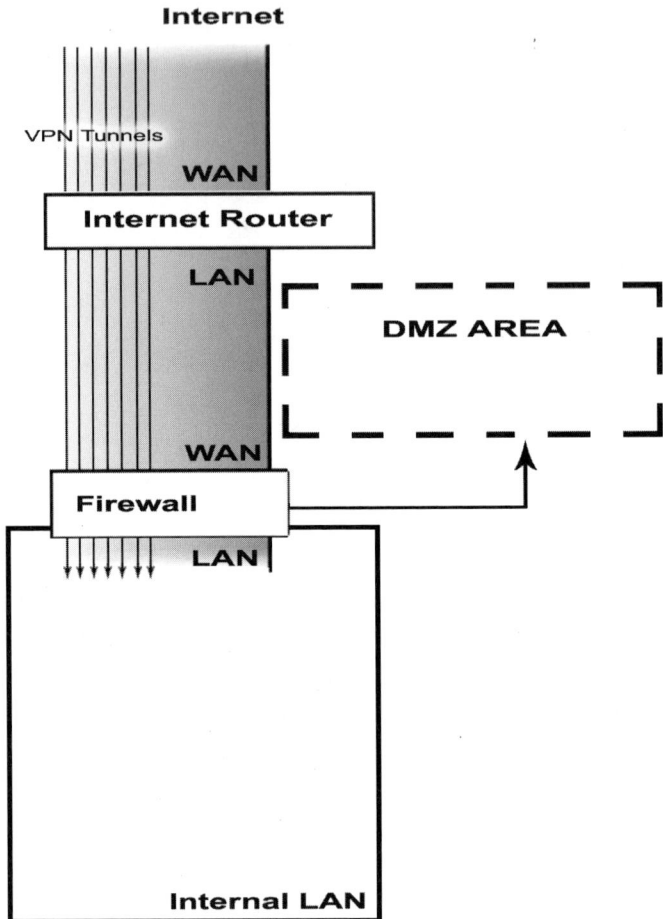

Figure 31-1. With today's high speed connections and advanced encryption algorithms, a possibility of Virtual Private Networking has been created that, traditionally, was accomplished by dial-up servers and modems.

easy to manage – the greatest obstacles to creating a VPN are: The technical abilities of the user, his understanding of the concept; and, Sensitivity of data [1].

Once these obstacles are conquered, and before the actual equipment purchase and integration, policy needs to be established. Questions such as these may arise:

- How sensitive is corporate data?
- How will decisions be made regarding access?
- At the individual server level?
- At the PC level?
- The workgroup or domain level [1]?

This is where the topology of the internal network plays a pivotal role. It can be very time consuming and difficult to arrange servers and information in ways that are particular to one user or even one group of users. Mapping drives is well and good, but can you map drives over a VPN? This is not a book about access control, however, but suffice it to say that yes, if permissions can be managed in the internal network, then the same administrative tools may be applied to the user that has authenticated across a VPN [1].

However, opening a VPN to the network in a certain way can often open a door to the network that allows the user access to everything. If it is a concern, then the method of authentication needs to be reviewed before allowing full, unrestricted access to all network resources. Most firewalls have the ability to create and manage user accounts that can be *enabled* for VPN access. These are generic accounts, and as such will often have the same level of access permissions to the network that the firewall enjoys. In access controlled areas, it is preferable to pass-through the VPN users to an ancillary authenticating server that has a better idea of user roles. Documents needed in one place may not be needed in another and, in fact, may even be restricted from certain users [1].

In any environment, it follows then that decisions must be made regarding who will have access to what, how the firewall will be positioned to allow access, what type of VPN will be used, how it will be setup, and will ancillary authentication be necessary. Furthermore, bandwidth usage must be considered. What sort of user activity will be typical? Running thin-clients? Accessing their Outlook exchange accounts? Moving large media files? Many of the firewall appliances discussed in the previous chapter are capable of tremendous throughput as well as tremendous numbers of VPN sessions. This can be very useful in WAN implementations where public communications systems may be used to establish a large, far reaching, network. Often times, in large enterprise deployments, a single (or several) server farm(s) will be centrally located and VPN technology will be used to link many thousands of remote locations [1].

Remote Office VPN

A VPN will allow organizations to leverage the backbone of the Internet o build their own secure WAN. For companies with many branch offices, the ability to build multiple, stable, Internet Protocol Security (IPSec) tunnels, is the ideal way to stay connected. A remote office VPN differs from a remote user VPN in that there exists, on each side of the connection, a firewall that has Remote Office VPN capabilities. Often times, internal subnets for an enterprise may have similar subnets; where remote user VPN's fail because of this, Remote Office VPN's may succeed. They also provide two way communication and visibility whereas remote user VPN creates a single point on the network and doesn't allow for connectivity between any machine accept the attached user device [1].

Remote User VPN

Remote User VPN describes a VPN circumstance where the remote PC uses an actual piece of client software to achieve the connection. Generally, the advantages of remote user VPN over PPTP VPN resides in the greater configurability and flexibility of the Client VPN to operate successfully in harsher network environments where a great level of convolution or complexity exists [1].

PPTP (Point to Point Tunneling Protocol) VPN

No Firewall solution worth its salt comes without PPTP support and passthrough support. PPTP settings will allow VPN passthrough (connection is passed to an internal VPN server for encryption and management). PPTP boasts ease of use – and as such it also fails the most easily and is the flakiest of the connections. Think "overcooked" fish. But it works, and for all intensive purposes, it works with the same level of security as Other Options. With PPTP VPN there is no need for additional software installation: Windows 98, Windows NT, Windows 2000 and Windows 2003 all come with PPTP VPN clients as part of the OS (Operating System). For additional security, strong encryption is available, however it must be configured when creating the connection on the user side – Windows clients connections must be set to use MS CHAP version 2.0 and 128-bit encryption [1].

Authenticating with a RADIUS ("Remote Access Dial-In User Service") Server

Many Firewalls Remote User VPN solutions offer RADIUS compatibility and an administrative screen may exist whereby the RADIUS server IP address and other configuration options may be entered. If this is the case, then the VPN users' authentication passes through to the Radius server for authentication. The firewall may or may not allow configuration of "password only" or "login and password" authentication from the RADIUS server [1].

•

FIREWALL POLICIES

Decide, and establish policies. Cordon off the restricted areas (if they aren't already), and create a written firewall policy. Many organizations create firewalls within firewalls within firewalls. There may be information that should never leave the office. There may be information so sensitive *you don't even want you to know* that you know about it. An effective Network Administrator has created a book to store information about the firewall (kept under lock and key in a safe location with a duplicate stored in a secure location offsite). A section of this notebook will outline VPN policy [1].

How Secure Is VPN Technology?

If they want it bad enough, they will get it, even if your policy is to never let it leave the office. Your secrets are more likely to walk out your front door in an employee's pocket or in a USB hard-drive in plain view on their keychain than they are to be stolen by someone who has hacked your VPN. With 128 bit encryption on all VPN traffic, it would take millions of years for a single computer to crack the code by guessing it [1].

Many firewall products are RADIUS compatible, and use keychain tokens and intrusion prevention for security. David Aylesworth, a Product Manager for eSoft, manufacturer's of Instagate, says, "[The] InstaGate can authenticate VPN, proxy, and mail users via RADIUS. I typically see customers using this so they don't have to duplicate their Windows user database on the InstaGate. Instead they run a RADIUS server on their Windows domain controller and have the InstaGate authenticate to it. Regarding password tokens, we do not support any natively, but many can be supported via RADIUS [1]."

Document Access

With the inherent difficulty in securing documents, many enterprises have turned to document management systems such as WORLDOX, iManage, and PCDocs to provide a comprehensive solution – one that will not only protect sensitive material from casual theft, but will also provide much needed sorting and categorizing elements [1].

A DMS (Document Management System) solution, such as WORLDOX, iManage, or PCDocs, has been shown to work quite well in assuring version control, location control, and safe access to documents by remote workers. Many DMS solutions also have web interface modules that can be used to emulate document interface at remote locations. Custom built solutions that provide a simple intranet with a documents solution so you can log usage, and then batten down the hatches and make it the only access route, are also effective. Microsoft's web server platform, IIS (Internet Information Service), has a built in user account that can be granted permission to a certain area of a server when others may not have access rights of any kind. It is, in essence, the primary operating principle of a web site – that the web server acts as an agent between the browser and the file system. Naturally, access to the server can be denied to anyone but the administrator. On a VPN, remote users at home or remote offices can surf the intranet just as they can on site [1].

Whether a Firewall is developed that allows users to VPN and have complete access or only access to terminal serve to the computer in their office, the virtual office place (complete with chat utilities to replace the traditional Water Cooler) is rapidly becoming as much of a reality as it is a necessity. With each day that passes, concerns over travel and time away from home and family become bigger issues and employers find that they must respond to the needs of employees. At the same time, they must ensure smooth functioning of their operation. With the installation of some equipment and some time to configure, A VPN, in combination with a solid firewall and a DMS, will increase productivity and profit – for for less than the cost of a new car [1].

SETTING UP A DEMILITARIZED ZONE (DMZ) – A VPN ALTERNATIVE?

Not really alternative in terms of the technology, but a so-called philosophical diametric to a VPN can be a DMZ. Philosophically, the purpose of both a DMZ and a VPN is to protect business data and resources from unauthorized access, and grant access to allowed functions to outside users. A DMZ, unlike a VPN, is an area that is like a bastion between the internal network, the firewall device, and the Internet. Historically, DMZs were created through the *layering* of firewall devices. However, with improvements in both electronics and firmware, setting up a Demilitarized zone can be as easy as plugging a CAT 5 (Ethernet cable) into an Ethernet port labeled "DMZ" on the firewall. Fig. 31-2 is a representation of a typical

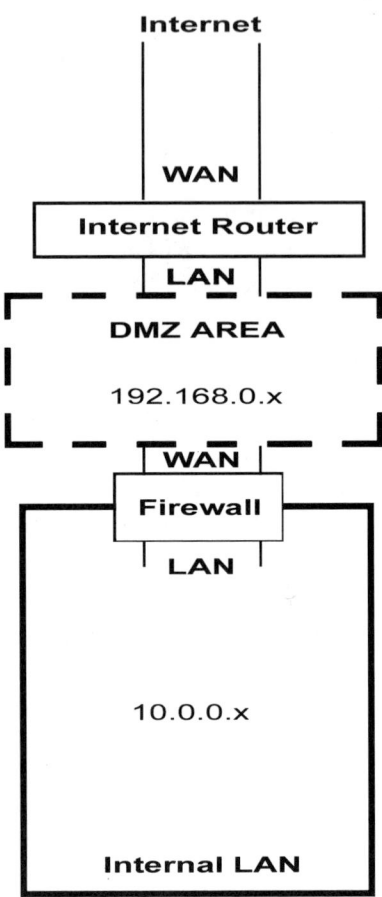

Figure 31-2. Simple DMZ Configuration.

firewall/DMZ arrangement [1]. Depending on configuration, interestingly, a VPN may even be used to connect to a DMZ.

Uses

A DMZ is a good place to put machines that need to be accessed via the external Internet when placing them in the internal network is too risky. This may be because the ports that need to be opened for certain types of functions (such as web and file serving) are more vulnerable, are hacker magnets, and, should a single machine on the internal network be compromised, it is a hacking waterfall and every other machine will be at risk or compromised in short order. Things such as FTP servers, file servers, web servers, and mail servers are often placed in a DMZ [1].

Theory of Operation

In its simplest terms, a DMZ is a separate network that sits between two "firewalls." It takes two devices to make a firewall because it is, definitively, the more vulnerable of two networks, sitting side by side. A good, clear definition would be: DMZ (Demilitarized zone) – the first of two networks, in series, with the first network separated from the Internet by a firewall or a router and the second network separated from the first by a firewall. Each network consists of a different subnet [1].

Typically, most modern firewalls have a DMZ setup where the firewall can control and create the DMZ. There are still two devices at work here – in the case of a firewall with DMZ capabilities, the second device is simply built into the firewall appliance and the firewall becomes a bidirectional bastion server. Many administrators take the approach of simply cordoning of an area between the modem/router and the firewall; the DMZ is then a separate subnet that sits between the modem router and the firewall. Fig. 31-2 is configured in this manner [1]. Configuration of port forwarding is accomplished at the router, and this can be accomplished in a number of ways, many of which are manufacturer specific. For example, some Speedstream models allow configuration of a DMZ on port 1 of the router network interface ports. It may require technical assistance from the manufacturer, but here is the target checklist:

- Router WAN: same as the external IP address.
- Router LAN IP: same as the DMZ subnet.
- DMZ has subnet of 10.0.0.xx or 172.[16-31].x.x or 192.168.x.x – these subnet addresses are private set-asides. They do not exist in the public domain.
- DMZ computer gateways: same as the Router LAN IP address.
- Firewall WAN is set to an address on the DMZ, with its gateway set to the Router LAN as well.
- NAT translation on the Router is enabled in this configuration. Configuring a DMZ with Network Address Translation (NAT) turned off may be considerably trickier to accomplish and may involve setting up pinholes [1].

The above configuration is well and good, but it may be very tricky (in other words, this author doesn't know how to do it) if not impossible to setup a true DMZ in this fashion AND allow for internal network VPN access. Using the DMZ port (if available) on a firewall may be an alternative configuration that will achieve the same results, or using a routing table (if such a feature is available on the router) to map addresses may be another, with the DMZ existing off of a firewall that is parallel to the private subnet firewall. One thing is certain, that if the above configuration is used, to enable VPN, the firewall will have to have a public IP address on its WAN port. For this to be accomplished, NAT must be disabled and the Router WAN and LAN must have the exact same, public, IP address. This is called a simple passthrough, but to put a DMZ between a router configured in this manner and the firewall would contradict the definition of DMZ. It would be more like a phalanx maneuver – one that will get its head lopped off. In this configuration, many routers offers absolutely zero packet filtering or stateful inspection. Check with manufacturer specifications to be certain [1].

Note: Some routers are more cooperative than others, and getting oneself locked out of a router is a most simple thing to do!

Managing Ports in a DMZ

There are 65535 ports that a computer uses; however, only the first thousand or so are actually used by anyone. In the range 1–1023, many services and software make use of these for communications and operations. The primary purpose of a firewall is to centralize all communication to and from a network so that unauthorized activities and requests to these ports may be monitored effectively. For the purposes of security, many of these ports are closed, or operate in a so-called stealth mode [1].

Through a number of methods, the firewall controlling the DMZ may allow certain types of traffic through, to, and from certain machines through IP address mapping. This is different than a routing table – a routing table in a router actually takes ALL the communication to one IP address and passes it to another. In Fig. 31-3, it is demonstrated that, through one IP address (the router) multiple machine ports are mapped to specific machines within the DMZ [1]. In a typical arrangement, configuration settings and administrative screens would reveal that port 80 for Web traffic is mapped to port 80 of a machine within the DMZ. This is useful because, should an attempt be made to open or "listen" or "scan" other ports on the internal machine, it won't happen because they aren't there – they don't exist. The machine, except for port 80, is entirely invisible to the Internet. Additional ports, such as port 21 for ftp (File Transfer Protocol) or port 25 for e-mail SMTP (Simple Mail Transfer Protocol) can also be mapped through the firewall.

A portion of this "hiding" may be achieved through Network Address Translation (NAT) where the headers of packets are converted to send IP packets bound for one address to another. It may also, in a more essential version of a DMZ, be achieved through port forwarding, where requests to a specific port on a machine are forwarded to that same port on another machine that, due to its configuration and services, may be more vulnerable to attack. The machine, a firewall, doing the forwarding should be considerably hardened. Port protection is very useful in that a machine simply sitting on the Internet is very vulnerable – it is actually impossible to close certain ports on a Windows machine [1]!

A DMZ may also be as simple as the subnet space that exists between a firewall and a router. A router has as its LAN address 10.x.x.1, pinholes are setup in the router to allow access to machines within the DMZ subnet, and the firewall sits between the DMZ and the private LAN [1].

DMZ Topology

Security, more than just a flavor of the day, is a constantly changing landscape and, as such, there are certain types of network addressing schemes that are so severely flawed that they hardly warrant mention – except, perhaps, to mention that they are inherently flawed. One such addressing scheme is called Standard Network Address Translation. Or, to be blunt, "May as Well be Full Blown Passthrough" would be more accurate. Don't laugh – there are networks out there, with firewalls, and with so-called DMZs, that actually have

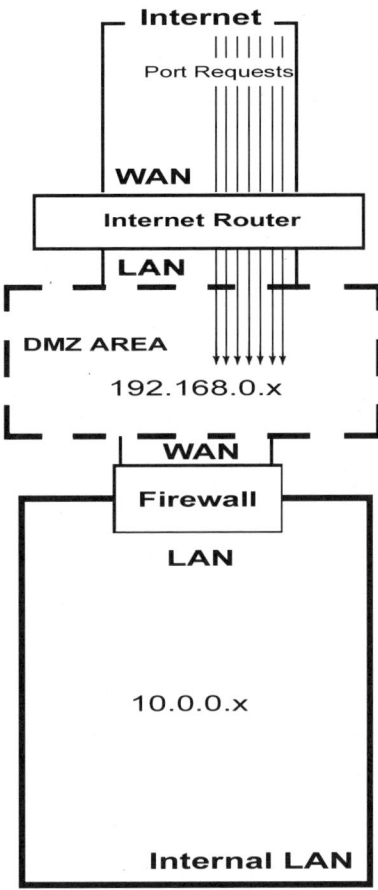

Figure 31-3. In this configuration, the router is setup to forward certain port requests to specific servers within the DMZ.

internal LAN machines configured with static IP addresses. These are typically small, or remote offices, where NAT, subnets, subnet masks, and firewalls are poorly understood or where the administrator is naïve and hails, perhaps, from a simpler time – the *golden era of the Internet* as it has been called (1991–1995). Or perhaps it is simply an office manager with some skill and little fear [1].

This author once had the experience of hooking up a new PC to one such network way back, back in the time of the Blaster Worm – within 30 seconds, the virus scan and the RPC service had been compromised. *Sometimes people aren't as familiar with the topology of their own networks as they like to think they are.* There is no doubt that, once cracked, these environments represents a secret gold mine opportunity for anyone of malevolent intent. A quick litmus test to determine if a network has standard addressing is easy. If the Router does not have NAT enabled, the LAN and WAN port are the same, and the firewall (if there is one) has NAT enabled and DHCP disabled, standard addressing must be in use [1].

Truly, the only legitimate reason that a network may have this configuration is for leading edge gaming where real-time responsiveness is required, where security has zero relevance, or where a firewall needs to be inserted with transparency in series with other devices that will negate the negatives of this architecture. The primary reason for setting up a network in this manner can often be attributed to the ease of setup, or Out of The Box (OTB) configurations that were never changed [1].

Standard Network Addressing Mode

This mode allows for the creation of a static subnet of public addresses on an internal LAN. It is not a recommended configuration and is listed here for identification and informational definition only [1]:

- Router has NAT Enabled or disabled. Some routers get confused if NAT is enabled and a LAN WAN IP address scheme is on the same public subnet. Many Routers will assume an IP spoofing attack is underway and throw errors.
- LAN PCs are configured with the Gateway as the firewall IP address
- LAN PC's are configured the same subnet mask as the firewall, and with static, public IP addresses
- Firewall LAN Subnet Mask is the same as the internal LAN
- WAN router address is the same as the firewall WAN address
- All subnet masks are the same, everywhere [1]

> **Note:** This is a sample; some firewall and router configurations may have more elaborate or less controls that will either achieve the same results in a different manner or be unable to configure standard mode at all.

The standard network addressing flaws are as follows:

- Ease of running continuous software directly against an IP to crack into it.
- Quickness of crackability on discovery of exploit.
- Ease of port listening to unencrypted traffic and associating that traffic with a specific user.
- Once cracked, ease of remote management and accessibility because the IP addresses never change and are completely unique on the entire network.
- Endless possibilities for reverse attacks (from the inside out).
- No restrictions, of any kind, on the sort of protocols emitted or received.
- Ease of tracking users' web browsing habits [1].

With a static IP, tracking a user's web browsing habits is so easy it truly is child's play. If an email is sent from a particular computer, with a static (never changing) public IP address, chances are good that the IP address was included in the email header. If a web user emailed a company, and they have a web site, chances are good they will harvest information on a large scale so that they may track the success of their marketing initiatives, attach demographics to browsing patterns, and subsequently know who people are when they are visiting. This is not necessarily a bad thing if it is just one company using the personal info and they protect your privacy. However, many do not, and in the current Internet environment, once discovered, a web surfer's name and IP address and other demographic data will hit the ground running. Making sense of all the data is not child's play, however, and large data manipulation mechanisms known as "Data Warehouses" are implemented for exactly this sort of thing [1].

Network Address Translation (NAT)

A lot has been said about NAT, some of it good, some of it bad, and some of it, simply put, untrue. NAT does not a firewall make. Most routers, in fact, do not a firewall make (and some do not even a router make). Digressions aside, NAT has its usefulness. Configuring NAT on a router means that the router will take all network traffic, coming and out, and alter the IP headers so that they go somewhere else. If, for example, inbound traffic is heading for 68.68.68.68, and the router is WAN IP configured to 68.68.68.68 with NAT turned on and a LAN side IP of 172.20.15.12, all IP traffic headed for 68.68.68.68 will be routed to 172.20.15.12. The two are intertwined without bias. Additionally, a router with the most recent firmware upgrades will provide updated defense, through packet inspection, of hacking attempts in the network layer [1].

Network Address Port Translation (NAPT)

This is the router equivalent of port forwarding as accomplished by firewalls. It allows the designation of a particular IP address and port number combination, such as 68.68.68.68:80 to be redirected, or *translated* to an internal IP, such as 192.168.0.1:80. Translations such as these are called "pinholes" and are defined through router administrative screens. Pinholes are also context sensitive in that they expect certain protocols and will limit the protocols used. Some routers are fussy about what protocols bind to which ports and may not, inherently, allow certain, more esoteric, applications to operate [1].

DMZ Drawback

Finally, a common drawback of the DMZ is not so much the reality, but the perception that the maintenance and administration of a DMZ involves a higher level of difficulty and complexity. Administering and setting up a DMZ is no more complex a task for a knowledgeable administrator than configuring a new PC on the network. However, it does take longer to setup than a VPN, requires more machine resources, and is, statistically, a greater security risk [1].

SUMMARY AND CONCLUSIONS

The amount of work involved in creating a unique, custom, tailored approach to firewall security and policy should never be underestimated. Likewise, the benefits to a corporation of investing in a quality approach are infinite – these are the tools and the methods that some of the largest enterprises in the world are implementing. DMZ and VPN represent scalability in its purest essence. It is a two edged sword and it can and it will cut both ways if it is not properly handled. There is a reason why martial arts masters will not allow inexperienced students to handle edged weapons and, likewise, there is a reason that inexperienced administrators should stay away from the cutting edge of the network. An improperly configured firewall, VPN, or DMZ, can gravely compromise critical and private data, can hammer the bandwidth to next to nothing, and can literally bring an operation to its knees while, at the same time, becoming a veritable. All ye who enter here: do not tread lightly. Look under every stone. Check every setting. Look at the log files. View the warnings. Change passwords often and change them frequently and then change them again. Implement RADIUS or similar technology. Finally, system administrators should be proven experts in RADIUS, tokens, card scanners (all of these are authentication methods) and above all, should have verifiable experience in the management of a written, secured, firewall policy [1].

REFERENCES

[1] John R. Vacca and Scott R. Ellis, Firewalls: Jumpstart for Network and Systems Administrators, Digital Press, 2005.

Chapter 32

SELECTING FIREWALL SECURITY TOPOLOGY POLICY

INTRODUCTION

Network administrators have increasing concerns about the security of their networks when they expose their organization's private data and networking infrastructure to Internet crackers. To provide the required level of protection, an organization needs a security policy to prevent unauthorized users from accessing resources on the private network and to protect against the unauthorized export of private information. Even if an organization is not connected to the Internet, it may still want to establish an internal security policy to manage user access to portions of the network and protect sensitive or secret information [3].

With regards to the Internet, many organizations have connected or want to connect their private LANs to the Internet so that their users can have convenient access to Internet services. Since the Internet as a whole is not trustworthy, their private systems are vulnerable to misuse and attack. A *firewall* is a safeguard one can use to control access between a trusted network and a less trusted one. A firewall is not a single component, it is a strategy for protecting an organization's Internet-reachable resources. Firewalls can also be used to secure segments of an organization's *intranet*, but this chapter will concentrate on the Internet aspects of firewall policy [3].

A firewall enforces a security policy, so without a policy, a firewall is useless. This chapter will help the responsible manager and firewall administrator create useful policy for the firewall. Throughout this chapter, the term *firewall* refers to the sum of the hardware, software, policy and procedures used to implement the firewall policy. A firewall is not necessarily a single piece of software sitting on a single computer system [3].

FIREWALL PROTECTION

The main function of a firewall is to centralize access control. A firewall serves as the gatekeeper between the untrusted Internet and the more trusted internal networks. If outsiders or remote users can access the internal networks without going through the firewall, its effectiveness is diluted. For example, if a traveling manager has a modem connected to his or her office PC that he or she can dial into while traveling (war-driving), and that PC is also on the protected internal network, an attacker who can dial into that PC has circumvented the firewall. Similarly, if a user has a dial-up Internet account with a commercial Internet Service Provider (ISP), and sometimes connects to the Internet from their office PC via modem, he or she is opening an unsecured connection to the Internet that circumvents the firewall. Firewalls provide several types of protection:

- They can block unwanted traffic.
- They can direct incoming traffic to more trustworthy internal systems.
- They hide vulnerable systems which can't easily be secured from the Internet.
- They can log traffic to and from the private network.
- They can hide information like system names, network topology, network device types, and internal user ID's from the Internet.
- They can provide more robust authentication than standard applications might be able to do [1].

Each of the preceding functions are described in greater detail next.

As with any safeguard, there are trade-offs between convenience and security. Transparency is the visibility of the firewall to both inside users and outsiders going through a firewall. A firewall is transparent to users if they do not notice or stop at the firewall in order to access a network. Firewalls are typically configured to be transparent to internal network users (while going outside the firewall); on the other hand, firewalls are configured to be non-transparent for outside network coming through the firewall. This generally provides the highest level of security without placing an undue burden on internal users [3].

FIREWALL ARCHITECTURES

Firewalls can be configured in a number of different architectures, providing various levels of security at different costs of installation and operation. Organizations should match their risk profile to the type of firewall architecture selected. This part of the chapter describes typical firewall architectures and sample policy statements:

- Multi-Homed Host.
- Screened Host.
- Screened Subnet [2].

Multi-Homed Host

A multi-homed host is a host (a firewall in this case) that has more than one network interface, with each interface connected to logically and physically separate network segments. A dual-homed host (host with two interfaces) is the most common instance of a multi-homed host [3].

A dual-homed firewall is a firewall with two network interfaces cards (NICs) with each interface connected to a different network. For instance, one network interface is typically connected to the external or untrusted network, while the other interface is connected to the internal or trusted network. In this configuration, a key security tenet does not to allow traffic coming in from the untrusted network to be directly routed to the trusted network – the firewall must always act as an intermediary [3].

> **Tip:** Routing by the firewall is usually disabled for a dual-homed firewall so that IP packets from one network are not directly routed from one network to the other.

Screened Host

A screened host firewall architecture uses a host (called a bastion host) to which all outside hosts connect, rather than allow direct connection to other, less secure internal hosts. To achieve this, a filtering router is configured so that all connections to the internal network from the outside network are directed towards the bastion host [3].

> **Tip:** If a packet-filtering gateway is to be deployed, then a bastion host should be set up so that all connections from the outside network go through the bastion host to prevent direct Internet connection between the organization network and the outside world.

Screened Subnet

The screened subnet architecture is essentially the same as the screened host architecture. But, the screened subnet architecture adds an extra strata of security by creating a network which the bastion host resides (often called a perimeter network), which is separated from the internal network [3].

> **Tip:** A screened subnet should be deployed by adding a perimeter network in order to separate the internal network from the external. This assures that if there is a successful attack on the bastion host, the attacker is restricted to the perimeter network by the screening router that is connected between the internal and perimeter network.

TYPES OF FIREWALLS

There are different implementations of firewalls which can be arranged in different ways. The various firewall implementations are discussed next and example policies presented. Table 32-1 depicts several firewall architectures and their ratings, as they would apply to low, medium and high risk processing environments [3]:

Table 32-1. Firewall Security Risk.

Firewall Architecture (if any one of these is being implemented)	High Risk Environment (Hospital)	Medium Risk Environment (University)	Low Risk Environment (florist shop)
Packet filtering	0	1	4
Application Gateways	3	4	2
Hybrid Gateways	4	3	2
Rating: Here are rating numbers, from recommended to unacceptable, for various firewall types: **4 – recommended choice** **3 – effective option** **2 – acceptable** **1 – minimal security** **0 – unacceptable**			

- Packet filtering.
- Application Gateways.
- Hybrid Gateways [1].

Packet Filtering Gateways

Packet filtering firewalls use routers with packet filtering rules to grant or deny access based on source address, destination address and port. They offer minimum security, but at a very low cost, and can be an appropriate choice for a low risk environment. They are fast, flexible, and transparent. Filtering rules are not often easily maintained on a router, but there are tools available to simplify the tasks of creating and maintaining the rules. Filtering gateways do have inherent risks including [3]:

- The source and destination addresses and ports contained in the IP packet header are the only information that is available to the router in making decision whether or not to permit traffic access to an internal network.
- They don't protect against Internet Protocol (IP) or Domain Name Server/Service (DNS) address spoofing.
- An attacker will have a direct access to any host on the internal network once access has been granted by the firewall.
- Strong user authentication isn't supported with some packet filtering gateways.
- They provide little or no useful logging [1].

Application Gateways

An application gateway uses server programs (called proxies) that run on the firewall. These proxies take external requests, examine them, and forward legitimate requests to the internal host that provides the appropriate service. Application gateways can support functions such as user authentication and logging. Because an application gateway is considered as the most secure type of firewall, this configuration provides a number of advantages to the medium-high risk site:

- The firewall can be configured as the only host address that is visible to the outside network, requiring all connections to and from the internal network to go through the firewall.
- The use of proxies for different services prevents direct access to services on the internal network, protecting the enterprise against insecure or misconfigured internal hosts.
- Strong user authentication can be enforced with application gateways.
- Proxies can provide detailed logging at the application level [1].

Application level firewalls should be configured such that out-bound network traffic appears as if the traffic had originated from the firewall (only the firewall is visible to outside networks). In this manner, direct access to network services on the internal network is not allowed. All incoming requests for different network services such as Telnet, File Transfer Protocol (FTP), Hyper Text Transfer Protocol (HTTP), Remote Login (RLOGIN), etc., regardless of which host on the internal network will be the final destination, must go through the appropriate proxy on the firewall [3].

Applications gateways require a proxy for each service, such as FTP, HTTP, etc., to be supported through the firewall. When a service is required that is not supported by a proxy, an organization has three choices:

- Deny the service until the firewall vendor has developed a secure proxy: This is the preferred approach, as many newly introduced Internet services have unacceptable vulnerabilities.
- Develop a custom proxy: This is a fairly difficult task and should be undertaken only by very sophisticated technical organizations.
- Pass the service through the firewall: Using what are typically called "plugs," most application gateway firewalls allow services to be passed directly through the firewall with only a minimum of packet filtering. This can limit some of the vulnerability, but can result in compromising the security of systems behind the firewall [2].

Low Risk

When an in-bound Internet service not supported by a proxy is required to pass through the firewall, the firewall administrator should define the configuration or plug that will allow the required service. When a proxy is available from the firewall vendor, the plug must be disabled and the proxy made operative [3].

Medium-High Risk

All in-bound Internet services must be processed by proxy software on the firewall. If a new service is requested, that service will not be made available until a proxy is available from the firewall vendor and tested by the firewall administrator. A custom proxy can be developed in-house or by other vendors only when approved by the CIO.

Hybrid Or Complex Gateways

Hybrid gateways combine two or more of the above firewall types and implement them in series rather than in parallel. If they are connected in series, then the overall security is enhanced. On the other hand, if they are connected in parallel, then the network security perimeter will be only as secure as the least secure of all methods used. In medium to high-risk environments, a hybrid gateway may be the ideal firewall implementation.

ISSUES

Now, let's look at some firewall policy issues. These issues consist of the following:

- Authentication.
- Routing Versus Forwarding.
- Source Routing.
- IP Spoofing.
- DNS and Mail Resolution [1].

Authentication

Router-based firewalls don't provide user authentication. Host-based firewalls can provide these kinds of authentication:

- Username/password: This provides the lowest level of protection, because the information can be sniffed off the network or shoulder-surfed.
- One-time passwords: One-time passwords using software or hardware tokens, generate a new password for each session. This means that old passwords cannot be reused if they are sniffed or otherwise borrowed or stolen.
- Digital Certificates: Digital certificates use a certificate generated using public key encryption [1].

Routing Versus Forwarding

A clearly defined policy has to be written as to whether or not the firewall will act as a router or a forwarder of Internet packets. This is trivial in the case of a router that acts as a packet filtering gateway: the firewall (router in this case) has no option but to route packets. Applications gateway firewalls should generally not be configured to route any traffic between the external interface and the internal network interface, since this could bypass security controls. All external to internal connections should go through the application proxies [3].

Source Routing

Source routing is a routing mechanism whereby the path to a target machine is determined by the source, rather than by intermediate routers. Source routing is mostly used for debugging network problems, but could also be used to attack a host. If an attacker has knowledge of some trust relationship between your hosts, source routing can be used to make it appear that the malicious packets are coming from a trusted host. Therefore, because of this security threat, a packet filtering router can easily be configured to reject packets containing a source route option. Thus, a site that wishes to avoid the problem of source routing entirely would write a policy [3].

IP Spoofing

IP spoofing is when an attacker masquerades his or her machine as a host on the target's network (fooling a target machine that packets are coming from a trusted machine on the target's internal network). Policy regarding packet routing has to be clearly written so that they will be handled accordingly if there is a security problem. It is necessary that authentication based on source address be combined with other security schemes to protect against IP spoofing attacks [3].

DNS And Mail Resolution

On the Internet, the Domain Name Service provides the mapping and translation of domain names to IP addresses, such as mapping server1.acme.com to 123.45.67.8. Some firewalls can be configured to run as a primary, secondary, or caching DNS server.

Deciding how to manage DNS services is generally not a security decision. Many organizations use a third party, such as an Internet Service Provider, to manage their DNS. In this case, the firewall can be used as a DNS caching server, improving performance, but not requiring your organization to maintain its own DNS database.

If the organization decides to manage its own DNS database, the firewall can (but doesn't have to) act as the DNS server. If the firewall is to be configured as a DNS server (primary, secondary, or caching), it is necessary that other security precautions be in place. One advantage of implementing the firewall as a DNS server is that it can be configured to hide the internal host information of a site. In other words, with the firewall acting as a DNS server, internal hosts get an unrestricted view of both internal and external DNS data. External hosts, on the other hand, do not have access to information about internal host machines. To the outside world, all connections to any host in the internal network will appear to have originated from the firewall. With the host information hidden from the outside, an attacker will not know the host names and addresses of internal hosts that offer service to the Internet [3].

> **Tip:** A security policy for DNS hiding might state: If the firewall is to run as a DNS server, then the firewall must be configured to hide information about the network, so that internal host data are not advertised to the outside world.

INTRANET

Although firewalls are usually placed between a network and the outside untrusted network, in large companies or organizations, firewalls are often used to create different subnets of the network, often called an Intranet. Intranet firewalls are intended to isolate a particular subnet from the overall corporate network. The reason for the isolation of a network segment might be that certain employees can only access subnets guarded by these firewalls only on a need-to-know basis. An example could be a firewall for the payroll or accounting department of an organization. The decision to use an Intranet firewall is generally based on the need to make certain information available to some, but not all internal users; or, to provide a high degree of accountability for the access and use of confidential or sensitive information [3].

> **Tip:** For any systems hosting organization critical applications, or providing access to sensitive or confidential information, internal firewalls or filtering routers should be used to provide strong access control and support for auditing and logging. These controls should be used to segment the internal organization network to support the access policies developed by the designated owners of information.

NETWORK TRUST RELATIONSHIPS

Business networks frequently require connections to other business networks. Such connections can occur over leased lines, proprietary Wide Area Networks, Value Added Networks, or over public networks such as the Internet. For instance, many local governments use leased lines or dedicated circuits to connect regional offices across the state. Many business use commercial VANs to connect business units across the country or the world [3].

The various network segments involved may be under control of different organizations and may operate under a variety of security policies. By their very nature, when networks are connected, the security of the resulting overall network drops to the level of the weakest network. When decisions are made for connecting networks, trust relationships must be defined to avoid reducing the effective security of all networks involved [3].

Trusted networks are defined as networks that share the same security policy or implement security controls and procedures that provide an agreed upon set of common security services. Untrusted networks are those that do not implement such a common set of security controls, or where the level of security is unknown or unpredictable. The most secure policy is to only allow connection to trusted networks, as defined by an appropriate level of management. However, business needs may force temporary connections with business partners or remote sites that involve the use of untrusted networks [3].

HIGH

All connections from the organization network to external networks must be approved by and managed by a Network Services Manager. Connections should be allowed only with external networks that have been reviewed and found to have acceptable security controls and procedures. All connections to approved external networks should pass through organization-approved firewalls [3].

Low-Medium

All connections from the organization network to external networks should be approved by a Network Services Manager. All connections to approved external networks should pass through organization-approved firewalls. To eliminate a major vulnerability, all connections and accounts related to external network connections should be periodically reviewed and deleted as soon as they are no longer required [3].

> **Tip:** Audit trails and system logs for external network connections should be reviewed weekly. Any accounts related to these connections that are not used on a monthly basis should be deactivated. A Network Services Manager should ask functional managers to validate the need for all such connections on a quarterly basis. When notified by the Network System Manager that the need for connection to a particular network is no longer valid, all accounts and parameters related to the connection should be deleted within one working day.

VIRTUAL PRIVATE NETWORKS (VPN)

Virtual Private Networks allow a trusted network to communicate with another trusted network, over untrusted networks such as the Internet. Since some firewalls provide VPN capability, it is necessary to define policy for establishing VPNs [3]. Firewall-based VPNs can be established in a number of different configurations.

> **Tip:** Any connection between firewalls over public networks should use encrypted Virtual Private Networks to ensure the privacy and integrity of the data passing over the public network. All VPN connections should be approved and managed by a Network Services Manager. Appropriate means for distributing and maintaining encryption keys must be established prior to operational use of VPNs.

FIREWALL ADMINISTRATION

A firewall, like any other network device, has to be managed by someone. Security policy should state who is responsible for managing the firewall [3].

> **Tip:** Two firewall administrators (one primary and secondary) should be designated by a Chief Information Security Officer (or other manager), and should be responsible for the upkeep of the firewall. The primary administrator should make changes to the firewall; and, the secondary should only do so in the absence of the former, so that there is no simultaneous or contradictory access to the firewall.

> **Tip:** Each firewall administrator should provide their home phone number, pager number, cellular phone number and other numbers or codes in which they can be contacted when support is required.

Qualification Of The Firewall Administrator

Two experienced people are generally recommended for the day to day administration of the firewall. In this manner availability of the firewall administrative function is largely insured. It should be required that information about each firewall administrator be written down so that he may contacting is possible in the event of a problem [3].

Security of a site is crucial to the day to day business activity of an organization. It is therefore required that the administrator of the firewall have a sound understanding of network concepts and implementation. For instance, since most firewalls are TCP/IP based, a thorough understanding of this protocol is compulsory [3].

An individual that is assigned the task of firewall administration must have a good hands-on experience with networking concepts, design, and implementation so that the firewall is configured correctly and administered properly. Firewall administrators should receive periodic training on the firewalls in use and in network security principals and practices [3].

Remote Firewall Administration

Firewalls are the first line of defense visible to an attacker. By design, firewalls are generally difficult to attack directly, causing attackers to often target the administrative accounts on a firewall. The username/password of administrative accounts must be strongly protected [3].

The most secure method of protecting against this form of attack is to have strong physical security around the firewall host and to only allow firewall administration from an attached terminal. However, operational concerns often dictate that some form of remote access for firewall administration be supported. In no case should remote access to the firewall be supported over untrusted networks without some form of strong authentication. In addition, to prevent eavesdropping, session encryption should be used for remote firewall connections [3].

Low

Any remote access over untrusted networks to the firewall for administration should use strong authentication. This would consist of one time passwords and/or hardware tokens [3].

Medium

The preferred method for firewall administration is directly from the attached terminal. Physical access to the firewall terminal is limited to the firewall administrator and backup administrator [3].

> **Tip:** Where remote access for firewall administration must be allowed, it should be limited to access from other hosts on the organization internal network. Such internal remote access requires the use of strong authentication, such as one time passwords and/or hardware tokens. Remote access over untrusted networks such as the Internet requires end to end encryption and strong authentication to be employed.

High

All firewall administration must be performed from the local terminal. No access to the firewall operating software should be permitted via remote access. Physical access to the firewall terminal should be limited to the firewall administrator and backup administrator [3].

User Accounts

Firewalls should never be used as general purpose servers. The only user accounts on the firewall should be those of the firewall administrator and any backup administrators. In addition, only these administrators should have privileges for updating system executables or other system software [3].

> **Tip:** Only the firewall administrator and backup administrators should be given user accounts on the ORGANIZATION firewall. Any modification of the firewall system software must be done by the firewall administrator or backup administrator and requires approval of the Network Services Manager

Firewall Backup

To support recovery after failure or natural disaster, a firewall like any other network host has to have some policy defining system backup. Data files as well as system configuration files need to be have some backup plan in case of firewall failure [3].

> **Tip:** The firewall (system software, configuration data, database files, etc.) should be backed up daily, weekly, and monthly so that in case of system failure, data and configuration files can be recovered. Backup files should be stored securely on a read-only media so that data in storage is not over-written inadvertently and locked up so that the media is only accessible to the appropriate personnel.

Another backup alternative would be to have another firewall configured as one already deployed. This firewall would be kept safely, so that in case there is a failure of the current one, this backup firewall would simply be turned on and used as the firewall while the previous one is undergoing a repair [3].

> **Tip:** At least one firewall should be configured and reserved (not-in-use) so that in case of a firewall failure, this backup firewall can be switched in to protect the network.

System Integrity

To prevent unauthorized modifications of the firewall configuration, some form of integrity assurance process should be used. Typically, checksums, cyclic redundancy checks, or cryptographic hashes are made from the runtime image and saved on protected media. Each time the firewall configuration has been modified by an authorized individual (usually the firewall administrator), it is necessary that the system integrity online database be updated and saved onto a file system on the network or removable media. If the system integrity check shows that the firewall configuration files have been modified, it should be known that the system has been compromised [3].

> **Tip:** The firewall's system integrity database should be updated each time the firewall configuration is modified. System integrity files must be stored on read only media or off-line storage. System integrity should be checked on a regular basis on the firewall in order for the administrator to generate a listing of all files that may have been modified, replaced, or deleted.

Documentation

It is important that the operational procedures for a firewall and its configurable parameters be well documented, updated, and kept in a safe and secure place. This assures that if a firewall administrator resigns or is otherwise unavailable, an experienced individual can read the documentation and rapidly pick up the administration of the firewall. In the event of a break-in, such documentation also supports trying to recreate the events that caused the security incident [3].

Physical Firewall Security

Physical access to the firewall must be tightly controlled to preclude any authorized changes to the firewall configuration or operational status, and to eliminate any potential for monitoring firewall activity. In addition, precautions should be taken to assure that proper environment alarms and backup systems are available to assure the firewall remains online [3].

> **Tip:** The organization firewall should be located in an controlled environment, with access limited to a Network Services Manager, the firewall administrator, and the backup firewall administrator.

> **Tip:** The room in which the firewall is to be physically located must be equipped with heat, air-conditioner, and smoke alarms to assure the proper working order of the room. The placement and recharge status of the fire extinguishers should be checked on a regular basis. If uninterruptible power service is available to any Internet-connected systems, such service should be provided to the firewall as well.

Firewall Incident Handling

Incident reporting is the process whereby certain anomalies are reported or logged on the firewall. A policy is required to determine what type of report to log and what to do with the generated log report. This should be consistent with incident handling policies discussed earlier in the chapter. The following policies are appropriate to all risk environments:

- The firewall should be configured to log all reports on daily, weekly, and monthly bases so that the network activity can be analyzed when needed.
- Firewall logs should be examined on a weekly basis to determine if attacks have been detected.
- The firewall administrator should be notified at anytime of any security alarm by email, pager, or other means so that he or she may immediately respond to such alarm.
- The firewall should reject any kind of probing or scanning tool that is directed to it so that information being protected is not leaked out by the firewall. In a similar fashion, the firewall should block all software types that are known to present security threats to a network (such as Active X, Java, etc. ...) to better tighten the security of the network [1].

Restoration Of Services

Once an incident has been detected, the firewall may need to be brought down and reconfigured. If it is necessary to bring down the firewall, Internet service should be disabled or a secondary firewall should be made operational – internal systems should not be connected to the Internet without a firewall. After being reconfigured, the firewall must be brought back into an operational and reliable state. Policies for restoring the firewall to a working state when a break-in occurs are needed [3].

> **Tip:** In case of a firewall break-in, the firewall administrator(s) are responsible for reconfiguring the firewall to address any vulnerabilities that were exploited. The firewall should be restored to the state it was before the break-in, so that the network is not left wide open. While the restoration is going on, the backup firewall should be deployed.

Upgrading The Firewall

It is often necessary that the firewall software and hardware components be upgraded with the necessary modules to assure optimal firewall performance. The firewall administrator should be aware of any hardware and software bugs, as well as firewall software upgrades that may be issued by the vendor. If an upgrade of any sort is necessary, certain precautions must be taken to continue to maintain a high level of operational security. Sample policies that should be written for upgrades may include:

- To optimize the performance of the firewall, all vendor recommendations for processor and memory capacities should be followed.
- The firewall administrator must evaluate each new release of the firewall software to determine if an upgrade is required. All security patches recommended by the firewall vendor should be implemented in a timely manner.
- Hardware and software components should be obtained from a list of vendor-recommended sources. Any firewall specific upgrades should also be obtained from the vendor. In addition, NFS should not be used as a means of obtaining hardware and software components. The use of virus checked CDROM or FTP to a vendor's site is an appropriate method.
- The firewall administrator(s) should monitor the vendor's firewall mailing list or maintain some other form of contact with the vendor to be aware of all required upgrades. Before an upgrade of any of the firewall component, the firewall administrator must verify with the vendor that an upgrade is required. After any upgrade, the firewall should be tested to verify proper operation prior to going operational [1].

Logs And Audit Trails: Audit/Event Reporting And Summaries

Most firewalls provide a wide range of capabilities for logging traffic and network events. Some security-relevant event that should be recorded on the firewall's audit trail logs are: hardware and disk media errors; login/logout activity; connect time; use of system administrator privileges; inbound and outbound e-mail traffic; TCP network connect attempts; and, in-bound and out-bound proxy traffic type [3].

Revision/Update Of Firewall Policy

Given the rapid introduction of new technologies, and the tendency for organizations to continually introduce new services, firewall security policies should be reviewed on a regular basis (see sidebar, "Example Of General Policies"). As network requirements change, so should security policy.

Example Of General Policies

The following policy statements are only examples. They do not constitute a complete firewall policy, and even if they did, they would not necessarily apply to your organization's environment. The statements are grouped into those applicable to Low-, Medium- and High-Risk environments. Within each category, they are divided into statements targeted toward users, managers and technicians. In general, all organizations would employ at least the Low-Risk policies.

Low-Risk Environment Policies: User

- All users who require access to Internet services must do so by using organization-approved software and Internet gateways.
- A firewall has been placed between your private networks and the Internet to protect your systems. Employees must not circumvent the firewall by using modems or network tunneling software to connect to the Internet.
- Some protocols have been blocked or redirected. If you have a business need for a particular protocol, you must raise the issue with your manager and the Internet security officer.

Low-Risk Environment Policies: Manager

- A firewall should be placed between the organization's network and the Internet to prevent untrusted networks from accessing the organization network. The firewall should be selected by and maintained by a Network Services Manager.
- All other forms of Internet access (such as via dial-out modems) from sites connected to the organization wide-area network are prohibited.
- All users who require access to Internet services must do so by using organization-approved software and Internet gateways.

Low-Risk Environment Policies: Technician

- All firewalls should fail to a configuration that denies all services, and require a firewall administrator to re-enable services after a failure.
- Source routing should be disabled on all firewalls and external routers (discussed earlier in the chapter).
- The firewall should not accept traffic on its external interfaces that appear to be coming from internal network addresses (discussed earlier in the chapter).
- The firewall should provide detailed audit logs of all sessions so that these logs can be reviewed for any anomalies.

- Secure media should be used to store log reports such that access to this media is restricted to only authorized personnel.
- Firewalls should be tested off-line and the proper configuration verified.
- The firewall should be configured to implement transparency for all outbound services. Unless approved by a Network Services manager, all in-bound services should be intercepted and processed by the firewall.
- Appropriate firewall documentation should be maintained on off-line storage at all times. Such information should include but not be limited to the network diagram, including all IP addresses of all network devices, the IP addresses of relevant hosts of the Internet Service Provider (ISP) such as external news server, router, DNS server, etc., and all other configuration parameters such as packet filter rules, etc. Such documentation should be updated any time the firewall configuration is changed.

Medium-Risk Environment Policies: User

When you are off-site, you may only access internal systems by using organization-approved one-time passwords and hardware tokens to authenticate yourself to the firewall. Any other means of accessing internal systems is prohibited.

Medium-Risk Environment Policies: Manager

- Strong authentication using organization-approved one-time passwords and hardware tokens is required for all remote access to internal systems through the firewall.
- The network security policy should be reviewed on a regular basis (every three months minimum) by the firewall administrator(s) and other top information (security) managers. Where requirements for network connections and services have changed, the security policy should be updated and approved. If a change is to be made, the firewall administrator should ensure that the change is implemented and the policy modified.
- The details of the organization internal trusted network should not be visible from outside the firewall.

Medium-Risk Environment Policies: Technician

- The firewall should be configured to deny all services not expressly permitted and should be regularly audited and monitored to detect intrusions or misuse.
- The firewall should notify the system administrator in near-real-time of any item that may need immediate attention such as a break-in into the network, little disk space available, or other related messages so that an immediate action could be taken.

- The firewall software should run on a dedicated computer - all non-firewall related software, such as compilers, editors, communications software, etc., should be deleted or disabled.
- The firewall should be configured to deny all services not expressly permitted and should be regularly audited and monitored to detect intrusions or misuse.

High-Risk Environment Policies: User

- All non-business use of the Internet from organization systems should be forbidden. All access to Internet services should be logged. Employees who violate this policy should be subject to disciplinary action.
- Your browser has been configured with a list of forbidden sites. Any attempts to access those sites should be reported to your manager.

High-Risk Environment Policies: Manager

All non-business use of the Internet from organization systems is forbidden. All access to Internet services should be logged. Employees who violate this policy should be subject to disciplinary action.

High-Risk Environment Policies: Technician

All access to Internet services should be logged. Summary and exception reports should be prepared for the network and security managers [1].

Example Service-Specific Policies

Connecting to the Internet makes a wide range of services available to internal users and a wide range of system accesses available to external users. Driven by the needs of the business or mission side of the organization, policy has to be clearly written to state what services to allow or disallow to both inside and outside networks [3].

There is a wide range of Internet services available. The most popular services, such as FTP, telnet, HTTP, etc. were discussed earlier in the chapter. Other common services are detailed here:

- Berkeley Software Distribution (BSD) UNIX "r" commands, such as rsh, rlogin, rcp, etc., are designed to allow UNIX system users to execute commands on remote systems. Most implementation do not support authentication or encryption and are very dangerous to use over the Internet.
- Post Office Protocol (POP) is a client-server protocol for retrieving electronic mail from a server. POP is a TCP-based service that supports the use of nonreusable passwords for authentication, known as APOP. POP does not support encryption – retrieved email is vulnerable to eavesdropping.

- Network News Transfer Protocol (NNTP) is used to support Usenet newsgroups. NNTP is a TCP-based service that implements a store and forward protocol. While NNTP is a relatively simple protocol, there have been recent attacks against common NNTP server software. NNTP servers should not be run on the firewall, but standard proxy services are available to pass NNTP.
- Finger and whois are similar functions. Finger is used to retrieve information about system users. Finger often gives out more information than is necessary – for most organizations, finger should be disabled or limited at the firewall. Whois is very similar and should also be disabled or limited at the firewall.
- The UNIX remote printing protocols lp and lpr allow remote hosts to print using printers attached to other hosts. Lpr is a store and forward protocol, while lp uses the rsh function to provide remote printing capabilities. In general, lp and lpr should be disabled at the firewall unless vendor supplied proxies are available.
- Network File System (NFS) allows disk drives to be made accessible to users and systems across the network. NFS uses a very weak form of authentication and is not considered safe to use across untrusted networks. NFS should not be allowed through a firewall.
- Real Audio provides for the delivery of digitized audio over TCP/IP networks – to take advantage of the multimedia capabilities of the World Wide Web, a number of new services have been developed [1].

Which Internet services to allow or deny must be driven by the needs of the organization. A sample security policy for some of these Internet services that might be required by a typical organization is illustrated in Table 32-2 [3]. Table 32-3 show the managerial-level concerns [3].

Table 32-2. Service Specific Policies.

Service	Policy				Sample Policy
	Inside to Outside		Outside to Inside		
	Status	Auth	Status	Auth	
FTP	y	n	y	y	FTP access should be allowed from the internal network to the external. Strong authentication should be required for FTP access from the outside to the inside.
Telnet	y	n	y	y	Telnet access should be allowed from the inside network to the outside network. For the telnet from the outside to the inside network, authentication should be required.
Rlogin	y	n	y	y	rlogin to ORGANIZATION hosts from external networks requires written approval from the Network Services Manager and the use of strong authentication.

HTTP	y	n	n	n	All WWW servers intended for access by external users should be hosted outside the ORGANIZATION firewall. No inbound HTTP should be allowed through the ORGANIZATION firewall.
SSL	y	n	y	y	Secure Sockets Layer sessions using client side certificates is required when SSL sessions are to be passed through the ORGANIZATION firewall.
POP3	n	n	y	n	The ORGANIZATION Post Office Protocol server is to be hosted inside the ORGANIZATION firewall. The firewall should pass POP traffic only to the POP server. The use of APOP is required.
NNTP	y	n	n	n	No external access should be allowed to the NNTP server.
Real Audio	n	n	n	n	There is currently no business requirement for supporting streaming audio sessions through the ORGANIZATION firewall. Any business units requiring such support should contact the Network Services Manager.
Lp	y	n	n	n	Inbound lp services are to be disabled at the ORGANIZATION firewall.
finger	y	n	n	n	Inbound finger services are to be disabled at the ORGANIZATION firewall.
gopher	y	n	n	n	Inbound gopher services are to be disabled at the ORGANIZATION firewall.
whois	y	n	n	n	Inbound whois services are to be disabled at the ORGANIZATION firewall.
SQL	y	n	n	n	Connections from external hosts to internal databases must be approved by the Network Services Manager and used approved SQL proxy services.
Rsh	y	n	n	n	Inbound rsh services are to be disabled at the ORGANIZATION firewall.
Other, such as NFS	n	n	n	n	Access to any other service not mentioned above should be denied in both direction so that only Internet services we have the need for and we know about are allowed and all others are denied.

Status (Y=Yes/N=No) = whether users can use the service

Auth (Y/N) = whether any form of authentication (strong or otherwise) is performed before the service can be used.

Table 32-3. Managerial Concerns.

Purpose	Protocols	What	Why
Email		Users have a single external email address.	Does not reveal business info.
[-12pt]	SMTP	A single server or cluster of servers provides email service for organization.	Centralized email is easier to maintain. SMTP servers are difficult to configure securely.
	POP3	POP users must use AUTH identification.	Prevents password sniffing.
	IMAP	Groups are encouraged to transition to IMAP.	Better support for travel, encryption.
USENET news	NTTP	blocked at firewall	no business need
WWW [-4pt]	HTTP	directed to www.my.org	Centralized WWW is easier to maintain. WWW servers are difficult to configure securely.
*	all others	routed	

SUMMARY AND CONCLUSIONS

An organization may wish to support some services without using strong authentication. For example, an anonymous FTP server may be used to allow all external users to download open information. In this case, such services should be hosted outside the firewall or on a service network not connected to corporate networks that contain sensitive data. Table 32-4 summarizes a method of describing such policy for a service such as FTP [3].

Table 32-4. Summarized Security Policy.

Policy	Non Anonymous FTP service	Anonymous FTP service
Put server machine outside the firewall	N	Y
Put server machine on the service network	N	Y
Put server machine on protected network	Y	N
Put server machine on the firewall itself	N	N
Server should be accessed by everyone on the Internet	N	Y

REFERENCES

[1] Barbara Guttman and Robert Bagwill, "Implementing Internet Firewall Security Policy," Computer Security Division, Information Technology Laboratory, National Institute of Standards and Technology, U.S. Department of Commerce, Gaithersburg, MD 20899-8930, April 13, 2001.

[2] John P. Wack and Lisa J Carnahan, "Keeping Your Site Comfortably Secure: An Introduction to Internet Firewalls," NIST Special Publications 800-10, National Institute of Standards and Technology, U.S. Department of Commerce, Gaithersburg, MD 20899-8930, April 2, 2000.

[3] John R. Vacca and Scott R. Ellis, Firewalls: Jumpstart for Network and Systems Administrators, Digital Press, 2005.

PART XIV

SECURITY MANAGEMENT SOLUTIONS AND FUTURE DIRECTIONS

Chapter 33

IDENTIFYING AND RESPONDING TO SECURITY VIOLATIONS

INTRODUCTION

It is imperative for Internet and security administrators to know exactly what is going on in their network. With a complete, real-time picture of the network, administrators can proactively protect their resources and quickly resolve any security incidents to strengthen their network security posture. Without proper visibility, administrators can be blindsided by attacks that they didn't even know they were vulnerable to and waste valuable resources researching, containing and responding to successful exploits [1].

Just obtaining a complete, on-demand picture of what is on the network, however, represents a significant challenge for most organizations:

- How does an administrator learn what servers, applications and devices have been added to the network?
- How do they find out about someone from finance suddenly accessing the R&D servers?
- How do they know when an employee downloads a new application from the Internet?
- How do they keep track of which software versions are loaded on each system?
- The answer to most of these questions is they often don't, until it is too late [1].

Generally this is because the person responsible for security may not be the same person who is responsible for the network, which may be separate from the IT administrator. Without tight integration and rigorous checks, it is highly probable that a new user, application, server or protocol will be introduced to the network without the security administrator knowing. Anything on the network that a security administrator doesn't know about represents a vulnerability [1].

Anything on the network, particularly changes to resources or activity, needs to be considered in the context of what it does to the organizations' overall Internet security posture. For example, someone connecting to a server that they have never connected to before may indicate a policy violation; a new application, such as P2P file sharing or Instant

Messaging, may open up holes that an attacker can use to get into the network; and desktops may be a risk until they receive the latest patch for a software version they are running. The security administrator needs to keep track of everything that is actively participating in or being used on the network to identify potential violations of the organization's policies or compromises in the organization's overall security stance [1].

To get this information, a security administrator has traditionally had to correlate disparate data derived from multiple sources and solutions. This often includes the manual aggregation and analysis of information from routers, firewalls, IDSes, IPSes and vulnerability scanners, which is a daunting, time consuming exercise that is virtually impossible to keep current. As a result, Internet security administrators regularly operate in a mode of catch up or spend their time researching and trying to resolve the most pressing Internet security incidents [1].

To give administrators the insight they need to understand what is going on in their network, they need an Internet security tool that passively monitors network activity and stores the data in a network profile. This profile can be used to provide administrators a comprehensive, on-demand view of network activity, for example what hosts, servers, applications and operating systems are currently on the network. This chapter very briefly describes this Internet security tool technology (as part of Internet security management solutions and future directions); and demonstrates how it can help administrators identify potential problems and make well-informed security decisions that strengthen the Internet's security posture [1].

THE PROFILER

An Internet security tool that passively monitors network activity and stores the data in a network profile should be designed to provide administrators the tools they need to identify changes to the network to ensure appropriate security policies are in place to enable the swift resolution of anomalies and exploits. This Internet security tool (IST) should also be an on-demand, searchable database that an administrator can use to quickly see the level of detail they need to understand what is going on in the network [1].

The database should also be integrated right into the log viewer to help administrators investigate and resolve security incidents. The database should also be available through the "profiler view," which an administrator can use to explore their network to help them predict where problems may arise, so they can make proactive security decisions [1].

There should also be at least three different views in the profiler to help administrators zero in on the information they need; as well as, a security violation view for pseudo firewall policies that help pinpoint what an administrator may not know about the network [1]. The IST should also passively monitor network activity and store the data in a network profile. Knowing where to look for important, relevant data that make up an interaction, IST should be provided with a record of all key network activity. The IST then stores this information, which includes any unique attempts, probes and successful connections, including the start, relevant service field information and end of the connection, in its searchable database. An administrator can then access this data as they perform investigative analysis to help identify potential problems in the network and resolve Internet security incidents [1].

HOW IST SHOULD WORK

The IST should be able to reassemble the packets on the network into the application message and remove any ambiguities to understand its intent. The IST then should perform a protocol analysis (for protocol anomaly detection) and classify portions of the traffic into their relevant service fields (for Stateful Signature attack pattern matching) [1].

Service fields relate to the functionality, or purpose, of that part of the communication. Service field examples for e-mail (SMTP) are TO: FROM: Attachment: Command line: line type, etc. The IST should be able to send a copy of the relevant service field information, as defined by the administrator, to be stored in the database. The administrator simply configures the IST to capture the service field information that he or she are interested in, for example, with e-mail, they can determine if they want to keep a record of usernames, attachment names, commands, etc. As a result, administrators can use the IST to quickly identify who is talking to whom and what they are doing during the conversation [1].

HOW IST CAN HELP

Administrators can use the IST to get the details they need to quickly assess what is going on and determine what is a true threat to their network security posture. They can find information, such as:

- What Windows users have logged in from a specific IP?
- What IPs has a specific user logged in from? (Based on Windows User ID, AIM Nick
- Name, MSN Nick Name, IRC Nick Name, etc.)
- What versions of SSH (clients & servers) have operated in the environment?
- What version of Microsoft Internet Explorer or IIS is being used on the network [1]?

In addition to identifying when hosts, servers and applications are active, it can also identify when they are idle on the network. For each entry in the database, the IST should be able to record the first and last seen time-stamps. By querying the IST for the last-seen time-stamp that is greater than a "xxx" number of days, administrators can quickly identify idle entries. An administrator can also use the IST's time-based filter and simply pick which data sync they want to use when comparing current data. In this way, administrators can quickly see changes, both activity and inactivity, and identify anything that may be suspicious and warrant further investigation. Ultimately, the information that an administrator gathers from the IST can be used to:

- Stay current on the hosts, servers and applications that are active on the network
- Identify software versions to facilitate effective security patching
- Quickly resolve security incidents through detailed investigations

- Quickly recognize the source of worms for containment
- Aid in validating and enforcing an organization's security policies [1]

IST REMOVING THE UNKNOWN: STAYING CURRENT ON HOSTS, SERVERS AND APPLICATIONS ON THE NETWORK

Anything on the network that the security administrator does not know about represents a possible vulnerability. Unknown servers, devices and applications deployed across the network can be holes in an organization's security posture, representing that which may be unprotected and not even considered in relation to how it potentially affects the network [1].

Many organizations have standards in terms of the technology they allow on the network (software versions, types of operating systems, etc.), and they scan for vulnerabilities and apply patches based on those standards. If a user introduces software or a server that the organization does not know about or that does not adhere to the company's standards, the appropriate measures needed to secure that system will not be taken, opening up a hole in the network that attackers can exploit [1].

QUICKLY RESOLVE SECURITY INCIDENTS THROUGH DETAILED INVESTIGATIONS

Understanding current Internet activity and then generating the level of detail necessary to make an informed security decision is often a challenge for administrators. Often, when an attack occurs, organizations don't have enough information to be able to efficiently resolve the incident. This is generally because the information available to an administrator is minimal, usually consisting of only one or two pieces of information [1].

Without enough data to make an immediate decision, the burden is on the administrator to investigate what they know and then extrapolate the relationship between the data and the security event and the relevance or impact on the Internet security posture. Ideally, administrators would be able to generate a high level view of attack activity and then quickly link data points to get additional specifics of what is going on in the network to effectively close out security events [1].

QUICKLY RECOGNIZE THE SOURCE OF WORMS FOR CONTAINMENT

Worms can wreak havoc on a network, which was painfully obvious for many organizations that were affected by any one of 2003's worms – Slammer, SoBig, Blaster, Nachi, etc. The biggest problem with worms is that they are often introduced to the network through ways that bypass traditional security measures and, once inside, they may steal data, bring down network resources or more generally burden business productivity. Administrators then spend countless hours, sometimes days, trying to figure out how the worm was introduced and which machines are infected.

The recent proliferation of worms demonstrated that many organizations did not have the visibility into the network they needed. Many were unable to effectively identify vulnerabilities to ensure their resources were adequately protected; the SQL Slammer worm hit some organizations whose policy it was to not "allow" SQL servers in their network. The primary reason it hit them so hard was because SQL applications were unknowingly installed as part of a Microsoft update. Because the applications were installed unknowingly, when SQL Slammer infected the network, organizations had trouble quickly identifying the source and effectively containing the attack to minimize impact. Many organizations wasted valuable resources investigating how the worms were introduced to the network, containing and then recovering from them [1].

Finally, another example is the Blaster worm, which exploited a vulnerability in Microsoft RPC, which is the foundation for Microsoft's networking that allows desktops to share files over a remote network. While corporate firewalls usually block filesharing traffic for control reasons (to protect sensitive corporate files from Internet users) on a local network, filesharing is a desirable feature and is usually enabled on desktops and allowed by personal firewalls. So it is quite easy to see, for example, how a user accessing the Internet through a café's wireless network could contract the Blaster worm from an infected user on that network. Because worms propagate by automatically scanning the network looking for other vulnerable systems to infect, that user's laptop would contract the Blaster worm because it is designed to allow RPC. That same user, when they return to the office and connect the laptop to the corporate network would introduce the worm and infect all of the other machines on the network that have RPC enabled. This is why Blaster was able to quickly propagate throughout the Internet and overwhelm many corporate networks [1].

SUMMARY AND CONCLUSIONS

An administrator must have a good understanding about the current network activity to be able to create and maintain a strong, effective Internet security posture. This poses a problem since the network is in a constant state of flux and the administrator may not even be privy to all of the changes that are taking place [1].

An IST should be able to continuously learn about the network and store that information in a searchable database, so administrators can proactively find the information they need to understand exactly what is going on in the network and make incremental adjustments to the security policies. Administrators can achieve a holistic view of the servers, clients, users and applications on the network seen by the IST to ensure appropriate security measures can be put in place. They can keep track of the changes that occur on the network to minimize the chance that something is introduced without the security team's knowledge [1].

With the IST, administrators should be able to identify areas that are vulnerable and be proactive about protecting critical resources. They can also quickly drill into detailed information for incident investigation and swift resolution of security events, including recognizing and protecting against worms on the network. The IST should also be able to provide an on-demand view of network activity to:

- Stay current on the hosts, servers and applications on the network to minimize exposure to Internet security vulnerabilities
- Identify software versions to facilitate effective security patching
- Conduct detailed investigations to quickly resolve security incidents
- Quickly recognize the source of worms for containment
- Aid in validating and enforcing an organization's security policies [1]

Now, with IST, administrators should have insight into the network, at different levels, so they can identify where they are vulnerable and predict what could potentially lead to a problem or attack, so that they can respond quickly. Now, administrators don't have to wait until they have a problem; with an IST, they should be able to have the information they need to be proactive and try to stop problems before they even start [1].

REFERENCES

[1] Sarah Sorensen, "Juniper's Enterprise Security Profiler (ESP)," Copyright © 2004, Juniper Networks, Inc., Juniper Networks, Inc., 1194 North Mathilda Avenue, Sunnyvale, CA 94089 USA, 2004.

Chapter 34

REAL-TIME MONITORING AND AUDITING

INTRODUCTION

The database community has begun to realize its role in a robust information security infrastructure. Traditionally there has been little concern for the security of relational database systems, and for the vast amounts of data they house. In the early days of relational databases, gaining access to a database was so difficult that the need for complex security features was irrelevant. Databases were housed in mainframes not accessible directly from the network. Slowly they were ported to other networked systems such as UNIX, Linux, and Windows, but even when this happened, the databases were kept far behind the firewall out of the reach of the typical Black Hat surfing the Internet [1].

As digital information has become more and more critical to how businesses and customers interact, firewalls, which once served as the walls of the fortress, have now become an archaic means of defense providing little real-world protection. Even the smallest of organizations have numerous entry points into their networks – wireless access, remote employees connecting through VPN, customers connecting through web applications, etc. As well, employees take home laptops, hook up to a home cable modem connection, get infected with a Trojan, and then return to work. This becomes a virtual "store and forward" attack that effectively gives the Black Hat a backdoor into an organization's internal network [1].

As the threats have changed, the responses must change as well. Rather than focusing protection solely on perimeter security, it is imperative you start looking at protecting data at the source – inside the database. The goal is to provide protection where it is most effective and cannot be circumvented. The database has come to be the de facto standard for housing an organization's most valuable information. The logical extension of these facts is that the database is where your strongest security needs to be in place [1].

Given the flurry of new information security related legislature that has arisen, there is a strong call to take extra steps to provide strong security at the database level. The need to protect sensitive information no longer needs to be driven by corporate strategy, federal laws are forcing organizations to put the proper defenses in place, with consequences for those who do not comply. Information security is focused on preserving the confidentiality, integrity, and availability (CIA) of the information system. Without maintaining these basics tenets, a database does not measure up to the requirements of handling commercial data [1].

Without real-time auditing and monitoring of data, CIA is impossible to maintain. While there have been many discussions on the need to provide some level of auditing and monitoring, there is little information to help organizations define what the appropriate auditing and monitoring strategy is for them. This chapter very briefly focuses on "theoretical best-practices" combined with "real-world practicality" to define a usable policy for the real-time auditing and monitoring of databases. By following the policies outlined in this chapter, you can properly implement a database system that will work well, and provide adequate security for the data it houses [1].

THE IDEAL MONITORING SOLUTION

Monitoring can be a complex task. Collecting data is the simple part of the job. An ideal solution needs to handle the tricky aspects of the job, as well as the simple ones. Some of the more difficult issues that need to be addressed by a monitoring solution include:

1. Deciding what to monitor for
2. Handling the volume of data that needs to be monitored
3. Detecting when something malicious has occurred
4. Ensuring the integrity of the audit data [1]

WATCHING THE DATABASE ADMINISTRATOR

Modern database technology is designed to be managed by database administrators, who are the unrestricted owners of the database. This architecture leaves an organization's most critical information entirely exposed to and controlled by a small handful of technologists, the Database Administrators or DBAs. This leaves both the DBA and the entire organization in a precarious position. The DBA is afraid that she or he will be blamed for any information leak, while the organization is forced to almost blindly trust a small number of people in the technology group [1].

One way to mitigate this risk is by properly auditing and monitoring the activities of the DBA. The amount of work that a DBA does on a production server is very limited. Auditing and monitoring this activity does not add significant overhead to the system [1].

How do you properly audit activity in a database? Native auditing fails here because it is fully under the control of the DBA. He or she can easily turn off auditing, clear the audit logs, manipulate an audit record, or even reconfigure auditing to filter out their own malicious activity. Auditing should ultimately provide a separation of duties. An ideal audit system would be intelligent enough to distinguish database administrative accounts, filter out noise and irrelevant events, and succinctly illustrate their activities. Auditing data should be written to a secure location, where even an administrator of the database would not have direct control over the recorded activity [1].

WATCHING TEMPORARY ACCOUNTS

Another type of activity that requires monitoring is the use of temporary and special accounts. Many companies have procedures through which the database administrator can request a temporary account for others or for themselves to manage databases if required. For instance, the DBA will request the operations team to create a temporary account for which to logon and manage the database when the database goes down or when backups need to be recovered. This account will be set to expire in several hours after which the account will be deleted [1].

This is a reasonable system for reducing exposure to a malicious database administrator. However, a window of exposure remains, in that it is difficult to track exactly what that administrator does while using the temporary account. An ideal monitoring and auditing system can provide real value in this situation. A system that can track the activity of the DBA's temporary account can be used to ensure that nothing malicious has occurred [1].

AUDITING ACCESS TO SENSITIVE DATA

An auditing system also needs to be able to monitor access to sensitive data in a subset of tables. A typical database contains massive amounts of data, some of which is not sensitive at all. Other pieces of data however could lead to disaster, if they fell into the wrong hands. Auditing all database activity is impractical, and can lead to information overload. For instance, suppose you have a lookup table to map products to product IDs. This table will likely be accessed regularly, possibly thousands of times each day. Tracking access to that lookup table won't catch any malicious activity; in fact the amount of noise this tracking would generate may very well bury a real attack in a sea of essentially meaningless data. While some tables are not sensitive, others probably are. Those that contain credit card numbers, payroll information, or social security numbers should be monitored, and the audit trail should be regularly reviewed [1].

In order to facilitate this type of auditing, database administrators or applications owner must decide what data is sensitive and define that in the auditing system. The auditing system should be able to accept and configure the list of databases, tables, objects, and columns that can be monitored, as well as being able to configure which actions on various objects to monitor. For instance, if you have static data that is public information, you will likely have no need to audit who selects from the table. At the same time, you may have a strong need to record who modifies the data. In that case you need the ability to audit any UPDATE, DELETE, or INSERT to the TABLE from any user [1].

THE FLEXIBILITY TO FILTER RESULTS

It is important to have the ability to filter out how data is audited based on who is accessing the data. For instance, there is a requirement within the HIPAA regulations stating that access to patient records be strongly accounted for. If an administrator in the system accessed patient Jane Smith's medical records on June 15th, there should be a record of the action to provide accountability for that data. On the other hand if the patient's doctor accesses the data twenty times in a day, there's little value in recording that activity multiple times. Auditing needs to be able to record unauthorized users attempting to access data, yet also needs to be flexible enough to keep the level of noise to a minimum. This can be accomplished by minimizing the recording of activity performed by authorized personnel. An ideal auditing solution should have the capability to perform granular filtering based on factors such as account name, source of activity, and the time of the activity [1].

ATTEMPTS TO CIRCUMVENT AN APPLICATION

Another common issue that needs to be monitored is users circumventing an application, and connecting directly to the database. This can be a problem if you are using two-tiered architectures, such as a Visual Basic executable connected directly to a database, or if you are using a three-tiered architecture, such as a web application connected to the backend database via an application server. Either way, there is a need to monitor for people using utilities such as Microsoft Access, Microsoft Excel, or even Query Analyzer to connect directly to the database. Someone doing this may simply be trying to make their job easier but are in effect opening up a security hole in the database. On many occasions, users have been discovered to have placed a linked Microsoft Excel spreadsheet on an open file share to allow other users to see the results of their work in the database. Unfortunately this linked spreadsheet can be manipulated to pull back information from the database other than the data for which it was intended [1].

Finally, there are two ways to audit for this problem. One way is to watch specifically for people using tools such as Microsoft Office to access the database. To do this effectively, you need to be able to list the most common applications that a curious, or well meaning user might employ. Another strategy is to audit any connections that do not come from the expected application. For instance, let's consider a database where users connect via an application called HRPayrollApp. An ideal auditing solution should be configurable to alert you when someone connects to the database using any application other than HRPayrollApp [1].

SUMMARY AND CONCLUSIONS

Monitoring of databases within an organization has become a critical component of a proper layered security approach, however to be useful, the monitoring must be done using the right combination of tools and best practices. Monitoring is not a replacement for the other layers in the security stack – it is a complementary piece that greatly decreases the likelihood of successful attacks. A major driver for the need to monitor and audit databases is the rise of government and industry regulations on how sensitive data is handled. These regulations include:

- VISA standards for credit card vendors
- Sarbanes-Oxley
- HIPAA (Health Insurance Portability and Accountability Act)
- European Union Data Protection Directive
- California's Database Security Breach Notification Act (California Senate Bill 1386)
- Gramm-Leach-Bliley Act [1]

Finally, there are security elements that go beyond monitoring which must be considered when creating a data security policy. Vulnerability assessment, encryption, and database integrity solutions help to ensure a solid security foundation for storing sensitive data. To provide effective and holistic security, be sure to incorporate defense mechanisms at all the different layers [1].

REFERENCES

[1] Aaron C. Newman, "Security Auditing In Microsoft SQL Server," © Copyright 2006. Application Security, Inc. All Rights Reserved. Application Security, Inc., 575 Eighth Avenue, Suite 1220, New York, NY 10018, 2006.

Chapter 35

LIMITING DAMAGE

INTRODUCTION

Why are current Internet security measures ineffective in detecting unknown malicious network-enabled applications? Each of the existing security measures, firewall, router, Anti-Virus etc., plays a vital role in protecting personal or business information. However, they are not effective against new and unknown network-enabled malicious applications, which are the fastest growing group of malicious applications [1].

Anti-Virus software can detect only known malicious applications, while the most damage is done by new and unknown programs. Even though Anti-Virus software manufacturers claim that it detects both known and unknown malicious programs, experience suggests otherwise [1].

The truth is that in a vast majority of cases Anti-Virus software can detect only known malicious applications, usually after damage has been done to thousands and some times millions of computers. If Anti-Virus software were truly capable of detecting unknown malicious applications using profiling – heuristic analysis, then there would be no need for a database. In fact heuristic analysis (profiling) is not reliable and in general is completely powerless against those unknown malicious applications that do not damage data but steal information or paralyze the network (network-enabled Trojans, worms, spyware etc). The recent worm barrage is a graphic example of Antivirus software's inability to deal with the "new and unknown [1]."

Many malicious applications designed to steal information will never be detected by Anti-Virus software. A worm attack is so massive that the assailing worm will inevitably be detected, sent to the Anti-Virus lab and eventually added to the database [1].

At the same time, today's profit-driven hackers use customized attacks against individuals and businesses. Customization means that a hacker designs a malicious application for a specific attack. As a result, this malicious program could exist in a very small number of copies (some times just in a single copy) and therefore has virtually no chance of being discovered by the user and sent to an Anti-Virus laboratory. Thus an unknown malicious program that shows no symptoms and does not propagate can exist through the life-time of the computer completely undetected stealing information even from the apparently most secured environment [1].

APPLICATION FIREWALLS

An application firewall requires an expert to be effective. But even for an expert without specialized tools (essentially an Anti-Virus laboratory) the decision will still remain an educated guess [1].

Even if an application firewall is able to stop the most sophisticated test, in real life, it has a low chance to prevent a malicious program from operating, because it relies solely on the end-user expertise. As a result, a malicious program is very unlikely be stopped unless it is called "iamreallybadatrojan.exe" and the user is warned in advance to lookout for it [1].

APPLICATION FIREWALLS WITH CENTRALIZED MANAGEMENT CONSOLE

An application firewall with a centralized management console allows an administrator to create a list of pre-approved applications for every computer on the network. As a result, in theory any application that is not approved will not be able to work [1].

However, realistically the centralized console will only lock *.exe files while dynamically linked libraries, representing the majority of executable code will not be controlled. Internet Explorer, for example, will have its *exe file locked, however its components (of which there can be as many as 60), will not be controlled [1].

Even though an option to lock components might be available, continued and constant updates of the operating system and applications make it impractical. An application firewall with a centralized management console creates an extremely restrictive environment for the end-user that can negatively affect productivity. Application firewalls are also not affordable for a vast majority of businesses due to the costs of their administration [1].

Perimeter firewalls or routers do not protect against attacks originating within a local network. The best corporate firewall or the best router will not prevent a malicious program from sending data outside the corporation, because the malicious application can use the same client type Internet connection as legitimate applications, such as Internet Explorer, messengers etc. [1].

TRAFFIC MONITORING INTRUSION DETECTION SYSTEMS

Similarly to perimeter firewalls traffic monitoring, intrusion detection systems are ineffective in detecting malicious applications. Why? Because, they do not know which application sends data, legitimate Internet Explorer or one of its malicious components [1].

THE PROBLEM WILL NOT GO AWAY

With more people around the world coming online every day, the number of attacks, particularly customized attacks, is increasing. In the virtual world a hacker does not need a visa or a ticket to travel. According to industry analysts, it is estimated that there are more than 60 million people worldwide capable of attacking another computer. Thus, exploiting the weaknesses of application control targeted hacker attacks are increasing at an alarming rate, becoming the most costly and devastating type of enterprise Internet security breach [1].

So, in keeping the preceding in mind, is it safe to send files for investigation outside your company? There are only two ways to find out if the file in question is malicious: ask experts to take a look and identify its intended function or risk a security breach [1].

Finally, today's malicious executables can be very sophisticated. Their analysis requires special hardware and software tools and experts with the "know-how" employed by software security companies. Also, the only files sent for investigation are executables that contain no personal or non-personal information. They are always encrypted while in transit [1].

SUMMARY AND CONCLUSIONS

The failure of the heuristic analysis of Anti-Virus software to detect unknown malicious network enabled applications has led to the development of application firewalls with a centralized management console. Unfortunately, an application firewall requires additional human resources to operate, creates a highly restrictive environment reducing productivity and, when set to highest security (components level), it becomes unmanageable [1].

Finally, enterprises need a system that operates only at the highest (components level) security level, but does not limit the user in the choice of applications to run. It also requires no additional human resources to maintain and is able to stop an unknown malicious application before it can inflict damage on a single computer. Thus, the key features of such a system to limit damage should be:

- Real-time protection from known and unknown malicious network-enabled programs and components
- Real-time protection not only from malicious applications, but also from legitimate applications that have dubious intent (spyware, etc.)
- The broadest possible range of protection without limiting the user's choice of applications to run
- No need to ever update the local database
- Deployment in a matter of minutes
- No additional human resources for maintenance
- Seamless integration into any existing security infrastructure
- Windows server and PC protection [1]

REFERENCES

[1] "Dedicated Application Control System: A New Frontier In Internet Security," © Copyright 2004. Internet Security Alliance Inc. All Rights Reserved. Internet Security Alliance Inc., 77 East Long Lake Road, Bloomfield Hills, MI 48302, 2004.

Chapter 36

KEEPING UP TO DATE ON NEW THREATS

INTRODUCTION

According to industry analysts, the Web filtering market continued to grow at a healthy pace in 2005, with 34% year-over-year growth reaching more than $544 million in world-wide software revenue. The demand and interest in Web filtering solutions remains strong, with rising corporate concerns about keeping up with Internet threats that reach beyond productivity, bandwidth, and liability issues and now into Web security. With the Internet becoming an increasingly complex threat vector for hackers, malicious applications, and vulnerability exploits, today's enterprises require a more holistic and integrated approach for Internet security (a Web security ecosystem) to combat emerging threats from the Internet. This chapter examines components of a comprehensive framework that enables organizations to enhance their threat-mitigation capabilities, while increasing the return on investment of existing information technology infrastructures. This chapter also looks at the role of a multilayered approach to building and maintaining an effective security ecosystem for enterprises [1].

SECURE CONTENT MANAGEMENT GROWS IN IMPORTANCE

Secure content management (SCM) is a term for a superset of several security areas that address many (but not all) of an organization's needs. The SCM market reflects enterprise needs for policy-based Internet management tools that manage Web content, messaging security, virus protection, spyware, and malicious code. SCM vendors enjoyed another strong year of growth in 2005. Industry analysts expect the worldwide revenue for SCM software to reach $7.7 billion in 2007. The market is forecast to increase to $21.6 billion in 2010 for a 19.8% compound annual growth rate (CAGR) for the period from 2005 through 2010 [1].

Major virus and worm outbreaks, explosive growth in phishing, and corporate deadlines for compliance with government regulations fueled the need for Web and messaging security solutions. Additionally spyware is new on the scene and quickly moving up the priority list of corporate security issues. What concerns corporate security departments the most is that spyware can also be used to monitor keystrokes, scan files, install additional spyware, reconfigure Web browsers, and snoop email and other applications [1].

Additionally, phishing attacks continue to be a key driver for multilayered, integrated solutions. Phishing and other Web-based frauds are an excellent example of how malicious content may be propagated through email and other messaging mediums, but must also be controlled by Web filtering and security solutions. Finally, government and industry regulations such as HIPAA, Sarbanes-Oxley, Gramm-Leach-Bliley, and various SEC regulations continue to pressure corporations to secure the use of all electronic forms of communications [1].

THE IMPERATIVE FOR SECURITY ECOSYSTEMS

The evolution of Web-based threats has not only highlighted the importance of keeping security solutions up to date, but it has also put a spotlight on the growing need for more proactive, integrated security solutions in the IT environment. The rapid infection rates of malicious attacks means that slow responding systems will cripple most customer environments because of the inability to get ahead of initial infections and far more serious re-infections [1].

Moreover, malicious hackers are getting more sophisticated at exploiting application vulnerabilities, increasingly using blended malware from multiple threat vectors – and more specifically the Internet. Instead of reactive responses from point solutions, today's threat-based environment requires a more holistic, integrated, and multilayered approach to security infrastructure (a Web security ecosystem) that can enable more centralized policy management and compliance auditing [1].

Organizations of all sizes require various products and services to support their IT security needs. Inevitably, the evaluation process for security solutions often leads to "best-of-breed" or "best-in-class" purchases based on how well the product or service satisfies the specific requirements for each customer environment. Once these best-in-class solutions are selected, a key challenge for IT managers is to maximize their return on investment by seamlessly integrating security solutions into their existing environment. Seamless integration of security components is critical because it:

- Lowers overall deployment costs
- Improves overall strength of security systems
- Increases the ROI of new and existing infrastructure investments

WEB FILTERING EXPANDS ITS ROLE

Web filtering software is an integral part of any enterprise security system and has accounted for the third-largest segment of the total SCM market in 2005. Recently, Web filtering has expanded its value proposition beyond objectionable and non-business related content to include malicious applications and Web sites. This increased demand for Web security in addition to traditional Web filtering has elevated the priority of Web filtering solutions within the IT security departments of enterprises of all sizes. The recent focus on Web filtering as a critical security component of the IT security infrastructure has created more extensive integration and interoperability requirements for Web filtering and security solutions [1].

Finally, according to industry analysts, in 2005, the worldwide Web filtering software market reached $544.6 million. Web filtering software will grow from $544.6 million in 2005 to $1.3 billion in 2010, representing a compounded annual growth rate of 17.6% [1].

SUMMARY AND CONCLUSIONS

Internet-borne threats to companies and organizations of all sizes continue to grow and become more complex. Although many security technologies have been deployed to protect these environments, hackers have increasingly focused on blended threats, a combination of malicious code keyed to exploit specific vulnerabilities. These blended attacks are specifically designed to circumvent point security mechanisms such as independent VPN, firewall, and antivirus products [1].

Finally, blended threats work against point solutions, but they have a high probability of failure when the security solutions are unified. According to industry analysts organizations need to develop and deploy holistic, integrated "security ecosystems" – systems that provide flexible best-practices security solutions for the future [1].

REFERENCES

[1] "Building a Web Security Ecosystem to Combat Emerging Internet Threats," © ©2005 IDC. All Rights Reserved. IDC, 5 Speen Street, Framingham, MA 01701 USA, September 2005.

Chapter 37

EMERGING TECHNOLOGIES

INTRODUCTION

This chapter examines differing views on how to deal with weaknesses in the Internet (specifically Internet security). This ranges from an effort at the National Science Foundation (NSF) to launch a $300 million research program on future Internet architectures (emerging technologies), to concerns that "smarter" networks will be more complicated and therefore error-prone [1].

THE DEVIL YOU KNOW

It's worth remembering that despite all of its flaws, all of its architectural kluginess and insecurity and the costs associated with patching it, the Internet still gets the job done. Any effort to implement a better version faces enormous practical problems: all Internet service providers would have to agree to change all their routers and software, and someone would have to foot the bill, which will likely come to many billions of dollars. But NSF isn't proposing to abandon the old network or to forcibly impose something new on the world. Rather, it essentially wants to build a better mousetrap, show that it's better, and allow a changeover to take place in response to user demand [1].

To that end, the NSF effort envisions the construction of a sprawling infrastructure that could cost approximately $300 million. It would include research labs across the United States and perhaps link with research efforts abroad, where new architectures can be given a full workout. With a high-speed optical backbone and smart routers, this test bed would be far more elaborate and representative than the smaller, more limited test beds in use today. The idea is that new architectures would be battle tested with real-world Internet traffic. You hope that provides enough value added that people are slowly and selectively willing to switch, and maybe it gets enough traction that people will switch over. Hopefully, ten years from now, how things play out is anyone's guess. It could be a parallel infrastructure that people could use for selective applications [1].

Still, skeptics claim that a smarter network could be even more complicated and less secure, and thus failure-prone than the original bare-bones Internet. Conventional wisdom holds that the network should remain dumb, but that the smart devices at its ends should become smarter. No one is happy with the current state of affairs. No one is happy with spam; no one is happy with the amount of vulnerability to various forms of attack. Therefore, it is easy to distinguish that the primary vectors causing a lot of trouble are penetrating holes in operating systems. It's more like the operating systems don't protect themselves very well. An argument could be made, why does the network have to do that [1]?

The more you ask the network to examine data (to authenticate a person's identity, say, or search for viruses) the less efficiently it will move the data around. It's really hard to have a network-level thing do this stuff, which means you have to assemble the packets into something bigger and thus violate all the protocols. That takes a heck of a lot of resources. Still, there is value in the new NSF initiative. The collapse of the Net, or a major security disaster, has been predicted for a decade now. And of course no such disaster has occurred – at least not at the time this writing [1].

The NSF effort to make the medium smarter also runs up against the libertarian culture of the Internet. The NSF program is a worthy one in the first instance because it begins with the premise that the current Net has outgrown some of its initial foundations and associated tenets. But there is a risk, too, that any attempt to rewrite the Net's technical constitution will be so much more fraught, so much more self-conscious of the nontechnical matters at stake, that the cure could be worse than the problem [1].

Still, there are hazards ahead if some sensible action isn't taken. The Internet's security problems, and the theft of intellectual property, could produce a counterreaction that would amount to a clampdown on the medium – everything from the tightening of software makers' control over their operating systems to security lockdowns by businesses. And of course, if a "digital Pearl Harbor" does occur, the federal government is liable to respond reflexively with heavy-handed reforms and controls. If such tightenings happen, you're bound to get an Internet that is, more secure – and less interesting [1].

But what all sides agree on is that the Internet's perennial problems are getting worse, at the same time that society's dependence on it is deepening. Just a few years ago, the work of researchers didn't garner wide interest outside the networking community. But these days, there is recognition that some of these problems are potentially quite serious. You could argue that they have always been there. But there is a wider recognition in the highest level of the government that this is true. Researchers are getting to the point where they are briefing people in the president's Office of Science and Technology Policy. As far as anyone knows, that's pretty new [1].

But, because you don't have power, there is a greater chance that you will be left alone to try. The goal of researchers today is to in call for a fresh design, and to free their minds from the current constraints, so they can envision a different future. The reason this should be stressed is that the Internet is so big, and so successful, that it seems like a fool's errand to send someone off to invent a different one. Whether the end result is a whole new architecture (or just an effective set of changes to the existing one) may not matter in the

Table 37-1. Major efforts to improve the Internet.

Institution	Location	Focus
PLANETLAB	Princeton University Princeton, NJ	Creating an Internet "overlay network" of hardware and software – currently 630 machines in 25 countries – that performs functions ranging from searching for worms to optimizing traffic.
EMULAB	University of Utah Salt Lake City, UT	A software and hardware test-bed that provides researchers a simple, practical way to emulate the Internet for a wide variety of research goals.
DETER/University of Southern	California Information Sciences Institute Marina del Rey, CA	A research test bed where researchers can safely launch simulated cyberattacks, analyze them, and develop defensive strategies, especially for critical infrastructure.
WINLAB (Wireless Information Network Laboratory)	Rutgers University New Brunswick, NJ	Develops wireless networking architectures and protocols, aimed at deploying the mobile Internet. Performs research on everything from high-speed modems to spectrum management.

end. Finally, given how entrenched the Internet is, the effort will have succeeded, if it at least gets the research community working toward common goals, and helps impose creep in the right direction [1].

SUMMARY AND CONCLUSIONS

The NSF's emerging effort to forge a clean-slate Internet architecture will draw on a wide body of existing research. Table 37-1 shows a sampling of major efforts aimed at improving everything from security to wireless communications [1].

REFERENCES

[1] David Talbot, "The Internet Is Broken – Part 3," © Copyright 2005. Technology Review [an independent media company owned by the Massachusetts Institute of Technology], One Main Street, # 7th Floor, # Cambridge, MA 02142, December 21, 2005.

Chapter 38

SUMMARY, CONCLUSIONS AND RECOMMENDATIONS

INTRODUCTION

In order to understand better how the security principles that were specifically covered in Chapter 2 and throughout the rest of this book can be applied, you need to understand the standard networking architecture and how the specific Internet Architecture fits this model. Then, you can see how the security principles that have just been discussed apply to the Internet model. This final chapter focuses on these security principles and presents a summary, conclusion and recommendation for each [1].

SUMMARY

The International Standards Organization (ISO), published an architecture in the early 1980s, whose primary philosophy is that different telecommunications functions should be handled by different standard and open "layers" of the architecture. This so called Open Systems Interconnect (OSI) model is constructed as follows [1].

ISO 7 Layer Model

The very lowest layer is the physical layer which is responsible for the physical transmission of the data from the computer to the network. Here, there are the electronic circuits and mechanical connectors which define how transmissions are to occur over coaxial ethernet, modems, FDDI or any other medium for transmitting data [1].

Next is the Data-link layer, which is responsible for the integrity of the bit stream between any two points. Here, there are standards for redundancy checks, parity, retransmission protocols, etc. to ensure that the same sequence of bits sent from point A is received at point B [1].

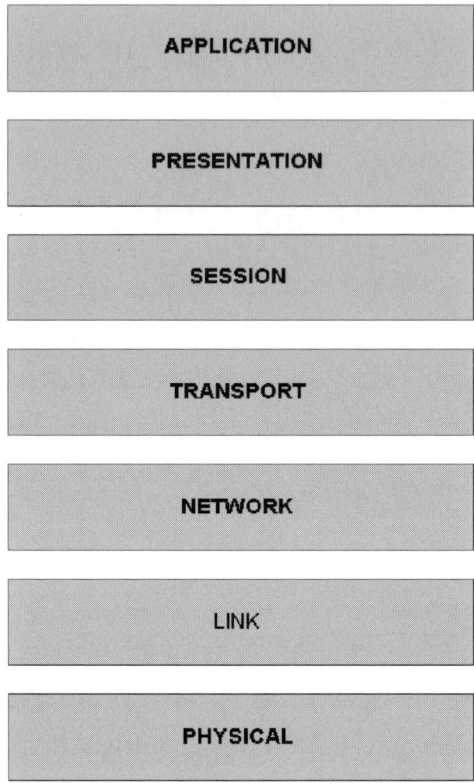

Figure 38-1. OSI model.

The Network layer extends the concepts of the Link layer into multiple networks, which may or may not be compatible. Internetworking also implies that this layer must be aware of different routes available to connect the sender with the recipient [1].

The Transport Layer ensures that different transmissions, which may be part of a sequence and which may have traversed the network via different paths, are appropriately resequenced at the receiver's site. The Session Layer manages the connecting and disconnecting of interactions between two computers and how the data is to be exchanged (duplex, simplex, etc.) [1].

Presentation determines what code sets will be used (ASCII, EBCDIC, international character sets, etc.). Finally, you come to the Applications Layer in which specific applications like FTP, Telnet, e-mail, Archie, and others reside [1].

The architecture of the OSI model is such that each layer uses services "below" it and provides services to those layers "above" it, giving the appearance of a stack. In fact, the model is known as a protocol stack and other architectures, such as TCP/IP, will also follow the stack model (see Fig. 38-1) [1].

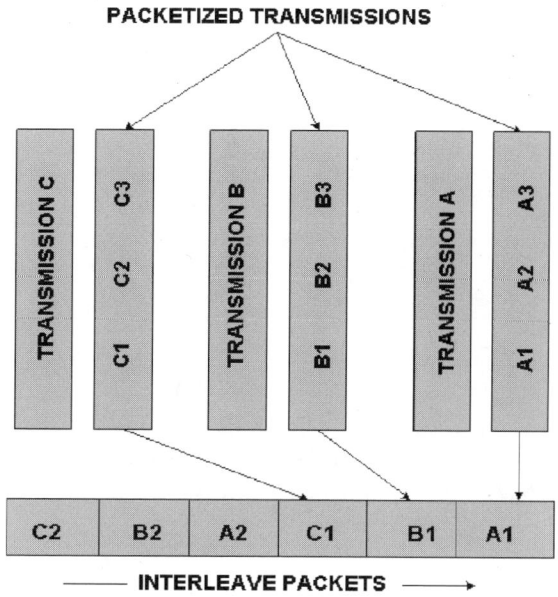

Figure 38-2. Packet transmissions.

Internet layers

At this point, the vast majority of people interested in the Internet are familiar with the acronym TCP/IP (Transmission Control Protocol/Internet Protocol), which form the foundation of communications for the net. This part of the chapter will cover the architectural constructs of the TCP/IP structure and their relationship to the Open Systems Interconnect model [1].

Packet Switched Networks

The Internet uses the concept of packets and packet switching to allow for simultaneous access by millions of people. Transmissions between any two points are broken into smaller transmissions known as packets as shown Fig. 38-2 [1]. By doing this, everyone's messages can be sent in an interleaved fashion so that all users see nearly the same level of performance [1].

Each connection to the Internet is designated with a unique Internet Address, usually written as four numbers determined by a standard Internet Protocol (IP). Packets are shipped to Internet destinations through routers, which use Transmission Control Protocol, or TCP. These fundamental layers of the Internet form the backbone upon which data can be sent from one point to another, with integrity [1].

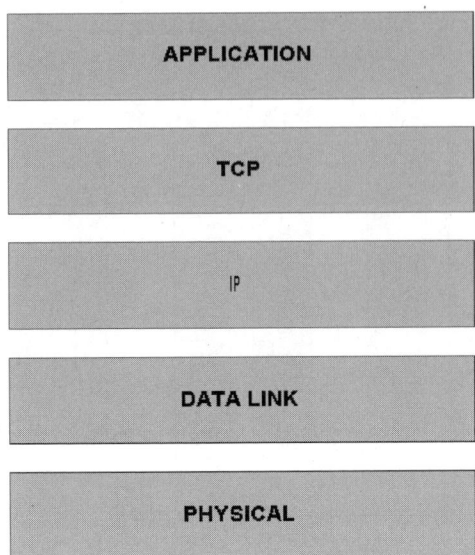

Figure 38-3. The OSI model minus session and presentation.

Applications Layer

Getting data from point A to point B is essential, but it is not enough. It is the equivalent of finding a telephone number in a phone book and being able to establish a telephone connection between the US and a foreign country. The individuals will not be able to communicate unless there is a common language. Similarly, on the Internet, as specified in the OSI model, there are other protocols and tools which are specific to the application layer and which correspond to these telephone analogies [1].

- File Transfer Protocol (FTP) is the oldest commonly used method to allow files transfer from one location to another. Using an anonymous FTP, a user can browse the files of a host, select appropriate files and have those files transferred to his or her own system.
- Telnet is an application and set of protocols that allows a user's Internet connected terminal to act as if it were directly connected to the host computer.
- E-mail applications use the Internet as an interconnecting infrastructure to allow messages to be transmitted among users. For example, AOL and CompuServe use the Internet to move e-mail traffic to and from each other [1].

As you can see in Fig. 38-3, the Internet layers roughly correspond to the OSI layers, with the exception of session and presentation [1]. This means that Internet applications must handle the tasks generally assigned to session and presentation in the OSI model [1].

To demonstrate how these layers work, Fig. 38-4 shows a PC connected to a Web server over a local ethernet connection [1]. In this environment, the PC has a coaxial connection for the physical layer, and uses ethernet as the link level control. The PC also will have a TCP/IP software protocol stack, and will likely use Netscape Navigator or Microsoft Explorer as its application software. On the server end, all of the bottom layers are identical, and the

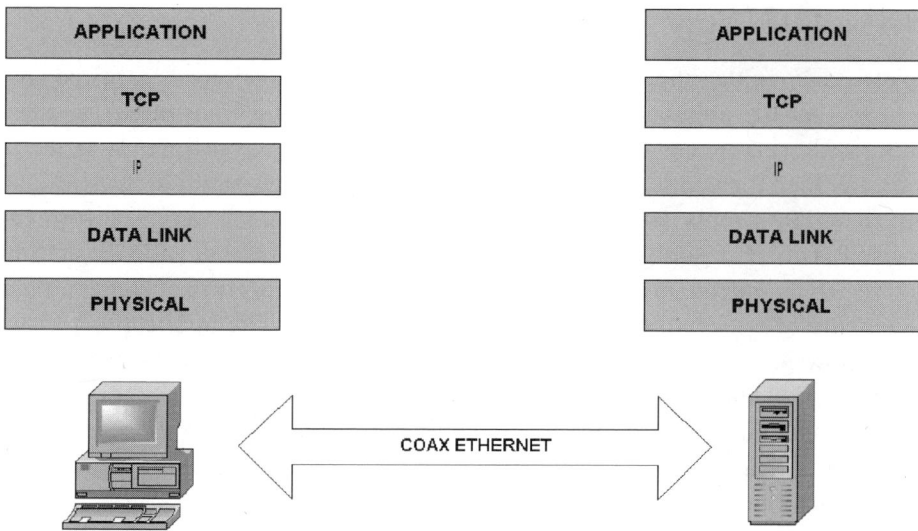

Figure 38-4. How the OSI model (minus session and presentation) works.

application will be the Web server and any custom software written, such as shopping or search engine applications. As mentioned earlier, each layer has its own set of dialogs and its own language in which to conduct those. For the application layer, for example, the language and protocol are contained within HTML commands and responses [1].

CONCLUSIONS

Given the architectures described earlier, where are the vulnerabilities, and specifically, what countermeasures can be taken to thwart potential attacks in this architecture? This part of the chapter examines the different tools which are available and where they are intended to be deployed for maximum protection. The placement of these security components will then constitute a Security Architecture for Internet configurations [1].

> **Note:** As in any architecture, the components are designed with a great deal of flexibility and depending on particular needs of specific situations, the selection of components and their interrelationships may vary significantly.

Two Approaches to Security

Over time, two distinct approaches have evolved to applying security countermeasures: networked coupled security and application coupled security. As the names imply, the first philosophy favors the use of securing the network infrastructure, while the second builds security into the applications themselves [1].

Network Coupled Security

In a Network coupled scheme, the focus is to make the network itself a trusted and secure subsystem so that the applications can assume the data being transmitted is safe, comes from authorized users and is being delivered to the appropriate recipients. If the network itself is secure, then the applications don't have to do anything special to operate in a secure environment – they simply assume that all security functions are being performed by the network itself. This philosophy is very similar to that of the Internet and OSI architectures. Applications which operate in the OSI and Internet environments do not concern themselves with sequencing of packets, validation of IP addresses, etc. The applications assume that the layers below in the supporting protocol stacks have done their job, and therefore the applications can concentrate on the data content. Similarly, in a secure network environment, applications can assume that the security is being handled by the lower levels [1].

The most significant advantage to network coupled security is that applications do not have to be security aware. Applications which are not security aware can be moved into a secure environment without modification. Less obvious, but equally important, is that the use of a consistent security mechanism within the network allows applications to interoperate from a security standpoint. There is no possibility that different applications will insist on different authentication schemes, key management schemes, etc. [1]

Application Coupled Security

Proponents of this scheme argue that the application knows best what kind of security is required for that application. Therefore, control of the security aspects should rest in the application layer. To these proponents, the need to create security aware applications is not a disadvantage, but rather a natural and reasonable consequence of the need to apply security at that level. Similarly, the potential for interoperability issues is seen as a flexibility advantage to the proponents of application- coupled security, who argue that a "one size fits all" approach in network security is insufficient for the broad range of security requirements [1].

Different Tools for Different Layers

There is no shortage of technology available to secure an organization's Internet connections. More appropriate questions have to do with which tools to use at which layers to effect the secure communications [1].

Early on, router manufacturers recognized the key role they could play in this endeavor, and have placed filtering capabilities in their products to establish a primary front line of defense. A router's ability to examine and discriminate network traffic based on the IP packet addresses is known as a "screening router". Some advanced routers provide the capability to screen packets based upon other criteria such as the type of protocol (http, ftp, udp), the source address, and the destination address fields for a particular type of protocol. This way, a communications manager can build "profiles" of users who are allowed access to different applications based on the protocols. Such a case is shown in Fig. 38-5 [1].

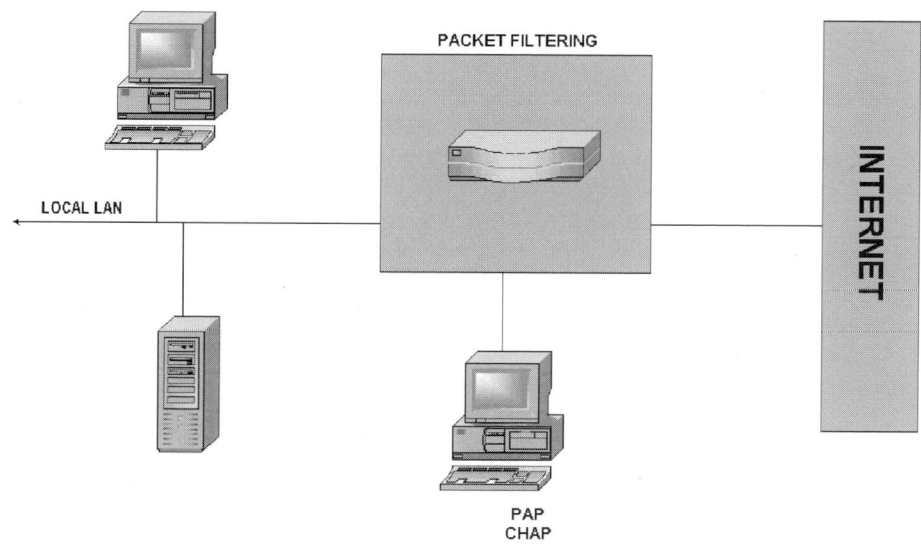

Figure 38-5. Profiles of users who are allowed access to different applications based on the protocols.

In Fig. 38-5, the packet filtering of the screening router is enhanced with authentication software which can add either password authentication or challenge authentication [1]. In the scenario described in Fig. 38-5, simple filtering, even with profiles, cannot authenticate that the individual on the other end of the connection is in fact the individual who should have access to the applications and data residing on the server connected to the local LAN [1]. Therefore, you need to add PAP/CHAP authentication to accomplish this, which provides another layer of security to the system. The screening router either alone or in combination with authentication, is known as a "Firewall", because it keeps the "fire" of unsecured communications outside a protective "wall".

Another popular configuration, particularly for organizations which have WWW presence, is the use of a so called "bastion host". Again borrowing from the medieval fortifications of cities, this concept consists of a double walled security layer. The outside wall, or perimeter wall, consists of a screening router which provides a first pass screen for the population of outside users who are allowed access to the Internet accessible applications in the Bastion Hosts, which sits in the "moat" between the two walls. A secondary router with or without authentication enhancements provides a second filter for those few privileged users who have access to the internal network. The bastion host concept is demonstrated in Fig. 38-6 [1].

Protecting against unauthorized access to the data via controlling who is allowed to communicate with the protected servers will guard against many of the vulnerabilities of networks. However, these schemes do not prevent espionage and theft of the data which may be captured en route between two validated correspondents. This is an area where the addition of encryption and key management, as defined in the SKIP standard, will provide effective countermeasures. By encrypting the data and properly managing the keys to the

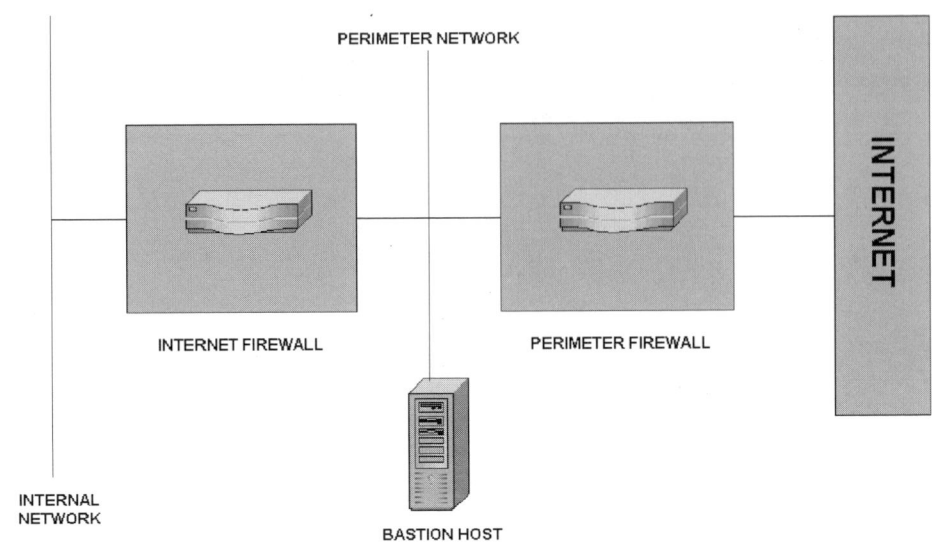

Figure 38-6. Profiles of users who are allowed access to different applications based on the protocols.

encryption and decryption, data which is intercepted is rendered unusable, and at the same time unmodifiable, thereby adding a further layer of protection for the data [1].

Beyond this level, additional security is still available coupled to the applications, as mentioned earlier. For example, database systems also have authentication capabilities with user names and passwords as well as profiles, access control lists, and the like. It is possible to add yet more layers of security beyond those discussed so far by adding similar technologies to the application layer. In these schemes, applications could also issue challenge passwords beyond those required to gain access to the network, thereby increasing the security of the data by decreasing the odds that a single error (lost password, etc.) could compromise the application or the data. One common form of application level security is the use of Secure Socket Layer (SSL) directly coupled with the application. In order for SSL to work, both the Browser client and the Server application must support its use, making the application security aware [1].

Managing the Risk

Network security is all about managing risks and using this risk management analysis to provide appropriate security at an affordable price. This part of the chapter explores a Risk Management tool which can be used to analyze the risks in your organization and take appropriate countermeasures [1].

Risk Determination

Risks can be characterized by two criteria: the likelihood that a particular attack will be successful, and the consequences of the results if the attack is successful. Security costs money, and therefore you must use that money wisely and only spend it where there is

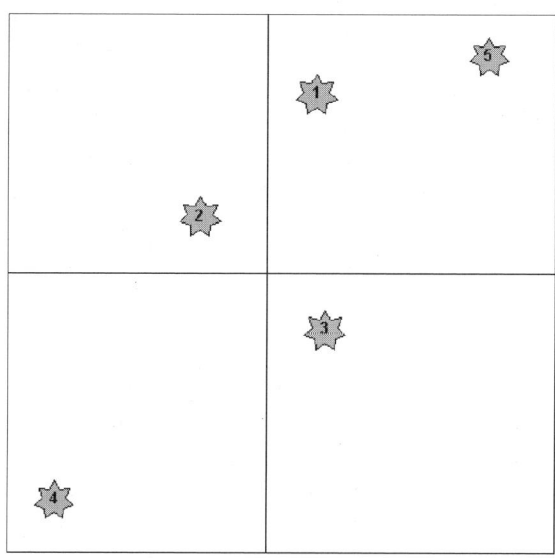

Figure 38-7. Plotting individual attacks.

a real likelihood of significant damage. Risk mitigation strategies then focus on either minimizing the likelihood of occurrence (by employing countermeasures), or by minimizing the consequences of the attack. One way to depict this is to characterize the risks along two axes, one indicating increasing likelihood of an attack succeeding, and a second indicating increasingly dire consequences. The individual attacks are plotted according to the two axes, and depending on where they fall, they can be characterized as worthy of defending or not (see Fig.38-7) [1]. If an attack is considered serious enough to defend against, countermeasures are developed to reposition the attack into the lower left hand quadrant [1].

In Fig. 38-7, five potential attacks are plotted in a hypothetical scenario to demonstrate this technique [1]. Attacks numbered one and five fall into the upper right hand corner, which means the analysis has shown them to be likely to succeed, and that the consequences are serious. Attack number three is somewhat likely to succeed, and the results appear to be moderately serious. Attack number four is not likely to succeed, and even if it did, the results would not be particularly damaging. Attack number two is also not likely to succeed, but if it did, the results would be damaging. Based on this analysis, an organization might opt to do nothing about attack number four, would definitely provide defenses against attacks one and five, and would optionally defend against number two and number three, depending on budget constraints [1].

Internet Security Toolkit

This part of the chapter describes the different technology tools available to deploy in developing a security architecture for any given network [1].

Secure Sockets Layer (SSL) And HyperText Transport Protocol Secure (HTTPS)

The SSL is inserted between the TCP protocol and the application protocol. The SSL protocol operates in two phases. In the first phase, the sender and receiver agree on the read and write keys to be used, and then in the second phase data is encrypted using the keys chosen in the first phase. Authentication and secure key exchange is also achieved using the RSA public key encryption algorithm. By layering a version of SSL between HTTP and TCP, Netscape has developed a secure version of HTTP as well [1].

Proxy servers

A proxy server is a firewall implemented in a hardware unit such as a workstation on a NT server, rather than in a router. This device looks at all of the data in each packet, not just address and headers. In most cases, the proxy examines the content and replaces the network address in the packet with proxy destinations that are known to be secure. Besides hiding the network from the outside world, they provide more control over the actual data at the application level. However, because they inspect all of the data in each packet, there have been reports of some significant performance degradations in high traffic areas [1].

Encryption

Encryption is a technique as old as the Romans. It is simply the scrambling of the transmitted text using a set of rules (algorithms, which in today's world means mathematical manipulations) which is known to the recipient, but hopefully to no one else. The recipient can then use the same set of rules in reverse to unscramble the coded text and read the intended message [1].

There are two classes of encryption algorithm. They are: Symmetric key and asymmetric key [1].

Symmetric Key

A symmetric key algorithm is one where the same key is used both to encode and decode the message. The most popular symmetric key algorithm is the Data Encryption Standard (DES), whose major advantage is that it is fast and widely implemented. Its major limitations are its relatively small key size (56 bits), which weakens the security of the algorithm, and the need to exchange a secret key between the communicating parties, before secure communication can be established. A variant of DES, Triple-DES or 3DES is based on using DES three times (normally in an encrypt-decrypt-encrypt sequence with three different, unrelated keys). Many people consider Triple-DES to be much safer than plain DES [1].

Asymmetric Key

It is a surprising fact that there are some algorithms which are difficult to reverse, even when the algorithm, the key, and the encrypted data are all available, unless some other piece of information is known. A public key encryption system is based on an algorithm of this type. Two keys are generated. One is kept private and the other can be made public. Two systems that want to hold a secure conversation can exchange their public keys. When one system sends to the other, it will encrypt the message using the other system's public key.

Even though an attacker might observe the exchange of keys and an encrypted message, the irreversiblity of the public key algorithm ensures that the data is secure [1].

The most popular public key algorithm is the RSA algorithm. The name RSA is derived from the first letters of the surnames of the algorithms inventors, Ron Rivest, Adi Shamir, and Leonard Adleman [1].

Although public key algorithms solve the key distribution problem, they are much slower than symmetric key algorithms. When implemented in hardware, DES is up to 10,000 faster than RSA. If efficiency is required, a public key system can be used to securely exchange symmetric keys which can then be used for the bulk of the data transfer [1].

Firewalls

The term "firewall" has become a generic term which encompasses a spectrum of technologies intended to provide protection from communications attacks on an organization. Screening routers, application gateways, proxy servers, authentication servers, are all examples of firewalls in use today. It is possible, and often desirable, to combine these different technologies according to the needs of the organization and their budget limitations [1].

Application Gateways

All packets are addressed to an application on the gateway that relays the packets between the two communication points. In most application gateway implementations, additional packet filter machines are required to control and screen the traffic between the gateway and the networks. Typically, this is a use of bastion hosts. These are secure but inefficient, since they are not transparent to users and applications [1].

Screening Routers

One of the most cost efficient and ubiquitous techniques for securing a network – a screening router, sometimes known as a packet filtering router, will allow known users (known by their IP addresses) to connect to specified applications (determined by their port address). Thereby, limiting the connections of even those users allowed to enter through the firewall, and completely denying any connections to those not authorized to access any applications [1].

Authenticating Servers

Authenticating Servers are often used in conjunction with Screening Routers to provide authentication services. This results in the verification of those users who claim to be originating from valid addresses, and are in fact who they say they are [1].

RECOMMENDATIONS

Okay, so now you've covered all of the building blocks and some examples of how they might go together. The question still might be on your mind: What should my organization do to be secure. The answer is "it depends." It depends on specific security needs and budget limitations of your organization. Very few enterprises, not even the Federal Government and the Military, can afford "security at any price." Eventually, you will be forced to stop building security features and learn to live with the residual risks of your system. Where you stop depends on how much you are willing to pay to get the amount of security appropriate to your application [1].

Finally, one typical and common sense approach is to develop a security infrastructure incrementally. Start inexpensively with packet filtering and authenticating routers as the beginning firewall. Many experts contend that over 90% of attacks can be successfully defended by integrated routers and firewalls. Later, if you still need more, you can add encryption and key management for further enhancements. At each point, determine where your vulnerabilities are, what the potential attacks might be, and what consequences would ensue from a successful attack. Many people find that the use of simple and inexpensive packet filtering and authentication "move their dots" into the lower left hand quadrant of the likelihood/consequence space, and they have no further need to add more sophisticated measures. Certainly, if more is required, and the cost implications are warranted, customers can move into application coupled systems to further enhance the security. The ultimate move, of course, is to go to private networks, where one eliminates the physical connection to the network from potential hackers. Finally, use the services of agencies such as the National Computer Security Agency (NCSA) and ISS, which offer security audits of sites to help you determine vulnerabilities and countermeasures, and help you decide whether the risks facing your operations warrant further expenditures of time and money [1].

REFERENCES

[1] "Internet Security Primer," copyright 2003/2004 ZZZ Online, ZZZ Online, 2004.

PART XV

APPENDICES

Appendix A

CONFIGURING INTERNET AUTHENTICATION SERVICE ON MICROSOFT WINDOWS 2003 SERVER WINDOWS 2003 / ENHANCED

INTRODUCTION

This appendix very briefly describes how to setup the Internet Authentication service (IAS) on a Microsoft Windows 2003 Server. As an example, with regards to configuration, this appendix walks the user through the steps to linking the SonicWALL security appliance and the IAS server up to respond on user authentication requests, and responds back with a filter-id, which can be used in rules and to VPN clients [1].

> **Disclaimer!** The author and publisher are not endorsing/promoting the SonicWALL security appliance tool. The use of the tool in this appendix is for illustration purposes only; and, was picked at random for that purpose.

This appendix contains the following topic areas:

- Configuring the Windows 2003 Server for IAS to Support RADIUS Clients
- Configuring the Windows 2003 Server for RADIUS User Management
- Configuring the SonicWALL Security Appliance to Support the Authentication Method [1]

CONFIGURING THE WINDOWS 2003 SERVER FOR IAS TO SUPPORT RADIUS CLIENTS

1. On the Windows 2003 Server, verify that you have applied the latest Service Pack and hotfixes. Also, verify that the "Remote Access and Routing Service" is running.
2. Open the control panel on the Windows server, find the add and remove software from the list, select windows components again find the Networking services and press details. Here you check Internet Authentication service and click OK.

3. After the installation, you can find the IAS under the administration tools. Start the IAS and select New RADIUS Client.
4. Enter the Name and IP of the SonicWALL security appliance the clients request could come from.
5. Select RADIUS Standard, (also the default option), enter a Shared secret. This shared secret is needed later on the SonicWALL security appliance, so note this for future reference.
6. Setup the access criteria for the users, right click on the Remote Access Policies and select New Remote Access Policy.
7. A wizard will emerge, click Next.
8. Select Set up a custom policy and enter a description for this access policy, click Next.
9. Click Add, a window with the different authentication criteria will pop up.
10. From this list, select Windows Groups, and click OK. By selecting Windows Groups, you can authenticate a user upon which group the user's a member of in the Windows AD, or Windows user group.
11. Click Add, then select and find the Windows Group that the user should be a member of, if he or she is to authenticate successfully. Click OK.
12. You could add more groups, but in this scenario you need to only be a member of one group, and you also need to send a specific filter-id back that represents this group on the SonicWALL security appliance.
13. Click Next.
14. This needs to be a Grant remote Access Permission policy. Click Next.
15. Click Edit Profile.
16. Select the Authentication tab, and uncheck any options except the Unencrypted authentication (PAP, SPAP).
17. Select the Advanced tab, and click Add.
18. A list of Attributes will appear, from this list we need the Filter-id option, Click Add.
19. In the subsequent windows, Add a text string that the IAS should send back to the SonicWALL security appliance along with a authentication successfully message. This text string should match a previous added User Group on the SonicWALL security appliance.
20. Enter the Group name (remark, it's case sensitive) on the SonicWALL security appliance. And click OK.
21. Click OK [1].

That completes the IAS configuration. If you have other groups on the AD that needs different access, you can add more Remote authentication policies [1].

CONFIGURING THE WINDOWS 2003 SERVER FOR RADIUS USER MANAGEMENT

1. Navigate to the user management on the Windows 2003 Server, in here you have a few things to check and edit on the users that suppose to authenticate through the SonicWALL and IAS.

2. Select the Dial-in tab, and check the Allow access option.
3. Select the Member Of tab, and either add or check that the user is in the correct group, it should be the same group as you added in the IAS under Windows Groups [1].

This completes the configuration for User Management on the Windows 2003 Server [1].

CONFIGURING THE SONICWALL SECURITY APPLIANCE TO SUPPORT THE AUTHENTICATION METHOD

1. Select the User menu, and select the settings item. Now select RADIUS at the Authentication Method and click Configure.
2. Enter the IP address of the IAS server, and enter the Shared Secret that you previously entered on the IAS.
3. In the RADIUS Users tab check the Use RADIUS Filter-ID attribute on RADIUS Server option, click Apply.
4. Navigate to the Test tab and enter the username and password of a user belonging to the SW group. It should now report back as the screen shot indicates below. In the Returned User Attributes box, the SW text string is returned to the SonicWALL security appliance along with a 'Succeeded' message [1].

The SonicWALL can now use the derived group membership or user information within Access Rules, GroupVPN Policies, or for Content Filtering policy application. So as you can see this provides a very flexible and highly controllable way of handling access rights for each user in an already existing Windows AD [1].

REFERENCES

[1] "Configuring Internet Authentication Service on Microsoft Windows 2003 Server Windows 2003 / Enhanced," Internet Security ® 2006 SonicWALL, Inc., SonicWALL, Inc., 1143 Borregas Avenue, Sunnyvale, CA 94089-1306, 2006.

Appendix B

INTERNET SECURITY MANAGEMENT, RESILIENCY AND SECURITY

INTRODUCTION

Modern organizations have a huge challenge on their hands, on a scale unlike anything they've seen since the Y2K crisis. They must "secure" the organization in the face of increasing complexity, uncertainty, and interconnection brought about by an unprecedented reliance on technology to accomplish their mission. They must also stay mindful of the heavy hand of regulation as legislators discover the importance of security. This appendix explores some of the challenges that organizations must overcome to be successful in this environment and introduces ways in which a change in perspective might be the impetus for an emerging mission-driven approach to security [1].

Let's start by recalling 9th grade biology class when you were introduced to the concept of a cell. You might remember that each cell in the body performs a specific function. To carry out this function, cells receive input from their environment, transform it, and create output – a continuous cycle that lasts throughout the cell's life. The success of the cell in performing this cycle is important to the larger environment in which it exists – the organs, systems, and functions of the body. Interestingly, this cycle can also be used to describe the basic functions of information systems and organizations as well. In particular, an organization can be described as an open system that gives and takes from its environment to exist, to be sustained, and to succeed [1].

It isn't such a leap to consider today's organizations in this context. Organizations are connected to their environment in an ever increasing way, particularly because technology is a pervasive force that enables business processes and strategies. This is apparent with respect to the use of the Internet. Not long ago, many organizations actively restricted the extent and type of Internet access provided to users; today, Internet access is a part of the baseline configuration of just about every user desktop and is an essential tool for performing job functions. In some ways, the use of the Internet (and all of its underlying technologies) has become the primary means by which the organization interacts with its environment.

While this brings tremendous opportunities, it also exposes the organization to new risks that must be identified, mitigated, and managed so as not to impede the organization's quest to meet its mission [1].

THE ORGANIZATION AS BENEFACTOR

Every cell in a living organism has a particular purpose or mission. All of the internal structures of a cell are employed in accomplishing this mission. Anything that impedes this process also interrupts the cell's ability to do its work, causing potential damage to the larger system or environment to which it belongs. Thus, ensuring that the cell can carry out its essential functions and maintain proper balance with the environment is paramount [1].

In the same way, the ultimate benefactor of the security activities that an organization undertakes should be the organization itself. Organizations deploy their internal structures – core assets and processes – with the goal of accomplishing their mission and providing benefits to stakeholders. As with the cell example, anything that impedes assets and processes from doing their jobs potentially derails the organization's ability to be successful. From this perspective, ensuring that assets and processes remain productive is the real benefit and focus of the organization's investment in security [1].

Managing security in the context of the organization's strategic drivers provides both advantages and conflict. On the one hand, this approach ensures that the goals of security management are forged from and aligned with the high-level goals of the organization. On the other hand, the strategic drivers and needs of the organization are often in conflict with the actions required to ensure that assets and processes remain productive. In addition, as the organization is exposed to more complexity and uncertainty (because of the increasing use of technology and the pace at which the organization's risk environment changes), keeping security activities and strategic drivers aligned becomes more difficult. In the end, finding the right balance between protecting the organization's core assets and processes and enabling them to do their job becomes a challenge for security management – and a significant barrier to effectiveness [1].

THE SCOPE OF SECURITY MANAGEMENT

Security as it is traditionally defined in organizations is one of the most pervasive problems that an organization must address. Rarely has there been an organizational issue, problem, or challenge that requires the mobilization of everyone in the organization to solve. (In this case, the Y2K effort comes to mind with one significant distinction – security is an ongoing issue that must be managed well beyond New Year's Eve!) The sheer expanse of any problem that traverses the entire organization poses many management challenges, particularly when the focus is security. First, the most important areas of the organization must be identified and targeted. This requires the organization to take an inventory to determine what needs to be protected and why. In a large, complex organization, this can result in the identification of hundreds of assets that are important to strategic drivers.

Second, to secure this collection of organizational assets requires many skills and resources that are typically scattered throughout the organization. Because security is a problem for the whole organization, it simply is no longer effective or acceptable to manage it from the information technology department. Chief Security Officers have the one of the most difficult jobs in executive-level management because their success depends on utilizing many of the organization's skills and resources. In effect, CSOs must mobilize many disparate parts of the organization to work together and to expand their core responsibilities to include security. This is not unlike a similar problem faced by U.S. automakers in the early 1980s. Faced with the need to improve quality to compete with their Asian counterparts, some U.S. automakers wisely focused on quality as a core element of their mission. As a result, quality became a part of every worker's core responsibilities and was integrated into key business processes, and thus, the entire organization worked together to overcome these deficiencies [1].

COMPLEXITY IS PERVASIVE

Connecting to a complex operational environment is not a choice for today's organizations. If the organization wants to compete and thrive, it must be willing to expose itself to operational and technical networks that enable it but also put it at risk. These networks are constantly changing and evolving, increasing the organization's exposure (but also its potential for growth). This problem is not limited to large organizations – virtually any organization that uses a modern operating system on its desktop computers or servers has inherited a complex and dynamically changing environment that must be actively managed [1].

This presents another challenge for managing security because the security strategy must be sufficiently dynamic to keep pace with the rate of organizational and technical change. On balance, security management must support the organization's quest to be sensing, flexible, and adaptive to its environment and must be able to make a measurable contribution to the organization's bottom-line and long-term resiliency [1].

SECURITY AS AN INVESTMENT

Dealing with a complex operating environment is costly and can significantly impact an organization's profitability. Protecting the financial condition and stability of an organization is one of the most important issues for management. The resulting pressures from managing to the bottom line are a rich source of challenges for many activities throughout an organization, especially for security management [1].

Expenditures receive much of the focus in organizations because they directly affect the organization's bottom line. Responsible financial managers scrutinize all expenses and make implicit, if not direct, risk-versus-reward decisions. Security management is no exception – it is often an expense-driven activity that can directly affect an organization's profitability. It is no wonder then that organizations are reluctant to view security as an investment that can generate benefits to the bottom line [1].

The view of security as overhead is an unfortunate outgrowth of the lack of inclusion of measurement and metrics as an essential element of security management. Organizations do not routinely require return on investment calculations on security investments, nor do they attempt to measure or gather metrics on the performance of security investments. Absent a set of established and accepted metrics for measuring security ROI, there is little an organization can do on its own in this area other than perform measurement in the context of incident avoidance or impact of a realized risk (the impact costs less than the control, and therefore provides a return). And organizations are faced with another problem: Which security investments should be measured? Technical controls, monitoring software, security staff, CSOs? The measurement dilemma is pervasive across the entire security community, and lacking specific guidance, organizations have become comfortable characterizing security activities as an expense on their balance sheets [1].

In much the same way that information technology investments are now commonly capitalized, the challenge for security management is to drive the organization in the same direction for security. The shift to characterizing security as an organizational investment promotes the view that security can, at a minimum, preserve an organization's bottom line, if not improve it. Consider this: an organization that successfully approaches security as an investment may increase its overall value in the marketplace, and may even be able to capture this value as "goodwill" on their balance sheet. In the future, a determinant of an organization's value may be the amount of goodwill on its balance sheet that is directly due to its ability to secure critical assets and processes and improveits resiliency. Certainly, an organization that can keep its core assets and processes in service in the face of an attack, accident, or failure (and actually improve their ability to adapt to future events) may be worth more than one that cannot, if only because of the competitive advantage they create. Until organizations shift their view away from security as a burden, the ability of security management to effectively do its job at the organizational level will be impeded [1].

TECHNOLOGICAL BIASES

The view of security as a financial impediment for the organization is often a consequence of the tendency of organizations to consider security as a technology-driven activity. The security industry itself contributes greatly to this characterization. Framing security in technical terms is a logical outgrowth of the expansive (and ever-increasing) number of technical products and services that are available to "help" organizations get a handle on security management. Worse yet, there is a propensity for organizations to frame security problems in technical terms, often ignoring the management and operational weaknesses that are root causes or contributing factors. The bias toward technological solutions or the framing of security issues in technical terms has done a great disservice to organizations in their pursuit of adequate security [1].

SECURITY IS A BUSINESS PROBLEM

Security is a business or organizational problem that must be framed and solved in the context of the organization's strategic drivers. However, many organizations adopt a technology-centric approach to security by default. There are several reasons why this has occurred. As stated previously, the largest contributor to the technology-centric view of security is the industry itself – there is a strong technology bias to security approaches and solutions, and even in the selection of skilled security personnel. Not only has this made organizations more likely to view security as a technical specialty, but it has also corrupted them into misplacing their most prized security resources in the IT department, further alienating them from connecting to and aligning with the organization's strategic drivers [1].

The evolution of a risk-based paradigm for security has made it clear that a secure organization does not result from securing technical infrastructure alone. A security approach that is mission-centric (based on strategic drivers) strives to secure the organization's critical assets and processes regardless of where they "live." This can be illustrated by examining the importance of information as an organizational asset. Information is frequently stored, transported, and processed through technical means, and therefore is considered a technical asset. However, this characterization is a distortion that can lead organizations inappropriately to a technical security approach. For example, an organization may store its product designs on paper or keep its medical records in paper form – both of which may be critical for meeting the organization's mission. Securing the organization's technical infrastructure will not provide a proper level of protection for these assets, nor will it protect many other information assets that are in no way dependent on technology for their existence or protection. Thus, the organization would be lulled into a false sense of security if they relied on protecting their technical infrastructure alone [1].

In the end, the "network" that most matters is the one that defines the organization and its related boundaries. The importance of the organization's technical network is established in its role in enabling the organization's assets and processes, but it provides little context for which of these assets and processes matter most to strategic drivers. It is only in the organizational network where the context for the importance of each asset and process is found, as well as the rationale for what needs to be protected and why it is provided [1].

REGULATORY BIASES

A final consideration for security management is the organization's regulatory environment. Just as the organization must expose itself to its environment to operate, so must it be willing to accept some of the limitations imposed on like organizations that operate in its competitive space. This brings another level of challenges that affects the organization's ability to be effective at security management [1].

Regulations reflect the need for organizations in a particular industry to look critically at their protection needs and to implement corresponding security strategies and controls. While this has had a positive effect in elevating the need to focus on security, for some organizations it can also be deleterious in that regulations can become an organization's security strategy by default. Regulations can draw the organization's focus away from organizational drivers and on to the compliance requirements of the moment. Complying with regulations is certainly an important activity in an organization, but it cannot substitute for a mission-focused, strategic security management process. Regulation is intended to improve the core industries on which it is focused, but compliance activities can give organizations a false sense of the overall effectiveness of their security programs. For example, compliance with HIPAA regulations may improve the security over core assets that are subject to the regulations, but other assets and processes are left unprotected. A compliance-driven approach to security can also cause costly and inefficient investments in protection mechanisms and controls to protect those assets and processes that are subject to regulation, when in fact this may not be the best use of limited resources for the organization [1].

Organization-centric approaches to security management consider the impact of risks and their effect on the organization to determine which security activities and practices are best for them. In effect, this allows the organization to focus on their true security needs. Security management that is subsumed by a need to comply with regulations can detour an organization from this strategy by diverting their attention away from what is best for their unique organizational context [1].

SECURITY AS A CORE COMPETENCY

Organizations want to focus their energy on their core competencies – those functions and activities that define the organization's existence and its value to stakeholders. The upsurge in outsourcing of horizontal business functions by organizations supports this claim. For many functions, such as payroll processing or benefits administration, this may be perfectly acceptable – if an organization cannot realize a strategic and competitive advantage from excelling at payroll processing, it may not make sense to develop a core competency in this area. However, this is why organizations may need to develop a core competency in security management based on their strategic drivers [1].

Security is so inextricably tied to the success of the organization in accomplishing its mission and improving its resiliency that it is in the organization's best interest to be competent at securing itself. Unfortunately, the high cost and limited availability of security resources (particularly technical resources) has made it cost-prohibitive for some organizations to develop this competency. The issues of cost and retention of key security personnel also has not made executive-level managers willing to embrace security as a legitimate long-term investment in the organization's strategic plan [1].

CONCLUSIONS

It is no wonder that security is so difficult to manage in modern organizations. The practice of security management continues to evolve inside organizations, and therefore has yet to garner its fair share of attention and resources. This is partially the consequence of the organization's inability to see the value of security outside of technical constraints and regulatory compliance. In addition, the industry's affinity for technology-based solutions alienates the "business people" in the organization. There is hope however that organizations and the security industry are evolving in this respect [1].

Many organizations are adopting a risk-based approach to security. The move to a risk based paradigm is a catalyst for moving security from a technical specialty to an organizational competency. Applying a risk perspective to security is a logical progression – risk management is a basic business function, and whether it is done implicitly or explicitly, it must be performed at an organizational level to be purposeful [1].

But even this paradigm for security has significant challenges to overcome, notwithstanding the many definitions of "risk" and the somewhat negligent way in which risk is bandied about as the new security buzzword. For example, the security industry offers many options and services for performing security "risk" assessments; however, at the nucleus of these offerings is usually a traditional vulnerability assessment with very little connection to risk drivers. Organizations must also be cognizant that a risk perspective alone is not a panacea for solving all of the issues that they face in elevating security to the level of other pervasive business problems [1].

In pursuit of addressing the challenges noted herein, the first obstacle that an organization must confront is to determine what they are trying to accomplish with their security activities. In essence, the organization must ask what benefits they get from "doing security." The organizational perspective is essential to determining these benefits and for setting appropriate targets for security [1].

One of the most important characteristics of cells and larger organisms is their ability to adapt to new or changing environments. Organizations, like cells, also must continually adapt to their environment and emerging risks – risks that are perhaps unknown until the organization is impacted by them. In order to do this successfully, organizations need to view security in the context of the larger picture – one of organizational or enterprise resilience. A resilient approach transforms the basic premise of security – that of "locking down" an asset so that it is free from harm – to one that positions security as a contributor to strengthening the organization's ability to adapt to new risk environments and accomplish its mission. Aiming to make the organization more sensing, agile, and prepared provides a clearer purpose, direction, and context for security management. Looking beyond security (to resiliency) may provide the change in perspective that organizations need to balance security and risk management with the organization's strategic drivers [1].

REFERENCES

[1] Richard A. Caralli and William R. Wilson. "The Challenges of Security Management," Copyright 2005 Carnegie Mellon University. CERT, Software Engineering Institute, Carnegie Mellon University, Pittsburgh, PA 15213-3890, U.S.A., 2006.

Appendix C

LIST OF TOP INTERNET SECURITY IMPLEMENTATION AND DEPLOYMENT COMPANIES

2AB Inc.
1700 Highway 31
Calera, AL 35040
www.2ab.com

2DL
454 West 44th St., Ste. G
New York, NY 10036
www.2dl.net

360 Degree Web Ltd.
2700 Augustine Dr., Ste. 175
Santa Clara, CA 95054
www.360degreeweb.com

3Com
5400 Bayfront Plaza
Santa Clara, CA 94583
www.3com.com

4FrontSecurity Inc.
11710 Plaza America Dr., Ste. 2000
Reston, VA 20190
www.4frontsecurity.com

8e6 Technologies
828 W. Taft Ave.
Orange, CA 92865
www.8e6.com

@mediaservice.net
via R. Cadorna, 47

Torino, TO 10137
Italy
(39) 011-3272100,
fax (39) 011-3246497

a.sys
Mariahilfer Strasse 45
Vienna, 1060
Austria
www.asys.at

ABC Unlimited
324 E. 52nd St.
New York, NY 10022
(212) 593-4606

ABI Software Development
1117-650 Queens Quay West
Toronto, ON M5V 3N2
Canada
www.abisoft.net

Above Security
1919 Lionel-Bertrand Blvd., Ste. 203
Boisbriand, Quebec J7H 1N8
Canada
www.abovesecurity.com

Absolute Software
111 Dunsmuir St., Ste. 800
Vancouver, BC V6B 6A3 Canada
www.absolute.com

Aceltech
100 Gilmore Rd.
Wrentham, MA 02093
www.aceltech.com

ACS Defense Services
6625 Selnick Dr.
Elkridge, MD 21075
www.acsassurance.com

ACT USA
707 E. Thousand Oaks Blvd.
Thousand Oaks, CA 91360
www.actusa.net

ActiveLane
11875 Dublin Blvd., Ste. D272
Dublin, CA 94568
www.activelane.com

Addison-Wesley
75 Arlington St., Ste. 300
Boston, MA 02116
www.awprofessional.com

Adhoc Security
Avenida Machupichu 11
Madrid, 28043
Spain
www.adhoc-security.es

ADTRAN Inc.
901 Explorer Blvd.
Huntsville, AL 35806
www.adtran.com

Advanced Software Products Group Inc.
3185 Horseshoe Dr. South
Naples, FL 34104
www.aspg.com

AEP Systems Inc.
30 Rowes Wharf
Boston, MA 02110
www.aepsystems.com

Aereous
9477 North Territorial
Dexter, MI 48108
www.aereous.com

Aladdin Knowledge Systems
2920 N. Arlington Heights Rd.
Arlington Heights, IL 60004
www.ealaddin.com

Alcatel
26801 W. Agoura Rd.
Calabasas, CA 91301
www.alcatel.com

Alchemedia Technologies
215 W. College St.
Grapevine, TX 76051
www.alchemedia.com

Alexander Allen Associates
Berry House, High St.
Limpsfield, RH8 0DT
United Kingdom
www.alexjobs.com

Aliroo
6 Hanagar St.
Kafar-Saba, 44425
Israel
www.aliroo.com

Allied Technology Group Inc.
1803 Research Blvd., Ste. 601
Rockville, MD 20850
www.alliedtech.com

AlphaShield
5945 Kathleen Ave., 6th Fl.
Burnaby, BC V5H 4J7
Canada
www.alphashield.com

Alta Associates Inc.
8 Bartles Corner Rd., Ste. 21
Flemington, NJ 08822
www.altaassociates.com

Alvaka Networks
5932 Bolsa Ave.
Huntington Beach, CA 92649
www.alvaka.net

AmberPoint Inc.
155 W. Grand Ave. Suite 404
Oakland, CA 94612

T 510-663-6300
F 510-663-6301
http://www.amberpoint.com

Amenaza Technologies Ltd.
550, 1000 8th Ave. SW
Calgary, AB T2P 3M7
Canada
www.amenaza.com

Analysts Int'l
3101 Technology Blvd., Ste. A
Lansing, MI 48910
www.analysts.com

Anfibia
Apdo de Correos 316
Cerdanyola, BCN 08290
Spain
www.anfibia.net

ANI Direct
13610 Midway Rd.
Dallas, TX 75244
www.anidirect.com

ANIXIS
9 Neilson Close
Glenmore Park, NSW 2745
Australia
www.anixis.com

Anti-Virus Information Exchange Network
RR 1
Braeside, ON K0A 1G0
Canada
www.avien.org

Anyware Technology
17837 Rowland St.
City of Industry, CA 91748
www.anywareusa.com

Application Security Inc.
117 E. 24th Street, Suite 2A
New York, NY 10010
www.appsecinc.com

Approva
1953 Gallows Rd., Ste. 525
Vienna, VA 22182
www.approva.net

Arbor Networks
430 Bedford St., Ste. 160
Lexington, MA 02420
www.arbornetworks.com

ARC IAI Inc.
4738 NW Loop 410
San Antonio, TX 78229
www.arcsa.org

Archer Technologies
13200 Metcalf, Ste. 300
Overland Park, KS 66213
www.archer-tech.com

Artech House Publishers
685 Canton St.
Norwood, MA 02062
www.artechhouse.com

Aspelle
41 E. 11th St., 11th Fl.
New York, NY 10003
www.aspelle.com

Assured Business Solutions Ltd.
Nicolford Hall, Norlands Lane
Widnes, Cheshire, WA8 5NA
United Kingdom
www.assuredltd.com

Astaro Corp.
67 S. Bedford St., Ste. 400W
Burlington, MA 01803
www.astaro.com

Audittindo Arin Prima PT
LISACO Bldg., 2nd Fl.,
Jl. Jati Baru Raya No. 28
Jakarta, 10160
Indonesia
www.audittindo.co.id

Authenex Inc.
333 Hegenberger Rd., Ste. 555
Oakland, CA 94621
www.authenex.com

Authentica Inc.
170 Tracer Lane
Waltham, MA 02451
www.authentica.com

Automated Total System Solutions Inc.
201 E. Sandpointe, Ste. 870
Santa Ana, CA 92707
www.atssi.biz

Avatier Inc.
111 Deerwood Rd.
San Ramon, CA 94583
www.avatier.com

Avatria
269 Gorwin Dr., Ste. 104
Holliston, MA 01746
www.avatria.com

Avaya Inc.
211 Mt. Airy Rd.
Basking Ridge, NJ 07920
www.avaya.com

Axiom Corp.
3490 Piedmont Rd., Ste. 1401
Atlanta, GA 30305-1743
www.axiom-corp.com

Backbone Security.com
66 Analomink St.
E. Stroudsburg, PA 18301
www.backbonesecurity.com

BAI Security
1548 N. Bond St., Ste. 112
Naperville, IL 60563
www.baisecurity.net

Baltimore Technologies
39 Parkgate St.
Dublin, 8
Ireland
www.baltimore.com

Barracuda Security Devices Int'l Inc.
22545 Kendrick Loop, Maple Ridge
BC, V2X 9W5
Canada
www.barracudasecurity.com

Barricade Lock, Safe & Alarms
32442 Dahlstrom Ave., Ste. 556, #9
Abbotsford, BC V2T 4Y4
Canada

(604) 825-8928
BearHill Security
411 Waverley Oaks Rd., Ste. 302
Waltham, MA 02452
www.bearhillsecurity.com

BeCrypt Ltd.
56 Dawlish Ave.
London, N13 4HP
United Kingdom
www.becrypt.com

Beginfinite Inc.
4520 St. Joseph Blvd., Ste. 700
Montreal, QC H8T 3P1
Canada
www.beginfinite.com

Bell Group PLC
Roding House, 970 Romford Rd.
London, E12 5LP
United Kingdom
www.bellgroupplc.com

Best Internet Security
26 Theodor Pallady Blvd.
Bucharest, Sector 3 07000
Romania
www.biss.ro

Beyond Security Australia
12 Columbia Way, Baulkham Hills
Sydney, NSW 2153
Australia
www.beyondsecurity.com.au

BigFix Inc.
5915 Hollis St.
Emeryville, CA 94608
www.bigfix.com

BindView Corp.
5151 San Felipe
Houston, TX 77054
www.bindview.com

BioconX Inc.
7400 Metro Blvd., Ste. 425
Minneapolis, MN 55439
www.bioconx.com

Biometric Advisors LLC
508 Twilight Trail, Ste. 101
Richardson, TX 75080
www.biometricadvisors.com

BioNetrix
1953 Gallows Rd., 5th Fl.
Vienna, VA 22182
www.bionetrix.com

BIOVISEC Inc.
575 Lexington Ave., 15th Fl.
New York, NY 10022
www.biovisec.com

Blade Software
3750 Scott St., Ste. 202
San Francisco, CA 94123
www.blade-software.com

Blockade Systems Corp.
2200 Yonge St., Ste. 1400
Toronto, ON M4S 2C6
Canada
www.blockade.com

Blue Lance
1700 W. Loop South, Ste. 1100
Houston, TX 77027
www.bluelance.com

Blue Ridge Networks
14120 Parke Long Ct., Ste. 201
Chantilly, VA 20151
www.blueridgenetworks.com

BLUEMX
318 Bear Hill Rd.
Waltham, MA 02451
www.bluemx.com

Bluesocket Inc.
7 New England Executive Park, 4th Fl.
Burlington, MA 01803
www.bluesocket.com

BMC Software Inc.
2101 CityWest Blvd.
Houston, TX 77042
www.bmc.com

Bodacion Technologies
18-3 Dundee Rd., Ste. 300
Barrington, IL 60010
www.bodacion.com

Boomerang Software
90 Concord Ave.
Belmont, MA 02478
www.boomerangsoftware.com

BorderWare Technologies Inc.
50 Burnhamthorpe Rd. West, Ste. 502
Mississauga, ON L5B 3C2
Canada
www.borderware.com

BostonNetSource Inc.
23 Main St., Ste. 300
Dover, MA 02030-2025
www.bostonnetsource.com

Brasfield Technology Inc.
P.O. Box 380006
Birmingham, AL 35238
www.brasfieldtech.com

Broadcom Corp.
16215 Alton Pkwy.
Irvine, CA 92618
www.broadcom.com

Brocade
1745 Technology Dr.
San Jose, CA 95010
www.brocade.com

BSI Inc.
12110 Sunset Hills Rd., Ste. 140
Reston, VA 20190
www.bsiamericas.com

Business Layers
365 W. Passaic St.
Rochelle Park, NJ 07662
www.businesslayers.com

bvba Woodstone
Houtemsesteenweg 306
Vilvoorde, BE 1800
Belgium
www.woodstone.nu

C-CURE
K. Rogierstraat 27
Antwerpen, B-2000
Belgium
www.c-cure.be

Cadre Computer Resources
255 E. Fifth St., Ste. 1200
Cincinnati, OH 45202
www.cadre.net

Callio Technologies BS7799
740 Galt Ouest, Suite 10
Sherbrooke (Quebec) Canada, J1H 1Z3
Tel: 1 (866) 211-8222
Fax: (819) 820-8222
http://www.callio.com

Callisma Inc.
1550 The Alameda, Ste. 305
San Jose, CA 95126
www.callisma.com

Cameron Communications Inc.
138 Orchard St.
Byfield, MA 01922
www.cameronpr.com

Canada Life Assurance Co.
330 University Ave.
Toronto, ON M5G 1R8
Canada
www.canadalife.com

Cap Gemini Ernst & Young
Gustavslundsvägen 131, P.O. Box 825
Stockholm, SE 16124
Sweden
www.cgey.com

Captus Networks
1680 Tide Ct., Ste. B
Woodland, CA 95776
www.captusnetworks.com

Caradas Inc.
639 Granite St., Ste. 300
Braintree, MA 02184
www.caradas.com

Carmichael Security LLC
215 Broadus St., Ste. 130
Sturgis, MI 49091
www.carmichaelsecurity.com

Catbird Networks
3140 Whisperwoods Ctr.
Northbrook, IL 60062
www.catbird.com

Cavium Networks
2610 Augustine Dr.
Santa Clara, CA 95054
www.cavium.com

CBE Technologies
50 Redfield St.
Boston, MA 02122
www.cbetech.com

Celeris Managed IT-Security
Studbachstrasse 13B
Hinwil, ZH 8340
Switzerland
www.celeris.ch

Celestix Networks Inc.
702 Brown Rd.
Fremont, CA 94539
www.celestix.com

CenturionSoft
2000 P St., Ste. 615
Washington, DC 20036
www.centurionsoft.com

Cenzic Inc.
3425 S. Bascom Ave.
Campbell, CA 95008
www.cenzic.com

CERT Coordination Center
Software Engineering Institute, 4500 Fifth Ave.
Pittsburgh, PA 15217
www.cert.org

Certeca Offshore
Heritage Ct., 41 Athol St.
Douglas, Isle of Man, IM99 1HN
British Isles
www.certeca.com

Certicom Corp.
5520 Explorer Dr., 4th Fl.
Mississauga, ON K2K 3G3
Canada
www.certicom.com

Cetis Ltd.
The Old Rectory, Main St.
Glenfield, Leicester LE3 8DG
United Kingdom
www.cetis.co.uk

CFSEC Security Architects
R. Senador Dantas, 76/502, Centro
Rio de Janeiro, RJ 20031-205, Brazil
www.cfsec.com.br

CGI Information Systems &
Management Consultants Inc.
1410 Blair Pl.
Ottawa, ON K1J 9B9
Canada
www.cgi.ca

Chameleon Consulting Inc.
392 Libbey Industrial Pkwy.
Weymouth, MA 02189
www.chamcon.com

Charon Systems
2 Gibbs Rd.
Toronto, ON M9B 6L6
Canada
www.charon.com

Check Point Software Technologies
3 Lagoon Dr., Ste. 400
Redwood City, CA 94065
www.checkpoint.com

Chrysalis-ITS
1 Chrysalis Way
Ottawa, ON K2G 6P9
Canada
www.chrysalis-its.com

Cigital Inc.
21351 Ridgetop Circle, Ste. 400
Dulles, VA 20166
www.cigital.com

CipherOptics
1401 Sunday Dr., Ste. 103
Raleigh, NC 27607
www.cipheroptics.com

CipherTrust
11475 Great Oaks Way, Ste. 210
Alpharetta, GA 30022
www.ciphertrust.com

Cisco Systems
170 West Tasman Dr.
San Jose, CA 95134
www.cisco.com

CISSP Ltd.
Eakring Rd.
Nottingham & London, NG22 8SX
United Kingdom
www.cissp.co.uk

Citadel Security Software
8750 N. Central Expressway, Ste. 100
Dallas, TX 75231
www.citadel.com

CK Global Inc.
1 Park Plaza, 6th Fl.
Irvine, CA 92614
www.ckcdglobal.com

Clarinet Systems Inc.
44040 Fremont Blvd.
Fremont, CA 94538
www.clarinetsys.com

CLEAN Communications
10201 Lee Highway, Ste. 520
Fairfax, VA 22030
www.cleancommunications.com

Clear Winds Technologies
100 Church Farm Rd.
Pell City, AL 35125
www.clearwinds.net

ClearPath Networks
222 N. Sepulveda Blvd., Ste. 1100
El Segundo, CA 90245
www.clearpathnet.com

Clearswift
15500 SE 30th Pl., Ste. 200
Bellevue, WA 98007
www.clearswift.com

CleverMinds Inc.
175 Maple St., Ste. 16
Stow, MA 01775
www.cleverminds.net

Cloakware Corp.
260 Hearst Way, Ste. 311
Kanata, ON K2L 3H1
Canada
www.cloakware.com

CMI VA Regional Office
4317 Palmer Rd.
McGaheysville, VA 22840
www.cmisales.com

CMS Peripherals Inc.
3095 Redhill Ave.
Costa Mesa, CA 92626
www.cmsproducts.com

Cobion
67 S. Bedford St., Ste. 400W
Burlington, MA 01803
www.cobion.com

Coda Creative Inc.
1230 Preservation Park
Oakland, CA 94612
www.codacreative.com

CodeTek Studios Inc.
1910 N. Federal Dr., Ste. 135
Urbana, IL 61801
www.codetek.com

Cogentric
195 New Hampshire Ave., Ste. 225
Portsmouth, NH 03801
www.cogentric.com

Colubris Networks Inc.
71 Second Ave., 3rd Fl.
Waltham, MA 02451
www.colubris.com

Columbitech
Box 38173
Stockholm, SW 10064
Sweden
www.columbitech.com

Com-Guard.com Inc.
2075 Corte del Nogal, Ste. R
Carlsbad, CA 92009
www.com-guard.com

Commissum
Quay House, 142 Commercial St.
Edinburgh, EH6 6LB
United Kingdom
www.commissum.com

Commonwealth Films Inc.
223 Commonwealth Ave.
Boston, MA 02116
www.commonwealthfilms.com

Communication Horizons LLC
65 High Ridge Rd., Ste. 428
Stamford, CT 06905
www.netlib.com

Communication Technologies Inc.
14151 Newbrook Dr., Ste. 400
Chantilly, VA 20151
www.comtechnologies.com

Communications Security
5315D FM 1960 West, Ste. 152
Houston, TX 77069
www.comsec-c3i.com

Complete Data Services
Corsham Media Park, Westwells Rd.
Corsham, SN13 9GB
United Kingdom
www.completedata.co.uk

Compufit Computer Corp.
485 Washington Ave.
Pleasantville, NY 10570
www.compufit.com

CompuSearch Int'l Division of MRI
1787 Old Earnhardt Rd.

Kannapolis, NC 28083
www.mrkannapolis.com

Computer Associates
One Computer Associates Plaza
Islandia, NY 11749
www.ca.com

Computer Breakthrough Inc.
101 Blanchard Rd.
Cambridge, MA 02138
www.cbi.net

Computer Communications Ltd.
Ste. 1, Academy House,
241 Chertsey Rd., Addlestone
Surrey, KT15 2EW
United Kingdom
www.ccl.co.uk

Computer Forensics NZ Ltd.
17 Albert St., City Central
Auckland, 100 1006
New Zealand
www.datarecovery.co.nz

Computer Peripheral Systems Inc. (CPS)
5096 Bristol Industrial Way , Ste. B
Buford, GA 30518
www.cpscom.com

Computer Sciences Corp.
132 National Business Pkwy., Ste. 400
Annapolis Junction, MD 20701
www.csc.com

Computer Security Institute
600 Harrison St.
San Francisco, CA 94107
www.gocsi.com

CompuVision Inc.
1421 State St., Ste. F
Santa Barbara, CA 93101
www.compuvision.com

ComTrust LLC
17570 West 12 Mile
Southfield, MI 48076
www.comtrust.com

Configuresoft Inc.
800 Research Dr., Ste. 150
Woodland Park, CO 80863
www.configuresoft.com

Connected Corp.
100 Pennsylvania Ave.
Framingham, MA 01701
www.connected.com

CONQWEST Inc.
84 October Hill Rd.
Holliston, MA 01746
www.conqwest.com

CONSUL Risk Management
30 Great Rd.
Acton, MA 01720
www.consul.com

Contingency Planning & OutSourcing Inc.
4530 Jackson Creek Rd.
Winnsboro, SC 29180
www.cpotracker.com

ContingenZ Corp.
227 Fowling St.
Playa del Rey, CA 90293
www.contingenz.com

Control Break Int'l
Peppelkade 46
Houten, UT 3992 AK
The Netherlands
www.safeboot.com

CopyTele Inc.
900 Walt Whitman Rd.
Melville, NY 11747
www.copytele.com

Core Competence Inc.
344 Valley View
Chester Springs, PA 19425
www.corecom.com

Core Security Technologies
44 Wall St., 12th Fl.
New York, NY 10005
www.coresecurity.com

Coresecure Inc.
318 Bear Hill Rd.
Waltham, MA 02451
www.coresecure.com

Corporate Technologies USA Inc., VICM
2000 44th St. SW, 1st Fl.
Fargo, ND 58103
www.corptech.net

Cosaint
1106 Harris Ave., Ste. 202
Bellingham, WA 98225
www.cosaint.net

Counterpane Internet Security
19050 Pruneridge Ave.
Cupertino, CA 95014
www.counterpane.com

Courion Corp.
1881 Worcester Rd.
Framingham, MA 01701
www.courion.com

CPLUS Multimedia Inc.
442 Young
Saint John, NB E2M 2V2
Canada
www.cplus.ca

Cranite Systems Inc.
6620 Via Del Oro, 2nd Fl.
San Jose, CA 95119
www.cranite.com

Credant Technologies
15305 Dallas Pkwy., Ste. 1010
Addison, TX 75001
www.credant.com

Critical IP
11250 Waples Mill Rd., Ste. 300
South Tower
Fairfax, VA 22030
www.criticalip.com

Critical Watch
14800 Quorum Dr., Ste. 330
Dallas, TX 75240
www.criticalwatch.com

Crius Inc.
4938 Hampden Lane, Ste. 350
Bethesda, MD 20814
www.crius.com

Crossbeam Systems
200 Baker Ave.
Concord, MA 01742
www.crossbeamsystems.com

Crown Technology
1900 Dunbarton, Ste. G
Jackson, MS 39216
www.crown-technology.net

Crucial Security Inc.
4094 Majestic Lane, Suite 320
Fairfax, VA 22033
www.crucialsecurity.com

Cryptek Inc.
1501 Moran Rd.
Sterling, VA 20166
www.cryptek.com

CRYPTOCard Corp.
300 March Rd., Ste. 304
Ottawa, ON K2K 2E2
Canada
www.cryptocard.com

Cryptomathic
Kannikegade 14
Aarhus, DK 8000
Denmark
www.cryptomathic.com

CryptoNet Spa
Via Vespucci, 2
Milan, MI 20124
Italy
www.cryptonet.it

CTitek Inc.
2670 Clarkson Rd.
Chesterfield, MO 63017
www.ctitek.com

Cyber Criminals Most Wanted LLC
P.O. Box 2878
La Belle, FL 33975
www.ccmostwanted.com

Cyber-Ark Software Inc.
270 Bridge St.
Dedham, MA 02026
www.cyber-ark.com

CyberGuard Corp.
2000 W. Commercial Blvd., Ste. 200
Ft. Lauderdale, FL 33309
www.cyberguard.com

CyberNet Defense
5807 Babcock Rd., Ste. 163
San Antonio, TX 78240
www.cybernetdefense.com

CyberSec Inc.
214 Jardin Vista
San Antonio, TX 78258
www.cybersec-inc.com

CyberShield Networks
563 Baywood Dr. South, Ste. 104
Dunedin, FL 34698
www.cybershieldnetworks.com

Cylant
121 Sweet Ave.
Moscow, ID 83843
www.cylant.com

Cylink Corp.
3131 Jay St.
Santa Clara, CA 95054
www.cylink.com

Daon
345 Park Ave., 17th Fl.
New York, NY 10154-0037
www.daon.com

Data Processing Sciences Corp.
10810 Kenwood Rd.
Cincinnati, OH 45242
www.dpsciences.com

Data Systems Analysts Inc.
10400 Eaton Pl., Ste. 500
Fairfax, VA 22030
www.dsainc.com

Datakey
407 West Travelers Trail
Minneapolis, MN 55337
www.datakey.com

DataMark Technologies Pte Ltd.
100 Jurong East, Ste. 21
609602 Singapore
www.datamark-tech.com

Dataway
180 Redwood St., Ste. 300
San Francisco, CA 94102
www.dataway.com

Datum-Trusted Time Division
10 Maguire Rd.
Lexington, MA 02421
www.datum.com/tt

Decru Inc.
275 Shoreline Dr., Ste. 450
Redwood City, CA 95065
www.decru.com

DeepNines Technologies
14643 Dallas Pkwy., Ste. 150
Dallas, TX 75254
www.deepnines.com

Deersoft Inc.
1660 Amphlett Blvd., Ste. 122
San Mateo, CA 94402
www.deersoft.com

Deloitte & Touche LLP
1633 Broadway
New York, NY 10019-6754
www.deloitte.com

Deloitte Consulting
(Soon to become Braxton)
25 Broadway
New York, NY 10004-1010
www.dc.com

Demarc Security Inc.
232 Anacapa St.
Santa Barbara, CA 93101
www.demarc.com

DigiDyne Inc.
2294 32nd Ave., Lachine
Quebec, H8T 3H4
Canada
www.digidyne.ca

DigiGAN
733 Summer St., 6th Fl.
Stamford, CT 06901
www.digigan.com

Digilog UK Ltd.
4 Ingate Pl.
London, SW8 3NS
United Kingdom
www.digilog.org

DigiSAFE Pte Ltd.
100 Jurong East, Ste. 21
609602 Singapore
www.digisafe.com

Digital DataTrust
309 Pirkle Ferry Rd., Ste. B-100
Atlanta, GA 30040
www.digitaldatatrust.com

Digital Security Int'l
2703 Arlington Blvd., Ste. 101
Arlington, VA 22201
www.dsiencryption.com

Digital Services Co.
96 Flintridge Dr.
Holbrook, NY 11741
www.computercrimeconsultants.com

Digital V6
4118 14th Ave., Unit 4
Markham, ON L3R 0J3
Canada
www.digitalv6.com

DigitalPersona Inc.
805 Veterans Blvd., Ste. 301
Redwood City, CA 94063
www.digitalpersona.com

Direct Corporate Source Inc.
310 N. Queen St., Ste. 101S
Toronto, ON M9C 5K4

Canada
(416) 239-9550,
fax (416) 239-4469

DirSec Inc.
5417 S. Hannibal Way, Ste. 100
Centennial, CO 80015
www.dirsec.com

Discount Safe
117 Grand Ave.
Palisades Park, NJ 07650
www.mediasafes.com

Diversinet Corp.
2225 Sheppard Ave. East, Ste. 1700
Toronto, ON M2J 5C2
Canada
www.diversinet.com

DLT Solutions Inc.
360 Herndon Pkwy., Ste. 700
Herndon, VA 20170
www.dlt.com

DogRiley
61 Cameron Ave.
Somerville, MA 02144
www.dogriley.com

DOMUS IT Security Laboratory
2220 Walkley Rd.
Ottawa, ON K1G 5L2
Canada
www.domusitsl.com

DynTek Inc.
18881 Von Karman Ave., Ste. 250
Irvine, CA 92612
www.dyntek.com

DYONYX
1235 North Loop West, Ste. 206
Houston, TX 77008
www.dyonyx.com

E*Maze Networks
Via Flavia 23/1
Trieste, TS 34148 Italy
www.emaze.net

E-Certify
350 Burnhamthorpe Rd. West, Ste. 302
Mississauga, ON L5B 3J1
Canada
www.e-certify.com

e-Security Inc.
295 Barnes Blvd.
Rockledge, FL 32955

E-witness Inc.
2950 Keele St., Ste. C
Toronto, ON M3M 2H2
Canada
www.e-witness.ca

Easy i Inc.
P.O. Box 1665
El Segundo, CA 90245
www.easyi.com

Ecora Software
500 Spaulding Tpke.
Portsmouth, NH 03802-3070
www.ecora.com

ECsoft
Stortorvet 10
Oslo, 0171
Norway
wwww.ecsoft.com

Ecutel Inc.
4401 Ford Ave., Ste. 1400
Alexandria, VA 22302
www.ecutel.com

Edgeos
P.O. Box 11594
Chandler, AZ 85248
www.edgeos.com

Edwards & Associates
P.O. Box 3151
Las Cruces, NM 88003
(505) 263-5796,
fax (435) 303-9474

eEye Digital Security
One Columbia
Aliso Viejo, CA 92656
www.eeye.com

Egroup Technologies Ltd.
Mourouzi 6th St. Athens Ct., Ste. 53
P.O. Box 27430
Nicosia, 1645
Cyprus
www.egroup.com.cy

ElcomSoft Co. Ltd.
2-171 Generala Antonova St.
Moscow, RU 117279
Russia
www.elcomsoft.com

Electronic Data Systems (EDS)
5400 Legacy Dr.
Plano, TX 75024
www.eds.com

Electronic Engineering Systems
1200 N. Battlefield Blvd., Ste. 120
Chesapeake, VA 23320
www.eescom.com

Element
Stoomtuigstraat 6
Gits, Wvl 8830
Belgium
www.element.be

Elron Software Inc.
7 New England Executive Park
Burlington, MA 01803
www.elronsoftware.com

Elytra Enterprises Inc.
5370 Canotek Rd., Unit 1
Ottawa, ON K1J 9E6
Canada
www.elytra.com

EMA Inc.
1501 W. Fountainhead Pkwy., Ste. 480
Tempe, AZ 85282
www.ema-inc.com

Emagined Security
2816 San Simeon Way
San Carlos, CA 94070
www.emagined.com

Emprise Technologies
3117 Washington Pike
Bridgeville, PA 15017
www.emprisetech.com

Encore Networks
45472 Holiday Dr.
Dulles, VA 20166
www.encorenetworks.com

Encryption Software Inc.
595 Bellemont Ct.
Duluth, GA 30097
www.encrsoft.com

Encryptopia
24 Center St.
N. Walpole, NH 03609
www.encryptopia.com

Endace Measurement Systems
Level 1, 13 Ronwood Ave., Manukau City
Auckland, NI 1702
New Zealand
www.endace.com

Enspherics
5675 DTC Blvd.
Greenwood Village, CO 80111
www.enspherics.com

Ensure Technologies
3526 W. Liberty Rd.
Ann Arbor, MI 48103
www.ensuretech.com

Ensuredmail
1708 Lovering Ave., Ste. 202
Wilmington, DE 19806
www.ensuredmail.com

Enterasys Networks
35 Industrial Way
Rochester, NH 03866-5005
www.enterasys.com

Entercept Security Technologies
1740 Technology Dr., Ste. 600
San Jose, CA 95110
www.entercept.com

Enterprise Risk Management
801 Brickell Ave., Ste. 900

Miami, FL 33131
www.emrisk.com

Enterprise Security & Availability
Group LLC (ESAAG)
3055 Treat Blvd., Ste. 37
Concord, CA 94518
www.esaag.com

Entrust Inc.
16633 Dallas Pkwy., Ste. 800
Addison, TX 75001
www.entrust.com

Equant
12490 Sunrise Valley Dr.
Mailstop VARESF0257
Reston, VA 20196
www.equant.com

Eracom Technologies
1098 Melody Lane, Ste. 301
Roseville, CA 95678
www.eracom-tech.com

Ernst & Young
5 Times Square
New York, NY 10036
www.ey.com

eSecurityOnline
12 West 12th St., Ste. 310
Kansas City, MO 64105
www.esecurityonline.com

ESET LLC
1317 Ynez Pl., Ste. C
Coronado, CA 92118
www.eset.com

eSoft Inc.
295 Interlocken Blvd.
Broomfield, CO 80021
www.esoft.com

ESTec Systems Corp.
17510 102nd Ave., 2nd Fl.
Edmonton, AB T5S 1K2
Canada
www.security.estec.com

Etek Int'l Corp.
7000 NW 52nd St.
Miami, FL 33166
www.etek.com

Eugene Barstow
2253 Stump Dr.
Oroville, CA 95966
(530) 699-0147

Eutron
via Gandhi 12
Treviolo, BG 24048
Italy
www.eutron.com

eVestigations Inc.
537 W. Boot Rd.
West Chester, PA 19380
www.itcso.com

Evidian
BP 68 Rue Jean-Jaurès
Les Clayes sous Bois, 78340
France
www.evidian.com

Evincible
14325 Willard Dr., Ste. 102
Chantilly, VA 20151
www.evincible.com

Executive Software
7590 N. Glenoaks Blvd.
Burbank, CA 91504
www.execsoft.com

Exodus, a Cable & Wireless Service
4650 Old Ironsides Dr.
Santa Clara, CA 95054
www.exodus.net

Extreme Logic
Two Concourse Pkwy., Ste. 500
Atlanta, GA 30328
www.extremelogic.com

F-Secure Inc.
675 N. 1st St., 5th Fl.
San Jose, CA 95112
www.f-secure.com

F5 Networks
401 Elliott Ave. W.
Seattle, WA 98119
www.f5.com

FatPipe Networks
4455 S. 700 East, 1st Fl.
Salt Lake City, UT 84107
www.fatpipeinc.com

Federal Trade Commission
600 Pennsylvania Ave. NW, NJ-2267
Washington, D.C. 20580
www.ftc.gov/infosecurity

Feitian Technologies
3F., No. 5 Building Jimen Hotel
Xueyuan Rd., Haidian District
Beijing, CN 100088
People's Republic of China
www.ftsafe.com

FERROD Systems
P.O. Box 300-244, JFK Airport Sta.
Jamaica, NY 11430
www.ferrodsys.com

Fifth Generation (India) Ltd.
1A, Jamasji Apartment, Sleater Rd.
Bombay, 400007 India
www.fgil.net

FilterLogix
3320 Peterson Rd., Ste. 105
Lawrence, KS 66049
www.filterlogix.com

Finjan Software
1720 Route 34, P.O. Box 1230
Wall, NJ 07719
www.finjan.com

First Consulting Group
111 W. Ocean Blvd., Ste. 1000
Long Beach, CA 90802
www.fcg.com

FishNet Security
1710 Walnut St.
Kansas City, MO 64108
www.fishnetsecurity.com

Flatrock Inc.
1505 SE Gideon, Ste. 600
Portland, OR 97202
www.flatrock.com

Fly-By-Day Consulting Inc.
4642 Bentley Pl.
Duluth, GA 30096
www.verysecurelinux.com

Forensics Explorers, a division of CTX
8229 Boone Blvd., Ste. 200
Vienna, VA 22182
www.forensicsexplorers.com

ForeScout Technologies Inc.
2755 Campus Dr., Ste. 115
San Mateo, CA 94403
www.forescout.com

Fortinet Inc.
3333 Octavius Dr.
Santa Clara, CA 95054
www.fortinet.com

Fortress Technologies
4025 Tampa Rd., Ste. 1111
Oldsmar, FL 34677
www.fortresstech.com

Forum Systems
95 Sawyer Rd., Ste. 110
Boston, MA 02453
www.forumsys.com

Foundstone Inc.
27201 Puerta Real, Ste. 400
Mission Viejo, CA 92691
www.foundstone.com

Fourth House Security Inc.
16467 Turnbury Oak Dr.
Odessa, FL 33556
www.4hsinc.com

Fox-IT
Haagweg 137
Rijswijk, ZH 2281 AG
The Netherlands
www.fox-it.com

Fujitsu Consulting
3141 Fairview Park Dr.

Falls Church, VA 22042
www.fujitsuconsulting.com

Funk Software Inc.
222 Third St.
Cambridge, MA 02142
www.funk.com

FutureSoft
12012 Wickchester Lane, Suite 600
Houston, TX 77079
www.dciseries.com

G. Swindon Consulting
6227 Drifter Dr.
San Jose, CA 95123
(408) 590-4199

Garcia & Associates LLC
271 E. Como Ave.
Columbus, OH 43202
www.garcia-associates.com

GatewayDefender LLC
5693 N. Main St.
Sylvania, OH 43560
www.gatewaydefender.com

GeCAD Software
223 Mihai Bravu Bd., Sector 3
Bucharest, RO 743391
Romania
www.ravantivirus.com

General Dynamics Decision Systems
8220 E. Roosevelt St., Mail Drop R7211
Scottsdale, AZ 85257
www.gd-decisionsystems.com

Genuity
225 Presidential Way
Woburn, MA 01801
www.genuity.com

GEOBRIDGE Corp.
11800 Sunrise Valley Dr., Ste. 400
Reston, VA 20191
www.geobridge.net

GeoTrust Inc.
40 Washington St., Ste. 20
Wellesley Hills, MA 02481
www.geotrust.com

Getronics Government Solutions
2525 Network Place
Herndon, VA 20171
www.getronicsgov.com

GFI Software Ltd.
5, Princeton Mews, 167-169 London Rd., Kingston-upon-Thames
Surrey, KT2 6PT
United Kingdom
www.gfi.com

Gianus Technologies Inc.
118 E. 60th St.
New York, NY 10022
www.phantomts.com

Gibraltar Software Inc.
1253 Lakeside Dr., Ste. 300
Sunnyvale, CA 94085
www.gilbraltarsoft.com

Gilian Technologies
1300 Island Dr., Ste. 102
Redwood City, CA 94065
www.gilian.com

Global DataGuard
5429 LBJ Freeway, Ste. 750
Dallas, TX 75240
www.globaldataguard.com

Global Systems
Information Exchange Corp.
11718 Critton Circle
Woodbridge, VA 22192-1019
www.ig6.org

Global Technologies Group Inc.
3108 Columbia Pike, Ste. 200
Arlington, VA 22204
www.gtgi.com

Global Technology Associates Inc.
3505 Lake Lynda Dr., Ste. 109
Orlando, FL 32817
www.gta.com

Gold Wire Technology
411 Waverley Oaks Rd., Ste. 3-31
Waltham, MA 02452
www.goldwiretech.com

Government Technology Solutions (gTech)
4110 Business Dr., Ste. A
Shingle Springs, CA 95682-7204
www.gtechonline.com

Granite Communications Inc.
116 School St.
Boylston, MA 01505
www.graniteco.com

Granite Island Group
127 Eastern Ave., Ste. 291
Gloucester, MA 01931
www.tscm.com

Greenidea Inc.
950 Page St.
San Francisco, CA 94117
www.greenidea.com

Greenwich Technology Partners
123 Main St., 8th Fl.
White Plains, NY 10601
www.greenwichtech.com

Griffin Technologies LLC
916 Massachusetts St., Ste. 200
Lawrence, KS 66044
www.griffintechnology.com

GROUP Software
321 Fortune Blvd.
Milford, MA 01757
www.group-software.com

Group1Internet
6830 Via Del Oro, Ste. 108
San Jose, CA 95119
www.group1internet.com

Guadagno Consulting
4462 Latting Rd.
Shortsville, NY 14548
(585) 703-6700

Guarded Networks Inc.
2525 Embassy Dr. South, Ste. 10
Cooper City, FL 33025
www.guardednetworks.com

GuardedNet
5901-A Peachtree Dunwoody Road, Suite 275
Atlanta, GA 30328
www.guarded.net

Guardent
75 Third Ave.
Waltham, MA 02451
www.guardent.com

Guardian Digital Inc.
165 Chestnut St., 2nd Fl.
Allendale, NJ 07401
www.guardiandigital.com

Guardian Technologies LLC
2325 Dulles Corner Blvd., Ste. 500
Herndon, VA 20171
www.guardiantek.com

Guidance Software
572 E. Green St., Ste. 300
Pasadena, CA 91101
www.guidancesoftware.com

Hackademia Inc.
2010 Crow Canyon Pl.
San Ramon, CA 94583
www.hackademia.com

Harriague & Associates
Bedoya 695
Cordoba, Cap 5000
Argentina
www.harriague.com.ar

Harris Corp.
STAT Operations Center, P.O. Box 8300
Melbourne, FL 32902-8300
www.statonline.com

Hart Systems
26904 West 12 Mile Rd.
Southfield, MI 48034
(248) 350-2409,
fax (248) 350-2409

HartGregory Group Inc.
20026 NE 190th Ct.
Woodinville, WA 98072
www.hartgregorygroup.com

HearSeeLearn
P.O. Box 98600
Tacoma, WA 98498-0600
www.hearseelearn.com

Hervè Schauer Consultants
4 bis, Rue de la Gare
Levallois-Perret, FR 92300
France
www.hsc.fr

Hewlett Packard
19111 Prunridge Ave.
Cupertino, CA 95014
www.hp.com

HexaLock Ltd.
P.O. Box 5007
Basking Ridge, NJ 07920
www.hexalock.com

High Tower Software
26870 Laguna Hills Dr., Ste. 200
Aliso Viejo, CA 92656
www.hightowersoftware.com

Holocon Inc.
2617 Countrywood Rd.
Raleigh, NC 27615
www.holocon.net

HP Ltd.
2 Kelvin Close, Birchwood Science Park N.
Warrington, WA3 7PB
United Kingdom
www.hp.com/security/index-windows.html

IATAC
3190 Fairview Park Dr.
Falls Church, VA 22042
www.dtic.mil

MailDefense: 6A
ibg (Internet Business Group)
201 Liberty Hill
Bedford, NH 03110
www.ibg.com

IBM
11501 Burnet Rd.
Austin, TX 78758
www.ibm.com

IDANETWORK
580 Lake Forest Dr., Ste. 1
Coppell, TX 75019
www.hipaaworld.com

Identico Systems
15 Charron Ave.
Nashua, NH 03063
www.identicosystems.com

Identix Inc.
3975 Fair Ridge Dr.
Fairfax, VA 22033
www.identix.com

IDG World Expo
3 Speen St., Ste. 320
Framingham, MA 01701
www.idgworldexpo.com

IGLOO Security Inc.
143-42 Wonbang Bldg. 6F, Samsung-Dong
Kangnam-Gu, Seoul 135-090
South Korea
www.igloosec.com

IGX Global
389 Main St.
Hackensack, NJ 07601
www.igxglobal.com

Imaging Automation
25 Constitution Dr.
Bedford, NH 03110
www.imagingauto.com

Imperito
1400 Fashion Island Blvd., Ste. 160
San Mateo, CA 94404
www.imperito.com

Inarma
70 W. Madison St., Ste. 1400
Chicago, IL 60602
www.inarma.com

Independent Commerce
301 30th St. NE, Ste. 110
Auburn, WA 98002
www.independentcommerce.com

Indicii Salus Ltd.
Indicii Salus House, 2 Bessborough Gardens

London, SW1V 2JE
United Kingdom
www.indiciisalus.com

InfoExpress Inc.
170 S. Whisman Rd., Ste. B
Mountain View, CA 94041
www.infoexpress.com

InfoGard Laboratories
641 Higuera St., 2nd Fl.
San Luis Obispo, CA 93401
www.infogard.com

Infoliance Inc.
101 First St., Ste. 725
Los Altos, CA 94022
www.infoliance.com

Information Security Architects
152 Hendrik Verwoerd Dr., Randburg
P.O. Box 78166
Johannesburg, Sandton 2146
South Africa
www.isa.co.za

Information Security Corp.
1141 Lake Cook Rd., Ste. D
Deerfield, IL 60015
www.infoseccorp.com

Information Security Magazine
85 Astor Ave., Ste. 2
Norwood, MA 02062
www.infosecuritymag.com

Information Security Solutions
Berkeley Square House, 2nd Fl.
Berkeley Square, Mayfair
London, W1J 6BD
United Kingdom
www.informationsecuritysolutions.com

Information Systems Audit and
Control Association
3701 Algonquin Rd., Ste. 1010
Rolling Meadows, IL 60008
www.isaca.org

InfoScreen Inc.
118 Prospect St., 2nd Fl.
Ithaca, NY 14850
www.infoscreen.com

InfoSec Group
264 Carroll St. NW
Washington, D.C. 20012
www.infosecgroup.com

InfoSec Law Group PC
101 First St., Ste. 725
Los Altos, CA 94022
www.infoseclaw.com

InfoSysSec
192 S. Benjamin Dr.
West Chester, PA 19382
www.infosyssec.com

InfoTek Security Consultants
Linden House, Willisham
Ipswich, Suffolk IP8 4SP
United Kingdom
www.infotek.co.uk

Infowest Systems Inc.
501-1340 W. 12th Ave.
Vancouver, BC V6H 1M5
Canada
www.infowest.ca

Infrasafe Inc.
1707 Orlando Central Pkwy., Ste. 350
Orlando, FL 32809
www.infrasafe.com

InfSecT Corp.
9051 Baltimore National Pike, Ste. 3E
Ellicott City, MD 21042
www.e-capsule.net

Ingrian Networks
475 Broadway St.
Redwood City, CA 94063
www.ingrian.com

INRANGE Global Consulting
11611 N. Meridian St., Ste. 800
Carmel, IN 46032
www.igc.inrange.com

Inside the Box Inc.
2307 Faith Lane
Aurora, IL 60504
www.insidethebox.com

Insight Consulting Ltd.
5 The Quintet, Churchfield Rd.,
Walton on Thames
Surrey, KT12 2TZ
United Kingdom
www.insight.co.uk

Integration Specialists Inc.
3001 Executive Dr., Ste. 180
Clearwater, FL 33762
www.isi-fl.com

Intelligent Connections LLC
25900 Greenfield Rd., Ste. 501
Oak Park, MI 48237
www.intelligentconnections.net

Intellitactics Inc.
305 King St. West, Ste. 800
Kitchener, ON N2G 1B9
Canada
www.intellitactics.com

Intense School
8211 W. Broward Blvd., Ste. 210
Ft. Lauderdale, FL 33324
www.intenseschool.com

Intergraph Solutions Group
170 Graphics Dr.
Madison, AL 35758
www.intergraph.com

Interliant Inc.
2 Manhattanville Rd.
Purchase, NY 10577
www.interliant.com

International Disaster Recovery Association (IDRA)
P.O. Box 4515
Shrewsbury, MA 01545
www.idra.com

International Information Systems Security Certification Consortium (ISC)2
860 Worcester Rd., Ste. 101
Framingham, MA 07102
www.isc2.org

International Security Technology Inc.
99 Park Ave., 11th Fl.
New York, NY 10016
www.ist-usa.com

Internet Security Blanket Corporation (ISBlanket)
Post Office Box 390841
Snellville, Georgia 30039
www.isblanket.com

Internet Security Systems
6303 Barfield Rd.
Atlanta, GA 30328
www.iss.net

Internet Threat Management
Technology LLC
5940 Tahoe Dr., Ste. 110
Grand Rapids, MI 49546
www.threatsmart.com

Interpact Inc.
11511 Pine St.
Seminole, FL 33772
www.getinsightnow.com

InterSec Communications Inc.
Grand Oak Business Park
860 Blue Gentian Rd., Ste. 245
Eagan, MN 55121
www.intersec.com

Interwork Technologies Inc.
294 Albert St., Ste. 601
Ottawa, ON K1P 6E6
Canada
www.interwork.com

Intranode Software Technologies
4 Place de Brazzaville
Paris, 75015
France
www.intranode.com

Intrusion Inc.
1101 E. Arapaho Rd.
Richardson, TX 75081
www.intrusion.com

IntruVert Networks
3200-A N. First St.
San Jose, CA 95134
www.intruvert.com

Iomart
Todd Campus
West of Scotland Science Park

Glasgow, Scotland G20 0XA
United Kingdom
www.netintelligence.com

IOTM
A52 Shiv Kirti Chincholi Bunder Rd.
Malad W
Mumbai, Maharashtra 400064
India
(91) 22-8738795

IPLocks Inc.
3393 Octavius Dr.
Santa Clara, CA 95054
www.iplocks.com

Iqon
17 Lorong Kilat, #02-10, Kilat Ct.
598139 Singapore
www.iqon-asia.com

Iridian Technologies Inc.
121 Whittendale Dr., Ste. B
Moorestown, NJ 08057
www.iridiantech.com

iSolve Ltd.
78A King St.
Knutsford, WA16 6ED
United Kingdom
www.i-solve.co.uk

Itillious Inc.
980 Hammond Dr., Ste. 850
Atlanta, GA 30328
www.itillious.com

ITSEC Associates Ltd.
24 Woodfield Rd., Oadby
Leicester, LE2 4HP
United Kingdom
www.itseca.com

ITSecure
32 Queen St.
St. Kilda East, VIC 3183
Australia
www.itsecure.com.au

J. Markowitz Consultants
5801 N. Sheridan Rd., Ste. 19A
Chicago, IL 60660
www.jmarkowitz.com

Janteknology Pty Ltd.
12 Columbia Way
Baulkham Hills, NSW 2153
Australia
www.janteknology.com.au

JANUS Associates Inc.
1010 Summer St.
Stamford, CT 06905
www.janusassociates.com

Jaycor
7929 Jones Branch Dr., Ste. G01S
McLean, VA 22102
www.jaycor.com

Jefferson Wells Int'l
825 N. Jefferson St., Ste. 200
Milwaukee, WI 53202
www.jeffersonwells.com

JETNET Internetworking Services Inc.
333 Preston St., Ste. 300
Ottawa, ON K1S 5N4
Canada
www.jetnet.ca

Jitlia Solutions Inc.
17100 Gillette Ave.
Irvine, CA 92614
www.jitlia.com

Joint Interoperability Test Command (JITC)
101 Strauss Ave., Bldg. 900
Indian Head, MD 20640
http://jitc.fhu.disa.mil

JTR Information Security Associates
4918 E. Cooper St.
Tucson, AZ 85711
(520) 881-4979

Kaspersky Labs
10 Geroyev Panfilovtcev St.
Moscow, 123363
Russia
www.kaspersky.com

Kasten Chase
5100 Orbitor Dr.
Mississauga, ON L4W 4Z4
Canada
www.kastenchase.com

KaVaDo Inc.
1450 Broadway, 18th Fl.
New York, NY 10018
www.kavado.com

Kensington Technology Group
2000 Alameda de las Pulgas
San Mateo, CA 94403
www.kensington.com

Kinder Shield Labs
6780 Northern Blvd., Ste. 100
E. Syracuse, NY 13057
www.kindermail.com

Appendix D

LIST OF INTERNET SECURITY PRODUCTS

Table D-1. List of Internet security products/tools and vendors/companies.

Product/Tool/Vendor	URL	Description
# Ad Zapper Popup Blocker	http://www.adzapper.net/	User friendly Popup Killer. Easily configured to allow popups from specific sites.
# Adeptech Systems, Inc	http://www.adeptech.com/	Provides information security, and network architecture services, and security analysis. Company profile, recent projects, and resource links.
# Altiris	http://www.altiris.com/	Integrated IT lifecycle management. Specializing in XP migration, patch management, backup and recovery, asset management, lifecycle management, imaging, software inventory, hardware inventory, software delivery, server deployment, systems management, and software license management.
# Apreo Inc.	http://www.surfcontrol.com/	Provides productivity tools to manage use filtering and endpoint security for games, MP3s, P2P swapping programs, or any file even if renamed to preserve network performance and security.
# Beepcard Inc.	http://www.beepcard.com/	Wireless authentication and verification systems for security and mass-market applications. Developed Comdot, a self-powered electronic card that performs wireless authentication without using a card reader.

# Argus	http://argus.tcp4me.com/	A system and network monitoring application which provides a facility for monitoring nearly all aspects of an Internet connected network.
# Ben's Online Web Utilities	http://www.phaster.com/find_info_net_traffic.shtml	Useful web interface for other network utilities, net traffic, and exploit search engine.
# Breach Security, Inc.	http://www.breach.com/	Provider of web application network security software, Breach Security products protect enterprise applications with an intrusion detection system (IDS). The Breach Adaption network security product is an automated and adaptive intrusion prevention system for SSL and security compliance.
# Cenzic, Inc.	http://www.cenzic.com/	Hailstorm Enterprise Solution has two product lines for Security Quality Assurance: Hailstorm Web and Hailstorm Protocol Modeler. Overview of products, services, and companies profile.
# Comodogroup	http://www.comodogroup.com/	Offers a range of internet security products, including SSL certificates, firewall, web servers, antivirus, and anti-spam.
# Create Accounts	http://www.createaccounts.com/	Free tool to create password protected web-site areas.
# Cypherpunks Tonga	http://www.cypherpunks.to/	A center for research and development of cypherpunk projects such as smartcards, onion routing, pgp, secure network tunnels, and anonymous services. Requires Secure Socket Layer capable browser.
# DeepFreeze	http://www.faronics.com/index.asp	Software which can help keep a stable system and prevent against viruses.
# DNA Key Security Company	http://www.dna-key.com/	Offers systems for networking security, authentication and access control.
# e-fense, Inc.	http://www.e-fense.com/	Provides full-life cycle network security support integrating security prevention and maintenance services with investigative and legal expertise.
# Firewall Test	http://www.auditmypc.com/	Online and downloadable tools that test for security vulnerabilities by scanning ports, checking browser security, and looking for spyware. Firewall and popup blocker downloads also available.

# Free Windows Firewall Downloads	http://www.iopus.com/guides/freefirewalls.htm	Attempts to list all free firewall software downloads on the Internet for the Windows Operating system.
# Gibson Research Corporation	http://www.grc.com/	Internet security resource featuring Shields Up-tests PC's ports for resistance against hacking and a CIH virus recovery tool.
# Gilian Technologies	http://www.breach.com/	Hardware solution that prevents web servers from publishing unauthorised or altered content, protecting against web site mutilation type attacks. Product and company information, customer case studies and contact details.
# GuardPrivacy	http://www.guardprivacy.com/	Offers popup blocker, IP blocker, port blocker, and other tools.
# Hackbusters	http://www.hackbusters.net/	Distributes the Linux tool LaBrea, a tarpit for worms that use IP scanning for spreading.
# Internet Guard	http://www.softforces.com/iguard.htm	Changes hidden settings in Windows registry in order to protect TCP/IP stack. This utility protects both server and desktop computers.
# iTools	http://www.itools.com/internet/	Collection of useful Internet tools
# Kasten Chase Applied Research Limited	http://www.kastenchase.com/	Assurency CipherShare enables any organization to protect, share and work with sensitive information, which is protected on the server, on the desktop and during transmission.
# LaBrea	http://www.hackbusters.net/LaBrea/	Application that puts unused IP addresses on a network to use, creating a "tarpit" which can stop or slow down scans of network address space.
# LockDown 2000	http://www.vastcity.com/lockdown2000/	Privacy and security software for Windows platforms, available to download.
# Magneto Software	http://www.magnetosoft.com/	Security software and development tools.
# MereSurfer	http://www.meresoft.com/products/meresurfer/	Stops pop-ups, erases tracks of Internet activity while web surfing and protects PC from DoS attacks.
# NetWolves	http://www.netwolves.com/	Makes Internet gateway solutions for LAN-to-Internet connectivity. The FoxBox is an e-business platform for distance learning, data-security, VPN networks.

# Network Security Technology Co.	http://www.nst.com.tw/	The NST product family includes complete PKI system operations, security applications and hardware cryptographic devices to secure business conduct over computer networks, whether for Internet, extranet or intranet applications.
# Online Security Guide	http://www.onlinesecurity-guide.com/	Find tools, software and articles to increase your online computer security.
# Oracle Phaos Products	http://www.oracle.com/technology/products/id_mgmt/phaos/index.html	Tools for enabling identity management security and standards-based cryptographic protocols.
# Phishing.net	http://www.phishing.net/	Anti-phishing software.
# Physq Hotlink Reverser	http://www.physq.com/	Physq offers scripts for webmasters. Hotlink Reverser is an advanced script that will protect your content against hotlinking.
# Pop Up Blocker test	http://www.auditmypc.com/freescan/popup-blocking.asp	Checks a PC for popups that may slip by the browser. Instructions on fixing discovered problems are provided.
# Proginet	http://www.proginet.com/	Enterprise-wide password synchronization, management and single sign-on. Secure, reliable, cost-effective file transfers of mission-critical data over your network and/or the Internet.
# Program Lock Pro	http://www.softdd.com/program-pc-lock-protect/index.htm	Lock and unlock any program on a PC so it cannot be used. Runs on all Windows systems.
# Protecteer LLC	http://www.protecteer.com/asp/home.asp	Desktop software combined with a web based service for managing website registration processes securely. Includes password and email address generation and management, automatic form filling and email screening. [Windows]
# Roe's Downloads	http://www.roe.ch/Main_Page	Freeware tools including Liberator (BO countermeasure), TCP/IP Connector, CAST-256 plugin for BO2K.
# Sanctum, Inc.	http://www.watchfire.com/securityzone/default.aspx	Solutions for securing web applications.
# Senforce Technologies, Inc.	http://www.senforce.com/	Manufacturer of software to assist Enterprise IT managers in policy enforced client security and wireless mobile security.
# ShareFix	http://www.kue.dsl.pipex.com/sharefix.htm	Utility to remove Windows default administration shares which pose a potential security problem.

# Skygate	http://www.skygate.co.uk/	Skygate specialises in IT security providing products, consultancy and software/application development to organisations. These include a two-factor authentication solution, BS7799 based security consultancy and audits, and Linux consultancy and development.
# Solo Antivirus software	http://www.antivirus-download.com/	Provides detection and removal tools. Also contains a powerful system integrity checker to block new Internet worms and backdoors.
# SPAM Blackout	http://www.spamblackout.com/	Blocks spam from your inbox. Safe and easy-to-use, has a powerful spam filtering Engine. Works with any email client program, such as MS Outlook. Can interface with your anti-virus Scanner. Works with Hotmail, POP3, and IMAP.
# SrvReport	http://srvreport.chosting.de/	Server monitoring tool that reports on network traffic, web server traffic, CPU usage, ftp logs, e-mail, authenticated users, server warnings, and tests for rootkits.
# 1st Internet Privacy Tool	http://www.privacywindows.com/ iptool/index.html	Utility that restricts access to Windows resources.
# StopITnow Modem Protection Software	http://www.stopitnow.com.au/	Software to protect and control of unauthorized access to your dial-up modem Internet connections.
# Tashilon Secure4Net	http://www.image-in.co.il/HTML/SEC4NET/	Implements the new AES encryption algorithm.
# Tiger Tools, Inc.	http://www.tigertools.net/	Tools for a professional security analysis.
# Tools-On.net	http://tools-on.net/	Free Network security and auditing tools from Alexander K. Yezhov, also security articles and archives.
# Tray Safe	http://www.fgroupsoft.com/Traysafe/	Password manager for web passwords automatic insertion of usernames and passwords into web forms [Win95/98/Me/NT/2000/XP].
# TruGeek	http://trugeek.com/Tools/	Online web based tools, software, and mailing lists.
# UBN	http://www.ubn.net/	Universal Business Network Inc. No 1 e catalogue exchnage center, Trading information exchange center, Global Security Information Key implement.

# Web Server Automatic Website Test Macros	http://www.iopus.com/imacros/	Automatically run link, form and download usability tests on web sites with this online macro recorder and form filler. Features extensive command line and batch file support.
# wINJECT	http://home19.inet.tele.dk/moofz/	Low-level packet builder/injector for win9x dialup users. It allows you to create custom packets with real or spoofed IP addresses.
# YouEncrypt.com	http://youencrypt.com/	Web Page Encryption is a tool to protect the content of your web page. It can protect your text, graphics or prevent others from copying your code or paypal links. With its help, spammers are stopped from extracting your email address from your web page so they can't send you spam emails.
# Yozons	http://www.yozons.com/pub/	Improves business processes with e-signatures and security.

Disclaimer! The Internet security product/tool information found in this appendix was supplied by the vendors/companies. This author and the publisher make no claims concerning their accuracy. Additionally, the listing or non-listing of a vendor/company or product/tool does not imply or infer any bias or endorsement on behalf of the author/publisher.

Appendix E

LIST OF INTERNET SECURITY STANDARDS

Table E-1. List of Internet security standards.

Mnemonic	Title	RFC#	STD#
USM-SNMPV3	User-based Security Model (USM) for version 3 of the Simple Network Management Protocol (SNMPv3)	3414	62
———	A Pseudo-Random Function (PRF) for the Kerberos V Generic Security Service Application Program Interface (GSS-API) Mechanism	4402*	
———	A Pseudo-Random Function (PRF) API Extension for the Generic Security Service Application Program Interface (GSS-API)	4401*	
———	Transport Layer Security (TLS) Extensions	4366*	
———	The Use of RSA/SHA-1 Signatures within Encapsulating Security Payload (ESP) and Authentication Header (AH)	4359*	
———	Datagram Transport Layer Security	4347*	
———	The Transport Layer Security (TLS) Protocol Version 1.1	4346*	
———	Improved Arcfour Modes for the Secure Shell (SSH) Transport Layer Protocol	4345*	
———	The Secure Shell (SSH) Transport Layer Encryption Modes	4344*	
———	Domain Name System (DNS) Security Extensions Mapping for the Extensible Provisioning Protocol (EPP)	4310*	
———	Using Advanced Encryption Standard (AES) CCM Mode with IPsec Encapsulating Security Payload (ESP)	4309*	
ESP	Cryptographic Algorithm Implementation Requirements for Encapsulating Security Payload (ESP) and Authentication Header (AH)	4305*	
———	Extended Sequence Number (ESN) Addendum to IPsec Domain of Interpretation (DOI) for Internet Security Association and Key Management Protocol (ISAKMP)	4304*	

ESP	IP Encapsulating Security Payload (ESP)	4303*	
IPSEC	Security Architecture for the Internet Protocol	4301*	
———	Pre-Shared Key Ciphersuites for Transport Layer Security (TLS)	4279*	
———	X.509 Certificate Extension for Secure/Multipurpose Internet Mail Extensions (S/MIME) Capabilities	4262*	
———	Common Open Policy Service (COPS) Over Transport Layer Security (TLS)	4261*	
———	Generic Message Exchange Authentication for the Secure Shell Protocol (SSH)	4256*	
———	Using DNS to Securely Publish Secure Shell (SSH) Key Fingerprints	4255*	
———	The Secure Shell (SSH) Connection Protocol	4254*	
———	The Secure Shell (SSH) Transport Layer Protocol	4253*	
———	The Secure Shell (SSH) Authentication Protocol	4252*	
———	The Secure Shell (SSH) Protocol Architecture	4251*	
———	The Secure Shell (SSH) Protocol Assigned Numbers	4250*	
———	The Simple and Protected Generic Security Service Application Program Interface (GSS-API) Negotiation Mechanism	4178	
———	Addition of SEED Cipher Suites to Transport Layer Security (TLS)	4162	
———	Addition of Camellia Cipher Suites to Transport Layer Security (TLS)	4132	
———	The Kerberos Version 5 Generic Security Service Application Program Interface (GSS-API) Mechanism: Version 2	4121	
———	The Use of Galois/Counter Mode (GCM) in IPsec Encapsulating Security Payload (ESP)	4106	
———	Additional XML Security Uniform Resource Identifiers (URIs)	4051	
———	Protocol Modifications for the DNS Security Extensions	4035	
———	Resource Records for the DNS Security Extensions	4034	
———	DNS Security Introduction and Requirements	4033	
———	The Advanced Encryption Standard (AES) Cipher Algorithm in the SNMP User-based Security Model	3826	
———	Security Considerations for Signaling Transport (SIGTRAN) Protocols	3788	
———	Transport Layer Security Protocol Compression Methods	3749	
———	Using Advanced Encryption Standard (AES) Counter Mode With IPsec Encapsulating Security Payload (ESP)	3686	
———	Generic Security Service Algorithm for Secret Key Transaction Authenticationfor DNS (GSS-TSIG)	3645	
———	PacketCable Security Ticket Control Sub-Option for the DHCP CableLabs ClientConfiguration (CCC) Option	3594	
———	IP Security Policy (IPSP) Requirements	3586	

	Transport Layer Security (TLS) Extensions	3546	
———	Transport Layer Security over Stream Control Transmission Protocol	3436	
———	Security Mechanism Agreement for the Session Initiation Protocol (SIP)	3329	
———	Advanced Encryption Standard (AES) Ciphersuites for Transport Layer Security (TLS)	3268	

Appendix F

LIST OF MISCELLANEOUS INTERNET SECURITY RESOURCES

Table F-1. Internet security resources.

Resource	URL
# Information Security Reading Room	http://www.sans.org/rr/
# SANS Security Policy Samples	http://www.sans.org/resources/policies/
# Webcasts	http://www.sans.org/webcasts/
# Newsletters	http://www.sans.org/newsletters/
# Guide To Popular Resources On Computer and Information Security	http://www.sans.org/resources/popular.php
# Intrusion Detection FAQ	http://www.sans.org/resources/idfaq/
# Malware FAQ	http://www.sans.org/resources/malwarefaq/
# S.C.O.R.E.	http://www.sans.org/score/
# Vendor Related Resources	http://www.sans.org/resources/#vendor
# Center for Internet Security	http://www.sans.org/resources/#cis
# Additional Resources	http://www.sans.org/resources/#additional

Appendix G

GLOSSARY

100Base-2 – The Institute of Electrical and Elec-tronic Engineers (IEEE) 802.3 specification for ethernet over thin coaxial cable.

10Base-T – The IEEE 802.3 specification for ethernet over unshielded twisted pair (UTP).

Access Control List (ACL) – Most network security systems operate by allowing selective use of services. An Access Control List is the usual means by which access to, and denial of, services is controlled. It is simply a list of the services available, each with a list of the hosts permitted to use the service.

Adapter – A board installed in a computer system to provide network communication capabilities to and from that computer system. Also called a Network Interface Card (NIC).

Alternate Routing – A mechanism that supports the use of a new path after an attempt to set up a connection along a previously selected path fails.

American Standard Code for Information Interchange (ASCII) – This is the code that most computers use to represent displayable characters. An ASCII file is a straightforward text file without special control characters.

AppleTalk – A networking protocol developed by Apple Computer for communication between Apple Computer products and other computers. This protocol is independent of what network it is layered on. Current implementations exist for LocalTalk (235 Kbps) and EtherTalk (10 Mbps).

Application Layer – Layer seven of the OSI Reference Model; implemented by various network applications including file transfer, electronic mail, and terminal emulation.

Application-Level Firewall – A firewall system in which service is provided by processes that maintain complete TCP connection state and sequencing. Application level firewalls often re-address traffic so that outgoing traffic appears to have originated from the firewall, rather than the internal host.

Asymmetrical Digital Subscriber Line (ASDL) – A new standard for transmitting at speeds up to seven Mbps over a single copper pair.

Asynchronous – Referring to two or more signals which, though they have the same nominal rates, actually operate at different rates.

Asynchronous Protocol – A type of transmission where information is sent at any speed and at random with no routing information.

Asynchronous Transfer Mode (ATM) – (1) The CCITT standard for cell relay wherein information for multiple types of services (voice, video, data) is conveyed in small, fixed-size cells. ATM is a connection oriented technology used in both LAN and WAN environments. (2) A fast-packet switching technology allowing free allocation of capacity to each channel. The SONET synchronous payload envelope is a variation of ATM. (3) ATM is an international ISDN high speed, high-volume, packet switching transmission protocol standard. ATM currently accommodates transmission speeds from 64 Kbps to 622 Mbps.

Authentication – The process of assuring that data has come from its claimed source, or of corroborating the claimed identity of a communicating party.

Authentication Token – A portable device used for authenticating a user. Authentication tokens operate by challenge/response, time-based code sequences, or other techniques. This may include paper-based lists of one-time passwords.

Authorization – The process of determining what types of activities are permitted. Usually, authorization is in the context of authentication: once you have authenticated a user, they may be authorized different types of access or activity.

B Channel – In ISDN, a full duplex, 64 Kbps channel for sending data.

Bandwidth – (1) Measure of the information capacity of a transmission channel. (2) The difference between the highest and lowest frequencies of a band that can be passed by a transmission medium without undue distortion, such as the AM band - 535 to 1705 kilohertz. (3)Information carrying capacity of a communication channel. Analog bandwidth is the range of signal frequencies that can be transmitted by a communication channel or network. (4) A term used to indicate the amount of transmission or processing capacity possessed by a system or a specific location in a system (usually a network system).

Bandwidth Balancing (BWB) – Method to reduce a station's access to a transmission bus, to improve fairness (802.6).

Bandwidth on Demand (BoD) – Dynamic allocation of line capacity to active users, inherent in FastComm FRADs.

Bandwidth On Demand Interoperability Group (BONDING) – Makers of inverse muxes.

Bastion Host – A system that has been hardened to resist attack, and which is installed on a network in such a way that it is expected to potentially come under attack. Bastion hosts are often components of firewalls, or may be "outside" Web servers or public access systems. Generally, a bastion host is running some form of general purpose operating system (e.g., UNIX, VMS, WNT, etc.) rather than a ROM-based or firmware operating system.

Bridge/Router – A device that can provide the functions of a bridge, router or both concurrently. Bridge/router can route one or more protocols, such as TCP/IP and/or XNS, and bridge all other traffic.

Broadcast Storm Firewalls – A mechanism that limits the rate at which broad-cast/multicast packets are forwarded through the system.

Challenge Handshake Authentication Protocol (CHAP) – Log-in security procedure for dial-in access.

Challenge/Response – An authentication technique whereby a server sends an unpredictable challenge to the user, who computes a response using some form of authentication token.

Channel Service Unit (CSU) – A CSU is a device that interfaces customer T1 (or E1) equipment to a carrier's T1 (or E1) service. At its most basic level, a CSU performs certain line-conditioning and equalization functions, and responds to loopback commands sent from the central office.

Channel Service Unit/Data Service Unit (CSU/DSU) – A digital interface unit that connects end user equipment to the local digital telephone loop.

Circuit – A two-way communications path. (2) A communication path or network; usually a pair of channels providing bidirectional communication.

Client/Server – A distributed system model of computing that brings computing power to the desktop, where users ("clients") access resources from servers.

Configuration – The phase in which the LE client discovers the LE Service.

D Channel – Full duplex 16 Kbps (basic rate) or 64 Kbps (primary rate) ISDN channel.

Data Encryption Standard (DES) – A popular, standard encryption scheme.

Data Terminal Equipment (DTE) – The part of a data station that serves as a data source, destination, or both, and that provides for the data communications control function according to protocol. DTE includes computers, protocol translators, and multiplexers.

Dial up – A type of communication that is established by a switched-circuit connection using the telephone network.

Digital Data System (DDS) – U.S. private data transmission network, established in 1974 by AT&T and based on AT&T's Dataphone data service. DDS is a digital overlay network built on the existing loop and trunking network.

DSU/CSU – Equipment used to terminate a Switched 56 line and convert a PC's digital data signal into a digital transmission signal.

Dynamic Bandwidth Allocation (DBA) – A process that optimizes overall network efficiency by automatically increasing or decreasing the bandwidth of a channel to accommodate changes in data flow from end-user equipment.

Dynamic Password Authentication Servers – Products consisting of server software that generates constantly changing passwords and two-factor, software or hardware-based password generators that teleworkers carry with them.

Dynamic Routing – Routing that adjusts automatically to changes in network topology or traffic.

Encryption – Applying a specific algorithm to data so as to alter the data's appearance and prevent other devices from reading the information. Decryption applies the algorithm in reverse to restore the data to its original form.

Ethernet – (1) A baseband LAN specification invented by Xerox Corporation and developed jointly by Xerox, Intel, and Digital Equipment Corporation. Ethernet networks operate at 10 Mbps using CSMA/CD to run over coaxial cable. Ethernet is similar to a series of standards produced by IEEE referred to as IEEE 802.3. (2) A very common method of networking computers in a local area network (LAN). Ethernet will handle about 10,000,000 bits per second and can be used with almost any kind of computer.

File Transfer Protocol (FTP) – (1) An IP application protocol for transferring files between network nodes. (2) An Internet protocol that allows a user on one host to transfer files to and from another host over a network.

Firewall – (1) Isolation of LAN segments from each other to protect data resources and help manage traffic. (2) Hardware or software that restricts traffic to a private network from an unsecured network.

Flash Memory – A technology developed by Intel and licensed to other semiconductor companies. Flash memory is non-volatile storage that can be electrically erased in the circuit and reprogrammed.

Fractional E1 – A carrier service that offers data rates between 64 kbps and 2.048 mbps (E1) in increments of 64 Kbps.

Fractional T-1 – A WAN communications service that provides the user with some portion of a T1 circuit which has been divided into 24 separate 64 Kb channels. Fractional E-1 is in Europe.

Frame Relay – High-performance interface for packet-switching networks. Considered more efficient than X.25 which it is expected to replace. Frame relay technology can handle "bursty" communications that have rapidly changing bandwidth requirements.

Frame Relay Forum – A voluntary organization composed of Frame Relay vendors, manufacturers, service providers, research organizations, and users. Similar in purpose to the ATM Forum.

Frequently Asked Questions (FAQ) – Usually appears in the form of a "read - me" file in a variety of Internet formats. New users are expected to read the FAQ before participating in newsgroups, bulletin boards, video conferences and so on.

Government Open Systems Interconnection Profile (GOSIP) – U.S. government version of the OSI protocols. GOSIP compatibility is a requirement in government networking purchases.

Home Page – The first page of a Web site or of a logical group of HTML documents.

Hyper Text Transfer Protocol (HTTP) – (1) The protocol most commonly used in the World-Wide Web to transfer information from Web servers to Web browsers. (2) The protocol that negotiates document delivery to a Web browser from a Web server.

Insider Attack – An attack originating from inside a protected network.

Integrated Digital Network (IDN) – The integration of transmission and switching functions using digital technology in a circuit-switched telecommunications network.

Integrated Services Digital Network (ISDN) – (1)The recommendation published by CCITT for private or public digital telephone networks where binary data, such as graphics and digitized voice and data transmission, pass over the same digital network that carries most telephone transmissions today. (2) An overall application of the technology to provide for both newer digital and more traditional telephone services in an integrated network and incorporates the new network and interfacing standards which are being adopted worldwide. (3) Method for carrying many different services over the same digital transmission and switching facilities. (4) A Digital telephone system made up of two 64kbps "B" channels for data and one "D" channel for message trafficking.

Interior Gateway Routing Protocol (IGRP) – Learns best routes through LAN Internet (TCP/IP).

Internation Organization for Standardization (ISO) – Best known for the 7-layer OSI Reference Model.

Internet – A collection of networks interconnected by a set of routers which allow them to function as a single, large virtual network.

Internet Access – The method by which users connect to the Internet.

Internet Address – Also called an IP address. It is a 32-bit address assigned to hosts using TCP/IP. The address is written as four octets separated with periods (dotted decimal format) that are made up of a network section, an optional subnet section, and a host section.

Internet Protocol (IP) – A Layer 3 (network layer) protocol that contains addressing information and some control information that allows packets to be routed. Documented in RFC 791.

Internet Service Provider (ISP) – (1) Any of a number of companies that sell Internet access to individuals or organizations at speeds ranging from 300bps to OC-3. (2) A business that enables individuals and companies to connect to the Internet by providing the interface to the Internet backbone.

Internetwork – A collection of networks interconnected by routers that function (generally) as a single network. Sometimes called an internet, which is not to be confused with the Internet.

Internetworking – General term used to refer to the industry that has arisen around the problem of connecting networks together. The term can refer to products, procedures, and technologies.

Intranet – A private network that uses Internet software and standards.

IP Spoofing – An attack whereby a system attempts to illicitly impersonate another system by using its IP network address.

ISDN BRI – A digital access line that is divided into three channels. Two of the channels, called B channels, operate at 64 Kbps and are always used for data or voice. The third D channel is used for signaling at 16 Kbps.

ISDN Centrex – A service provided by local telephone companies to customer premises, in which a central office digital switch performs in lieu of a customer PBX in an ISDN system. ISDN Centrex uses one B channel and one D channel to provide an array of digital voice and data capabilities.

ISDN Integrated Access Bridge/Router – A remote access device that connects your computer to an ISDN line, performs bridging and/or routing and supports analog devices such as phones or faxes.

ISDN PRI – Based physically and electrically on an E1 circuit, but channelized so that two channels are used for signaling and 30 channels are allocated for user traffic. ISDN PRI is available in E1 and T1 frame formats, depending on country.

Modem – Contraction of modulator-demodulator. A device which modulates and de-modulates signals transmitted over communication facilities.

Multi-homed Host – A computer connected to more than one physical datalink. The data links may or may not be attached to the same network.

Network – A collection of computers and other devices that are able to communicate with each other over some network medium.

Open Systems Interconnection (OSI) – A 7-layer architecture model for communications systems developed by ISO and used as a reference model for most network architectures.

Packet – (1) A logical grouping of information that includes a header and (usually) user data. (2) Continuous sequence of binary digits of information is switched through the network and an integral unit. Consists of up to 1024 bits (128 octets) of customer data plus additional transmission and error control information.

Packet Buffer – Storage area to hold incoming data until the receiving device can process the data.

Packet Filtering – A second layer of filtering on top of the standard filtering provided by a traditional transparent bridge. Can improve network performance, provide additional security, or logically segment a network to support virtual workgroups.

Packet Switch Node (PSN) – The modern term used for nodes in the ARPANET and MILNET. These used to be called IMPs (Interface Message Processors). PSNs are currently implemented with BBN C30 or C300 minicomputers.

Packet Switching – Type of data transfer that occupies a communication link only during the time of actual data transmission. Messages are split into packets and reassembled at the receiving end of the communication link. (2) A transmission technique that segments and routes information into discrete units. Packet switching allows for efficient sharing of network resources as packets from different sources can all be sent over the same channel in the same bitstream.

Password – A group of characters assigned to a Staffware User by the System Administrator and used to sign off some Forms.

Password Authentication Protocol (PAP) – A simple password protocol that transmits a user name and password across the network, unencrypted.

Path – One or more Sonet lines, including network elements at each end capable of accessing, generating, and processing Path Overhead. Paths provide end-to-end transport of services.

Perimeter Firewall – There are two types of perimeter firewalls: static packet filtering and dynamic firewalls. Both work at the IP address level, selectively passing or blocking data packets. Static packet filters are less flexible than dynamic firewalls.

Port – The identifier (16-bit unsigned integer) used by Internet transport protocols to distinguish among multiple simultaneous connections to a single destination host.

Profile – A set of information about a User, such as name, password or department, set up by the System Administrator.

Protocol – (1)A formal description of a set of rules and conventions that govern how devices on a network exchange information. (2) Set of rules conducting interactions between two or more parties. These rules consist of syntax (header structure) semantics (actions and reactions that are supposed to occur) and timing (relative ordering and direction of states and events).(3) A formal set of rules.

Protocol Address – Also called a network address. A network layer address referring to a logical, rather than a physical, network device.

Protocol Stack – Related layers of protocol software that function together to implement a particular communications architecture. Examples include AppleTalk and DECnet.

Proxy – The mechanism whereby one system "fronts for" another system in responding to protocol requests. Proxy systems are used in network management to avoid having to implement full protocol stacks in simple devices, such as modems.

Remote Access – The process of allowing remote workers to access a corporate LAN over analog or digital telephone lines.

Remote Access Server – Access equipment at a central site that connects remote users with corporate LAN resources.

Remote Bridge – A bridge that connects physically disparate network segments via WAN links.

Route – A path through an internetwork.

Routed (Route Daemon) – A program that runs under 4.2 or 4.3BDS UNIX systems (and derived operating systems) to propagate routes among machines on a local area network. Pronounced "route-dee."

Routed Protocol – A protocol that can be routed by a router. To route a routed protocol, a router must understand the logical internetwork as perceived by that routed protocol. Examples of routed protocols include DECnet, AppleTalk, and IP.

Router – (1) An OSI Layer 3 device that can decide which of several paths network traffic will follow based on some optimality metric. Also called a gateway (although this definition of gateway is becoming increasingly outdated), routers forward packets from one network to another based on network-layer information. (2) A dedicated computer hardware and/or software package which manages the connection between two or more networks.

Router Cluster – Private, high-speed switched links to each building in a campus. They are used to expand interbuilding bandwidth.

Routing – The process of finding a path to the destination host. Routing is very complex in large networks because of the many potential intermediate destinations a packet might traverse before reaching its destination host.

Routing Bridge – MAC-layer bridge that uses network layer methods to determine a network's topology.

Routing Information Protocol (RIP) – An IGP supplied with Berkeley UNIX systems. It is the most common IGP in the Internet. RIP uses hop count as a routing metric. The largest allowable hop count for RIP is 16.

Routing Metric – The method by which a routing algorithm determines that one route is better than another. This information is stored in routing tables. Metrics include reliability, delay, bandwidth, load, MTUs, communication costs, and hop count.

Routing Protocol – A protocol that accomplishes routing through the implementation of a specific routing algorithm. Examples of routing protocols include IGRP, RIP, and OSPF.

Routing Table – A table stored in a router or some other internetworking device that keeps track of routes (and, in some cases, metrics associated with those routes) to particular network destinations.

Routing Update – A message sent from a router to indicate network reachability and associated cost information. Routing updates are typically sent at regular intervals and after a change in network topology.

Secure HTTP (S-HTTP) – An extension of HTTP for authentication and data encryption between a Web server and a Web browser.

Security – Protection against unwanted behavior. The most widely used definition of (computer) security is security = confidentiality + integrity + availability.

Security Policy – A security policy is the set of rules, principles and practices that determine how security is implemented in an organization. It must maintain the principles of the organization's general security policy.

Simple Mail Transfer Protocol (SMTP) – Protocol governing mail transmissions. It is defined in RFC 821, with associated message format descriptions in RFC 822.

Subnetwork – Collection of OSI end systems and intermediate systems under the control of one administrative domain and using a single network access protocol. For example, private X.25 networks, a series of bridged LANs.

Switched FDDI – A technique of transparently connecting separate FDDI networks at full 100 Mbps wire speed.

Synchronous Transfer Mode (STM) – B-ISDN communications method that transmits a group of several traffic streams synchronized to a single reference clock. This is the standard method carriers currently utilize to assign channels within a T1/E1 line.

T1 – (1) Digital transmission facility operating with a nominal bandwidth of 1.544 Mbps. Also known as Digital Signal Level 1 (D1). Composed of 24 DS-0 channels in many cases. The T1 digital transmission system is the primary digital communication system in North America. (2) A high-speed 1.5 mbits/sec leased line often used by companies for access to the Internet.

Transmission Control Protocol/Internet Protocol (TCP/IP) – (1) The common name for the suite of protocols developed by the U.S. Department of Defense in the 1970s to support the construction of world-wide internetworks. TCP and IP are the two best-known protocols in the suite. TCP corresponds to Layer 4 (the transport layer) of the OSI reference model. It provides reliable transmission of data. IP corresponds to layer 3 (the network layer) of the OSI reference model and provides connectionless datagram service. (2) The collection of transport and application protocols used to communicate on the Internet and other networks.

U Interface (ISDN BRI) – The two-wire interface that connects to the NT1 on a user's premises. In North America it can be integrated into the customer premises equipment. In other countries, it is typically supplied by the local carrier.

Use File – a file designated as a Use File resides in a special area, and is read into the active Form each time it is created.

Virtual Private Network (VPN) – A network service offered by public carriers in which the customer is provided a network that in many ways appears as if it is a private network (customer-unique addressing, network management capabilities, dynamic reconfiguration, etc.) but which, in fact, is provided over the carrier's public network facilities.

INDEX

Note: Citations derived from figures are indicated by an *f*; citations from tables are indicated by a *t*.